# COSTA RICA

Yves Séguin
Francis Giguère

**Authors**
Yves Séguin
Francis Giguère

**Collaboration**
Marie-Josée Guy
François Brodeur

**Translation**
Traci Williams
Christina Poole
Sarah Kresh
Danielle Gauthier
Suzanne Murray
Tracy Kendrick
Janet Logan

**Series Director**
Claude Morneau

**Production Supervisor**
Pascale Couture

**Editing**
Tara Salman
Stephanie Heidenreich

**Layout**
Stephanie Heidenreich
Tara Salman

**Cartography**
André Duchesne
*Assistants*
Patrick Thivièrge
Isabelle Lalonde

**Cover Photograph**
Margaret Mead (Image Bank)

**Interior Photographs**
Claude-Hervé Bazin
Stéphane G.-Marceau
Roger Michel
Didier Raffin

**Design**
Patrick Farei
(Atoll Direction)

**Illustrations**
Sophie Matteau
Lorette Pierson
Marie-Annick Viatour.

**Thanks to** Ricardo Bolaños, Jeff Crandall, Loic Dervieu, Daisy Arroyo Sánchez, Mariette Daignault, Natalie Ewing, Estela Fuentes Alvarado, Marc Fournier, William Granados, Susana Guevara, Manfred Gutiérrez, Rafael Gutiérrez Rojas, Bill Hemmer, Isabelle Miralles, Edgar Neidhardt, Elizabeth Newton, Alfredo Oporta, Pierre Perron, Patrick Pinzelli, Alexander Quesada, Luis F. Quesada, Didier Raffin, James Remes, María Amalia Revelo, Ireth Rodríguez, Silvio Trevisan, Marjorie Washburn Calvo, Jan and Pilar Westra, Sylvia and Claude.
Instituto Costarricense de Turismo (ICT), Area de Conservación Guanacaste, Costa Rica Expeditions, Ecotours, Fundación de Parques Nacionales, Ministerio de Ambiente y Energia (MINAE), Prego Rent a Car, Sistema Nacional de Areas de Conservación (SINAC), Fundación Museos Banco Central, Wilson Botanical Garden, Grupo ProImagen and the Costa Rican Consulate in Montréal.

## DISTRIBUTORS

**AUSTRALIA**: Little Hills Press, 11/37-43 Alexander St., Crows Nest NSW 2065, ☎ (612) 437-6995, Fax: (612) 438-5762

**BELGIUM AND LUXEMBOURG**: Vander, Vrijwilligerlaan 321, B-1150 Brussel, ☎ (02) 762 98 04, Fax: (02) 762 06 62

**CANADA**: Ulysses Books & Maps, 4176 Saint-Denis, Montréal, Québec, H2W 2M5, ☎ (514) 843-9882, ext.2232, 800-748-9171, Fax: 514-843-9448, www.ulysses.ca

**GERMANY AND AUSTRIA**: Brettschneider, Fernreisebedarf, Feldfirchner Strasse 2, D-85551 Heimstetten, München, ☎ 89-99 02 03 30, Fax: 89-99 02 03 31, Brettschneider_Fernreisebedarf@t-online.de

**GREAT BRITAIN AND IRELAND**: World Leisure Marketing, Unit 11, Newmarket Court, Newmartket Drive, Derby DE24 8NW, ☎ 1 332 57 37 37, Fax: 1 332 57 33 99

**ITALY**: Centro Cartografico del Riccio, Via di Soffiano 164/A, 50143 Firenze, ☎ (055) 71 33 33, Fax: (055) 71 63 50

**NETHERLANDS**: Nilsson & Lamm, Pampuslaan 212-214, 1380 AD Weesp (NL), ☎ 0294-494949, Fax: 0294-494455, E-mail: nilam@euronet.nl

**PORTUGAL**: Dinapress, Lg. Dr. Antonio de Sousa de Macedo, 2, Lisboa 1200, ☎ (1) 395 52 70, Fax: (1) 395 03 90

**SCANDINAVIA**: Scanvik, Esplanaden 8B, 1263 Copenhagen K, DK, ☎ (45) 33.12.77.66, Fax: (45) 33.91.28.82

**SPAIN**: Altaïr, Balmes 69, E-08007 Barcelona, ☎ 454 29 66, Fax: 451 25 59, altair@globalcom.es

**SWITZERLAND**: OLF, P.O. Box 1061, CH-1701 Fribourg, ☎ (026) 467.51.11, Fax: (026) 467.54.66

**U.S.A.**: The Globe Pequot Press, 6 Business Park Road, P.O. Box 833, Old Saybrook, CT 06475, ☎ 1-800-243-0495, Fax: 800-820-2329, sales@globe-pequot.com

Other countries, contact Ulysses Books & Maps (Montréal), Fax: (514) 843-9448



**Canadian Cataloguing in Publication Data**


Printed in Canada

*"Vivían en valles verdiazules,*
*con cielos transparentes*
*y aires olorosos a cedro.*
*Entre esplendores de selvas*
*y augustas soledades."*

Cary Sagot Salazar de Carmiol,
*Cuando Lala enloquecia*

*"They lived in the green and blue valleys*
*where the skies were clear*
*and the air was scented with cedars.*
*Between the splendours of the forest*
*and an imposing solitude."*

# TABLE OF CONTENTS

## WRITE TO US

The information contained in this guide was correct at press time. However, mistakes can slip in, omissions are always possible, places can disappear, etc. The authors and publisher hereby disclaim any liability for loss or damage resulting from omissions or errors.

We value your comments, corrections and suggestions, as they allow us to keep each guide up to date. The best contributions will be rewarded with a free book from Ulysses Travel Publications. All you have to do is write us at the following address and indicate which title you would be interested in receiving (see the list at the end of guide).

**Ulysses Travel Publications**
**4176 Rue Saint-Denis**
**Montréal, Québec**
**Canada H2W 2M5**
**www.ulysses.ca**
**E-mail: guiduly@ulysses.ca**

## CATALOGUING

**Canadian Cataloguing in Publication Data:**

Giguère, Francis
Costa Rica
(Ulysses Travel Guide)
Translation of: Costa Rica
Includes index.
ISBN 2-89464-144-3
1. Costa Rica - Guidebooks. I. Séguin, Yves, 1961 - . II. Title. III. Series
F1543.5.B5213 1999 917.28604'5 C98-941547-3

"We acknowledge the financial support of the Government of Canada through the Book Publishing Industry Development Program (BPIDP) for our publishing activities." We would also like to thank SODEC for their financial support.

## LIST OF MAPS



## MAP SYMBOLS

| | | |
|---|---|---|
| Tourist Information | National Parks | Beach |
| Hospital | Wildlife Sanctuary | Camping |
| Airport, Airfield | Volcano | Post Office |
| Bus Terminal | Mountain | Cathedral |
| Car Ferry | Lookout | Church |
| Passenger Ferry | Pedestrian Walkway | |

## SYMBOLS

| | |
|---|---|
| (ship symbol) | Ulysses's favourite |
| ☎ | Telephone number |
| ⇄ | Fax number |
| ≡ | Air conditioning |
| ⊗ | Fan |
| # | Screen |
| ≈ | Pool |
| ℜ | Restaurant |
| ⊛ | Whirlpool |
| ℝ | Refrigerator |
| K | Kitchenette |
| ◙ | In-room safe |
| ⌂ | Sauna |
| ⊝ | Exercise room |
| hw | Hot water |
| cw | Cold water |
| tv | Colour television |
| ctv | Cable television |
| pb | Private bathroom |
| sb | Shared bathroom |
| ps | Private shower |
| bkfst | Breakfast |
| fb | Full board (lodging + three meals) |
| ½b | Half board (lodging + two meals) |

### ATTRACTION CLASSIFICATION

| | |
|---|---|
| ★ | Interesting |
| ★★ | Worth a visit |
| ★★★ | Not to be missed |

### HOTEL CLASSIFICATION

| | |
|---|---|
| $ | US$15 or less |
| $$ | US$15 to US$25 |
| $$$ | US$25 to US$50 |
| $$$$ | US$50 to US$75 |
| $$$$$ | US$75 to US$120 |
| $$$$$$ | US$120 or more |

### RESTAURANT CLASSIFICATION

| | |
|---|---|
| $ | US$5 or less |
| $$ | US$5 to US$10 |
| $$$ | US$10 to US$20 |
| $$$$ | US$20 to US$40 |
| $$$$$ | US$40 or more |

**All prices in this guide are in US dollars.**

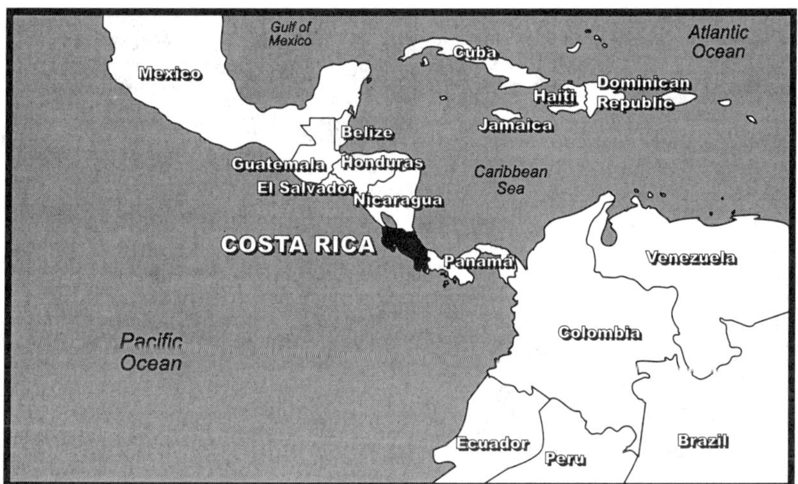

*Where is Costa Rica ?*

**Costa Rica**

**Capital :** San José
**Area :** 50 700 km²
**Population :** 3 500 000 inhab.
**Languages :** Spanish, English, Creole
**Currency :** colón

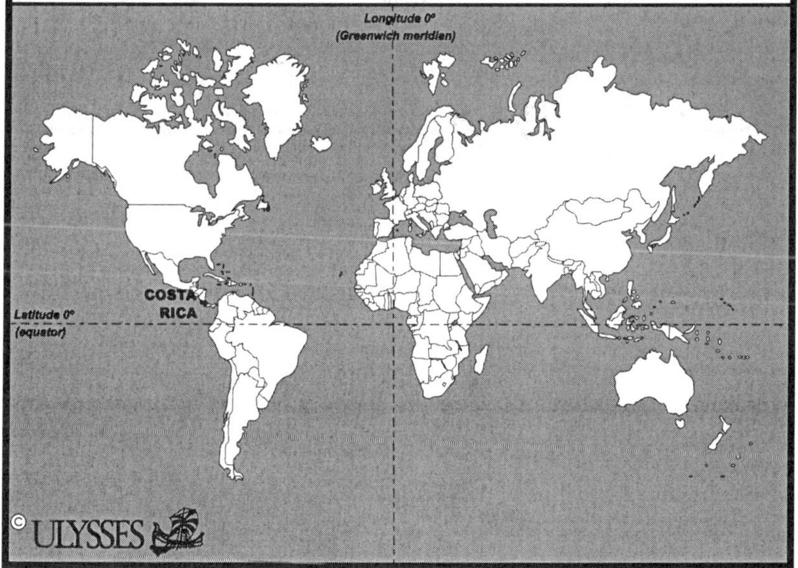

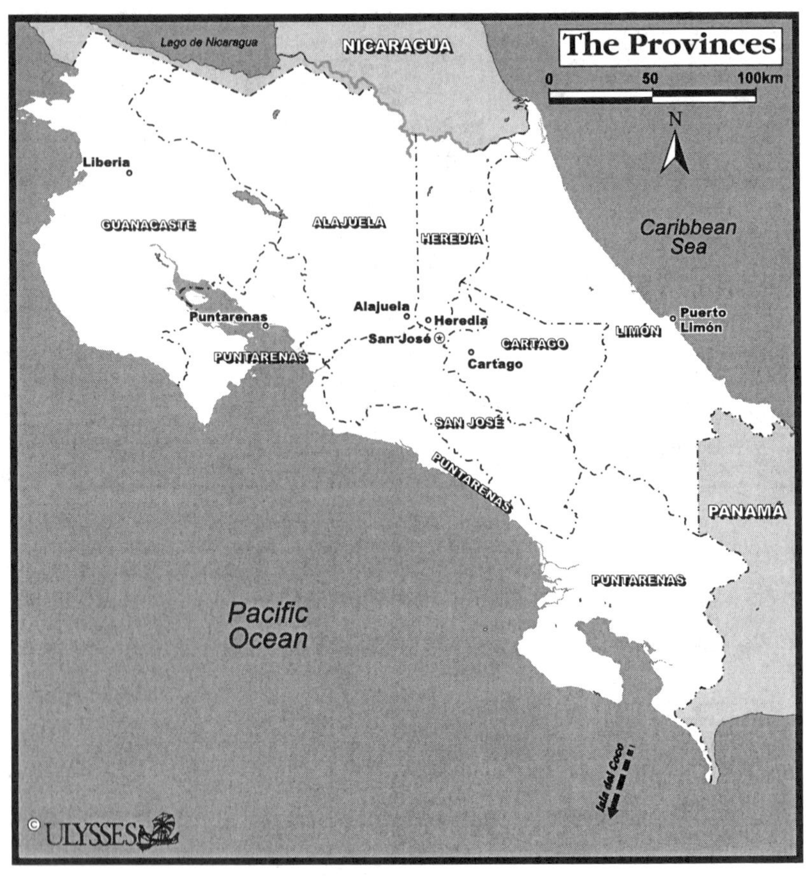

The Provinces
0
50
100km
N
Lago de Nicaragua
NICARAGUA
Liberia
GUANACASTE
ALAJUELA
HEREDIA
Caribbean
Sea
Alajuela
Heredia
San José
Puntarenas
PUNTARENAS
CARTAGO
Cartago
LIMÓN
Puerto
Limón
SAN JOSÉ
PUNTARENAS
PANAMÁ
PUNTARENAS
Pacific
Ocean
Isla del Coco
© ULYSSES

# PORTRAIT

How do you describe Costa Rica, a country with so many natural treasures? Perhaps the best way to start would be with its name, which means "the rich coast".

"Coast" comes first, not only because it is the first word in the name, but also because this part of Central America is bordered by two long, sinuous coasts with kilometres of idyllic beaches: the eastern side is bathed by the Caribbean Sea with its many coral reefs, and the western side by the calm, vast Pacific Ocean.

And the region between these coasts can only be described as "rich". Since it is located on the isthmus separating the Americas, Costa Rica is the natural habitat for many species of flora and fauna found in both northern and southern continents. The microclimates of its mountains and rivers, valleys and plains, and dry tropical and rainforests favour the existence and continual growth of this abundant plant and animal life. In its lush vegetation, you can smell the heady scent of flowers, hear the birds whose songs are as lovely as their plumage, see multicoloured butterflies fluttering through the fields, and glimpse endangered species in the forest: Costa Rica's natural beauty is mesmerizing. However, its culture and people are just as fascinating, the warm and welcoming *Ticos* have contributed greatly to Latin American society.

No matter how long you stay, this rich coast is sure to seduce you!

## GEOGRAPHY

Although Costa Rica has an area of only 50,700 square kilometres, it is not the smallest country in Central America; it is larger than both El Salvador (21,040 km²) and Belize

(22,960 km²). The area of Costa Rica is comparable to that of the states of Vermont and New Hampshire combined (49,079 km²), the Midi-Pyrenees region of France (45,602 km²), Denmark (43,070 km²) or Switzerland (41,288 km²). And with its high plateaus, stable political system and abolished army (1949), Costa Rica is dubbed the "Switzerland of Central America". Costa Rica is 380 kilometres at its longest point and 270 kilometres at its widest. Its narrowest point between the two coasts measures only 120 kilometres. With its many bays, coves and two peninsulas (Nicoya and Osa), the Pacific Coast is 1,016 kilometres long. The Atlantic Coast is far shorter, only 212 kilometres long.

Costa Rica is bordered on the north by Nicaragua and on the south by Panama. The Interamericana Highway which runs 534 kilometres north to south through Costa Rica, from the Nicaraguan border (Peñas Blancas) to the Panamian border (Paso Canoas). Costa Rica is located between 8° and 11° latitude north and between 82° and 86° longitude west. Isla del Coco (25 km²) 500 kilometres off Pacific Coast (5 30' N. and 87 05' W.), belongs to Costa Rica and is also a national park.

Costa Rica is divided into seven provinces: San José, Heredia, Alajuela, Cartago, Limón, Puntarenas and Guanacaste. Each province has the same name as its capital city, except Guanacaste, whose capital is Liberia. The provinces of San José, Heredia, Alajuela and Cartago are all found in the Central Valley. The other three provinces are divided according to their geographic location in relation to the Central Valley (one on both coasts and one in the north).

With a population of 330,000, at an altitude of 1,150 metres, and in the middle of Costa Rica and the Central Valley, San José is not only the largest city, but also the natural capital.

## Sea and Mountains

No matter where you are in the country, warm, salty water (Caribbean Sea or Pacific Ocean) is often less than an hour away, and rarely more than three. Thus, you can spend the morning in the mountains (exploring volcanoes, hiking, rafting, birdwatching, etc.) and the afternoon by the sea (swimming, scuba diving, surfing, fishing, etc.).

The mountain range, or cordilleras, divide Costa Rica into two distinct regions: the Caribbean (Atlantic) and Pacific. The slopes on the Atlantic side are less steep than those of the Pacific side where summits rise between 1,500 metres to 3,819 metres in altitude. It is possible to see the typical vegetation of the lower, middle and higher mountains on the western slopes.

The long mountain range, stretching across the country from the northwest (Nicaragua) to southeast (Panama), is made up of four distinct mountain chains: Guanacaste, Tilarán, Central and Talamanca. In the north, the newer **Guanacaste Cordillera** consists of young volcanic, rock and has several active volcanoes including Orosí (1,487 m), Rincón de la Vieja (1,895 m), Santa María (1,916 m) and Miravalles (2,028 m). To the south, near Arenal Lake, the **Tilarán Cordillera** is home to the Arenal Volcano (1,633 m), one of the most active volcanos in the world, and one of the most popular attractions in the country. At nightfall, from a safe distance, you can hear the volcano rumbling and admire the red lava flowing from it.

In the middle of the country, the **Central Cordillera** has some of the highest and most accessible volcanos in Costa Rica. The Poás (2,704 m), Barva (2,906 m), Irazú (3,432 m) and Turrialba (3,328 m) volcanos are a complete change of scenery, and a sight to behold only 60 kilometres from the capital. The Central Cordillera shelters part of the Central Valley (Valle Central or Meseta Central), which ranges from 800 metres to 1,600 metres in height. With 3,500 square kilometres of fertile land, this valley is blessed with a temperate climate – cooler and less humid than on the coasts – and has quickly become the place to enjoy the "good life". It is no wonder that almost two-thirds of the Costa Rican population lives in this mountainous region, where most of the major cities are found, including the country's capital, San José (330,000 inh.), located at an altitude of 1,150 metres.

In the south, the **Talamanca Cordillera** is a plicated rock mass of limestone and igneous rock. It boasts Cerro Chirripó (3,819 m), the highest point in Costa Rica, and more than a dozen summits over 3,000 metres, high including Urán (3,600 m), Terbi (3,720 m), Ami (3,295 m), Ena (3,126 m), Cabécar (3,030 m), Eli (3,097 m) and Dúrika (3,280 m).

Although Costa Rica has many impressive mountains and volcanos, there are also lower-lying areas. The largest plain is on the northeast coast, along the Caribbean Sea. These immense, and often swampy area extends from the Nicaraguan border to the city of Limón, covering 20% of the country.

On the Pacific side, the mountains are much closer to the coast, alternately forming capes, cliffs, bays and creeks. There are also two large gulfs: in the north, the Gulf of Nicoya with a peninsula bearing the same name; and in the south, the Golfo Dulce and the Osa Peninsula. These two gulfs bathe the shores of the province of Puntarenas, where there are many highly prized tourist attractions, the biggest towns being Jacó, Quepos and Montezuma.

Costa Rica has very few natural freshwater lakes. Apart from small lakes, such as Cachi (San José), Astillero (Heredia) and Caño Negro (Alajuela), the country's only lake of any significant size is Arenal (Guanacaste). This magnificent body of clear water (39 km x 5 km) lies just west of the famous Arenal Volcano. Highly valued by swimmers and fishers alike (especially for its rainbow perch, called *guapote*), Lake Arenal is also a paradise for windsurfers who come from all over to tackle its winds.

Although it is a country of mountains – some of them very high – Costa Rica also harbours many waterways, some emptying into the Pacific, others zigzagging towards the Caribbean Sea. There are about fifteen major rivers, the most popular being the Tempisque, Sarapiquí, Revontazón and Pacuare. The last two have earned an international reputation for great rafting and kayaking.

## Geological Formation

Costa Rica's current territory only came into being three million years ago. A million years before the formation of the actual land mass, the sea still occupied this region between North and South America. At this time, however, a string of volcanic islands on the Pacific side already existed, as evidenced by volcanic rock and sediment dating back about 100 million years that were discovered on the Nicoya Peninsula in this century.

The relatively sudden appearance of Costa Rica three million years ago was due to tectonic forces, which caused the Cocos plate to begin drifting eastward and collide with the Antillean plate, sliding under it at a rate of 10 centimetres a year. The friction between the two plates raised the bedrock, causing numerous volcanic eruptions. This formed a land bridge between the two continents. At that point, Costa Rica was made up of about 100 volcanoes, but most have levelled off, leaving only about a dozen perfectly conically shaped ones, mostly in the northwest and centre of the country.

Costa Rica lies on the Pacific "Rim of Fire" which consists of approximately 60 volcanoes, seven of which are still active in Costa Rica. Some of the most active volcanoes – Poás (2,704 m), Rincón de la Vieja (1,895 m) and especially Arenal (1,633 m) – have become major tourist attractions.

The collision of the Cocos and Caribbean plates has also caused a number of earthquakes. Though most have been minor, some earthquakes, such as the one that occurred in April 1991, measuring 7.4 on the Richter Scale (see p 134), warn of the ever-present potential for a natural disaster.

## CLIMATE

Costa Rica has a tropical climate with two seasons: the dry season and the rainy season (or green season). Several microclimates also exist, depending on the region and altitude. Basically, four climatic zones can be discerned: The Caribbean Coast's is wet, and has the highest rate of precipitation year-round. On the Pacific Coast, Guanacaste province and the Nicoya Peninsula have an arid climate, and during the dry season weeks can pass before it rains. The reverse is true for the mountains where it can rain two out of three days during the rainy season. In the Central Valley and San José, it is spring year round, with steady temperatures averaging between 22° and 25°C.

The rainy season lasts from May to November. Costa Ricans call this wet season *invierno* (winter), which is nothing like the snowy, intensely cold winter in North America and Europe. The rainy season is referred to as the "green season" by Costa Ricans, because this is when plants begin to sprout. Most people prefer to visit the country during the rainy season for the incredible blossoming flora, the reduced number of tourists and the significantly lower prices. The dry season lasts from December to April and is known as *verano* (spring). March and April are generally the warmest months.

Temperatures tend not to fluctuate in Costa Rica, except between altitudes. On the coasts, the mercury regularly rises above 35°C. On the Caribbean Coast, these high temperatures can be attributed to the humidity, whereas on the Pacific Coast, particularly in the province of Guanacaste, they are the result of the very dry and arid climate. Some parts of this province might not see a single drop of rain between January and May!

The higher you go, the cooler it gets (temperatures drop by 1°C for every 150 m in altitude). At the top of the highest mountains, such as Mount Chirripó (3,819 m), temperatures can fall to the freezing point. The coldest temperature ever recorded was - 9°C, on Mount Chirripó.

For the past few years, climatic conditions have been irregular and unpredictable, probably due to deforestation and El Niño. But since Costa Rica is a small country with many climates, every tourist will find some place that matches his or her comfort level. People who do not like very hot and humid weather should stay in the Central Valley, where it rains less than in other regions, and where the temperature is almost always cool and comfortable.

## FLORA AND FAUNA

Approximately three million years ago, the two American subcontinents (North America and South America) were connected by a narrow strip of land, creating a land bridge or isthmus. This bridge has been crossed not only by humans, but also by the flora and fauna from both subcontinents. Thus, Costa Rica with its varied climates and location between the two land masses, is a natural "biodome" with a diverse plant and animal life.

### Flora

According to a vegetation classification system devised by the biologist L.H. Holdridge in 1947, there are some 116 life zones on earth. These observations are based on the different types of climates, temperature changes, precipitation and seasonal changes. Due to the great diversity in climatic conditions and the very rugged terrain of Costa Rica, 12 life zones and 8 transition zones have been identified. Lagoons, marshes, herbaceous zones, mangroves, plains, tropical dry forest and high-altitude subalpine plains (*páramos*) make up the Costa Rican landscape, depending on the altitude or region. The country's high mountains have the some of the lowest temperatures in Central America, and their rivers flow into the Atlantic and Pacific Oceans.

Although Costa Rica represents only 0.03% (3/10,000ths) of the Earth's surface, it is home to 5% of all existing vegetation and animal species. Therefore, approximately 10,000 species of plants and more than 1,000 tree species live side by side with 1,400 orchid species, including the national flower, *guaria morada*, a lilac-coloured "Cattleya" orchid.

#### The Tropical Dry Forest

The tropical dry forest has practically disappeared in Central America. Only 2% of its original area is left, most of it in Costa Rica, in the northwestern province of Guanacaste.

***Orchid***

Where the forests of Guanacaste once stood proudly, there are now huge cleared tracts of land and pastures. The former open woodland and savannah cannot be replaced, because deforestation has impoverished the soil so it can no longer retain water. This intensified the dry and rainy seasons, making the dry season, which runs from December to April, a truly desert-like climate, where rain is almost unheard of. This drought, which can last for several months, has forced trees to adapt by shedding their leaves.

The rainy season brings relief and makes this desert bloom again. The grass becomes green, flowers try to outdo each other with their brilliant displays of colour, the trees blossom with white, yellow, red or pink flowers. Even the majestic *guanacaste* (*Enterolobium cyclocarpum*), Costa Rica's national tree for which its northwestern province is named, shows off its white flowers and green foliage.

**The Tropical Rainforest**

The tropical rainforest is very diverse in Costa Rica, both on the Atlantic (Caribbean Sea) and the Pacific coast, and even in the centre of the country. It is called "rainforest", because, like the Amazon, at least 2,000 millimetres of rain falls there every year, sometimes as much as 6,000 millimetres, especially in the province of Limón on the Atlantic coast. Humidity is also very high, and the annual temperature is almost steady with an average of approximately 24°C.

A constant supply of clean water is therefore essential to the survival of the tropical rainforest. Also, since the tropical rainforest recycles 75% of its water through evaporation, it sucks up plant and animal nutrients from the soil. Termites and mushrooms then decompose the dead vegetation so the trees can replenish it with the lost nutrients through their roots.

Altitude also affects the rainforest's vegetal composition. Vegetation gets sparser the higher you go. Between 1000 and 3000 metres, the forest is extremely dense with mosses, lichens, lians, vines, bushes and trees whose canopy is shrouded in mist. Between 3000 and 4000 metres, another type of vegetation grows, which is characteristic of the cold and wet high plains: the *páramo*. The northern end of the Andean *páramo* is in Costa Rica. Here, only vegetation that can adapt to the harsh climate grows, such as stunted bushes. You can see this type of vegetation by climbing above the tree line in the high mountains of the Talamanca Cordillera, especially on the Chirripó (*cerros*) (3,819 m) and Muerte (3,491 m) mountains.

**Deforestation**

Before the Spanish conquistadors set foot on its shores in the 16th century, Costa Rica was almost entirely made up of rich natural forests. Only small sections had been deforested by the natives to grow corn and cassava, among other crops. When the Spanish colonized the country, they began clearing forested areas to make way for towns and later for crops, such as bananas and coffee, or for pastures.

Deforestation proceeded at a relatively moderate rate until the mid-20th century when it took off at a drastic pace. In 1950, 75% of Costa Rica was still forested; in 1978, this percentage dropped to close to 35%, and to 26% in 1985. In 1993, the percentage of forested areas was less than 20%. If this trend continues, the rainforest may completely disappear. Thus, it is extremely important to protect the existing forests and implement an efficient reforestation policy. If not, the deforestation of tropical rainforest will cause an ecological disaster and it will take tens, if not hundreds, of years before anything can grow again.

Deforestation has done more than just deface some of the most beautiful natural landscapes in Costa Rica. Soil erosion has actually created deserts in the province of Guanacaste, where the average temperature has increased by approximately 10°C. During the dry season, water for domestic and industrial consumption becomes scarcer. Some rivers dry up, endangering much of their flora and fauna. During the rainy season, floods cause the most extensive damage.

**Environmental Conservation**

Starting in the sixties, many grassroots environmental movements sprang up worldwide to counteract mass deforestation, realizing the importance of protecting natural resources. These groups viewed the United States National Park System as the basic model for conservation. However, since the population of tiny Costa Rica doubled within 20 years (1950-1970) and was distributed evenly throughout the country, the forest conservation project was seen as a threat to the prosperity of farmers and breeders. Therefore, environmentalists had to find a good reason for the population to cooperate in protecting the forest, while maintaining their livelihood. Tourism was the answer. Tourism and farming were seen as more profitable than farming alone and, and blending the two could better protect nature. These economic activities were thus combined in long-term resource management or "sustainable development", in which most of the population of Costa Rica is involved.

And so, since the 1970s, protecting nature has become a national priority. Almost 25% of the territory is now protected (through parks and reserves), which corresponds to the percentage of uncleared or unused territory. Costa Rica is ranked first in the world for having the highest percentage of protected land and one of the first countries in the world to have practiced ecotourism.

## Fauna

Because of its microclimates and geographical location on the Central American isthmus, Costa Rica has the greatest variety of animal species in the world. Biodiversity or the variety of animal species, is measured by counting the number of species per 10,000 square kilometres. Thus, according to the *World Resources Institute* (1995), Costa Rica is the biodiversity capital of the world, with 615 species (mammals and birds) identified in 10,000 square kilometres. Even a country as large as the United States (104 species) has six times fewer varieties of animal species in a given territory than Costa Rica.

Thus, you don't have to go too far in Costa Rica to observe animals fully adapted to and thus thriving in their environment. In this tiny corner of the planet, you can discover some of the 15,000 species of butterfly, 850 species of birds (a true birdwatchers' paradise), 208 species of mammals, 220 species of reptiles, 34,000 species of insects, 130 species of freshwater fish and 160 species of amphibians. Some of these species are indigenous to Costa Rica: 41 species of amphibians, 24 species of reptiles, 16 species of freshwater fish, 6 species of birds and 5 species of mammals.

Some of the many animals that you may see in Costa Rica include monkeys (white-faced capuchins, howler monkeys and spider monkeys), sloths, agoutis, coatis, white-tailed deer, iguanas, lizards, toads, vermillon-coloured poison dart frogs, crocodiles and caimans. Timid mammals such as coyotes, anteaters, tapirs and large felines (jaguars, pumas, ocelots) flee at the sight of humans, but sometimes leave their tracks behind. The country also has several species of snakes, including vipers, boa constrictors and the fearsome "spearhead", known as *terciopelo* in Costa Rican.

Four species of sea turtles visit the beaches: the leatherback turtle, the largest sea turtle in the world; Ridley's turtle; Hawksbill turtle and the Pacific green turtle. It is fascinating to watch a female leatherback turtle lay its eggs on the Playa Grande of the Parque Nacional Marino Las Baulas (Guanacaste).

Just like tourists, several species of bird from North America head south to Costa Rica for the winter; including swallows, warblers, bunting and thrushes.

Costa Rica has so many birds that new species are identified each year. Toucans and parakeets come in all shapes and sizes, and their colourful plumage is dazzling. The saffron toucanet and majestic scarlet macaws are some of the most beautiful birds in the world, and are easy to spot in certain regions of the country. But the bird that turns the most heads is the beautiful quetzal. Indeed, many of the world's ornithologists travel to Costa Rica just to observe it. This relatively large bird (almost 35 cm tall), with its long emerald tail measuring up to 60 centimetres, lives high up in the canopy of the rainforest, such as in the Monteverde region.

# HISTORY

## The Pre-Columbian Period

When one imagines pre-Columbian settlements in Central America, what comes to mind most often are the Mayan pyramids of the Yucatan Peninsula, or the pomp and circumstance surrounding the Aztec ruler in the capital of Tenochtitlan (Mexico). The empires built up by these civilizations were located in territories much further north than Costa Rica. However, this does not mean that Costa Rica didn't have any great civilizations before the arrival of the Spaniards – in fact, quite the contrary was true.

Humans first settled in what is now Costa Rica occurred over 10,000 years ago. Different native civilizations with their own social and economic structure came from either north or south (via what is now Nicaragua and Panama), and gradually settled in the area. Nomadic hunters roamed the east coast, while sedentary groups settled in the interior and on the west coast. These last people practised agriculture and acquired advanced craftsmanship techniques, especially those in the interior, as is evidenced by pottery, metal and gold objects found during 20th-century excavations. In fact, there were goldsmiths in Costa Rica 1,000 years before the Spaniards had even discovered gold.

These groups were never very numerous, and there were barely more than 20,000 native people by the time the Europeans arrived. This low population was probably due to the nature of the land: at times mountainous, at times swampy, it did not make Costa Rica a very hospitable environment to support a large population. Geographical features also explain why there was almost no mixing between the populations of the north and south of this part of the Central American isthmus.

Unfortunately, little else is known about these pre-Columbian civilizations, nor is there any trace of written records or conflicts that could have led one tribe to defeat another and set up the basis for an empire. Therefore, retracing these their way of life is more a task for archeologists than for historians, and a matter of speculation rather than a narrative.

The country's most interesting archeological site, Monumento Nacional Guayabo (see p 119), is about 50 kilometres from San José. The site contains the remains of an ancient city, which existed many centuries before the common era, and was first inhabited by one or more nomadic groups, then the Corobicis, and finally by the most advanced society of the Nahuatl, who came from Mexico. At its peak, the city had a population of 10,000.

Archeologists are puzzled by the different-sized, perfectly spherical granite spheres found in the southwest of the country, particularly on Isla del Caño and in the Palmar region (see p 346). Although some claim that they are the work of the Chibchas (a group that lived in the southern part of the Pacific coast), no one is entirely sure of their origin or purpose.

Archeological findings in the northwestern part of the country, more particularly in the Nicoya peninsula, reveal that the local population traded with the more northerly civilizations well before the common era. The development of trade inevitably led to the settlement of this area by Costa Rica's largest native civilization, the Chorotegas. Their culture is similar to that of the Aztecs and Mayas, and not surprisingly so, since the Chorotegas fled from southern Mexico around 1325 (*chorotegas* means "runaway"). They practised agriculture and grew mainly legumes, corn and squash, but unlike Costa Rica's previous civilizations, the Chorotega had a written language as well as a calendar. They also had a complex social system in which priests and nobles formed the ruling class. At the very bottom of the social scale were slaves snatched from neighbouring tribes who were forced to perform hard labour or, even worse, used as human sacrifice. Chorotega art is among the country's most interesting, known particularly for its stylized jade pieces. Many of these have been preserved and most are on display in San José's jade museum (see p 76).

## After Christopher Columbus

After being commissioned by King Ferdinand and Queen Isabella of Spain to find a westward passage to the orient and all of its riches, Christopher Columbus accidentally discovered the Americas when he landed on the island of Santo-Domingo (Hispanola) in 1492. In 1502, while on his fourth expedition, a storm damaged his rig and forced him land at Cariari Bay.

This is how Central America and Costa Rica were "discovered", though natives had been there for a thousand years preceding the arrival of the Spanish. Columbus was surely impressed by the lush vegetation, because he baptized the country *Huerta*, which means "garden" in Spanish. The coastal natives gave him a warm welcome, and showered him with gifts of a certain precious yellow metal coveted by Europeans: gold.

Ferdinand of Spain decided to colonize the new territories and convert the natives to Christianity in order to procure their gold. In 1506, he named Diego de Nicuesa governor of the new colony and put him at the head of a new expedition. However, things took a turn for the worst the minute Nicuesa and his men landed in Panama. They had to head north, across impossible terrain and through inhospitable climate. Their morale fell quickly, and many troops either mutinied or died of tropical diseases. To make matters worse, relations between the natives and Spaniards worsened, and the latter were subject to repeated surprise attacks. Spain did not gain anything from Nicuesa's efforts, other than the realization that this region of Central America would be difficult to conquer.

In 1522, Gil González Davila tried to conquer and colonize the region. At first, his expedition met with more success than Nicuesa's, because he managed to find gold. Convinced that he had found Eldorado, he changed the country's name from La Huerta to *Costa Rica*, the "rich coast". However, Davila was unable to colonize the area, because disease and hardship claimed the lives of many of his men.

These failed early expeditions caused the Spanish conquistadors to lose interest in Costa Rica for a while. Instead, they colonized the empire's other possessions, which they deemed Eldorados; namely Peru and Mexico. Colonizing Costa Rica only resumed in the second half of the 16th century, when King Philip II of Spain sent missionaries to convert the natives to Christianity. However, this proved to be no easy task, since the native population had decreased significantly during the Spanish absence from Costa Rica. Defenceless against the viruses brought over by the Europeans, they had been decimated by smallpox and tuberculosis. Those who managed to survive fled to the valleys hidden deep in the interior. In fact, only the Chorotegas of the Nicoya Peninsula remained when Costa Rica's new governor, Juan Vásquez de Coronado, arrived in 1562.

## Coronado

The new governor, Juan Vásquez de Coronado, showed more interest in Costa Rica than his predecessors. He explored the country's interior and discovered the Central Valley, which he decided to colonize because of its better climate and fertile volcanic soil. Thus, in 1563, he built Cartago, Costa Rica's first town.

The priests accompanying Coronado were not the only people frustrated by the lack of natives, whom they sought to convert. The soldiers also needed more slave labour to make lands granted to them under the *Encomienda* system profitable. Because they could not find enough natives to work the land and were far from the slave markets, the governor and settlers had to work the land themselves. They practised subsistence agriculture, unlike the thriving plantations of neighbouring colonies.

The Coronado colony was also very isolated geographically. In other regions of Central America, the Spanish were concentrated along the coasts, which provided trade routes. Costa Ricans, on the other hand, lived in the country's interior, several hours or days from the coast. Mountains and forests further hindered contact with the outside world. This isolation even forced the settlers to use cocoa beans as currency for some time. The Spaniards soon discovered that, unlike other New World colonies, Costa Rica had very few precious metals in its soil.

Not surprisingly, the colony grew slowly. In fact, it was to take over 250 years for its population to reach 70,000. Once again, Spain lost interest in Costa Rica and abandoned its flock of settlers in the midst of the jungle. Cut off from the outside world, Costa Ricans developed their own society, more egalitarian than those of other Spanish colonies. This was primarily the result of having no social classes, since almost everyone in the Central Valley made a living from farming. While other regions in Central and South America eventually achieved the status of intendants (*intendencias*) under the Spanish crown, Costa Rica remained under the rule of the Captaincy-General of Guatemala and of the Bishopric of León in Nicaragua. Just to show how isolated these settlers were, for over a century and a half, Cartago was the only town in the Central Valley!

Gradually, however, other towns were established. Heredia and Cubujuquie were founded in 1717, and San José twenty years later. Alajuela was not established until 1782.

The coastal regions of Costa Rica, experienced a somewhat different development. On the west coast, Nicaragua directly controlled Guanacaste. This allowed large agricultural plantations, similar to those in colonies further north, to be set up. On the Caribbean coast, settlers grew cocoa, and then tobacco. These very profitable crops could have made the region rich, but harvests would have had to be exported, which became impossible in 1665, when Spain closed down all the region's ports in an attempt to discourage piracy. The result was exactly the opposite of what was intended, since the coast was then clear for pirates and smugglers to thrive.

## The 19th Century

Sparsely populated, difficult to access, and with no riches to speak of, Costa Rica never really interested colonial authorities, be they from Guatemala, Mexico, or Madrid. Costa Rica's towns were thus left to the country's elite to govern. This relative indifference did not bother settlers, who never really made a formal demand for independence. There was not even much excitement in the streets of San José when the news spread of the liberation of Spanish colonies starting on September 15, 1821. Costa Rican settlements were still so isolated that the news, brought by mule, was only heard a month later.

The initial response of Heredia and Cartago to the liberation movement was to join the new empire of Mexico. But, in 1823, the other former colonies of Central America opted for the creation of a federation with Guatemala City as its capital. The issue of joining the empire became a hot debate in Costa Rica. In San José and Alajuela, a Republican party called for joining the new federation. Heredia and Cartago opposed this. Talks broke down and a civil war broke out the same year, from which the Republicans in Ochomogo emerged victorious. The towns of Costa Rica therefore joined the federation, but remained fully autonomous. The Republicans chose San José as the capital of the new province, putting an end to Cartago's two-and-a-half century reign. A year later, Guanacaste separated from Nicaragua and joined Costa Rica.

The first head of the new province, Juan Mora Fernández, ruled for 12 years, during which he ushered in peace and laid the foundations for Costa Rican independence. To stimulate the local economy, Fernández took a risk in growing coffee and managed to attract foreign buyers, particularly from Great Britain. However, an uprising in 1835 pitted San José against the province's other towns. The capital city, headed by a new dictator, Braulio Carillo, won. In 1838, he led Costa Rica to independence. Carillo was not the head of state for long, since he was ousted by Honduran General Francisco Morazán in 1842. The latter turned out to be even less fortunate than his predecessor; his military ambitions led to his overthrow and execution less than a year later.

In the meantime, Costa Rican coffee was successfully breaking into the market, and the response was exceptionally good. The development of the country's ports on both the Pacific and the Caribbean coasts was necessary to export the coffee harvest. The coffee bean was seen as the *grano de oro*, or "golden bean", and coffee plantations sprang up all over the country. The success of the coffee industry led to the modernization of Costa Rica. However, it also made the coffee barons, or *cafetaleros*, so powerful that they were able to seize political control of the country, replacing Costa Rica's first elected president, José Maria Castro, with one of their own, Juan Rafael Mora.

It is argued that it was only during President Mora's second mandate that Costa Rica really assumed its national identity. This was precipitated by a very bizarre crisis: the excessive ambition of an adventurer from the United States by the name of William Walker, who tried to conquer Central America (see p 23). President Mora was not any more successful than Morazán, the latter of whom Costa Ricans remember with resentment. Instead of dealing with the cholera epidemic that killed one out of every 10 Costa Ricans, he tampered with ballot boxes to stay in power. But when he attempted to break the coffee barons' monopoly on the nation's finances, they ran him out of power and executed him when he attempted to regain it.

Shortly thereafter, rivalry for political control of the country broke out between the coffee barons. In April 1870, General Tomás Guardia seized power and held onto it for 12 years. His dictatorship was considered very beneficial for Costa Rica, because he managed to curb the coffee barons' power by taxing them and using that money toward the common good. Guardia was also responsible for social innovations; most notably, he abolished the death penalty and made primary schooling free and compulsory for everyone. Thus, it became evident to Costa Ricans that peace brought prosperity.

Guardia also wanted to build a railway between the Central Valley and the Caribbean Sea to replace transportation by mule. However, such a large-scale project was beyond the country's finances, and foreign capital was sought.

The project interested Henry Meigg, a financier from the United States who raised the necessary funds to begin construction of the railway. Due to a lack of local manpower, cheap labour was imported from China, Italy and Jamaica. Despite these efforts, Meigg could not complete the project: climate, topography, dense forests and wild animals stood between the central plateau and the coast. In addition, the

## The Era of William Walker

Of all the people who played major roles in Central American history, few have gained as much notoriety as William Walker. Academically gifted, Walker attended universities in the United States and Europe. He became a lawyer, a doctor, and then gold prospector. Around 1850, he finally found his true vocation – as a mercenary. During this era, disagreements between slave-owners and abolitionists were tearing the United States apart. Walker sided with the former, and set out to conquer territories where he would legalize slavery to reinforce the position of the states of the Union, where this practice was tolerated.

He first conquered the Baja Peninsula in Mexico, where he declared himself president. He remained there for a year, but soon returned to the United States, where he was arrested for violating the peace with Mexico. However, thanks to friends in high places, he was acquitted.

He re-established contact with his sponsors, this time for an even more daring plot: to conquer Central America and build a canal in southern Nicaragua, which would link the Atlantic and Pacific Oceans. Eventually, the conquered territories were to be annexed to the United States. The idea of opening a canal won him the support of President Buchanan and financier Cornelius Vanderbilt.

Walker landed in Nicaragua in 1855 with approximately 50 men. Things got off to a bad start, and he had to wait for reinforcements from California before succeeding in conquering the country and declaring himself its president. President Mora of Costa Rica saw the invasion as a threat to the young country's independence. He was not alone in his thinking, and within a week, 5,000 men from various backgrounds answered his call to arms with old rifles, machetes, and pickaxes. Though they were not trained soldiers, they reached Guanacaste after two weeks and defeated 200 Americans at the Hacienda Santa Rosa, on March 20, 1856. The militia then pursued Walker through Nicaragua. Cornered, Walker finally found asylum aboard an American warship.

Walker didn't stay in exile for long, however, and attempted to conquer Honduras in 1860. This time his luck completely ran out. The Hondurans put an end to his career – and his life. William Walker is still reviled throughout Central America – his enormous ambition resulted in the deaths of nearly 200,000 people.

state found itself heavily in debt. Construction stopped until Meigg's nephew, Minor C. Keith, arrived on the scene and proposed an innovative solution. He paid off the government's debt in exchange for land along the railway, which finally opened in 1890. But what did he do with this land? The answer – bananas! Keith used the land to plant bananas, which quickly became Costa Rica's second most valuable export.

Minor C. Keith founded the United Fruit Company, notorious for its economic and political role throughout Central

America. His and several other major international corporations quickly bought up the entire banana market, creating stiff competition for small local producers.

## The 20th Century

There is one event that singlehandedly changed political behaviour in Costa Rica before the turn of the century: in 1889, Joaquín Rodríguez won the national elections fair and square, but the outgoing president, Bernardo Soto, refused to give up his seat. The people took to the streets in protest, and Soto relinquished his position. For the first time in the country's history, democracy had been achieved in its truest form. But democracy wasn't Rodríguez's strongest point, nor was it that of his immediate successors, Rafael Iglesias and González Visquez. They had the habit of dissolving the legislature, appointing their successor and exiling their rivals – anything for the *presidente* to stay in power longer.

The first real "test" of democracy occurred in 1913, when none of the candidates acquired a majority in the elections through direct suffrage. Consequently, the legislative assembly appointed Alfredo González Flores as president, even though he was not a candidate. General Federico Tinoco Granados, wouldn't hear of this and seized power in 1917. His dictatorship quickly rendered him unpopular, and even the United States refused to recognize his authority. The army and the navy successfully overthrew him in 1919.

Democracy prevailed again when Rafael Calderón Guardia became president in 1940. He approved a new labour code, improved the social system, and managed to expand industry for the war effort. However, like his predecessors, he became power-hungry. The elections saw Teodoro Picado, a weaker candidate, come to power – probably through a setup. In 1948, Calderón lost the election and claimed electoral fraud, but he could not prove it because a fire destroyed the ballots, and Picado nullified the results.

The controversy over the elections of 1948 sparked a short but bloody civil war, which claimed the lives of several thousand people. This was the opportunity that "Don Pepe" José Figueres Ferrer, Calderón's longtime opponent, was waiting for. Don Pepe overthrew his rival and proclaimed himself president. He used his presidency to improve the democratic system by adopting new social measures: nationalization of the banks, universal right to vote, company taxes, etc. Tired of having the army interfere in politics and disturb the general peace, he abolished it. Military barracks were transformed into fine arts museums, and the army's budget was re-allocated to education. Once his reforms were implemented, he gave back power to the real elected president, Otilio Ulate. Like any good democrat, he waited to run for president in the 1953 elections. He won and was even re-elected a second time (1970-1974). He died a national hero in 1990.

The Civil War of 1948 allowed Costa Rica to consolidate its democracy after decades of abuse. Calderón took this opportunity to run for a second presidency in 1962. He lost, however, because the electorate was from a newer generation.

More stable, the Costa Rican government was able to play a greater role in the country's social and economic affairs. The government set up a welfare state system based on that of other democracies. This steered the country in the right direction economically during the 1960s and 1970s, but Costa Rica made the same mistake as its Latin American neighbours by borrowing foreign money for its national development projects.

Costa Rica was doubly hard hit by the second oil crisis of the 1970s, which caused coffee and banana prices to fall drastically. An agricultural crisis ensued, and the government, heavily in debt, could no longer afford to keep up its overinflated bureaucracy.

At the same time, Central American peace was rapidly collapsing. Costa Rica's neighbours were swept up by a wave of political turmoil and terrorism. Each time a government was overthrown by a military junta in either Nicaragua, Guatemala or El Salvador, refugees poured into Costa Rica. The country simultaneously welcomed certain guerilla groups to use its soil as a training ground. President Luis Alberto Monge's policy of neutrality became very strained and, in 1985, Costa Rica even froze diplomatic relations with Nicaragua.

The following year, Oscar Arias Sánchez, a political scientist, became president. He immediately began working on a solution to the problems plaguing his country and this region of the Americas. He proposed a peace plan to his neighbours in February 1987, which they reluctantly accepted. It came into affect in August 1987. Shortly thereafter, Sánchez received the Nobel Peace Prize for his treaty.

Economically, Costa Rica was not recovering very well from the recession brought on by the oil crises of the '70s. Sanchez temporarily suspended payments on the debt, which hovered around US$5 billion, and asked his creditors to restructure the repayment schedule. On the eve of the millennium, Costa Rica has become a solid democracy, but one whose economy is still very shaky.

## POLITICAL ADMINISTRATION

Although Costa Rica is a small country, it has seven provinces: San José, Alajuela, Cartago, Heredia, Limón, Puntarenas and Guanacaste. These provinces are sub-divided into cantons, which are further sub-divided into districts. The provinces have very limited powers and cannot levy taxes, and are headed by a governor, appointed by the president. Therefore, Costa Rica is considered to be a strongly centralized federation.

Costa Rice has a presidential government system. Every four years, a president of the republic, 2 vice-presidents and 57 representatives who will make up the legislative assembly are elected. In order to prevent potentially explosive situations such as the ones that occurred in 1948 and keep any political party from getting too powerful, the president can no longer run for a second term, either immediately following the first term, or later. In fact, there is very little difference in ideology between the two major parties who alternately take control: the PLN (Partido de Liberación Nacional) is a type of social democratic party, and the PUSC (Partido Unidad Social Cristiana) is a Christian democratic party.

The Costa Rican constitution is based on the principle of separating the powers of government between the executive, legislative and judiciary. As in most western democracies, there is much friction between the executive and legislative branches of the state.

According to the constitution, the legislative assembly adopts laws, controls the budget, and has the power to veto presidential decisions with a two-thirds majority vote. As a result, many presidents have had to rule by decree as a last resort in order to govern effectively. The advantage of such a system is that it forces the parties to work on solutions together.

The legislative assembly also appoints 24 judges to Costa Rica's supreme court. A judge has an eight-year mandate, which is automatically renewed at the end of the term unless the assembly votes against it. In turn, these judges name magistrates to the lower courts.

In Costa Rica, one out of four employed persons works for the government. The country's public employees are well known for their love for bureaucratic red tape. Having to line up at a series of counters can try tourists' nerves. To avoid this problem, hire a *despachante*, a person who is very familiar with the workings of government bureaucracy and who will take your place and stand in the right lines for you. Unfortunately, corruption is still a real problem, even if it has not reached the proportions found elsewhere in Latin America.

Since its very beginnings, Costa Rica has worked toward the democratic ideal, even though it has been a bumpy ride. Its main advantage over its neighbours is that the distinctions between the different social classes are not as evident. Whereas other Spanish colonies exploited the population by establishing overlords and enslaving the poor, Costa Rican society has been a place where everyone has had to earn his or her own lot.

Costa Rica also differs from its neighbours because it was the first Latin American country to abolish slavery and establish a democracy right after obtaining its independence in 1838. Fifty years later, honest and free elections were held, and it will be years before the neighbouring republics can make a similar claim. Since February 1998, the country has been run by Manuel Rodríguez and his party, the PUSC (Partido Unidad Social Cristiana).

## ECONOMY

Its political system, society, history and economy have made Costa Rica the country with the most egalitarian distribution of weallh in Latin America. Costa Rica's social security system is the most elaborate in Central America, and is so efficient that the country's life expectancy rate is the highest in the region: 72 years for men, and 77 for women.

Each region of Costa Rica has a different economic activity: the coffee industry is concentrated in the Central Valley, the banana industry on the Caribbean coast, cattle rearing for meat production (which accounts for a modest percentage of Costa Rican exports) in the province of Guanacaste, and palm oil in the southern part of the Pacific coast. Consumer goods, such as clothing, ornamental plants and cut flowers are mostly produced in the urban areas of the Central Valley.

The coffee industry is not dominated by a few large coffee-producing corporations; it is mostly carried out by many small coffee farmers. In fact, over half of the coffee producers are small family operations. This is in stark contrast with the banana industry, which is run by a few big multinationals. Bananas and coffee still represent over 40% of Costa Rica's exports.

## The Flower Industry

The flowers and ferns that decorate the bouquets that you buy at florists in North America and Europe probably came from Costa Rica. Indeed, these plants usually grow on the mountainsides at altitudes too high for coffee cultivation. These dense crops, grown in greenhouses covered in green and black tarpaulins to protect them, can be seen on the road to the Poás Volcano.

Costa Rica's foreign currency revenues fluctuate greatly due to the limited range of export products. Markets are very volatile in the country's vital sectors, i.e., banana and coffee growing. It's a buyers' market in which suppliers have very little impact on the prices. This is why Costa Rica's national debt reached almost US$5 billion at the end of the 1980s: a fortune with respect to the country's ability to repay.

For the last few decades, the country has been trying to diversify its economy. Although mineral resources are abundant, lots of capital is needed to exploit them. As of yet, only small deposits have been tapped into. Christopher Columbus's dreams of mountains of gold seem to be just that – dreams.

Forests are still being cut down at an alarming rate. Today, only one-third of the original forest remains, the area having been cleared primarily for pasture and agricultural purposes. Deforestation has had a serious impact on the country's climate. In Guanacaste, for example, the dry season is getting progressively longer and more severe.

Despite deforestation, Costa Rica harbours and incredible wealth of natural ecosystems. Over 5% of the world's biodiversity is found here. In the last 20 years, many officials have become more aware of the importance of protecting the country's many waters and green spaces. Forests, marshes, nesting areas for endangered species, coral seabeds and other ecosystems are now rigorously protected. Thanks to these efforts, ecotourism has really taken off in Costa Rica, and is developing at about the same rate as leisure tourism. Vacationers mostly come for the beaches: Costa Rica has about 1,200 kilometres of coastline and the water is reportedly always warm and pleasant in both the Pacific Ocean and Caribbean Sea. Therefore, it is not surprising that every region in the country is undergoing a boom in tourism. In 1993 alone, tourists spent over US$600 million in Costa Rica.

Moreover, because leisure tourism developed later than in some other countries of the region, it is relatively cheaper here than in the Caribbean, for example. But Costa Rica is reluctant to develop large-scale resorts, such as those in Cancún or Acapulco, Mexico. Any proposal to build one of these complexes in Costa Rica would cause a lot of controversy because of the harmful effects it might have on the environment. This is why small tour agencies, which provide accommodation, food and recreational services, account for a very significant percentage of the tourist industry. Tens of thousands of North Americans who have moved to Costa Rica have also contributed to this steadily developing market based on the country's wonderful climate. The ICT (Instituto Costaricense de Turismo) and Pro

Imagen, a private tourism association in Costa Rica, are presently trying to turn ecotourism into a sustainable development.

Costa Rica is also trying to improve its economic ties with other countries. Costa Rica's main trading partner is the United States, for both exports and imports. However, so as not to become entirely dependant on this trading partner, and to expand its markets, Costa Rica signed a free-trade agreement with Mexico in 1995.

Finally, the Costa Rican government has begun to exploit another priceless resource: its population. Costa Rica's education system has created a well-educated and highly skilled work force. And because Costa Ricans are willing to work for less than their North American and European counterparts, they are being increasingly sought out by major companies that are changing the world economy, such as the communications technologies company, Intel. Other markets are also being developed, including recycling: tests are currently being conducted to transform banana- and palm-tree leaves into paper products.

One day, Costa Rica will see the fruits of its economic endeavours, but this day must come soon: Costa Rica must quickly find a way to balance its trade deficit (more imports than exports), or its social welfare system, which has been painstakingly developed for over a century, could collapse.

## PEOPLE AND RELIGION

### Population

Costa Rica has a population of approximately 3,500,000 people, over half (50.2%) of which is urbanized. Costa Rica's ancestry is very different from that of other Central American countries: 80% are of European descent (mainly from Spain), 15% are *mestizo* (a mix of European and native ancestry), 3% are Afro-Caribbean (found mostly on the Caribbean coast, in the Province of Limón) and 2% are Asian. Natives make up less than 1% of the population: they number about 15,000, are scattered in twenty-two communities, and are isolated from large urban centres and mainstream society.

With 69 inhabitants per square kilometre, Costa Rica has the third highest population density in Central America after El Salvador (275.5 inh./km²) and Guatemala (100.4 inh./km²). Its population density is much higher than that in Canada (2.98 inh./km²) and the United States (28.8 inh./km²), but lower than France's (106.6 inh./km²). Approximately 60% of the population lives in the Central Valley, where the largest cities in the country are located (San José, Cartago, Heredia and Alajuela).

Spanish is the most widely spoken language in the country. Because elementary education is free and compulsory, under 10% of the population is illiterate today, ranking Costa Rica with industrialized countries. Lastly, life expectancy of Costa Ricans is 76.3 years, one of the highest in the world.

### Religion

Catholicism is still the most practised religion (95%), followed by Protestantism in a distant second place (3%). Although the Catholicism is the state religion (the Catholic Church is still funded by public money), religious tolerance was made official by the constitution of 1873.

## ARCHITECTURE AND LANDSCAPING

Costa Rica is still building itself architecturally. Costa Rican buildings (hotels, houses, clinics, commercial spaces, office buildings) are set up in such a way as to bring the outdoors inside, even more so in the countryside. Urban residential dwellings, especially the more traditional ones, often have "closed yards", with the living room facing a small atrium.

Urban planning is rather simple, especially in the oldest parts of the city. In the middle of the city, there is a central plaza laid out with green spaces, which serves as a social meeting place and is surrounded by a church and administrative and commercial buildings. Streets follow a consistent grid-like pattern (city blocks of 100 m), making it easy to find your way around. Instead in numbered addresses, addresses are given by intersections or by distances of metres from a certain landmark.

The landscaping of the central square follows a standard design: an architectural structure at the centre of the park reserved for shows and festivities, a French garden around it (geometrical, with formal separation of spaces) spreads all the way to the street with numerous benches, paved surfaces for strolling and green spaces for rest and relaxation. Certain streets around this park may be closed to traffic during festivities. Parks confer a certain charm upon Costa Rica's lively town centres, but the construction of North-American-style shopping centres outside the downtown core is threatening the traditional way of life by luring Costa Ricans away from the central plazas.

Apart from San José, which has a handful of high-rises, most cities in Costa Rica are of modest size. Due to the social system, there are few if any shantytowns, but many places reflect their lack of prosperity in their simple architecture and poor landscaping. Plus an elaborate architecture may not be such a big concern in Costa Rica because of the many earthquakes that have destroyed much of the country's architectural heritage (which is the case for Cartago). But there are still many beautiful things to discover.

In certain areas, land that was once jungle has been turned into farmland for grazing and agriculture. So don't expect to walk out of the Liberia airport and into lush tropical forest! In Guanacaste, you have to travel for miles for this – but it's well worth the trip!

Like many countries in the world, Costa Rica is being largely urbanized. The number of cars is constantly growing. The government is trying to deal with these new realities as best it can. For now, the highway system is still in its initial stages and concentrated around the capital, whereas the rest of the roads in the country are of varying condition, from the relatively well-maintained two-lane highway (which is primarily the Interamericana) all the way down to the dirt road linking a hotel, a park or a village, which is often impassable during the rainy season. Sometimes you have to ford a river or cross a waterway on an incredibly narrow bridge (sometimes single lane). City roads are not necessarily any better – so watch out!

## ART AND CULTURE

Costa Ricans' fondness of art and culture is evident in the many cultural centres and museums found throughout the country, especially in San José. These include the Museo Nacional (see p 76), the Museo de Arte Costarricense (see p 72), and the basement level of the Plaza de la Cultura (see p 76). Costa Rica has a rich Latin American and *Tican* artistic and cultural scene, and immersing yourself in it is a great way of getting to know the country and region. The Costa Rican Department of Culture contributes (despite its budget constraints) to the development of cultural activities by funding most forms of art (theatre, music, opera, dance, literature, poetry, sculpture, painting, cinema, etc.)

Musically, Costa Rica has all the warm, steamy rhythms of Latin-American music – salsa, merengue, cumbia, reggae and Latino rock – so you can let loose! Costa Rica has also carved out its place in classical music with the great 19th century tenor, Melicio Salazar. Since then, classical music has grown in popularity and the country even has two symphony orchestras that became internationally renowned in the 1970s: the National Symphony Orchestra and the National Youth Orchestra.

Costa Rica has produced some famous names in the literary world, such as poets Roberto Brenes Mesén, Carmen Naranjo and Eunice Odio; writers Carlos Gagini, Quince Duncan and José León Sánchez; authors Manuel González Zeledón and Pio Víquez in costumbrismo (short stories based on local legends) and Carmen Lyra for children's stories. Their works are widely available in bookstores throughout the country.

Because of centuries of isolation during the colonization of Latin America, Costa Rica has produced an original style of painting and sculpture, which is reflected in the works of artists Luisa González de Saenz, Enrique Echandi and Juan Rafael Chacón.

### Language

Costa Rican Spanish is the same as that spoken all over Latin America, but with a different accent and expressions unique to the country. Nevertheless, people here will still understand you if you speak the Spanish from one of the regions of Spain. If you do not speak Spanish, Costa Rica has several language schools where you can learn it. Some people speak English, which is taught as a second language in highschool, mainly in the tourist areas. In this guide, we have tried to point out places where you can be understood in English.

If you would like to give your Spanish a try, refer to the small conversation guide at the end of this book on p 376.

# PRACTICAL INFORMATION

This chapter contains all the information you need to plan your trip to Costa Rica, and to get by once you are there.

## ENTRANCE FORMALITIES

To enter Costa Rica, citizens of Canada, the United States and the European Union only need a passport that is valid for the length of their stay. No visas are necessary for stays of under 90 days. Citizens of other countries are advised to consult the nearest Costa Rican embassy or consulate. Because entrance requirements can change without notice, it's a good idea to get the most up-to-date information before you leave.

Officials can ask to see your passport or tourist card at any time during your stay. It is therefore a good idea to keep a photocopy of the key pages of your passport and other important papers, and to write down your passport number and its expiry date. This way, the documents will be much easier to replace if they are lost or stolen. If this should occur, contact your country's consulate or embassy to have a new passport issued.

### Departure Tax

Each person leaving Costa Rica must pay a departure tax of US$16. The tax is collected at the airport when you check in for your return flight. Remember to have this amount in cash, because credit cards are not accepted.

# EMBASSIES AND CONSULATES

## In Costa Rica

All embassies in Costa Rica are in San José.

**Australia**
Plaza Polanco Torre B, Col. Los Morales, Mexico P.F., ☎395-9092.

**Austria**
Av. 4, Calle 36/38, ☎255-3007.

**Canada**
Calle 3, Av. 1, ☎255-3522.

**Germany**
Rohrmoser, ☎232-5533 or ☎232-5450.

**Great Britain**
Edificio Centro Colón, Paseo Colón, Centro Colón, ☎258-2025.

**Guatemala**
Guadeloupe, ☎233-5283.

**Italy**
White house on the corner, 5th entrance of the Barrio Los Yoses, ☎224-9415, 234-2326 or 224-6574.

**Mexico**
Calle 5, Av. 5, ☎233-8874.

**Netherlands**
Los Yoses, ☎234-0949.

**Nicaragua**
La California, ☎233-8747.

**Panama**
San Pedro, ☎225-0667.

**Spain**
Calle 32, between Avenida 2 and Paseo Colón, ☎222-1933, 221-7005 or 222-5745.

**Sweden**
La Uruca, ☎232-8549.

**Switzerland**
Centro Colón, ☎233-0052.

**United States**
Apartado 920-1200 Pavas, ☎220-3939.

## Costa Rican Embassies and Consulates Abroad

**Australia**
30 Clarence Street, Sidney NSW 2000, mailing address; PO Box 2513 NSW 2001 Sidney, ☎(612) 9261-1177, ⇄(612) 9261-2953.

**Austria**
Schloegasse 10/2, A-1120 Vienna, ☎(431) 804-0537, ⇄(431) 804-9071.

**Belgium**
489 Av. Louise, Box 13, 1050 Brussels, ☎(02) 640-5541 or 640-5969, ⇄(02) 648-3192.

**Canada**
135 York Street, Suite 208, Ottawa, Ontario, ☎(613) 562-2855, ⇄(613) 562-2582.

1825 Boulevard René-Lévesque, Montréal, Québec, ☎(514) 393-1057, ⇄(514) 393-1624.

**Germany**
Langenbachstrasse 19, 53113 Bonn, ☎(228) 54.00.40, ⇄(228) 54.90.53.

**Great Britain**
Flat 1, 14 Lancaster Gate, London W2 3L, ☎(441) 71-706-8844, ⇄(441) 71-706-8655.

**Italy**
Via Bartolomeo Eustachio 22, Roma 00161, ☎(6-4) 425-1046 or 425-1042, ⇄(6-4) 425-1048.

**Norway and Sweden**
Skippergarten 33, 0154 Oslo, Norway, ☎(22) 425-823, ⇄(22) 330-408.

**Spain**
Paseo de la Castellana 164, 17-A 28046 Madrid, ☎(91) 345-9622 or 345-9521, ⇄(91) 345-6807.

**Switzerland**
Thunstrasse 150 E, 3074 Berne, ☎(31) 952-6230, ⇄(31) 952-6457.

**United States**
2112 "S" Street NW, Washington, DC 20008, ☎(202) 328-6628, ⇄(202) 265-4795.

## ENTERING THE COUNTRY

### By Plane

**Airports**

Costa Rica has two international airports: the Aeropuerto Internacional San Juan Santamaría and the Aeropuerto Daniel Oduber.

**Aeropuerto Internacional Juan Santamaría**

The Aeropuerto Internacional Juan Santamaría *(☎441-4737)* is the country's main airport. Located in the middle of Costa Rica, it is near the capital and receives flights from most major international airlines.

The airport is located on the General Cañas Highway which leads directly to San José, the country's capital, which is only about 20 kilometres to the southeast. The airport is well-linked to the country's major transportation routes, so you can also easily access the beaches on the central Pacific coast to the west via this highway, or head directly to Guanacaste province on the Inter-American Highway. There are restaurants, a small souvenir and magazine shop, and a currency exchange counter at the airport. Taxis are always available: the fare to San José is about US$10. Hotel shuttle buses pick up passengers on time. Things generally run smoothly, and you'll be able clear customs and get out into the Costa Rican sunshine with no major hassles.

**Aeropuerto Daniel Oduber**

The Aeropuerto Daniel Oduber *(every day from 6am to 9pm, ☎667-0199 or 667-0032, ⇄667-0000)* is smaller and located in the country's northwest, in Guanacaste. It is only 17 kilometres south of the region's capital, Liberia, along the Santa Cruz highway. The airport has all the standard services (customs, narcotics inspection, bank services, etc.). Some airlines have connecting flights from the Juan Santamaría airport in the Central Valley. Some chartered flights from North America also land here, which saves travel time for visitors who only come for the beaches in this area.

**Other Airports**

Costa Rica has several other landing strips used mostly by domestic flights. The **Tobias Bolaños** airport *(☎232-8049)* in Pavas, a suburb of San José, is one of these, but there are several others near cities in remote areas (such as the Golfito airport in the south) or popular bathing areas along the coast (such as Playa Carrillo, near Playa Sámara in Guanacaste). These airfields are listed in the chapters of the regions in which they are located.

**Airlines**

The sales offices of **LACSA** *(Calle 1, Av. 5, Edificio Numar, ☎257-9444 or 296-0909, ⇌232-3372)* airlines are located near the intersection of Calle 1 and Avenida 1 in San José. This company flies to the major international destinations.

**Major International Airlines in San José**

**Air France**: Av. 1, Calle 4/6, ☎222-8811, ⇌223-4970.

**American Airlines**: Edificio Centro Cars, Calle 42, Av. 5, ☎257-1266, ⇌223-5213.

**British Airways**: Av. 7, Calle 7, ☎223-5648, ⇌223-4863.

**Continental Airlines**: 200 metres south, 300 metres east, and 50 metres north of the American embassy, ☎296-4911, ⇌296-4920.

**Copa**: Calle 1, Av. 5, ☎222-6640, ⇌221-6798.

**KLM**: Edificio Oficentro Ejecutivo, 50 metres south of the Contraloría, ☎220-4111, ⇌220-3092.

**Taca**: Calle 40, Av. 3, ☎222-1790, ⇌223-4238.

**United Airlines**: Sabana Sur, 50 metres south of the Contraloría, ☎220-4844, ⇌220-4855.

**Major Domestic Airlines**

Two large airlines handle most domestic flights in Costa Rica: **Sansa** *(Calle 24, Av. Ctl/1, ☎221-9414, ⇌255-2176)* is state-owned and uses the international airport, while **Travel Air** *(Terminal Internacional, Tobias Bolaños airport, ☎220-3054, ⇌220-0413)* is a private enterprise and flies out of the smaller Tobias Baños airport, in the suburbs west of the capital. Both companies have reasonable rates for visitors who want to travel around the country quickly. **Aero Costa Rica** *(west side of the Juan Pablo Segundo bridge, La Uruca, ☎296-1111, ⇌290-5848)*, **Aero Costa Sol** *(Juan Santamaría airport, ☎441-0922 or 441-1444, ⇌441-2671)* and **Aerotour** *(Tobias Bolaños airport, ☎323-1248, ⇌232-9192)* also offer domestic flights.

## By Boat

Costa Rica has major ports in each of its coastal regions. On the Pacific coast, the port of Caldera is 8 kilometres south of Puntarenas. In fact, it also just reopened its port to receive large cruise ships. Limón is the main port on the Caribbean coast. Yacht owners can also dock at various other marinas along the coast.

# FINDING YOUR WAY AROUND

## By Car

Travelling by car is the most feasible form of transportation, since you don't have to plan around bus schedules and you can always get exactly where you want to go.

Costa Rica has a good network of roads, even though there are few highways once you get further away from the capital. The secondary roads usually have two lanes, which occasionally merge as the road crosses a bridge. Other roads are often in poor condition, especially in villages, parks, and around the beaches, so it's important to drive with caution.

# Table of distances (km/mi)

## Via the shortest route

© ULYSSES

1 mile = 1.62 kilometres
1 kilometre = 0.62 miles

| | Ciudad Quesada | Golfito | Jacó | Liberia | Nicoya | Paso Canoas (Frontera Sur) | Peñas Blancas (Frontera Norte) | Puerto Limón | Puerto Viejo de Sarapiquí | Puntarenas | Quepos | San Isidro de El General |
|---|---|---|---|---|---|---|---|---|---|---|---|---|
| Ciudad Quesada | | | | | | | | | | | | |
| Golfito | 385/239 | | | | | | | | | | | |
| Jacó | 146/91 | 272/169 | | | | | | | | | | |
| Liberia | 186/115 | 465/288 | 193/120 | | | | | | | | | |
| Nicoya | 212/131 | 442/274 | 162/100 | 83/51 | | | | | | | | |
| Paso Canoas (Frontera Sur) | 389/241 | 53/33 | 284/176 | 470/291 | 452/280 | | | | | | | |
| Peñas Blancas (Frontera Norte) | 221/137 | 524/325 | 263/163 | 77/48 | 160/99 | 536/332 | | | | | | |
| Puerto Limón | 181/112 | 447/277 | 243/151 | 345/214 | 331/205 | 448/278 | 425/264 | | | | | |
| Puerto Viejo de Sarapiquí | 57/35 | 393/244 | 184/114 | 272/169 | 264/164 | 402/249 | 383/237 | 126/78 | | | | |
| Puntarenas | 111/69 | 334/207 | 79/49 | 136/84 | 118/73 | 355/220 | 211/131 | 246/153 | 173/107 | | | |
| Quepos | 119/74 | 195/121 | 78/48 | 265/164 | 243/151 | 209/130 | 334/207 | 337/209 | 254/157 | 154/95 | | |
| San Isidro de El General | 213/132 | 186/115 | 251/156 | 351/218 | 336/208 | 186/115 | 428/265 | 264/164 | 205/127 | 249/154 | 329/204 | |
| San José | 76/47 | 309/192 | 114/71 | 220/136 | 202/125 | 321/199 | 306/190 | 130/81 | 67/42 | 118/73 | 192/119 | 130/81 |

Example : The distance between Liberia and Puntarenas is 136km/84mi.

PRACTICAL INFORMATION

The **Inter-American Highway** (Carretera Interamericana) runs north and south through the country. This road begins on the west coast, but veers inland around San José. It is much used and well maintained.

Road conditions are variable: sometimes whole roads are unpaved, sometimes only sections are. Also, heavy downpours during the rainy season can affect the road surface and levelling, and road conditions can deteriorate rapidly.

Entrances to tourist attractions are not always easily visible from the road: you'll have to watch for them carefully. The same can be true for popular hotels and parks, which might also be badly signed out, or accessed by small, nondescript paths.

Keep in mind that "traffic" can include many different things in Costa Rica – not just cars! You might well find yourself sharing the road with single or herds of cows and sheep, people on horseback, cyclists and other unexpected companions. People often walk along the road, even on the shoulder of major thoroughfares. Also, watch for vehicles stopping suddenly right in front of you: buses often pick up passengers along roads, including highways. Be careful if you decide to stop somewhere along the way yourself (to admire the view or stretch your legs), since there are usually no shoulders or rest areas along the road.

If possible, avoid driving at night. The streets are not lit, and destinations are poorly signed out.

Service stations were once scarce in some areas, but this is most often no longer the case. However, it's a good idea to fill up your tank before setting off, just in case! A full tank of gas costs about US$15.

The finishing touches are being put on a new road that will make it easier to travel to the south. The Dominical-Palmar road runs along the Pacific coast, and is a blessing for truckers and anyone else in the transport industry because it makes it possible to avoid the many ups and downs of the older road through the central cordillera.

### Driving and the Highway Code

You will notice frequent signs along the road that warn *"Puente angosto adelante"* (narrow bridge ahead), so be careful! Also, respect all *"Ceda el paso"* (yield the right of way) and *"No hay paso"* (do not enter) and stop signs. One-way streets are indicated by arrows painted onto the pavement in the cities.

The word *"escuela"* (school) frequently appears on signs in villages, and is often accompanied with the added warning to *"despacio"*, or slow down.

Direction signs are not always consistent. They might suddenly discontinue, or appear right at the last minute. The numerous holes in the Inter-American Highway are not necessarily well indicated, either.

It is rare for cities to have special signs to indicate their names, so watch for the blue ICE signs which have the name of the town, as well as directions to public telephones or other regional means of communication, written on them.

### Parking

Try to park in busy, well-lit areas. In San José, however, take a taxi (very affordable) or park your car in one of the many *parqueos publicos* (public parking areas). Careful, though: some are open 24 hours a day, while others are not. Also, prices can vary from place to place.

Several establishments, especially in San José, provide patrolled parking areas. It is standard to tip the guard about 200 colons.

**Renting a Car**

Renting a car in Costa Rica is easy, and you can even do so at the airport as soon as you arrive. During the holidays, however (Christmas, Easter, etc. see p 50), it is important to reserve well in advance, especially for four-wheel drive vehicles. The legal driving age is 18, but most agencies will only rent to people 21 years old or more. It costs about US$275 to rent a basic car for a week. A four-wheel drive vehicle can cost up to $500 per week, which includes insurance coverage with a $750 deductable. Many agencies ask for an added $1,500 deposit (generally through your credit card). Some offer insurance plans without a deductable for an extra $8 to $10 a day. **Prego** *(☎221-8680, ⇌255-4492, pregomot@sol.racsa.ca.cr)* is a Costa Rican agency that has some inexpensive package deals.

Which vehicle you should choose depends on the length and nature of your trip. For example, if you take a two-week trip to remote and difficult to access areas, a vehicle with high suspension and good shock absorbers and traction (ideally, four-wheel drive) is essential. If you are only going between cities and stay on the better roads, a regular car will do.

If you want to switch cars along the way, you don't need to return to San José. You can have the rental agency deliver a car to you for a fee between $45 and $100, depending on where you are in the country.

Some cars have a registration tag in the rear window instead of a license plate. This includes many rental cars, as it makes it more difficult for potential thieves to identify whether the car is being driven by foreigners or not.

Car rental agencies in San José:

| | |
|---|---|
| Avis | ☎293-2222 |
| Budget | ☎223-3284 |
| Discovery | ☎293-2866 |
| Hertz | ☎221-1818 |
| National | ☎233-4044 |
| Prego | ☎221-8680 |
| Thrifty | ☎257-3434 |
| U-Haul | ☎257-8283 |

## By Train

Train travel was discontinued in Costa Rica in 1991, because of earthquakes and financial difficulties.

## By Bus

The public transportation system is efficient, well-maintained and much used in Costa Rica. Bus service runs from the cities to even the smallest towns, and there are many departures daily. The buses are usually quite comfortable, even if they are sometimes so crowded that they seem ready to burst!

For a list of the routes, pick up a copy of *Costa Rica Today*, published annually.

Usually, you can go directly to the bus terminal and purchase your ticket just prior to your departure. Each city has a central bus depot, but San José has several, so check beforehand from which one your bus departs (see p 68). Here is a list of bus companies that run from San José to the country's major cities:

**Autotransportes Blanco** *(Calle 12, Av. 9, ☎771-2550)*, to Puerto Jiménez;
**Autotransportes Ciudad Quesada** *(Coca Cola bus depot, ☎255-4318)*, to Ciudad Quesada;
**Autotransportes Mepe** *(Calle Ctl., Va. 9/11, ☎221-0524)*, to Bribrí, Cahuita and Sixaola;
**Coopelímon** *(Av. 3, Calle 19/21, ☎223-7811)*, to Puerto Limón;
**Empresa Alfaro** *(Calle 14, Av. 3/5, ☎222-2750)*, to Nicoya, Santa Cruz and Filadelfia as well as Sámara and Tamarindo;
**Empresarios Unidos de Puntarenas** *(☎222-0064)*, to Puntarenas;
**Pulmitan** *(Calle 14, Av. 1/3, ☎222-1650)* to Playa del Coco and Liberia;
**Sacsa** *(Calle 5, Av. 18, ☎233-5350)*, to Cartago;
**Tracopa** *(Av. 18, Calle 4, ☎221-4214)*, to Ciudad Neily, Palmar, Norte, Golfito and San Vito;
**Tracopa Empresa Alfaro** *(Calle 14, Av. 3/5, ☎222-2750)*, to San Vito;
**Tralapa** *(Calle 20, Av. 3, ☎221-7202)*, to Playa Flamingo;
**Transportes La Cañera** *(Calle 16, Av. 1/3, ☎222-3006)*, to Cañas;
**Transportes Morales** *(☎223-5567)*, to Quepos and Manuel Antonio;
**Transportes Musoc** *(Calle 16, Av. 1/3, ☎222-2422)*, to San Isidro and El General;
**Transtura** *(Av. 16, Calle 13, ☎556-0073)*, to Turrialba;
**Tuasa** *(Av. 2, Calle 12, ☎222-5325)*, to Alajuela;
**Tuasur** *(☎222-9763)*, to San Isidro and El General.

## On Foot

Costa Rica's urban layout is quite easy to understand: almost every town has a central park surrounded by many public and commercial establishments, such as churches, hotels, banks, restaurants and shops. For the most part, the idea of putting large commercial centres at the peripheries of a city has not caught on yet in Costa Rica. Street blocks are usually 100 metres long, making it easy to use distances in giving directions and addresses. For more on the system of addresses, see p 46.

Be careful when exploring the cities on foot, since they were often not built with pedestrians in mind. You will come across sidewalks in all kinds of conditions, and the traffic lights are often difficult to see.

## By Taxi

Taxis are easy to spot: they're all painted red! There are plenty of taxis around, even in small villages, but the cars are in various conditions. You can nearly always hail one in the street, even at night. In fact, it often takes less time to hail a cab than to call for one and wait for it to arrive. Taxi stands exist, mostly near busy places like parks, public squares and even hotels and bars.

Taking a taxi is inexpensive. In San José, cab fare shouldn't cost more than $5, although the trip to the airport costs about $10.

# TOURIST INFORMATION

Great efforts are being made to improve Costa Rica's tourist infrastructure. The **Instituto Costarricense de Turismo** (**ICT**) *(Apartado postal 777-1000, San José, ☎223-1733 or 800-012-3456 from Costa Rica, ⇒223-5452)* has set up tourist information offices in the most frequented places; the main one is at the Juan Santamaría international airport. However, these offices can close without warning (like the ICT on San José's Plaza de la Cultura). Before leaving the capital, head to the ICT on Avenida 4, between Calles 5 and 7. Also, many organizations, both public and private, publish information about all sorts of sites and activities that could interest tourists. Hotel receptions often have several of these useful brochures available. Some of the more popular hotels can give you good advice; it is worthwhile to consult them.

If you want a guided visit of a national park, city or region, see the beginning of the San José chapter on p 69 for listings of good **tourist agencies** that offer excursions throughout the country.

## CLIMATE AND PACKING

### Climate

Costa Rica's various microclimates can undoubtedly be considered among the country's many riches (see also p 14), and have helped shape its rich and diverse fauna and flora. Generally, however, Caribbean coast and the southern part of the Pacific coast have a humid, tropical climate with high temperatures and plenty of rainfall. The central area of the country has a more temperate climate, with cooler temperatures the higher you go. Guanacaste and the Nicoya Peninsula have a hot, dry climate with very little precipitation during the dry season.

Costa Rica has two seasons: the dry season from December to April, and the rainy or "green" season, from May to November, which has plenty of precipitation, especially from September onwards. However, the weather has been unpredictable for the last few years: in 1997, the year of El Niño, the country experienced a drought, especially in Guanacaste. The following year, however, it was hit by torrential rains that followed Hurricane Mitch; fortunately, Costa Rica was spared the devastation suffered by Honduras and Nicaragua, its neighbours to the north.

### What to Pack

Given the many different climates of Costa Rica, what you pack will depend on which regions you are planning to visit. In the mountains and volcanic regions a windbreaker will come in handy, and a set of warm clothes is indispensable if you want to do some hiking in these areas. On the other hand, pack light cotton clothes if you are staying on the coast, and don't forget a hat and sun screen. It's "eternal spring" in the Central Valley which lies at an elevation that is between these two regions. Here, it becomes quite cool in the evenings, and it might even seem chilly if you're coming from the coast. If you visit during the rainy season, be sure to bring along a "good" umbrella, as sudden downpours are frequent.

## INSURANCE

### Health Insurance

Health insurance is the most important type of insurance for travellers and should be purchased before your departure. A comprehensive health insurance policy that provides a level of coverage sufficient to pay for hospitalization, nursing care and doctor's fees is recommended. Keep in mind that health care costs are rising quickly everywhere. The policy should also have a repatriation clause in case the required care is not available in Costa Rica. As patients are sometimes asked to pay for medical services up front, find out what provisions your policy makes in this case. Always carry your health insurance policy with you when travelling to avoid problems if you are in an accident, and get receipts for any expenses incurred.

### Cancellation Insurance

This type of insurance is usually offered by your travel agent when you purchase your airplane ticket or tour package. It covers any non-refundable payments to travel suppliers such as airlines, and must be purchased at the same time as initial payment is made for air tickets or tour packages. This insurance allows you to be reimbursed for the ticket or package deal if your trip must be cancelled due to serious illness or death. This type of insurance can be useful, but weigh the likelihood of your using it against the price.

### Theft Insurance

Most residential insurance policies in North America protect some of your goods from theft, even if the theft occurs in a foreign country. To make a claim, you must fill out a police report. Usually the coverage for a theft abroad is 10% of your total coverage. If you plan on travelling with valuable objects, check your policy or with an insurance agency to see if additional baggage insurance is necessary. European visitors should take out baggage insurance.

### Life Insurance

By purchasing your tickets with certain credit cards you will get life insurance. Several airline companies offer a life insurance plan included in the price of the airplane ticket. However, many travellers already have another form of life insurance and do not need extra insurance.

## HEALTH

Hospitals and medical centres are generally well-equipped in Costa Rica, thanks to the large sums of money pumped into health care over the last few years. Doctors and health workers are competent, and usually take the time to understand your problem. Of course, medical services outside the big centres might seem more modest. In tourist areas, you can usually find an English-speaking doctor. If you need a blood transfusion, make sure that the blood has been tested and is safe.

Insufficiently treated water, which can contain harmful bacteria, is the cause of most of the health problems you are likely to encounter, such as stomach upset, diarrhea or fever. Although the drinking water in most cities and towns in Costa Rica is treated and presumably safe, always ask about it before you drink it. Signs posted at the entrance of many cities and towns indicate whether the water is safe to drink or not. Drinking only bottled water which is available in stores and restaurants throughout the country, is the best way to avoid catching anything. Make sure the bottle is well-sealed when you buy it. In addition, fresh fruits and vegetables that have been washed but not peeled can also pose a health risk. Make sure that the vegetables you eat are well-cooked, and peel your own fruit. Remember: cook it, peel it, or forget it.

If you do get diarrhea, soothe your stomach by avoiding solids; instead, drink carbonated beverages, bottled water, or weak tea (avoid milk) until you recover. As dehydration can be dangerous, drinking sufficient quantities of liquid is crucial. Pharmacies sell various preparations for the treatment of diarrhea, with different effects. Pepto Bismol and Imodium will stop the diarrhea, which slows the loss of fluids, but they should be avoided if you have a fever as they will prevent the necessary elimination of bacteria. Oral rehydration products, such as Gastrolyte, will replace the minerals and electrolytes which your body has lost as a result of the diarrhea. In a pinch, you can make your own rehydration solution by mixing one litre of pure water with one teaspoon of sugar and two or three teaspoons of salt. After, eat easily digested foods like rice to give your stomach time to adjust. If symptoms become more serious (high fever, persistent diarrhea), see a doctor as antibiotics may be necessary.

Nutrition and climate can also cause problems. Pay attention to food's freshness (especially fish and meat) and the cleanliness of the preparation area. Good hygiene (wash your hands often) will help avoid undesirable situations.

It is best not to walk around bare-foot as parasites and insects can cause a variety of problems, the least of which is athlete's foot.

Costa Rica is a wonderful country to explore; however, travellers should be aware of and protect themselves from a number of health risks associated with the region, such as malaria, typhoid, diphtheria, tetanus, polio and hepatitis A. Cases of these diseases are rare but there is a risk. **Travellers are therefore advised to consult a doctor (or travellers' clinic) for advice on what precautions to take.** Remember that it is much easier to prevent these illnesses than it is to cure them and that a vaccination is not a substitute for cautious travel.



## Illnesses

Please note that this section is intended to provide general information only.

### Malaria

Malaria (paludism) is caused by a parasite in the blood called *Plasmodium sp.* This parasite is transmitted by anopheles mosquitoes, which bite from nightfall until dawn. Hardly any cases of malaria have been reported in Costa Rica in the last few years. The risk is minimal and anti-malaria drugs are not necessary. It is nevertheless a good idea to take measures to prevent mosquito bites (see p 42).

The symptoms of malaria include high fever, chills, extreme fatigue and headaches as well as stomach and muscle aches. There are several forms of malaria, including one serious type caused by *P. falciparum*. The disease can take hold while you are still on holiday or up to 12 weeks following your return; in some cases the symptoms can appear months later.

#### Hepatitis A

This disease is generally transmitted by ingesting food or water that has been contaminated by faecal matter. The symptoms include fever, yellowing of the skin, loss of appetite and fatigue, and can appear between 15 and 50 days after infection. An effective vaccination by injection is available. Besides the recommended vaccine, good hygiene is important. Always wash your hands before every meal, and ensure that the food and preparation area are clean.

#### Hepatits B

Hepatitis B, like hepatitis A, affects the liver, but is transmitted through direct contact of bodily fluids. The symptoms are flu-like, and similar to those of hepatitis A. A vaccination exists but must be administered over an extended period of time, so be sure to check with your doctor several weeks in advance.

#### Typhoid

This illness is caused by ingesting food that has come in contact (direct or indirect) with an infected person's stool. Common symptoms include high fever, loss of appetite, headaches, constipation and occasionally diarrhea, as well as the appearance of red spots on the skin. These symptoms will appear one to three weeks after infection. Which vaccination you get (it exists in two forms, oral and by injection) will depend on your trip. Once again, it is always a good idea to visit a travellers' clinic a few weeks before your departure.

#### Diphtheria and Tetanus

These two illnesses, against which most people are vaccinated during their childhood, can have serious consequences. Thus, before leaving, check that your vaccinations are valid; you may need a booster shot. Diphtheria is a bacterial infection that is transmitted by nose and throat secretions or by skin lesions on an infected person. Symptoms include sore throat, high fever, general aches and pains and occasionally skin infections. Tetanus is caused by a bacteria that enters your body through an open wound that comes in contact with contaminated dust or rusty metal.

#### Other Health Tips

Cases of illnesses like Hepatitis B, AIDS and certain venereal diseases have been reported; it is therefore a good idea to be careful.

Remember that consuming too much alcohol, particularly during prolonged exposure to the sun, can cause severe dehydration and lead to health problems.

### Mosquitoes

A nuisance common to many countries, mosquitoes are no strangers to Costa Rica. They are particularly numerous during the rainy season. Protect yourself with a good insect repellent. Repellents with DEET are the most effective. The concentration of DEET varies from one product to the next; the higher the concentration, the longer the protection. In rare cases, the use of repellents with high concentrations (35% or more) of DEET has been associated with convulsions in young children; it is therefore important to apply these products sparingly, on exposed surfaces, and to wash it off once back inside. A concentration of 35% DEET will protect for four to six hours, while 95% will last from 10 to 12 hours. New formulas with DEET in lesser concentrations, but which last just as long, are available.

To further reduce the possibility of getting bitten, do not wear perfume or bright colours. Sundown is an especially active time for insects. When walking in wooded areas, cover your legs and ankles well. Insect coils can help provide a better night's sleep. Before bed, apply insect repellent to your skin and to the headboard and baseboard of your bed. If possible, get an air-conditioned room, or bring a mosquito net.

Lastly, since it is impossible to completely avoid contact with mosquitoes, bring along a cream to soothe the bites you will invariably get.

## Snakes

Among a country's rich and diverse fauna, there are bound to be some species that are less congenial than others. Accordingly, Costa Rica is home to several kinds of snakes, some of which are poisonous. There is no need to get too alarmed, as you are unlikely to cross paths with one during your visit. Nevertheless, it is important to keep your eyes open and watch where you step. In the forest, look around before you lean against something or sit down somewhere. When hiking, be careful as you part the foliage that sometimes hangs across the path, and check the shores as well as the surface of the water if you go swimming in a river. Some people think they are faster than a snake and tease it, or poke it to see if they can make it move; needless to say, this is not a good idea! The presence of snakes should not prevent you from exploring everything that Costa Rica has to offer. Like most wild animals, snakes avoid contact with humans as much as possible.

## The Sun

Its benefits are many, but so are its harms. Always wear sunscreen (SPF 15 for adults and SPF 30 for children) and apply it 20 to 30 minutes before exposure. Many creams on the market do not offer adequate protection; ask a pharmacist. Too much sun can cause sunstroke (dizziness, vomiting, fever, etc.). Be careful, especially the first few days, as it takes time to get used to the sun. Take sun in small doses and protect yourself with a hat and sunglasses.

## First Aid Kit

A small first-aid kit can prove very useful. Bring along sufficient amounts of any medications you take regularly as well as a valid prescription in case you lose your supply; it can be difficult to find certain medications in the small towns. Other medications such as anti-malaria pills and Imodium (or an equivalent), can also be hard to find. Finally, don't forget self-adhesive bandages, disinfectant cream or ointment, analgesics (pain-killers), antihistamines (for allergies), an extra pair of sunglasses or contact lenses, contact lens solution, and medicine for upset stomach. Though these items are all available in Costa Rica, having them on hand can certainly make life easier.

## SAFETY AND SECURITY

Costa Rica hasn't had an army since the 1940s, but the police is still very powerful and has a strong presence, especially on the roads outside the cities. Also, there is a kind of private militia whose main purpose is to combat the drug trade and prevent illegal immigrants from entering the country.

They operate mainly along the borders with Panama and Nicaragua. You can recognize them by their insignia of crossed rifles, and it is not advisable to bother them for nothing, since they mean business.

Theft is common, especially in the cities, and every establishment with any kind of a reputation to uphold has its own parking lot attendant, often armed with a bat.

Generally, the country is really quite safe. By taking the usual precautions, you shouldn't run into any problems, even in San José. Nevertheless, avoid walking by yourself through dimly lit areas after dark. Remember, the sun sets at about 6pm! On the Caribbean coast (see p 133), the crime rate is higher. Theft is more frequent, but this shouldn't stop you from enjoying this beautiful region, as long as you're careful.

## MONEY AND BANKING

### Currency

The currency in Costa Rica is the colon. Since the currency is quite weak, the smaller denominations (coins) are not worth much, and you will find yourself using paper money almost exclusively.

Since the value of the colon can change rapidly, prices in this guide are given in US dollars. Some restaurants and hotels also chosen advertise their rates in US dollars.

### Banks

The Banco de Costa and the Banco Nacional are the country's most popular financial institutions. Both banks have at least one outlet in every city. As in North America, banks are open Monday to Friday, from 9am to 3pm.

Automatic teller machines (ATMs) are quite common, efficient, and easy to find, especially in San José. The money you withdraw from your account will be given to you in the local currency.

### Credit Cards

Most credit cards, especially Visa and MasterCard, are accepted in a large number of businesses, including hotels and restaurants. While the main advantage of credit cards is that they allow you to avoid carrying large sums of money, using a credit card also makes leaving a deposit for a rental car much easier. In addition, the exchange rate with a credit card is usually better.

Credit cards also let you avoid service charges when exchanging money. By overpaying your credit card (to avoid interest charges), you can then withdraw against it. You can thus avoid carrying large amounts of money or traveller's cheques. Withdrawals can be made directly from an automatic teller if you have a personal identification number (PIN) for your card.

### Exchange Rates

| | | | | | |
|---|---|---|---|---|---|
| 10 colones | = | $0.04 US | $1 US | = | 268.29 colones |
| $1 CAN | = | $0.66 US | $1 US | = | $1.51 CAN |
| 1 EURO | = | $1.13 US | $1 US | = | 0.88 EURO |
| 1 £ | = | $1.64 US | $1 US | = | 0.61 £ |
| 1 FF | = | $0.17 US | $1 US | = | 5.79 FF |
| 1 DM | = | $0.58 US | $1 US | = | 1.73 DM |
| 1 SF | = | $0.71 US | $1 US | = | 1.41 SF |
| 10 BF | = | $0.28 US | $1 US | = | 35.62 BF |
| 100 PTA | = | $0.68 US | $1 US | = | 146.92 PTA |
| 1,0000 ITL | = | $0.58 US | $1 US | = | 1,709.73 ITL |



ATMs can be found at the many branches of the **Banco Popular y de Desarrollo de Costa Rica** throughout the country, and at branches of **A Toda Hora** (**ATH**) and **Ben Crescen**, which have small streetside locations. Costa Rica has a good automated banking network, so you don't have to worry about getting stranded without any money. ATMs are a fast, practical and safe way to get money, and they give the same exchange rates as banks.

### Traveller's Cheques

It is always best to keep most of your money in traveller's cheques, which are accepted in some restaurants, hotels and shops (those in American dollars are most widely accepted). They are also easy to cash in at banks and exchange offices. Always keep a copy of the serial numbers of your cheques in a separate place; that way, if the cheques are lost, the company can replace them quickly and easily. Do not rely solely on traveller's cheques, always carry some cash.

## TELECOMMUNICATIONS

Costa Rica's telecommunications system is still being developed. Seven-digit telephone numbers were introduced several years ago to increase the network's capacity. The country's area code is **506**, and there are no regional codes. To call Costa Rica, dial the number for the international operator (011 in Canada and the United States, for example), followed by 506 and the number you want to reach.

There are two types of public telephones in the country: rotary dial phones accept 5, 10 and 20 colon pieces, while the touch-tone telephones require a special phone card that you can buy. The latter have a small screen that explains how to use them; the instructions will appear in English if you press the right buttons.

To make an international call from Costa Rica, dial **00**, followed by the country code, the area or city code (if needed), and the number of the person you want to reach.

For instance, to call **Canada** or the **United States**, dial 00-1, the area code, and the number. Canada Direct *(☎0-800-015-1161)* is a free service that connects you with a Canadian operator. If you are using a public telephone, you will still have to insert a phone card or money to get a dial tone.

Some Other Country Codes:

United Kingdom: 44
Australia: 61
New Zealand: 64
Belgium: 32
Italy: 39
Germany: 49
Netherlands: 31
Switzerland: 41

## MAIL

Apart from numbered PO Boxes, the country uses an address system based on geographic orientation from a specific point, such as an intersection, important building, central plaza or park. Thus, the postal address of a hotel might be: 100 metres south and 300 metres west of the central park. The government is currently working out the details of a costly shift to the more commonly used international system, with numbered buildings. Some buildings are marked with a number, but addresses are not officially designated this way yet. Currently, addresses are given as: Calle 4, Avenida 3/4 or Avenida 4, Calle 2. This means that the place is located on 4th Street, between 3rd and 4th Avenues, or on 4th Avenue, near 2nd Street. Traditional addresses have not been provided in this guide for the small villages in order to make the text more clear and concise. To write to one of these places, simply indicate the name of the establishment, the name of the city or town and the name of the region, followed by the name of the country, of course. This is all the information needed for your letter to arrive!

Postage is inexpensive in Costa Rica: sending a letter to Europe only costs 32¢, while mailing a postcard costs 5¢ less.

## MEDIA

### Newspapers

***La Nación*** includes a calendar of cultural activities around the country (movies, performances and art shows). ***La República***, ***El Día*** and ***La Prensa Libre*** are national newspapers published in Spanish.

The ***Tico Times*** is an English-language newspaper published by Costa Rica's English-speaking community. It deals with political issues similar to those in *La Nacíon* and *La Prensa Libre*. A section on cultural activities and movie listings is also included.

### Magazines

***Costa Rica Today*** is a bilingual English and Spanish magazine published with tourists in mind. It is sold at stands, but you can pick up a free copy at most hotels and airports. It contains a calendar of events.

***Guide*** is also targeted at tourists, and is distributed at airports.

In addition to tourist publications, Costa Rica also has its own special interest magazines for women, businesspeople, etc. ***Gente 10*** is a local gay publication that can be found at various locations throughout the country.

## Radio

There are radio stations for all tastes, especially if you're staying in the Central Valley. In the regions on the other side of the mountains, however, you might have difficulties picking up the FM broadcasts without an antenna (i.e. on the car).

For music from the 1960s and beyond, tune in to **Radio 2** at 99.5 FM; the DJs speak in both English and Spanish.

For classical music, turn your dial to 96.7 FM, **Radio Universidad**.

Latin (Latin-American or Spanish) and North-American music can be found on **Estereo Azul**, at 99.9 FM.

## Internet

Costa Rica' main Internet service provider is **Radiográfica Costarricense** *(Calle 1, Av. 5, San José, ☎287-0087, ⇌223-1609)*, a subsidiary of the ICE. You can surf the net at its offices from 8am to 10pm for $3 an hour.

Here are some sites with useful information about Costa Rica:

www.cr
www.tourism-costarica.com/
www.centralamerica.com/cr/maps
http://photo.net/cr/index.html
www.incostarica.net/centers/visitor
www.worldheadquarters.com/costarica.html
http://catalog.com/calypso/
www.city.net/countries/costarica/
members.aol.com/aaguila/hatillo2.htm
www.nacion.co.cr/
www.tuanis.com/costarica/parks/parks.html
www.casapres.go.cr/

# ACCOMMODATIONS

There are several types of accommodations in Costa Rica, from luxury hotels with a wide array of services, to small, charming bungalows with a more local feel.

Prices listed in this guide are for one double-occupancy room in high season:

| | |
|---|---|
| *$* | less than US$15 |
| *$$* | $15 to $25 |
| *$$$* | $25 to $50 |
| *$$$$* | $50 to $75 |
| *$$$$$* | $75 to $120 |
| *$$$$$$* | more than $120 |

The 13% general tax is included in the price of the hotel room, but a tourist tax of about 3% (rate varies) is not.

## Types of Accommodations

**Hotels**

Small, inexpensive hotels usually have a room with a bed, with no extra amenities. Bathrooms are often shared, and do not always have running water. This type of hotel costs under $15.

The big luxury hotels at the other end of the scale have seemingly limitless facilities. Designed for wealthy tourists, business people and celebrities, they are often (but not always) vast complexes with spacious grounds and many services, such as casinos, large restaurants, bars, swimming pools, refrigerators in the rooms, etc.

All beaches belong to the state, so no one has the right to claim the exclusive right to any specific stretch of the

PRACTICAL INFORMATION

coast. Sometimes, however, a beach can only be accessed through private property. Thus, certain hotels have taken advantage of this so their guests can enjoy a serene seaside experience.

Because tourism has grown so quickly in Costa Rica, there wasn't enough time for accommodations between these two categories to develop until recently. Gradually, more mid-range establishments are opening their doors, offering travellers a variety of services at a moderate price.

Patios and other outdoor areas attached to a room are not necessarily private. Most hotels have small safes available to store your valuables. Most bathrooms only have showers.

"***Cabinas***" are an alternative to the traditional hotel room. They are small, detached bungalows which usually consist of only one room, and sometimes have a private bathroom. Occasionally they come with a kitchenette and small livingroom. This type of lodging is also known as "*habitación*".

### *Apart-hotels*

*Apart-hotels* are like hotels in that they offer all the services, but like apartments because rooms include kitchenettes equipped with dishes and utensils. This is a very economical option for longer stays.

### Bed & Breakfasts

Bed & Breakfasts, where you stay with a family in their home, are very popular, and the atmosphere is much warmer than in a hotel! However, the charm of staying at a Bed & Breakfast lies primarily in the decor and the friendliness of the welcome, which can vary from place to place. The owners can often help you plan your excursions in an informal way, and help you out with any problems you might encounter during your stay.

Staying in someone's home is the perfect way to fully experience life in another country, with everything this may entail. Although Costa Ricans are known for their hospitality, living conditions vary from one place to the next. You will also be living with the daily habits of your hosts; the incessant sounds of the television or radio are not uncommon. Also, Costa Ricans tend to go to bed early. Inquiring about these details beforehand can make the difference between an "okay" vacation and the one of your dreams. In addition to the establishments listed in this guide, language schools, some churches, classified advertisements or chatting with people at the University of Costa Rica can all be sources of information about interesting Bed & Breakfasts.

### Camping

You can camp in several parks in the country. Facilities are rustic, but there are often washrooms nearby. See the descriptions of the parks or the "Accommodations" section of each chapter for more detailed information about specific sites. There are few official campgrounds to speak of, but many hotels allow travellers to camp on their grounds. Inquire about this possibility at the local tourist offices. Alternately, you can join Costa Rican campers who pitch their tents under the trees along the beach. Of course, no services are available here – and be respectful of the natural surroundings.

Wilderness camping is possible in most parks, but reserve in advance.

## RESTAURANTS AND FINE FOOD

Costa Rica has many different types of cuisine, thanks to the numerous waves of immigration, all of which have contributed to its variety. You will even find some Chinese restaurants around. However, apart from the large cities in the Central Valley, it is still difficult to find upscale restaurants or non-Costa Rican specialized cuisine. You can find some real gems in the countryside, but these are quite sparse, especially if you stay in remote areas where tourism is just beginning to take hold. In these areas, the restaurants found in hotels are your best bet.

Breakfasts and lunch are the main, and most substantial, meals of the day. Some of the smaller restaurants close early in the evening.

International restaurant chains are no strangers to Costa Rica: Pizza Hut, MacDonald's and the like have franchises here. However, fans of these commercial giants should note that these restaurants are found only in the large cities of the Central Valley. On the other hand, some kinds of fast food abound throughout the country. **Pop's** and **Mönpik** restaurants, specializing in ice cream, and **AS**, a 24-hour chain that serves light meals, are among these. There are also slightly more upscale chains, like **Rosti Pollos**, where you can have Costa Rican-style chicken at the counter or in a sit-down dining room.

Most menus are in Spanish and English. The bill usually includes a 10% tip and the 13% tax.

There is no such thing as a non-smoking section in Costa Rican restaurants, though some vegetarian establishments prohibit smoking altogether.

Prices listed in this guide are for a meal for one person:

| | |
|---|---|
| *$* | less than $5 |
| *$$* | $5 to $10 |
| *$$$* | $10 to $20 |
| *$$$$* | $20 to $40 |
| *$$$$$* | over $40 |

### Types of Restaurants

A ***soda*** is a small neighbourhood restaurant that generally serves local cuisine and fast food (hamburgers, sandwiches, etc.). At lunch, they often serve a *plato del día* (daily special), sometimes referred to as the *ejecutivo*.

A ***pulpería*** is something like a small corner store. These are found in even the smallest villages and provide a slew of basic necessities: canned goods, beverages, toiletries, bread, milk, and sometimes sandwiches and other quick snacks.

***Panaderías*** (bakeries) and ***pastelarías*** (pastry shops) sometimes serve small meals, sandwiches and drinks in addition to their usual wares.

Local **cafés** are much the same as those found elsewhere: small establishments where you can relax, chat or read while enjoying a coffee or a light meal in a laid-back atmosphere.

**Vegetarian restaurants** are popular in Costa Rica, especially in San José. They prepare tasty meals that really let you savour the many fruits and vegetables that grow here! Also, the meals are usually quite inexpensive.

PRACTICAL INFORMATION

## Costa Rican Cuisine

Contrary to what you'd expect if you've only ever had Mexican food, not all Latin American cuisine is spicy! Costa Rican cooking is generally quite mild, and while hot peppers are often served on the side, they are rarely used in food preparation. Fresh coriander, on the other hand, is used in almost everything!

***Gallo pinto*** is Costa Rica's national dish. A mixture of rice and red or black beans, it is often served with eggs, meat or vegetables. It can be served for any meal of the day, or for all three! Of course, it's not the real thing unless it's accompanied by **tortillas**; small, thin cornmeal pancakes.

Chicken, or ***pollo***, is very popular. Prepared in many different ways, it is the mainstay of many restaurants.

***Tamales*** are small cornmeal pastries stuffed with meat and vegetables. They are usually served at Christmas.

***Tres leches*** cake is an incredibly smooth, creamy, sweet indulgence: ***arroz con leche*** (rice pudding) is another popular dessert.

Freshly squeezed fruit juices (***frescos*** and ***jugos***), mixed with water or milk, are very popular, and are sold everywhere. Made with sun-ripened fruits, these drinks are a real treat!

## WINE, BEER AND SPIRITS

Costa Rica is neither a wine producer nor a big importer of wine. Nevertheless, you shouldn't have any difficulty finding a bottle of red or white wine (*vino tinto, vino blanco*). Larger restaurants, especially those specializing in French cuisine, all have a good selection of vintages.

The country's national alcoholic beverage is ***guaro***, made from sugar cane. Quality rum and coffee liqueurs are also produced here.

### Beer

If you order a beer, you might be surprised to find that it is served on ice! This only makes it cooler and more refreshing, though. Home-brewed beer is also popular: it generally tastes like light, blond American beers.

## ENTERTAINMENT

Most of the nightlife is found in the Central Valley, especially in San José, where bars, nightclubs, theatres, cinemas, and other diversions abound. You shouldn't have any problems finding things to do in the other regions, either. Although cinemas and theatres are rarer in the outlying areas, you will be hard pressed to find a place that doesn't have a bar or a dance club! Bars sometimes serve an appetizer called "*bocas*" with your drink.

Gambling is also common in Costa Rica, and you can find casinos in many places, including some hotels.

## FESTIVALS AND PUBLIC HOLIDAYS

Costa Rica has many holidays, both civil and religious. In addition, there are several regional festivals that are only celebrated in certain parts of the country.

### Public Holidays

**New Year's Day**: January 1
***Semana Santa***: March 29 to April 4, 1999; April 17 to 23, 2000; April 9 to 15, 2001
**Festival of Juan Santamarína**: April 11
**Labour Day**: May 1
**Anniversary of the Annexation of Guanacaste Province**: July 25
**Mothers' Day**: August 15
**Independence Day**: September 15
**All Souls Day**: November 2
**Christmas Day**: December 25

### Major Festivals

**January**
*Fiesta Patronales* (Alajuela)
*Fiestas de Santa Cruz* (Santa Cruz)

**February**
Agricultural Fair (San Isidro de El General)

**March**
Book Fair (San José)
*Festival Internacional Los Artes* (San José)

**April**
Festival of Juan Santamarína (Alajuela)

**May**
Oxcart Parade (Escazú and San Isidro de El General)

**July**
Guanacaste Festival (Liberia and Santa Cruz): folk dances, music and rodeos
*Festival Internacional de Música (☎282-7724)* (national)

**August**
*Festival Internacional de Música (☎282-7724)* (national)
Festival of the Virgin of Los Angeles (Cartago, August 2): religious procession

**September**
Independence Day (national, September 15): parades, fireworks and all kinds of celebrations

**October**
Puerto Limón Carnival: parades, dances
*Día de la Raza* (October 12): commemorates Christopher Columbus' arrival in America

**November**
All Souls Day (November 2): religious processions, pilgrimages
*Festival Internacional de Teatro* (San José): theatre performances, street theatre, and other entertainment

**December**
*Fiesta de Los Negritos* (Boruca, December 8): costumed dances
*Immaculada Concepción* (national, December 8): fireworks
*Fiesta de la Yeguita* (Nicoya, December 12): processions, fireworks, concerts
*Las Posadas* (national, December 15)
*Fiestas de fin de año* (San José, December 26): procession of horses, parades

## SHOPPING

You can find almost everything in Costa Rica, especially in the Central Valley. Specialty stores, department stores and more can be found in all urban centres. Few of the large international chains have opened stores in Costa Rica, though you might come across some familiar North American names in the shopping centres that have recently opened in the San José area. Every town has a ***pulperia*** (see p 49), a type of convenience store.

There are people selling fruit, clothing and knickknacks along the road, even though this is officially prohibited in

Costa Rica, at least on the larger routes. Note that bargaining is **not** customary in Costa Rica.

Here are some of the main stores you will find in Costa Rica:

**Mas X Menos** (More or Less) is a very popular chain of supermarkets. There are locations throughout the country, but most are found in the Central Valley (in San José, there is one on Paseo Colón, corner of Calle 26).

The **Automercado** is a supermarket similar to Mas X Menos. One of its locations is in San José on Calle 3, between Avenida 4 and 5.

**La Gloria** is a large chain store. The San José outlet is somewhat run down, but other locations are clean and modern.

Every urban centre has its own **central market** (*mercado central*). This is a great place to walk around and mingle with the locals to get a taste of what everyday life is like in the country – and of the food, as well!

It is illegal to buy Pre-Columbian artifacts and goods made from animals that are on the endangered species list. If someone offers to sell you either of these, they are either illegal, or fake.

The 13% sales tax is included in the prices marked on items.

## What to Bring Back

Colourful **summer clothing** (T-shirts, dresses, blouses) and **accessories** (scarves, hats) with lively patterns make charming souvenirs.

**Reproductions of Pre-Columbian objects** also make great gifts.

**Wood carvings** are wonderful mementos. They come in all shapes and sizes, and can be bought retail, wholesale, or directly from artisans. Sarchí (see p 107) is a town in the Central Valley that is particularly renowned for its wood carvings.

**Costa Rican coffee** is practically a must, whether you buy the beans, ground coffee, coffee liqueur (Café Rica), or coffee essence. It is available just about everywhere, but some specialized souvenir shops carry all of the above under one roof.

Several shops in San José specialize in imported cigars.

## TIME CHANGE

Costa Rica is six hours behind the Greenwich meridian in Britain, and seven hours behind the rest of Europe. It is in the Central Time Zone (Chicago, Houston, Winnipeg), one hour behind the Eastern Time Zone (Montreal, Toronto, New York). It does not observe daylight saving time.

## BUSINESS HOURS

Banks are open Monday to Friday from 9am to 3pm. Government offices are open Monday to Friday from 9am to 4pm, while private offices are usually open until 6pm.

Stores are usually open Monday to Saturday from 9am to 6pm, and are closed Sundays.

## GAY AND LESBIAN LIFE

Costa Rica has a reputation of being more open towards gays and lesbians than its neighbouring countries. An association to bring more gays into the tourist industry was formed recently. Also, some hotels and businesses now openly welcome a gay clientele. Thus, it is becoming much easier for gay and lesbian travellers to find establishments that cater specifically to them. The gay magazine ***Gente 10*** is available at select locations across the country.

## IDENTITY AND CULTURE SHOCK

Before going on vacation, we pack our luggage and get the necessary vaccinations and travel documents, but rarely do we prepare for culture shock. The following text explains what culture shock is and how to deal with it.

In a nutshell, culture shock can be defined as a certain anxiety that may be experienced upon arriving in another country where everything is different, including the culture and language, making communication as you know it very difficult. Combined with jetlag and fatigue, the strain of orienting yourself in a new cultural context can lead to psychological stress that may throw you off track.

Culture shock is a frustrating phenomenon that can easily turn travellers setting out with the best of intentions into intolerant, racist and ethnocentric ones – they may come to believe that their society is better than the new, and seemingly incomprehensible, one. This type of reaction detracts from the whole travel experience.

People in other countries have different customs and lifestyles that are sometimes hard for us to understand or accept. We might even find ourselves wondering how people can live the way they do when their customs run contrary to what we deem to be "normal". In the end, however, it is easier to adapt to them than to criticize or disregard them.

Even though this is the era of globalization and cultural homogenization, we still live in a world of many "worlds", such as the business world, the worlds of different continents, suburbia, and the world of the rich and the poor. Of course, these worlds intersect, but each has its own characteristic set of ideas and cultural values. Furthermore, even if they are not in direct contact, each has at least an image of the other (which is often distorted and nothing more). And if a picture is worth a thousand words, then our world contains million upon millions of them. Sometimes it is hard to tell what is real and what isn't, but one thing is certain: what you see on television about a place is not the same as when you get there.

When people interact with each other, they inevitably make sense of each other through their differences. The strength of a group, human or animal, lies in its diversity, whether it be in genetics or ideas. Can you imagine how boring the world would be if everyone were the same?

Travelling can be seen as a way of developing a more holistic, or global, vision of the world; this means accepting that our cultural fabric is complex and woven with many different ethnicities, and that all have something to teach us, be it a philosophy of life, medical knowledge, or a culinary dish, which adds to the richness of our personal experience.

Remember that culture is relative, and that people's social, technological and financial situations shape their way of being and looking at the world. It takes more than curiosity and tolerance to be open minded: it is a matter of learning to see the world anew, through a different cultural perspective.

When travelling abroad, don't spend too much energy looking for the familiar, and don't try to see the place as you would like it to be – go with the flow instead. And though a foreign country might seem difficult to understand or even unwelcoming at times, remember that there are people who find happiness and satisfaction in life everywhere. When you get involved in their daily lives, you will begin to see things differently – things which at first seemed exotic and mystifying are easily understood after having been explained. It always helps to know the rules before playing a game, and it goes without saying that learning the language will help you better understand what's going on. But be careful about communicating with your hands, since certain gestures might mean the opposite of what you are trying to say!

Prepare yourself for culture shock as early as possible. Libraries and bookstores are good places for information about the cultures you are interested in. Reading about them is like a journey in itself, and will leave you with even more cherished memories of your trip.

## HANDICAPPED TRAVELLERS

Tourist facilities everywhere are becoming more and more responsive to the needs of travellers who have difficulties getting around, and Costa Rica is no exception. However, aside from establishments that cater specifically to tourists, buildings and public spaces are not really designed with these considerations in mind.

## WOMEN TRAVELLERS

Women travelling alone should not encounter any problems. For the most part, people are friendly and not aggressive. Generally, men are respectful toward women, and harassment is uncommon, although Costa Rican males do have a tendency to flirt. Of course, a certain level of caution should be exercised; avoid making eye contact, ignore any advances or comments and do not walk around alone in poorly-lit areas at night.

## MISCELLANEOUS

### Religion

Although Costa Rica is officially a Catholic country, freedom of religion exists. Ask hotel staff for a list of local places of worship, or check the newspaper for the times of the services. Of course, the further you go from the Central Valley, the fewer non-Catholic religious establishments you will find. The Caribbean coast has a number of Protestant churches, though.

### Electricity

Like in North America, wall sockets take plugs with two flat pins and work on an alternating current of 110 volts (60 cycles). Sockets do not always have the third hole that grounds the current, so bring along the appropriate adaptor.

## Some Interesting Associations

The following is a short list of associations and special interest groups that have offices in Costa Rica:

**Ornithological Club of Costa Rica**
☎267-7191;
**Œnological Club of Costa Rica**
☎228-9666;
**Canadian Club of Costa Rica**
☎282-5580.

## Weights and Measures

Costa Rica uses the metric system. The following conversion table may be helpful.

**Weights**
1 pound (lb) = 454 grams (g)
1 kilogram (kg) = 2.2 pounds (lbs)

**Linear Measure**
1 inch = 2.2 centimetres (cm)
1 foot (ft) = 30 centimetres (cm)
1 mile = 1.6 kilometres (km)
1 kilometres (km) = 0.63 miles
1 metre (m) = 39.37 inches

**Land Measure**
1 acre = 0.4 hectare
1 hectare = 2.471 acres

**Volume Measure**
1 U.S. gallon (gal) = 3.79 litres
1 U.S. gallon (gal) = 0.83 imperial gallon

**Temperature**
To convert °F into °C: subtract 32, divide by 9, multiply by 5.
To convert °C into °F: multiply by 9, divide by 5, add 32.

PRACTICAL INFORMATION

## Some Useful Terms...

*Pura vida*: this is the favourite *tica* expression. It is a very positive expression, used when things are going well, similar to "wonderful" or "great."

*Tico*, *Tica*: short for *Costariccense*, which is the colloquial term for Costa Ricans.

*Tuanis*: is the second most popular expression, and is used to express appreciation, happiness, etc. For instance, if a place is *tuanis*, it comes highly recommended.

*Mae* (or *Maje*): means "man." Young people use it all the time.

*Jale*: means "let's go!"

*Upe*: what you would call out in an empty building or area, similar to "is anyone there?"

*Tucán*: like in Canada, where one-dollar coins are often called "loonies" after the bird that is engraved on them, *Ticos* sometimes call 5,000 *colones* coins *"tucán"*; you can see why....

*Vos*: In Costa Rica, *vos* is most often used when speaking to people. It refers to the second person singular ("you") and should be conjugated as such.

# OUTDOORS

Costa Rica is a nature lover's paradise where you can take part in almost every kind of outdoor activity imaginable. The country has modern services to help you actively enjoy its vast open spaces, and nearly all of the agencies we went with were highly professional, punctual, safety-conscious, respectful of the environment and receptive to clients' questions and comments. Costa Ricans are proud, honest and courteous, and determined to make whichever outdoor activity you choose to do a highly enjoyable experience.

Suggested outdoor activities in each region, as well as names of agencies and places where "nature" and "adventure" invariably go together (mostly national parks) are listed in the various chapters of this guide. However, here is an overview of the main outdoor activities available in this country where the favourite local expression *Pura vide* (pure life) takes on a whole new meaning.

## PARKS

Costa Rica has 23 national parks, which make up 12% of the country's total area. In addition, there are 9 ecological reserves, 30 national wildlife reserves, 12 forest reserves, 30 protected zones and 12 swamps. The total of all these protected areas covers 25% of the country's area. If you include the constantly growing number of private reserves, the percentage of the country's land found in conservation areas is the highest in the world.

The system of national parks has been completely restructured since 1995, in order to support decentralized regional planning. The parks are managed by the **SINAC** (Sistema Nacional de Areas de Conservación), a committee formed from the **MINAE** (Ministerio de Ambiante y Energía). The country is divided into 11 regions which correspond to the 11 conservation

Top Ten Visited Parks (1996)

| | Parks | Number of visitors |
|---|---|---|
| 1 | Parque Nacional Volcán Poás | 174 630 |
| 2 | Parque Nacional Manuel Antonio | 104 807 |
| 3 | Parque Nacional Volcán Irazú | 104 347 |
| 4 | Parque Nacional Santa Rosa | 54 001 |
| 5 | Reserva Biológica Carara | 28 234 |
| 6 | Parque Nacional Arenal | 27 166 |
| 7 | Parque Nacional Tapantí | 26 243 |
| 8 | Parque Nacional Cahuita | 23 925 |
| 9 | Parque Nacional Rincón de la Vieja | 22 173 |
| 10 | Parque Nacional Corcovado | 18 974 |

areas (*areas de conservación*) in which the parks are found. There is usually an information centre in one of the larger cities in each region.

If you visit several of Costa Rica's national parks, you will notice that they are all quite different. Therefore don't expect the quality of services to be the same from one park to another, as you would in Canada or the United States where park infrastructure is more consistent. The quality of park entrances, accommodations, camping facilities, picnic areas, maps and hiking trails vary considerably, as do the access roads leading to them, which are often unpaved and only passable with a four-wheel drive vehicle.

Of course, each national park has its own unique features and natural splendours. However, because some of them really deserve a special mention, they have been star-rated like tourist attractions (★, ★★ or ★★★) to help you decide which ones to include in your itinerary. **Rincón de la Vieja**, **Chirripó**, **Tortuguero**, **Corovado** and **Irazú** are absolute musts, and are sure to amaze you with their beauty and rich variety of flora and fauna.

Some parks are busier than others. In 1996, Parque Nacional Barra Honda received only 1,265 visitors (ranking 21st in popularity), while Parque Nacional Volcán Poás welcomed close to 175,000 (ranking No. 1). Together, the parks had a total of 658,657 visitors, of which 389,883 were Costa Ricans while 268, 774 were foreigners. The parks of the Poás volcano, Manuel Antonio, and the Irazú volcano accounted for half of the visitors.

Admission to some parks and reserves is limited, to protect these natural habitats from suffering too much damage. The parks of the Poás volcano, Manuel Antonio, the Irazú volcano, Tortuguero, and Carara all have quotas of how many visitors they allow to enter the park and use the trails.

Entrance fees to the parks is **$6** per person for foreign visitors, and 85¢ for Costa Ricans. Rights of access to these areas were vehemently contested in 1994, when park entry fees jumped from under $2 per person to $15 per person! Travellers refused to pay this price and avoided going to the parks, causing the number of visitors to decline drastically. In April 1996, the

## Parks and Nature Reserves

0 50 100km

1. Estación Biológica La Selva
2. Jardín Botánico Las Cusingas
3. Parque Internacional La Amistad
4. Parque Nacional Arenal
5. Parque Nacional Barra Honda
6. Parque Nacional Braulio Carrillo
7. Parque Nacional Cahuita
8. Parque Nacional Chirripó
9. Parque Nacional Corcovado
10. Parque Nacional Guanacaste
11. Parque Nacional Isla del Coco
12. Parque Nacional Juan Castro Blanco
13. Parque Nacional Manuel Antonio
14. Parque Nacional Marino Ballena
15. Parque Nacional Marino Las Baulas de Guanacaste
16. Parque Nacional Palo Verde
17. Parque Nacional Rincón de la Vieja
18. Parque Nacional Santa Rosa
19. Parque Nacional Tortuguero
20. Parque Nacional Volcán Irazú
21. Parque Nacional Volcán Poás
22. Refugio Nacional Bahía Junquillal
23. Refugio Nacional de Fauna Silvestre Barra del Colorado
24. Refugio Nacional de Fauna Silvestre Curú
25. Refugio Nacional de Fauna Silvestre Golfito
26. Refugio Nacional de Fauna Silvestre Isla Bolaños
27. Refugio Nacional de Fauna Silvestre Ostional
28. Refugio Nacional de Fauna Silvestre Tapantí
29. Refugio Nacional de Vida Silvestre Caño Negro
30. Refugio Nacional de Vida Silvestre Gandoca-Manzanillo
31. Refugio Silvestre Peñas Blancas
32. Reserva Biológica Bosque Nuboso Monteverde
33. Reserva Biológica Carara
34. Reserva Biológica de Nosara
35. Reserva Biológica Hitoy-Cerere
36. Reserva Biológica Isla del Caño
37. Reserva Biológica Isla Guayabo
38. Reserva Biológica Isla Negrito
39. Reserva Biológica Isla Pájaros
40. Reserva Biológica Lomas Barbudal
41. Reserva Biológica Oro Verde
42. Reserva del Bosque Nuboso del Colegio de Santa Elena
43. Reserva Natural Absoluta Cabo Blanco
44. Wilson Botanical Gardens

government lowered the rates to $6, which is much more reasonable, although many still find the two-tiered system unfair, arguing that foreign visitors should not be charged more than locals.

Here is a price list for the services found in the various parks:

- Overnight stay in one of the parks or at the park keeper's house ($2 per person)
- Overnight stay in dormitory-style accommodations in the Parque Nacional Santa Rosa ($14.60 per person per night)
- Camping ($1.25 per person per day)
- Booking a conference room ($14.60 per day)
- Using a computer hook-up ($1.70 per day)
- Using a laboratory ($1.70 per day)
- Obtaining an underwater diving permit in protected zones ($4.20 per person per day)
- Parking (car 45¢, minivan 65¢, bus $1.05 per day), when not included in the entrance fee
- Hiring a guide from the national park service ($5 per hour)

**Please note**: the telephone numbers for the visitor centres and park administration offices are listed in the chapters corresponding to the region in which the parks are found.

In Costa Rica, call ☎**192** (toll free) for general information about all national parks. You can also contact the offices of **SINAC** *(☎283-8004, ≠283-7343, Sistema Nacional de Areas de Conservación)* in San José.

The **Fundación de Parques Nacionales**, or FPN, *(Mon to Fri 8am to 5pm; Av. 15 and Calle 23/25, near the Santa Terisita church, ☎257-2239, ≠222-4732)* is an excellent source of information about visiting the various national parks. The staff is friendly and dedicated, and some speak English (ask for Alexia).

## OUTDOOR ACTIVITIES

### Swimming

Costa Rica has dozens of idyllic beaches perfect for swimming. The salty waters of the Pacific Ocean and Caribbean Sea are warm – sometimes almost too warm! Some beaches are known around the world for their excellent surfing conditions: the waves are often high and very powerful. Keep in mind that these are not the best places for family swimming.

Also, be very cautious of the undertow (strong seaward current) created by the breaking waves: it claims several victims in Costa Rica each year. If you feel yourself being dragged by the current, don't resist it as this is futile. Rather, take a deep breath, relax your muscles and let yourself drift (only for a few seconds) until the current subsides and releases you. You can then swim back to the beach, which will suddenly be quite a distance away!

If you go to the beach with children, it is strongly recommended that you always accompany them into the water, or at least keep a close watch on them. In some places, the waves break almost on the beach itself, and children, as well as adults, can easily be knocked down by a sudden wave.

### Rafting

If you've never gone rafting before, this is your perfect opportunity to try it, since Costa Rica's rivers are among the best in the world for this sport. Because some sections of the river are very calm while others are quite violent, you have plenty of choices – everything from a pleasant excursion through the surrounding scenery to a wild and unforgettable adventure that will get your adrenalin pumping.

The **Río Pacuare** is considered one of the most spectacular rivers in the tropics. Running through untamed forest, and comprising several waterfalls along the way, the river narrows as it enters a picturesque canyon that has some perfect spots for bathing. The trip is ranked moderately difficult (classes III and IV), but beginners in good physical shape and with a taste for adventure will enjoy it. Unfortunately, the canyon is threatened by a huge hydro-electric dam that is scheduled to be built soon, and will definitely put an end to rafting in the area.

Another river that is renowned for its rafting possibilities is the **Río Reventazón**, which runs parallel to the Río Pacuare, slightly to the north-west. It has an easy stretch (classes II and III) that is perfect for beginners, as well as very difficult sections (classes IV and V) that will make even the most seasoned adventurers sweat a little.

In addition, the **Río Corobicí**, **Río Sarapiquí**, **Río Peñas Blancas** and **Río Chirripó** are also good for rafting. The **Río Corobicí**, located in Guanacaste, has a long easy section that is a real boon for birdwatchers, since its leisurely pace gives them time to observe dozens of species of birds, as well as iguanas, monkeys and caymans.

## Horseback Riding

You will be surprised by the number of horses in Costa Rica, especially in Guanacaste, which is sometimes called the "Far West" of Costa Rica. Because cars are relatively expensive, roads are rutted or in generally poor condition, and distances between villages are quite short, many Costa Ricans use horses to get around in the mountains and the countryside.

As a result, it is easy to find places that rent horses. However, caution is advised: while Costa Ricans are excellent riders, visitors are often novices. Look around (hotels are good places to start) for horses that are calm and used to being ridden.

Also, Costa Ricans do not usually use bits, a metal piece that is put in a horse's mouth to help direct it. Some tourists find that without it, they do not feel they have absolute control over the animal. Also, remember that it can get extremely hot (about 35° C) on the beaches and along the coast, and that horses, like people, are susceptible to dehydration. If you plan to ride for several hours, ask the attendant about rules regarding rests, water, etc. and set the pace accordingly.

## Golf

Like in North America and Europe, more and more people are discovering the pleasure of this sport in Costa Rica. While hardly any facilities existed several years ago, four new golf courses were built between 1996 and 1998, and there are plans for several more in the next few years. Some greens are located in the Central Valley near San José, while others, such as the **Playa Tambor**, **Playa Grande** and

**Playa Conchal** courses are magnificently situated by the sea.

To find out more about the various golf courses, and for the most up-to-date information about the newest additions, contact **Costa Rica Golf Adventures** *(☎/≠446-5547, golf@centralamerica.com)*.

## Kayaking

Costa Rica's many rivers will set any kayak-lover's heart aflutter. The **Río Pacuare** and the **Río Reventazón** near the city of Siquirres (Limón province), the **Río Corobicí** near Cañas (Guanacaste), the **Río Sarapiquí** near Puerto Viejo (Heredia), the **Río Peñas Blancas** and the **Río Chirripó** near San Isidro de El General (Puntarenas) are all ideal places to practice this sport. However, since these rivers are also popular with rafters, you will sometimes find whole groups of river enthusiasts sharing the waterway with you.

Sea kayaking is becoming increasingly popular in Costa Rica. Since the country is situated between two oceans (the Atlantic and Pacific) and has 1,228 kilometres of shoreline, the potential growth for this sport is enormous. While few opportunities exist as of yet, the **Nicoya Peninsula** (north Pacific coast) and the **Osa Peninsula** (south Pacific coast) have calm waters where beginners can discover this wonderful sport that brings you close to the sea.

## Wildlife Observation

The rules are simple: keep your eyes open, your ears alert and remain absolutely still! Costa Rica is the perfect place to observe wild animals, which will enchant you and give you a deeper appreciation for nature and the importance of preserving natural habitats. Monkeys, giant sea turtles, agoutis, sloths, white-tailed deer, iguanas, lizards, caymans, crocodiles, frogs and butterflies are among the most frequently spotted animals in the country, and are especially abundant in the national parks and reserves.

Although there are thousands of mammals, butterflies, reptiles, insects, fish and amphibians in Costa Rica, some visitors leave complaining that they didn't see any wildlife during their stay, even in the remote regions of the country. This is because many of these animals have developed highly effective forms of camouflage, stay well out of the way of humans, or only come out of hiding at night. Thus, we **strongly recommend that you go with a nature guide** who knows the best times and places to see dozens of animals and can answer your questions.

## Birdwatching

With 850 bird species, Costa Rica is undoubtedly one of the best places in the world for birdwatching. People come from around the world to see the famous **resplendent quetzal** *(Pharomachrus mocinno)*, which inhabits the **Monteverde** reserve, as well as the brilliantly coloured **scarlet macaw** *(Ara macao)*, which is found almost exclusively at the **Carara** reserve and on the **Osa Peninsula** (in the Parque Nacional Corcovado).

Hiring the services of a nature guide will allow you to see the largest number of bird species during your excursion, since the forest is very dense, the trees covered in moss, creepers and all sorts of epiphytic plants, making it extremely difficult to see certain kinds of birds. Above all, don't forget your binoculars!

## Fishing

With its numerous mountain rivers and lakes, including Lake Arenal, which is the largest in the country, Costa Rica provides many possibilities for freshwater fishing, including rainbow trout and rainbow perch.

With the Pacific Ocean on one side, and the Caribbean Sea on the other, Costa Rica has also made a name for itself in deep sea fishing. You can catch swordfish, tarpon, pike, marlin, shark, sailfish, mackerel, tuna and daurade, among others. **Tarpon**, which is usually caught between January and May on the Caribbean coast, is said to be best near Tortuguero. This enormous fish weighs over 35 kilos on average and is extremely ferocious, putting up a good fight that is as exhausting as it is memorable!

## Windsurfing

Windsurfers from around the world come to experience the superb **Lake Arenal**, just west of the Arenal volcano (1, 633 m), which is one of the planet's most active volcanoes. Measuring 39 kilometres in length, and 5 kilometres in width, the lake is the largest in Costa Rica. Favourable winds make Lake Arenal the best freshwater place to windsurf in Central America.

## Scuba Diving and Snorkelling

With its 1, 016-kilometre Pacific coast and its 212 kilometre Atlantic coast, Costa Rica has many beaches and underwater escarpments from which you can go snorkelling and scuba diving. The southern section of the Atlantic coast, between Cahuita and Manzanillo, has superb coral reefs. Certain islands in the Pacific, such as Isla del Caño, Isla del Coco, Isla Ballena and Isla Tortuga, as well as the countless bays of the Nicoya Peninsula (Guanacaste), are ideal places for snorkelling and scuba diving. Several agencies offer introductory courses and sea excursions.

## Hiking

Hiking is one of the best ways to explore Costa Rica's parks, reserves and wildlife conservation areas. Since the country is small and mountainous, there are plenty of spectacular mountain hikes which pass by the major volcanoes (Rincón de la Vieja, Arenal, Irazú, Poás, etc.), as well as some mountains with altitudes of over 3, 000 metres (Chiripó, Urán, etc.). Some parks have scenic trails along the coast (Corcovado, Manuel Antonio, Cabo Blanco, Santa Rosa, Cahuita, Gandoca-Manzanillo, etc.). Though they are not very steep, these paths are strenuous because of the stifling heat and humidity. Luckily, there is almost always a beach where you can refresh yourself.

Many of the parks and reserves we visited have a small network of pathways, but few have extensive hiking trails. However, we found that **Chirripó**, **Rincón de la Vieja**, **Corcovado**, and **Monteverde** are some of the country's best places for hiking.

## Bungie Jumping

Bungie jumping only caught on in Costa Rica several years ago. If you long to launch yourself from a bridge with your feet firmly attached to an elastic cord,

OUTDOORS

call Tropical Bungee *(☎233-6455)*, the only company offering this service. Jumps take place from the bridge spanning the **Río Colorado**, about an hour's drive from San José. It costs $45 for the first jump, and $25 for additional ones.

## Surfing

Costa Rica has numerous beaches where you can go surfing, both on its Pacific and Caribbean coast. While some are well-suited for beginners, others attract die-hard surfers from around the world with their incredible waves.

Among the most popular beaches, where you can watch expert surfers in action, are **Salsa Brava**, **Naranjo** (Witch's Rock), **Tamarindo**, **Mal País**, **Hermosa**, **Dominical**, **Matapalo** and **Pavones**. The last beach has some of the longest waves in the world.

## Cycling

Costa Rica's smaller roads are perfect for cycling. Paradoxically, the many potholes work in cyclists' favour, as they slow down traffic, making conditions safer. Many of these roads are unsurfaced, so mountain bikes are your best bet. However, once you leave the Central Valley, temperatures can get very high, preventing even the most determined cyclists from undertaking long excursions. If you really want to put yourself to the test, tackle the **Irazú volcano** (1, 432 m), about 30 kilometres north of the city of Cartago (Central Valley).

## Canopy Tours

Tours of the forest canopy are very popular in Costa Rica. They involve climbing to solid platforms found at the top of one or several of the highest trees in a certain area. Some agencies have a pulley system rigged between the platforms, allowing you to travel from one to the next along cables. For the less adventurous, there are also tours that stay on one platform from which the surrounding flora and fauna (monkeys, parrots, toucans, orchids, etc.) can peacefully be observed. These usually last about five hours. Canopy tours are available in several of the country's regions, most notably around Monteverde, the Parque Nacional Rincón de la Vieja, the Dominical region and on the Osa Peninsula.

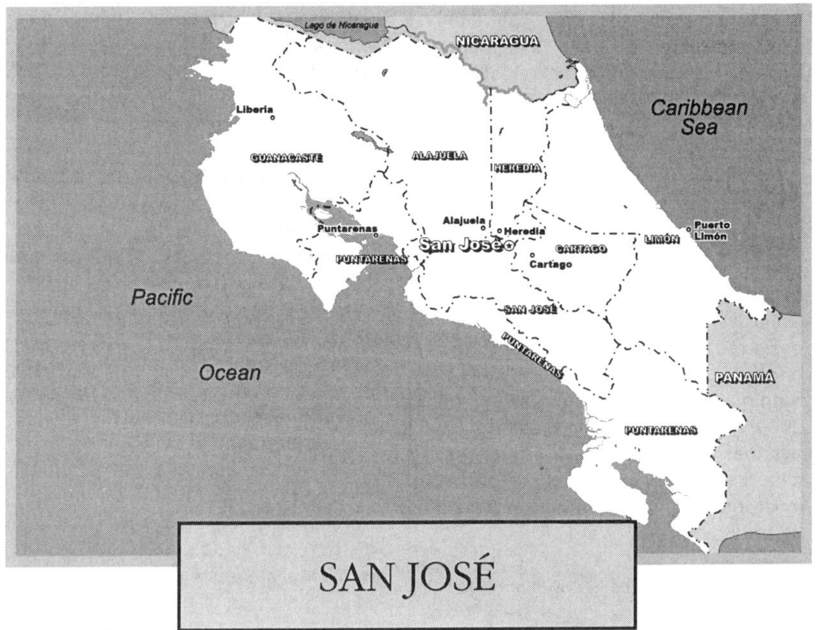


# SAN JOSÉ

The first thing that will strike you about the capital of Costa Rica is the feeling of being removed from nature – something you are not likely to experience elsewhere in the country. Indeed, at first sight **San José ★★** seems noisy, smoky and generally unremarkable. To discover its character, the city must be experienced over a certain period of time. Of course, it does not quite have the charm of old colonial cities, nor the sleek look of a North American megalopolis. But San José is a vibrant place with no shortage of people to mingle within a safe environment. Here, you can go out every night, enjoy a delicious ice cream in the pedestrian zone with swarms of people streaming past, delve into the country's cultural scene, and succumb to the delights of its international cuisine.

San José only became the nation's capital in the 19th century, when it supplanted the older and more historic city of Cartago following a short-lived civil war that led to the country's independence. Since the beginning of the 20th century, the city has grown steadily, and today its million inhabitants (suburbs included) constitute almost a third of the country's population. San José is still a constantly expanding city – the largest in the country – and has the energy and restlessness that goes along with it.

It seems appropriate that San José, the nation's capital, should lie in the middle of everything. Its urban sprawl is the point of convergence in the Central Valley, as it is centrally located amid the region's other major cities. This region, in turn, lies in the heart of the country as a whole. Furthermore, San José plays an integral role in the country's economy, transportation system and cultural life, all of which are centred around it.

In addition to all this, San José is only a short distance from the Central Valley's national parks. It is definitely worthwhile to visit this city, around which much of the country's life revolves.

## FINDING YOUR WAY AROUND

Finding your way around San José is easy. Most of the city is laid out in a basic grid, with *calles* (streets) running north and south and *avenidas* (avenues) running east and west. Furthermore, almost all of the city streets and avenues are numbered, starting at the city centre where Avenida Central intersects Calle Central, and increasing as they extend outwards.

This orderly system is especially useful since houses are generally not numbered (see p 38). Instead, addresses are given in metres in relation to specific intersections of streets and avenues, and you will have to find your way according to these. Costa Ricans often use popular landmarks (for instance, "at Calle 5 and Avenida 7, behind the Holiday Inn") when giving directions.

Avenida Central, which becomes Paseo Colón, a pedestrian zone downtown, and Avenida 2 are the main roads leading into the capital from the west, via the highway from the airport.

The **Coca Cola** district that borders San José's central market is noisy and lively, but poor, and should be avoided after dark. Conversely, **Barrio Amón**, in north-central San José, is the city's charming historic district – it is even designated as such by the authorities – with some of the finest little hotels in the capital, as well as many cultural activities and night spots. You would be hard-pressed to find a completely quiet street, however. The calmer **Aranjurez** district is also close to the heart of the city, and some of its residences are being converted into hotels.

**Escazú** is one of San José's affluent suburbs where wealthy homeowners have taken up residence in the foothills just west of the city. This district boasts a certain number of high quality hotels and restaurants in a natural setting. **Pavas** (where the American embassy is located) has a few hotels and restaurants, but **Sabana** has many more and also contains La Sabana, a huge recreational park. **Rohrmoser** is another of the capital's posh tranquil neighbourhoods but has few hotels.

On the east side, **San Pedro** and **Los Yoses** are also quite fashionable San José districts. The former contains the University of Costa Rica and a few good, quiet hotels, while the latter boasts several embassies, restaurants and comfortable accommodations. Lastly, **Tournón**, just north of downtown, encompasses the popular little **El Pueblo** shopping centre and a few hotels.

The stretch of the General Cañas Highway leading to the international airport, located outside San José, is dotted with a whole series of large hotels that make use of the sizeable plots of land and their convenient location on the expressway. In this area, you will find the **Cariari** district.

Like in other major cities around the world, prostitution exists in San José. The south part of Morazán Park and the Coca Cola district are the so-called "red-light districts", as is the stretch of Calle 7 between Avenidas 1 and 3.

If you want to lose yourself in a crowd, stroll along the downtown stretch of Avenida Central that is closed off to

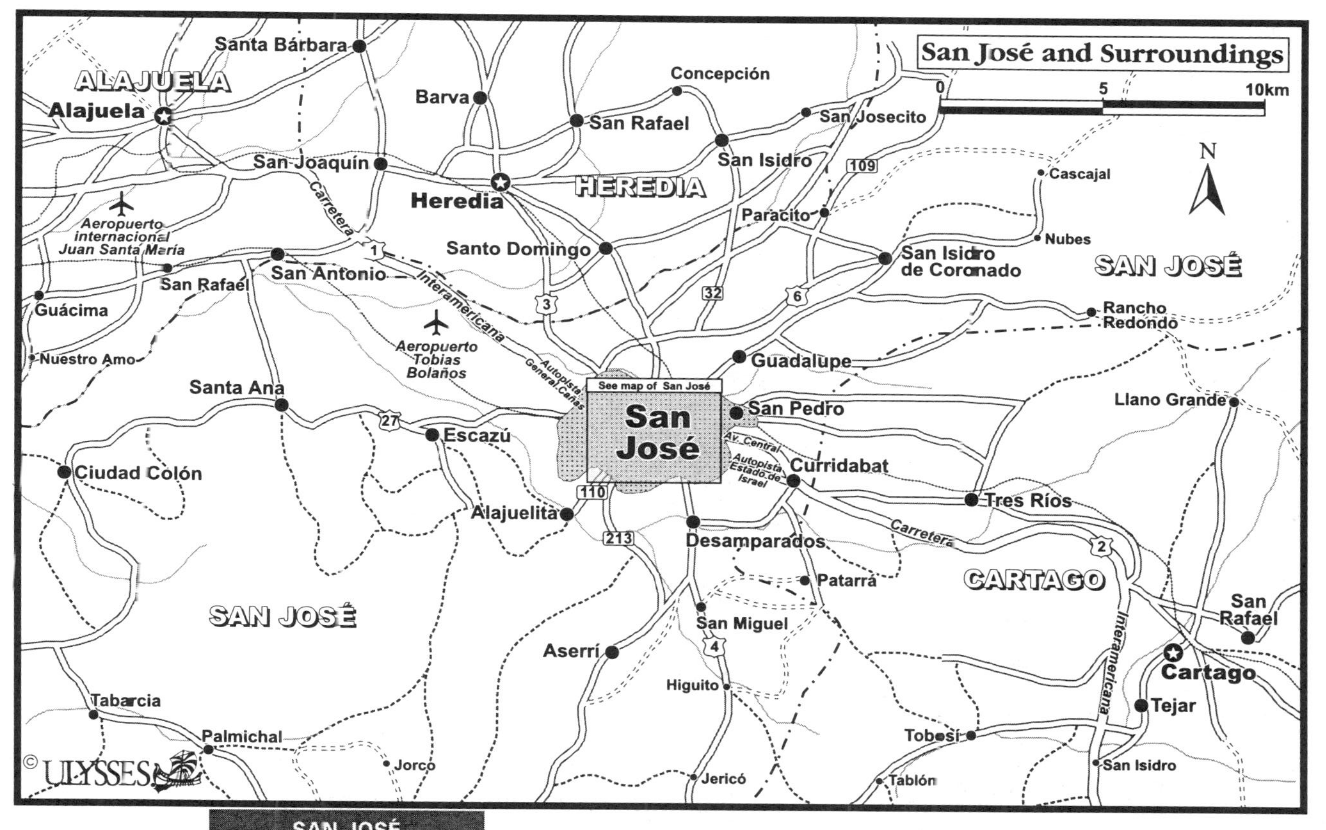
San José and Surroundings
0
5
10km
N
ALAJUELA
Alajuela
Santa Bárbara
Barva
San Rafael
Concepción
San Josecito
San Isidro
San Joaquín
Heredia
HEREDIA
109
Cascajal
Aeropuerto internacional Juan Santa María
Carretera
Paracito
Nubes
Santo Domingo
San Isidro de Coronado
SAN JOSÉ
1
San Antonio
San Rafael
Guácima
Interamericana
3
32
6
Rancho Redondo
Aeropuerto Tobías Bolaños
Nuestro Amo
Autopista General Cañas
Guadalupe
See map of San José
San José
Santa Ana
San Pedro
Llano Grande
27
Escazú
Av. Central
Autopista Estado de Israel
Curridabat
Ciudad Colón
110
Tres Ríos
Alajuelita
Carretera
213
Desamparados
2
CARTAGO
Patarrá
SAN JOSÉ
San Miguel
San Rafael
Interamericana
Aserrí
4
Cartago
Tejar
Higuito
Tabarcia
Palmichal
Tobosi
Jorco
© ULYSSES
Jericó
Tablón
San Isidro

traffic; it is often bustling with people and activities.

## By Bus

San José is the hub where most of Costa Rica's inter-city, regional and international bus routes converge.

There are many departures from the Coca Cola district, located just west of the city centre and Mercado Central. The bus stops are scattered along main thoroughfares around the **Terminus Coca Cola**, located on Avenida 1 between Calles 16 and 18. For example, the coaches bound for the suburb of **Escazú** as well as **Nicoya** and Guanacaste-area beaches stop at the quadrilateral just west of the terminus. Those heading to **San Isidro de El General, San Ramón, Liberia** and **Playa del Coco** are found just east of the terminus. Buses for the **Volcán Poás, Alajuela** or **Heredia** are a little farther south, on Avenida 2, by the San Juan de Dios hospital. If you are not using the hotel shuttle, you can take the regular Alajuela-bound bus which also goes to the **international airport**. Along northbound Calle 12 are the coaches for **Tilarán, Monteverde, Puerto Jiménez, Guápiles, Puerto Viejo de Sarapiquí, San Vito, Playa Sámara, Playa Tamarindo, Playa Panamá** and **Playa Hermosa**. Departures for **Quepos, Manuel Antonio** and **Playa Jacó** as well as **Ciudad Quesada** (San Carlos) leave from the Coca Cola terminal.

Departures for **Irazú** *(Av. 2, near the Teatro Nacional)*, **Cahuita** *(Calle Central, Av. 9/11)*, **Puerto Limón** *(Av. 3, Calle 19, east of Parque Nacional)*, **Turrialba** *(Calle 13, Av. 6)* and **Puntarenas** *(Calle 16, Av. 10)* are at other locations around the city, but still downtown.

South of the Coca Cola bus terminal, the Tracopa company *(Av. 18, Calle 4, ☎221-4214)* offers several daily departures for southern Costa Rica: **Ciudad Neily, Golfito, Palmar Norte** and **San Vito**. A one-way trip to the south of the country should cost you around US$10.

The Sacsa company *(Calle 5, Av. 18, ☎233-5350)* has daily departures for **Cartago**, in eastern Costa Rica. Travel within the Valley only costs a few dollars, no matter how far away the destination.

For a list of addresses for the other main bus companies, see p 38.

To obtain an up-to-date list of the **city bus** routes (i.e. those to the suburbs), head to the ICT (see further below). Buses run frequently and make many stops, but you won't have to use them to visit the city centre, as everything is within walking distance.

## By Taxi

There is no shortage of taxis in San José. There are many taxi stands (on Avenida 2, near the Ministerio de l'Economía, for example) and you can flag one down in the street any time of day or night. All taxis are red (see also p 38).

# PRACTICAL INFORMATION

## Tourist Information

Tourist information is available at the head office of the **Instituto Costarricense de Turismo** (ICT) *(Av. 4, Calle 5/7)*, since their outlet on Plaza de la Cultura closed down. However, the institute's administrators are aware of the inconvenience this causes, and are considering reopening an information office on Plaza de la Cultura. It may be worth checking out whether this location has in fact been reopened, as it is much more convenient and pleasant.

**Guided Tours**

Here are a few agencies in and around San José that offer guided tours or outdoor activities. You can make arrangements over the phone with most companies, saving yourself the trip to the offices. Also, most of San José hotels have numerous brochures and can make the reservations for you.

**Aventuras Naturales** *(Av. Central, Calle 33/35, ☎225-3939, ⇒253-6934)* offers rafting excursions on the Río Pacuare and the Río Reventazón.

Since 1975, **Calypso Tours** *(Av. 2, Calle 1/3, in the Las Arcadas building, Oficina 11, ☎256-2727, ⇒233-0401)* has been organizing very popular boating excursions (aboard the catamarans *Calypso* or *Manta Raya*) through the Gulf of Nicoya, and particularly to Isla Tortuga.

A quick stop at the agency **Costa Rica Expeditions** *(every day 5:30am to 9pm; souvenir shop; Calle Central, Avenida 3, ☎257-0766 or 222-0333, ⇒257-1665, costaric@expeditions.co.cr)*, right in the middle of downtown San José, should be enough to convince you that Costa Rica has become one of the world's top destinations for ecotourism and adventure-tourism. This agency, generally thought of as having pioneered nature tourism in Costa Rica, provides very professional service. Whether you go on a half-day, one-day or overnight excursion (hiking, rafting, canopy tours, horseback riding, birdwatching, sightseeing and more: their brochure is 82 pages long!), you will be accompanied by experienced and qualified naturalist guides. Moreover, the agency goes all over the country and owns the Monteverde Lodge (North), the Tortuga Lodge (Caribbean coast) and the Corcovado Lodge Tent Camp (South), as well as two luxury hotels and a heavenly campground, all for a memorable stay. And the hearty meals served in their restaurants are invariably fresh.

**Costa Rica Sun Tours** *(Av. 7, Calle 5/7, ☎255-3418, ⇒255-4410)* offers a host of guided tours in and around the greater Central Valley region, and manages the Arenal Observatory Lodge and the Tiskita Lodge.

**Ecole Travel** *(Calle 7, Av. Central/1, ☎223-2240, ⇒223-4128)* offers guided tours (Isla Tortuga, Manuel Antonio, Monteverde, Arenal, Corcovado, Tortuguero, etc.) for budget travellers.

**Ecoscape Nature Tours** *(☎297-0664, ⇒297-0549)* and **Marbella Travel & Tours** *(☎259-0055, ⇒259-0065)* will take you on a one-day tour of the Volcán Poás and Braulio Carrillo parks, as well as the Río Sarapiquí, Cataratas La Paz and Selva Verde Lodge.

**Expediciones Tropicales** *(Calle 3B, Av. 11/13, ☎257-4171, ⇒257-4124)* offers guided tours of the Central Valley's main volcanoes (Irazú, Poás, Barva, Orosí).

**Geotur** *(☎/⇒227-4029)* takes visitors on tours of the Parque Nacional Braulio Carrillo and the Reserva Biológica Carara

**Horizontes** *(Calle 28, Av. 1/3, ☎222-2020, ⇒255-4513)* offers rafting on the Rió Pacuare and the Rió Reventazón, as well as guided family tours.

**Agencia de Viajes La Cruz** *(☎679-9276, ⇌226-5581)* is managed by Ricardo Bolaños, a first-rate tour guide. The agency organizes trips throughout the country, but specializes in the Guanacaste region, particularly the northern part of the province. Visits to this region's parks and reserves (Rincón de la Vieja, Santa Rosa, etc.) as well as sea excursions such as snorkelling and outings to beaches, are offered. The talkative Ricardo, who speaks English, will be happy to answer your questions – at great length!

Run by Manfred Gutiérrez, **Maguines Travel Service** *(☎/⇌283-4510, manfredg@sol.racsa.co.cr)* organizes customized packages for short and extended stays in various regions of the country (hotel and car reservations and all kinds of activities).

**Ríos Tropicales** *(Calle 32, Av. 2, ☎233-6455, ⇌255-4354)* specializes in rafting, as well as river and sea kayaking.

**Swiss Travel Service** *(☎282-4898, ⇌282-4890)* and **Fantasy Tours** *(☎326-8279 or 220-2126, ⇌220-2393)* organize many different guided tours (San José, volcanoes, rafting, Isla Tortuga, etc.) in the greater Central Valley region.

**Tikal Tours** *(Av. 2, Calle 7/9, ☎223-2811, ⇌223-1916)* specializes in ecotourism and offers guided tours of several regions of the country.

Since 1985, **Vesa Tours** *(☎220-0260 or 290-6603, ⇌220-2779, vesatour@sol.racsa.co.cr)* has been organizing expeditions that explore the country's natural, as well as cultural and historical, attractions. Among these, the guided tour of San José is particularly interesting, and will introduce you to the production of coffee and handicrafts, take you on various outdoor excursions like rafting and horseback riding and, of course, visit the national parks. The staff is experienced and conscientious.

## Banks and Foreign Exchange Offices

There are many banks in San José, especially downtown. Many of them have ATMs (automatic teller machines), so you don't have to wait in the long lines for the tellers. Avoid making bank transactions on the street at night. Exchange rates and bank administrative fees are reasonable in Costa Rica, so it is not worth taking the risk of using money changers on the street.

## Health

The **Hospital San Juan de Dios** *(Av. 2, Calle 14, ☎257-6282)* is a very large general hospital in downtown San José. Health care costs are much lower in Costa Rica than in most of North America and Europe, and there are many private medical clinics and pharmacies. Your country's consulate can best advise you where to turn should you need medical services. You can also consult the *Costa Rica Guide*, published yearly by the *Tico Times*, which can recommend clinics to treat most health problems.

As in most of North America, dial **☎911** for all emergencies. For a Red Cross ambulance, call **☎128**; in case of fire, dial **☎118**.

## Mail, Fax, Telegraph and Internet

San José's main post office is the Correo Central *(Calle 2, Av. 1/ 3; Mon to Fri 8am to midnight, Sat 8am to noon)*. The mail boxes for out-going

San José
ATTRACTIONS
1. Parque La Sabana
2. Museo de Arte Costarricense
3. Centro Costarricense de la Ciencia y la Cultura
4. University of Costa Rica Campus
ACCOMMODATIONS
1. Americano del Este
2. Amstel Escazú
3. Aparthotel El Sesteo
4. Aparthotel La Sabana
5. Aparthotel Los Yoses
6. Aparthotel María Alexandra
7. Aparthotel Ramgo
8. Ara Macao
9. Bergerac
10. Casa Las Orquideas
11. Colours
12. Corobici
13. Cristina
14. D'Galah
15. Don Fadrique
16. Don Paco Inn
17. Hampton Inn
18. Herradura
19. Irazu
20. Jacques et Helena
21. La Granja
22. Marriot
23. Melia Cariari
24. Palma Real
25. Parque del Lago
26. Pico Blanco Inn
27. Pine Tree Inn
28. Posada El Quijote
29. Puesta del Sol
30. Radisson
31. Residencias de Golf
32. Rincón del Valle
33. San José Palacio
34. Tennis Club
35. Toruma
36. Villa Tournón
RESTAURANTS
1. Angus Steak House
2. El Chicote
3. Il Bagatto
4. La Esquina de Los Mariscos
5. La Masia
6. Las Tunas
7. Lukas
8. Pastelaría Giacomín
9. Supermercado Yaohan
SAN JUAN DE TIBAS
SAN VICENTE DE MORAVIA
GUADALUPE
CINCO ESQUINAS
URUCA
MONTELIMAR
LEÓN XIII
CUATRO REINAS
VUELTA VIRILLA
PEREGRINA
BAJOS DEL TORRES
MONTSERRAT
ROHRMOSER
LILAS
MÉXICO
See map of City Centre
PASO DE LA VACA
CARMEN
MANTICA
COCA COLA
MERCED
SOLEDAD
SAN FRANCISCO
LAS VEGAS
PASEO COLÓN
SAN BOSCO
DOLOROSA
MILFLOR
ANGELES
PACÍFICO
CUBA
CRISTO REY
GONZÁLEZ VIQUEZ
MONTE ALEGRE
CALDERÓN MUÑOZ
JIMENEZ
ESCALANTE
EMPALME
YOSES
SAN PEDRO
ZAPOTE
CURRIDABAT
HATILLO
SAGRADA FAMILIA
SAN SEBASTIÁN
ALAJUELITA
La Sabana Padre Chapui
Parque La Paz
Av. Las Américas
Av. Campos
Paseo Colón
Av. Central
Calle Central
Av. San Martín
Av. San Martín (10)
San José Periférica
Autopista General Cañas
Autopista Estado de Israel
Interamericana
Heredia, Alajuela Juan Sta.María Airport, Interamericana
Tobías Bolaños Airport, Escazú
Cartago
Río Virilla
Río Torres
Río María Aguilar
Río Tiribí
Río Ocloro
Quebrada
Quebrada Barreal
Rivera
Chiquita
0 1 2km
© ULYSSES

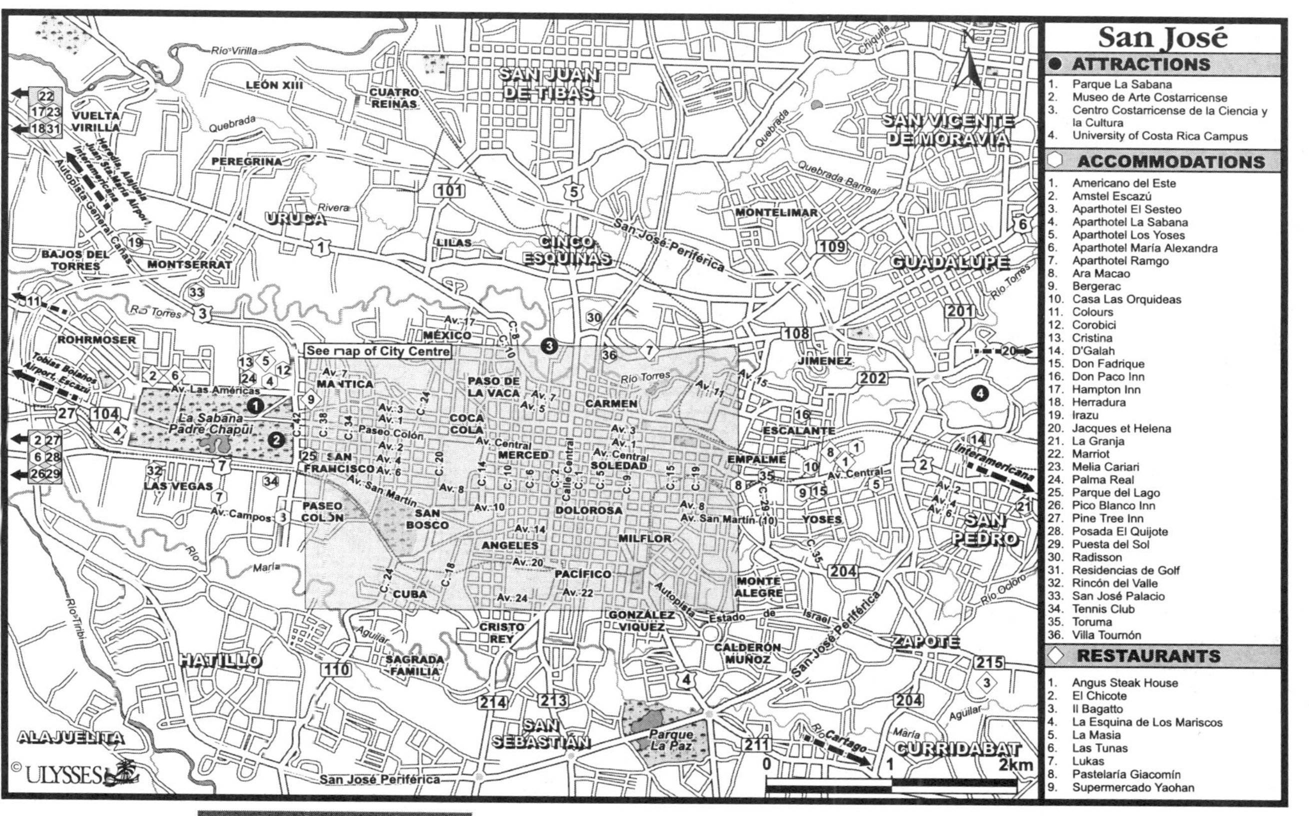

SAN JOSÉ

letters and postcards are at the entrance, on the left.

You can dispatch telegrams and send or receive faxes at **Radiográfica** *(Av. 5, Calle Central/1)*. Long-distance phone calls can also be made here, or from phone booths on the street.

More and more major hotels are providing Internet service. In addition, the **Net Café** *(8:30am to 5:30pm; on the General Cañas Highway service road, opposite the San José 2000 shopping centre)* cybercafé has many Internet work stations. Unfortunately, it is located quite far from downtown.

### Newspapers, Magazines and Books

The small magazine store next to the **Supermercado Yaohan** *(opposite the Corobici hotel)* sells many of the major Western newspapers and all kinds of periodicals: *El País, Le Monde, Le Figaro, The Wall Street Journal, USA Today*. It also has a good Costa Rican book section.

A few major hotels offer a selection of newspapers, as does **Librería Lehmann** *(Av. Central, Calle 1/3)*.

## EXPLORING

We suggest you start your tour San José's west end, on the fringes of La Sabana Metropolitan Park. Proceed through the northern part of the city to the centre of town, and then continue east through Barrio Amón, and eventually return to downtown. The tour ends with a stroll through the Paseo de los Estudiantes district, on the south side.

*Josefinos* love their **Parque La Sabana** ★★★. Many recreational activities are possible in this vast green space, right in the capital. It has numerous sports facilities (an Olympic-size pool; footpaths and jogging tracks; tennis, volleyball and basketball courts; fúbol and baseball fields; a palaestra, stadium and more) and many tree-shaded picnic and rest areas and an artificial lake, all of which are unique to San José. Furthermore, the Museo de Arte Costarricense is located in the park, on Paseo Colón, which runs into the city. It is surprising to know that this extraordinary green space is located on the spot where the city's former airport used to be. In fact, the park has become such a central facet of life that the whole surrounding district has been named after it.

The **Museo de Arte Costarricense** ★★ *($2; Tue to Sun 10am to 5pm; Calle 42, opposite Paseo Colón in La Sabana Park)* exhibits works by the best artists in the country. Chamber music concerts are sometimes held in the museum's Salón Dorado.

Established in 1855, the large **Hospital San Juan de Dios** *(Calle 14, opposite Av. 2)* is in the middle of San José, and marks off the west side of the city centre, an area which can easily be toured on foot. This neighbourhood's more recent development blends well with the older Manueline-style architecture.

The **Iglesia de la Merced** *(Av. 2, Calle 10/12)* was being renovated during our visit. A panel in front explains the history of this eclectic Gothic-style church, which was built in 1894. Unfortunately, a wire fence bars access to the vast verdant grounds, which are very rare in the city centre.

The **Mercado Central** ★★ *(Av. 1/Central, Calle 6/8)* is a fairly crowded indoor market where masses of people swarm through a warren of arrow passages, closely hemmed in by *sodas* and other little stalls that sell everything from clothing and accessories to groceries and flowers, etc. This place is always busy, and provides an excellent opportunity to immerse yourself in everyday Costa Rican life. Plaques at the market's southeast entrance *(Av. 1, Calle 6)* honour the memory of key political figures in Costa Rican history.

Opposite the Mercado Central is the **Mercado de Carnes** (meat market), which has a series of small delicatessen and butcher's stalls.

If you look north down Calle 4 from Avenida 5, there is a beautiful view of San José's former prison, which now houses the new Costa Rican museum and cultural centre: the **Centro Costarricense de la Ciencia y la Cultura ★★★**. With its crenellated walls and towers flanking the entrance, this veritable fortress is a lovely scene at night, when the whole building is illuminated. The centre's brand-new children's museum, the **Museo de los Niños** *(Wed to Fri 10am to noon and 2pm to 5pm, Sat and Sun 10am to 1pm and 2pm to 5pm)*, is unique in Central America, and is even worth the trip for adults. Its many vivid thematic hands-on exhibits that cover many different fields of knowledge make it a real learning experience! The centre also boasts exhibition halls, and a library and large auditorium will soon be added.

**Librería Lehmann** *(Av. Central, Calle 1/3)* is located in a Beaux Art-style building that could use some fixing up.

The downtown outlet of the **La Gloria** *(Av. Central, Calle 4/6)* chain of department stores is worth a visit for its classic 1960s-style decor.

The main building of the **Banco de Costa Rica** *(Av. 2, Calle 4/6)* is a fine example of the international monumental architecture of the 1960s and 1970s, whose domination of the urban landscape was meant to demonstrate the company's stature. The black marble façade makes the building all the more imposing. An elevator will take you to the eighth floor, from which there is a good view of San José, which is hard to come by since the city has few skyscrapers.

Art exhibitions are sometimes held at the **Banco Nacional** *(Av. 1, Calle 2/4)*.

Stamp collectors can visit the **Museo Filatélico** *(Mon to Fri 9am to 2pm; Calle 2, Av. 1/3)*, on the second floor of the Correo Central (central post office) to admire Costa Rican commemorative stamps.

The building of the **Alianza Francesa ★** *(Calle 7, Av. 5)* is one of San José's beautiful and well-preserved colonial-style buildings. Its media library and exhibition halls are open to the public.

Surrounded by busy thoroughfares, the well-landscaped **Parque Morazán** *(Av. 3, Calle 5/9)* is a quiet spot for locals and tourists to relax. Like many Costa Rican city parks, it has a concert bandstand.

The **Edificio Metálico ★** *(Av. 5, Calle 9)*, which now houses a school, stands opposite Parque Morazán. The building materials for this unique and interesting green steel structure were imported from France.

The **Aurola Holiday Inn** *(northwest corner of Parque Morazán)* is a popular landmark in San José's urban landscape. This huge building stands out from its neighbours with its mirrored exterior, and thus serves as a

## ATTRACTIONS

1. Hospital San Juan de Dios
2. Iglesia de la Merced
3. Mercado Central
4. Mercado de Carnes
5. Centro Costarricense de la Ciencia y la Cultura
6. Librería Lehman
7. La Gloria
8. Banco de Costa Rica
9. Banco Nacional
10. Museo Filatélico
11. Alianza Francesa
12. Parque Morazán
13. Edificio Metálico
14. Aurola Holiday Inn
15. Del Rey
16. Parque Zoológico Simón Bolívar
17. Spyrogyra
18. Parque España
19. Museo del Jade
20. Casa Amarilla
21. Centro Nacional de la Cultura
22. Museo Nacional
23. Plaza de la Democracia
24. Serpentarium
25. Plaza de la Cultura
26. Museo del Oro precolombino
27. Museo de Numismática
28. Teatro Nacional
29. Café Ruiseñor
30. Teatro Melico Salazar
31. Parque Central
32. El Paseo de los Estudiantes
33. Liceo de Costa Rica
34. Iglesia de Nuestra Señora de la Saludad
35. Parthenon

## ACCOMMODATIONS

1. Ambassador
2. América
3. Amón Park Plaza
4. Aparthotel San José
5. Aranjuez
6. Asia
7. Aurola Holiday Inn
8. Balmoral
9. Bellavista
10. Bienvenido
11. Boruca
12. Britannia
13. Casa 429 El Paso
14. Casa Ridgway
15. Casa Verde
16. Centro Americano
17. Cocori
18. Costa Rica Morazán
19. Del Rey (R)
20. Diana's Inn
21. Diplomat
22. Doña Ines
23. Dunn Inn
24. Fleur de Lys (R)
25. Gran Hotel Costa Rica
26. Gran Hotel Imperial
27. Gran Via
28. Grano de Oro (R)
29. Hemingway Inn
30. Johnson
31. Joluva Guesthouse
32. Kekoldi
33. La Gema
34. Mansión de Braulio
35. Marlyn
36. Napoleón
37. Pensión de la Cuesta
38. Petit Hotel
39. Petit Victoria
40. Presidente
41. Quality Hotel Centro Colón
42. Rey Amón
43. Rosa del Paseo
44. San José Best Western
45. Santo Tomás
46. Talamanca
47. Taylor's Inn
48. Torremolinos
49. Vesuvio

(R): Restaurant

## RESTAURANTS

1. Alpino da Rodrigo
2. Amón Coffee Shop
3. Café parisien
4. Café Ruiseñor
5. Chelles
6. Delicias Vegetarianas
7. Don Wang
8. El Balcón de Europa
9. Esmeralda
10. Feliz Feliz
11. France
12. Goya
13. Kasbah
14. La Amistad
15. La Cañada
16. La Cocina de Bordolino
17. La Esquina del Café
18. La Hacienda
19. La Pizza Metro
20. La Vasconia
21. Lobster's Inn
22. Machu Picchu
23. Marolo's
24. Mercado Central
25. Morazán
26. Pasta Factory
27. Pizzería Italiana Peperoni
28. Pollo Campesino
29. Restaurante Cafetería La Criollita
30. Sant Jordi
31. Shakti
32. Soda La Perla
33. Spoon
34. Suizo
35. Tar Zan
36. Taska Al Andalus
37. Tin Jo

geographical reference point for anyone trying to find their way in the area. The same is true of the candy-pink **Del Rey** hotel, located a stone's throw away, on the other side of Parque Morazán.

Though it is relatively small and doesn't house any particularly fascinating species, the **Parque Zoológico Nacional Simón Bolívar** *(Tue to Fri 8am to 4pm, Sat and Sun 9am to 5pm; Av. 11, Calle 7, Parque Bolívar)* can make spot for a pleasant and instructive stroll.

Also on the north side of Parque Bolívar, by the zoo, is **Spyrogyra** *($5; every day 8am to 3pm; 100 m east and 150 m south of El Pueblo, just north of downtown, near the Guapiles hwy., 10 minutes' walking distance; take the "Calle Blancos" bus at Calle 3 and Av. 5, get off at the El Pueblo shopping centre and follow directions from there or, if you're coming from Paseo Colón, take the downtown-bound "Periférica" bus to Centro Colón, or take the same bus from the Saprissa stop facing the Mönpik ice cream shop to the University of Costa Rica, ☎222-2937)*, a butterfly garden where you can admire these beautiful creatures, as well as hummingbirds, in their natural

San José
City Centre
Parque Zoológico Simón Bolívar
Río Torres
PASO DE LA VACA
MANTICA
COCA COLA
AMÓN
SAN FRANCISCO
MERCED
SOLEDAD
DOLOROSA
MILFLOR
ANGELES
PACÍFICO
PASEO COLÓN
SAN BOSCO
CUBA
Hospital San Juan de Dios
Cementerio General
Paseo Colón
Av. Central
Calle Central
Av. San Martín
Av. San Martín (10)
Paseo de Los Estudiantes
Autopista Estado de Israel
© ULYSSES

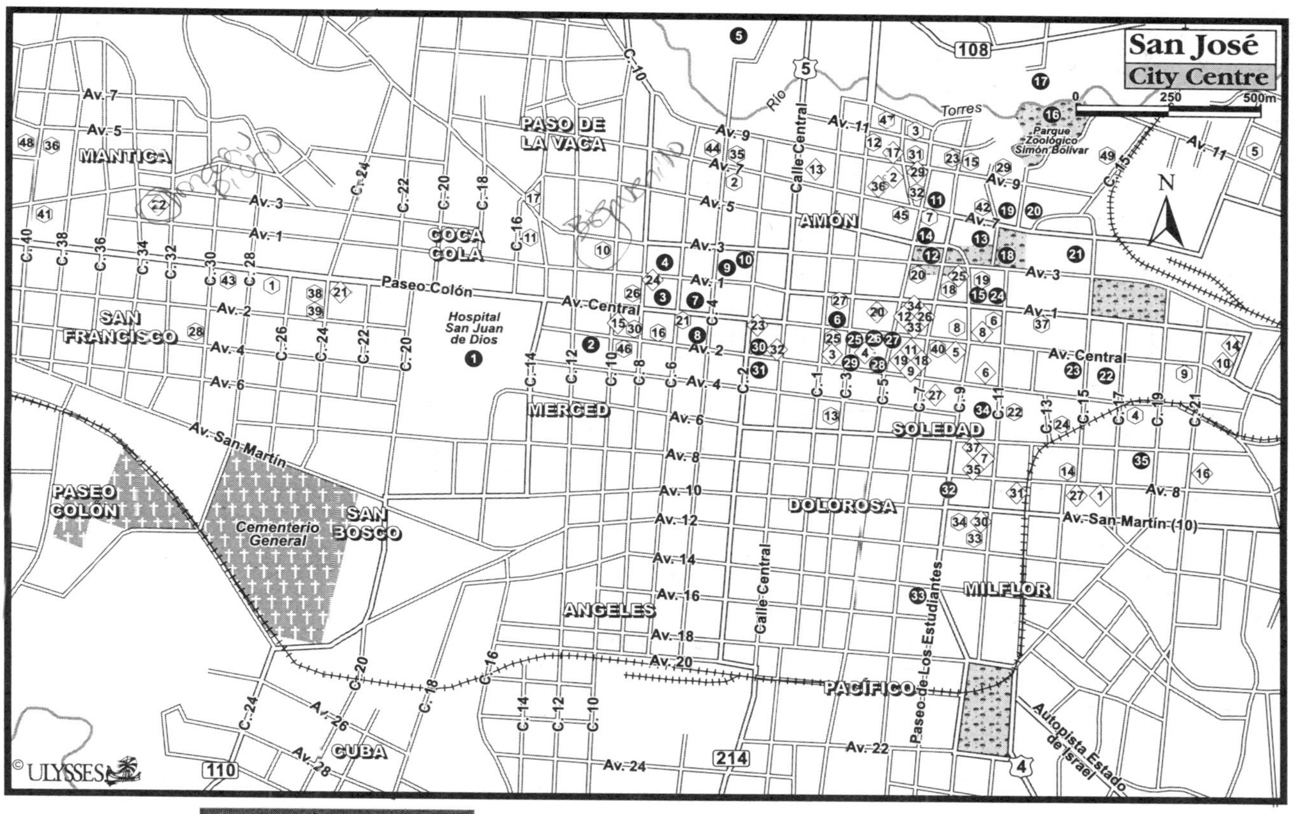

SAN JOSÉ

surroundings. There are other butterfly gardens in the country (in the Central Valley and in Monteverde), but this one is an excellent introduction to Costa Rica's natural history, and is conveniently located near downtown.

**Parque España** *(Av. 3/7, Calle 9/11)* is another beautiful and peaceful park. The beautiful, fully-grown landscaping is inviting and is more natural than that found in most of the other parks in the city.

The **Museo del Jade** *(Mon to Sat 8am to 4:30pm; on the 3rd floor of the Instituto Nacional de Seguros, Calle 9, Av. 7)* has a lovely collection of artifacts made from the magnificent green stone, and also provides a beautiful view over the city.

The **Casa Amarilla** ★ *(Av. 7, Calle 11)* is one of the capital's most elegant buildings. Bequeathed to the nation by Andrew Carnegie, the rich and famous American philanthropist, the "Yellow House" now houses the Department of Foreign Affairs

The **Centro Nacional de la Cultura** ★★ *(every day 10am to 5pm)* recently established itself in one of the city's oldest industrial facilities (the former National Liquor Factory, built in 1856). It is home to the national Ministry of Culture, Youth and Sports, the Museum of Contemporary Art and Design, the Hispano-American cultural centre, the Colegio de Costa Rica, the national dance company's rehearsal studios and performance spaces, etc. This beautifully renovated building no longer produces liquor since the state distillery has been relocated in Grecia.

The **Museo Nacional** ★★ *(Tue to Sun 9am to 5pm; Av. 2, Calle 17)* is housed in the former Bellavista fortress (used in the Civil War of 1948), which has been renovated into a museum that exhibits a permanent collection of pre-Colombian gold and ceramic artifacts, as well as religious art works. The museum also has a display of the nation's history. The **Plaza de la Democracia** *(Calle 15, Av. Central/2)* adjoining the museum was laid out in the late 1980s to mark the occasion of a major international conference hosted by Costa Rica.

The **Serpentarium** *(Mon to Fri 9am to 6pm, Sat and Sun 10am to 5pm; Av. 1, Calle 9/11, ☎225-4210)* is *the* place to learn everything there is to know about the Costa Rica's reptiles. There are live specimens from all over the world, including the deadly cobra and the famous piranha, which is fed every Monday, Wednesday and Friday at 5pm.

**Plaza de la Cultura** ★★ *(Av. Central, Calle 3/5)* can be considered the most central of San José's downtown squares, if such a thing is possible! It is always bustling with young people, students, lovers and businesspeople – in short, of everyone! Numerous shops line the lovely terraced space. The Gran Hotel Costa Rica's café and the Teatro Nacional's Café Ruiseñor and the Avenida Central pedestrian zone also border the square, so it is really not surprising that it is such a popular place to hang out at any time of day!

Below the Plaza de la Cultura *(Av. Central, Calle 5)* are a whole series of museums run by the Fundación Museos del Banco Central de Costa Rica *(☎223-0528 or 257-0987)*. The **Museo del Oro Precolombino** ★★★ *(Tue to Sun 10am to 4:30pm)* houses a dazzling collection of precious gold objects from the pre-Colombian era to the time of Spanish Conquest. The **Museo de Numismática** ★ *(Tue to Sun 10am to 4:30pm)* relates the history of Costa Rican paper money. The complex also has spaces for temporary fine-arts and pottery exhibits.

The architecture of the **Teatro Nacional** ★★★ *(Mon to Sat 9am to 4:30pm; Plaza de la Cultura, Calle 3, Av. 2)* is similar to that of the Paris Opera house. The national theatre was built when prima donna Andelina Patti refused to perform in Costa Rica, for want of an appropriate venue. It was inaugurated in 1897, and is now the headquarters of the **Orquesta Sinfónica Nacional y Juvenil** (National Symphony and Youth Orchestra). The building was classified as an historic monument in 1965, and it has undergone renovation and restoration work over the last few years to mark its centenary.

The **Café Ruiseñor** *(inside the Teatro Nacional)* regularly presents temporary exhibitions.

The **Teatro Melico Salazar** ★★ *(Av. 2, Calle Central; opposite Parque Central, ☎222-2653)* is not only a theatre hall, but also the place where Costa Rica's independence came into being. Popular bands (including Emerson, Lake & Palmer in 1997) perform here on their Central American tours. The hall was named in honour of world-famous Costa Rican tenor Melico Salazar.

**Parque Central** *(Calle Central/2, Av. 2/4)* is quite well-kept, but would be more accurately described as a square than a park, since much of its surface is paved. This centrally located park has a lot of character with its lovely terraced design and large rotunda with voluted classical columns crowned with a cupola. If you want to stand beneath the cupola, be warned: neighbourhood pigeons like to roost on the inside edges.

Calle 9 is also known as **El Paseo de los Estudiantes** (the students' route), as it leads south to the **Liceo de Costa Rica**, one of the largest and oldest high schools in the country. During the school year, many students can be seen coming and going, clad in their school uniforms. Some of the Liceo's buildings are of architectural and historical interest.

The **Iglesia de Nuestra Señora de la Saludad** *(Calle 9, Av. 6)*, on Paseo de los Estudiantes, is very well-kept and newly renovated. The church has beautifully made and very colourful lateral stained-glass windows. The white interior is has a pleasant and almost magical feel to it, and its architecture as a whole makes it a worthwhile stop if you are passing through the neighbourhood.

Opposite the Iglesia de la Saludad, at Calle 9, north of Avenida 6, the small Paseo de los Estudiantes square is delightfully ornamented with plants. There are also commemorative plaques honouring Carlos Gardel, an ambassador of Argentinian culture who died under tragic circumstances.

A small, very lovely white classical parthenon stands on Calle 19, on the northwest corner of the grounds of the Museum of Criminology. Illuminated at night, it is the site where future president Oscar Arias Sanchéz gave the inaugural speech of the University of Costa Rica in 1941.

Farther east, in the San Pedro district, the very large campus of the **Universidad de Costa Rica** ★ is a lovely place for a quiet walk. The grounds include features, a beautiful tree-lined path almost two kilometres long.

## ACCOMMODATIONS

The rooms at the **America** *($; hw, sb; Av. 7, Calle 4, ☎221-4116)* hotel are clean, but offer minimal comfort. The windows do not open very wide.

The **Asia** *($; sb/pb; Calle 11, Av. Central/1, ☎223-3893, ⇌283-7957)* hotel offers very basic rooms with single beds and a shared bathroom (only one room has a private bathroom). None of them have windows. However, the hotel is well-kept.

The **Bienvenido** *($; pb; Calle 10, Av. 1/3, ☎233-2161, ⇌221-1872)* hotel is much better than the Asia. It is cleaner and friendlier, and its inexpensive rooms are airy and fairly quiet. It also has a good location near the Mercado Central.

The rooms at the **Boruca** *($; hw, sb; Calle 14, Av. 1/3, ☎223-0016)* are small (really small!), poorly decorated and have no windows. However, the place is clean. Beware: you might have to share your room with one of the people who live in the house! Conveniently located near numerous bus stops.

The reception desk at the **Centro Americano** *($; hw, pb, ☎, ℜ, ◙, ♿, bar, laundry service, souvenir shop; Av. 2, Calle 6/8, ☎221-3362)* hotel is down a corridor, at the back of the building. The rooms face small interior courtyards, providing a great deal of peace and quiet despite the fact that the hotel is situated on one of the busiest streets in San José; indeed, guests are asked to be extremely quiet after 9pm. The decor is not particularly charming, but the hotel is clean and wheelchair accessible.

The **Gran Hotel Imperial** *($; hw, sb/pb; Calle 8, Av. Central/1, ☎222-7899)* touts itself as the best in its class and, strictly speaking, this may be true for budget travellers who wish to stay in the capital. Though the level of comfort is basic, the building is quiet and guarded for your safety. The welcome is gracious, and the hotel very popular with young people and students. A balcony runs the whole length of the hotel. The adjacent restaurant has a simple, low-priced menu.

The **Johnson** *($; hw, pb, ℜ, tv lounge, laundry service; Calle 8, Av. 2/Central, ☎223-7633 or 223-7827, ⇌222-3683)* hotel is extremely pleasant, clean and inexpensive if you want to stay in the popular neighbourhood around the central market. However, the establishment's style is somewhat outdated. Though it is always fairly busy, the hotel is nevertheless known for its tranquillity, which is rare in this area.

The **Marlyn** *($; sb/pb; Calle 4, Av. 7/9, ☎233-3212)* hotel has small and clean rooms that face an interior courtyard, but are furnished only with a bed. Very popular with budget-conscious travellers. Friendly staff.

The **Bellavista** *($$ bkfst incl.; hw, pb; Av. Central, Calle 19/21, ☎223-0095, ⇌223-8385)* hotel is quiet, which is its main advantage. The rooms are clean, though very simple and sombre as their windows face a central corridor. The welcome is fairly pleasant, and you can enjoy sandwiches and refreshments at the in-house snack bar.

The **Casa Ridgway** *($$; hw, sb, laundry service; along Av. 6, Calle 15, ☎233-6168)* is the quintessential youth hostel. Located right next to the Centro de Amigos para la Paz, it is a lively and sociable place. Guests can stay in dormitories or private rooms, and have access to the kitchen and library. Special rates for groups of eight or more people.

The **Cocori** *($$; hw, pb; Calle 16, Av. 3, ☎233-0081, ⇌255-1058)* is a basic but very decent hotel, with clean and comfortable rooms. The building is simply yet tastefully designed, and located in the vicinity of the Coca Cola bus terminal and the Hospital San Juan de Dios (unfortunately, not the most attractive of neighbourhoods).

Peace and quiet prevail at the **D'Galah** *($$; K; opposite the gardens of the Universidad de Costa Rica campus, San Pedro, ☎/⇌234-1743 or 253-7539)* thanks to its extensive verdant grounds that shelter it from the university across the street.

Run by a friendly family, the eight-room **La Granja** *($$; discounts for Hostelling International cardholders; hw, K, ℜ, free P, laundry service; Av. Central, 50 metres south of Antiguo Higuerón, San Pedro, ☎/⇌225-1073 or 280-6239)* hotel is a good place to keep in mind.

The very decent **Jacques et Helena** *($$ bkfst incl.; hw; Urbanización Carmiol, Calle 8, Casa 811, Sabanilla, ☎224-596)* Bed & Breakfast is located in a quiet neighbourhood some 10 minutes from the city centre.

Run by mother and son, the **Petit Hotel** *($$ bkfst incl.; hw in a few rooms, sb/pb; Calle 24, Av. Central/2, ☎233-0766, ⇌233-4794)* has simple and clean rooms, though the furnishings are somewhat old-fashioned.

The **Toruma** *($$-$$$ bkfst incl.; discount for Hostelling International cardholders; sb, access to kitchen and laundromat; Av. Central, Calle 31/33, ☎224-4085)* is the unofficial headquarters of the Costa Rican youth-hostel network.

The **Aparthotel Ramgo** *($$$; hw, pb, ☎, tv; 200 metres west and 100 metres south of the tennis club, on the south side of La Sabana Park, ☎232-3366, ⇌232-3111)* has large and clean, though sombre, apartments whose seventies' decor is outdated. There is a room in which guests can hand-wash and dry their clothes.

A small entrance separates the **Aparthotel San José** *($$$; hw, pb, ctv, ☎, ℝ, K; Av. 2, Calle 17/19, ☎221-2191, ⇌221-6684)* from noisy Avenida 2. The apartments are clean, but not very attractive with their seventies' furnishings. Some apartments can accommodate up to six people. The hotel is very well situated, near the Museo Nacional.

The main asset of the **Aparthotel El Sesteo** *($$$; hw, pb, ctv, K, ℜ, ≈, ⊛; in the continuation of the General Cañas Highway toward the south side of La Sabana Park, ☎296-1805, ⇌296-1865)* is its location, only a short distance from La Sabana Park and the highway leading to the international airport. The building's amenities (common rooms and guest rooms) are very basic, but the interior courtyard, with a swimming pool, whirlpool and garden, is lovely and quite private. However, the apartments around this courtyard are too close together, which can be a nuisance with noisy neighbours and children.

Like the El Sesteo, the **Aparthotel La Sabana** *($$$ bkfst incl.; hw, pb, tv, ≈, ℜ, △, K, laundromat; Sabana Norte, 50 metres west and 150 north of Burger King, ☎220-2422, ⇌231-7386)* is only steps away from La Sabana Park and the highway to the international airport.

The apartment hotel **Ara Macao** *($$$ bkfst incl.; K, ℝ, laundromat; 50 m south of Avenida Central, opposite Pizza Hut, in Barrio California, right before Los Yoses, ☎233-2742,*

*⇒257-6228)* has fine apartments with balconies. The common rooms are pleasant: a small dining room sheltered from the rain in a central atrium, and a patio where you can have barbecues while observing small turtles crawling in the fountain and frogs frolicking in the aquarium. A quiet place.

Located in the very quiet neighbourhood of the same name, **Hotel Aranjuez** *($$$ bkfst incl.; hw, pb, ctv, ℜ, P, hair dryers, laundry service; Calle 19, Av. 11/13, ☎223-3559, ⇒223-3528)* is a lovely surprise: while its exterior is unassuming, the building's interior turns out to be very spacious. The rooms and bathrooms are large and clean, and the common living rooms are spacious, as are the gardens. Moreover, the owners are environmentally conscious (recycling, solar heating, etc.). Special weekly and monthly rates available. Children under 10 years of age stay for free.

Do not judge **Diana's Inn** *($$$; hw, pb, ☎, tv, ≡; Calle 5, Av. 3, ☎223-6542, ⇒233-0495)* by its entrance. The rooms upstairs are simply decorated but clean. The common rooms are quite lovely and bright. Moreover, it is right in the heart of the city, just opposite Morazán Park.

The **Diplomat** *($$$; pb, ☎; Calle 6, Av. Central/2, ☎221-8744 or 221-8133, ⇒233-7474)* hotel has clean rooms offering basic comfort. Some windows open onto a shaft that allows air to circulate, making them cooler. The common areas are clean.

The **Doña Ines** *($$$; hw, pb, ☎, tv, laundry service; Calle 11, Av. 2/6, ☎222-7443 or 222-7553, ⇒223-5426)* is Italian through and through: its ornately scrolled interior leaves no doubt as to the owner's country of origin. The place is spotless.

The very charming **Dunn Inn** *($$$ bkfst incl.; hw, pb, radio-alarm clock, ctv, ⊗, ☎; Calle 5, Av. 11, ☎222-3232 or 222-3426, ⇒221-4596)* has a very peaceful interior decor, particularly in its "atrium restaurant."

**La Gema** *($$$; hw, pb, tv, ☎; Av. 12, Calle 9/11, ☎257-2524, ⇒222-1074)* is a simple little hotel with rather small rooms, some of which are stuffy. It has a pool table.

You would be hard-pressed to find a better hotel than the **Gran Hotel Costa Rica** *($$$; hw, pb, ctv, ℜ, bar, casino, laundry service; Calle 3 and Av. Central/2, ☎221-4000, ⇒221-3501)* in the centre of San José. Though its charm is somewhat faded (renovation work is currently under way), the place is clean and still very popular.

The **Gran Via** *($$$; hw, pb, ☎; Av. Central, Calle 1/3, ☎222-7737, ⇒222-7205)* has been around for nearly 30 years and is one of the capital's oldest hotels. It shows its age, but the rooms are clean. Moreover, it is superbly located in the downtown pedestrian zone, and rooms with balconies cost only a little more.

The small, comfortable **Joluva Guesthouse** *($$$ bkfst incl.; hw, pb, ctv, VCR rental; along Calle 3, Av. 9/11, No. 936, ☎223-7961, ⇒257-7668, joluva@sol.racsa.co.cr)* welcomes a gay clientele. However, its hospitality is not always first-rate.

The **Kalexma** *($$$ bkfst incl.; hw, sb/pb, K, P; 50 m south of the Juan Pablo II Bridge, ☎/⇒232-0115)* is a rather humble, uncharming Bed & Breakfast in a quiet neighbourhood a fair distance from downtown, but close to the General Cañas Highway, which runs to the airport.

The **Hotel Kekoldi** *($$$ bkfst incl.; hw, pb, ⊗, ☎, laundry service; Calle 3 Bis, Av. 9, ☎223-3244, ⇄257-5476, kekoldi@sol.racsa.co.cr)* is decorated in striking pastels (the work of Helen Eltis), which is at once cheerful and relaxing. This charming, colourful little hotel offers large rooms with king-size beds and lovely little shared living rooms. Close to all the downtown attractions. Some rooms are noisier than others because of the traffic, so ask for a quiet room when you check in.

The **Pensión de la Cuesta** *($$$ bkfst incl.; hw, access to kitchen, ctv in living room; Av. 1, Calle 11/15, ☎256-7946, ⇄255-2896)* is very decent for the price. Housed in a colonial-style building, its rooms are somewhat sombre, but the general liveliness of the place will cheer you up, particularly in the common living rooms where guests gather to chat.

The **Pico Blanco Inn** *($$$; ℜ; San Antonio de Escazú, ☎228-1908, ⇄289-5189)* is a small, clean and pleasant mountain inn (rather hard to reach) where you can hear the parrots that live in the surrounding area. The view over the valley is breathtaking.

The **Pine Tree Inn** *($$$ bkfst incl.; hw, pb, ctv, ☎, ≈, P, laundry service; on a residential street opposite the Quiubo restaurant, in the Urbanización Trejos Montalegre district, Escazú, next to the Aparthotel María Alexandra, ☎289-7405, ⇄228-2180)* has around fifteen comfortable rooms in a very quiet neighbourhood in Escazú. Gymnasium and racquetball nearby.

The fairly quiet **Rey Amón** *($$$ bkfst incl.; hw, pb, ctv; Av. 7, Calle 7/9, ☎233-3819, ⇄233-1769)* has small but clean rooms that are plainly furnished. Friendly welcome.

The **Talamanca** *($$$ bkfst incl; hw, pb, ☎, ctv, ⊗, room service, bar; Av. 2, Calle 8/10, ☎233-5033, ⇄233-5420)* is a clean, modern hotel with a somewhat too predictable style. The bar on the top floor affords a splendid view of the city.

The main advantage of the **Tennis Club** *($$$ bkfst and welcoming cocktail incl.; hw, pb, ≡, ☎, ctv, ≈, ℜ, P, bar; in the south end of La Sabana, next to the pyramidal Controlaría General de la República building, ☎232-1266, ⇄232-3867, hotel@crtennis.icr.co.cr)* hotel lies in the many activities guests can participate in at one of the oldest sports club in San José: tennis, bowling, sauna, gym, pool and recreation grounds are available to the clientele 24 hours a day. The rooms, however, are not very attractive and the beds are uncomfortable.

The **Vesuvio** *($$$ bkfst incl.; hw, pb, ctv, ☎, ⊗, ℜ, P; Av. 11, Calle 13/15, Barrio Otoya, ☎/⇄221-7586, 221-8325 or 256-1616)* hotel is clean and modern, but relatively small. The common spaces may be somewhat lacking in warmth, but the establishment is located right near the zoo, in a quiet neighbourhood with lovely architecture.

The **Amstel Escazú** *($$$$ bkfst incl.; hw, pb, ctv, ≈, P, bar, access to kitchen; 200 m south of the El Cruce shopping centre, a little past the Santa Ana d'Escazú intersection, ☎228-1764, ⇄228-0620)* is a residential building that has been converted into a hotel. One of its main advantages, for those who do not like the city, is its location outside San José, in the lovely region of Escazú.

The **Aparthotel Los Yoses** *($$$$; hw, pb, ⊗, ≡, tv, ≈, laundry service; on the main street, 150 metres west of Fuente de la Hispanidad, Los Yoses,*

*☎225-0033 or 225-0044, ⇌225-5595)* has large, clean, fully equipped and well furnished apartments, each of which has an adjacent washer and dryer outlet. Parking and babysitting available.

**Aurola Holiday Inn** *($$$$; hw, pb, ☎, ctv, ≈, ℜ, △; Avenida 5, Calle 5, opposite Morazán Park, ☎233-7233 or 233-7036, ⇌255-1036, aurola@sol.racsa.co.cr)* is a San José institution, because it is one of the tallest skyscrapers in the downtown, and the only one with mirrored windows. Sauna, gymnasium, casino, boutique and newsstand. You won't find another hotel of this scale with a better location in the heart of the city.

**Hotel Balmoral** *($$$$; hw, pb, ctv, ≡, P, △, casino, babysitting service; Av. Central, Calle 7/9, ☎222-5022, ⇌221-1919)* is one of those modern hotels that were popular in design a few years ago. However, the place is very clean and the service is gracious.

The rooms at the **Hotel Le Bergerac** *($$$$ bkfst incl.; hw, pb, ctv, ☎, ⊗, ⊛, P, ℜ for hotel guests only, hair dryers, laundry service, bar, meeting room; Calle 35, 50 m south of Avenida Central, ☎234-7850, ⇌225-9103, bergerac@sol.racsa.co.cr)* are lovely and elegant, as is the rest of the hotel. The lavish gardens are perfect to relax in. The management is French, and the welcome proves it.

**Casa 429 El Paso** *($$$$; hw, pb/sb; Calle 3, Av. 4/6, 150 m south of the Teatro Nacional, ☎222-1708, ⇌233-5785)* is a former downtown residence that has recently been renovated and converted into a hotel. It is comfortable and fairly quiet, with spacious and tastefully decorated rooms.

The pleasant, emerald-green **Casa Las Orquideas** *($$$$ bkfst incl.; hw, pb, tv, ☎, ⊗, P, laundry service; Av. Central, Calle 33/37, 75 m west of the Automercado Los Yoses, Los Yoses, ☎283-8203, ⇌234-8203)* is clean and very charming, with wood and ceramic accents in the decor, lovely little rest areas and skylights. The delightful restaurant is slated to be turned into a small bar.

The **Corobici Hotel** *($$$$; hw, pb, ctv, ≡, hair dryers, ≈, ⊛, ℜ, ⊘; the beginning of the General Cañas Hwy., past Avenida Sabana Norte, ☎232-8122, ⇌231-5834, corobici@sol.racsa.co.cr)* is a major hotel, even in terms of size. The main part is impressive, with a huge "cathedral roof" that crowns the common spaces in the middle of the complex (casino, restaurant, meeting rooms, conference rooms, etc.). The hotel houses two good speciality restaurants: Japanese and Italian (see p 93).

The design of the **Costa Rica Morazán** *($$$$; hw, pb, some with bath, ≡, tv, ☎, ℜ; Calle 7, Av. 1, ☎222-4622, ⇌233-3329)* dates from the seventies. Though its rooms are rather small, they all have airconditioners – a necessity in this busy neighbourhood where you will have to sleep with the windows closed. Discounts for guests over 60 years of age.

The **Aparthotel Cristina** *($$$$ bkfst incl.; hw, pb, ♿, K, ℝ, ctv, P, ≈; 300 m north of ICE, Sabana Norte, ☎231-1618 or 220-0453, ⇌220-2096)* essentially caters to businesspeople. The apartments are clean and have a simple design.

The **Del Rey** *($$$$; hw, pb, ctv, ☎, ⊗, ≡ in some rooms, bath, non-smoking rooms, ℜ, casino; Calle 9, Av. 1, ☎221-7272 or 257-3130, ⇌221-0096)* is a large hotel whose kitschy-pink exterior is hard to miss in the neighbourhood. The place is very popular nonetheless, with its central location amid the bustle of downtown. Though the common living rooms are pleasant, the rooms facing inwards are badly ventilated. Moreover, only some of the units have a balcony. The City Café, next to the hotel, is open day and night (see p 89).

**Hotel Don Fadrique** *($$$$ bkfst incl.; hw, pb, ☎, ⊗, ctv, bar, laundry service; Calle 37, Av. 8, Los Yoses, ☎225-8186, ⇌224-9746)* is a remodelled 19th-century villa surrounded by gardens that insulate it from its surroundings, and makes it a lovely spot for intimate dinners. Some rooms have direct access to the gardens. The hotel also houses a collection of Costa Rican art and the portrait of a very colourful national figure; Don Fadrique himself.

The charming **Don Paco Inn** *($$$$ bkfst incl.; hw, pb, ctv; Calle 33, Av. 11, ☎/⇌283-2012 or 283-2033)* is in a large building that once housed United Nations offices. It has since been renovated but has preserved its colonial style. The rooms are stylish and very comfortable. The hotel is located in an extremely quiet residential neighbourhood, and is a fair distance from the downtown core.

The **Fleur de Lys** *($$$$ bkfst incl.; hw, pb, natural ventilation, bath in most rooms, radio-alarm clock; Calle 13, Av. 2/6, ☎222-4391, 223-1206 or 257-2621, ⇌257-3637, florlys@sol.racsa.co.cr)* has a great deal of style, evident in the inviting, pleasantly furnished common rooms throughout the building and in each of the guest rooms. Though it is right downtown, the establishment is in a quiet area. A tiny, pleasant bar and a good restaurant (see p 91) complete the amenities. The hotel also has a very good travel agency.

The **Hotel Grano de Oro** *($$$$; hw, pb, ctv, P, laundry service; Calle 30, Av. 2/4, ☎255-3322, ⇌221-2782, granoro@sol.racsa.co.cr)*, located in a quiet neighbourhood close to downtown, is a superbly renovated turn-of-the-century manor that exudes character and panache! The rooms are inviting, with elegant bathrooms and fine wood furnishings. There is a delightful rooftop terrace with deckchairs and whirlpools, as well as a lovely garden with fountains. All rooms are non-smoking. The Hotel Grano de Oro is very popular, even in the off-peak season. Its restaurant (see p 93) is one of the best in the country, according to a Central American gourmet association.

The **Hampton Inn** *($$$$ bkfst incl.; hw, pb, ≈; General Cañas Hwy. service road, two minutes from the Juan Santamaría Airport, ☎443-0043, ⇌442-9532)* offers North American standards of comfort, and is part of the chain of the same name. Its main asset is its location, just two minutes from San José's international airport. Children as well as the third and fourth person sharing a room stay for free.

The **Hemingway Inn** *($$$$ bkfst incl.; hw, pb, ctv, radio-alarm clock, laundry service, ⊛, complementary afternoon cocktail; Av. 9, Calle 9, ☎/⇌221-1804)* is owned by a Canadian who is involved with ecotourism, so feel free to ask him about the subject. The lovely little Spanish manor harbours fine rooms with all the modern conveniences. The rosewood decor blends harmoniously with the surrounding greenery. Guests get a $10 discount on the shuttle from the airport.

The recently renovated **Irazu Hotel** *($$$$; hw, pb, ctv, ≈, ≡, ☎, ⌂, ♿, casino, tennis; next door to the San José 2000 shopping centre, along the General Cañas Hwy., ☎232-4811, ⇄232-4549)* belongs to the Best Western chain. Many rooms have a balcony overlooking the pool or the garden, and some are wheelchair accessible. Try not to get a room on the main floor near the common areas, as the commotion of the many tour groups coming and going may disturb you.

The **Mansión de Braulio** *($$$$; hw, pb, ctv in common room; Av. 10, Calle 9, ☎222-0423, ⇄222-7947)* is located on the top floor of a lovely building. Its rooms are clean, though their furnishings are a bit worn. The common living rooms are relatively well fitted-out, but the staff is not overly friendly.

The brand-new (early 1997) **Palma Real** *($$$$; hw, pb, ⊛, ℜ, bar; 200 metres north of ICE, Sabana Norte, ☎290-5060, ⇄290-4160, fiesta@sol.racsa.co.cr)* hotel essentially caters to a business clientele; facilities include meeting and conference rooms, as well as a business centre. The modern rooms have a standard design, but are very comfortable. The restaurant serves international cuisine.

The **Petit Victoria** *($$$$; hw, pb, ctv, ℜ; Calle 24, Av. 2, ☎233-1812 or 233-1813, ⇄233-1938)* offers stylish rooms in its very charming Victorian building. However, traffic around the hotel can sometimes get noisy.

The American owners of the **Posada El Quijote** *($$$$ bkfst incl.; hw, pb, ☎, ctv; take the first exit to Bello Horizonte and drive 1.3 km south, then 200 m west, 25 m south and finally 25 m east, Bello Horizonte de Escazú, ☎289-8401, ⇄289-8729, quijote@sol.racsa.co.cr)* purchased this magnificent residence from the United States embassy, which gives you a pretty good idea of what the place is like. It offers flawless comfort, and a superbly decorated interior. The rooms are spacious, and the bay windows in the living rooms afford a magnificent view over the Central Valley. The gardens are wonderfully relaxing. Shuttle service between the airport and San José available. The road leading to the *posada* can be rather rough going.

The **Presidente** *($$$$; hw, pb, ctv, ≡, ☎, ⌂, ⊛, bar, casino; Av. Central, Calle 7, ☎222-3022, ⇄221-1205, hotpres@sol.racsa.co.cr)* is very well situated, in the heart of the city. Its modern layout guarantees good comfort, but makes for standard rooms.

The **Puesta del Sol** *($$$$; hw, pb, ☎, ≈, ℜ, ctv; 100 metres east and 75 metres south of Antigua Fabrica Intex, Escazú, ☎289-6581 or 289-8775, ⇄289-8766)* is new to the hotel scene and does not quite fill up in the high season. Nevertheless, the facilities, located in the mountains of Escazú on the former property of a European ambassador, are very lovely (as well as secluded). You can also rent a cottage here. The owner can easily recommend the sights worth seeing in the country, as he writes on that very subject. Moreover, hotel guests have access to a delightful private reserve.

The **Rincón del Valle** *($$$$ bkfst incl.; hw, pb, hair dryers, ctv, ≡, ☎, radio-alarm clock, laundry service, P; 50 m east and 50 m south of the Colegio de Médicos, on the south side of La Sabana Park, ☎231-4927 or 231-7881, ⇄231-5924, susana@sol.racsa.co.cr)* hotel is brand-new. Its dark reddish wood gives it a tasteful, classical touch. The rooms have a North American level of comfort, and the service is attentive. Guests have access to a pool, a gymnasium and tennis courts next door. Located in a quiet neighbourhood, the establishment is quite far from the town centre. There are conference facilities in the Quiubo restaurant in Escazú.

**Hotel Rosa del Paseo** *($$$$ bkfst incl.; hw, pb with bath, ctv, ☎, radio-alarm clock, ⊗, laundry service; Paseo Colón, opposite the Banco Anglo, between Calles 28 and 30, ☎257 3258, ⇌223-2776)* is the former residence of a *cafetaleras* (coffee baron) that has been painstakingly renovated to preserve the unique style of each of its rooms (including the guest rooms), while adding touches of comfort.

The **Quality Hotel Centro Colón** *($$$$; hw, pb, ≡, ☎, ctv, casino, ℜ, P, bar; Av. 3, Calle 40, ☎257-2580, ⇌257-2582)* is primarily a hotel for businesspeople. Its style and comfort conform to the norms of international hotel chains. However, its location near La Sabana Park, the Museo de Arte Costarricense and the airport-bound city exit is quite far from the centre of town.

The **Santo Tomás** *($$$$ bkfst incl.; hw, pb, bath in some rooms, ☎, ctv, ⊗, bar, laundry service; Av. 7, Calle 3/5, ☎255-0448, ⇌222 3950, hotelst@sol.racsa.co.cr)* hotel offers spacious and elegant rooms, much like the building as a whole, for that matter. Sure value for a certain number of years now in San José, especially because it is located in one of the best neighbourhoods in the heart of the city, namely Barrio Amón.

The **Best Western San José** *($$$$ bkfst incl.; hw, pb, ctv, ≡, free P, ℜ; Av. 7, Calle 6, ☎255-4766, ⇌255-4613, garden@sol.racsa.co.cr)* provides the type of comfort typical of this hotel chain. The layout of the common spaces, notably the pool and garden area, is rather lovely, and the balconies overlooking them are most pleasant. The hotel is situated on the fringes of a less interesting neighbourhood than its neighbour, Barrio Amón; the building's architecture looks out of place in this environment. Free shuttle service between the airport and San José, free parking and complementary cocktail!

**Taylor's Inn** *($$$$ bkfst incl.; hw, pb, ctv, non-smoking rooms; Calle 3, Av. 11, ☎257-4333, ⇌221-1475)*, a decent little Bed & Breakfast, occupies a former residence with a dozen tidy rooms filled with wicker furniture.

**Torremolinos** *($$$$; hw, pb, ☎, ctv, ≈, ⊗, bar, ℜ, P, radio-alarm clock, laundry service; Calle 40, along Av. 5, near La Sabana, ☎222-5266, ⇌255-3167, torremolinos@centralamerica.com)* is a modern establishment located in a peaceful neighbourhood quite far from downtown. Its classical streamlined decor (rooms and lobby alike) is attractive.

The modern **Villa Tournón** *($$$$; hw, pb, ctv, ≈, ⊗, ℜ, P; ☎233-6622, ⇌222-5211)* is located just on the outskirts of downtown, to the north, in Barrio Tournón. The rooms are pleasantly furnished and comfortable. Children under 12 years of age stay in their parents' room for free.

Though it has a good reputation, the **Hotel Ambassador** *($$$$-$$$$$; hw, pb, ctv, ℜ; Paseo Colón, Calle 26/28, ☎221-8155, ⇌255-3396)* is showing its age. Everything from the narrow corridors to the colour scheme, carpets and furniture, obviously dates from the sixties. The ceilings are low, and the small rooms lack character. Moreover, the rooms are not necessarily made up each day. Some rooms overlook noisy

Paseo Colón. Variety shows are held at the hotel.

The **Americano del Este** *($$$$$ bkfst incl.; hw, pb, hair dryers, tv, ☎, ≈, bar, P; 175 m north of the Subaru dealership, Los Yoses, ☎224-2455, ⇄224-2166)* is located at the end of a quiet street in the fashionable Los Yoses district, and was being expanded at the time of our visit. The standard design may be more suitable for people who are just passing through on business.

The new **Amón Park Plaza** *($$$$$; hw, pb, ctv, ☎, hair dryers, P, casino; Av. 11, along Calle 3, ☎257-0191, ⇄257-0284, amonpark@sol.racsa.co.cr)* is classic and modern at the same time. Though it is designed to cater specifically to businesspeople, it may also appeal to tourists. The rooms are clean and well furnished. The hotel has a large restaurant that serves international cuisine in the evenings *(5pm to midnight)*, and light meals in its main lobby day and night.

The **Aparthotel María Alexandra** *($$$$$; hw, pb, ctv, ℝ, microwave oven, dishwasher, radio-alarm clock, VCR, P; on a residential street across from the Quiubo restaurant, in the Urbanización Trejos Montalegre district, Escazú, ☎289-5192)* is located in a very quiet, upscale residential district. Amenities include a laundromat, a beauty salon, a sauna, a barbecue area and a video-rental counter. The overall design is luxurious, and the apartments are fully equipped. The hotel also has a very good restaurant (see p 92).

The beautiful hotel **Britannia** *($$$$$ bkfst incl.; hw, pb, bath in some rooms, ⊗, ctv, ℜ, bar; Calle 3, Av. 9/11, ☎223-6667, ⇄223-6411, britannia@sol.racsa.co.cr)* occupies a Victorian house whose charm has been successfully preserved. The large guest rooms and common rooms are inviting. Social and cultural events are sometimes held in the lobby. The hotel is located in Barrio Amón, one of the best areas if you want to stay right downtown. Airport shuttle service.

The **Casa Verde** *($$$$$ bkfst incl.; hw, pb, ctv, ☎, ⊗, radio-alarm clock, △, patio; Calle 7, Av. 9, ☎/⇄223-0969 or 257-1054)* was built in the Victorian era and has been so well restored that it has won several awards. The common areas are appealing, as are the guest rooms. It is worth a visit, even if you don't stay here.

**Colours** *($$$$$ bkfst and evening cocktail incl.; hw, pb/sb, ⊗, ⊛, ≈, ℜ, bar; Rorhmoser Blvd., El Triangulo, ☎296-1880 or 232-3504, ⇄296-1597 or 305-534-0362, newcolours@aol.com)* is somewhere between a Bed & Breakfast and a small, intimate hotel. It is elegantly designed, and has a North American level of comfort. The establishment caters to a gay clientele, and is located in a very quiet neighbourhood that is quite far from downtown. The managers are very dynamic, and frequently organize activities for tourists and the local gay community. They are also very well informed about gay life in Costa Rica.

The **Herradura** *($$$$$: hw, pb, ☎, ctv, ≡, ⊛, △, ⊘, casino; Cariari hotel district, Cariari, ☎239-0033, ⇄239-2292, hherradu@sol.racsa.co.cr)* is located halfway between San José and the international airport. A first-class complex with a wealth of services, including three restaurants (Japanese, Spanish and international, the latter open 24 hours a day), access to the neighbouring golf club and about ten tennis courts. Tennis lessons are also available. Sportfishing excursions can also be organized here. Some of the rooms have a private balcony and terrace. Free for children under 12 years of age sharing a room with their parents.

The brand-new **Marriott** *($$$$$; hw, pb, ctv, ≈; San Antonio de Belén, ☎298-0000, ⇄298-0011)* provides the luxury expected of this famous chain. Attention to detail is evident in the rooms and common areas, including the spacious lobbies and outdoor spaces. Elements of the 16th-century colonial style are evident in the design, which creates some interesting effects in such a huge modern complex. Free shuttle service to and from the airport and downtown. Amenities include a golf course (with driving range), a health club, saunas, whirlpools, jogging tracks, two swimming pools, a casino and conference reception facilities.

The **Melia Cariari** *($$$$$; hw, pb, ≡, ☎, hair dryers, ctv, ≈, ℜ, ⊘, tennis, golf; along the General Cañas Hwy., between the airport and San José, at the San Antonio de Belén intersection, ☎239-0022, ⇄239-3007)* is on a vast 55-hectare property. However, a large part of it encompasses a golf club. This superior-grade hotel is part of the Sol Melia chain, and functions both as a golf resort and a conference centre. The decor is tasteful and conservative.

The **Napoleon** *($$$$$ bkfst incl.; hw, pb, hair dryers, ☎, ctv, ⊛, ≡, ≈, P; Calle 40, Av. 5, 200 m north of the Banco de Costa Rica, Paseo Colón, ☎222-2278 or 223-4750, ⇄222-9487, napoleon@sol.racsa.co.cr)* caters to business executives and has a unique decor. The neighbourhood is quiet, but very close to the downtown core.

The classic **Parque del Lago** *($$$$$ bkfst incl.; hw, pb, ctv, ≡, ☎, hair dryers, ℜ, P; Av. 2, Calle 40/42, ☎257-8787, ⇄223-1617, parklago@sol.racsa.co.cr)* caters primarily to businesspeople, with amenities such as work and meeting rooms and a business centre.

The **Radisson** *($$$$$; hw, pb, ctv, radio-alarm clock, ℝ, ≈, ⊘, casino, ℜ, bar; Guapiles Highway, Barrio Tournón, ☎257-3257, ⇄257-8221)* is another of the capital's major hotels, and is located in Barrio Tournón, in north-central San José, just north of Barrio Amón, near the El Pueblo shopping centre. It is the kind of place that is better suited to the business clientele (with conference rooms and *ejecutivos* suites) or tourists who are just passing through.

You wouldn't guess it from the outside, but the **Residencias de Golf** *($$$$$; hw, pb, ≡, ctv, radio, K, ⊛, ≈, P; between Residencial Los Arcos and the Cariari hotel, in the Cariari district, ☎239-2272, ⇄239-2001, residgo@sol.racsa.co.cr)* has a large, peaceful interior courtyard, which is something to keep in mind when choosing your room. All the rooms are attractive and very comfortable. Guests have access to the Cariari Country Club. Free airport shuttle.

The **San José Palacio** *($$$$$; hw, pb, ≡, ☎, hair dryers, ctv, radio, ≈, △, ⊘, tennis and racquetball courts, ⊛, ℜ, casino, P; on the General Cañas Hwy., between La Sabana and La Uruca, ☎220-2034, ⇄220-2036)* is a major hotel that belongs to the Spanish Barcelo chain. Its design and decor conform to North American tastes.

## RESTAURANTS

The restaurants of the major hotels generally offer good international cuisine, and are your best bet if you have your heart set on an American continental-style breakfast.

You can purchase all kinds of food at the numerous sidewalk kiosks lining the streets of San José: commercial or freshly prepared beverages, fruits, little pastries – and more daring types can try the fried food, sandwiches and meats cooked on the spot.

Most of the major fast food chains can be found in the San José area, so you should have no difficulty finding your favourite one.

To sample typical Costa Rican fast food, try the small **AS** restaurant chain, which serves quick regional meals in an atmosphere similar to McDonald's. There is an outlet on Avenida 2, between Calle 1 and Calle Central.

Some restaurant chains prepare more elaborate meals. Among these is **Rosti Pollos**, a favourite among Costa Ricans. This restaurant chain serves very good chicken – cooked just about any way you like. Take-out service is also available.

Most restaurant menus are in Spanish and English.

The **La Cañada** *($; 11am to 11:30pm; Av. 2, Calle 8/10)* inexplicably won our hearts. Though its decor is not particularly remarkable, and the staff is not *exceptionally* friendly, the place is clean, popular (even among young people) and, above all, its *boca* dishes (with fries) are generous for the price, which means you can easily eat here for under $5! Moreover, the place is off the tourist circuit and really feels like a "neighbourhood restaurant." A good opportunity to mingle with the city's local population.

**Restaurante Cafetería La Criollita** *($; 6am to 8pm; Av. 9, along Calle 3/5, ☎233-0128)* is a small establishment where patrons are served full, lavish and very good meals for a pittance. The restaurant is thus very crowded at lunchtime, particularly on the main floor.

The **La Cocina de Bordolino** *($; Calle 21, Av. 6)* is a cheap but decent little *soda* that serves Argentinian-style empanadas in a setting that includes the always noisy television set.

The **Chelles** *($; Av. Central, Calle 9)* is a small and unpretentious *café-soda-bar* that has, among other things, a long counter for those in a hurry. Clean and inexpensive.

**Cafeterías Panaderías Deli City** *($)* is a chain whose outlets have spread throughout San José and in certain other cities in the region. Light meals and pretty decent pastries. Ignore the late-1970s interior decor and colour scheme.

The **Soda Mauren** *($; Av. 4, Calle 3)* is a small *soda* where local workers gather to eat. Very clean and pleasant.

The **Mercado Central** *($; Av. Central/1, Calle 6/8)* is another place that serves small, inexpensive meals.

The **Morazán** *($)*, located opposite the park of the same name, celebrated its 100th anniversary in 1997. Pleasant, unpretentious and very popular, it offers all kinds of different beverages, all displayed along the walls, and serves very good *bocas*. The restaurant prides itself on serving the best "gourmet coffees." A great meeting place for Costa Ricans, students and foreigners alike. However, the Morazán resounds with the sounds of a jukebox and two or three televisions. Alcoholic beverages are served from 10am to midnight. Cuban cigars and cigarillos are sold here, as well.

The **Papa Brava** *($; every day until 2am; Carretera Prospero Fernández service road, opposite La Sabana Park, ☎220-7414) restaurant-soda* is a great find. The staff is young and friendly, and the place is ideal to go to after exploring La Sabana Park or playing a game of tennis at the sports club (whose young clientele often gets together here). The house speciality is *papa brava*; a delicious dish of potatoes stuffed with different ingredients. The restaurant also draws local businesspeople.

**Pollos Titanic** *($; Av. 5, Calle 4)* sits kitty-corner from the Panadería Durand, and serves fried chicken (so common in Costa Rica) and cheap beer. The place is clean and very popular. Moreover, prices are reasonable.

Ill-assorted tables covered with waxed tablecloths make **La Vasconia** *($; Calle 3, Av. 1, ☎223-4857)* a simple, unpretentious *restaurant-soda* that draws a crowd from San José. The place offers all kinds of very reasonably priced *ceviches*.

You have to try the **Vishnu** *($; Calle 1, Av. 4; Av. 1, Calle 1/3; Calle 14, Av. Central/2)* vegetarian restaurants at least once. Tasty and original lunches for under $5 are prepared with whole-grain flour and other healthy ingredients. There are many different dishes, whose presentation alone will rouse your tastebuds. The desserts are excellent. Moreover, the place is spotless. Note, however, that all three outlets are generally very busy; you may well have to wait a little while before finding a seat.

The cafeteria of the **Supermercado Yaohan** *($; opposite the Corobici hotel, Sabana Este)* is also an excellent place for a good, fast meal served in very clean surroundings.

**Il Bagatto** *($$; Tue to Sat noon to 3pm and 7pm to 11pm, Sun noon to 3pm; Zapote, Curridabat, opposite the Registro Nacional, ☎224-5297)* offers home-made Italian cuisine at inexpensive prices. A worthwhile choice.

Right by the Del Rey hotel, **El Balcón de Europa** *($$; Calle 9, Av. Central/1, ☎221-4841)* is a very pleasant restaurant whose walls are covered in old photographs. Open since 1909, the establishment has earned itself a solid reputation in the capital. Even Sunday nights can be packed with a lively crowd, and pleasant background music adds to the atmosphere. A delicious Italian cheese platter is served as a starter.

The **City Café** *($$; Av. 1, Calle 9, ☎221-7272)* is located in the Del Rey hotel (see p 82). The place is open day and night and serves good lunches in a fine ambiance, with photographs from the twenties on the walls.

**Delicias Vegetarianas** *($$; Av. 2, Calle 9/11, ☎256-7392)* is, as its name indicates, a vegetarian deli (*"natural, macrobiotic and ecological,"* the managers proclaim) that offers all kinds of tasty little dishes, as well as whole grain flour-based breads, desserts, all sorts of incense and more.

**La Esquina de Los Mariscos** *($$; Mon to Fri 11am to 10:30pm, Sun 11am to 9pm; on the street along the west side of La Sabana Park, ☎443-8077)* is a good, inexpensive seafood restaurant that is very popular with Costa Ricans – always a good sign!

Specializing in Chinese cuisine, **Feliz Feliz** *($$; Calle 23, Av. 1, next to the La Amistad restaurant)* has a varied menu that attracts families, particularly on Sundays. It has the simple, ordinary decor of a family restaurant. The *tacos chinos* (egg rolls) are very good, and the staff is fairly affable. One drawback is the that the television set at the back of the room is always on.

**Kasbah** *($$; Mon to Fri 11am to 11pm, Sat and Sun 11am to midnight; Calle Central, Av. 7/9)* serves good *ceviches*, among other things, in a somewhat Moorish interior with a pleasant, relaxed ambiance. The restaurant, which is popular with a gay clientele, is also a bar.

**Mac's American Bar & Grill** *($$; at the San Rafael and Escazú junction)* is a small, unpretentious bar-restaurant with a decor to match. The place is always busy, with a crowd looking for a meal (North American fare) or a beer.

The very simply decorated **Machu Picchu** *($$; Mon to Sat 11:30am to 3pm and 6pm to 10pm; Calle 32, Av. 1, ☎222-7384)* serves Peruvian cuisine of excellent quality for the price.

The **Pasta Factory** *($$; Mon to Sat 11am to 10:30pm; Av. 1, Calle 7, ☎222-4642)* offers fresh pasta as well as pizza in a pleasant atmosphere.

Inside the Teatro Melico Salazar, **Soda La Perla** *($$; 24 hours a day; Calle Central and Av. 2)* is a very clean and popular restaurant with a varied lunch and after-hours menu. The *hamburguesa La Perla* is delicious. The restaurant's windows are large enough to take in the bustling city centre. However, what with the television and radio added to the mix, this restaurant may not be the best choice for a quiet meal.

The **Pollo Campesino** *($$; every day 11am to midnight; Calle 7, Av. 2/4)* is a rotisserie (take-out available). You can see the chicken cooking on enormous rotating spits. The decor, however, is rather ordinary and somewhat cheesy like that of 1970s fast food restaurants (plywood, booths, etc.).

The popular **Pollo Frito Pio-Pio** *($$; Av. 2, Calle 2)* serves fried chicken, as does the **Campero** *($$)*, which has an outlet on Plaza de la Cultura.

**Shakti** *($$; Mon to Fri 7am to 4pm; Calle 13, Av. 8, right near the Fleur de Lys hotel, ☎222-9096)* is a lovely little restaurant recommended for its macrobiotic cuisine. However, it closes very early.

**Spoon** *($$; several locations: downtown, Av. Central, Calle 5/7; Los Yoses, 100 m south and 100 m west of Cancún; Pavas, opposite the American embassy; western suburb, Multi-Plaza shopping centre, opposite the Camino Real hotel)* offer a rather extensive menu and have a much better reputation than Deli City (see p 88). The pastries here are absolutely delicious!

**Lamm's Steak House** *($$; main street, Escazú)* has two simply decorated rooms, one of which is right on the street. Prices are reasonable, given the quality of the meals.

**Tar Zan** *($$; Calle 11, Av. 6/8, ☎223-1537)* specializes in Americanized Chinese cooking. Its family atmosphere (with the television set always playing) means the food here is cheaper than in the neighbouring restaurants of the same kind. Clean.

**Las Tunas** *($$; open late at night; Sabana Norte)* "restaurant-complex" (*complejo*) has a varied menu. The place is made up of several small dining rooms and a covered terrace, unified by an overall "cathedral" design. Of course, there is a television set in all four corners of the room. A convenient place for late-night victuals.

**Alpino da Rodrigo** *($$$; 11:30am to 2:30pm and 6:30pm to 10:30pm, closed Wed; Av. 8, opposite Calle 17, ☎222-4950)* is a charming Italian restaurant that was the first in the country (1961) to offer pizza and Italian cuisine. The inviting interior has an Italian atmosphere, with blue-and-red tablecloths and wood decor. The wonderful aroma of tomatoes, spices and sauce fills the air. The establishment is composed of a restaurant (with television, unfortunately) and a dining room.

**La Amistad** *($$$; Calle 23, Av. 1, right next to the El Cartel de la Boca del Monte bar, ☎221-0559 or 223-8876)* specializes in Chinese cuisine. Its decor is simple and its service unpretentious.

**Los Antojitos** *($$$; several outlets, including one in the Rohrmoser district, on Route 104, ☎231-5564)* serves very good Mexican cuisine and has a great holiday ambiance, with Mexican singers and musicians trying hard to outdo each other!

The newly opened **Bihagua** *($$$; ☎225-0613)* is a real find. Its famous chef, Isabel Campabadal, cooks for visiting dignitaries. She is one of the people behind Costa Rican nouvelle cuisine (blending traditional food with international flavours), and a brand-new addition to the country's culinary landscape. The restaurant has a simple yet distinguished charm, which goes hand in hand with the renowned clientele it welcomes.

**El Chicote** *($$$; every day 11am to midnight; Av. Las Américas, 400 m west of the ICE building, Sabana Norte, ☎232-0936 or 232-3777)* is a first-rate restaurant well-known for its grill dishes. It has a terrace and a bar. The *crema de pejiballe* and *pollo Chicote* are delicious.

**Don Wang** *($$$; Calle 11, Av. 6/8, ☎233-6184 or 223-5925)* serves authentic Cantonese and Szechwan cuisine in a stylish and tasteful decor. For a serious and distinguished clientele not necessarily willing to splurge.

**El Exotico Oriente** *($$$; closed Sun; main street, Escazú, opposite the Mas X Menos supermarket, ☎228-5980)* specializes in Thai food. The place has a lovely, very simple ambiance, and the staff is both friendly and attentive.

The Victorian decor of the **Fleur de Lys** *($$$; every day 11am to 2pm and 6pm to 10pm; Calle 13, Av. 2/6, ☎223-1206, in the hotel of the same name, see p 83)* is as appealing and inspiring as the chef's international and Costa Rican cuisine.

Named after the famous Spanish painter, **Goya** *($$$; lunch specials; Mon to Sat 11am to 2:30pm and 5:30pm to 11pm; Av. 1, Calle 5/7, next to the Suizo restaurant, ☎221-3887)* has a classy decor. *Paellas* and *tortillas* are the menu's highlights.

**La Hacienda** *($$$; Calle 7, Av. 2)* is a steakhouse whose architecture (resembling a barn) distinguishes it from the surrounding buildings. Relatively new, it offers steaks, of course, but also salads and chicken.

**Lukas** *($$$; 24 hours a day; the El Pueblo shopping centre, in the*

*Tournón district, north of downtown, ☎233-8145)* serves good, diverse cuisine in a newly established restaurant. It is all the more appealing because it is open day and night.

The **María Alexandra** *($$$; Mon to Sat 11:30am to 2:30pm and 5:30pm to 11:30pm; the apartment hotel of the same name, in Escazú, on the street opposite Quiubo, in the Urbanización Trejos Montalegre district, ☎228-4876)* restaurant brings together a convivial clientele in an intimate setting.

**Marolo's** *($$$; 24 hours a day; Av. Central, Calle Central/2, ☎221-2041 or 222-2234)* has a wonderful, lively atmosphere with its own musicians performing every night of the week *(from 7pm to 9pm)*. Though the place is very popular, finding a table should not be too difficult as the restaurant has a huge upstairs dining room as well as a terrace.

**La Pizza Metro** *($$$; closed Mon; Av. 2, Calle 5/7, next to the La Esmeralda restaurant, ☎233-0306)* is a very pleasant little Italian restaurant. Though it is rather small, the place is well fitted-out, with its distinctly Italian (scrolled, etc.) design. The lovely little wooden tables and lamps make it just the place for a romantic dinner. And the pizzas are excellent! The patrons even eat quietly until late into the evening on weekends.

**Pizzeria Italiana Peperoni** *($$$; Av. 8, Calle 15)* features very good Italian dishes. It also offers free one-hour parking.

**Ponte Vecchio***($$$; every day 11am to 2:30pm and 6pm to 10:30pm; 200 m west of the San Pedro church, and 25 metres farther north, ☎225-9399)* offers patrons warm and friendly service. The chef, a New Yorker, has done everything to ensure that his restaurant is recognized as one of the 100 best in Central America.

**Quiubo** *($$$; main street, Escazú, ☎228-4091 or 289-9335)* offers steaks and international cuisine (mainly Mexican and Costa Rican) in a pub-like atmosphere. The service is very friendly and attentive. Conference rooms. The restaurant pays the taxi fare of guests from the Rincón del Valle hotel.

**Sant Jordi** *($$$, $5 daily menu; Mon to Sat 11:30am to 3pm and 6pm to midnight, closed Sun; Av. 10, Calle 9, beneath the La Mansión de Braulio hotel)* offers reasonably priced Spanish specialities.

**Suizo** *($$$; 11:30am to 2:30pm and 6pm to 10pm, closed Sun; Av. 1, Calle 5/7)* is easy to recognize by its Swiss-chalet architecture, which makes it stand out from its surroundings. Interior decor to match. It has set the standard for Swiss cuisine for several years now.

**Taska Al Andalus** *($$$; Calle 3, Av. 7/9, ☎257-6556)* is very pleasant and quite simple. It has a cozy and vaguely Hispanic atmosphere and serves excellent Spanish cuisine, most notably *paella*, the house speciality.

**Tiffany's** *($$$; 24 hours/day; Herradura hotel, Ciudad Cariari, ☎239-0033 or 293-0136)* serves international fare in a classy environment. Open day and night.

**Tin Jo** *($$$; Mon to Sat 11:30am to 3pm and 5:30pm to 11pm, Sun 11:30am to 10pm; Calle 11, Av. 6/8, ☎221-7605)* is a very good restaurant that serves Thai, Indian, Chinese and vegetarian cuisine. A stylish and tasteful establishment. Its decor is inspiring, as are the aromas greeting you as you enter.

The big **Angus Steak House** *($$$$; Av. Central, Calle 41, Los Yoses)* serves excellent steak and is popular with the area's wealthy residents.

Right next door to the Herradura hotel, in Ciudad Cariari, **Antonio's** *($$$$; Mon to Fri noon to 11pm, Sat 5:30pm to 11pm, closed Sun; ☎239-1613 or 293-0622)* is an Italian restaurant that lives up to its country's romantic reputation. The classical atmosphere (with piano) that prevails here is perfect for fine dining.

**Esmeralda** *($$$$; buffet and lunch menu available; 11am to 5pm; Av. 2, Calle 5/7, ☎233-7386)* is a huge restaurant with a lovely decor where a great variety of food is offered. The *mariachis* who perform here draw many people, particularly at night.

The interior of **France** *($$$$; 11:45am to 2pm and 6pm to 10:30pm, Sat 6pm to 10:30pm, closed Sun; Calle 7, north of Av. 2, ☎222-4241)* is plastered with posters of Toulouse-Lautrec, and the main language on the menu confirms this establishment's French allegiance. Scallop of seafood with Pernod, blanquettes of veal, rabbit pâté with green pepper and cognac as well as shrimp with lime are just some of the dishes offered by this stylish restaurant.

**El Fuji** *($$$$; Mon to Sat noon to 2:30pm and 6pm to 11pm; ☎232-8122)*, at the Corobici hotel (see p 82) is an elegant restaurant that specializes in Japanese food.

Also at the Corobici hotel, **Gondola** *($$$$; lunch, dinner from 6:30pm)* is an Italian restaurant where the veal vies with the pasta in a gourmet setting.

The cuisine at the **Grano de Oro** *($$$$; 6am to 10pm; Calle 30, Av. 2/4, ☎255-3322)* restaurant, in the hotel of the same name (see p 83), combines classic Costa Rican and European cuisine. The resident chef, Francis Canal, has done so well that the establishment is identified by some as one of the best restaurants in the country. The decor is enchanting and soothing with its many plants.

**Hostario Cerutti** *($$$$; on the road from San Rafael to Escazú, past the junction)* is the place for fine dining – where Italian cuisine, seafood and steaks are the stars of the menu. It also has a streetfront terrace.

**The Lobster's Inn** *($$$$; Paseo Colón, Calle 24)* is, as its name suggests, a seafood restaurant, and a very popular one at that. Its elegant decor is perfect for fine dining. Attentive service.

**La Masia** *($$$$; Tue to Sat 11:30am to 2pm and 6:30pm to 10:30pm, Sun 11:30am to 3:30pm; 100 m east of ICE and 175 m north, in the Casa España's building, Sabana Norte, ☎296-3528)* is a high-class restaurant that specializes in Spanish cuisine, as you will tell its decor and service. It is also home to the Casa España, a Spanish social club that has been offering its members a host of activities for over 100 years. Just the place for a stylish evening out.

**Rias Bajas** *($$$$; Mon to Sat noon to 3pm and 6:30pm to midnight; ☎221-7123)* specializes in seafood. Though delicious, meals are expensive.

**Sakura** *($$$$; Mon to sat 11:30am to 3pm and 6pm to 11:15pm, Sun 12:30pm to 11pm; Ciudad Cariari, ☎239-0033 or 293-0130)*, in the Herradura hotel (see p 86), is a very well-maintained Japanese restaurant with an Asian decor.

**Sancho Panza Tasca** *($$$$; Mon to Sat 11:30am to 3pm and 6pm to 11:15pm,*

*Sun 12:30pm to 11pm; Herradura hotel, Ciudad Cariari, ☎239-0033 ext. 265)* serves Spanish cuisine in an old-style Spanish ambiance, reminiscient of *Don Quixote* (hence the name). The place has received very good reviews.

## Cafés, Bakeries, and Pastry and Ice-Cream Shops

There are a good number of cafés, bakeries, and pastry and ice cream shops in the region, providing you with ample opportunities to have a little snack or to take a break from your explorations!

In Escazú, the **Cafetería Portofino** *($; next to the Aparthotel María Alexandra, on the street facing Quiubo, in the Urbanización Trejos Montalegre district)* offers excellent Italian ice cream. The style and decor are more refined than those of the Pop's chain, which has an outlet nearby.

Also in Escazú is the **Chocolatería San Simón** *(main street, Escazú)*, a chocoholic's dream come true.

There are two cafés opposite Hotel Kekoldi, in Barrio Amón: **La Esquina del Café** and the **Amón Coffee Shop** *($; along Calle 3, Av. 9)*, where you can savour this exalted beverage and its every conceivable accompaniment in the charming setting of a truly delightful little café.

There are many **Mus Anni** *($) panderías* in San José. These bakeries and pastry shops are not excessively refined, but their substantial and rich treats will give you a taste of Costa Rican baking. Moreover, the names of each item (*quesadilla, pan de cebolla, strudel de manzana, enchillada, pan de ajo*) are enough to tempt you to sample every last one of them.

**Panadería El Caballito** *($; opposite the central market, on Av. 1)* is a very good bakery and pastry shop that has been around since 1955. It sells all kinds of bread and pastries, as well as cheese, chocolate bars and refreshments. Prices are very reasonable and the staff is friendly.

Open day and night, **Panadería Durand** *($; Calle 4, Av. 5)* offers a wide variety of pastries and breads. The place is both pleasant and clean. This is a popular spot, and gets quite lively at night.

In the Los Yoses district, the **Pastelaría Giacomín** *($; Mon to Sat 8am to noon and 2pm to 7pm; near the Automercado de Los Yoses, on Avenida Central between Calles 39 and 41, ☎225-0356)* sells some of the best pastries, which are especially good with a coffee.

Clean and inexpensive, **Mönpik** serves all kinds of ice cream. This chain has outlets on Avenida 3, between Calles 3 and 5, and on the corner of Avenida Central and Calle Central

**Pop's** is another very popular Costa Rican ice cream shop. There are many locations throughout the country, and their cool treats are very refreshing after walking around in the sun. You should have no trouble finding one in San José (there is one on Avenida Central between Calles 3 and 5, for instance).

**Café Ruiseñor** *($$; Mon to Fri 10:30am to 6pm; Av. 2, Calle 5, at the main entrance of the Teatro Nacional)* is a very lovely coffee shop with excellent food. It is just the place for late afternoon relaxation in the centre of town. Costa Rican art works are sometimes exhibited here.

In the very heart of downtown, you can't miss the **Café Parisien** *($$; Av. 2, Calle 3, opposite the Teatro Nacional, ☎221-4000)*, located on the main floor of the Gran Hotel Costa Rica, on the square. This charmingly tranquil yet bustling café (it is located on the public square, after all!) has long drawn a large clientele. It is a fashionable place to go for 5 o'clock tea.

In Escazú, **Delimundo** *($$; in the basement of the Plaza Colonial Escazú shopping centre, on the main street)* is a small restaurant that serves bagels, sandwiches, natural juices, salads and a selection of very good breads (i.e. pumpernickel). Its interior, however, is somewhat cold and sterile.

## ENTERTAINMENT

### Bars and Nightclubs

As you might expect, San José is hardly lacking in nightspots. The best way to get anywhere at night is by taxi. They are affordable and you won't have to walk through unsafe areas. You will find lovely places to have a drink or mingle with the night owls if you stroll around the downtown core. The area north of Avenida 2 and east of Calle 4 is one of its safest. The Amón district (*barrio*) has an especially interesting nightlife.

**Art** *(in the El Cruce shopping centre, at the San Rafael de Escazú junction)* bar is the number one hot spot for the young crowd.

The **Bavaria** *(Calle 21, Av. 4/6)*, along with the **Akelarre** next door, occupies an enormous white turn-of-the-century private residence. This charming, streamlined Victorian house is surrounded by beautiful gardens, and is one of those trendy bars that fills up with Costa Rican youth on warm summer nights. The bar has a large terrace in the back.

The popular **El Balcón de Europa** *(Calle 9, Av. Central/1)* restaurant is a good place for a drink, and its reputation is well deserved.

A little north of El Balcón de Europa and not far from the Del Rey hotel is the **Beatle Bar** *(Calle 9, Av. Central/1)*, where photos of the Beatles cover the walls. The crowd is rather young and very lively. The place has a very American ambiance.

**Café Plantter's** *(Escazú, on the main highway)* attracts such a large crowd of young people on Friday nights that some end up on the street, beer in hand.

Everyone knows **El Cuartel de la Boca del Monte** *(Mon to Fri noon to 2:30am, Sat and Sun 7pm to 2am; Av. 1, Calle 21/23, ☎221-0327)* for its good daytime meals as well as for its nighttime ambiance. Even during the week, you will often have to make your way through a tightly packed crowd in the evenings. Most of San José's youth hangs out in this very pleasant establishment. Meals are served late into the night, which is rare in the city.

Go see (and especially hear!) the *mariachis* at the **Esmeralda** *(11am to 5am; Av. 2, Calle 5/7, ☎233-7386)*; they literally sing at the top of their lungs! The songs (lyrics and music) are sung in their entirety; these *mariachis* stay true to the originals! Indeed, they gather on the sidewalk in front of the restaurant at night, blocking the flow of pedestrian traffic somewhat.

**El Pueblo** *(in Barrio Tournón, on the Guapiles hwy., north of downtown, opposite the Bougainvillea hotel)* is a complex of shops and offices housed in small dwellings recreating a small Spanish colonial village (*pueblo*), with narrow winding streets. The restaurants stay open fairly late (Lukas restaurant, see p 91) and there are bars such as **Cocoloco** *(Tue to Sat; ☎222-8782)* in which to relax or dance.

**The Loft** *(at the San Rafael and Escazú junction)* is a bar located above Mac's restaurant. A hip and friendly clientele shoots pool in its laid-back ambiance. The bar offers "2-for-1" specials.

The top-floor bar of the **Talamanca** hotel *(Av. 2, Calle 8/10)* provides its quiet clientele with an interesting view over the city.

**Las Tunas** *(Sabana Norte)* (see p 91) has a nightclub on weekends.

### Gay Bars and Nightclubs

**La Avispa** *(Tue to Sun; Calle 1, Av. 8/10)* has been attracting a gay and lesbian crowd for 18 years now. A mix of Pop and the tropical rythms of Latin music is played here.

**Le Boys Bar** *(Complejo Convoy, Antiguo Kilates, Tibas, north of San José)* is the Costa Rican version of Panama's Boys Bar.

**Café Mundo** *(Mon to Sat; Av. 9, Calle 15, in the bend)* is a rather quiet European-style restaurant that turns into a bar at night.

Featuring techno-pop mixed with Spanish hits, **Deja Vu** *(Wed to Sun; Calle 2, Av. 14/16)* is described as the best club in Central America. Mixed crowd.

The Moorish-style bar-restaurant **Kasbah** *(11am to 11pm, Fri and Sat until midnight; Calle Central, Av. 7/9)* sometimes turns into a dance club at night.

## Casinos

If you want to try your luck at games of chance, there are many casinos in San José, most of which are open 24 hours a day. In addition to the many hotel gaming clubs, the **Casino Colonial** *(24 hours a day; Av. 1, Calle 9/11, right near the Del Rey hotel, ☎258-2807)* is an independent, high-class gambling house, as evidenced by its interior decor (vast spaces with high ceilings, ceramic-tiled floors, matching colours, and stately columns) and the doorperson in attendance. The building's façade is easily recognizable, with its columns, pediment and portico. The casino also houses a restaurant *(**$$$**)* with a North American atmosphere.

## Cultural and Artistic Activities

Most of the nation's newspapers (the *Tico Times* and *La Nación* in particular) will provide you with information about the cultural and artistic activities being held in the capital.

## Theatres

**Teatro La Aduana, Teatro Fanal** and **Teatro 1987** *(Calle 25, Av. 3/5, ☎221-5205 or 257-0005)*.

**Teatro del Angel** *(Av. Central, Calle 13/15, ☎222-8258)*.

**Teatro Carpa** *(Moravia, ☎234-2866)*.

**Teatro La Comedia** *(Av. Central, Calle 13/15, ☎222-4376)*.

A veritable paradise for birds and plants, the Monteverde region attracts ornithologists as well as tourists for its rare quetzals.
- *Roger Michel*

The small village of Montezuma on the Nicoya Peninsula boasts magnificent, seemingly endless beaches.
- *R. M.*

The stork, one of the country's many winged species.
*- D. R.*

Sugar cane fields dance in the wind as far as the eye can see.

*- Stéphane G. Marceau*

**Teatro Eugene O'Neill** *(Centro Cultural Costarricense Norteamericano, in the Dent district, Calle Los Negritos, ☎253-5527)*.

**Teatro Laurence Olivier** *(Av. 2, Calle 28, ☎223-1969 or 222-1034)*.

**Teatro La Mascara** *(Calle 13, Av. 2/4, ☎255-4250)*.

**Teatro Melico Salazar** *(Av. 2, Calle Central/2, ☎221-4952)*.

**Teatro Nacional** *(☎233-6354)*.

**Teatro Vargas Calvo** *(Calle 5, Av. Central/2, ☎222-1875)*.

## Cinema

**Sala Garbo** *(Av. 2, Calle 28)* screens international films with Spanish subtitles.

**Teatro Laurence Olivier** *(Av. 2, Calle 28)* presents plays and films. The complex also has an art gallery and a café.

The **Universidad de Costa Rica**, in San Pedro, presents modestly priced films in the auditorium of the **Estudios Generales** pavilion. Like at other North American universities, the films shown here are generally recent, often repertory, and intended primarily for the student population. However, screenings are also open to the general public.

## SHOPPING

In addition to Costa Rican chain department stores, San José has the large, popular, Japanese-owned **Supermercado Yaohan** supermarket located opposite the Corobici hotel, in Sabana Este.

The **Librería Universal** is a very large bookshop and stationer's with one outlet in the heart of the city *(Av. 1, Calle Central/1, ☎222-2222 ext. 320, ⇌222-2992)*, and another on the Prospero Fernández Highway service road, which runs along the south side of La Sabana Park. A good place to pick up books about Costa Rica (photo and fact books) as well as popular books (business, etc.).

The **Librería Lehmann** *(Av. Central, Calle 1/3)* is another major bookshop located in the heart of the city.

The **Librería Internacional** *(300 m west of Taco Bell, in the Dent district, San Pedro, ☎283-6965, ⇌283-7857)* sells English, French, Spanish and German language books.

There are several small bookshops, many of which sell used books, on or near Paseo de los Estudiantes. **Chispas Books** *(9am to 6pm; Calle 7, Av. Central/1, ☎256-8251)* has a fine selection of English language books.

There are also numerous bookshops near the Universidad de Costa Rica campus, in San Pedro.

Certain shopping centres are also worth checking out such as the upscale **Centro Comercial Multi-Plaza**, right next to the Camino Real hotel. **El Pueblo** *(in Barrio Tournón, on the Guapiles hwy., north of downtown, opposite the Bougainvillea hotel)*, a reconstruction of an old colonial village, is also worth a visit.

The bustling **Mercado Central** *(Av. Central/1, Calle 6/8)* also merits a visit to pick up certain consumer goods (clothing, accessories, all kinds of food, flowers, etc.) while immersing yourselves in a pleasant and completely Costa Rican atmosphere.

If you want to buy cigars, there are two places of interest around Parque Morazán. The first is the **Cigar Shoppe** *(Calle 5, Av. 3)*, a small chic place on the main floor of Diana's Inn that offers Cuban, Honduran and Nicaraguan cigars. The second is the unpretentious **Morazán** restaurant, which stocks cigars and cigarillos near the cash register.

For arts and crafts, head to **Artesanías El Pueblo** *(at the El Pueblo shopping centre, in the Tournón district, north of downtown, ☎222-5938)*, which carries souvenirs, handicrafts and works by famous artists such as Bolívar García and Amighetti. The **Mercado Central** also has kiosks selling handicrafts.

San José, of course, has several places where you can stock up on **coffee**: first and foremost, at the Mercado Central and in supermarkets, but also at souvenir and coffee shops scattered throughout the capital. **La Esquina del Café** as well as the **Amón Coffee Shop** *(near the corner of Calle 3 and Av. 9, Barrio Amón)*, located almost next to each other, are also worth checking out. They have displays of coffee and its many uses; it's amazing what can be done with *granos de oro* these days! Both places feature all kinds of ideas for gifts to bring back. There are also a certain number of merchants that sell coffee, which they describe as *100% puro*, around Avenida 1 on the few blocks northwest of the Mercado Central.

The **shop at the Museos del Banco Central de Costa Rica** *(Calle 5, Av. Central)* also offers visitors a golden opportunity (literally and figuratively) to do some great shopping. The boutique is part of the underground museum complex located beneath Plaza de la Cultura that comprises, among other institutions, the Museum of Numismatics and the Museo del Oro Precolombino (Pre-Colombian Gold Museum). Sold here are gold reproductions of pre-Colombian and other art works, as well as beautifully crafted art and history books.

The **Mercado Nacional de Artesanía** and **CANAPI** *(Av. 1, Calle 11)* sell handicrafts.

Lastly, **ANDA** *(Av. Central, Calle 5/7)* sells handicrafts made by Costa Rica's native people.

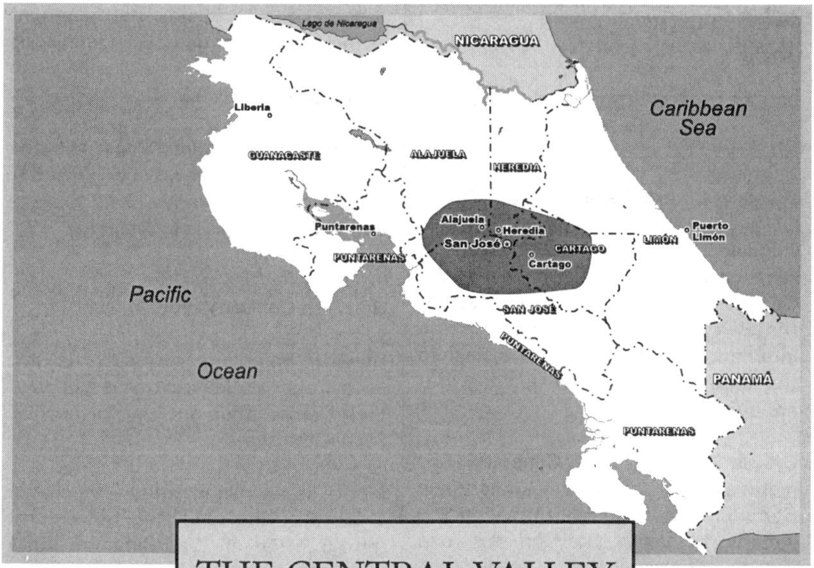

# THE CENTRAL VALLEY

Cradled between mountains in the middle of the country, the Central Valley provided a fertile terrain for the country's economic development. Thus, the country's first cities sprang up here, including the national capital, San José and three of the provincial capitals: Alajuela, Heredia and Cartago.

Today, the Valley attracts travellers for two different reasons. The larger, historic cities are home to many of the nation's cultural and artistic activities. Because these cities are more developed, they also have many of the country's best hotels and restaurants, as well as a thriving nightlife.

In addition to the cultural attractions, there is the extraordinary natural beauty of the Central Valley. The weather here is always temperate, and the fields, plantations and pastures in the countryside almost extravagantly green. Lush forests and dense tropical jungle cover hillsides in tiers. And the entire valley is encircled by majestic volcanoes and mountain chains. Perhaps the best way to describe the Central Valley is to say it is like heaven on earth!

The fact that all of this natural beauty is concentrated in a small area makes the Central Valley a great place to stay. The whole 50-by-20-kilometre region can be travelled from one end to the other in one day. The dramatic changes in elevation provide many strikingly beautiful views that combine all of the valley's most scenic elements: fields, forests, cliffs, volcanoes and cities.

While this chapter offers some suggested activities, feel free to head off to do some random exploring on the roads in the area. Whichever direction you take, they lead to delightful surprises!

## By Car

### Western Central Valley

**Alajuela**: it is very easy to get to Alajuela from San José. Simply take the General Cañas highway, which starts at the Parque La Sabana, towards the international airport. Alajuela is close to the airport, and the signs leading to it are quite clear.

**Ojo de Agua**: take the General Cañas highway west. Past the Cariari and Herradura hotels, turn left towards San Antonio de Belén. Stay on this road until Ojo de Agua.

**Atenas**: this town is off the General Cañas highway, a few kilometres past Alajuela if you are coming from San José. This is also an alternative route to Jacó, on the Pacific Coast (the other way is via Puntarenas). There is usually a fair amount of traffic, especially on weekends. On the other hand, it is a pretty drive through magnificent, hilly countryside.

**The Butterfly Farm**: take the General Cañas highway (west of the Hotel Cariari) towards San Antonio de Belén. In San Antonio, turn right after the church, then left after the first block of houses. Stay on this road, which passes through the villages of San Rafael and La Guácima. Bear left at the fork in the road at Hacienda Los Reyes. Follow the signs to the nearby farm.

**Madame Butterfly Garden**: start as if going to the Butterfly Farm. Take the General Cañas to San Antonio de Belén. Turn right after the church, then left after the first block of houses. Stay on this road through the villages of San Rafael and La Guácima. Then bear right at the fork in the road at Hacienda Los Reyes. Turn left at the Las Vueltas bridge after La Guácima.

**Parque Nacional Volcán Poás**: take the Interamericana Highway to Alajuela. Then take the secondary road through San Pedro de Poás and Fraijanes.

### Northern Central Valley

**Heredia**: Heredia is very close to San José. Take the General Cañas highway; there is more than one exit to the city. Follow the signs.

**Monte de la Cruz**: to get to Monte de la Cruz, take the road that goes north from San Rafael. (San Rafael is just a few kilometres northeast of Heredia).

**Parque Nacional Braulio Carrillo** and **Rainforest Aerial Tram**: from San José, take Calle 3 north. This road becomes the Autopista Braulio Carrillo (or Guápiles) *(85¢ toll)*. It takes about 20 minutes to get to the park, and about 45 minutes to get to the Aerial Tram.

### Eastern Central Valley

**Cartago**: this city is found along the Interamericana Highway, which goes south to Cerro de la Muerte and the southern region of the country. This major highway has four lanes most of the way from San José to Cartago.

**Parque Nacional Volcán Irazú**: take the Interamericana to Cartago. Continue through the village of San Rafael and follow the signs to the park.

**Refugio Nacional de Fauna Silvestre Tapantí**: go to Cartago via the Interamericana. From there, take the

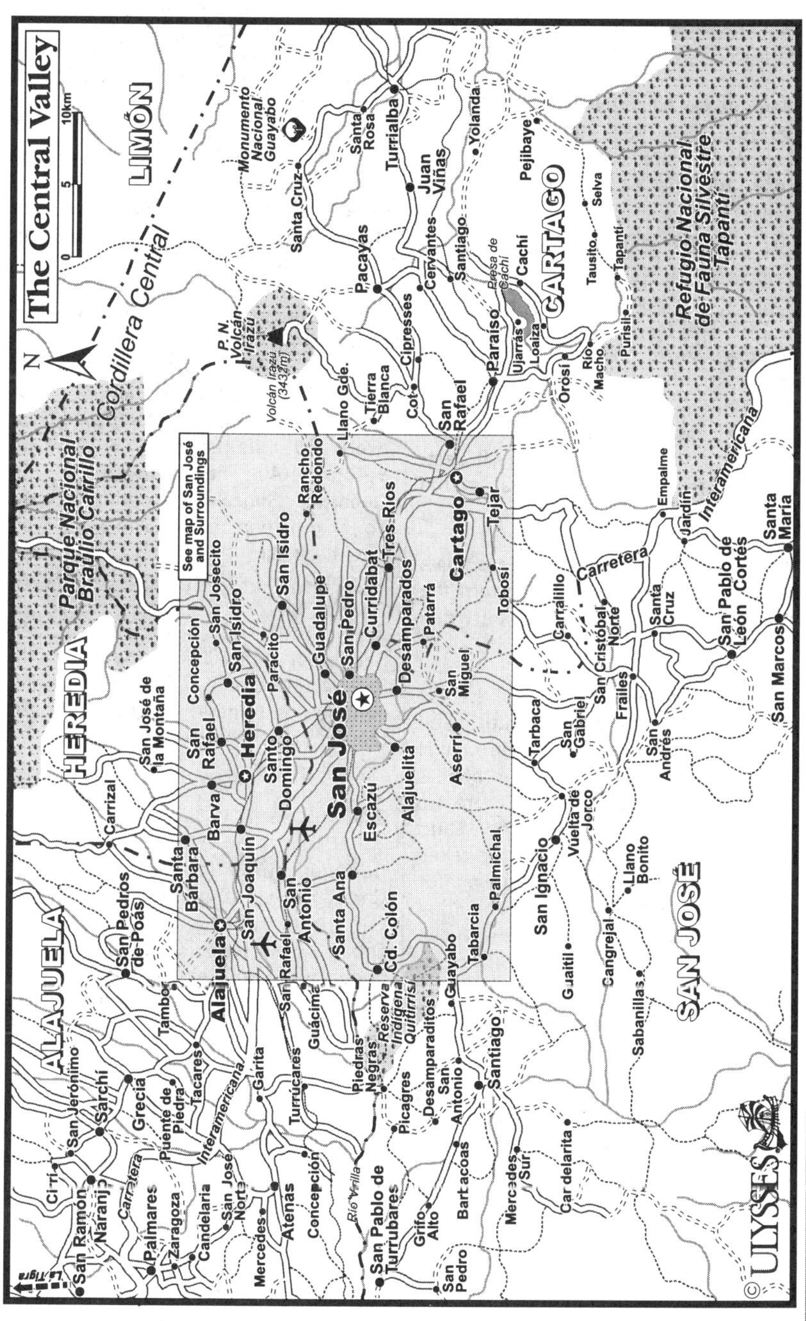

The Central Valley
0
5
10km
N
LIMÓN
HEREDIA
ALAJUELA
CARTAGO
SAN JOSÉ
Cordillera Central
Parque Nacional Braulio Carrillo
Refugio Nacional de Fauna Silvestre Tapantí
Monumento Nacional Guayabo
P. N. Volcán Irazú
Volcán Irazú (3432m)
See map of San José and Surroundings
San José
Heredia
Alajuela
Cartago
Turrialba
Santa Rosa
Santa Cruz
Pacayas
Juan Viñas
Cervantes
Santiago
Yolanda
Pejibaye
Cachí
Presa de Cachí
Paraíso
Ujarrás
Loaiza
Orosi
Río Macho
Purisil
Tapantí
Tausito
Selva
Cipresses
Cot
Tierra Blanca
Llano Gde.
San Rafael
Rancho Redondo
San Isidro
San Josecito
Concepción
Guadalupe
San Pedro
Curridabat
Tres Ríos
Desamparados
Patarrá
Tobosí
Tejar
San Miguel
Paracito
Santo Domingo
Barva
San José de la Montaña
Carrizal
Santa Bárbara
San Joaquín
San Antonio
Escazú
Alajuelita
Aserrí
Santa Ana
Cd. Colón
Guayabo
Tabarcia
Palmichal
San Rafael
San Pedros de Poás
Tambor
Guácima
Reserva Indígena Quitirrisí
Desamparaditos
San Ignacio
Vuelta de Jorco
Tarbaca
San Gabriel
Frailes
San Cristóbal Norte
Carralillo
Carretera Interamericana
Jardín
Empalme
Santa María
San Pablo de León Cortés
Santa Cruz
San Marcos
San Andrés
Llano Bonito
Cangrejal
Guaitil
Sabanillas
Santiago
San Antonio
Desamparaditos
Picagres
Piedras Negras
Turrúcares
Garita
Tacares
Puente de Piedra
Grecia
Sarchí
San Jerónimo
Ciruí
Naranjo
San Ramón
Palmares
Zaragoza
Candelaria
San José Norte
Mercedes
Atenas
Concepción
Río Virilla
San Pablo de Turrubares
Grifo Alto
Bart acoas
Mercedes Sur
Car delarita
San Pedro
La Tigra
© ULYSSES

secondary road through Paraíso, Orosí, Río Macho and Tapantí.

**Monumento Nacional Guayabo**: go to Cartago, then pass through Paraíso, Juan Viñas and Turrialba. Follow the signs for the Monumento Nacional Guayabo.

## By Bus

### Western Central Valley

**Alajuela**: departures from San José are frequent. Buses leave from Avenida 2, between Calles 12 and 14. In Alajuela, the bus depot is to the west of the market and the central park.

**Ojo de Agua**: in San José, buses leave for Ojo de Agua every hour from the stop on Avenida 1, between Calles 18 and 20.

**The Butterfly Farm**: in Alajuela, the bus stop is 100 metres south and 100 metres west of the Tikal supermarket. Make sure the bus is marked "La Guácima abajo." There are four buses to the Butterfly Farm between 6am and 2pm. The trip takes about 40 minutes. Ask the driver for "La Finca de Mariposas." From San José, there are two buses every day except Sunday. The buses leave at 11am and 2pm from the stop on Avenida 1 between Calles 20 and 22 that says "Ojo de Agua/San Antonio." Stay on the bus until the last stop of the hour-long trip. From the school just follow the signs for 300 metres to the farm. The bus returns to San José at 3:15pm. However, there are three direct buses to The Butterfly Farm every day. For information and reservations, call the Farm at ☎438-0400.

**Parque Nacional Volcán Poás**: buses run only on Sundays and holidays at 8:30am *($1.25; Calle 12, Av. 2/4)*.

### Northern Central Valley

**Heredia**: buses leave San José for Heredia every 10 minutes. The trip takes about 25 minutes.

**Barva**: buses leave Heredia for Barva every 30 minutes.

**Parque Nacional Braulio Carrillo**: buses leave from San José *(Calle 12, Av. 7/9)* every 30 minutes from 5:30am to 9:45pm. Ask the driver for the Quebrada González reception centre. To take the bus back to San Jose, wait for it near the road. Transport Empresarios Guapilenos *($1.55, ☎223-1276)*.

**Rainforest Aerial Tram**: the buses for Parque Nacional Braulio Carrillo continue on to here. Ask the driver for the Rainforest Aerial Tram.

### Eastern Central Valley

**Cartago**: buses leave San José for Cartago every 10 minutes.

**Orosí**: buses leave Cartago for Orosí about every hour and a half, between 6am and 10pm, Monday to Friday. The return trips depart between 4:30pm and 6:30pm.

**Turrialba**: buses leave San José for Turrialba and Guayabo every hour, between 5am and 10pm. The return buses follow the same schedule for the 50-minute trip.

**Parque Nacional Volcán Irazú**: there is bus service to the park on Saturdays and Sundays only. Departure time is

8am *($4.20; Av. 2, Calle 1/3, ☎272-0651)*.

**Refugio Nacional de Fauna Silvestre Tapantí**: take the bus to Cartago, where you transfer to the bus for the Orosí Valley *(☎551-6810)*. This bus takes you as far as the Río Macho (just past Orosí), about nine kilometres from the entrance to the park. From there, you can take a taxi *(about $6)* to the park.

**Monumento Nacional Guayabo**: take the bus to Turrialba, and transfer to the bus that goes to the monument *(☎556-0583)*.

## PRACTICAL INFORMATION

The Central Valley is home to almost half of the population of Costa Rica, and is thus highly urbanized. And because the three provincial capitals are only a few kilometres from the national capital, you should not have any trouble finding the basic services anywhere in the region.

### Western Central Valley

**Alajuela**: all the major national banks can be found in Alajuela. They are concentrated in the Parque Central area, and most have automated teller machines.

The San Rafael hospital *(Calle Central, Av. 9, ☎441-5011)* is north of the downtown area.

The departure area for most buses is two streets west of the Mercado Central, on Avenida 1.

### Northern Central Valley

**Heredia**: there are several banks around the Parque Central and on Avenida 6.

The major bus stops are also around the Parque Central, on Calle Central.

San Vicente de Paul hospital *(☎261-0091)* is located west of the downtown area, at the end of Avenida 8, on Calle 14.

### Eastern Central Valley

**Cartago**: most of the large national banks have branches in Cartago: Banco Popular is located near the south side of the Parque de Las Ruinas.

The Max Peralta hospital *(☎551-0611)* is located to the south of Parque Central (and of Parque de Las Ruinas) on Avenida 5.

The bus stops are situated either on Calle 4, or, nearby Avenida 3.

## EXPLORING

### Western Central Valley

West of the Mexico hospital, between San José and the Juan Santamaría airport, **Pueblo Antiguo ★** *(☎296-2212 or 231-2001, ≠296-2212)* is a restoration of an historical village that shows what life in Costa Rica was like at the end of the last century. In addition to the village and old-fashioned countryside, there are performances by professionals *(music and dance, Fri, Sat and Sun at 6:30pm, and period craftsmanship, Sat and Sun at 10am)*.

**Ojo de Agua ★** *(5 km west of San Antonio, which is 3 km from the*

*General Cañas highway, between Alajuela and San José)* is a recreational complex with underground springs that attracts people from all parts of the Valley. In addition to lakes, facilities include playgrounds, an amphitheatre and green spaces, with picnic areas planned for the near future. A babysitting service is available. However, this public facility can get crowded, particularly on weekends.

Coffee plantations and fields of decorative plants are fairly common sights in the Valley, particularly north of Alajuela (from Quebradas to San Isidro de Poás) and in the Atenas Valley.

***Coffee tree***

**The Alajuela Region**

**Alajuela** ★, the capital of the province of the same name, is somewhat warmer than San José because of its lower altitude. Its main advantage is that it is only five minutes away from the airport. However, thanks to the General Cañas highway, San José is also easy to reach from here. Alajuela is the province's transportation hub, but the modern highway makes it possible to bypass the town and visit most of the province's tourist attractions starting from San José.

The architecture of the **Alajuela cathedral** *(Calle Central, Av. Central/1)*, with its classical porch with pilasters, and the cupola in the centre of the transept, is vaguely Portuguese-Gothic. However, the **Iglesia La Agonia** *(Calle 9, Av. Central/1)* is probably more attractive, and has a pretty little park with a fountain and an enormous tree next to it.

The shady **Parque Central** in Alajuela is a very popular meeting place for the locals. Like most of Costa Rica's urban central parks, it has a pavilion for concerts, traditional festivals or neighbourhood theatrical productions.

The **Museo Juan Santamaría** (free admission; Tue to Sun 10am to 6pm; one block north of Parque Central, inside a former prison) retells the famous events of the mid-19th century, in which William Walker tried to invade Costa Rica and set up a pro-slavery political regime, but failed (see p 23).

**Los Chorros** ★ *(a few km north of Tacares, which is 15 km from Alajuela)* are two lovely falls, about 25 metres high, which are protected by the national park service. Although this is officially private property and has a fence that everyone seems not to see, there are some amenities for visitors (parking, toilets and places for washing feet). The view from the path going down to the falls, accompanied by the sound of the river, is lovely. Walk down the slope, then follow the trail. Visiting Los Chorros is certainly a pleasant outing, and it's very popular with *Ticos* on weekends.

**The Atenas Valley Region, between La Garita and San Mateo**

In **La Garita, Zoo Ave** ★★ *($7 adults, $1 children; every day 9am to 5pm; 3 km from the Atenas exit off the Interamericana, ☎433-8989, ⇾433-9140)* is a zoo that was originally an ornithological garden (*ave* means "bird" in Spanish). It now includes monkeys, reptiles and many varieties of plants. This zoo unique because the animals were either abandoned, injured or were confiscated by the authorities. Since 1995 it has been recognized by the Costa Rican government as an official animal shelter.

Further south in **La Guácime** is the largest and oldest enterprise of its kind in Costa Rica, **The Butterfly Farm** ★★★ *($5 adults, $2 children; every day 9am to 3:30pm; across from the Los Reyes Country Club, ☎438-0400, ⇄438-0300)*. The owners mainly raise butterflies for export, but added an educational aspect to it with an enlightening two-hour guided tour that explains the whole process of raising and selling butterflies (host plants, predators, potential buyers, etc.). There is an optional video presentation after the tour. Having a meal at the farm's restaurant or picnicking on the grounds are a nice way to round out the visit.

**Madame Butterfly Garden** *(every day 8am to 4pm; ☎255-2031 or 255-2262)* is a greenhouse garden similar to The Butterfly Farm. One greenhouse is for raising butterflies, and the other is for reproducing them. The owner has studied the subject for more than three years and can explain it in English. Because it is relatively new, this establishment is less frequented than The Butterfly Farm.

People say that the region of **Atenas** enjoys the best climate in the world. This, together with its geography, makes it is one of the most beautiful places to visit in the entire country. Between La Garita and Atenas there are many magnificent panoramas of the fairly steep mountains and the rivers that run between them. There is only one real drawback to area's lack of commercial development: there are no roadside restaurants where you can stop to eat while admiring the view.

**Cooperativa Agropecuaria Industrial y de Servicios Multiples de Atenas** *(☎446-5141)* is a coffee-producing co-op that offers a tour of its facilities if you make advance reservations, which is definitely worth it!

Between **Atenas** and San Mateo the chain of mountains that separates the Central Valley from the Pacific Coast dominates the breathtakingly beautiful scenery. But pay attention to the narrow and winding road demands the driver's full attention because it goes up one side of the mountain range and comes down the other, with some steep sections along the way. Unfortunately there are few places to stop and admire the view, except for a rudimentary and not too clearly indicated lookout (*mirador*) at Alto del Monte, not far past the Linda Vista bar near Atenas. This is an ideal trip – from a passenger's point of view!

### The San Ramón and Zarcero Areas

**Bosque Nuboso Los Angeles** ★★ *(between San Ramón and La Tigra, signs to it are fairly clear)* is a magnificent private reserve, literally nestled in the clouds, because you will actually be walking through them at certain points during your visit! Former President Rodrigo Carazo owns this 800-hectare nature reserve. There are guided excursions on foot or on horseback and exploring the trails without a guide is also possible. Bosque Nuboso is easy to get to from San José, and there are a growing number of services here, such as the Villablanca hotel (see p 124).

The route to the reserve turns off the San Ramon-La Tigra road, and passes through lovely countryside with valleys and pastures. About five kilometres south of the dam between La Tigra and Los Angeles, there are some picturesque little waterfalls that make interesting viewing – for your passengers, of course!

There are three outstanding places to visit in **San Ramón**, the "city of presidents and poets": the market, the San Ramón museum and the José Figueres historic and cultural centre. With a population of 50,000, San Ramón is a decent-sized town whose main attraction is its **market** ★. Saturday is market day, and it is especially worth checking out because few tourists go. The country's horticultural and agricultural products. The farm produce is just as varied and abundant at the public indoor market in San Ramón, located between pedestrian-zoned streets that, lined with businesses that make for pleasant shopping. There are also a few interesting commercial streets near the church.

**Museo de San Ramón** *(free admission; Mon to Fri 1pm to 5pm; next to the former courthouse square, facing the park, San Ramón)* has displays explaining the region's history, including its important historical figures.

The brand-new **Centro Cultural y Histórico José Figueres** *(Mon to Sat 9am to 11:30am and 1:30pm to 5:30pm, closed on holidays; on the same street as the church, San Ramón)* was built in honour of Don Pepe (three-time President of Costa Rica), who was born in San Ramón in 1906. It is on the same street as the city's museum.

**Mariposas y Orquideas de San Ramón** *(free admission; 1 km west of the San Ramón exit on the Interamericana, ☎445-4887)* is another, albeit less well-known, place to learn all about butterflies and perhaps buy a cocoon...

Coffee plantations give way to pine forests as the altitude increases on the way to **Zarcero** ★★. Driving through the region is very enjoyable.

Zarcero is one of the prettiest little towns in Costa Rica, and it has a marvellous climate. Because the town is at an altitude of 1,700 metres, the weather is always slightly cool. The pastoral countryside is magnificent, and so is the landscaping of the town. The central park is famous for its bushes which are trimmed into various shapes. The brilliant white church that faces the park has an equally beautiful, colourful interior. Because the city is full of open spaces, every outing is a pleasure, whether on foot, by bike or by car. Zarcero's water is safe to drink, and the place is so clean that there is no reason to fear eating in the local restaurants, especially those around the church and park squares. The people in Zarcero show their civic pride during their town's annual festival in February, which is the perfect time to visit it.

**Bosque de Paz** ★ *(between Zarcero and Bajos de Toro, ☎234-6676 or 225-0203)* is a private tropical rainforest reserve that forms a sort of natural corridor between the Poás and the Juan Castro Blanco national parks. It is becoming a highly acclaimed centre for ecotourism that compares favourably with La Selva in Monteverde (see p 185). There are ten different nature interpretation trails with differing themes and degrees of difficulty. The reserve very popular with amateur birders and ornithologists who keep tabs on the number of bird species. There is a restaurant here as well. The Britt coffee producers are associated with Bosque de Paz and offer passes to the reserve, but reservations are always required.

*Carreta*

**Naranjo, Sarchí and Grecia**

On the way back from Zarcero you can pass through **Naranjo ★**, a little town at an altitude of 1,000 metres. Its interesting Manueline-style church, with its many scrolled decorations, can be seen from a great distance. Next to the church is a large archway of shrubbery which leads into a grotto devoted to the Virgin Mary. The overall effect is very aesthetically pleasing. The municipal building is also interesting, as is the central park, which has French gardens that surround a space used for ceremonies, concerts and theatrical productions. The city centre overlooks the residential areas in the valley around it, and affords splendid views of the coffee plantations, vegetable gardens and fields in the countryside.

**Sarchí ★★**, east of Naranjo, has a very pretty little church and town square. The general layout of the town is aesthetically pleasing, mostly because the buildings are well proportioned, clean and well maintained. The central park in Sarchí is part garden, part public square, and the site of the **Monumento a la Carreta**. Finished in 1994, this monument represents one of the typical carts that were used in the last century to transport coffee across mountains and valleys from the centre of the country to the Pacific Coast. The city's overall atmosphere is pleasant, especially in the late afternoon when the air is cooler and everything is calm. Sarchí is known for its woodworkers and traditional carts, so it is not surprising that there are many shops and handicrafts studios all over town.

**Grecia**, south of Sarchí, is the cleanest town around. It has even been named as the cleanest town in Latin America, and its residents are proud of this: they have even posted signs all over Grecia promoting respect for the environment. The town also has a lovely church with a handsome red metal roof.

**Jewels of the Rainforest ★** *(small admission fee; every day 9am to 5pm; municipal museum of Grecia, ☎244-5006)* is a fascinating museum, showcasing more than 50,000 species of insects from tropical rainforests all over the world. The collection was assembled by a couple from the United States over their lifetime.

In the region of Grecia, **El Bosque del Niño de la Reserva Forestal Grecia ★** *(small admission fee; closed Mon; follow the signs to it from Grecia, which are the same as those to Los Trapiches)* is a pretty little forest where you can go for pleasant walks. Camping is permitted.

In the same area, **Los Trapiches ★** *(between Santa Gertrudis Sur and Santa Gertrudis Norte, ☎444-6656)* will satisfy your sweet tooth. The *trapiche* (sugarcane press) on display here dates back to the 1860s and is probably the only one left in the country. Here, you can learn how sugar is produced (the cane crushed, the extract boiled, and the cooked product moulded into shape). You can grab a bite at the restaurant, or have a picnic on the grass. It is also pleasant to stroll on the lawns or go for a swim in one of the pools. Costa Ricans come here to enjoy the simple pleasures of life on weekends, so it can get a bit crowded.

**El Mundo de las Serpientes** *(every day 8am to 4pm; on the road leaving town towards Alajuela, across from the Poró saw mill, Grecia; ☎494-3700)* is a serpentium (snake zoo). Indigenous snakes and species from other parts of the world, such as the rare albino Birman python, are displayed in large cages. Guided tours are available in English and Spanish. This relatively new establishment is only two minutes from downtown Grecia.

In the middle of Grecia, facing the park, the pretty pastel-coloured **church of San Isidro de Poás** adds a nice touch to the urban landscape. You can get a lovely view of this ensemble from the top of the hill.

## Parque Nacional Volcán Poás

With a record attendance of 175,000 people in 1996, **Parque Nacional Volcán Poás ★★★** *($6; every day 8am to 4pm; ☎290-1927 or 232-5324)* is the most popular park in Costa Rica. This is mainly because of its proximity to San José (37 km) and the excellent paved road that goes all the way there (and even right up to the volcano). Also, the drive there is pleasant in itself, passing through lovely countryside and the towns of Alajuela and San Pedro de Poás. Keep in mind that the park is swarming with tourists on Sundays.

Despite being crowded, there is a lot to see and do at the Poás Volcano national park: craters, lakes, short trails and an interpretation centre. There is a slide show about the volcano at the information centre, where there are also toilets, snack bar, a café, a souvenir shop, and a small butterfly museum. There are also large signs and models explaining the formation of volcanoes in Costa Rica and elsewhere. Several photos and models illustrate the history of the Poás Volcano, with its several significant periods of activity. The first well-documented eruption was in 1747. The most famous occurred in 1910, when the explosion sent lava 4,000 metres into the air and volcanic ash as far away as Puntarenas, 70 kilometres to the west. The park has been forced to close several times since 1989, when the volcano started spewing out cinders again.

This national park was created on January 25, 1971 to protect the 2,708-metre-high volcano and the dense forests around it. In 1993, the 6,506-hectare park has incorporated the Cerro Congo mountains in the south. The annual precipitation is rather heavy at 3.5 metres. Even during the dry period, which lasts from December to April, it is best to visit the park in the morning because clouds often obscure the view of the crater by afternoon. The average temperatures is a cool 14°C and can get as low as -6°C, and only goes up to 21°C, so always bring warm clothes and rain gear.

It is an easy 400-metre walk to the star attraction of the park: the **main crater of the Poás Volcano**. One and a half kilometres wide and 300 metres deep, it is one of the largest craters in the world. The greenish water at the bottom of the crater is very acidic and sulfurous. As the water evaporates, it produces sulfur deposits and acid rain. This constant release of gasses probably reduces the volcano's internal pressure so that a devastating eruption is unlikely in the near future. Nevertheless, the state of the volcano is closely monitored and constantly analysed since this volcano has more than one crater: nine have been counted so far.

Returning from the main crater, take the **Laguna Botos** (one km round trip) trail, which goes to the pretty little lake that gave it its name. The trees along the trail are stunted and twisted because of the occasionally glacial temperatures, strong winds and acid rain. Lake Botos is actually one of the volcano's craters that has filled up with rainwater. It is 400 metres wide and 14 metres deep. The water temperature is always between 10°C and 14°C. Although this trail is connected to the Escalonia trail on the park map, we had to turn around and backtrack. Returning to the information centre via the **Escalonia** (560 m) trail is interesting because of the interpretive signs that describe the native flora in this high volcanic region, specifically the *poás magnolia* and *escalonia* trees, as well as different varieties of oak. Along this trail you can also observe some of the 79 species of birds that have been seen in the park, including hummingbirds and the famous quetzal.

## Northern Central Valley

The town of **Heredia**, called "Ciudad de las Flores", was founded in 1706. At a slightly higher elevation than San José, it has a somewhat cooler climate and is also less frenetic. It has the attractive urban landscape of a former colonial city, and its proximity to San José makes it an ideal place to visit. Don't miss the beautiful **colonial church** ★★ which dates back to 1796. It is one of the three churches that can be toured in the centre of Heredia, the most modern of which is in the Art Deco style. The parks in front of these churches are ideal for relaxing. The covered central market is a great place to meet the owners of downtown businesses and to locals including students from the Universidad Nacional (east of town).

The **museum of the Centro de Investigaciones del Instituto de Café (CICAFE)** *(400 m north of the colonial church in Heredia)* was closed for renovations during our visit. It is scheduled to reopen in 1999, but inquire before you head out. One of the exhibits includes a collection of coffee mills.

Built at the end of the last century, the **Gothic church at San Isidro de Heredia** ★★ has a beautifully detailed carved wood interior. It is worth the short detour to this village just east of Heredia.

**North of Heredia**

The area north of Heredia is very interesting to explore. A magnificent alpine atmosphere extends all the way to the top of the highlands of **Monte de la Cruz** ★★ with green pastures and enormous trees. Because it is close to the capital, the region of Monte Cruz includes excellent recreational parks, hotels, restaurants and a high-class residential area. The area is still under development.

The views from the **Monte de la Cruz recreational park** are sensational, especially from its famous cross. You'll feel like you're on top of the world! The park is a great place for a stroll or a picnic. There is also a restaurant, but the menu is limited.

The lovely church in **Barva** ★ has an interesting vaulted interior. Despite the laudable restoration efforts to preserve the 18th-century buildings downtown, the houses are rather basic. Overall, the town looks dreary.

**Britt coffee production centre** *(presentations, Mon to Sat 9am, 11am, 3pm; store, every day 8am to 5pm in high season; follow the signs on the road from Heredia to Barva, ☎260-2748, ⇒238-1848, info@cafebritt.com)* produces excellent coffee for export, but that's not all that is produced here! The owner had the ingenious idea of offering guided tours of the facility, complete with actors presenting information about coffee production in an engaging manner. At the end of the tour the coffee is sampled. A small shop on the premises sells coffee, and you can subscribe to Britt coffee here and receive it at home on a regular basis. Transportation from San José is available, and the visit can include an excursion to Bosque de Paz.

The **Butterfly Park** *($5; every day 8am to 4pm; beside the Autopista Braulio Carrillo, ☎382-3953)* is located three kilometres past the Río Sucio bridge, just before the Rainforest Aerial Tram. There are 35 varieties of butterflies and five frog species displayed in large aviaries. The tour explains the life cycle of butterflies, their methods of reproduction and their role in the ecology of the forest. Behind the park, you can take a trail through the forest and a dip in the nearby river.

**Rainforest Aerial Tram** ★★ *(adults $47.50, under 18 and students $23.75; every day 6am to 3:30pm; ☎257-5961, ⇒257-6053)* is a cable car that travels above the rich and diverse tropical rainforest, giving you the chance to admire the plant and animal life of the canopy. Only an hour's drive from San José, this is the ideal place to learn about the tropical rainforest in a short amount of time. If you are unable to visit the country's many parks, or have only one day to explore the forest, you should definitely come here!

The Rainforest Aerial Tram is part of a 450-hectare private nature reserve just a few minutes away from the Parque Nacional Braulio Carrello (see below). Donald Perry, a biologist from the United States, came to Costa Rica in 1974 to study the extraordinary wealth of flora and fauna in the forest canopy. In order to spend hours comfortably observing plants, mosses, ants, insects, larva and reptiles in trees that are more than 30 metres high, he devised various methods of installing himself in the canopy, including platforms. Then, he had the audacious idea of creating a cable-car ride that would allow visitors from all over the world to discover this hidden universe without disrupting the forest's ecosystem. Donald Perry has written a book about his research, entitled *Life Above the Jungle Floor* (2nd edition, Don Perro Press, San

José, 1991, 170 pages), which is available at the souvenir shop here and in most large bookstores in San José.

It took 65 people two years to set up the 250,000 kilograms of equipment for the project. Helicopters were used to install the 12 steel towers that support the cables. The tramway finally opened in 1994.

The best time of the day to visit is early in the morning, before the parking lot fills up. The park opens at 6am every morning except Monday, which is reserved for maintenance of the cable cars (6am to 9am). First, there is a short walk or a gondola ride from the parking lot to the reception centre (large room, food, souvenir shop, toilets), where the tour is explained and a video about Donald Perry and his project is shown.

Next, small groups tour the forest on foot (1 to 1.5 hours) with a guide who explains the main features of the tropical rainforest's natural phenomena. Then, four or five people and a guide get into one of the ten cable cars for the 2.6-kilometre ride through the canopy. With frequent stops for observing, asking questions and taking photographs, the tour takes about an hour and a half. The cable car starts out at mid-tree level and then goes up to the canopy, which is teeming with life. It rains frequently here, so rain gear is a must.

## Parque Nacional Braulio Carrillo

Just 20 kilometres from San José, **Parque Nacional Braulio Carrillo ★★** *($6; every day 8am to 4pm; ☎290-1027 or 232-5324)* encompasses lowland plains and high mountains. These mountains are the main source of water needed for agricultural and domestic purposes in the Central Valley, Costa Rica's most densely populated region. In spite of being so close to urban centres, the park is still very wild and largely unexplored. This is due to the height of the mountains, the density of the forest and the lack, until quite recently, of good roads going to it.

With an area of 45,899 hectares, this is the largest park in the Central Valley. It is named after the third president of Costa Rica, Braulio Carrillo, who governed from 1837 to 1842. Carrillo overthrew the elected president, and proclaimed himself "President for life". He was eventually deposed and exiled to El Salvador, where he was assassinated. Although this president was a merciless dictator, he is credited with conceiving the idea of building a road from the Central Valley to the Caribbean Coast to make it easier to ship coffee to Europe. A small road to the coast was only completed in 1882. However, it was superceded by the railway between San José and Limón in 1891, and was subsequently abandoned after several bridges on it were destroyed.

It was only in 1977 that the project of building a road to the coast was revived. Because it was feared that building the road would lead to the destructive encroachment of settlements and massive deforestation, the Parque Nacional Braulio Carrillo was created to protect the area on April 15, 1978. The road, **Autopista Braulio Carrillo ★★**, was finished in 1987. It is certainly one of the most spectacular in the country (note that it is sometimes called the Guápiles highway or the Siquirres highway), and provides easy access to protected virgin tropical rainforest just a few kilometres from San José. This park is important to Costa Rica because the country lost two thirds of its forest since the

***Jaguar***

1950s. It is important to drive cautiously through the park: is rains every day in the mountains, so roads are very slippery and traffic is heavy. Also, don't get too close to the edge of the road, even if you get out of your car to take pictures, because landslides have happened.

With an abundant 4.5 metres of precipitation per year, plant life thrives in the park. There are seven different ecological life zones, ranging from tropical rainforest to high altitude rainforest. The flora is exceptionally diverse because of this broad range of altitudes and climates. Some 6,000 species of plant life have already been counted. The lowest area of the park lies 36 metres above sea level, while the highest altitude is 2,906 metres at the top of the Barva Volcano. The average temperature varies between 25°C and 30°C in the low lying areas, and drops to an average of 15°C in the mountains. Although it rains very often, there is less rain during the dry season, from January to April.

Animal life in the park is also very diversified. There are over 100 species of reptiles and amphibians, and 135 species of mammals, including pumas, ocelots, jaguars, capuchin and howler monkeys, tapirs and sloths. Among the 350 birds species are toucans, aras, eagles and the famous quetzal.

Parque Nacional Braulio Carrillo is divided into five sectors of which the northernmost two are rarely visited (Ceibo and Magsasay). The Autopista Braulio Carillo runs to the other three sectors – Zurquí, Quebrada González and Barva – so they are easy to access. The Barva park district is hardest to reach of the three, but is the only one with camp sites and a shelter. Note that the toll for cars that drive through the park is only 85¢ per vehicle. However, if you stop at the reception centre at one of the sectors, you must pay a $6 entrance fee to the hiking trails.

**Zurquí Sector ★**

This sector is only 20 kilometres from San José, via the Autopista Braulio Carrillo. The reception centre is on the right, one kilometre before the Zurquí tunnel. Behind the reception area there is a short 250-metre trail through the surrounding forest. On the other side of the road, a second trail climbs through primary forest and leads to the tunnel. On the way back, the trail follows the road. This 2.5 -kilometre loop takes less than two hours on foot and is said to be excellent for birdwatching.

**Quebrada González Sector ★**

This sector also borders on the Autopista Braulio Carrillo, but it is 43 kilometres from San José. It has a reception centre and a parking area with a guard, as does Zurquí. The **Las Palmas** trail starts near the reception centre and makes a 1.6-kilometre loop through dense tropical rainforest. The lush vegetation thrives on the approximately six metres of rain that this part of the park receives annually! The trail is very beautiful, and there is a pamphlet that explains the flora at 12 interpretation points found along the way. The fifth interpretation point deals with the palm trees after which the trail is named. Another part of the trail goes along the González stream (for which the Quebrada González sector is named). It takes a little more than an hour to do the whole trail. The **Botarama** trail (1.2 km) starts on the other side of the road and goes towards the Río Sucio. It is named after a species of tree that grows in this region.

**Barva Sector ★★**

With its trails, lookouts, picnic area and camp sites, this sector has the most to offer nature enthusiasts. It is also the most difficult to get to by car. The 32-kilometre trip from San José to the reception area should take about an hour and a half – if everything goes well. However, because there are no signs pointing it out along the way, finding it can be difficult. The route goes through Heredia, Barva, San José de la Montaña, Porrosatí (or Paso Llano) and Sacramento. After Sacramento, there are only four kilometres to go, but the road is so rocky that only a four-wheel drive vehicle can negotiate it. The park rangers at the reception centre *($6)* are very welcoming and will answer any questions about the trails over a hot cup of tea or coffee. At this elevation of over 2,800 metres, the temperature goes down to 10°C at night. The campsites *($1.25/person/night)*, and the shelter that accommodates four *($4.20/person/night)*, are next to the reception centre. You can make reservations for the campsites or the shelter from San José *(☎283-5906)*.

The total distance of the trails in this park district is 12.3 kilometres. Since there are very few hills, most hikers can easily cover all of them in one day. The highest point in the park (2,906 metres) is at the top of the extinct **Barva Volcano**. This summit is completely different from the Irazú and Poás craters: trees have grown over it and there is no outward sign of its volcanic origin. The most beautiful view in the Barva park district is at the **Mirador Varva Blanca**, 1.5 kilometres farther along the trail. From this lookout (mirador) you can see fields of cultivated ferns stand out in startling black patches because of the canvases that cover them. The Poás Volcano (2,704 m) is the salient feature on the opposite side of the valley.

This sector's other star attraction is **Laguna Barva**, three kilometres from the reception centre. The trail that climbs gradually up to Laguna Barva is a former service road. Plants with leaves that are one metre wide *(Gunnera insignis)* grow alongside the path. They are more commonly known as *sombrilla de pobre*, which means "poor man's parasol." Tracks of Baird's tapir can often be seen in this region. This animal looks like a pig with a trunk-like snout, and can weigh up to 300 kilos! Laguna Brava is only 70 metres wide, but is located at an altitude of 2,840 metres. The water temperature hovers around 11 °C. The trail continues 200 metres past the lake to lookout with a scenic view of the lake and the valley to the north.

There is a trail from Laguna Barva that ends at **Laguna Copey** two kilometres away. Its one scenic view is of the eastern valley and the Irazú Volcano (3,432 m) with its distinctive transmission towers. The lake itself is something of a disappointment: it is only 40 metres wide and 4 metres deep. At 2,620 metres above sea level, it is slightly lower than Laguna Barva. There is no cleared area or scenic lookout near the lake.

Many hikers just do Mirador Varva Blanca and Laguna Barva, a total distance of 8.3 kilometres, which takes less than half a day. When we were there, the park ranger informed us that the 40-kilometre trail to the Magsasay park district was not officially open to the public. Rarely cleared and difficult to get to, the Magsasay takes three or four days to complete. Hikers who want to attempt it should find out ahead of time if it is open, by contacting either the park or the bureau of national parks in San José *(☎192 or 283-8004, ⇌283-7343)*.

## Eastern Central Valley

The little town of **Moravia** (or San Vicente de Moravia) is just 7 kilometres east of San José. It is a popular for its handicrafts, particularly leather-work (see p 131).

Slightly farther east, there are some inviting areas for side trips to explore the natural beauty of this part of the Central Valley. **Rancho Redondo** and its lookout, **San Isidro de Coronade** and its festival on May 15, and **Las Nubes** and its pastures are especially worthwhile.

### Cartago and the Orosí Valley

**Cartago** ★ was the capital city of Costa Rica for several centuries, but its important historical buildings were destroyed by the numerous earthquakes over the centuries. Two buildings remain that are worth seeing. First, the **ruins** *(Calle 2/4, Av. ½)* of the church in front of the central park. It was abandoned in mid-construction because of an earthquake. The ruins are in the centre of a charming little park that is an ideal place to relax and take in the modern urban scene. Also, there is the **Basílica Nuestra Señora de los Angeles** ★★★ *(Calle 16, Av. 2/4)*, to which thousands of pilgrims flock every year on August 2, some of them coming from San José, 22 kilometres away, to pay homage to La Negrita (Our Lady of the Angels). The statue of La Negrita was found at the site of the present basilica. It is said to have mysteriously reappeared there after having been taken away, and many miracles have been attributed to it. Each year, people claiming to have been healed by the statue leave symbols of the part of them that was healed at the foot of the statue. Our Lady of the Angels has become the

*Ujarras ruins*

patron saint of Costa Rica. The basilica itself is lovely, built in a somewhat Byzantine style.

Between Cartago and Paraíso are the **Lankester Gardens** ★ *($2.50; every day 8:30am to 3:30pm; 6 m east of Cartago)*, created by Charles Lankester, a British botanist. There are over 800 orchid species on display here (February, March and April are the best months to see them in bloom). There is also an arboretum with plants and trees from the differing ecosystems found in Costa Rica. The gardens are now managed by the University of Costa Rica and are open to the public.

The **Orosí Valley** ★★ starts at Paraíso and stretches out south of Cartago. It is a beautiful, fertile valley, and well worth visiting. Four places are specifically recommended: Ujarras, Lake Cachi and its Charrarra tourist complex, and the city of Orosí.

**Ujarras** ★ *(7 km east of Paraíso)* is actually the ruins of a city that was abandoned after a flood at the beginning of the 19th century. The walls of the 17th-century church are still standing, but its roof has disintegrated. Landscaping surrounds the ruins. There are washroom facilities and a large parking area at the site.

**Lake Cachi** is an artificial lake that is perfect for canoeing. It offers lovely views of the surrounding region.

**Charrarra** *(50¢; 8am to 5pm, closed Mon; a few km west of Ujarras)* is a tourist complex on the lake that is run by the Instituto Costarricense du Turismo. It has a swimming pool, basketball court and hiking trails. Boating is available. There are also a picnic area and a restaurant.

On the lake's south shore, on the road between the dam and Orosí, **Casa del Soñador** *(every day 8am to 6pm; 2 km from Represa Rumbo in Orosí;*

*☎533-3297)* is filled with wooden sculptures, and even has some delightful scenes carved right into its wooden walls! The original artist Macedonio Quesada Valerín is now deceased, but others who were inspired by his work, including his sons, have transformed this residence into a studio for wood sculpting. Miguel, one of his sons, speaks a little English.

The city of **Orosí** is named after an native leader during the Spanish Conquest. This is the country's most intact colonial city, despite the frequent earthquakes that are common to the region. It is well worth seeing the oldest surviving colonial church, built in the first half of the 18th century. There is a small museum of religious history annexed to the church *(every day 9am to 12pm and 1pm to 5pm).*

#### The Turrialba Region

**Turrialba** used to be a commercial link on the railway from San José to Limón. Now that the Guápiles highway has been built, Turrialba has transformed itself into a tourist town. Advantageously located near the tumultuous Pacuare and Reventazón rivers, the town itself attracts kayaking enthusiasts from all over the world, especially during the winter months, when town becomes a thriving community with plenty of activity. Check out the central market across from the railroad station.

One of the most important centres for the study of tropical agriculture in the world is located in the Turrialba area. **Centro Agronómica Tropicao de Investigación y Enseñanzab**, or **CATIE** ★★ *(☎556-6431),* has a triple mission: to increase the productivity of food crops, to preserve the genetic diversity of tropical flora and to develop methods of agriculture that are consistent with sustainable development in the tropics. Ten thousand hectares of land are consecrated to the study centre, which also has one of the world's most complete library collections in the field of tropical agriculture. In addition to the greenhouses, a dairy processing plant, fields of experimental crops, an herb garden and a seed bank, there is housing for personnel and people who come to study at the centre. CATIE furnishes seeds for fruit trees and other tropical species, but special licenses are needed to export them. You can roam the paths of the complex at your leisure, but you must make arrangements with the centre for a guided tour of the facility.

### Parque Nacional Volcán Irazú

Like the Poás Volcano, **Parque Nacional Volcán Irazú** ★★★ *($6; every day 8am to 4pm; ☎290-1927 or 232-5324)* is very popular with visitors, and for many of the same reasons. Over 100,000 people come here every year, most from Cartago (31 km) and San José (53 km), which are relatively close by. Although there is no interpretation centre or real hiking trails, the road goes all the way to the top of the volcano whose spectacular beauty, impressive height and awe-inspiring craters make it a highlight of any trip to the Central Valley. Moreover, the little road (Route 8) that winds its way from Cartago to the park passes through vast plains serves up superb views of the Central Valley. There are attractive farms with green pastures and forests of oak trees that are comparable to those in the English countryside. Drive carefully, because horses and cows share this road.

The Costa Rican conservation movement achieved one of its first successes on July 30, 1955 when 2,309 hectares of land around the Irazú Volcano became a protected area with the creation of Parque Nacional Volcán Irazú. The name is a variation on the Amerindian word *istarú*, which means "shaking and thundering mountain." As early as 1563, Spanish settlers noted that this high mountain (3,432 m) occasionally spewed out fire and ashes. Irazú's first recorded full-blown eruption of was in 1723.

The volcano's most famous eruption occurred on March 19, 1963. It coincided with the official visit of US President John F. Kennedy to Costa Rica. The eruption was so intense that tons of volcanic ash, up to 40 centimetres deep, covered the entire valley, including the cities of San José and Cartago. People had difficulty removing it from the roofs and sweeping it up from the streets, and began carrying umbrellas, especially on windy days, to protect themselves from the ash. This volcanic activity continued sporadically for two years. Since then, there have been only mild earthquakes and occasional emissions of gases and steam. The Irazú Volcano is not believed to be dangerous at the present time. The soil is enriched by deposits of volcanic ash so the earth in the Central Valley is exceptionally fertile.

### The Craters

The parking area at the top of the volcano is over 3,400 metres above sea level and the weather is much cooler than in the valley. The average temperature is only 11°C and the wind can be blustery at times, so warm clothing is essential. Next to the parking area there are some picnic tables with roofs and a mobile *soda* that sells hot coffee to people who are trying to get warm.

The three largest craters are close to each other. The first, 100 metres from the parking lot, is called **Diego de la Haya** in honour of one of the early 18th-century governors of Costa Rica. This crater is 690 metres wide and 80 metres deep, and has a small amount of water in its centre. The path around it consists of black volcanic earth, which makes the area resemble a lunar landscape.

Next to first crater is the immense **principal crater**, which is 1,050 metres in diameter and 333 metres deep. At the bottom of the crater is an emerald green lake, which shows that the volcano has been dormant for quite a while. Prior to the eruption, the volcano had a forest-covered peak – just try to imagine the incalculable force it took to explode the top of the mountain and create such a deep crater! The ruins of a foundation are all that remain of the main building that scientists used to observe the volcano prior to the 1963 eruption. A sign at the end of the crater warns visitors not to proceed any further, although dozens of hikers climb the rim of the volcano seeking a better view!

The third main crater is difficult to recognize. It consists of a large sandy area that begins south of the other two craters and extends west of the parking area and little reception building. It is called **Playa Hermosa**, or "beautiful beach". **La Laguna** and **Piroclastico** are east of the three main craters, and are much smaller and less interesting. On a beautiful clear day lovely scenic views of the Valley can be had from the top of the nearby peak where the transmission towers are installed (2 km hike there and back). Incidentally, Parque Nacional Volcán Irazú is known as one of the few places in Costa Rica from which it is possible to see both the Pacific and the Atlantic Oceans. However, the sky is rarely clear enough to see that far, even in the morning. Nevertheless, under ideal conditions and using a telescope, it is possible to identify Lago de Nicaragua, northeast of Costa Rica's border.

## Refugio Nacional de Fauna Silvestre Tapantí

**Refugio Nacional de Fauna Silvestre Tapantí** ★★ *($6; every day; ☎771-3297, ☎771-3155)* is not far from San José (50 km) and borders on the superb Orosí Valley (by way of Cartago and Paraíso). It is the perfect place to explore a peaceful, unspoiled wilderness. It is best to get here by car, as no overnight stays are permitted in the park and the closest bus stop is nine kilometres away in Orosí. While you can take a taxi from the bus stop to the park, or to walk the distance, this time is better spent on the trails. There are roads that go through the park, with parking areas at the beginning of the trails.

The area was originally a national wildlife reserve covering some 6,080 hectares of dense tropical rainforest, until April 23, 1992, when it officially became the Refugio Nacional de Fauna Silvestre Tapantí. It receives an average annual rainfall of 6.5 metres, but sometimes gets as much as 8 metres. Four ecological life zones are found at different altitudes between 1,220 and 2,560 metres. The best time to visit the refuge is between December and April. October has the heaviest rains. Rain gear including rain boots or waterproof hiking boots is necessary all year round, since the trails are always wet and muddy.

The area's heavy rainfall has helped the incredibly dense and varied flora to grow: on a single hectare of land there are 160 different species of trees. The number of orchids, bromeliads, ferns and other epiphytic plants is simply amazing, and there are 72 different kinds of moss! The fauna is also exceptional, with 45 mammalian species, including some that are endangered, such as the ocelot and the *jaguarundi.* There are 33 amphibian species and 28 species of reptiles. Because of the constant humidity, the park is crawling with snakes, salamanders and frogs. This is a famous area in the Central Valley for birdwatching, since it has over 250 listed species of birds including eagles, falcons and the magnificent quetzal.

### Scenic Attractions

In response to requests from birders and other nature lovers, the Refugio Nacional de Fauna Silvestre Tapantí opens earlier, at 6am. Information about the trails and activities in the park is available at the reception centre at the park entrance near the administration buildings. A detailed plan of the trails costs 65¢. Both camping and fishing are prohibited.

A few kilometres from the reception centre is the park's first scenic attraction, the **Mirador.** A very short trail (100 m) climbs to this lookout from which you can see miles of vibrant green forest. In the lowest valley, the Río Orosí makes its way through the dense vegetation. About 500 metres in front of the lookout, an elegant waterfall, some 30 metres long, cascades from midway down a mountain.

Heading back towards the main road, the short **La Pava** trail (800 m round trip) goes down to a spot on the Río Grande Orosí where you can have a picnic or go for a dip in the river. Once back on the main road, continue to the next parking area, about two kilometres away. Here, there are two trails on opposite sides of the road. It is best to take **Natural Arboles Caído** (2 km loop) first, because it goes up and is the more difficult of the two. It starts on the southern side of the road (towards the Mirador), across from the parking area. It is a steep but relatively short climb that leads to tropical rainforest. Going down, the trail comes out on the road that leads back to the parking area.

Starting on the same side of the road as the parking area, the **Oropéndola** (1.2 km loop) leads to the Río Grande Orosí where former camp sites have been turned into fairly secluded picnic areas. There are washrooms and drinking water here. At the end of the path beside the river is a small beach, perfect for relaxing or swimming (the water is cool).

If you have a few hours to spare after visiting the Refugio Nacional de Fauna Silvestre Tapantí, we highly recommend stopping at **Agua Thermales de Orosí** *($1.50)*, next to Los Patios restaurant. There are two swimming pools filled with naturally-heated volcanic mineral water. The soothing water is a warm 41°C in one and 51°C in the other.

## Monumento Nacional Guayabo

**Monumento Nacional Guayabo ★★** *($6; every day 8am to 4pm; ☎290-1927, ≠232-5324)* is the most important archeological site in Costa Rica, as well as a pleasant place to hike or relax. Nineteen kilometres northeast of Turrialba, it is more than 80 kilometres from San José (about a 2-hour drive). There is a bus between Turrialba and Guayabo (see p 102). The site has a reception area, campsites, washrooms and drinking water. The site also varies in elevation between 960 and 1,300 metres, and the weather is warm and humid, with over 3.5 metres of rainfall per year.

It was Don Anastasio Alfaro, a local naturalist, who first discovered the site at the end of the 18th century. However, real archeological research only began in 1968, under archeologist Carlos Aguilar Piedra. Digs uncovered a number of rooms as well as signs of urban development. The need to protect the area led to the creation of the *monumento nacional* on August 13, 1973. Today, it is part of the national park service. Of the 218 hectares consigned to the site, 20 hectares have been excavated so far.

Excavations and research have concluded that the site was inhabited for approximately 2,400 years, from 1000 BC until the 15th century. The structures and infrastructures that have been uncovered so far date back to the period between the fourth and eighth centuries AD. The reason for the demise of this well-structured and long-established community is still unknown. Some people believe that a large-scale war or a devastating disease put an end to this two-millennium-old social organization.

Some of the pottery and other items excavated from the site are on display at the Museo Nacional in San José (see p 76). You can also see the stone roads, mounds, bridges, foundations, support walls, aqueducts, water reservoirs, tombs and petroglyphs (pictograms) that have been uncovered. They were built with both round and large flat stones and level with the different elevations in the terrain.

### The Sites

In order to help people understand the significance of these archeological excavations, the personnel of the Monumento Nacional Guayabo have set up a self-guided tour at the site. This tour is called **Los Montículos** and forms a 1.2-kilometre loop with 15 interpretation points where signs refer to explanations in the pamphlet (in Spanish or English) distributed at the entrance. There are stops at a monolith, petroglyphs, tombs, a paved road, and a grass-covered mound. The social organization of the people of this period and its evolution are also explained. Beside the trail there is a little hill (with a lookout) that offers a good view of part of the excavations.

Another trail at the site, **Los Cantarillos**, makes for a pleasant stroll in the rainforest. An easy (1.1-km) loop, it goes through abundant vegetation that conceals diverse wildlife: armadillos, sloths, coatis, kinkajous, toucans, woodpeckers, hummingbirds, and other animals. The trail leads to the bank of the Río Lajitas, a pretty river about five metres wide, and returns to its starting point near the reception centre.

If you have a four-wheel drive vehicle, there is an unpaved road that you can take to get back to San José without retracing your route. It runs northwest of the national monument, through mountain scenery dotted with farms and houses. It ends, after 15 kilometres, at San Antonio. From there, continue northwest on the paved roads through Santa Cruz and Pacayas to Cartago.

## OUTDOOR ACTIVITIES

### Hiking

The Central Valley contains many parks and other outdoor locations where the best way to explore the rich dense tropical forest is on foot. **Parque Nacional Braulio Carrillo** (see p 111) has very short trails in the Zurquí and Quebrada González sectors. The Barva sector offers longer (12 km) and more interesting trails, and camping is permitted there.

**Parque Nacional Volcán Poás** (see p 108) has short trails to the craters and the lovely lake Botos, and through the magnificent forest where there are many bird species.

**Refugio Nacional de Fauna Silvestre Tapantí** (see p 118) is very wild and less crowded than the Poás or Irazú volcanoes. Four trails allow hikers to penetrate the tropical rainforest, admire a splendid panorama and picnic beside or swim in Río Grande Orosí.

**Monumento Nacional Guayabo** (see p 119) has two short trails; one is an educational tour of the archeological excavations, while the other goes through the surrounding forest.

Starting from **Chalet Tirol** (see p 126) hotel, just a few kilometres before the **Monte de la Cruz** park, there are hiking and horseback riding trails, including some that lead into the park. This is also a good spot for birdwatching.

### Rafting

Costa Rica's two most fabulous rivers, Río Reventazón and Río Pacuare, are internationally known for rafting and kayaking. The rivers start near Turrialba in the Central Valley and flow to Siquirres in Limón province and the Atlantic Ocean.

Anyone, from beginner to expert, can spend a pleasant day without too much excitement travelling down the **Río Reventazón ★★** (class III, 15 km) and through its scintillating green valleys. Other sections of the river are much wilder (class IV-V) and demand greater expertise.

**Río Pacuare** ★★★ (class III-IV) is a magnificent river that goes through wild tropical rainforest. It is among the ten most exciting rivers in the world for kayaking and rafting. However, this river is not just for experts: anyone in good physical condition can experience the thrill of this run with competent guides who know how to safely and skilfully navigate through the rapids. You can even take a dip in the river towards the end of the trip. The ride finishes with a slow glide down the river, between high rocky cliffs.

Most rafting and kayaking excursions start in San José (or Turrialba) and last all day (6am to 7pm). The price (about $85) includes transportation (from your hotel), breakfast, lunch, all equipment, a certified guide and an introductory course. During the trip, the rafts are constantly surrounded by kayakers who rescue anyone who falls overboard. Often, photographers in kayaks take pictures of the rafters in action that cost only a few dollars and will be delivered to your hotel.

**Some Agencies**

Costa Rica Expeditions (White Water); ☎257-0766, ⇄257-1665.
Aventuras Naturales; ☎225-3939, ⇄253-6934.
Ríos Tropicales; ☎233-6455, ⇄255-4354.
Pioneer Raft; ☎253-9132, ⇄253-4687.
Aguas Bravas; ☎292-2072, ⇄229-4837.

## Cycling

In the San José region, several agencies offer cycling tours in the Central Valley. Many of these excursions (road or mountain) last all day and include transportation, bicycle rentals and an accompanying guide. The most popular cycling trips are to the Irazú and Poás volcanoes, Monumento Nacional Guayabo, Refugio Nacional de Fauna Silvestre Tapantí and through the magnificent Orosí valley. Other bicycle rides, from two to ten hours, allow you to peacefully explore the mountains and valleys inhabited by laid-back, friendly people.

**Some Agencies**

Aventuras Naturales; ☎225-3939, ⇄253-6934.
Río Tropicales; ☎233-6455, ⇄255-4354.
Costa Rica Tropical Cycling ☎255-2011, ⇄255-3529.
Eco Treks Adventure; ☎228-4029, ⇄289-8191.
Geoventuras; ☎221-2053, ⇄282-3333.
Horizontes; ☎222-2022, ⇄255-4513.

## Golf

In San José, the **Cariari Country Club** *(☎293-3211)* has a superb 18-hole golf course.

West of San José, the little town of **Escazú** has a nine-hole golf course, the **Costa Rica Country Club** *(☎228-9333)* that allows members' guests to play.

Still farther west, in **Santa Ana**, **Parque Valle del Sol** *(☎282-9222)* has opened a nine-hole golf course and plans to add nine more holes in the near future.

## ACCOMMODATIONS

The Central Valley offers an excellent choice of places to stay outside the city. As mentioned at the beginning of the chapter, everything is relatively close by in the region and the highway system is excellent. While the capital is at the geographical centre of the area, there is no problem getting to other places in the region, even if you don't stay in San Jose.

It can be just as practical – and twice as pleasant – stay amidst beautiful natural surroundings, such as a picturesque plantation or up on a hill with a breathtaking view of the town's lights twinkling below.

Even if you are leaving from San José's Juan Santamaría airport, there is no need for you to change hotels the night before departing, as it is easy to reach from anywhere in the Valley.

### Western Central Valley

#### Alajuela

**Mango Verde Hostel** *($$; pb, hw in the shower, common tv room, access to the kitchen; Av. 3, Calle2/4, 25 m west of the Juan Santamaría museum; Alajuela, ☎441-6330, ⇌443-3814)* rents very clean, small rooms.

**Pensión Alajuela** *($$; sb/pb; Av. 9, on the south side of the courthouse, Alajuela, ☎441-6251)* is an economical option in the city centre.

**Villa Real** *($$; sb, hw; Calle 1, Av. 3, 100 m south of the post office, Alajuela, ☎441-4122)* is in a renovated wooden house that could have been a pleasant inn, but has been neglected. Both cleanliness and furniture are minimal. Guests have access to the kitchen.

**Charly's Place** *($$$; sb/pb; 200 m north and 25 m east of the central park, Alajuela, ☎441-0115)* is a small urban hotel with clean rooms. The owner is very friendly.

**La Guaria Inn** *($$$ bkfst incl.; pb, hw, ℝ; 225 m east of Juan Santamaría park, Alajuela, ☎/⇌441-9573)* is clean, but plain. It is conveniently located right downtown.

Also in downtown Alajuela, **Hotel 1915** *($$$ bkfst incl.; common room with cable tv; three blocks from the central park, Alajuela, ☎/⇌441-0495)* is one of the best places to stay. It is quiet, very clean, and the bedrooms and common areas have a certain charm. It is run by an dignified, older lady who has a pleasant personality.

**Islands B&B** *($$$ bkfst incl.; common tv room, laundry service, P; Av. 1, Calle 7/9, 50 m west of the Agonia church, Alajuela, ☎442-0573, ⇌442-2909)* rents very simply furnished but clean rooms. It is small but quiet, in spite of being right downtown. Student discounts are available.

Three kilometres northwest of Alajuela, **Michele's Hotel** *($$$ bkfst incl.; between Alajuela and Grecia, 200 m north on the road to Poás, ☎/⇌433-9864)* is a relatively new 14-room establishment on a large property with some lovely views of the surroundings. The rooms are spacious and handsomely decorated, but overall, it isn't quite as attractive as its next-door neighbour Las Orquideas Inn (see further below). When we were there, the owners were planning to add a swimming pool and restaurant.

**Paraíso Tropical Hotel** *($$$ bkfst incl.; laundry service, free shuttle to the* *airport; 200 m north of the Punto Rojo factory on the road to Tuetal, Alajuela, ☎441-4882)* is new and not very well-known. It has a real family atmosphere. The somewhat dark, but clean and modern rooms are in a separate building from the main house. The grounds are well laid out, and the owner will do anything to give her guests the best service possible.

**B&B Pura Vida** *($$$ bkfst incl.; hw, pb; 1,500 m from the Punto Rojo factory, at the intersection of the Tuetal Norte and Sur roads, ☎441-1157)* is extremely pleasant. The owner, originally from France, goes out of her way to make her customers' stay enjoyable. The house is clean and the rooms are cozy. There is also a little bungalow for rent on the spacious grounds.

**Tuetal Lodge** *($$$; sb/pb, solar-heated water; Tuetal Norte, ☎441-1804)*, two kilometres from Alajuela, rents four *cabinas* and has a campground. The large residential lot is beautifully landscaped.

Conveniently located on the way to the airport, **Villa Dolce** *($$$; hw, pb, ☎, tv, ℝ, ≈, laundry service; on the road to Jacó, 7 km form the Alajuela airport, Alajuela, ☎433-9832)* rents six clean rooms in a well-run establishment.

The *posada* **Canal Grande** *($$$$ bkfst incl.; pb, hw, ctv, ≈, △, bar, ℜ, laundry service; Piedades de Santa Ana, west of San José, at the end of the Autopista Prospero Fernández, ☎282-4089 or 282-4101, ⇌282-5733)* is near the capital. The 12 rooms are relatively large and soberly furnished, but share a terrace. This establishment is in a small complex with a pool in the middle.

Next to Michele's Hotel, **Las Orquideas Inn** *($$$$ bkfst incl. sb/pb, ≈; no children; on the road to San Pedro de Poás, between Alajuela and Grecia, ☎443-9346, ⇌443-9740)* is charming in every way. The common rooms and the bedrooms are consistently stylish. The gardens surrounding the property set it back from the road, making it very relaxing. The popular Marilyn Monroe bar has an inviting atmosphere.

Six kilometres north of Alajuela, **Xandari** *($$$$$ bkfst incl.; ℝ, ≈, ⊛, ℜ, ⊘, video screening room, massage available, library, ☎443-2020, ⇌442-4847)* is idyllically situated on a coffee plantation! Two sets of eight pretty, well-decorated villas are built on a hillside. Each villa has a private terrace and also shares the common terrace which has a panoramic view and two swimming pools. Fruit, vegetables and herbs from the garden find their way into the restaurant's cuisine. The coffee is homegrown, too, of course. There are three kilometres of hiking trails and five natural waterfalls where you can swim. The shuttle to the airport is free.

### Atenas Valley and La Garita

**Apartementos Atenas** *($$$ bkfst incl.; ≈, K, ⊘, tennis court, laundry service; Atenas, ☎446-5792)* are pretty cottages in the forest, owned by a very welcoming German couple.

**Villas de la Colina** *($$$ bkfst incl.; K; Atenas, ☎446-6635)* are attractive cottages nestled in a hillside near Atenas. The friendly owner can organize trips to the nearby coffee cooperatives or motorbike trips.

**Cafetal Inn** *($$$$ bkfst incl.; ≈; Santa Eulalia de Atenas, ☎/⇌446-5785)* is a little Bed & Breakfast in a mode house on a coffee plantation. In addition to attractive rooms, it has a coffee bar where you can buy coffee products.

**Chatelle** *($$$$ bkfst incl.; ≡, ctv, ☎, ℝ, ≈, K, ℜ; La Garita, 1 km from the Fiesta del Maíz restaurant on Bulevar de Las Flores, ☎487-7781, 487-7271 or 487-7050, ⇄487-7095)* is a tastefully decorated country resort complex with a subdued architectural style; the pink trim blends well with the brick walls and the wood *casitas.* The rooms and *casitas* (with kitchenettes) are spacious, and all open onto the pool area overlooking the La Garita countryside.

### San Ramón and Zarcero

**Don Beto** *($$$; sb/pb, on the north side of the Zarcero church, Zarcero, ☎463-3137)* is a charming little hotel right in the centre of the village. It is very clean and its rooms are attractively decorated in an old-fashioned, flowery style that is very relaxing.

**La Posada** *($$$ bkfst incl.; 50 m east of the Nueva Imagen vision centre, San Ramón, ☎445-7359)* is a brand-new Bed & Breakfast in San Ramón. The bathrooms are shared, but everything is very clean and the hostess is friendly. Lunch and dinner are available.

**Hotelera San Lorenzo** at **Valle Escondido Lodge** *($$$$; hw, pb, bar, ℜ, ≈, ⊛; between San Ramón and Bajo Rodríguez, ☎231-0906, ⇄232-9591)* is isolated from the rest of the world in its own hidden valley (hence *"valle escondido"*).There are a lot of interesting activities to do here, such as swimming in the river, horseback riding and biking. The view is magnificent. The rooms are standard and clean.

**Hotel Villablanca** *($$$$$ bkfst incl.; hw, bathtub; next to Bosque Nuboso Los Angeles, between San Ramón de Alajuela and La Tigra, ☎228-4603 or 289-6569, ⇄228-4004)* is a hotel complex still under development in the Bosque Nuboso Los Angeles reserve, and therefore seems far from civilization. It has a series of charming *casitas* with fireplaces, situated on a large property with the main pavilion in the centre. The restaurant is in the main building, and the chefs can prepare special meals (vegetarian, salt-free, etc.). The hotel can also accommodate large groups, and week-long retreats are also possible. The service is excellent. While we were there, some low budget accommodations were being built (essentially, for student ecotourists), but we were assured that these new units would be set up in a way that the presumably livelier students who might stay here do not disturb the regular clientele.

### Naranjo, Sarchí and Grecia

**Hotel Sarchí** *($$; across from the ICE, between the central park and the church plaza, Sarchí, ☎454-3309)* rents out four quite plain motel rooms in downtown Sarchí.

**Rancho Mirador** *($$$; ≈, ℜ, bar; San Miguel de Naranjo, ☎451-1302, ⇄451-1301)* consists of clean, simple little cottages perched on a hill above the General Cañas highway, affording interesting views of the vast Naranjo region. You can't miss it: just look for the thatched-straw roof on the *rancho*'s restaurant.

The Tropical Spa in the **Healthy Day Inn** *($$$; ⊛, ⊘, Turkish bath, △, ≈, ℜ; 800 m northeast of the Grecia church on the road to Sarchí, ☎444-5903)* offers several kinds of natural therapies (massage, thalassotherapy, iridology, hydrotherapy, etc.). The concept of the hotel is excellent, and it is the only spa-resort in Costa Rica. The rooms are quite comfortable, but could be better decorated. You can use the exercise room and equipment without being registered as a guest. There are even facilities for children to use while their parents exercise. The grounds are pleasantly landscaped, but the lot is rather small. There is a macrobiotic restaurant.

**Villa Sarchí Lodge** *($$$ bkfst incl.; fb or ½b also available, ≈, ℜ; 500 m north of the service station west of town, Sarchí Norte, ☎454-4006)* is a clean little motel very close to Sarchí. The rooms are standard but afford lovely view of Sarchí. The friendly owners even offer Spanish lessons. Free shuttle service to the airport is available. The restaurant is inviting.

## Parque Nacional Volcán Poás

On the road to the Poás Volcano **Hotel Buena Vista** *($$$$; ℜ, ≈; Las Pilas de San Isidro, 6 km north of Alajuela, ☎442-8595, ⇄442-8701)* is a recently built Spanish colonial-style hotel but with North American standards of comfort . It is on a coffee plantation at an elevation of 1,300 metres, so the views are magnificent, especially from the rooms with balconies. Children under 12 can share their parents' room for free.

## Northern Central Valley

### Heredia

The hotel **America** *($$$ bkfst incl.; hw, pb, ☎, ctv in the hotel's snack-bar; 100 m south of the central park, Heredia, ☎260-9292 or 260-9293, ⇄260-7540)* is in a former movie theatre and the decor is interesting, since certain elements from the building's past have been preserved. The hotel is modern, with clean, contemporary-style rooms. The bar and restaurant are open night and day.

**Apartotel Roma** *($$$; 100 m west of Universidad Nacional, Heredia, ☎260-0127 or 238-3705, ⇄260-6339)* rents very clean and practical, fully equipped apartments right in downtown Heredia. What's more, its staff is friendly and helpful. Weekly or monthly rates available.

**Apartotel Vargas** *($$$; ℝ, K, tv, P, laundry service; 750 m north of Colegio Santa Cecilia, Heredia, ☎237-8526 or 238-1810, ⇄260-4698)* rents clean, fully equipped apartments in a concrete building lacking in style. Some of the apartments have a pretty view, which helps; others are rather dark, but all have small balconies. Some single rooms open onto the outdoor walkway.

**Debbie King's B & B Inn** *($$$ bkfst incl.; pb, hw, use of the kitchen permitted; San Rafael de Heredia, ☎/⇄268-8284)* belongs to a former Hollywood restaurant owner who can name several celebrities who have stayed at the inn, attesting to its allure. The inn is also attractively located on a small coffee plantation. The establishment offers warm, personalized hospitality and the rooms are appealing. It might be hard to find, so call ahead for directions.

**Casa Monticello** *($$$$ bkfst incl.; sb/pb, hw, ℜ; 3 km north of Heredia, ☎237-8570, ⇄260-4618, monticello@cafebritt.com)* is perched at an altitude of 1,300 metres, surrounded by coffee plantations and fruit trees. It comprises four large, clean and comfortable rooms, as well as a spacious dining room. The Belgian managers, Dominique Manet and Daniel Beissel, cook wonderful traditional European dishes, and can tell you all about the country.

**Posada de La Montaña** *($$$$ bkfst incl.; sb/pb, hw, ≈, bar; 1.5 km north of San Isidro de Heredia, ☎/⇌268-8096)* has bright, attractive, clean rooms, as well as cottages with kitchens and fireplaces. There is a common living room with a television, a fireplace, and a covered veranda where you can enjoy the scenery. The extensive grounds are well landscaped and include a covered barbecue area. Weekly or monthly rates available.

**Rosa Blanca** *($$$$$ bkfst incl.; pb, hw ℜ; near Santa Bárbara de Heredia, ☎269-9392, ⇌269-9555)* is a classy hotel. The owners have added their personal touch to the decor of the rooms. Drive carefully: the road to the hotel becomes more and more difficult to negotiate as it slowly narrows into a dirt road.

**Valladolid** *($$$$$; pb, hw, ≈, ≡, ctv, ☎, K, hair-dryer; Calle 7, Av. 7, Heredia, ☎260-2905, ⇌260-2912)* offers all the comforts of a large hotel, but on a reduced scale proportionate to the small city of Heredia. Nevertheless, it is probably the highest building in this city. Each room has a kitchenette. There are a whirlpool, a sauna, a solarium and a bar on the upper floors of the hotel, providing excellent views of the Central Valley.

### North of Heredia

**Chalet Tirol** *($$$$; pb, hw, fireplace, bathtub, hair-dryer, ☎, tv, tennis courts; in the residential neighbourhood of Del Monte, Monte de la Cruz, ☎267-7371 or 267-7070, ⇌267-7050)* is a five-star hotel complex. All the buildings are in a uniform Tyrolean style appropriate to the area's alpine climate. The landscaping is as stylish as the building. The hotel is in a chic residential neighbourhood, which is in the middle of protected rainforest next to Parque Nacional Braulio Carrillo. The service is high class. The French restaurant is highly recommended (see p 129). There is also a Salzburg concert-café , which presents classical music concerts during Costa Rica's international music festival, which draws famous Costa Rican and international guests.

Just before the fork in the road where one branches off to the Del Monte residential park and the other to the Mirador de Monte de la Cruz is the new **Hotel Occidental La Condesa** *($$$$$; pb, ≈; ☎260-4092)*. It is part of a chic chain, Groupe Occidental Hotels. There are a hundred rooms and suites, three conference rooms, and two restaurants. All sorts of outdoor activities are offered on its splendid site.

## Eastern Central Valley

### Cartago and the Orosí Valley

In the village of Orosí, **Montaña Linda** *($; bkfst. available, hw, K; ☎533-3640, ⇌533-3132)* is a little place that rents inexpensive rooms. It is very near the town's hot springs swimming pool ($1 for clients of Montaña Linda). The owner will gladly suggest various activities for your enjoyment.

The owners of **Albergue Montaña Orosí** *($$;sb, hw, K, Orosí, ☎533-3032)* can also recommend all sorts of places to see and activities in the region. The rooms in the *albergue* are simple and clean.

In Cartago itself, **Los Angeles Lodge** *($$$ bkfst incl.; hw, pb; on the north side of Plaza de la Basílica, ☎551-0957)* is the best place to stay in terms of location.

**Albergue y Cabinas Mirador de Quetzales** *($$$; hw, ℜ; at km 70 on the Interamericana, after Empalme, ☎454-4746 or 543-4415)* claims to be the best place to observe that most famous of birds, the quetzal. There are rooms in the main house, and two *cabinas* that can each accommodate six. On the whole, it's pretty rustic.

**Albergue Tapantí** *($$$$; pb, hw, heater on request, ℜ; at km 62 on the Interamericana, south of Cahén, ☎/⇄232-0436)* is on a little private reserve at the far edge of the Central Valley. There are two-bedroom cottages (not very attractive) dispersed on the grounds, each with a private terrace. Rooms with single beds are also available in the inn. The restaurant is worth checking out (see p 130).

### Turrialba

**Hotel Interamericano** *($; sb/pb; near the railroad station, Turrialba, ☎556-0142)* is an economical place to stay in downtown Turrialba.

If you have to stay in Turrialba, **Turrialtico** *($$; pb, hw; 8 km east of town, on top of a hill, ☎556-1111)* offers decent accommodations. The rooms are clean, comfortable and inexpensive. The restaurant is fabulous (see p 130).

**Albergue de Montaña Pochotel** *($$$; pb, hw; 11 km from Turrialba towards Limón, ☎556-0111, ⇄556-6222)* is above the village of Paves. A lookout tower (the view is magnificent) and a playground for children round out the facilities of this highly recommended little hotel. Camp sites are available.

Right in downtown Turrialba, **Hotel Wagtail** *($$$; hw, tv, ℜ, ≈; 150 m west of the central park, Turrialba, ☎556-1566, ⇄556-1596)* has pretty little clean rooms.

**Casa Turire** *($$$$$; pb, bathtub, ℝ, hair-dryer, ☎, ctv, ≈, ℜ; 20 km southwest of Turrialba, ☎531-7111 or 531-1111, ⇄531-1075)* is a luxury hotel that is associated with five others in Costa Rica (including Grano de Oro, in San José, see p 83). All are small-scale, high-class hotels with character. Casa Turire is built in the style of a plantation manor. The fields of coffee, macadamia nuts and sugar cane that surround it have belonged to the same farming family for 50 years. The hotel has meeting rooms and is close to Río Reventazón. They also offer many excursions in the area including kayaking trips and archeological tours.

## Refugio Nacional de Fauna Silvestre Tapantí

In the Orosí region, but on the road to Tapantí park, **Kiri Lodge** *($$ bkfst incl.; fb also available, pb, hw; ☎533-3040)* rents large simple rooms with comfortable beds.

## Monumento Naciona Guayabo

Near the Monumento Nacional Guayabo, **La Calzada** *($$$; sb/pb, hw, ℜ; 400 m before the entrance to the national monument, ☎556-0465, ⇄556-0427)* is a highly recommended hotel (comfortable, bright rooms), and the owners are very helpful in planning activities in the region.

## RESTAURANTS

### Western Central Valley

**Alajuela**

There are some fast-food chains in Alajuela.

**Trigo Miel** *($; Calle 3, Av. Central/1, Alajuela, ☎221-8995)* is a popular, friendly *panadería-soda-pastelaría*. Great for a small, quick bite to eat.

The pizzeria **Italiana** *($$; 100 m north of the Agoya church, Alajuela)* serves good pizzas in a simple little dining area.

**La Jarra** *($$$; 200 m west of Plaza Feria, Alajuela, ☎441-6708 or 441-5913)* is a bar-restaurant that serves a variety of Costa Rican dishes. The outdoor bar, in a small hut, contributes to the atmosphere and general layout of the place.

**El Cencerro** *($$$$; every day 11am to 10pm; on the south side of the central park, above McDonald's, Alajuela)* is the most popular steak house and grill in Alajuela. It has an attractive dining room.

**The Atenas Valley**

**La Fiesta del Maís** *($$; Fri to Sun; on the road to La Garita, on the corner of the road to Bosque Encantado)* is a great place to try all sorts of home-made corn-based Costa Rican dishes. The large dining room is noisy.

**La Lora Verde** *($$$$; no credit cards; on the road between La Garita and the Interamericana, ☎487-7846)* serves international cuisine in pleasant surroundings, and is ideal for more formal occasions.

**San Ramón and Zarcero**

There are few "real" restaurants in San Ramón de Alajuela. There are three decent and inexpensive *sodas* upstairs in the public market, just next to the church: **Bella Visa**, **Piri** and **Julia**.

**Naranjo, Sarchí and Grecia**

In Sarchí, the bakery *(panadería)*, **Super Pan** *($; ☎454-4121)* is a super spot to buy bread or pastries, or to have a coffee or sandwich. The premises are very clean. It is the perfect place to relax, people-watch, admire the surroundings and enjoy the slow pace of life of this charming little town.

Across from Super Pan is **De Negocios** *($$; Sarchí Norte)*, a very clean little *soda* that serves typical Costa Rican food in an appealing environment.

On the road running along the east side of the recreational park in Sarchí is another little *soda* that is worth trying. It is very popular with the locals, and is busy until late at night.

In Los Trapiches, take advantage of the convenient hours kept by **La Chimenea** *($$; 8am to midnight; ☎494-1988 or 444-6656)*. The menu is varied, but it features *tico* dishes.

**Coco's Bar Restaurante** *($$; Naranjo)* serves rotisserie-style grilled chicken.

Inside the **tourist centre El Río** *($$; at the end of Sarchí, on the road to Naranjo, ☎454-4980)* is an outdoor restaurant with the same name. It has a round hut-style roof and a simple, modern set up. The menu has *tico* and Italian selections in all price ranges.

**Restaurante El Mirador** *($$; Tue to Sun 6am to 8pm; ☎451-1959)* is a great place to stop between Naranjo and Zarcero. It is a pleasure to eat in the attractive wooden building (with terrace), and customers can also buy jellies and snacks for the road. The view from the lookout is fantastic. There is even a telescope to get a closer look at the surroundings.

## Parque Nacional Volcán Poás

The restaurant in the **Hotel Buena Vista** *($$$; Las Pilas de San Isidro, on the road to the Poás Volcano, 6 km north of Alajuela, ☎442-8595)* is a convenient breakfast stop on the way to the volcano. The view is also terrific, since the restaurant is located at an altitude of 1,300 metres. The restaurant serves good, energizing Costa Rican food.

## Northern Central Valley

### Heredia

**El Rancho del Fofo** *($$; Av. Central, Heredia)* is a little restaurant that has live *mariachi* music on some nights. **La Choza** and **El Bulevar** *(Av. Central, Calle 7, Heredia)* are small, friendly bars that are very popular with students.

**Le Petit Paris** *($$$; Tue to Sun 11am to 10pm; Calle 5, Av.2/Central, Heredia, ☎238-1721)* serves wonderful French cuisine. There are also a library and paintings by different Central American artists every month. There are two dining rooms: one is indoors and decorated with posters, while the other is in a covered tropical garden that even includes some hummingbirds. Situated in the heart of Heredia, right on the university campus, this is a great starting point for a walking tour of the town!

### North of Heredia

**Las Fresas** *($$; between Sabana Redonda de Poás and Fraijanes, north of San Pedro de Poás, ☎448-5567)* is recommended for Italian food, especially the pizza cooked in a wood-burning, brick oven. There are also well-prepared Costa Rican specialties.

The restaurant at the **Country Club El Castillo** *($$$; Monte de la Cruz, San Rafael de Heredia, ☎267-7111 or 267-7112)* is open to the public and provides first class service and a splendid view of the club grounds and the Central Valley. The El Castillo Country Club was created for the well-to-do of Costa Rica. Everything has been done here to induce recreation, relaxation and contemplation (the site is ideal because of its location overlooking the Central Valley). After 25 years, it is still the largest and chicest recreational centre in the country (5,000 members). Permission to use the facilities of this private club must be requested at the manager's office. The name, El Castillo, comes from the small castle (*castillo,* in Spanish) on the grounds that now houses a museum exhibiting objects from earlier Costa Rican cultures. (If you want to see the museum or go to the restaurant, you must specify this at the entrance to the club).

**Le Barbizon** *($$$$; Mon to Sat 11:30am to 10:30pm; Monte de la Cruz, ☎267-7449)* is a high-class French restaurant on top of a hill. The beautifully constructed building is surrounded by pastures that contain a little lake to attract waterfowl.

The hotel-restaurant at **Chalet Tirol** *$$$$; every day 8am to 10pm, Sun*

*8am to 6am; Monte de la Cruz, ☎267-7371)* serves exquisite food. It belongs to the prestigious French gourmet association, "La chaîne des rôtisseurs." The restaurant's distinguished tone, welcoming personnel, tasteful decor and beautiful natural surroundings will completely seduce you before you've even tasted the culinary delights!

## Eastern Central Valley

### Cartago and the Orosí Valley

**Coto** *($; central plaza, Orosí)* is an attractive little *soda* that belongs to the owners of Albergue Montaña Orosí.

The restaurant in the **Albergue Tapantí** *($$; at km 62 on the Interamericana, south of Cahén, ☎232-0436)* radiates warmth with its inviting alpine charm. The menu lists a variety of dishes, but trout is a specialty.

The restaurant at **Kiri Lodge** *($$; between Orosí and the Refugio Nacional de Fauna Silvestre Tapantí, ☎533-3040)* also specializes in trout.

For an original meal, try **Posada de la Luna** *($$$; west of the Cervantes church, halfway between Turrialba and Cartago)*. This restaurant serves excellent *tico* specialties and is a veritable museum with all sorts of items on display: old swords and rifles, archeological and pre-Columbian objects, and others. This place is very popular with outdoor enthusiasts on their way to go rafting or kayaking on the nearby rivers.

### Turrialba

There are very few good restaurants in Turrialba proper, except for **Kingston** *($$; leaving Turrialba for Limón, ☎556-1613)* where the chef prepares *tico* dishes with a Jamaican accent, and the very good restaurant at **Hotel Wagelia** *($$$; 150 m west of the central park, Turrialba, ☎556-1566 or 556-1596)*.

The restaurant at **Turrialtico** *($$$; 8 km east of Turrialba towards Limón, ☎556-1111)* also serves good *tico* dishes in tasteful decor with a stunning view of the surroundings.

The restaurant at **Albergue de Montaña Pochotel** *($$$; 11 km east of Turrialba towards Limón, ☎556-0111)* serves Costa Rican cuisine from its elevated location with a panoramic view of this beautiful region. There is also an observation tower on the premises.

## Parque Nacional Volcán Poás

On the road to the Irazú Volcano, **Linda Vista** *($$)* has a pretty view of the valley from the dining room, though the inexpensive food is rather ordinary.

## Monumento Nacional Guayabo

The restaurant at the **Hotel La Calzada** *($$$; 400 m before the entrance to Monumento Nacional Guayabo, ☎556-0465, ≠556-0427)* serves Costa Rican country-style food.

# ENTERTAINMENT

## Western Central Valley

### Alajuela

**Marilyn Monroe** *(on the road to San Pedro de Poás, between Alajuela and*

*Grecia, ☎443-9346)* is a popular and friendly bar at the Los Orquideas Inn.

**La Jarra** *(200 m west of Plaza Feria, Alajuela, ☎441-6708)* is a lively outdoor bar under a hut-style roof.

### Northern Central Valley

**Heredia**

The hotel bar at the **America** *(100 m south of the central park, Heredia, ☎260-9292 or 260-9293)* is open 24 hours a day.

## SHOPPING

### Western Central Valley

**Alajuela**

**Alajuela** has an indoor central market not far from the central park. All sorts of things, from meats to clothing, are for sale here. Also, a shop that sells religious articles is open during the day in the Alajuela cathedral annex.

**Naranjo, Sarchí and Grecia**

**Sarchí** is known for its handicrafts and typical Costa Rican carts. There are little shops and artisans' workshops just about everywhere in town, both in Sarchí Norte and in Sarchí Sur. Take a shopping tour of them on foot. Among others, there is the *Fabrica de Carretas* **Chaverri** which has been making *carretas* in Sarchí since 1903. Next to the Muebleria El Sueño, there is a large store selling locally made handicrafts. **La Plaza de la Artesanía**, in the heart of downtown, is a huge shopping mall, with a unique and appealing architecture, inside and out. It has a large number of stores and shops that sell crafts, furniture and souvenirs. **Valle de Mariposa**, a little farther along, is also an interesting crafts and souvenir shop.

On the road to Naranjo, just outside of Sarchí, the **El Río** tourist centre consists of a large store that sells of handcrafted furniture and wooden souvenirs.

**Tierra Linda** *(on the road between Grecia and Sarchí, ☎454-4934)* is another handicrafts centre, with a small jewellery store.

### Northern Central Valley

**Heredia** has a covered central market not far from the central park. It sells almost everything.

### Eastern Central Valley

In **San Vicente de Moravia** (or simply, Moravia, as the *Ticos* call it) there are some good leather items for sale at **Caballo Blanco** *(opposite the central park, Moravia, ☎235-6797)*. Moravia is good for last-minute shopping before you leave Costa Rica, because it is located only a few kilometres east of the national capital. **Artesanía Bribrí**, in the same area, sells hand-crafted items made by the Bribrí on the Atlantic coast. There is also the **Mercado de Artesanías Las Garzas** *(every day 8:30am to 6pm; 100 m south, and 75 m east of the town hall, ☎236-0037)*, a small shopping centre which, like the one in Sarchí, sells local handcrafted articles.

The Caribbean Coast
0 15 30km
N
NICARAGUA
HEREDIA
CARTAGO
LIMÓN
PANAMÁ
Caribbean Sea
Río Toro
Río San Juan
Refugio Nacional de Fauna Silvestre Barra del Colorado
Barra del Colorado
Río Colorado
Puerto Viejo de Sarapiquí
Río Chirripó
Río Sucio
Las Horquetas
Río Frío
Cariari
Tortuguero
Río Tortuguero
Agua Fría
Parque Nacional Tortuguero
Rita
Roxana
Guápiles
Zancudo
Siete
Jardín Botánico Las Cusingas
Jiménez
Villa Franca
Guácimo
Río Jiménez
Jaloba
Suerre
Pocora
Parismina
Germania
Reventazón
Cairo
Santa Cruz
Monumento Nacional Guayabo
Río Pacuare
San Rafael
Siquirres
Pacuarito
Turrialba
Lajas
Juan Viñas
Peralta
Batán
Pavones
Matina
Saborío
Pejibaye
La Suiza
Reserva Indígena Barbilla
Tuís
Platanillo
Reserva Indígena Alto Y Bajo Chirripó
Refugio Nacional de Fauna Silvestre Tapantí
Moín
Portete
Piuta
Puerto Limón
Chirripó del Atlántico
Cerro Blanco (3800m)
Parque Nacional Chirripó
Cerro Chirripó (3819m)
Reserva Indígena Tayní
Cerro Terbi (3760m)
Reserva Indígena Telire
Reserva Biológica Hitoy-Cerere
Penshurst
Parque Nacional Cahuita
Bocuares
Cahuita
Puerto Vargas
Cordillera de Talamanca
Río Telire
Río Carbón
Comadre
Parque Internacional La Amistad
Reserva Indígena Talamanca-Bribri
Uatsi
Bribri
Chase
Puerto Viejo de Talamanca
Bratsi
Katsi
Res. Indígena Kekoldi
Pta.Uva
Yorkin
Reserva Indígena Ujarras-Salitre
Margarita
Refugio Nacional de Vida Silvestre Gandoca-Manzanillo
Río Sixaola
Manzanillo
Buenos Aires
Reserva Indígena Cabagra
Sixaola
© ULYSSES

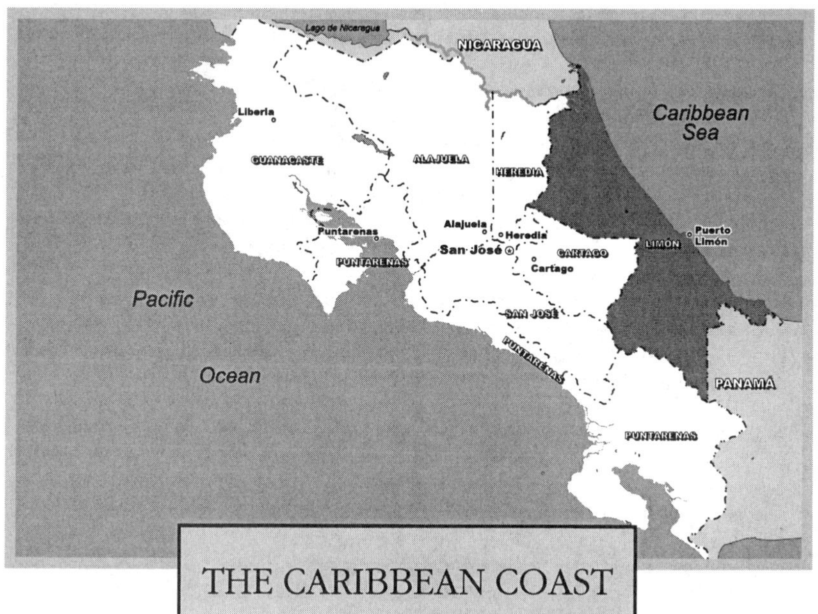


# THE CARIBBEAN COAST

The Caribbean coast encompasses the whole province of Limón; the port city of Puerto Limón is the region's capital, and its largest town. Washed by the waters of the Caribbean sea, the coast stretches 212 kilometres between Nicaragua in the north and Panama in the south, while the Pacific coast is almost five times longer (or 1,016 km). The Caribbean coast is unique because of its more humid climate, the flatter and swampy terrain, and the cultural and linguistic differences.

This region is home to a proud and fascinating people, many of whom originate from the West Indies (more specifically Jamaica), but also from China, Europe, and North America. Even *Joséfinos* (residents of San José) will admit to feeling out of place when they visit this part of Costa Rica. This is mostly due to the distinctive language used on the coast – a mix of Creole and English.

We should also mention that the people of the Caribbean coast have acquired an unsavoury reputation throughout the entire country. When we announced our intentions of visiting the Caribbean coast, no matter where we were, people often warned us to *"Be careful, because the people are poor, violent, and thieves!"* But when asked when they had last set foot in the region, the most common response was *"Well, I've never been there..."*

However, it is true that you must be careful, especially after sunset, in the areas of Cahuita and Puerto Viejo. The cool and relaxed atmosphere of the coast sometimes seduces unwary tourists into forgetting to keep an eye on their money, passport, jewellery, etc. Drug use is also more widespread here than in other parts of the country,

### One April 22...

On April 22, 1991, at around 4pm, a violent earthquake that measured 7.4 on the Richter scale shook the country, especially Limón province. The epicentre was in the small community of Pandora, not far from Cahuita. Fortunately, this natural disaster claimed few lives, probably between 30 and 50 if you include those who died of ensuing heart attacks. Although the capital, San José, suffered little damage, more than 3,000 buildings were destroyed in the province of Limón, leaving more than 12,000 homeless.

Many buildings, roads and bridges completely collapsed, bringing things to a standstill in certain areas. The popular railway between San José and Puerto Limón, dubbed the "jungle train" by Costa Ricans and tourists, was so badly damaged that authorities decided to shut it down.

A Costa Rican friend told us that he travelled to the area several days after the earthquake and was horrified to see that the sea level had gone down 1.5 metres! He later learned that this was not the case, but rather that the shoreline itself had been thrust up 1.5 metres! This massive upheaval also damaged a large part of the coral reefs by exposing them to the air, thereby weakening their structure. The elevated coral reef made the canals between Moín and Barra del Cororado (100 km) shallower and totally impassable at certain points.

which means that the crime rate is higher, even among tourists.

In general, it is cheaper to stay on the Caribbean coast than elsewhere in Costa Rica. It is relatively easy to find a double room in a small, decent hotel near the beach for less than $25 per night. A full meal can often be had for about $5, and if you look around a bit, you can find a plate of rice and chicken (*arroz con pollo*) fairly easily for about $3. Caribbean coast cuisine is delicious and refined, with excellent fish and seafood dishes. Many foods are of Afro-Caribbean origin, and prepared with coconut milk. Rundown (a fish and vegetable stew) and Pan Bon (a fruit and spice bread) are not only delicious, but nutritious as well.

The warm ambience in the southern part of this region is reflected in the reggae and calypso music that plays in the restaurants, bars, and hotels. It is not uncommon to be greeted with a laid-back "Hi, brother" by a dreadlocked Rasta calmly strolling down the street in Cahuita or Puerto Viejo, or on the beach, singing to himself. Hats, bracelets, belts, and other items with the African colours are readily available from a street vendor or in one of the local shops.

Most people visit the Caribbean coast for its magnificent black and white sand beaches lined with palm trees, where the word "vacation" takes on its full meaning. The beaches of this region are considered among the most paradisiacal in all of Costa Rica, and some of them are among the most beautiful in the world.

In addition to its Fantasy-Island-like beaches, the Caribbean coast also has huge tracts of wilderness with an abundant flora and fauna. In the south, the coral reefs in the Parque Nacional Cahuita and the Refugio Nacional de Vida Silvestre Gandoca-Manzanillo are natural wonders. The Reserva Biológica Hitoy Cerere and the various indigenous reserves are fascinating places, and off the beaten track. Parque Nacional Tortuguero in the north is only accessible by plane or boat and one of the country's small hidden treasures that should not be missed.

The Caribbean coast is synonymous with abundance. Nature is as diversified as it is omnipresent. There are 450 families of plants, with some 2,500 species. Birds abound, with about 500 species belonging to 58 distinct families, accounting for more than half of all the species found in the country. The Tortuguero region alone is home to toucans, egrets, trogons, parakeets, herons, and other water birds. You can also see a variety of other animals including howler and white-faced capuchin monkeys, sloths, sea turtles (four species), fresh-water turtles, crocodiles, iguanas, lizards, poison-arrow frogs.

**Native Reserves**

The first native reserves (Cocles, Bribrí, Cabécar, Telire, Teyni) were established in the Talamanca region between 1976 and 1977. The **KéköLdi** reserve which extends into the mountains south of Puerto Viejo de Talamanca, was created in 1976 to protect this part of the country, home to about 200 Bribrí and Cabécar descendants. The reserve was first named Cocles after the river of the same name which runs through its territory. It was renamed KéköLdi (*KéköL* means tree essence; *di* means water or river) in 1989, and refers to a sacred tree growing on the banks of the Río Cocles, whose wood was used to make sacred ceremonial lances for shamen. It is said that the first native peoples were created by the god Sibö from grains of corn. Sibö came to the Talamanca region to explain how he created the earth, sea, plants, and animals, and to instruct the people in how to live their lives. This fundamental knowledge has been passed down by oral tradition to the present day.

For tourists passing through the region, it is relatively difficult to visit these reserves and encounter the people. Most of the reserves are located deep in the forest and are difficult to access, even with a four-wheel drive vehicle. Often, the only way to get there is on foot or horseback. Also, since these people live in isolation, communication can be difficult. Thus, it is better to contact a guide who knows how to get there, make contact with the natives, and teach you about their lifestyle. **ATEC** (see p 145) and **Terra Aventuras** (see p 145) in Puerto Viejo de Talamanca, as well as **Cahuita Tours** (see p 143) in Cahuita, offer guided tours of KéköLdi and several of the region's other reserves.

You can find out more about the past and present of the ecologically-minded natives of the KéköLdi reserve by reading ***Taking Care of Sibö's Gifts*** *(Paula Palmer, Juanita Sánchez and Gloria Mayorga, Editorama, Costa Rica)*, a wonderful little book available at ATEC, among other places.

## FINDING YOUR WAY AROUND

### By Plane

The isolated regions of Tortuguero or Barra del Colorado are reachable either by boat or by plane with **Travelair** *(☎220-3054, ⇌220-0413)* and **Sansa**

*(☎221-9414, ≠255-2176)* airlines in San José. It costs $90 for a return ticket. Many hotels in the region include the flight in their packages.

## By Bus

**Puerto Limón:** buses leave every 30 minutes from the Parque Nacional in San José *(Avenida 3, Calle 19/21)* between 5am and 7pm. The trip takes approximately 2.5 hours. Companies such as Coopelimón *(regular: $2.20, express: $2.70; ☎223-7811)* and Transportes Caribeños *(regular: $2.60, express: $3.20; ☎257-0895)* go to this popular destination. The schedule is similar for the return trip *(Puerto Limón, Calle 2, Avenida 1/2)*.

**Cahuita** and **Sixaola:** buses leave daily from San José *(Calle Central/1, Avenida 11)* at 6am, 1:30pm and 3:30pm for regular service, and 10am and 4pm for express service. The trip to Cahuita takes about 3 hours *($4.60)* and another hour *($6.25)* to Sixaola with Transportes Mepe *(☎257-8129)*.

**Puerto Viejo de Talamanca** and **Manzanillo:** Daily departures from San José *(Calle Central/1, Avenida 11)* at 10am and 4pm. The trip to Manzanillo takes about 4.5 hours *($6)* with Transportes Mepe *(☎257-8129)*.

**Puerto Limón – Cahuita – Puerto Viejo de Talamanca:** Buses leave from Puerto Limón *(Avenida 4, Calle 3)* at 5am, 10am, 1pm and 4pm. It takes an hour to get to Cahuita *($1)* and about another half hour to Puerto Viejo de Talamanca *($1.25)* with Transportes Mepe *(☎758-1572 or 258-3522)*.

## By Car

The quickest way to get to the Caribbean coast is through the magnificent Parque Nacional Braulio Carrillo *(toll: 85¢)*. From San José, take Calle 3 north to the Guápiles Highway, built in 1987. The road through the park goes up a very steep hill, then winds downward and can become congested with traffic. Be careful because roads may be slippery: it rains almost every day in the high mountains of the park, and there may be fog. But don't worry, it becomes hot and sunny again toward the Atlantic plain. The road to **Puerto Limón** is well maintained, so you can drive at a steady speed, but don't go too fast – there are police radar stations, especially active on Sundays! After Siquirres, the villages make way for fields of banana plantations, which are the main source of economic activity in the region. The trip between San José and Puerto Limón (162 km) takes two to three hours.

If you have more time (at least 4 hours) on your hands to travel between San José and Puerto Limón, you can take the absolutely charming country road past Cartago, Paraíso, Cervantes, Juan Viñas, Turrialba and Pavones, and then on to Siquirres, where there are magnificent valleys of coffee plants and macadamia trees, mountainside villages and lovely rivers, including the famous Río Reventazón, a rafter's paradise.

You can get to **Moín**, seven kilometres northwest of Puerto Limón, by passing Puerto Limón. On the road to Puerto Limón, there will be a sign indicating which road to take (the one to the left) to reach Moín and its port.

From Puerto Limón, the road heads directly south to **Cahuita**. This road is

43 kilometres, in pretty good condition, and runs along the Caribbean Sea and its beaches. It takes about 45 minutes to get to Cahuita.

**Puerto Viejo de Talamanca** is about 20 minutes, or 18 kilometres, south of Cahuita. After 12 kilometres you will come to a fork in the road: go straight on the unpaved road (and not to the right on the paved road which will take you to Bribrí and Sixaola) to get to Puerto Viejo de Talamanca. There is a police station on the road, to discourage smuggling between Costa Rica and Panama. You will be signalled either to stop and be searched, or to continue on your way, depending on the officer's mood. From Puerto Viejo de Talamanca to **Manzanillo**, the 13-kilometre road is unpaved, but in fairly good condition.

## By Boat

Most vacationers who want to visit Tortuguero or Barra del Colorado either go through an agency in San José or reserve a room in one of the region's hotels, whose packages include a return trip from San José by minibus and boat. If you go on your own, you will have to go to **Moín** and take a boat to Tortuguero. Note that this type of boat transportation is not regulated, and you will have to arrange the terms and conditions of your passage. At the Moín Quay, ask which boats go to Tortuguero, when they leave (varies according to the water level in the canal) and how much it costs. It takes anywhere between 2.5 and 4 hours for the trip, depending on the speed of the boat and how many stops are made to admire the vegetation along the canals. Prices are negotiable, especially for groups.

The guided package offered by tour agencies in **Cahuita** or **Puerto Viejo de Talamanca** is a good deal. It costs around $55 (2 days/1 night) or $65 (3 days/2 nights) and includes a guide and the return boat trip.

## PRACTICAL INFORMATION

The **Tony Facio Hospital** *(north of Puerto Limón, near the sea, ☎758-2222)* is the only hospital on the Caribbean coast.

In Puerto Limón, there is also the **Clínica Santa Lucía** *(Calle 2, Avenida 4/5, ☎758-1286)*. You will find a few **pharmacies** in downtown Puerto Limón, between Calle 2, Calle 4, Avenida 2 and Avenida 4.

South of Puerto Limón, there is a medical clinic in the small village of **Bribrí**.

For **emergencies**, call ☎758-0580 or 911.

The **Banco de Costa Rica** *(Avenida 2, Calle 1)* and **Banco Nacional de Costa Rica** *(Avenida 2, Calle 3)* are located in downtown Puerto Limón.

There are no banks south of Puerto Limón, and you will have to go to **Bribrí**, where there is the **Banco Nacional de Costa Rica**.

Many hotels can convert traveller's cheques or American currency into *colones*. In Cahuita, the **Cahuita Tours** agency (see p 143) also offers this service.

## EXPLORING

### The Guápiles Region

The plain resurfaces after the mountains of Parque Nacional Braulio Carillo. The small town of **Guápiles**, about 60 kilometres from San José, is an important banana shipping centre. East of the town, towards Guácimo, is the **Jardín Botánico Las Cusingas** *($5; 4 km south of the main road, ☎382-5805)*, owned by Jane Segleau and Ulyses Blanco. It contains a variety of medicinal plants (80 species), ornamental plants (80 species of orchids and 30 species of bromeliad) and fruit trees. The 20-hectare site protects a portion of the humid tropical forest, and ensures reforestation. There are guided tours that describe the plants and their medicinal uses, as well as general nature tours. Small paths crisscross the surrounding forest; one of them leads to the Río Santa Clara. A hundred or so bird species have already been identified. A small rustic *cabina* with two rooms and a kitchenette for four people can be rented (see p 155). During the rainy season, the road leading to the botanical gardens is more easily accessible with a four-wheel drive vehicle.

Twelve kilometres east of Guápiles, in the village of **Guácimo**, is the Escuela de Agricultura de la Región Tropical Húmida, or simply **EARTH** *(east of Guácimo, ☎255-2000)*. The school offers specialized university-level courses on tropical agriculture that attract students from all over Latin America. Guided tours are also offered to the public. The site includes an experimental banana plantation, which uses environment-friendly methods of cultivation, and a 400-hectare rainforest reserve with hiking trails; the

***Banana blossom***

school also runs a hotel on the premises (see p 156).

North of Guácimo, the 120-hectare **Finca Costa Flores** *(☎716-6457, ⇄716-6439)* grows over 600 species of heliconias and tropical plants, some of which are exported. Guided tours (*$15*) explain this type of crop. The farm also includes lovely landscaped gardens with footpaths and marshes, as well as a restaurant.

The small town of **Siquirres** used to be a major railway centre. But ever since the arrival of the Guápiles Highway in 1987, which goes through Parque Nacional Braulio Carrillo, and the abandonment of the San José-Limón railway following the 1991 earthquake, Siquirres has become a quiet little town where few visitors linger. The charming road that passes through Cartago, Paraíso, Cervantes, Juan Vinas, and Turrialba eventually arrives at Siquirres.

The exhilarating rafting descent on the very popular **Río Pacuare** (see p 154) ends on the outskirts of Siquirres, underneath the bridge of the main road. Another well-known rafting and kayaking paradise, the **Río Reventazón**, runs just north of Siquirres.

Between Siquirres and Puerto Limón (58 km), you will come across a number of small villages with names like Bristol, Boston, Stratford, Venecia, Buffalo, and Liverpool - names that have nothing to do with banana plantations!

## The Puerto Limón Region

**Puerto Limón** ★, or simply Limón, is the capital of the province of the same name. When Christopher Columbus set foot here on September 18, 1502, the town was an indigenous village called Cariari. Columbus spent several days there to have his boats repaired.

According to popular legend, the town and its surroundings were once prey to numerous epidemics of yellow fever and other tropical diseases. The only lemon tree in the region, located where city hall now stands, apparently possessed miraculous healing powers. The inhabitants would come to pick the ripe fruit, as well as the green ones whose leaves were used to make therapeutic infusions for curing yellow fever. Because of the tree's increasing popularity (it even served as a town landmark), the name El Limón gradually replaced that of Cariari. However, it was only in October 1852 that the town officially adopted the name Puerto Limón. The canton of Limón was created in 1892 and became a province on August 6, 1902.

Today, Puerto Limón is the country's largest port, but its level of activity has diminished considerably over the past few years. At the beginning of the century, the town was one of the prettiest in Costa Rica, with attractive architecture, spacious docking facilities, a magnificent park, and the country's first paved roads. However, unemployment, partly due to the withdrawal of United Fruit Company in the 1940s, and the earthquake in 1991, have left the town in a state of neglect.

Puerto Limón's only real tourist attraction is its **Carnaval** ★★, attended by 100,000 people annually from all over Costa Rica. The carnival officially starts on October 12, the day Christopher Colombus landed in the Americas, and continues for several days. Music of all kinds, parades, dancing, and flamboyant costumes liven up the town. Make your hotel reservations long in advance, or you will have great difficulty finding a decent place to stay.

The popular **Mercado Central** *(Avenida 2, Calle 3/4)*, which is surrounded by *sodas*, restaurants and inexpensive hotels, is the busiest place in town. The population has a mixed Spanish, Chinese and West Indian ancestry. The central market and the downtown area are also favourite hangouts of pickpockets and thieves, so be on your guard at all times.

You can learn more about the history and culture of the region's people at the **Museo Etno-Histórico** *(Tue to Sat 9am to 5pm; Calle 4, Avenida 2, ☎758-3903)*, near the Mercado Central.

There is a pretty park on the outskirts of town. **Parque Vargas** ★ *(Calle 1, Avenida ½)* is named after the Governor of Limón, Don Balvanero Vargas, whose bust is located in the centre of the park. The busts of Christopher Columbus and his son Fernando face the ocean, commemorating their arrival in Puerto Lima. Large palm trees and lush greenery were planted here at the beginning of this century to beau-

the city. Vargas also put up a **sea wall** ★, by filling a section of sea with earth. The powerful waves apparently used to reach all the way to the central market! A stroll along the sea wall is pleasantly refreshing.

**Isla Uvita**, where Christopher Columbus landed in 1502, is located approximately one kilometre from town. This small island can be visited by boat: inquire at your hotel or at one of the hotels that organize tours.

The closest swimming beach to Puerto Limón is **Playa Bonita** ★★, four kilometres northeast of town, towards Moín. It is surrounded by lush vegetation and is very popular with tourists for relaxing, swimming, and picnicking. Playa Bonita is also considered a good beach for surfing.

## Reserva Biológica Hitoy Cerere

Sixty kilometres south of Puerto Limón, the **Reserva Biológica Hitoy Cerere** ★

*($6; every day; ☎283-8004 or 758-3996)* was established in April 1978. It is the least visited park in the region, and has only the most basic tourist facilities. However, nature-lovers will enjoy its wild countryside, with its abundant rivers, flora and fauna, including 115 species of birds. Terra Aventuras (see p 145) in Puerto Viejo de Talamanca, organizes safe guided tours of the reserve.

The name of the reserve, which comes from Amerindian words meaning 'bed of moss' (*Hitoy*) and 'clear water' (*Cerere*), perfectly describes this humid region with its incredibly dense vegetation. The 9,155-hectare reserve covers entire valleys and mountains, with the highest peak at Mount Bitarkara (1,025 m), in the western part of the park. With annual rainfalls exceeding 3.5 metres, there are many rivers and waterfalls formed by the runoff from the mountains. The Río Hitoy and Río Cerere join together in the valley.

Hiking is without a doubt the most popular activity in the reserve. Wilderness abounds, to the delight of ornithologists and botanists alike. It is best to go on a guided hiking excursion, because the network of trails is poorly signed and thus confusing. The 1991 earthquake also left its mark, felling numerous trees. Most of the trails run along the rivers.

To get to the reserve, go through the Valle de la Estrella via Penshurst (20 km). The many small roads make it difficult to access, and four-wheel drive vehicles are essential. This area of the mountains receives a lot of rain year-round, so there really is no ideal time to visit. Migratory birds pass through the reserve between September and December.

## The Cahuita Region

The small village of **Cahuita ★**, located 43 kilometres south of Puerto Limón, is picture-perfect, with its sand-covered streets, small hospitable hotels and restaurants, and the Caribbean Sea as a backdrop. The atmosphere is relaxed, and tourists wander around and socialize with each other at some of the more popular bars and restaurants.

Most of these tourists are young people who come to relax and have a good time, since Cahuita and Puerto Viejo are two of the least expensive places to stay in Costa Rica. It is easy to find a double-occupancy room for under $25 a night, and prices can be negotiated for groups and longer stays. For dinner, several small restaurants serve excellent local, Caribbean-style cuisine, where fish and coconut milk are featured prominently and where you will often pay less than $5 for a full meal.

Originally settled by Jamaicans in mid-nineteenth century, Cahuita was a small, quiet village for many decades. The name Cahuita is derived from two native words, *kawe* (mahogany) and *ta* (point), and refers to the point in the Parque Nacional Cahuita. Until the mid-1980s, When the Guápiles highway was built, getting to this region was an adventure in itself. First, you would have to take a narrow road to get from San José to Puerto Limón. The second part of the trip between Puerto Limón and Cahuita required a good half-day, because there were neither roads nor bridges linking the towns. You had to take the train to Penshurst, cross the Río Estrella in a canoe, and complete the last leg of the trip in an old bus along an unpaved road. Nowadays, it takes less than 45 minutes to get from

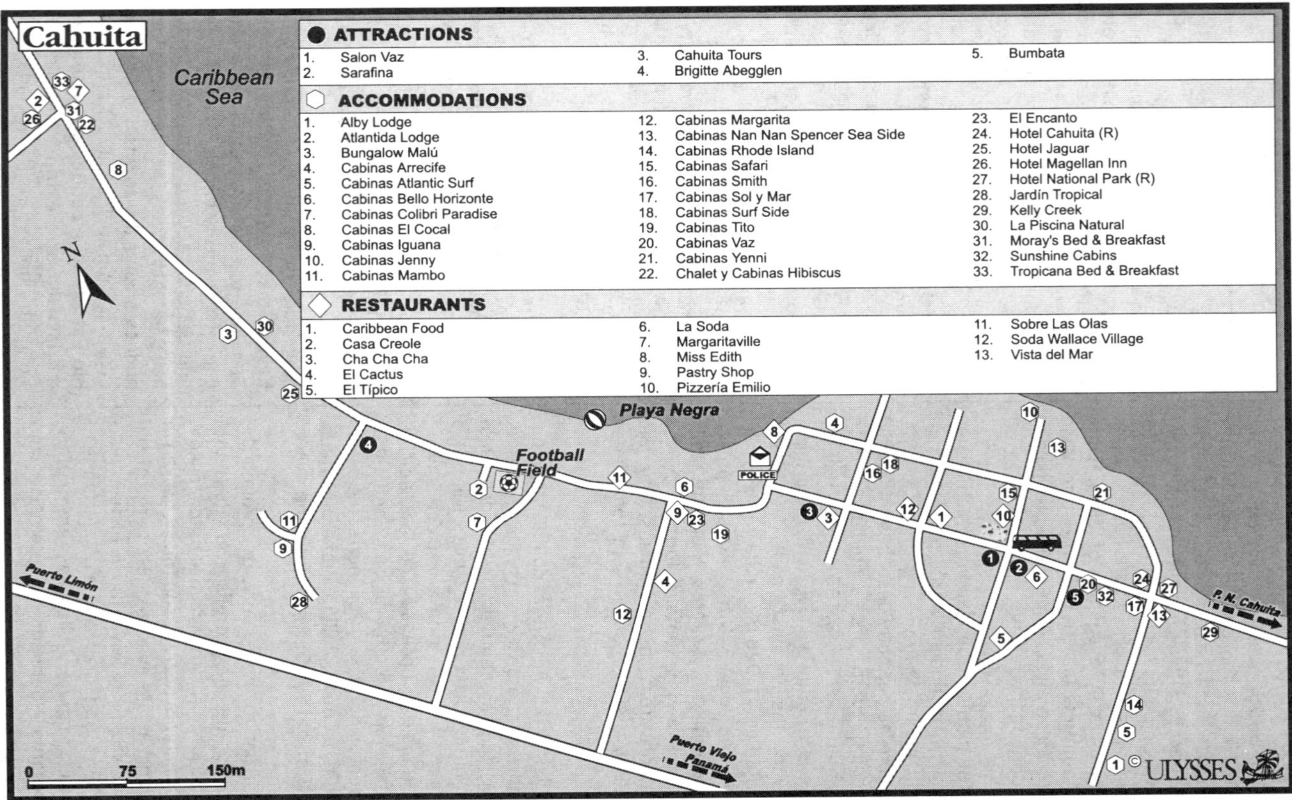
Cahuita
ATTRACTIONS
1. Salon Vaz
2. Sarafina
3. Cahuita Tours
4. Brigitte Abegglen
5. Bumbata
ACCOMMODATIONS
1. Alby Lodge
2. Atlantida Lodge
3. Bungalow Malú
4. Cabinas Arrecife
5. Cabinas Atlantic Surf
6. Cabinas Bello Horizonte
7. Cabinas Colibri Paradise
8. Cabinas El Cocal
9. Cabinas Iguana
10. Cabinas Jenny
11. Cabinas Mambo
12. Cabinas Margarita
13. Cabinas Nan Nan Spencer Sea Side
14. Cabinas Rhode Island
15. Cabinas Safari
16. Cabinas Smith
17. Cabinas Sol y Mar
18. Cabinas Surf Side
19. Cabinas Tito
20. Cabinas Vaz
21. Cabinas Yenni
22. Chalet y Cabinas Hibiscus
23. El Encanto
24. Hotel Cahuita (R)
25. Hotel Jaguar
26. Hotel Magellan Inn
27. Hotel National Park (R)
28. Jardín Tropical
29. Kelly Creek
30. La Piscina Natural
31. Moray's Bed & Breakfast
32. Sunshine Cabins
33. Tropicana Bed & Breakfast
RESTAURANTS
1. Caribbean Food
2. Casa Creole
3. Cha Cha Cha
4. El Cactus
5. El Típico
6. La Soda
7. Margaritaville
8. Miss Edith
9. Pastry Shop
10. Pizzería Emilio
11. Sobre Las Olas
12. Soda Wallace Village
13. Vista del Mar
Caribbean Sea
Playa Negra
Football Field
POLICE
P. N. Cahuita
Puerto Limón
Puerto Viejo Panamá
N
0 75 150m
© ULYSSES

Cahuita to Puerto Limón, and under four hours from San José.

There is nothing much to see in Cahuita. The beaches are located at either end of the village. **Playa Negra** is a black-sand beach, good for swimming, which runs several kilometres northwest of the village. Two other white-sand beaches are located to the east of the village in the Parque Nacional Cahuita (see further below). The first beach is at the Cahuita National Park Hotel. Access to this part of the park is free.

**Cahuita Tours** *(7am to 8pm, north of the main road, ☎755-0232, ⇌755-0082)* is a good place to go for general information on the region, including hotels, restaurants, indigenous culture, etc. There are a currency exchange counter, taxi, telephone, and fax services; bus tickets for San José are sold and bicycle and snorkelling equipment can be rented. This tour operator also offers guided tours of the region: glass-bottomed boat excursions out to the coral reef (*$20*); guided hikes in Parque Nacional Cahuita (*$10*); birdwatching expeditions along the coast (*$40*); guided hikes of the Bribrí native reserve (*$45*); and river-rafting down the Río Reventazon (*$65*) or Río Pacuare (*$85*). They also offer inexpensive trips to Tortuguero: 2 days/1 night for $55 and 3 days/2 nights for $65, including the guide and transportation there and back.

**Roberto Tours** *(☎755-0117, ⇌755-0092)* and **Turística Cahuita** *(☎755-0071)*, in the centre of town, also offer a number of guided tours of the area, and rent bicycle and snorkelling equipment at approximately the same prices as Cahuita Tours.

To know more about the fascinating history of Cahuita's inhabitants and the Talamanca coast, Paula Palmer's excellent book ***What Happen*** (*Publications in English: San José, Costa Rica, 1993, 264 pages*) gives an interesting account of these descendants of the original Caribbean island settlers, and of their traditions. This book can be purchased in several places along the coast (Cahuita Tours), and in the large bookstores of San José.

## Parque Nacional Cahuita

**Parque Nacional Cahuita** ★★★ *(free entry or $6 depending on the sector; camping; ☎755-0060)* became a national monument in 1970, and then a national park in April 1978. The park was created primarily to protect the magnificent coral reef surrounding Punta Cahuita. With a total surface area of 1,067 hectares on land, and more than 600 hectares of ocean, the park encompasses a superb tropical rainforest as well as two magnificent white-sand beaches.

This coral reef is one of the largest and most fully grown in the country. There are approximately 35 coral species (some of which are about 2 m in diameter), 123 species of fish, 44 species of crustaceans, 140 species of molluscs and 128 species of seaweed.

However, this unique habitat is threatened with extinction by the deforestation of the surrounding areas and the waste being dumped into the rivers that flow through the banana plantations. The coral was severely damaged by the 1991 earthquake, when the shoreline was raised by as much as a metre in certain places, exposing and killing much of the reef. Some coral still sticks out of the water. Despite everything, the reef is still one of the best snorkelling spots in Costa

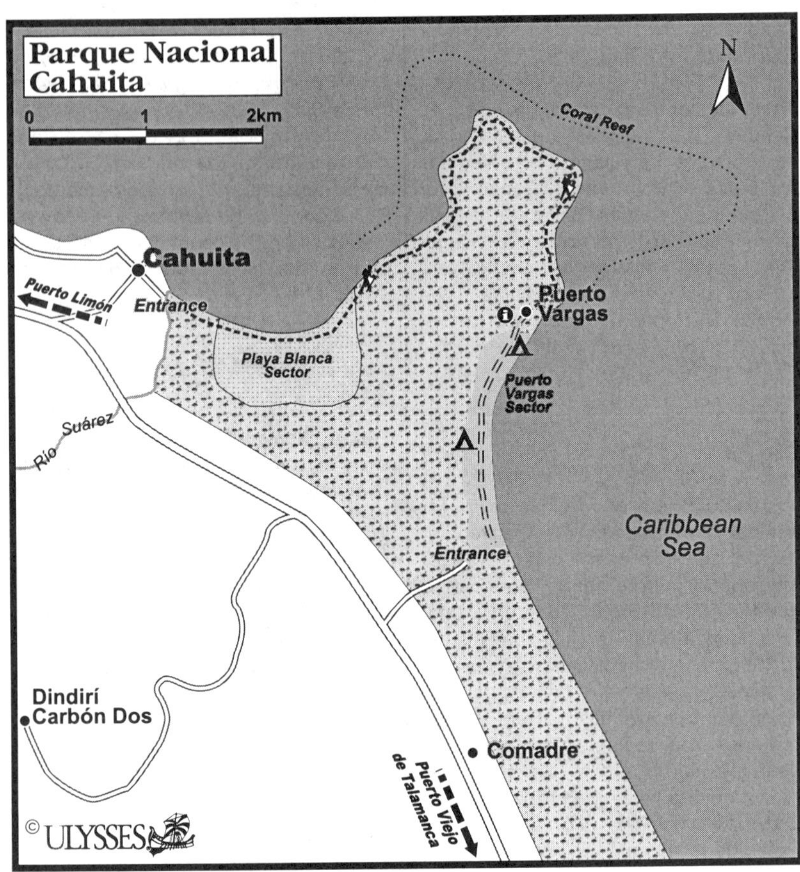


Rica. Several of the region's tour operators, including **Cahuita Tours** in Cahuita and **Terra Aventuras** in Puerto Veijo de Talamanca, organize glass-bottomed boat excursions as well as snorkelling in the park.

Parque Nacional Cahuita is bordered by the Río Suarez to the north, Río Carbon to the south, and the road between Cahuita and Puerto Viejo runs along its west side. There park has two sectors. The first is called **Playa Blanca** and encompasses the actual village of Cahuita and its superb white-sand beach. Access to the beach is now free, thanks to the efforts of the residents of the village who not only saw the beach as theirs, but considered the admission fee harmful towards their town's tourist industry. The second sector, **Puerto Vargas** *($6)*, is five kilometres south of the village, and includes the administrative buildings, as well as magnificent beach-side camp sites (see p 157).

Since the park receives almost three metres of rain a year, it is better to visit during the drier seasons from February to May or from August to October, when the average temperature is a balmy 25°C.

In addition to swimming, snorkelling, beach sports, and nature observation, hiking is an excellent way of getting from one sector of the park to the other.

## The Puerto Viejo de Talamanca Region

**Puerto Viejo de Talamanca** ★ (see map on p 162) is a small, lively village where tourists, primarily young North Americans and Europeans, stay longer than planned to fully enjoy the marvellous white sand beaches, the small inexpensive hotels and restaurants, and especially the "cool" reggae music-playing atmosphere.

Just a few years ago, Cahuita was the place to stay for its tourist amenities. However, Puerto Viejo has rapidly been gaining ground in recent years. An added attraction is the beach, which literally borders the village and is within walking distance. In addition to the white-sand one, a black-sand beach stretches for several kilometres to the west of the village. It is even possible, albeit strenuous, to walk the entire 18 kilometres along the beach to Cahuita.

The village of Puerto Viejo, also known as Puerto Viejo de Talamanca so as not to confuse it with Puerto Viejo de Sarapiquí in the north, is the gateway to the Talamanca Coast, which extends all the way to the Panamanian border to the south (via Cocles, Playa Chiquita, Punta Uva, Manzanillo and Gandoca). For more information about the region, consult the little newspaper ***Talamanca's Voice*** *(☎750-0062, ⇄223-7479, wolfbiss@sol.racsa.co.cr)*, which is chock-full of cultural, historic, and other information of interest to tourists. The quarterly newspaper was founded by Wanda Bissinger (the current editor) and Robin Short in 1996, and provides a contemporary perspective on this rich southern part of the Caribbean coast.

At the centre of the village, in front of the Tamara *soda*, the Associación Talamanqueña de Ecoturismo y Conservación, or **ATEC** *(open every day from 7am to 7pm; on the main street, ☎/⇄750-0188, atecmail@sol.racsa.co.cr, www.greencoast.com/atec.htm)*, is a good place for information about environmental protection and regional culture. This non-profit grassroots organization was established in 1990 to encourage local guides, businesses, restaurants, and hotels to do their part for the environment. Educational programs and courses on environmental issues are available for local residents. Groups from various universities are also welcome.

ATEC offers excursions and guided tours of the region. These tours focus, among other things, on indigenous communities, Afro-Caribbean culture, the environment, history, hiking, bird-watching, snorkelling, and fishing. The guides are very qualified and professional. We are told that a good part of the money goes directly to them, so that they earn more money than if they worked for a large tour operator.

The likeable Juan Carlos at **Terra Aventuras** *(beside the Comisariato Manuel Leon, near the beach, ☎750-0004)* will be able to give you information on the region's hotels, restaurants, bars, and boutiques. Inside you will also find native and Afro-Caribbean crafts from the region of Talamanca for sale. Terra Aventuras also organizes guided tours to Refugio Nacional de Vida Silvestre Gandoca-Manzanillo (*$35*), Reserva Biológica Hitoy Cerere (*$50*), Parque Nacional Cahuita *(in a glass-bottomed boat, $35)*, Parque Nacional Tortuguero

*(2 days/1 night, transport and guide included, $55)*, river rafting on the Río Pacuare (*$85*), and horseback riding on the beach and in the mountains (*$25)*. Snorkelling equipment can also be rented here.

Here are two of the region's better guides: **Harry** (originally from Germany, but a longtime resident of Costa Rica and owner of Cabinas Tropical), who offers several excursions in the region and the rest of the country, and **Juppy** (whose real name is Roberto Hansel) who knows the mountains of Talamanca, the region's fauna and flora (particularly medicinal plants) and the traditional life of the Bribrí better than anyone.

On the side of the black-sand beach (Black Beach), the **Botanical Gardens ★** *($3; Thu to Sun, 10am to 4pm)*, whose entrance is located 200 metres north of Pizote Lodge, has a wide variety of ornamental plants, fruit trees and spices. The location is excellent for observing the tiny, colourful poison-arrow frogs, sloths, and many bird species. Guided tours *($8)* are available.

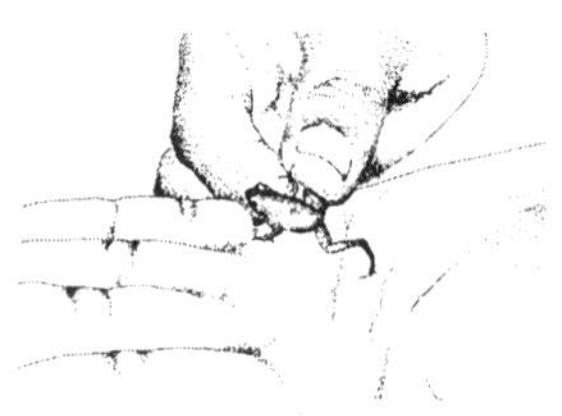

***Tiny frog***

To see experienced surfers bravely riding the waves, go to **Playa Salsa Brava ★★**, just southeast of the village. The waves of this internationally renowned beach are at their best and most challenging from December to March or in June and July. The main danger lies in the coral reef underneath, where, we were informed, many surfers have smashed up their boards and severely injured themselves. Outside of these peak surfing months, the sea is quite calm and swimming is good.

Between Puerto Viejo and Manzanillo, the coast is interspersed with gorgeous white sand beaches that are among the best in the country for swimming and relaxing. However, you should inquire about swimming conditions before you go, because at certain times of the year the waves and currents are too strong for safe swimming.

The little unpaved road linking Puerto Viejo to Manzanillo is pleasant to cycle along, not only to soak up the beauty of the scenery, the beaches and the sea, but also to stop at a *pulpería,* café, or restaurant to chat with the local people, particularly the older crowd, who always have interesting tales to tell! A small detour to **Punta Uva ★**, via a small road branching to the left, leads to a pleasant resting place beneath the coconuts or on the beach, where you can contemplate the magnificent point jutting into the sea. This is one of the coast's best places for swimming.

## The Manzanillo Region

**Manzanillo** has not yet been invaded by tourists, but the number of hotels along the road from Puerto Viejo de Talamanca to Manzanillo is growing, which means that within a few years this small coastal village will become a prime tourist destination. For now, there is little tourist infrastructure, only a *pulpería*, a restaurant-bar, and a few *cabañas*. This peaceful village, with its happy children playing on the road or beach, is only rivalled by the wild beauty of the scenery. **Aquamor Adventures** *(☎391-3417, aquamor@sol.racsa.co.cr)* offers guided tours, boat tours (dolphins), and scuba diving courses and excursions, and rents kayaks and snorkelling equipment.

**Willy Burton**, a friendly, experienced guide, lives in a small house at the end of the village, close to the entrance of the Refugio Nacional de Vida Silvestre Gandoca-Manzanillo. Willy can take you fishing or snorkelling in the park's coral reefs by boat. You can also park your car at his house before walking down the path to Punta Una.

## Refugio Nacional de Vida Silvestre Gandoca-Manzanillo

The **Refugio Nacional de Vida Silvestre Gandoca-Manzanillo** ★★ was established in October 1985 to protect one of the most beautiful areas of Costa Rica from harmful tourist development. The park encompasses 5,013 hectares of land and 4,436 hectares of sea, and runs south of Puerto Viejo de Talamanca, up to the Río Sixaola, near the border of Panama.

Rarely visited by tourists, probably due to the lack of facilities, the park is still an exceptional site that protects threatened flora and fauna. It is home to immense coral reefs (Punta Uva, Manzanillo and Punta Mona), an oyster bed, a mangrove swamp, fields, a rich, dense tropical rainforest, and breathtakingly beautiful white-sand beaches bordered by coconut trees. There are some 360 species of birds, including pelicans, toucans, parakeets and eagles, as well as howling monkeys, capuchins, sloths, tapirs, caimans and crocodiles. The park also has four species of turtles, including the impressive leatherback turtle, the largest turtle in the world, which lays its eggs between March and July.

The park was named after the tiny villages of Manzanillo and Gandoca, which are located in the southern part of the park and existed before this region became a protected territory. If you decide to explore this park on your own, stop first at the small information office *(oficina de información)* in Manzanillo. Camping is allowed in the park, but there are no facilities (no parking or washrooms). Furthermore, with the heat, the mosquitoes and the snakes, you may prefer the accommodations at the beach or in the village.

Since there is so much to discover here, we strongly recommend that you join a tour group or hire an experienced guide who knows all the secrets of this natural reserve (see above, under "Manzanillo" and "Puerto Viejo").

The main park activities are hiking and snorkelling, and you can do both on the same day. Or you can try reeling in a feisty tarpon near the Río Sixaola! The main trail runs from Manzanillo to Punta Mona, and is 5.5 kilometres one way. Remember to bring enough water and insecticide. This trail runs through the forest to several small isolated and idyllic beaches, where you can snorkel to an incredibly beautiful coral reef. The coral here abounds with captivating marine life and is apparently in better shape than in Cahuita, since there is less pollution. However, the waves and currents are rather strong. But thanks to these geographical conditions, many beautiful seashells can be found along the beach. Back in the forest, it is very easy to spot the toucans and small, brightly-coloured poisonous frogs. The trail ends at Punta Mona (Monkey Point), where there is a lovely beach and a view of Panama.

## The Bribrí Region

**Bribrí**, located about a dozen kilometres from Puerto Viejo de Talamanca, has few tourist attractions, because it serves primarily as the administrative centre of this region of green valleys. There are a bank, offices, a clinic, and a few businesses. A 34-kilometre road winds south of here, through the banana plantations to the little border village of **Sixaola** and into Panama.

## The Tortuguero Region

This region includes the village of Tortuguero, an extensive network of canals, and Parque Nacional Tortuguero, and has some of the most spectacular flora and fauna in the country. Because it is not very easily accessible (only by boat or plane), the area is virtually unspoilt and nature still dictates the inhabitants' way of life. Things might change soon because this destination, just 250 kilometres from San José and 80 kilometres from Puerto Limón, is becoming more popular and already has a number of hotels.

A minimum stay of three days (and two nights) is needed to navigate along the canals, wander through the village, relax on the beach, visit the sea-turtle museum and leave time to sit back in a hammock and contemplate the lush green surroundings. Also keep in mind that the boat trip (from Moín, or by bus and boat from San José) takes at least a half-day.

The canals of the Tortuguero region were built so that the local inhabitants wouldn't have to sail out on the rough sea in their small boats. The 100-kilometre canal network runs from **Moín**, near Puerto Limón, to Barra del Colorado, and was completed in 1974. Since the 1991 earthquake, however, the shoreline has risen in numerous places, which sometimes makes navigation difficult. We got stuck in **Parismina** because our flat-bottomed boat was scraping the bottom of the canal – one of the passengers even had to get into the water and guide the boat through the deepest parts of the canal! The guide told us that sometimes it is impossible to get through, and that the boat must then stop at the closest village and wait for the water level to rise before continuing.

The Tortuguero region has an especially abundant flora and fauna due to its favourable climate. It receives over 5,000 millimetres of rain annually – one of the highest rates of precipitation in the world! There is no dry season per se, although less rain does fall in February, March, and September. It is therefore extremely important to bring along boots (hiking or rubber), as well as a raincoat. Many of the region's hotels provide ponchos for their guests. An umbrella is also very useful, not only for the rain, but also against the sun, which shines more intensely after a sudden rainfall. The region also has high humidity, but it rarely get hot enough to be stifling. The average annual temperature is 26°C and the nights are cool. If you plan on walking in the forest, remember to bring along your insect repellent, or you will be too busy swatting at these pesky creatures to get any really good photos of the many brightly coloured frogs!

Swimming in the Tortuguero region is somewhat risky. The ocean waves and currents are often very powerful, and sharks have occasionally been sighted. The brown water in the canals is not at all inviting, and have crocodiles living in them. However, close to Tortuguero village, there are often children

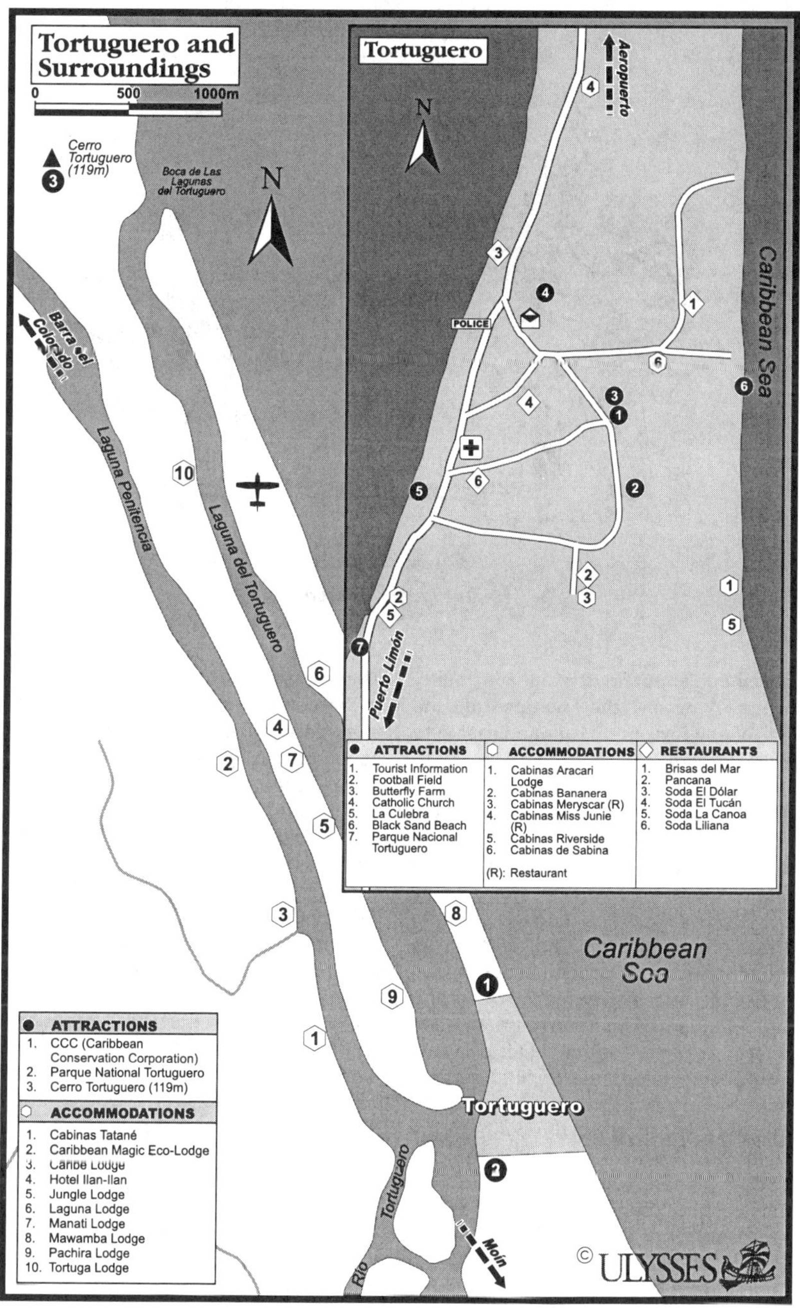
Tortuguero and Surroundings
0
500
1000m
Cerro Tortuguero (119m)
Boca de Las Lagunas del Tortuguero
N
Barra del Colorado
Laguna Penitencia
Laguna del Tortuguero
Caribbean Sea
Tortuguero
Río Tortuguero
Moín
ATTRACTIONS
1. CCC (Caribbean Conservation Corporation)
2. Parque National Tortuguero
3. Cerro Tortuguero (119m)
ACCOMMODATIONS
1. Cabinas Tatané
2. Caribbean Magic Eco-Lodge
3. Caribe Lodge
4. Hotel Ilan-Ilan
5. Jungle Lodge
6. Laguna Lodge
7. Manati Lodge
8. Mawamba Lodge
9. Pachira Lodge
10. Tortuga Lodge
Tortuguero
Aeropuerto
N
POLICE
Caribbean Sea
Puerto Limón
ATTRACTIONS
1. Tourist Information
2. Football Field
3. Butterfly Farm
4. Catholic Church
5. La Culebra
6. Black Sand Beach
7. Parque Nacional Tortuguero
ACCOMMODATIONS
1. Cabinas Aracari Lodge
2. Cabinas Bananera
3. Cabinas Meryscar (R)
4. Cabinas Miss Junie (R)
5. Cabinas Riverside
6. Cabinas de Sabina
(R): Restaurant
RESTAURANTS
1. Brisas del Mar
2. Pancana
3. Soda El Dólar
4. Soda El Tucán
5. Soda La Canoa
6. Soda Liliana
© ULYSSES

***Tortuguero church***

splashing about in the canal's murky waters, or in the waters of the Caribbean Sea, but it is not advisable to imitate them.

The little village of **Tortuguero** ★★ was founded in the 1920s, but did not have electricity until the beginning of the 1980s. It is bordered on one side by the Río Tortuguero and on the other by the Caribbean Sea. The 500 or so inhabitants lead a peaceful and tranquil life, and the majority make their living from tourism. The tourist information booth, near the football field, provides information about the original settlers and the history of the village up to the present day. At press time, a butterfly farm was being set up close to the booth. The village has a few picturesque, unpaved streets, which are less than one metre wide. The small yellow **Catholic church** stands in the centre of town. There are also some friendly neighbourhood restaurants and two souvenir shops.

The most popular attraction in the area is the canal, which you can sail along to explore the surroundings in a dugout canoe rented (with or without a guide) from the village (available at La Culebra, the *pulpería*, at the entrance of Parque Nacional Tortuguero, or at most of the hotels).

The Caribbean Conservation Corporation, or **CCC** ★★ *(voluntary donation; Mon to Sat 10am to 5:30pm, Sun 2pm to 5pm; ☎224-9215)* north of the village, near the Río Tortuguero, has a natural history museum highlighting sea turtles. The CCC has been involved in sea turtle conservation projects since 1959. Four species are found in the region (green, leatherback, Hawksbill, and loggerhead turtles). The museum opened in 1994 and presents information on the various species of turtle and educates visitors on how to protect their natural habitats. An 18-minute video also explores the region's flora and fauna. A small on-site souvenir shop selling books, videos, T-shirts, and more finances the museum.

A **black-sand beach** starts at the village and stretches five kilometres north along the lagoon, all the way to the mouth of the Tortuguero River. Strolling next to its lush forest is very pleasant. Along the way, you will be able to see Tortuguero's small airport, busy each morning between 7 and 8 o'clock. At the end, at the mouth of the lagoon, there are often fishermen in the water up to their knees, trying to catch enormous fish. On the western side of the lagoon is Cerro Tortuguero, the region's highest peak.

**Cerro Tortuguero** ★★ stands 119 metres tall and is located 5 kilometres from the village. It is accessible only by boat, from the mouth of the lagoon. Then, a short but steep path leads to its summit. It takes about 30 minutes to make it to the top, which will give you plenty of time to stop and admire the monkeys, small, colourful poison-arrow frogs, and great variety of plants and trees in the forest. At the top, there is a view of the canals, the forest and the vast ocean; and if you look straight down, you can clearly see the mouth of the Laguna Tortuguero at the bottom of the hill.

## Parque Nacional Tortuguero

The **Parque Nacional Tortuguero** ★★★ *($6; ☎719-2929, ⇌710-7673, the Cuatro Esquinas entrance, south of Tortuguero; or the Jalova entrance, south of the canal, near Parismina)* is one of the most popular sites on the Caribbean coast. It is not that crowded because visitors are spread out along different canals and over the many places of interest (river, beach, trails, etc.). The quality and quantity of flora and fauna is incredible, and the sloths hanging from branches, howler monkeys or capuchins, freshwater turtles, iguanas, lizards, venomous frogs and even camouflaged caimans can be safely observed from the narrow canal.

Tortuguero's turtles have been hunted for their eggs (tortuguero means "turtle hunter" in Spanish), which are a delicacy, ever since people first lived in the region. Their over-hunting for overseas markets in the 20th century has threatened the survival of this species. This led Dr. Archie Carr, a marine biologist and founding member of the CCC (see p 150), to wage a global public-awareness campaign against hunting these turtles, which still goes on. The organization has managed to turn many turtle hunters into excellent tour guides, who have given up poaching to work for the park or for the region's hotels.

If you want to see turtles lay their eggs on the beach, you will have to go with a guide and respect certain rules (no talking, disturbing the turtle, flash photography, etc.) so as not to disrupt the process. A female turtle will lay between one and six sets of eggs, 10 to 14 days apart, every two to four years at sundown, when the tide is high. Green turtles lay eggs between July and October, and leatherback turtles lay theirs between February and June.

In addition to the four species of turtle found in the Tortuguero region, there are 107 other reptile species, 57 species of amphibians, 55 species of freshwater fish, 60 species of mammals and over 300 species of birds, including toucans, trogons,

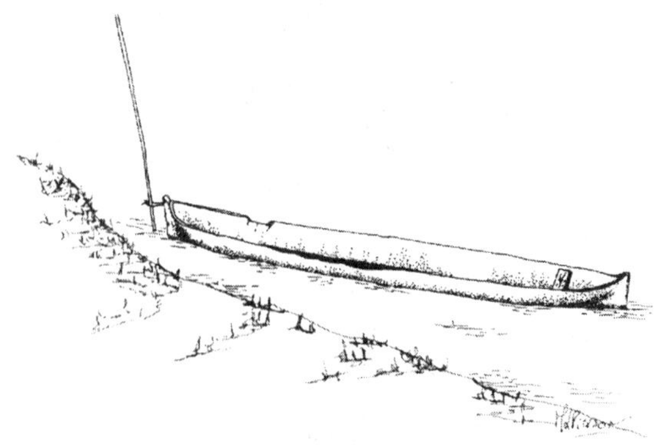

***Dugout Canoe***

parakeets, herons and other egrets, which can easily be observed up close, provided you have the proper equipment. In fact, walking along the canals of Tortuguero without binoculars is a bit like fishing without a rod! There are also great hiking trails near the Cuatro Esquinas entrance, by Tortuguero, and around Jalova, south of the park (see p 153).

## Barra del Colorado

North of Tortuguero, the wild Barra del Colorado region has many canals, lagoons and rivers, and has been relatively untouched by tourists. It is renowned for its excellent sport fishing; many lodges have been set up for this purpose and all sorts of packages are available. Although this region is one of the most remote in Costa Rica, about 2,000 people live here.

This region has been protected since 1985, when it was incorporated into the **Refugio Nacional de Fauna Silvestre Barra del Colorado ★**. With an area of 92,000 hectares, it is the largest national wildlife reserve in the country. This reserve is primarily made up of swamps and tropical rainforest, and runs north to Río San Juan, the natural border between Costa Rica and Nicaragua. The Río Colorado runs west to east through the park and empties into the Caribbean Sea, north of the small airport in the village of Barra del Colorado and south of Machuca Island.

If you want to stay in the area, you should make reservations, because there is little tourist infrastructure, and hotels are far and few between. Also, accommodations are expensive and organized activities mainly involve fishing. The region is internationally renowned for its tarpon fishing. If you want to travel along the canals with a guide to explain the flora and fauna, we recommend that you specify this when you reserve, because some hotels do not offer this or, if they do, they usually hire external guides for sports fishing excursions.

## OUTDOOR ACTIVITIES

### Cycling

One of the loveliest rides in the region is along the small, unpaved road between Puerto Viejo de Talamanca and Manzanillo (13 km), past incredible white-sand beaches where you can stop to rest and swim. There are also small restaurants, *sodas* and *pulperías* along the road. In Cahuita, **Cahuita Tours** *(7am to 8pm; north of the main street, ☎755-0232, ≠755-0082)* rents out bicycles.

### Hiking

The **Reserva Biológica Hitoy Cerere** (see p 140) has three hiking trails that will take you through the rainforest in the area around the administrative building, which is also used as a reception centre: the **Tepescuintle** trail involves approximately one hour of hiking, and passes by the Río Cerere; the **Espavel** trail requires just over two hours and takes you through a dense, rich forest with 50-metre-tall trees; and the **Bobócara** trail, which takes 2.5 hours and winds through the tropical rainforest's abundant epiphytic plants, such as ferns, orchids and bromellads.

The 7-kilometre (one-way) trail in the **Parque Nacional Cahuita** (see p 143) starts in village of Cahuita (free entry) and finishes at the beach at Puerto Vargas. The trail is wide, well maintained and practically flat. It runs along a beautiful forested white-sand beach, where you will be able to see splendid flora and fauna. The park is home to many species, including howler monkeys and capuchins, *pizotes* (badgers), coatis, raccoons and sloths which you can see as long as you don't do anything to scare them off.

Halfway there, the trail runs along the Punta Cahuita, where one of the largest coral reefs in the country is located. The fine sand is composed of millions of tiny pieces of coral. The trail ends by the park's administrative offices and camping sites, near an incredible beach which runs further south. If you do not have transportation back to Cahuita, you can either return via the trail, or leave the park at the Puerto Vargas exit and wait for the bus (or a taxi), or walk along the main road to the village (7.5 km). **Warning:** The main road attracts many thieves who hide in the forest waiting to rob hikers of their cameras, jewellery and money. Therefore, we recommend that you leave any valuables behind and undertake this excursion in groups. Most of the region's hotels, as well as Cahuita Tours, can help you form a group.

The main trails of **Refugio Nacional de Vida Silvestre Gandoca-Manzanillo** (see p 147) runs 5.5 kilometres (one way) from Manzanillo to Punta Mona.

The **Cerro Tortuguero** (see p 151), 5 kilometres from the village of Tortugeuro, overlooks the region from a height of 119 metres. It can only be accessed by boat. The trail that goes to the summit is short, but steep. It will take you approximately 30 minutes to get to the top.

The main activity in the **Parque Nacional Tortuguero** (see p 151) are boat tours of the flora and fauna, but there are also some hiking trails. Near the Cuatro Esquinas entrance and the village of Tortuguero, the **Gavilán Trail** (2 km, 30 min) will take you through the tropical rain forest and the beach where turtles come to lay eggs at nightfall (from July to October). **La Ceiba** (500 m, approx. 2 hours) is a pleasant trail over land and water: you have to cross the small Chiquero canal by canoe to get to the entrance of this short trail, from which you will see many different kinds of tropical plants, and maybe even monkeys (howler and capuchin), butterflies, bats, venomous frogs and jaguar tracks. Near Jalova, further south, the **El Tucán Trail** (1.5 km, 30 min) runs through the exceptional vegetation in this part of the park where more than 50 species of freshwater fish thrive.

For guided hikes in the regional parks, contact **Cahuita Tours** *(☎755-0232, Cahuita)*, **ATEC** *(☎750-0188, Puerto Viejo)* or **Terra Aventuras** *(☎750-0004, Puerto Viejo)* for information about the different tours they offer.

## Rafting

Two rivers in the Siquirres Region, the **Río Pacuare** and **Río Reventazón**, are great for rafting. Although most whitewater rafting companies are located in San José, this sport is also offered on the Caribbean coast. In Cahuita, **Cahuita Tours** *(7am to 8pm; north of the main road, ☎755-0232, ⇄755-0082)* offers day-long trips on the Río Reventazón *($65)* or the Río Pacuare *($85)*. In Puerto Viejo, **Terra Aventuras** *(beside the the Comisariato Manuel León, on the beach, ☎750-0004)* also organizes excursions on the Río Pacuare *($85)*.

## Kayaking

Whitewater kayaking can be done on the Río Pacuare and Río Reventazón. In Manzanillo, **Aquamor Adventures** *(☎391-3417)* offers guided tours and kayak rentals.

## Surfing

Four kilometres northwest of Puerto Limón, towards Moín, **Playa Bonita** is known as one of the best surfing beaches on the coast.

In Cahuita, **Black Beach** has become a favourite with surfers.

But the most famous surfing beach on the Caribbean coast by far is **Playa Salsa Brava**, just southeast of Puerto Viejo de Talamanca. This internationally renowned beach has foaming, challenging waves between December and March, and in June and July.

## Fishing

Most hotels in the **Tortuguero** region, and even more around **Barra del Colorado**, offer fishing packages. These regions have an excellent reputation for ocean and river sports fishing, especially when it comes to tarpon.

In Puerto Viejo, **ATEC** *(☎/⇄750-0188)* organizes fishing trips.

In Manzanillo, **Willy Burton** can take you deep-sea fishing on his boat. Just stop by his house, the last one in the village near the trail to Punta Mona, if you're interested.

## Scuba Diving and Snorkelling

In Cahuita, **Cahuita Tours** *(7am to 8pm; north of the main street, ☎755-0232, ⇄755-0082)* rents snorkelling equipment.

In Puerto Viejo, **ATEC** *(☎/⇄750-0188)* organizes snorkelling excursions. **Terra Aventuras** *(beside the Comisariato Manuel León, by the beach,*

*☎750-0004)* rents out snorkelling equipment.

In Manzanillo, **Aquamor Adventures** *(☎391-3417)* offers excursions and courses in scuba diving, and rents snorkelling equipment. **Willy Burton,** also in Manzanillo, will take you out to the coral reefs by boat so that you can go snorkelling. To contact him, go directly to his house, the last one in the village, near the trail to Punta Mona.

## Swimming

The closest beach to Puerto Limón is at **Playa Bonita**, four kilometres northwest of the city.

The southern part of the coast, especially between Cahuita and Manzanillo, has many black-sand and white-sand beaches perfect for swimming. These beaches are some of the country's most beautiful. However, you have to be careful in some area, since there are coral reefs.

## Horseback Riding

In Cahuita, **Brigitte Abegglen** *(50 m west of the Ancla Restaurant, Playa Negra, ☎755-0053)* rents out horses *($10/hour)* and offers two guided tours: one in the mountains to 10-metre waterfalls where you can swim *(5 hours, $35)* and the other along a trail on the beach and the forest *(3 hours, $25)*.

In Puerto Viejo, **Terra Aventuras** *(next to the Comisariato Manuel León, beside the beach, ☎750-0004)* offers horseback riding on the beach or in the mountains *(3 hours, $25)*.

# ACCOMMODATIONS

## The Guápiles Region

### Guápiles

The **Happy Rana Lodge** *($$$ bkfst incl.; pb, hw; 8 km west of Guápiles, ☎710-6794, ⇌710-2301)* is a Bed & Breakfast focussing on nature and relaxation in the forest. The *cabinas* are rustic, very large and comfortable. On the terrace, there are hammocks shaded by the tropical rainforest. The owners, Heidi and Alvaro Monge, offer different activities such as guided hiking tours, horseback riding and rafting.

At the **Jardín Botánico Las Cusingas** *($$$; pb, K; ☎382-5805)* (see p 138), you can stay in a rustic, but comfortable, two-bedroom *cabina* complete with kitchenette, livingroom and wood stove. Perfect for families.

The pleasant Bed & Breakfast **Casa Río Blanco** *($$$$ bkfst incl.; pb, hw; 6 km west of Guápiles, take the short road to the right, past La Ponderosa Restaurant, ☎/⇌382-0957, crblanco@sol.racsa.co.cr)* is owned by Thea Gaudette and Ron Deletetsky, who will show you the wonders of this region. The rooms are clean and comfortable. There are trails throughout the forest and the river is perfect for swimming. Guided tours, including morning hikes, are offered.

The **Hotel Country Club Suerre** *($$$$$; pb, hw, ≡, ⊛, ctv, ℜ; Guápiles, ☎710-7551, ⇌710-6376)* is a big North American-style hotel with air-conditioning in the rooms and an elaborate sports complex. There are an Olympic swimming pool, a wading pool for children, water slides, a children's play area, tennis and basketball courts, and a sauna, as well as several hiking trails in the neighbouring reserves and gardens. The 30 rooms are spacious and comfortable.

**Guácimo**

**EARTH** (see p 138) has its own hotel *($$; pb, hw, ⊘, ⊗, ≈; ☎255-2000*) with simple, but clean rooms. There are also a pool and exercise equipment.

**Hotel Río Palmas** *($$$; pb, hw, ⊗, tv, ≈, ℜ; ☎760-0305, ⇄760-0296)* is located just over half a kilometre past EARTH, east of Guácimo. Although it is on Limón's busy road, it is an excellent choice for anyone who does not want to go directly to the Caribbean coast or San José. Rooms are spacious, clean, comfortable and tastefully decorated. Its restaurant has an excellent reputation. There are also a pool and short hiking trails.

## The Puerto Limón Region

Unfortunately, Puerto Limón is not the safest city around, nor the most pleasant. Most vacationers who visit this city tend to stay in Cahuita or Puerto Viejo, to which they return in the evening. However, Puerto Limón has many places to stay, for all tastes and budgets. Surfers and anyone else wishing to visit Tortuguero by boat should stay around the Playa Bonita, Portete and Moín, less than seven kilometres from Puerto Limón.

**Hotel Cariari** *($; sb; Avenida 3, Calle 2, Puerto Limón, ☎758-1395)* is one of the cheapest hotels in town, but the rooms have neither airconditioning, nor fans.

**Hotel Oriental** *($; sb, ⊗; Calle 4, Avenida 3/4, north of the market, Puerto Limón, ☎758-0117)* is also inexpensive and relatively clean.

**Hotel Palace** *($-$$; sb/pb, ⊗; Calle 2, Avenida 2/3, Puerto Limón, ☎758-0419)* has different types of rooms that are of good value for the price.

**Hotel Acón** *($$; pb, hw, ≡, ℜ; Avenida 3, Calle 3, near the market, Puerto Limón, ☎758-1010, ⇄758-2924)* has 39 rooms, a restaurant and a nightclub, so it gets noisy on weekends.

**Hotel Miami** *($$; pp, ≡, ⊗, tv; Avenida 2, Calle 4/5, west of the market, Puerto Limón, ☎758-0490, ⇄758-1978)* has 30 well-maintained, air-conditioned rooms, but no hot water.

In Moín, the **Hotel Moín Caribe** *($$; pb, hw, ⊗, ≈, ℜ, P; Moín, ☎/⇄758-1112)* has 15 simple rooms. Its nightclub is very popular on weekends.

The **Hotel Tete** *($$; pb, hw, ≡, ⊗; Avenida 3, Calle 4, Puerto Limón, ☎758-1122, ⇄758-0707)* is located near the market and has 14 clean rooms. Rooms with a balcony facing the street are noisier than those without.

The **Nuevo Internacional** *($$; pb, hw, ⊗, ≡, P; Avenida 5, Calle 2/3, Puerto Limón, ☎758-0662),* north of the village, has very clean rooms, available with or without airconditioning.

The old-fashioned **Hotel Park** *($$-$$$; pb, hw, ≡, tv, P; Avenida 3, Calle 1, north of Parque Vargas, Puerto Limón, ☎758-3476, ⇄758-4364)* is one of the most popular places to stay in Puerto Limón. Right on the beach near Vargas Park, it has different types of rooms, the cheapest of which do not have hot water. Obviously, the rooms with an ocean view, hot water and television are the best and most expensive. Hotel Park also has a good restaurant.

Northwest of Puerto Limón , towards the Playa Bonita, **Apartotel Cocori** *($$-$$$; pb, ≡, ⊗, K, ≈; Playa Bonita, ☎/⇌758-2930)* has 21 clean rooms with kitchenettes, available with or without airconditioning. The view of the sea from the restaurant is spectacular.

Opposite the Apartotel Cocori, the 16 rooms of **Hotel Matama** *($$$$; pb, hw, ≡, ≈, ℜ; Playa Bonita, ☎758-1123, ⇌223-6378)*, are attractive and very clean. The location is beautiful with its tropical gardens and magnificent view.

The hillside **Hotel Maribú Caribe** *($$$$-$$$$$; pb, hw, ≡, ≈, ℜ; Playa Bonita, ☎758-4543, ⇌758-3541)*, three kilometres from Puerto Limón, near Playa Bonita, definitely has the best view in the region. The 17 circular *cabinas* are very pretty and clean. There are also a casino, an open-air restaurant with a great view, two pools and the opportunity to partake in one of the many organized excursions.

**South of Puerto Limón**

Ten kilometres north of Cahuita, and one kilometre from Río Estrella, **Los Aviarios del Caribe** *($$$$/day; pb, hw, ⊗; ☎/⇌382-1335)* is a private wildlife sanctuary (75 ha), home to over 250 species of birds, monkeys, sloths, caimans, river turtles, venomous frogs, etc. Small hiking trails lead to a rich, dense forest. Guided tours, usually in canoes, for birdwatching and nature study. The rooms are modern, clean and tastefully decorated. The site managers, Judy and Luis Arroyo, will be pleased to share their knowledge with you.

Halfway (22 km) between Puerto Limón and Cahuita, the **Hotel Selva Mar Club Campestre** *($$$$ bkfst incl.; pb, hw, ≡, ⊗, ≈, ℜ, tv; ☎/⇌758-2861)* has 51 rooms and a wide range of activities (fishing, kayaking, hiking, volleyball, etc.), all less than 200 metres from an incredible beach.

The **Selva Bananito Lodge** *($$$$/day; pb, hw; ☎253-8118, ⇌224-2640, costari@netins.net)* is in the middle of the forest, at the foot of the Talamanca mountain range. To get to this private reserve (850 ha), take the small trail west towards the Río Bananito. This trail is in very poor condition, so it is best to telephone ahead of time and have someone come and pick you up. The *cabinas* are lovely and have solar-powered water heaters. The terraces have hammocks and a magnificent view of the tropical forest. Activities include walking in the forest and along the river to the waterfalls, horseback riding and a forest canopy tour.

## Cahuita

The tiny village of Cahuita has about forty hotels, *cabinas* and Bed & Breakfasts ranging in price from $7 to $75 for a room for two people. Therefore you should have no trouble finding a room to fit your budget. Many hotels and *cabinas* outside of the village will pick you up at the village bus stop. Just tell them when you will be arriving when you make your reservations.

At the **Parque Nacional Cahuita** *($1.25/person/day)*, there are 50 very good camping sites next to the fine-sand beach; some have fire pits for cooking and sheltered picnic tables.

There are showers and washrooms behind the sites, near the building.

The **Cabinas Atlantic Surf** *($; ⊗; ☎755-0086)* and **Cabinas Rhode Island** *($; ⊗; ☎755-0264)*, behind the Sol y Mar Restaurant, have six and eight plain, inexpensive rooms respectively.

Opposite the El Encanto Bed & Breakfast, the **Cabinas Bello Horizonte** *($; sb/pb, hw; ☎755-0206)* has inexpensive rooms and *cabinas*, as well as a "café-soda".

Near the school, the **Cabinas Smith** *($; sb, hw, ⊗; ☎755-0068)* has six clean rooms that won't break the bank.

The **Cabinas Sol y Mar** *($; sb, hw, ⊗; ☎755-0237)*, opposite Hotel Cahuita, rents out 11 reasonably priced rooms. There is also a *soda* that serves breakfast.

The **Cabinas Surf Side** *($; pb, hw, P; ☎755-0246)* are directly opposite the school. There are 23 clean rooms, plus a private parking lot with a guard. At $5 per person or $15 for three people, it is definitely the cheapest place to stay in Cahuita.

The **Cabinas Vaz** *($; hw, ⊗, ℜ; ☎755-0218)* are located in the heart of the village. The establishment has 14 adequate, inexpensive rooms, but gets noisy when the restaurant blares the music.

The **Hotel Cahuita** *($; ℜ, ≈; ☎755-0233)* has nine simple, cheap rooms next to the main building, all side by side on one floor like a motel. There are also a bar and restaurant.

**Cabinas Jenny** *($-$$; pb, hw, ⊗; ☎755-0256, ⇌755-0082)* has recently re-opened after closing for a few months due to the owner's poor health. Three friendly, young Quebeckers now run the place, which is one of the best budget establishments in Cahuita. Literally right on the sea, with a view of the headland and the spectacular beach of Parque Nacional Cahuita, Cabinas Jenny has eight rooms with private washrooms, hot water, hammocks, etc. It is worth spending a few more dollars for one of the four upper rooms with balconies overlooking the ocean.

**Cabinas Nan Nan Spencer Sea Side** *($-$$; pb, ⊗; ☎/⇌755-0027)*, right beside Cabinas Jenny, is a great place to stay in the village, since it is close to the sea. The rooms are airy, comfortable and perfect for relaxing, and some of the higher priced ones have kitchenettes.

The **Cabinas Margarita** *($-$$; pb, hw, ℜ; ☎755-0205)*, just off the road, near the El Cactus pizzeria, has ten simple and inexpensive *cabinas*.

**La Piscina Natural** *($-$$; pb, ec, ⊗)* is named for the natural cavity on its beach in which water gets trapped when the tide goes out. It is 1.5 kilometres from the village, on Playa Negra, and has five rooms, a garden and hammocks.

The inexpensive **Cabinas Arrecife** *($$; pb, hw, ⊗, ℜ; ☎/⇌755-0081)* has ten rooms and a lovely view of the sea. Brand new, the rooms are clean and well kept. Sometimes a refreshing sea breeze blows in the area.

The **Cabinas El Cocal** *($$; pb, ⊗, K; ☎755-0034)* is near Playa Negra, two kilometres from the village. The two *cabinas* have fully equipped kitchens, including utensils.

The **Cabinas Mambo** *($$; pb, hw, ⊗, ℜ)* has four charming rooms with balconies.

The **Cabinas Safari** *($$; ⊗; ☎755-0078)* rents seven rooms with cooking facilities.

The **Cabinas Yenni** *($$; pb, hw, ⊗; ☎755-0256)* are 200 metres west of the park, facing the sea. There are seven rooms with private bathrooms, hot water, balconies and hammocks.

The **Jardín Tropical** *($$; pb, hw, ⊗, ℝ, K; ☎/⇄755-0033)*, located outside the village, south of the Cabinas Iguana, has three *cabinas* that can accommodate a handful of people. All have kitchen facilities. Jimi and Arlene run the place, as well as the small *soda* and a popular bar.

The **National Park Hotel** *($$; pb, hw, ⊗, ℜ; ☎755-0244)* has one of the best locations in Cahuita. A hop, skip and a jump from Cahuita national park and its magnificent beach, this hotel has 13 rooms, some with a view of the sea. There are also a restaurant and bar.

**Moray's Bed & Breakfast** *($$ bkfst incl.; pb, ⊗, ℜ; ☎755-0038)*, on Playa Negra, approximately 2 kilometres from the village, has four rooms and a natural coral pool. The restaurant, Margaritaville (see p 171), is excellent. At $25 a night for two people, including breakfast, it is a good place to stay if you do not mind walking to the village.

The **Cabinas Iguana** *($$-$$$; pb/sb, ≈, ℝ, K; ☎755-0005, ⇄755-0054)*, owned by a Swiss couple, Christina and Martin, has small cottages with kitchenettes for five people, *cabinas* with private bathrooms and refrigerators, and three rooms with a shared bathroom. There are also an organic garden, a small library, and a nice pool, all along a 200-metre stretch of the beach.

**La Rocalla** *($$-$$$; pb, ⊗, ℝ, K; ☎755-0291)* has two small houses with terraces and hammocks.

**Bungalow Malú** *($$$; pb, hw, ⊗; ☎755-0006)* has seven round wooden bungalows, just up the road from the Jaguar Hotel.

**Cabinas Colibri Paradise** *($$$; pb, hw; ☎755-0055)* is just outside the village, behind the football field. To get there by car, take the main road and not the road along Playa Negra. There are four attractive *cabinas* (the old kitchenettes have been removed). The owner, Mario, from Quebec, has opened two camping sites *($4/day)*, each with a terrace and kitchen.

Outside Cahuita near Playa Negra are **Cabinas Tito** *($$$; pb, ⊗; ☎755-0286)*, four clean and well-maintained *cabinas*.

**El Encanto** *($$$ bkfst incl.; pb, hw, ⊗; ☎755-0113)* is a Bed & Breakfast with three wooden, clean and very comfortable *cabinas*, run by Michael and Karen Russell. It is far enough away (300 m) from the village to relax, but still close to the action.

**Kelly Creek** *($$$; pb, hw, ℜ; ☎755-0007)* is just a few metres from the entrance of Parque Nacional Cahuita. The attractive wooden *cabinas* are very clean and cosy. Kelly Creek also has a Spanish restaurant.

The **Sunshine Cabins** *($$$; pb, hw, ⊗, K; ☎755-0368)*, near Sol y Mar, has four *cabinas* with kitchenettes.

The **Tropicana Bed & Breakfast** *($$$ bkfst incl.; pb, hw, ⊗, P; ☎755-0059, borgato@sol.racsa.co.cr)*, on Playa Negra and about two kilometres from the village, has five rooms with balconies overlooking the sea, a terrace and hammocks.

**Villas Exoticas Cahuita** *($$$; pb, ec, ℝ, K; ☎755-0005)* are 11 small houses near the Parque Nacional Cahuita. When the owners are away, they rent their houses by the day or week. Each house has a kitchen and a bathroom with hot water.

The **Alby Lodge** *($$$; pb, hw, ⊗, ♯; ☎/⇌755-0031)* rents out beautiful wooden *cabinas* with thatched roofs, which can accommodate four people. Since they are located only 200 metres from Cahuita national park, the *cabinas* are surrounded by trees and tropical gardens.

As its name indicates, **Chalet y Cabinas Hibiscus** *($$$-$$$$; pb, hw, ℝ, K, ≈, P; ☎755-0021, ⇌755-0015)* rents lovely wood *cabinas*, as well as two fully equipped cottages. Located over two kilometres from Cahuita, on Playa Negra, this establishment also has a pool, a volleyball court, a pool table and a bar.

The **Hotel Jaguar** *($$$-$$$$ bkfst incl.; pb, hw, ≈, ℜ; ☎755-0238, ⇌226-4693, jaguar@sol.racsa.co.cr)*, with 45 rooms, is the largest hotel in Cahuita. Located just over a kilometre from the village, on Playa Negra, it has clean, airy rooms, half of which are luxury suites. There are also a restaurant, a bar, a pool, a few short hiking trails and a floral garden.

The **Atlantida Lodge** *($$$$ bkfst incl.; pb, hw, ⊗, ≈, ℜ; ☎/⇌755-0213, atlantis@sol.racsa.co.cr)*, beside the football field, is a mini-hotel complex containing 30 rooms, managed by French Canadian Lucas Généreux. The rooms are attractive and comfortable and are surrounded by a tropical garden. There are also a restaurant, which serves local and international cuisine, a bar, a gym, a pool and a medical clinic. The Atlantida Lodge offers different guided tours of the region.

Over two kilometres from Cahuita, near the Playa Negra, **Magellan Inn** *($$$$ bkfst incl.; pb, hw, ⊗, ≈, ℜ; ☎/⇌755-0035)* has a calm, relaxing and warm environment. There are six lovely, large, very clean and airy rooms with private terraces and deckchairs. Breakfast is served on the poolside terrace, which is surrounded by trees and exotic plants. The landscaping has been so thoughtfully laid out that it even attracts various species of birds! A small path leads to an excellent restaurant, La Casa Creole (see p 171), run by Terri and Hervé, daughter and son-in-law of Elizabeth Newton, the friendly hotel owner.

## The Puerto Viejo de Talamanca Region

Like Cahuita, the village of Puerto Viejo de Talamanca has plenty of hotels and restaurants. For the past few years, the number of establishments has been on the rise, especially along the road to Manzanillo.

Contact the **Terra Aventuras Tourist Information Centre** *(☎750-0004)* or the **ATEC** *(☎/⇌750-0188)* for a list of hotels in the area. Before this hotel boom, it was difficult to find a vacancy without a reservation. The competition has also served to lower the prices of rooms.

### Puerto Viejo de Talamanca

In the village of Puerto Viejo de Talamanca, you can camp right beside the **Cabinas Salsa Brava**. **Hotel Puerto Viejo** may have camping sites available, but it is best to inquire ahead of time.

Two of the cheapest places to stay in Puerto Viejo are the **Hotel Kiskadee** *($; sb)*, just a few minutes' walk from the football field, and **Cashew Hill** *($-$$; sb)*, right next to the field. They are like youth hostels, with dormitory-style rooms, access to the kitchen and a friendly atmosphere.

The **Cabinas Diti** *($; pb)*, near the Hotel Maritza, has four *cabinas* with private bathrooms and are among the cheapest in the area.

The **Cabinas Zully** *($; sb)* are located near the Black Sand Beach, approximately two kilometres west of Puerto Viejo de Talamanca. The area is quiet, the rooms relatively plain, and there is a stove available for cooking.

**Los Almendros** *($; pb; ☎750-0099)* is located behind the Terra Aventuras tourist information centre. Rooms are plain, but clean and comfortable.

The **Cabinas Salsa Brava** *($-$$; pb, ⊗)* are among the only affordable *cabinas* with private bathrooms and ocean views. There is also a café, open all day.

In the middle of the village, **Hotel Puerto Viejo** *($-$$; pb/sb)* has thirty inexpensive rooms, some with private bathrooms. Since the hotel is popular with surfers, it can get rather noisy at times. The upstairs rooms are better.

**Cabinas Black Sand** *($$; sb, ℝ, K, #; ☎750-0124)* is an inexpensive place, about two kilometres west of the village, on the beach. The small *bribrí*-style house has four rustic rooms and a shared kitchen where you can prepare your own meals. Whether you are in a group (better deal) or on your own, the Californian owners Darcy and Victor will do everything to make your stay a pleasant one.

The **Cabinas Chimuri** *($$; sb; ☎750-0119)* is in the mountains, over two kilometres from Puerto Viejo de Talamanca, and quite well-known. There are rustic *bribrí*-style *cabinas* made out of bamboo with thatched roofs and a shared kitchen. If the manager is around, he can tell you all about traditional *bribrí* culture.

West of the village, on a small, quiet road leading to the Botanical Gardens, there are the **Cabinas Maribe** *($$; ⊗; ☎750-0182)*, with simple, but decent rooms, and **Cabinas Playa Negra** *($-$$; pb, K; ☎556-1132)*, with small two- or three-room houses with kitchens. Prices are more than reasonable for groups of four to six.

The new **Coco Loco Lodge** *($$; pb, hw, ⊗, #; ☎750-0188, atecmail@sol.racsa.co.cr)*, is located just outside the village. The two friendly Austrian owners, Sabine and Helmut, tastefully decorated the three attractive *cabinas* which are surrounded by lush vegetation.

The **Hotel Maritza** *($$; pb, hw, ⊗, ℝ, P; ☎/≠750-0003)* is in the centre of Puerto Viejo de Talamanca, but faces the sea, and has plain but comfortable rooms.

The **Hotel Pura Vida** *($$; sb/pb, hw, ⊗, P; ☎/≠750-0002)* has ten lovely, clean rooms. You can also make use of their kitchen. The hotel's large terrace and garden make it an excellent choice in downtown Puerto Viejo de Talamanca.

The **Cabinas Casa Verde** *($$-$$$; sb/pb, hw, ⊗, #, P; ☎750-0015, ≠750-0047, www.greenarrow.com/x/casaverd.htm)* is one of the area's best-priced hotels in terms of quality. Very clean and

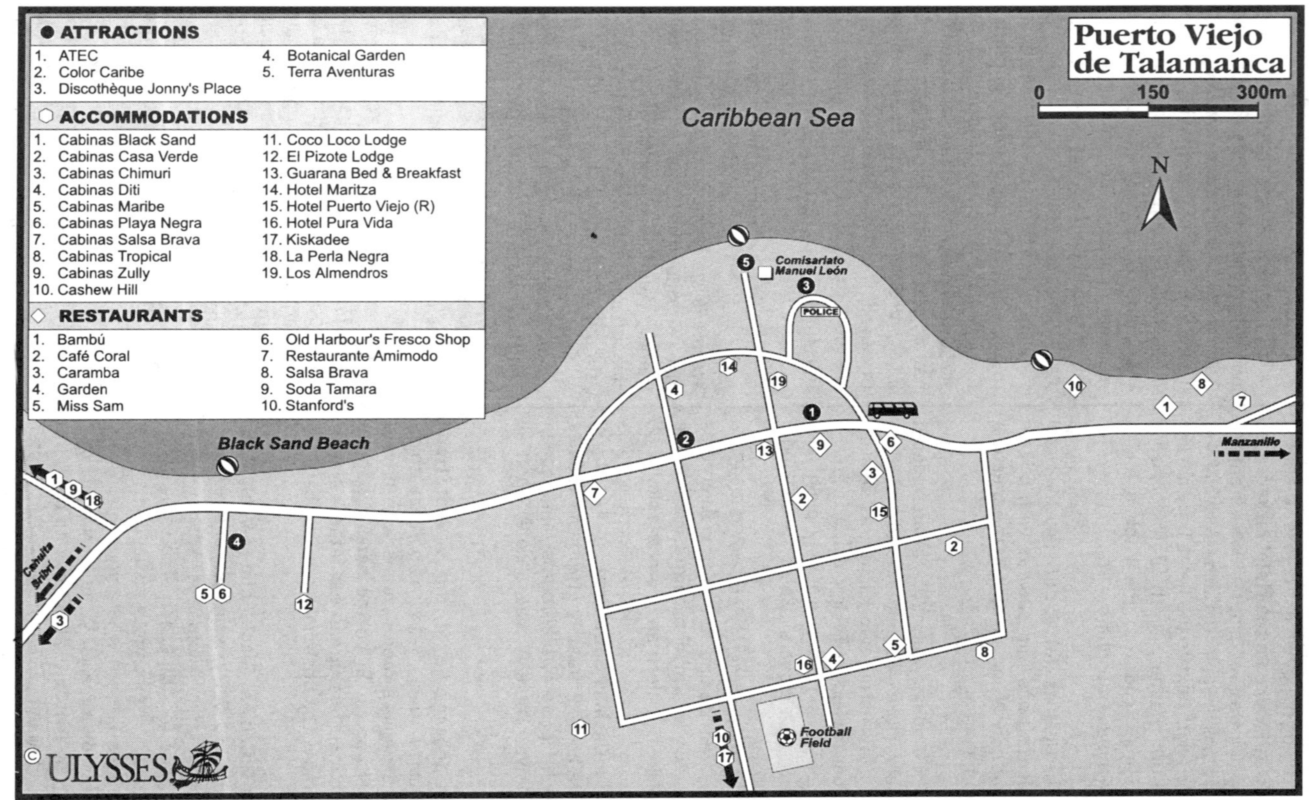
● ATTRACTIONS
1. ATEC
2. Color Caribe
3. Discothèque Jonny's Place
4. Botanical Garden
5. Terra Aventuras
ACCOMMODATIONS
1. Cabinas Black Sand
2. Cabinas Casa Verde
3. Cabinas Chimuri
4. Cabinas Diti
5. Cabinas Maribe
6. Cabinas Playa Negra
7. Cabinas Salsa Brava
8. Cabinas Tropical
9. Cabinas Zully
10. Cashew Hill
11. Coco Loco Lodge
12. El Pizote Lodge
13. Guarana Bed & Breakfast
14. Hotel Maritza
15. Hotel Puerto Viejo (R)
16. Hotel Pura Vida
17. Kiskadee
18. La Perla Negra
19. Los Almendros
◇ RESTAURANTS
1. Bambú
2. Café Coral
3. Caramba
4. Garden
5. Miss Sam
6. Old Harbour's Fresco Shop
7. Restaurante Amimodo
8. Salsa Brava
9. Soda Tamara
10. Stanford's
Puerto Viejo de Talamanca
0
150
300m
Caribbean Sea
N
Comisariato Manuel León
POLICE
Black Sand Beach
Manzanillo
Cahuita
Bribri
Football Field
© ULYSSES

soberly decorated, rooms have a balcony where you can relax in a hammock. A small, affordable house with a kitchen is also for rent. To complete the picture, there is a tropical garden with tiny venomous frogs.

In the centre of Puerto Viejo de Talamanca, near Mr. Pratt's Bakery, the brand-new **Guarana Bed & Breakfast** *($$-$$$ every day; pb, hw, ♯, P; ☎750-0034, ⇌750-0188)* has 12 very clean and comfortable rooms with balconies. The owners speak French, English and Italian, as well as Spanish.

The **Hotel La Perla Negra** *($$$; pb, hw, ⊗, ℜ, ≈; ☎750-0111, ⇌750-0114)*, is two kilometres west of the village, along a black-sand beach, and has three attractive, wooden buildings, each housing spacious, clean rooms with balconies. With a pool facing the sea, a restaurant and a bar, all in a tranquil setting, this hotel is a great choice outside of the village.

**Cabinas Tropical** *($$$; pb, ⊗)* has five clean and well-kept rooms. The buffet-style breakfast *($)* will help you start your day off right. Rates go down for longer stays. The owner, Harry, is a well-known guide throughout the region and organizes several outings in the area, the country and even to the magnificent islands in Parque Nacional Bastimentos Marine in Panama.

**El Pizote Lodge** *($$$-$$$$; pb/sb, ⊗, ℜ; ☎221-0986 or 750-0088, ⇌223-8838)* is one kilometre west of the village, amidst tropical gardens and wilderness. There are eight rooms, six *cabinas* and a house. The owners plan to build a large pool and luxury houses. A bar and restaurant complete the picture.

**Between Puerto Viejo de Talamanca and Playa Salsa Brava**

Just before Escape Caribeño (see further below), a large, pink house called the **Coconut Grove** *($$; pb, hw; ☎/⇌750-0093)* offers clean rooms, a shared kitchen and free coffee.

**Cabinas Calalú** *($$-$$$; pb, K, ℜ; ☎750-0042)* come with kitchenettes. All are clean and comfortable, and surrounded by luscious tropical vegetation.

With the large sign on its fence, you can't miss **Cabinas David** *($$-$$$)*. The eight clean and attractive attached *cabinas*.

Across the street from Cabinas David, **Cabinas Yucca** *($$-$$$; pb)* has four bungalows with king-size beds and a veranda facing the beach.

The **Costa de Papito** *($$$; pb, ⊗; ☎/⇌750-0080, www.greenarrow.com/x/papito.htm)* rents four charming *cabinas* in lush greenery.

The **Escape Caribeño Bungalows** *($$$; pb, hw, ⊗, ♯; ☎750-0103)* has pretty little *cabinas* with a ceramic-tiled terrace, mosquito net and hammock.

**Cariblue Bungalows** *($$$$ bkfst incl.; pb, hw; ☎/⇌750-0057)* are run by an Italian couple, Sandra and Leonardo. The *cabinas* are simple, but comfortable, and set in a garden with fruit trees.

**Playa Salsa Brava and Playa Cocles**

The **Cabinas Surf Point** *($-$$; sb/pb, ⊗; ☎750-0123)* are owned by Nelida, a local woman. Half of the six *cabinas* have private washrooms. All look out onto the world-famous surf beach,

Salsa Brava, and are therefore popular with surfers.

The three brand-new **Cabinas Eltesoro** *($$$; pb, hw; ☎750-0128)* sleep two to five people each, and are huge and clean. Home-made bread is served for breakfast (not included). Carmen, one of the owners, also sells jewellery that she makes.

**Isla Inn** *($$$; pb, hw, ⊗; ☎750-0188)* is a large wooden house with four rooms (one downstairs and three upstairs), an expansive veranda, hammocks and a wonderful view. At press time, the house was up for sale.

### Playa Chiquita

Near Playa Chiquita, you can go **camping** beside the dirt-cheap **Irie Cabinas** *($)*.

**Cabinas Villa Paraíso** *($$$; pb, hw)* has eight bungalows surrounded by a garden, all beside the La Paloma Café Restaurant.

Surrounded by a lovely garden, **Hotel Kashá** *($$$; pb, hw; ☎288-2563 or 750-0127, ⇄222-2213)* has six rooms and two houses for rent. The rooms are large and clean, with hammocks on the terrace. The Reef Café serves breakfast and drinks.

The hotel-restaurant **Yaré** *($$$; pb, hw, ⊗, ℜ; ☎/⇄750-0106)* rents 21 *cabinas* and a big house. The brightly coloured *cabinas* are clean and well maintained. The *cabinas* are connected by raised wooden walkways which go through dense, peaceful vegetation.

The **Playa Chiquita Lodge** *($$$ bkfst incl.; pb, ⊗; ☎/⇄750-0062, wolfbiss@sol.racsa.co.cr)* rents wooden *cabinas* that blend in perfectly with their natural surroundings, only 50 metres from the sea and a spectacular white-sand beach. Each *cabina* is very clean and has a private bathroom plus a veranda with hammocks and rocking chairs for relaxation. There are also three well-equipped houses for rent. They plan to open a "jungle health spa". The manager, Wanda Bissinger, is also the founding editor of a very interesting little newspaper, *Talamanca's Voice* (see p 145).

**Cabinas La Caracola** *($$$$; pb, hw, ⊗, K; ☎750-0135)*, facing the sea, has colourful double rooms with kitchens.

The brand-new **Casa Camarona** *($$$$; pb, hw, ℜ; ☎750-0151 or 224-3050, ⇄750-0151 or 222-6184, camarona@ticonet.co.cr)* has 18 lovely rooms with an ocean view. The wonderful restaurant, Lapalapa, is in another building (see p 172).

The **Best Western Hotel Punta Cocles** *($$$$; pb, hw, ≡, ⊗, ≈ ℜ, ⊛, ctv; ☎234-8055, ⇄234-8033)* has 60 air-conditioned rooms, a pool, whirlpool, children's play area and a private section of the beach just 500 metres from the hotel, where there are also showers, a bar, and a restaurant. Your typical large, chain hotel.

The **Miraflores Lodge** *($$$$ bkfst incl.; pb/sb, ⊗; ☎750-0038 or 233-2822, mirapam@sol.racsa.co.cr)* has eight rooms, some quite large with private bathrooms. This Bed & Breakfast is tastefully decorated, even on the outside with exotic plants and countless heliconias. Pamela Carpenter, the owner, is very interested in the environment, agriculture and culture of the region. She organizes outings to the Kéköldi reserve.

**Villas del Caribe** *($$$$; pb, hw, ⊗; ☎233-2200, ⇄221-2801)* has

12 apartments with a spectacular view of the beach from their balconies.

The 12 enormous palm-roofed *cabinas* at the **Hotel Shawandha** *($$$$$ bkfst incl.; pb, hw, ℜ; ☎750-0018, ≠750-0037)* are perfect for rest and relaxation. Each is tastefully decorated in its own particular style and has a bright bathroom by French ceramist Filou Pascal. El Rancho, the restaurant, serves refined cuisine (see p 172). A short 200-metre trail leads to a beautiful white-sand beach.

### Punta Uva

Although **Selvin's Restaurant & Cabinas** *($; sb, ℜ)* has modest rooms, the restaurant is said to be one of the best in the region (see p 172).

Not far from Punta Uva, **Cabinas Casa Angela** *($$-$$$ bkfst incl.; pb, hw; ≠750-0144)* are owned by Angela, a very friendly Swiss woman, who makes sure that everything runs smoothly.

The former Las Palmas hotel is now two separate hotels: Palm Beach and Talamanca Caribe. The **Palm Beach** *($$$$-$$$$$; pb, hw, ≡, ℝ; ☎255-3939, ≠750-0049)* has been turned into a luxury hotel. The **Talamanca Caribe** *($$$$; pb, hw, ≡, ⊗, ≈, ℜ, tv; ☎750-0181, ≠750-0196, talamanc@sol.racsa.co.cr)* has 40 spacious rooms, a restaurant and many open-air facilities (pool, tennis courts, basketball courts, etc.) For sportive types.

## The Manzanillo Region

Camping is permitted at the Refugio Nacional de Vida Silvestre Gandoca-Manzanillo, but since there are neither designated sites nor services, most people prefer to sleep in the village of Manzanillo or in Puerto Viejo de Talamanca.

**Maxi's Cabinas** *($; sb; near the bus stop)*, located in the small village of Manzanillo, rents out rooms and has a restaurant, bar and nightclub (open on weekends). This place is definitely not one of the quietest on the Caribbean coast!

The **Almonds and Corals Lodge Tent Camp** *($$$$; pb, ⊗, ℜ; 8 km south of Puerto Viejo, ☎272-2024, ≠272-2220, almonds@sol.racsa.co.cr)*, 300 metres off the road to the beach, deserves a four-star rating for camping. The 20 *cabinas* are nothing more than a roof covered by a giant mosquito net, under which there are a tent, table, washroom and hammock. Each *cabina* is connected to the others by a wooden walkway, which also leads to the restaurant and superb white-sand beach. This establishment belongs to Geo Expediciones, a tour operator that organizes outdoor excursions on land and water.

## The Tortuguero Region

There are sites for camping near the entrance to the **Parque Nacional Tortuguero**. Because it rains a lot in this region, you might want to rent one of the reasonably priced *cabinas* near the park, instead.

Since the Tortuguero region, which includes Parismina and Barra del Colorado, is difficult to access (airplane or boat only), you should reserve a place to stay ahead of time. Most of the local hotels offer two- or three-day all-inclusive packages (transportation, accommodation, food, guided activities, etc.). Many tourists have told us that in retrospect they regretted having opted for the 2 day/1 night package (with boat transport) instead of the 3 day/2 night one, which would have allowed them to see more of the region. Furthermore, the boat trip also includes a long bus trip, so getting to Tortuguero takes the better part of a day.

If you want to go to Tortuguero on your own and stay in one of the village's low-budget hotels, you can take the boat from Moín (near Puerto Limón).

On the second canal, on the Penitencia Lagoon, a few minutes from the village by boat, the **Cabinas Tatané** *($; sb; ☎223-2240)* are nothing fancy, but cheap.

The **Caribe Lodge** *($$; sb, ℜ; ☎224-3348, pager 233-3333)*, on the Penitencia Lagoon, has nine very rustic *cabinas* with a shared bathroom for up to 30 people. Transportation to the village is free, and excursions along the different canals costs $5 per person.

The new owner of **Caribbean Magic Eco-Lodge** *($$$; pb, hw, ⊗, ≈, ℜ; ☎258-3536)* wants to completely redo this 16-room hotel. A lovely garden surrounds the small pool. A room for two people costs $45, while a stay of three days and two nights is $245 per person (including bus and boat transportation, room and meals).

The small **Manati Lodge** *($$$ bkfst incl.; pb, ⊗, ℜ; ☎383-0330)* was built in 1980. Its six rooms are plain, but pleasant, and very affordable for a hotel right on the Tortuguero canal. The owner, Fernando Figuls, offers excursions along the canals and in Parque Nacional Tortuguero. This lodge also has a games room for the whole family and a small bar.

**Hotel Ilan-Ilan** *($$$$ fb; pb, ⊗, ℜ; Agencia Mitur, ☎255-2262 or 255-2031, ⇄255-1946, mitour@sol.racsa.co.cr)* is located about three kilometres from the village in the middle of lush tropical vegetation. The hotel was built in 1989 and named for a tree, the *Cananga odorata*, which is almost exclusive to the area and produces pretty yellow flowers. There are 24 clean and comfortable *cabinas* in a row. A 3 day/2 night stay costs $220 per person (including bus and boat transportation, room and meals).

The **Jungle Lodge** *($$$$; pb, hw, ⊗, ℜ; ☎233-0133 or 233-0155, ⇄233-0778, cotour@sol.racsa.co.cr)* is a bit outdated, but charming. Its 50 rooms are clean and comfortable. There are also several activities such as hiking on the 400-metre trail near the hotel. Three days and two nights costs $235 per person (including bus and boat transportation, room and meals), whereas two days and one night is $175.

The **Laguna Lodge** *($$$$; pb, ⊗, ℜ; ☎225-3740 or 280-7843, ⇄283-8031)* is one of the only two lodges near the village, and has direct access to the beach. There are 27 attractive and very clean rooms, divided into 7 sections of 4 rooms. This lodge is peaceful and well kept. A three day/two night package costs $235 per person (including bus and boat transportation, room and meals).

The **Mawamba Lodge** *($$$$; pb, hw, ⊗, ≈, ℜ; ☎223-7490 or 223-2421, ⇄222-5463, mawamba@sol.racsa.co.cr)* is the only lodge within walking distance of the village (approx. 1 km). There is a short trail to the beach. The 36 wood-built rooms are extremely pleasant and clean. Mawamba also has a restaurant, a bar, a souvenir shop and a conference room, where slide shows of the regional flora and fauna are presented. The centrepiece of this lodge is its fanciful pool with its small bridge, where you can relax between excursions organized by the hotel. Three days/two nights costs $250 per person (including bus and boat transportation, room and meals).

The **Pachira Lodge** *($$$$; pb, hw, ⊗, ℜ; ☎256-7080, ⇛223-1119)* is just outside the village of Tortuguero. It is one of the most attractive and charming hotels in the region, with 34 clean rooms, tastefully decorated in pastels. The hotel was mainly built of wood, and still smells like freshly chopped timber (built in 1995). It also has a superb restaurant, a bar, a small souvenir shop, a games room and two short hiking trails. They plan to add a pool soon. The cost is $260 per person for 3 nights/2 days (including transportation by bus and boat, room and meals).

The **Tortuga Lodge** *($$$$$; pb, hw, ⊗, ℜ; ☎257-0766 or 222-0333, ⇛257-1665, costaric@expeditions.co.cr)* is owned by the famous Costa Rica Expeditions. The tour agency lives up to its reputation by offering a hotel with unparalleled ambience, rooms, food and service. Here, they pull out all the stops to insure a pleasant and memorable stay. They also plan to put in a pool in early 1999. In 1996, the rooms and landscaping were redone to blend in better with the natural surroundings. The impeccable rooms, four per building, are luxurious and spacious and have huge windows on three walls. The bathrooms are large, practical and luxurious. Rooms on the upper floors share a large covered terrace spanning the entire exterior, where you can take in the serene view of the canals and the forest. A small trail behind the hotel (remember to bring your insect repellent!) leads through the dense, enchanting forest. Some of the many species you may encounter include the magnificent small, brightly coloured, venomous frogs. The stylish restaurant, with its long terrace, is located on the waterfront, and serves some of the best meals in the country – one evening, we were even served gargantuan plates of all-you-can-eat fresh shrimp! The large tables are close together, making it easy to meet fellow travellers. The Tortuga Lodge also has some of the best guides in the region, from whom you will certainly learn a lot about the impressive flora and fauna. The organized activities are many, from sea turtle watching to tarpon fishing, to nature watching along the canals and climbing the Cerro Tortuguero. A stay of three nights and two days costs $459 per person (including transportation by airplane and boat/bus, accommodation, meals, and a guided tour of the canals). For $105 per person, you can stay an additional night (three meals included).

### Tortuguero Village

The **Cabinas Aracari Lodge** *($; pb; ☎798-3059)*, behind the football field, has rooms with private bathrooms for as little as $10.

The **Cabinas de Sabina** *($; sb/pb, ℜ)* has several rooms, three with private bathroom. **Cabinas Meryscar** *($; sb)* has very simple rooms that costr next to nothing. The **Cabinas Riverside** *($$; pb)* and **Bananera** *($; sb)* also have modest rooms at modest prices.

At the northern end of the village, the **Cabinas Miss Junie** *($$$; pb, ⊗; ☎710-0523)* have very clean rooms with private bathrooms, as well as an excellent restaurant (see p 173).

**Parismina**

A stay at **Chito's Lodge** *($$$$; pb, hw, ≈, ℜ; ☎768-8636)* includes transportation, room and board starting at $75 per day per person. The rooms are clean, and the gardens around the pool are very pretty. You can also take a day-long nature excursion *($45/person)* about local flora and fauna.

The **Caribbean Expedition Lodge** *($$$$$; pb, hw, ℜ; ☎512-992-5753, ⇄512-884-8740)*, located at the mouth of the Río Parismina, offers fishing packages, including transportation, room and board, and the excursion starting at $230 per day per person.

The **Río Parismina Lodge** *($$$$$; pb, hw, ≡, ℜ, ≈; ☎257-3553)* offers good fishing packages. A three-day stay including transportation, room, and fishing excursions costs approximately $1,500 per person. The 12 rooms are very clean and comfortable. The lodge also has magnificent tropical gardens and a few short hiking trails through the forest.

## Barra del Colorado

The **Tarponland Lodge** *($$-$$$; pb, hw, ⊗; ☎383-6097, ⇄710-6592)*, on the south side of the Río Colorado, is definitely the cheapest place to stay in the region and offers fishing and nature expeditions.

North of the Río Colorado, the **Tropical Tarpon Lodge** *($$$; pb, ⊗; ☎242-2701)* has lovely, simple rooms at competitive prices. Horseback riding excursions are offered on the Agua Dulce beach, and to other places in the area. The hotel is open between December and April, and the month of September.

Less than 10 kilometres south of Barra del Colorado, the **Samay Lagoon Lodge** *($$$-$$$$; pb, hw, ℜ; ☎284-7047, ⇄234-0646)* sets itself apart from others with its combination hiking and fishing excursions. A boat will take you to the lodge via Puerto Viejo de Sarapiquí. A stay of 3 days/2 nights costs at least $200 a person (including boat transportation, room, meals and guided tour).

The **Río Colorado Fishing Lodge** *($$$$; pb, hw, ≡, ⊗, ℜ; ☎232-8610, ⇄231-5987, tarpon4u@cyperspy.com)*, on the south side of the river of the same name, is the most famous hotel in the region. Founded by Archie Fields, but now managed by Dan Wise, it is one of the best places to relax, eat well, and, in particular, go on guided fishing expeditions *($360/person/day)* to catch one of the famous gigantic tarpons for which the area is known. The non-fishing "nature" package *(2 days/1 night, $196 per person)* includes meals, accommodation and boat transportation from Puerto Viejo de Sarapiquí to Barra del Colorado on the first day, then on to the hotel in Moín (near Puerto Limón) after visiting the Parque Nacional de Tortuguero on the second day.

The **Casa Mar Fishing Lodge** *($$$$$; pb, hw, ⊗, ℜ; ☎433-8834, ⇄433-9287)*, north of Barra del Colorado, on the Agua Dulce Lagoon, has clean, comfortable *cabinas*. This hotel offers one-week fishing trips ($1,995 a person, all-inclusive, including air transportation from San José), but also has a number of shorter packages. The hotel is only open during the fishing seasons (January to mid-March and September to October).

Just south of the Casa Mar Fishing Lodge, **Isla de Pesca** *($$$$$; pb, hw, ⊗, ℜ; ☎223-4560, ⇄221-5148)* has 20 A-frame *cabinas* with thatched roofs. Packages are available from three to seven days for both fishing ($1,000 to $1,400) and nature observation, which will take you mostly around the Parque Nacional de Tortuguero.

The ***Rain Goddess*** *($$$$$; sb, hw, ≡, ℜ; ☎231-4299, ⇌231-3816)* is a luxurious 20-metre-long houseboat belonging to Dr. Alfredo López. There are six spacious, comfortable *cabinas* and a well-equipped "restaurant"-kitchen that serves refined cuisine. There are fishing and nature excursions. A 3 day/2 night package starts at $475 per person (including transportation by car from San José to Puerto Viejo de Sarapiquí, transportation by boat to the *Rain Goddess*, room, meals, drinks and return trip to San José).

The **Silver King Lodge** *($$$$$; pb, hw, ⊗, ≈, ℜ; ☎/⇌381-1403)*, south of the Río Colorado Fishing Lodge, has a great reputation in the area for fishing, and for its comfortable hotel. The rooms are very clean and large. The restaurant serves high-quality food, and the hotel adds some extra touches (free soft drinks, beer and coffee, coffee makers in the rooms, etc.) to make your stay all the more enjoyable. The hotel rents out guides and boats for fishing excursions, mostly for tarpon, which the area is known for. A four night/three day fishing package costs $1,300 per person, including airplane, hotel in San José, accommodation at the Silver King Lodge, meals, drinks and the fishing excursion. Canoes, with or without guides, can be rented to explore the natural surroundings.

## RESTAURANTS

### Puerto Limón

In Puerto Limón, there are many quaint restaurants and *sodas*, which mostly serve Caribbean cuisine and cheap fish dishes. Several hotels have restaurants, which are open to everyone.

Three of the most popular *sodas* with residents and travellers alike are **La Estrella** *($-$$; Calle 5, Avenida 3)*, where the atmosphere, service, food and prices are excellent; the very pretty **Soda Mares** *($; Avenida 2, Calle 3/4)* with a varied, low-priced menu, and the exciting atmosphere of the nearby *mercado*; and the inexpensive **Soda Yans** *($; Avenida 2, Calle 5/6)*, a local hangout.

**Brisas del Caribe** *($-$$; Calle 1, Avenida 2)*, beside Vargas Park, is the place to go for a reasonably priced sandwich or a *casado* (rice, beans, tomatoes, cole slaw, egg and meat), or just a coffee. At the end of the day, music takes you into the evening.

**Arrecife** *($$; ☎758-4030)* is a good seafood restaurant on the way to Playa Bonita.

A bit further along the road to Playa Bonita is **Springfield** *($$; ☎758-1203)*, popular for its savoury Caribbean, fish and seafood dishes.

**Kimbambú** *($$-$$$)*, facing Playa Bonita, is a good place to try Caribbean specialties, including fish, soup, chicken and *ceviche* dishes.

## Cahuita

The small village of Cahuita has about two dozen restaurants for all tastes and budgets. Most of these serve local Caribbean-style cuisine with lots of fish and coconut. Some also have international cuisine, such as Chinese, French, Italian, Swiss, Spanish and German dishes.

In addition to the restaurants below, many hotels also have a restaurant or *soda*.

If you have a craving for a good cake or pastry, stop by the **Pastry Shop** *($; 9am to 6pm; ☎755-0275)*, near Playa Negra, approximately 350 metres from the village.

**Wallace Village** *($; 7am to 7pm)*, a *soda* in front of the Turística Cahuita, serves Creole cuisine.

**El Cactus** *($-$$; 5pm to 10pm; ☎755-0276)* is a pizzeria which serves good pasta, just outside the village.

You can enjoy good pizza, pasta and other Italian dishes for little money at the **Delle Alpi** *($-$$; every day noon to 10pm; ☎755-0230)* at the Cahuita Hotel.

The restaurant at the **Hotel National Park** *($-$$; 7am to 10pm; ☎755-0244)* serves Costa Rican and international dishes at reasonable prices. People mostly come here for a drink during happy hour while taking in the incredible vista of the sea.

**Miss Edith** *($-$$; 7am to 9pm, closed Sun; ☎755-0248)*, near the post office and police station, is quite well-known and somewhat busy, and with good reason: it serves excellent, cheap local dishes. The decor is pretty basic, with a few closely placed wooden tables, but the place is clean, and freshly painted orange.

**Pizzería Emilio** *($-$$; 4pm to 11pm; ☎755-0063)*, beside the municipal park, serves pizzas and other fast food. Also near the municipal park, but right on the main street, **Caribbean Food** *($-$$; 7:30am to 7pm)* serves delicious low-priced local cuisine.

The tiny downtown restaurant **La Soda** *($-$$; every day 7am to 8pm; ☎755-0055)* has terrific breakfasts with fresh fruit, prepared by Quebecker Mario, who lives right beside it. From lunch until closing, two chefs, one an amusing Italian, the other a Costa Rican from the area, prepare good, inexpensive local specialties. They sing and joke with their guests while preparing tasty piña coladas.

**Sobre Las Olas** *($-$$)*, 600 metres from the village, serves international continental cuisine. With windows everywhere, you can enjoy a superb view of the sea, making this place very popular at happy hour.

Southwest of the village, **El Típico** *($-$$; 5pm to 10pm; ☎755-0118)* serves affordable Caribbean and international cuisine.

**Vishnú** *($-$$; 7am to 4pm; ☎755-0263)* specializes in Italian food. Therefore it does not belong to the San José restaurant chain of the same name, but it does serve great vegetarian breakfasts with homemade bread.

At the **Vista del Mar** *($-$$; 7:30am to 10pm; ☎755-0008)*, near the entrance to Cahuita national park, you can eat a gigantic plate of Chinese food for next to nothing. However, the service is often very slow.

**Cha Cha Cha** *($$-$$$; evenings only)*, next to Cahuita Tours, is owned by a Quebecker. It specializes in *del mundo* cuisine, including pasta, seafood and steak. Although the place is tastefully decorated in blue and white, the chairs made of tree trunks are quite uncomfortable.

The **Margaritaville Restaurant** *($$-$$$; evenings only, closed Wed; 2 km west of the village, Playa Negra, ☎755-0038)*, in Moray's Bed & Breakfast (see p 159), is undeniably charming. It is located on the second floor, completely finished in wood, has an open-air kitchen and a friendly, family atmosphere. Run by Canadian Sandra Simla, the restaurant makes typical Caribbean and Canadian dishes from home-grown produce.

The **Casa Creole** *($$$-$$$$; evenings only, closed Sun; ☎755-0104)* is two kilometres from the city, and about half a kilometre from Playa Negra. If you are looking for great food in a warm ambiance, this is the place to go. Owned by Hervé and Terri, La Casa serves delicious Creole and French cuisine, with many fish dishes, especially the succulent *ceviche*. The desserts are hard to resist, especially the *profiteroles* and homemade sorbet.

## The Puerto Viejo de Talamanca Region

### Puerto Viejo de Talamanca

At the **Bambu Restaurant** *($; as you leave the village towards Manzanillo, next to Stanford's Restaurant)*, fresh food is always available, but people come here especially to spend a few hours listening to the reggae music.

The **Café Coral** *($; one street west of the ATEC, then south)* serves the best breakfast in town. You can savour the delicious homemade bread, yogurt, muesli and crepes. Their chocolate cake is supposedly divine.

The **Monchies** *($)* is a pastry shop that opens at 6am and serves excellent whole-wheat bread and breakfasts.

At **Miss Sam** *($; one street east and two streets south of the ATEC)*, you can enjoy reasonably priced Caribbean specialties such as fish, rice and beans. Good value for the money.

The **Old Harbour's Fresco Shop** *($)*, opposite the bus stop, serves tasty breakfasts with homemade whole-wheat bread. You can also order cheap, tasty fish dishes.

Next to the Bambu Restaurant, the restaurant-café **Salsa Brava** *($)* now serves breakfast.

**MexiTico** *($-$$)* at the Puerto Viejo Hotel (see p 161) prepares great Mexican and vegetarian cuisine.

**Stanford's Restaurant** *($-$$; as you exit the village towards Manzanillo, near the sea)* serves reasonably-priced seafood and Caribbean cuisine. It has a popular nightclub, open on weekends.

**Tamara** *($-$$; in front of the ATEC)* is a *soda* that serves breakfasts and local dishes, such as the Rundown, a seafood soup. You can also eat good lobster dishes without spending too much.

**Caramba** *($$; one street east of the ATEC, on the right)* serves gigantic pizzas and good desserts.

The **Garden Restaurant** *($$)*, near the football field, is a favourite with tourists and locals. It serves Caribbean, Asian and vegetarian dishes, as well as good desserts and fresh fruit.

The **Restaurante Amimodo** *($$)*, near the western end of the village, specializes in Italian food, as well as fish and seafood. The owner is in the process of opening up a new restaurant in town, so he left his son in charge of the restaurant in Puerto Viejo.

#### Playa Salsa Brava and Playa Cocles

Beside the Cabinas Surf Point, opposite the world-class Salsa Brava surfing beach, **Beach Creak** *($-$$, Playa Salsa Brava)* serves breakfast and sandwiches.

**Extravaganzia Art Café** *($-$$; Playa Cocles)* prepares excellent Italian food at a good price, all in a relaxed ambiance and decor. Creations of local artists are also on display.

The incredible restaurant **Lapalapa** *($$-$$$; Playa Cocles, ☎750-0151 or 224-3050)* is in a new building next to La Casa Camarona Hotel. The large terrace is decorated in matte and subdued tones. On the menu are fresh fish and seafood as well as typically Caribbean and Jamaican dishes.

#### Playa Chiquita

**Elena's Restaurante** *($-$$)*, owned by Elena Brown, is recommended for its tasty fish and local dishes.

Also on the Playa Chiquita, the **Paloma Café** *($-$$; next to the Cabinas Villa Paraiso)* has Caribbean and international cuisine as well as seafood.

Nearby, the **Soda Aquarius** *($-$$)* is open for breakfast and dinner, but with reservations only.

**El Rancho** *($$$; ☎750 0018)*, at the Shawandha Hotel (see p 165), serves simple yet refined tropical French cuisine in a warm and pleasant atmosphere.

#### Punta Uva

**Soda y Restaurant Naturales** *($-$$; right before Punta Uva, coming from Puerto Viejo de Talamanca)* is just off the main road and has an incredible view of the sea. You can eat breakfasts complete with homemade bread, as well as other dishes, and admire the local crafts that decorate the restaurant.

**Selvin's Restaurant** *($-$$; Wed to Sun)* is one of the best in the region. It is good and cheap, and serves the most delicious Caribbean and fish dishes. This open-air restaurant is rather small, but a pleasant atmosphere prevails.

Across from the Punta Uva *pulpería*, just before the small trail leading to the magnificent summit, **El Duende Feliz** *($$-$$$)* is good value for Italian dishes. Moreno and Fabrizio assure a great atmosphere and service.

In Manzanillo, the restaurant-bar **Maxi** *($$-$$$; near the bus stop)* serves fresh seafood.

### The Tortuguero Region

For a village as small as Tortuguero, it is surprising to find eight *sodas*, or small restaurants, in addition to the restaurants, hotels and lodges located in the surrounding area. *Sodas* such as **El Dólar** *($-$$; near Tienda de Artesanía)*, **El Tucán** *($-$$; north of the medical clinic)*, **Liliana** *($-$$; near the medical clinic)* and **La Canoa** *($-$$; near the Parque Nacional Tortuguero information centre)*, and restaurants such as **Brisas del Mar** *($-$$; behind* *the school)* and **Meryscar** *($-$$; southwest of the football field)*, serve excellent homemade Caribbean food, as well as North American dishes such as sandwiches. **Miss Junie** *($-$$; north of the village)* prepares great chicken, fish and steak, whereas **Pancana** *($-$$; southwest of the football field)* offers sandwiches and other dishes, such as excellent homemade brioches.

## ENTERTAINMENT

### Cahuita

The most popular spot in Cahuita, especially on a Saturday night, is the **Vaz**, where you can listen to reggae music as well as salsa and merengue.

**Jimmy's** is a very popular spot to play pool. You can also play chess or checkers while listening to rock 'n roll and blues.

The other hip place in town is the **Sarafina**, which plays international music and serves reasonably-priced food, including pizza.

### Puerto Viejo de Talamanca

The **Bambú** *(as you leave the village towards Manzanillo)* is a bar that plays reggae music.

The locals hang out at **Stanford's** *(as you leave the village, past the football field, near the sea)*, a nightclub mixing reggae, calypso and salsa.

The most popular nightclub among tourists in the region is **Jonny's Place** *(near the police station)*, which plays international music. It gets packed after 10pm.

**Manzanillo**

The **Maxi** bar *(near the bus stop)* becomes a dance club on weekends.

## SHOPPING

### Puerto Limón

**Helennik Souvenirs** *(Calle 3, Avenida 4/5)* sells local crafts and clothing.

### Cahuita

T-shirts, original clothing, jewellery and many reggae-style items are sold at: **Bumbata**, **Cahuita Soul** and **Coco Miko**.

### Puerto Viejo de Talamanca

**Color Caribe** *(main street, ☎750-0075)* sells original T-shirts, jewellery, hammocks and crafts. **ATEC** *(main street, ☎750-0188)* sells some books, maps and other documentation on the area. **Terra Aventuras** *(beside the Comisariato Manuel León, by the beach, ☎750-0004)* also sells local crafts.

### Tortuguero

**Paraíso Tropical**, **Jungle Shop** and **Tienda de Artesanía**, all downtown, sell regional souvenirs.

The natural history museum **CCC** *(just outside the village)* (see p 150) has a small souvenir shop inside (documentation, videos, books, etc).

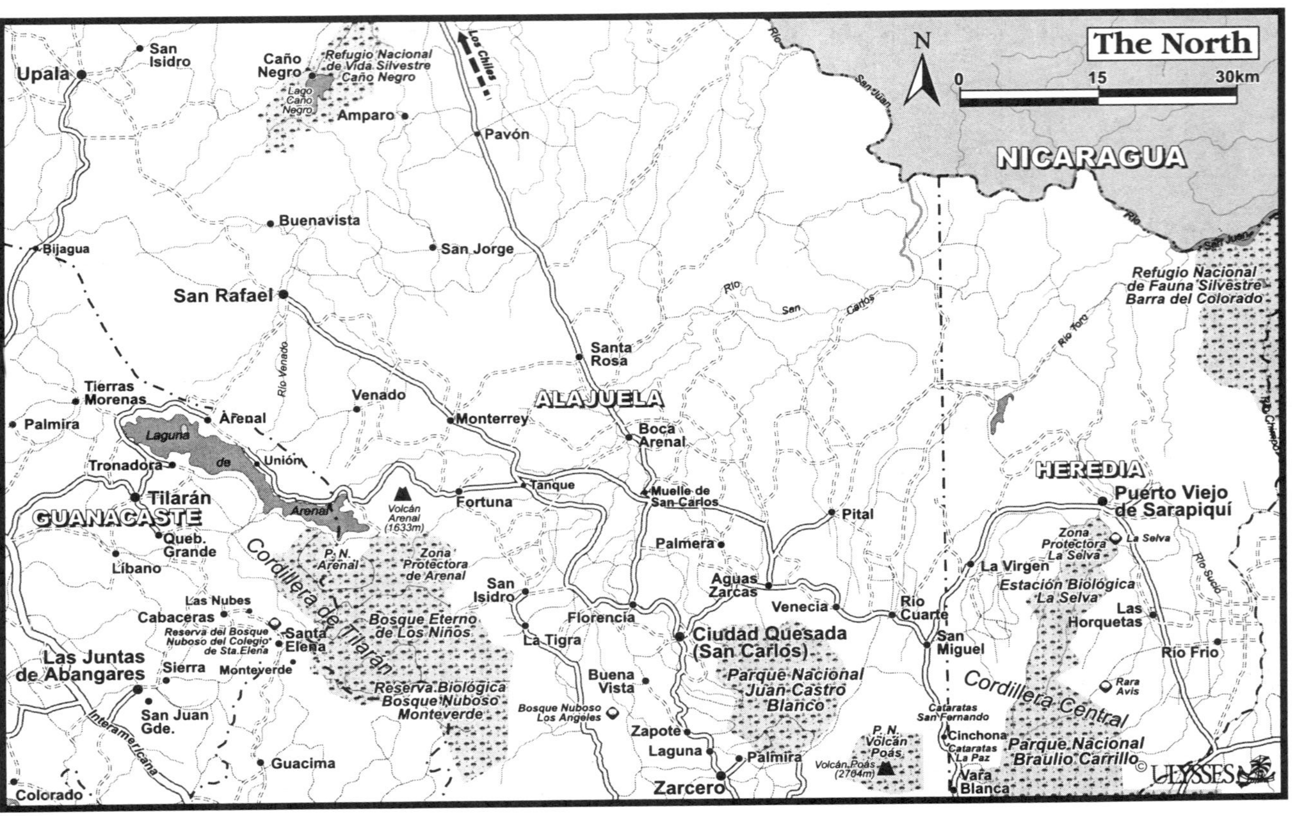

The North
N
0
15
30km
NICARAGUA
ALAJUELA
HEREDIA
GUANACASTE
Upala
San Isidro
Caño Negro
Refugio Nacional de Vida Silvestre Caño Negro
Lago Caño Negro
Amparo
Los Chiles
Pavón
Buenavista
San Jorge
Bijagua
San Rafael
Río Venado
Río San Carlos
Río San Juan
Santa Rosa
Tierras Morenas
Venado
Arenal
Palmira
Monterrey
Boca Arenal
Laguna de Arenal
Unión
Tronadora
Tilarán
Tanque
Fortuna
Muelle de San Carlos
Volcán Arenal (1633m)
Pital
Quebr. Grande
Líbano
P. N. Arenal
Zona Protectora de Arenal
Cordillera de Tilarán
Palmera
San Isidro
Aguas Zarcas
Las Nubes
Cabaceras
Reserva del Bosque Nuboso del Colegio de Sta. Elena
Santa Elena
Monteverde
Bosque Eterno de Los Niños
Florencia
La Tigra
Venecia
Ciudad Quesada (San Carlos)
Río Cuarte
San Miguel
Las Juntas de Abangares
Sierra
San Juan Gde.
Interamericana
Guacima
Colorado
Reserva Biológica Bosque Nuboso Monteverde
Buena Vista
Bosque Nuboso Los Angeles
Zapote
Laguna
Zarcero
Palmira
Parque Nacional Juan Castro Blanco
P. N. Volcán Poás
Volcán Poás (2704m)
Cataratas San Fernando
Cinchona
Cataratas La Paz
Vara Blanca
Cordillera Central
Parque Nacional Braulio Carrillo
Refugio Nacional de Fauna Silvestre Barra del Colorado
Río Toro
Puerto Viejo de Sarapiquí
Zona Protectora La Selva
La Selva
La Virgen
Estación Biológica La Selva
Río Sucio
Las Horquetas
Río Frío
Rara Avis
© ULYSSES

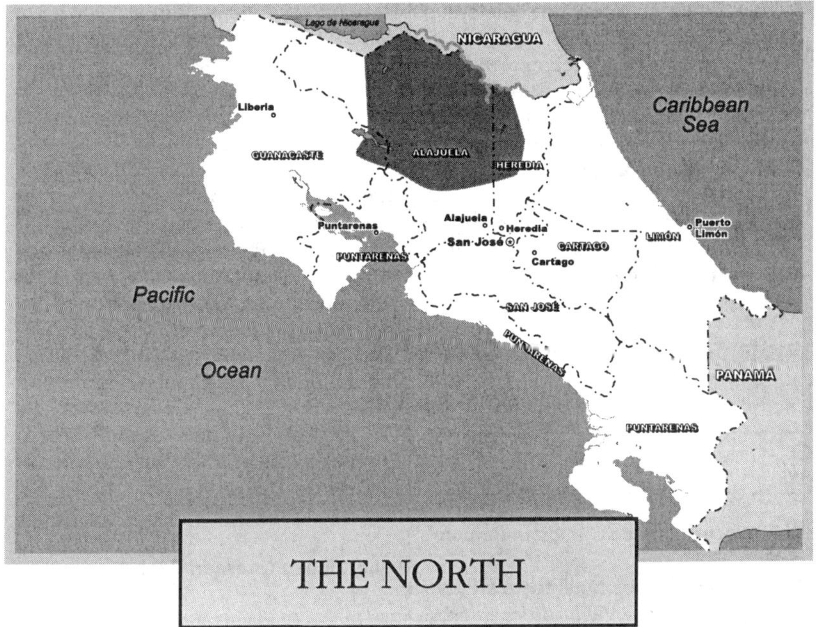


# THE NORTH

Northern Costa Rica is an often overlooked part of the country. It wasn't on the most popular tourist routes for many years, but this is in the process of changing. Though there are no beaches in the region, the north boasts the largest lake in the country, known for the best windsurfing in Central America! And where else can you see a volcano in the process of erupting? It is also in the north that visitors will find some of the most beautiful reserves of virgin forest in all of Costa Rica!

The area described in this chapter is made up of four large regions, northwest of the Valle Central. The regions of Puerto Viejo de Sarapiquí, Monteverde, and Caño Negro (in the far north, bordering on Nicaragua) are known for their large protected green spaces. The region of Arenal, in the middle, is interesting to visit because of its still-active volcano and immense artificial lake. This last region is part of the vast San Carlos *llanura* (lowland plains), a dairy farming and crop-raising region with Ciudad Quesada (also to be described) as its main town.

The vast region of the north, beyond the Cordillera Central and the Cordillera de Tilarán, has several distinct climates. There is something for everyone: hot, rainy Sarapiquí, the humid San Carlos *llanura*, the cooler Monteverde, and the drier, more windy extreme northwest, in the region of Arenal. The entire region was once an immense forest. The vast area of the San Carlos *llanura* was transformed into fields and pastures (or banana plantations in the region of Sarapiquí). Although the conversion of the forest to agricultural land certainly has had consequences on the region's environment, the patchwork quilt pattern of pastures and fields under cultivation is lovely to travel through.

Mostly thanks to a few ecologists and dedicated nature lovers, the other regions of the Costa Rican north have retained large expanses of dense tropical rainforest which shelter uncounted numbers of unidentified birds, plants and animals.

Though it is little known, this region has certain advantages. After all, it is much less crowded for anyone who ventures here!

## FINDING YOUR WAY AROUND

### By Car

**The Puerto Viejo de Sarapiquí Region**

**Puerto Viejo de Sarapiquí:** there are two roads to Puerto Viejo de Sarapiquí from the Central Valley. One starts north of Heredia and Alajuela, runs between the Barva and Poás Volcanoes, and then heads east to Puerto Viejo after passing through San Miguel and La Virgen. This is a very pretty route with some scenic stops along the way, such as the Poás Volcano and some magnificent waterfalls, including those at La Paz. The trip takes approximately 2.5 hours, non-stop.

The second and faster way is to take the Guapiles Highway towards the Caribbean Coast, and go through the magnificent Parque Nacional Braulio Carrillo. Then, turn left near Santa Clara and head almost due north. This route passes within two kilometres of the La Selva ecological reserve, which is about four kilometres south of Puerto Viejo.

If you are coming from Guanacaste, La Fortuna, or Ciudad Quesada (all on the same route), simply go northeast to Puerto Viejo in the Central Valley, passing by Ajuas Zarcas and San Miguel (north of the Poás Volcano) and La Virgen.

**Rara Avis**

Rara Avis is some fifteen kilometres southwest of Las Horquetas, which is southeast of Puerto Viejo de Sarapiquí. Arrange transportation to Rara Avis well ahead of time, because the road going there is extremely rough and hilly and parts of it must be navigated by tractor or on rented horses. Four-wheel drive vehicles can travel 12 of the 15 kilometres to the reserve, but no more. It takes at least two hours to get there from Las Horquetas.

**The Ciudad Quesada Region**

To get to **Ciudad Quesada** (San Carlos), take the General Cañas Highway to the Naranjo exit, which is about 25 km west of Alajuela, and drive due north through Naranjo and Zarcero.

**The Arenal Region**

**La Fortuna:** The road to La Fortuna goes through Zarcero and San Carlos (Ciudad Quesada), then heads directly north to Muelle. Once at Muelle, turn left and go due west. The scenery is attractive with the Arenal Volcano rising above the lowland plains of the San Carlos *llanura.*

There is a small road between **Monteverde** and La Fortuna. Starting from Monteverde, head to Santa Elena. From there, take the unpaved road north to Tilarán. This road zigzags between high valleys with splendid panoramic views of the region, and is sometimes impassable – check its condition before you go. Shortly before Tilarán, the road becomes paved. At

Tilarán, go north to Lake Arenal and follow the road along the northern shore of the lake. Past the village of Arenal, the road is in bad shape for some ten kilometres, then it suddenly becomes excellent again. When we took it, part of the road had been swept away by the river. We were forced to take a very steep side road to detour around it (again, ask about the condition of this road before taking it). The 117-kilometre trip will take four to five hours.

**Nuevo Arenal**: you can get to Nuevo Arenal from Guanacaste (west of Lake Arenal), or from La Fortuna (east of the lake). From Guanacaste, the road goes through Tilarán and follows the west side of the lake, which is windier and is good for water sports. The eastern route follows the shore for almost the whole length of the lake. The road is in pretty good condition until the last few kilometres before Nuevo Arenal. From there on, it is unpaved and barely passable. Travelling it at night is to be avoided.

### Parque Nacional Arenal

The entrance to the Parque Nacional Arenal is located on the south side of the Arenal volcano, fifteen kilometres (about 30 minutes) from the village of La Fortuna, on the east side. Take the road around the volcano, close to the Tabacón hot springs, and then, near the lake, take the small, unpaved, poorly maintained road to the park and the Arenal Observatory Lodge.

### The Monteverde Region

From San José, take the Inter-American Highway north towards Puntarenas. At the intersection near Puntarenas, stay on the highway and head towards Cañas, rather than turning off towards Puntarenas. Less than 20 kilometres further, at Rancho Grande, there is a sign on the right indicating the road to Monteverde. It is 32 kilometres long and usually in terrible condition, with many steep pitches and heavy traffic. The long climb ends at the village of Santa Elena. From there, the road descends for about five kilometres to Monteverde and the reserve of the same name. The drive takes about four hours, depending on the season, the state of the road and the vehicle (a four-wheel drive is ideal).

### Refugio Nacional de Vida Silvestre Caño Negro

This reserve is located 165 kilometres from San José and 21 kilometres from Los Chiles. From San José, the highway passes through Naranjo, Zarcero, Ciudad Quesada (San Carlos), Floriencia, Muelle de San Carlos and Los Chiles. From the province of Guanacaste, you can get to the park via the small town of Upala, which is 36 kilometres west of Caño Negro. From Upala, take the road going to San Rafael and after about 10 kilometres, at Colonia Puntarenas, take the small road indicated by the sign to Caño Negro.

## By Bus

### The Puerto Viejo de Sarapiquí Region

**Puerto Viejo de Sarapiquí**: At least six buses per day go from San José to Puerto Viejo. They leave from Avenida 11 between Calles Central and 1. Some buses take the road to Heredia, others take the Guapiles Highway. The trip lasts about four hours. Some of the buses that travel along the highway stop in Río Frío, making the trip longer.

There are three departures daily from **Heredia.** Buses leave almost every two hours from **San Carlos** for **Puerto Viejo de Sarapiquí.** The trip takes at least one hour.

### The Ciudad Quesada Region

**Ciudad Quesada**: there is excellent bus service to this destination from San José (Coca Cola bus terminal). In fact, there are hourly departures from 5am to 7pm. The trip takes three hours.

### The Arenal Region

**La Fortuna**: There are three departures every morning from San José to La Fortuna, leaving from the Coca Cola bus terminal. There is a mid-afternoon return trip to San José. The trip takes at least 4.5 hours. Buses leave **Ciudad Quesada** for La Fortuna practically every two hours. The trip takes about one hour.

**Nuevo Arenal**: Two buses per day leave Ciudad Quesada for Arenal-Tilarán: one in the morning and one in the afternoon.

### The Monteverde Region

There are two buses daily from San José *(Calle 14, and Avenidas 9/11)*, at 6:30am and 2:30pm. The trip takes about four hours *($5.30; Transportes Tilarán, ☎222-3854)*.

### Refugio Nacional de Vida Silvestre Caño Negro

There are two buses daily from San José *(Calle 12, and Avenida 9)*, at 5:30am and at 3:30pm. The trip from San José to Los Chiles takes about 2.5 hours *($2.20; Autotransportes, ☎460-5032)*.

## PRACTICAL INFORMATION

## Travel Agencies

**Aventuras Arenal** *(☎479-9133, ⇌479-9295)*, on the main street of La Fortuna, organizes all sorts of excursions in the region: by car, by bicycle, on foot or on horseback. You can also visit the Caño Negro Park or go fishing on Lake Arenal with them.

**AveRica** *(☎479-9076, ⇌479-9456)* in La Fortuna organizes birdwatching expeditions around Lake Arenal, Refugio Nacional de Vida Silvestre Caño Negro, the Río Frío and Parque Nacional Juan Castro Blanco.

**Albergue Tío Henry** *(San Rafael de Guatusi, north of Nuevo Arenal; ☎464-0211)* offers guided tours of the Refugio Nacional de Vida Silvestre Caño Negro, the Río Celeste waterfalls (on horseback), and the two-mile-long Cavernas de Venado – and even visits a caiman and Ujuminican crocodile farm!

**Ecotours** *(Playa Hermosa, on the corner of Guanacaste, ☎/⇌672-0175)* organizes guided birdwatching in the **Refugio Nacional de Vida Silvestre Caño Negro** where there are many different bird species. The tour costs $75 per person, including transportation, breakfast, entrance permit and a guide. If you have your own car it costs $60 per day plus expenses, no matter how many people are in the vehicle. One of the guides, Quebecker Marc Fournier, will gladly share his love for Costa Rica's nature with you.

**Stable** *(3 km west of Nuevo Arenal; ☎694-4092)* offers horseback riding excursions for all levels.

**Tilawa Windsurf Spots & Boat Rental** and **Tico Winds Windsurf Spot & Equipment Rental**, both at the western end of Lake Arenal, provide services and equipment for various water sports.

## EXPLORING

### The Puerto Viejo de Sarapiquí Region

A visit to the Puerto Viejo region will help you better understand the fragile ecology of our planet. The region's reserves, parks and other undeveloped areas help preserve entire ecosystems that shelter thousands of species of flora and fauna. But don't expect sunny, cool weather: most of this area lies in the hot and humid Caribbean zone of the country. However, it is this tropical climate that fosters the luxuriant growth of the rainforest.

From the looks of it, **Puerto Viejo de Sarapiquí** doesn't seem very interesting, but it was once the country's most important port. In the era before modern transportation links were constructed, boats used to sail north on Río Sarapiquí to get to Río San Juan (the natural border between Costa Rica and Nicaragua) and the Atlantic Ocean.

A few kilometres southwest of Puerto Viejo is **MUSA** ★ *(El Tigre, on the road to Horquetas)*, a local women's co-operative farm where herbs are grown for medicinal, cosmetic and other commercial purposes. A small donation is requested from visitors. The palce is both pleasant and educational to visit. Everyday products containing these herbs are sold here.

There are three noteworthy waterfalls in the region. The first is the spectacular **Catarata San Rafael** ★ in La Cinchona, a little spot about halfway between San José and Puerto Viejo.

**Cataratas La Paz** ★, on the river of the same name, is located on the road from Poás to Puerto Viejo de Sarapiquí. By crossing the river via the bridge you can get a beautiful view of what looks like one waterfall but is actually two superimposed. The mist produced by the waterfall is a refreshing break from the heat. The falls are lit up at night and look lovely, with the surrounding greenery also illuminated. It is not safe to go behind the waterfalls because the path is extremely slippery.

**Cataratas San Fernando** ★, a little farther north along the road going from Poás to Puerto Viejo de Sarapiquí, are also worth seeing. The falls can be admired from **El Parador**, a private house that is open to the public. The owners feed a bevy of hummingbirds that are interesting to watch, especially when they drink energy-giving sugar-water from feeders outside the house.

### Rara Avis

**Rara Avis** ★ *(☎/☏253-0844)* is a private nature reserve established by American Amos Bien who first visited Costa Rica in 1977. Fascinated by the rich ecosystems in this part of the world, he soon realized that they were threatened by clear-cutting and the excessive burning of the rainforest to make pasturage, as seen in Guanacaste and along the Río Sarapiquí. Therefore, in 1983, he created the Rara Avis reserve next to the La Selva reserve and the Braulio Carrillo national park. The

1,300-hectare terrain was meant to demonstrate that it was possible to use Costa Rica's ecological resources in an economically viable way without destroying them. As a functioning centre for research and nature preserve, this reserve is relatively far from the tourist-beaten path and therefore ideal for adventurous types with a passion for nature. There are several reasons we say this: firstly, because the road leading into the reserve is really pretty terrible and requires considerable patience and endurance (see p 176). Secondly, it rains non-stop. Lastly, the standards of the accommodations provided are nowhere near those of a large hotel. However, if you decide to make the trip, you will be rewarded with a fascinating variety of animals and plants. There is also a magnificent 55-metre-high waterfall in the reserve's jungle. The trails can be explored alone or with a guide.

## La Selva

**La Selva** ★ *(3 km south of Puerto Viejo de Sarapiquí, ☎740-1515, ⇋740-1414, or via OTS ☎240-6696, ⇋240-6783)* is a 1,600-hectare ecological reserve managed by the Organisation for Tropical Studies (OTS), which is dedicated to the study of tropical and subtropical green spaces. Its members hail from universities and research centres across the United States, Puerto Rico, and Costa Rica. The reserve is essentially a research and study centre that attracts specialists and students from all over the world, and facilities have been set up to do fieldwork at the site. It is, however, possible to visit, or even stay at the reserve, if reservations are made in advance. It should be kept in mind that, while it is more accessible than Rara Avis, La Selva's climate is just as hot and rainy, and requires special clothing. The number of plant and animal species that have been identified here impressive. In fact, the reserve is home to more than 400 species of birds – not bad for 1,600 hectares! To explore the reserve, you must be accompanied by one of their guides *($20/adult, discount for children)*. This is done so as not to disturb the scientific research going on. The trails are, however, in excellent condition and wheelchair-accessible most of the way.

Overnight stays are possible with advance reservations (see p 196). By staying here, you'll come to appreciate the admirable, ecological ideals of the people running the station.

## The Ciudad Quesada Region

The region of **Cuidad Quesada** (called **San Carlos** by its residents) is located in the San Carlos *llanura* (lowland plains), which run all the way to the Nicaraguan border in the north. It is one of the most productive agricultural regions in Costa Rica, and you'll certainly notice this if you're coming from San Ramón and Zarcero.

The **region between Zarcero and Ciudad Quesada** ★★ has some magnificent landscapes with valleys and rivers, fields of crops and cows grazing in pastures, making it hard to concentrate on the road. There are too few places to stop and admire the scenery!

Though Ciudad Quesada is a fair-sized town with a population of 35,000, people mostly come here for the surrounding countryside and tourist resorts.

Ciudad Quesada is also a good place to stop midway between San José and the Arenal region. You have to pass through it if you want to get to the region of Puerto Viejo de Sarapiquí without taking the road to the Poás Volcano.

The region of **Zarcero** is described in the chapter on the Central Valley (see p 106).

## The Arenal Region

The region of Arenal is characterized by two geographical formations: its active volcano and its lake, the largest in the country. Both contribute to the imposing landscape of the flatlands in the east and the gentle valleys in the west. In addition, the roads to the region are being improved every year.

On the way to Arenal from Ciudad Quesada, via Muelle, you'll see the **Arenal Volcano** rising up in the distance. With a height of 1,633 metres and a perfectly conical shape, often with a plume of white smoke, the volcano certainly dominates the plains. It is the perfect image of a stereotypical volcano, with rumbling subterranean explosions sending a halo of smoke and fire to the surface. With a little luck (if the weather is good and the volcano is in an active period), the nighttime spectacle is breathtaking. Sometimes you can even see lava flowing down the crater. A better volcano would be hard to find (see also p 183).

The Arenal Volcano has only been active since the late 1960s. The last time it erupted there were 68 deaths, and the towns of Pueblo Nuovo and Tabacón were destroyed. The giant awoke with earthquakes, rockslides, smoke and noxious gases, and covered the lush vegetation on the mountainside with a thick layer of volcanic ash. Since then, the volcano rumbles and spits periodically during the year.

People have capitalized on the volcano's reawakening and the new lake nearby has a whole slew of interesting activities and facilities for visitors. All this makes it more pleasant to stay in this region longer.

### The La Fortuna Region

Although it is the closest city to the volcano, **La Fortuna** is not very attractive. It was originally an agricultural centre, but, thanks to the popularity of the nearby volcano, it quickly became a tourist town with more and more businesses opening up in the city and on the road leading to the volcano. Therefore, you should have no problem finding comfortable and reasonably priced accommodations. Since the rate of tourism in Costa Rica has levelled-off somewhat in recent years, the many new hotels and *cabinas* must keep prices down to remain competitive. There are almost too many places from which to choose in every price category. One thing that might make your decision a little easier is to choose one with a pool right beside your *cabina*, because La Fortuna is relatively hot, since it is only 250 metres above sea level. Outings in the surrounding areas are easy to arrange through several tourist agencies in the city, and many other organisations and hotels. All kinds of sports equipment can be rented in the area as well.

Five and a half kilometres south of La Fortuna is the **Catarata La Fortuna** ★ *(take the first street west of the church, which crosses the Río Burío)*, accessible by car, on horseback or even on foot. Pay attention to the road, as it can get difficult in places (especially during the rainy season).

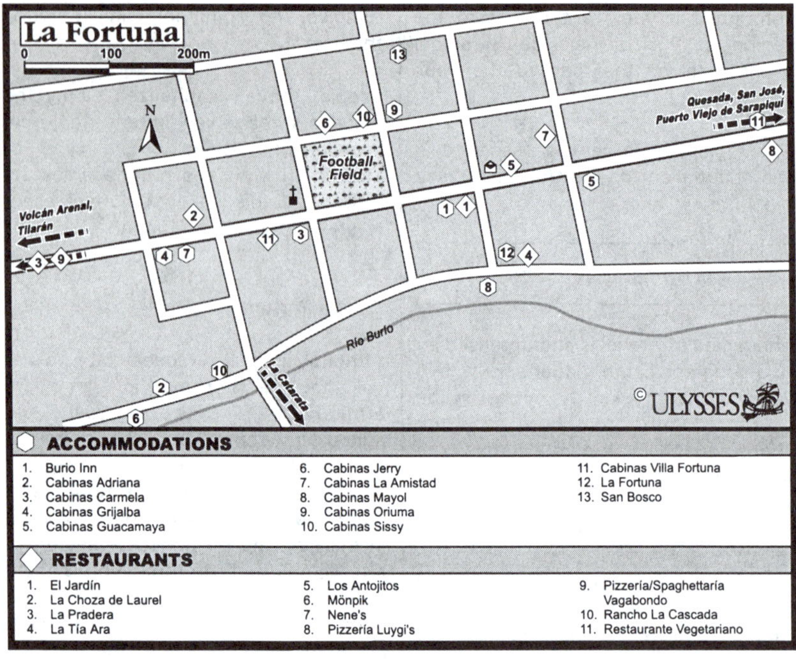


Also, the way to the falls is not clearly marked. The waterfall is very beautiful, cascading down the rock face in tiers. It can be seen from the parking lot, but you can get closer to it by taking a steep path to the foot of the falls. Some people swim there, but the strong current can be dangerous.

The **Tabacón Resort** ★★★ *($14/day, $20 admission to the restaurant; every day 10am to 10pm; 13 km west of La Fortuna en route to the Arenal Volcano, ☎222-1072 or ☎233-0780, ⇄221-3075)* hot springs are superbly designed: ten swimming pools with thermally heated water from the Río Tabacón, waterfalls, two restaurants (see p 206) and two bars (one actually in a swimming pool) provide true relaxation! Each swimming pool is set at a specific temperature, from 23 degrees to 40 degrees Celsius. It is a fun little place surrounded by lush tropical forest, and with an attractive view of the volcano. Try the waters or the restaurant at night when it is dark, or even foggy, outside. It is usually crowded, even during the low season. Therapeutic massages and volcanic mud masks are available. There are plans to build a first-rate hotel here in the near future.

Across the road from the Tabacón Resort, there is a less expensive way to enjoy the **hot springs** in the area. Less structured and glamorous, the entrance fee is only $5. There are bathrooms, a changing room and a little *soda (every day 9:30am to 10pm)*.

**Around Lake Arenal**

Head west from Tabacón Resort and the park road to get to the dike that retains the newer part of **Lake Arenal ★**. Originally smaller, the lake is in fact a large reservoir that provides water for irrigation systems in the area and electricity for the country. The water is clean, *guapotes* (rainbow perch) are plentiful, and there is constant wind, particularly in the western part of the lake. It is not surprising that swimmers, fishermen, boaters and windsurfers are often seen on the lake. The road runs parallel to the shore and offers glimpses of the superb view of the lake with the volcano rising above it. Because the scenery is so beautiful and there are so many possibilities for recreational activities in the area, some hotels have been built on the beach and on hills overlooking the lake in recent years.

**Cavernas de Venado** *($15; the road starts a few km east of Nuevo Arenal)*, one hour from Lake Arenal, form a grotto some two kilometres in length. During the guided tour of the caves, all the expected geological forms, such as stalactites and stalagmites, can be seen – as well as bats!

**Lake Coter** is also to the north of Lake Arenal *(4 km)*, and only accessible via a road a few kilometres west of Nuevo Arenal. All sorts of water sports are practiced here, especially swimming (see "Lago Coter Eco-Lodge", p 201).

**Jardín Botánico Arenal ★** *($4; every day 9am to 5pm; on the road between La Fortuna and Tilarán, 5 km east of Nuevo Arenal and 25 km west of the Lake Arena dike, ☎694-4273, ≠694-4086)* is a lovely little botanical garden. Its paths wind through more than 1,200 plants from all over the world. Several species of birds and butterflies are regular visitors here. There is even a small butterfly farm on the premises. It can be toured without a guide.

The area around **Nuevo Arenal** *(midway between La Fortun and Tilarán)*, on the northwest shore of the lake, enjoys a better climate than La Fortuna, where it is almost always oppressively hot and humid. This village, which is also referred to simply as Arenal, was built when the original site was submerged due to the artificial expansion of the lake: hence "Nuevo". The town has grown somewhat, but it is still quiet. To date, there are not many establishments that can accommodate tourists. It is a pleasant place to take a stroll and have a good, simple meal at one of its more established restaurants.

The closer you go to the western end of Lake Arenal, the windier it gets. Because of this, the nights are cool. From the south shore to the western end of the lake there are many windmills, putting this constant and economical source of energy to a good use. The Arenal-Tilarán road, which runs along the northwest side of the lake, provides a good vantage point from which to admire the arresting landscape created by these dynamic, silent giants cresting the hills. This part of Lake Arenal is the most popular for windsurfing. There are a few places where the public can access the lake, such as at the government-owned wharf *(just past the Rock and Surf hotel, about 4 km towards Tilarán)*.

## Parque Nacional Arenal

The Arenal Volcano is the archetypical erupting volcano: its elegant, conical form makes it stand out from the neighbouring mountains, and it is not part of the mountain range. With an altitude of 1633 metres, it can be

## The Reawakening of Arenal

The Arenal Volcano wasn't always a fire-and-stone-spitting monster. In fact, until the end of the 1960s, the mountain was quiet, and people living around it believed it to be extinct. Then, on July 29, 1968, the mountain suddenly awoke. A very violent explosion blew off the top of the cone, and sent tons of rock flying into the air. Then lava started flowing down its sides. The impact of the eruption was so powerful that it destroyed the villages of Pueblo Nuevo and Tabacón, and a large part of the surrounding forest. Seventy-eight people were killed, and hundreds of others had to evacuate the area. The explosion was so violent that the tremors from it could be felt as far as Boulder, Colorado, in the United States!

spotted easily from all directions, most particularly from the west, with Lake Arenal in the foreground. It is also the image of a "real" volcano because it is one of the most active in the world. People come from all over the planet to admire its boiling crater. They hope for a clear night so that they can see glowing lava flowing down its sides.

In 1994, 12,016 hectares were added to the Area de Conservación Arenal, which was then renamed **Parque Nacional Arenal** ★★ *($6; every day, 8am to 10pm; ☎460-1412 or 695-5908, ⇄460-0644)*. The park was created to protect the region and inform the public about this very active volcano. Overly adventurous people are park tries to dissuaded from climbing up to the crater of the volcano: over the years, there have been dozens of accidents here, some of them fatal. Hikers who were a little too curious, probably got too close to the volcano and fell in.

At the entrance to the park there is a reception area with a parking lot, toilets, telephones, drinking water, maps of the park, and so on. The park authorities have a learning centre and other tourist facilities in mind for the future.

Most visitors to the park go to the **Mirador** observation point, about 1.3 kilometres from the entrance. It is accessible via a footpath or by car, and there is parking available. Since this observation point is at the foot of the volcano, it is probably the best place to see, hear and feel the volcano's power. From here, you can see the lava that flows to the base of the mountain, destroying everything in its path. On some days, ash explodes from the top of the volcano. And don't be startled if you feel the earth shaking and hear a loud rumbling, as though the Arenal wanted to demonstrate its power and destructive force.

Park employees have cleared trails to the base of the volcano and the lava flows. The **Las Heliconias** trail (1 km) goes to the Mirador observation point. Different species of plants that have managed to grow after the eruption of 1968 can be found along this path. This trail also branches off onto the **Las Coladas** trail (2 km) which leads to the area where only lava flows. Along the trail at different points are scenic views of the Chato Volcano to the east, the Lake Arenal dike to the west, and the Arenal Volcano itself. Another trail, **Los Tucanes** (2 km), winds its way through exotic flora and fauna including toucans, monkeys, and *armadillos*. The last trail, **Los Miradores**

(1.2 km), next to Lake Arenal, used to be a service road to the hydroelectric dam.

Located at the edge of Parque Nacional Arenal, the **Arenal Observatory Lodge** ★★ *($1.50; bar-restaurant, ☎257-9489, ⇗257-4220; past the park, follow the signs)* (see also p 199) is a fantastic spot for volcano-watching. For the first 25 years after it exploded, the hotel was exclusively used by researchers from the Institute of Seismology at the national university of Costa Rica. Now, anyone can spend a memorable day, or an even more extraordinary evening here, enjoying the best possible vantage point for observing the volcano. On clear nights, if the volcano is spitting fire, the visitors go out on the terrace of the hotel to better admire the spectacle put on by the roaring monster. Most of the excellent nighttime photographs of the volcano emitting huge amounts of glowing, orange lava, were taken from this terrace. A network of trails has been set up from the hotel so visitors can explore the rich, dense vegetation in this part of the rainforest. This is a great place to spend a day, or more. The road to the hotel is very bumpy and fords a river. If your vehicle does not have four-wheel drive, call ahead to ask about road conditions.

## The Monteverde Region

The region of Monteverde is made up of vast forests which cover large valleys and mountains that are between 800 and 1,800 metres high. Just getting there by car or by bus is an experience in itself, and will give you the impression of going to the end of the earth. But after two hours of snaking along the little ribbon of a road, you actually arrive in a region with a whole gamut of hotels and nature-related activities. This is a popular destination for people from all over Costa Rica and the world. A veritable botanical and ornithological paradise, the region of Monteverde is a year-round attraction for nature lovers, some of whom are scientists while others are ordinary tourists, hoping to see the rare **quetzal**, a superb, large, emerald-and-red bird that lives at high altitudes in the tropical rainforest.

For centuries, the region of Monteverde was an extremely wild and remote area with only a few isolated family farms. Then, in 1951, 44 settlers arrived, determined to live in harmony with nature. They were a group of 11 **Quaker** families who fled the United States during the early 1950s to escape imprisonment in their native Alabama for refusing military service. These pacifists chose to live in Costa Rica because the country has no standing army and is politically stable. To secure their freedom and live out their convictions, they bought land in the region of Monteverde, which, at that time, was accessible only by horse and buggy.

**Monteverde** is not built like a typical village with a grid-like pattern of streets and central square. Instead, its houses, hotels, restaurants and stores line the five-kilometre stretch of unpaved road that runs from the village of Santa Elena to the Monteverde reserve.

It is easy to understand why the residents refuse to pave their road: the village receives enough tourists on foot or horseback, by bicycle and car. If the road which connects them to the Inter-American Highway were to be paved, even more tourists would come – by the busloads! – disturbing the tranquil way of life.

THE NORTH

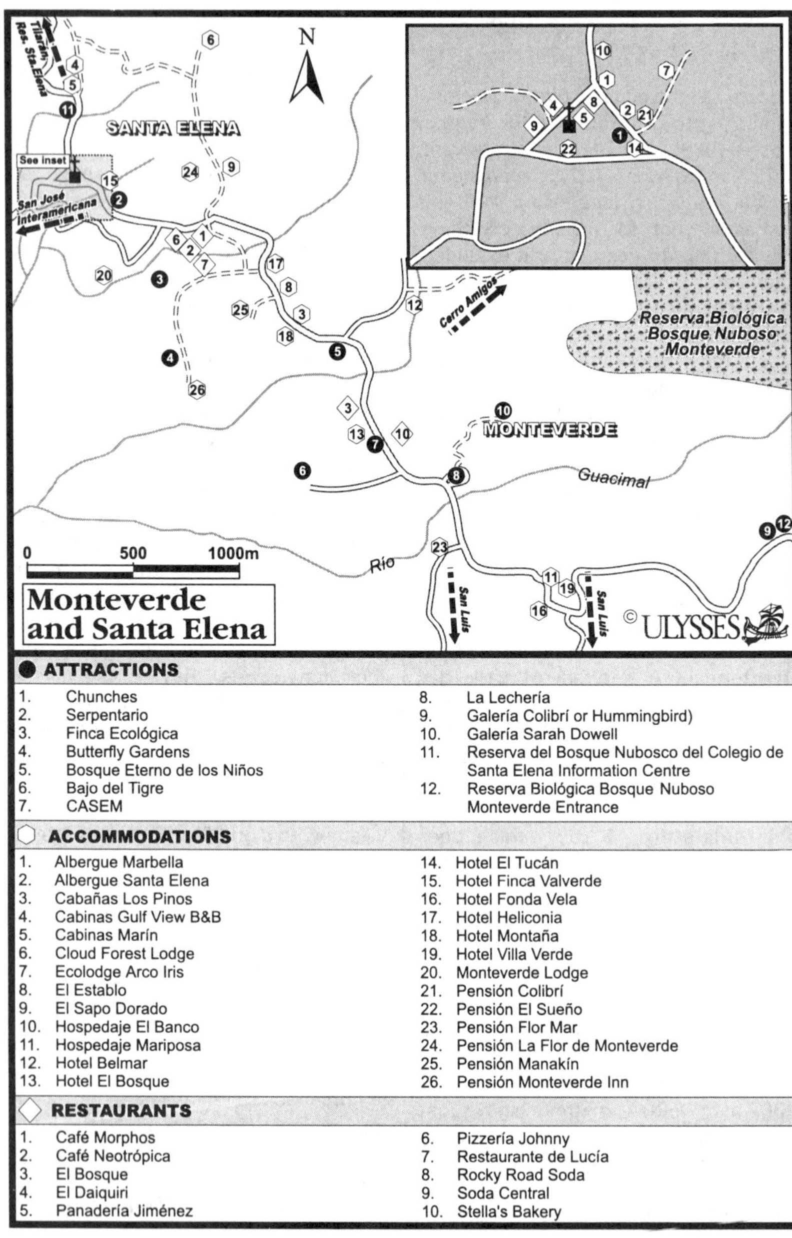


## Monteverde and Santa Elena

### ● ATTRACTIONS

1. Chunches
2. Serpentario
3. Finca Ecológica
4. Butterfly Gardens
5. Bosque Eterno de los Niños
6. Bajo del Tigre
7. CASEM
8. La Lechería
9. Galería Colibrí or Hummingbird)
10. Galería Sarah Dowell
11. Reserva del Bosque Nubosco del Colegio de Santa Elena Information Centre
12. Reserva Biológica Bosque Nuboso Monteverde Entrance

### ⬡ ACCOMMODATIONS

1. Albergue Marbella
2. Albergue Santa Elena
3. Cabañas Los Pinos
4. Cabinas Gulf View B&B
5. Cabinas Marín
6. Cloud Forest Lodge
7. Ecolodge Arco Iris
8. El Establo
9. El Sapo Dorado
10. Hospedaje El Banco
11. Hospedaje Mariposa
12. Hotel Belmar
13. Hotel El Bosque
14. Hotel El Tucán
15. Hotel Finca Valverde
16. Hotel Fonda Vela
17. Hotel Heliconia
18. Hotel Montaña
19. Hotel Villa Verde
20. Monteverde Lodge
21. Pensión Colibrí
22. Pensión El Sueño
23. Pensión Flor Mar
24. Pensión La Flor de Monteverde
25. Pensión Manakín
26. Pensión Monteverde Inn

### ◇ RESTAURANTS

1. Café Morphos
2. Café Neotrópica
3. El Bosque
4. El Daiquiri
5. Panadería Jiménez
6. Pizzería Johnny
7. Restaurante de Lucía
8. Rocky Road Soda
9. Soda Central
10. Stella's Bakery

## Quakers

Quakers are a Protestant sect founded by an English cobbler, George Fox (1624-1691), who believed he had been called by the Holy Spirit and began preaching in 1647. His followers called themselves the "Religious Society of Friends", but became known as quakers with reference to Fox's expression to 'quake before the word of God'. Because the central facet of the Quaker faith is the presence of the Holy Spirit in the individual, they have no clergy or liturgy.



The church, post office, bank, medical clinic, grocery store, public telephone, and most of the low-cost hotels and rooms for rent in the region are found in the village of **Santa Elena.**

A visit to **Chunches** *(Santa Elena, ☎/≠645-5147)* can be very convenient. It is a café and laundromat that sells new and second-hand books. The friendly owners, Wendy and Jim Standley, know all about the activities, hotels and restaurants in the region.

The private 80-hectare **Reserva Sendero Tranquilo** *($15, including guided tour; information at the El Sapo Dorado hotel, ☎645-5010)* lives up to the meaning of its name in Spanish, providing a peaceful part of the forest for visitors to explore. A mandatory guide leads each group of two to six people on silent, but enriching, excursions.

With its elevated walkways and suspended bridges, **Sky Walk** *($8; every day, 6am to 5pm; ☎/≠645-5238)* rises above the treetops of the tropical rainforest. Open since March of 1997, the trail was designed for visitors to take quiet walks into the lush forest where every tree is covered with lianas, mosses and flowering epiphyte plants. Along the two-kilometre loop, there are five suspended bridges, which are approximately one metre wide, 100 metres long and 40 metres above the ground. To get there, go north on Santa Elena's main street to the Colegio Santa Elena, and follow the signs from there.

On the outskirts of the village, near the Finca Valverde hotel, the **Serpentario** *($3; every day 9am to 5pm; ☎645-5238)* exhibits snakes of Costa Rica, but focusses on those found in the Monteverde region. The aim is not to frighten, but rather to teach people how to recognise the most dangerous species, which include poisonous vipers such as the formidable Central American fer-de-lance *(Bothrops asper)*. Now you will know how to react if you happen to encounter one of these dangerous reptiles in the wild!

Just before the butterfly garden, the **Finca Ecológica** *($5; every day 7am to 5pm; ☎645-5222)*, a private, 17-hectare ecological reserve, gives you the chance to observe a large variety of birds (a list is provided) and butterflies. Many wild animals can also be seen, such as coatis, agoutis, sloths and white-faced capuchin monkeys. Because the place is located at a lower altitude, it receives less rain than the tropical rainforest, and the vegetation is consequently less dense. There are even a few small banana trees and coffee plants. Four pedestrian paths cover the area of the reserve, and lead to different scenic views, including a waterfall. There is a 10-minute path from the very elegant Monteverde Lodge (see p 204) to the farm.

***Sloth***

The **Butterfly Garden** ★★ *($6, including guided tour; every day 9:30am to 4pm; picnic area, souvenir shop; ☎645-5512)* is the ideal place to observe the unique and beautiful butterflies of the tropical forest. The guides are very friendly and explain the complicated and fascinating stages in the life of a butterfly. Inside the interpretation centre is a large collection of butterflies, and each is identified by its shape and colours. Some have distinctive markings referred to as "eyes" on their wings, to frighten predators. Others are camouflaged like leaves, so that their enemies will overlook them. In one of the showcases, you can actually see caterpillars weaving themselves into chrysalides, and you might even be lucky enough to see a new butterfly emerge from its cocoon and take its first flight!

After the visit to the interpretation centre there is a tour of the aviary, which houses three distinct gardens. Each garden has climatic conditions and plant varieties similar to those found in the natural habitat of several species of butterflies. The gardens are home to hundreds of butterflies, from the 40 or more local species. It is a great place to take photographs! One of the most spectacular butterflies is the "blue morpho". Measuring about 10 centimetres in length, its wings are pure blue, bordered with brown and white speckles on one side, and with "eyes" on the other. Though the tour takes only an hour, we recommend that you bring a lunch and stay half a day: you can stroll through the gardens again, picnic next to the interpretation centre, or relax in the sunshine and observe the many different birds that share the premises. You will be amazed by the grace and beauty of the brilliantly coloured butterflies which provide a captivating spectacle.

**Bosque Eterno de los Niños** *(every day 8am to 5pm; across from the service station, ☎645-5003, ⇄645-5104)*, or the Children's Eternal Forest, is a brilliant conservation project that protects the environment by purchasing the forests around the Reserva Biológica Monteverde. The League for the Conservation of Monteverde was formed in 1986. Thanks to a donation from Swedish children, it began buying land around the reserve in 1987 – and the eternal forest has not stopped growing since! Today, it covers more than 18,500 hectares. The organization's goal is to create a natural corridor so that the exceptional fauna and flora in the region of Monteverde can survive.

Since the project's beginning, children and adults from 44 countries have collected funds to safeguard a part of the tropical rainforest for future generations. Working in concert with local communities, the League for the Conservation of Monteverde is also involved in research and education. It has two education centres deep in the forest: Poco Sol and San Gerardo. These have facilities for housing, classrooms and laboratories, as well as networks of well-maintained hiking trails. Both centres are on the Atlantic side of the Cordillero de Tilarán Divide. The line runs just east of Monteverde and Santa Elena.

Easier to access, **Bajo del Tigre** ★ *($5; every day 8am to 4:30pm; near the CASEM)* is also associated with the League for the Conservation of Monteverde. This network of short trails (3.3 km) goes through forest that is less dense than the Bosque Eterno, but just as teeming with plant and animal life. Part of the Pacific Divide of the Cordillera de Tilarán, it affords lovely views of the Gulf of Nicoya. A visit here starts at the nature interpretation centre with an explanation of what there is to see and do in the surroundings. Educational games for children introduce them to the ecology of the tropical forest. Among other things, the area is considered an excellent place for ornithology. More than 200 bird species have been listed. Before setting out on the trails, which lead to the Río Máquina canyon, visitors are given an excellent booklet about the 22 interpretation points that explain the flora and fauna to be observed along the way.

Several women in the region of Monteverde have united to form a local handicrafts cooperative called **CASEM** *(every day 8am to 5pm; ☎645-5190, ⇄645-5262)*. They create handmade items, including clothing, decorated with motifs of the region's flora and fauna. Profits from the sale of these handicrafts foster the artisan tradition in the Monteverde community.

Halfway between Santa Elena and the reserve is a cheese factory, **La Lechería** *(every day 7:30am to 4pm, except Sun until 12:30pm; ☎645-5136)*, founded by Quakers in 1953. Visitors can see the manufacturing process for many different kinds of cheese (edam, gouda, emmenthal, cheddar, etc.), including the very famous and popular, *monterico*. The factory's output, which started at 10 kilograms per day in the 1950s, has grown to 1,000 kilograms per day. The cheese is distributed to all parts of the country, and more than 100 people are employed by the factory.

There is a hummingbird gallery just at the entrance to the reserve. **Galería Colibrí** ★ *(every day 10am to 4:30pm, ☎645-5030)* displays the work of the famous English photographers Michael and Patricia Fogden, who used to live in the area. In addition to slides and photographs, the shop sells all sorts of art objects, articles of clothing and jewellery, mostly inspired by plant and animal themes. At 4:30 there is a slide show presentation by a local biologist *($3)*. Feeders hung outside the gallery attract dozens of hummingbirds, representing the nine indigenous species. It is a unique experience to see these tiny birds darting around, buzzing like bees. This may be the only chance you'll ever have to take photographs of these charming little birds.

## La Reserva del Bosque Nuboso de Colegio de Santa Elena

If the Monteverde Reserve is too large for you, visit the rainforest at the smaller **Reserva del Bosque Nuboso del Colegio de Santa Elena** ★★ *($6; every day 7am to 4pm; ☎645-5390, ≠645-5014)*. This 310-hectare reserve is located 6.5 kilometres from the village of Santa Elena, where there is an information bureau about the reserve. At an altitude of 1,670 metres, the reserve receives a lot of precipitation, so dress accordingly (rain boots can be rented at the reserve).

Originally, this area was supposed to be turned into an experimental farm for research and educational purposes, but the plans didn't work out. Then, in 1989, with the support of Youth Challenge International, a Canadian non-profit organisation, it was turned into a tropical rainforest reserve. It is now administered by the college in Santa Elena, with profits (from entrance fees, boot rentals, guide services, souvenirs, transportation, etc.) going to preserve this precious territory, and to improve the environmental education of the region's students. Moreover, many groups of students from several countries, as well as volunteers from Canada and the United States, come to help maintain the trails and the visitor reception centre.

To get to the reserve, go north on Santa Elena's main road to the Colegio Santa Elena, and follow the signs from there. The reserve is 6.5 kilometres north of the village, which has an information bureau that provides transportation to the reserve *($1.70; departure every day at 7am)*. At the reserve, there are a reception and information centre, a snack bar, a souvenir shop and toilets. Documentation about the reserve is also available.

The reserve has four hiking trails that total 12 kilometres. Each trail makes a loop that takes between 45 minutes and four hours to complete, and has some scenic lookouts *(miradores)* along the way. Among others, there is a view of the famous Arenal Volcano (1,633 m), one of the most active volcanoes in the world, though the views from the lookouts are often obstructed by clouds or fog. However, according to Eduardo Venegas, the reserve's friendly administrator and owner of Pensión La Flor de Monteverde (see p 202), on a clear day you can see not only Lake Arenal and its volcano, but also the Tenorio (1,916 m), Miravalles (2,028 m) and Rincón de la Vieja (1,895 m) volcanoes in the northwest, and the Gulf of Nicoya to the south!

One of the trails, called **The Youth Challenge** (0.8 km), is very educational. There is a guide booklet that explains what there is to see at the 15 interpretation points along the path, which goes through primary and secondary forests, displaying a wealth of fauna and flora. Eighty percent of the Santa Elena reserve is primary forest. The other 20 percent is secondary forest, with smaller and shorter trees that let in more sunlight.

## The Quetzal

The best time to spot the quetzal *(Pharomachrus moccinno)* at the Monteverde reserve is between March and May. This is mating season, when the birds make their nests high in the trees, some ten metres above the ground. At other times of the year, the bird is harder to spot. However, an experienced guide can show you the most frequented areas. This is how, in early December, we were able to observe both a male and a female quetzal. The quetzal is a member of the trogon family and is remarkably large. They are 35 centimetres tall on average and have an extraordinary emerald green train, or extension to the tail, that can be up to 60 centimetres long! The quetzal makes its home in the tropical rainforest from southern Mexico to Panama, at elevations between 1,200 and 3,000 metres.

It takes approximately 80 years for the younger trees of the secondary forest to mature and be classified as primary forest.

Though it is unlikely that you will spot an animal, it is quite common to see tracks left by peccary, kinkajou, ocelot and puma. Birds are also numerous. Because this reserve is smaller than that of Monteverde, some ornithologists argue that this makes it quieter and thus better for observations. And, like at Monteverde, you might come across one of the fabulous quetzals that live in the region.

## Reserva Biológica Bosque Nuboso Monteverde

The **Reserva Biológica Bosque Nuboso Monteverde** *($8; every day 7am to 4pm; reception centre, restaurant, souvenir shop, guides, explanatory material, rain boot rentals; ☎645-5122, ⇒645-5034, montever@sol.rasca.co.cr)* is deservedly the main tourist attraction in the region for its outstanding natural features. The Monteverde reserve is actually a private ecological reserve, owned by the Centro Científico Tropical de San José. This non-profit organisation carries out scientific research and ecological education.

Through the reserve, the organization manages to raise visitors' awareness about the need to preserve the national treasure that is the tropical rainforest which, in addition to protecting flora and fauna, is a source of water for many of the surrounding valleys.

The concept of preserving this tropical rainforest entered the minds of scientists George and Harriet Powell in 1972, when they visited the region. With the help of a local resident, Wilford Guindon, they publicised the urgency of setting aside land to create a reserve to protect the rainforest. The Centro Científico Tropical de San José finally bought the land and created protected zones. The reserve began with 328 hectares. Then, in 1975, they received another 554 hectares from the Quaker community. Today, the reserve covers over 10,500 hectares of the tropical rainforest and, along with the Children's Eternal Forest (*Bosque Eterno de los Niños*) (see p 189) around the reserve, and the other nearby reserves and protected forests, the region of Monteverde can be seen as a model for environmental protection.

The Continental Divide runs through the park: rivers to the west of it flow toward the Pacific Ocean, and those to the east empty into the Caribbean. The Continental Divide is about two kilometres east of the reception and information centre. Because of this line there is great geographical and climatic diversity in different parts of the park, which can be experienced without having to travel long distances. While hiking along the trails in the reserve, be prepared for changeable weather conditions (rain, sun, wind, more rain, extreme humidity, etc). Bring a change of clothing, rain boots, a raincoat, or other rain gear, as well as a camera, insecticide – and don't forget your binoculars! The reserve is in the mountains (the reception centre is at an elevation of 1,530 m), so mornings can be quite cool and humid. The average temperature is around 17 degrees Celsius, and the annual precipitation exceeds three metres.

The landscapes change according to altitude. The lowest section, at 600 metres, is near the Río Peñas Blancas. The highest point is at the summit of Cerro Tres Amigos (1,842 m), in the northwest part of the reserve. Between these two extremes, the vegetation consists of rich forests with sometimes enormous trees covered in mosses, lianas and thousands of epiphytes that prevent the sun from reaching the ground. Among the approximately 2,500 plant species, there are no fewer than 420 kinds of orchids. The reserve is divided into six different horticultural zones, and the biodiversity of each is so complex that new scientific discoveries are constantly being made.

The reserve is also home to a hundred mammal species, including the jaguar, the ocelot and Baird's tapir. Though they are hard to spot, they sometimes leave their paw marks in the ground. On the other hand, mischievous howling and capuchin monkeys make themselves visible, or at least heard! And let's not forget amphibians and reptiles. Finally, over 400 bird species make the reserve a birdwatcher's paradise!

#### The Trails

The Monteverde reserve has seven hiking trails with a total length of 12.4 kilometres (not including the trails where access is limited). Only 120 visitors are allowed on the trails at one time. It is best to reserve your admissions ticket a night in advance (most hotels can do this and hire a guide for you) so you can arrive early

Sunset over magnificent Panamá beach, a tropical forest hideaway.
*- R. M.*

A church in the Central Valley surrounded by lovely magenta bougainvillaea.
*- D. R.*

Ox carts are still used in some parts of the country.
*- D. R.*

the next morning and get in a few hours for birdwatching. You can also spend the night in one of the three shelters off the trails, or in the shelter right at the entrance to the reserve (priority is given to groups and researchers). It is highly recommended to take the reserve's guided nature tour to learn more about the flora and fauna here. The **guided tour** *(day or evening at 7:30pm, reservations recommended, $15/person, plus entrance fee)* lasts about three hours. It begins at the Galería Colibrí (Hummingbird Gallery) with a short (10 minutes) slide presentation. It continues along a series of very short trails where the guide explains the diversity of the plant and animal life. After the tour, you can either attend another longer slide presentation (30 minutes) at the Galería Colibrí, or roam freely on designated trails through the reserve.

The very well-signed and maintained hiking trails in the reserve make it easy to explore the tropical rainforest (a map of the trails is included in the entrance fee). The most popular trails form a triangle (El Triangulo) to the east. The **Río** trail leads to Río Cuecha and its little waterfalls. The **Chomogo** trail climbs to an altitude of 1,680 metres and accesses the scenic lookout on the **Roble** trail. Finally, the nature interpretation trail, **Bosque Nuboso** (booklet available at the reception centre) consists of 28 numbered interpretation points that explain the reserve's flora and fauna. This trail ends at the scenic lookout, **La Ventura**, where the view extends for miles in all directions.

It's a two to six hour hike to the **three shelters** *($3.50/person/night, by reservation only)* that can accommodate up to ten hikers each, and come with electricity, a stove, cooking utensils, drinking water and a shower.

## Refugio Nacional de Vida Silvestre Caño Negro

**Refugio Nacional de Vida Silvestre Caño Negro** ★ *($6; every day 8am to 4pm; ☎460-1412, ⇛460-0644)* is in the extreme north of the country, near Nicaragua. The 9,969-hectare reserve is popular mostly for its 800-hectare lake. Actually, the size of the lake varies: during the rainy season it expands and sometime swells the Río Frío, whereas during the dry season, between January and April, it gradually shrinks, and sometimes even disappears!

Ornithologists, biologists and other naturalists are the most frequent visitors to this reserve, but more and more organized groups are coming to spend the day observing the exceptionally large number of animals in the reserve. In fact, Quebecker Mark Founier, a guide with Ecotours, actually prefers to bring his groups here, rather than to the Palo Verde reserve, because there are fewer tourists and thus more wildlife to be seen.

Most visitors enjoy exploring the reserve by boat or canoe along the Río Frío, starting from Los Chiles. During the excursion, caimans, turtles, iguanas, monkeys and other animals can be spotted. Among the abundant avian species you might see are American anhingas *(Anhinga anhinga)*, roseate spoonbills *(Ajaia ajaja)*, white ibises *(Eudocimus albus)*, American jacanas *(Jacana spinosa)*, American wood storks *(Mycteria Americana)*, whistling ducks *(Dendrocygna autunmalis)* and American jabirus *(Jabiru mycteria)*. The reserve is also home to the largest colony of olive cormorants *(Phalacrocorax olivaceus)* in Costa Rica, and the only colony of Nicaraguan grackles *(Quiscalus Nicaraguensis)*.

Apart from boat rides and observing the fauna, there is little to do in the way of outdoor activities at the reserve. When the lake dries up during the first half of the year, it can be explored on foot. Camping is permitted. The small park rangers' house is also the reception and information centre. We strongly recommend visiting the reserve through a tourist agency (in San José or in La Fortuna), or with a guide from Los Chiles.

## OUTDOOR ACTIVITIES

### Hiking

**Parque Nacional Arenal** (see p 183) has short, but extremely interesting trails that lead to excellent viewpoints of the volcano and lava flows.

Right next to the park, **Arenal Observatory Lodge** (see p 185) also has a network of hiking trails and an incredible view of the volcano.

The region of **Monteverde** has everything an experienced hiker could desire. The flora and fauna of the tropical rainforest attract people from all over the world. The trails in the Santa Elena reserve, the Finca Ecológica, the Children's Eternal Forest and the Sendero Tranquilo reserve are also accessible to visitors.

### Birdwatching

The region of **Monteverde** has over 400 bird species, including the rare quetzal (see p 191).

Ornithologists consider the **Refugio Nacional de Vida Silvestre Caño Negro** (see p 193) one of the best-kept secrets of Costa Rica. Avian fauna here is abundant and diverse. There are several species of water birds.

### Rafting

**Aguas Bravas** *(☎229-4837 in La Fortuna, or ☎292-2072 in San José)* offers white-water rafting on Río Sarapiquí (class III) or on the Haut Sarapiquí (class IV and V) in the area of Puerto Viejo, as well as on Río Peñas Blancas (class II and IV) near the Arenal Volcano.

### Horseback Riding

In the region of **Monteverde** you can go horseback riding with or without a guide. Renting a horse costs between $8 and $12 per hour. Just ask at the hotel, or call Chunches in Santa Elena *(☎645-5147)*. Also, **Meg's Stables** *(☎645-5560)* gives guided horseback rides *($10/hour or $35 for 5 hours)* that are very popular with tourists.

### Canopy Tours

On the **Canopy Tour** *($40; starting times are 7:30am, 10:30am and at 2:30pm; reservations suggested during the high season, ☎645-5243 or 257-5149)* you can pretend you are Tarzan swinging from treetop to treetop in the forest, only you are wearing a harness attached to a pulley system. The activity consists of hoisting yourself onto a platform at the top of an enormous tree, then sliding along cables from one treetop to another. This is a unique way to observe the dense vegetation from 30 metres up in the air! The tour lasts about 2.5 hours, including the short walk through the forest to the starting point. The organizers are busy constructing a longer course that should be even more thrilling.

## ACCOMMODATIONS

### The Puerto Viejo de Sarapiquí Region

**Puerto Viejo de Sarapiquí**

**Cabinas Monteverde** *($; pb, ⊗, ☎766-7236)* offers the basic comforts to travellers on a tight budget, and is near a popular restaurant.

**Mi Lindo Sarapiquí** *($$; hw, pb, ⊗, ℜ; on the south side of the football field, ☎766-6281 or 766-6074)* is another reasonably-priced hotel in Sarapiquí. The rooms are bright and clean, but simply decorated. It has a good little restaurant (see p 205).

**El Bambu** *($$$$ bkfst incl.; pb, hw, ⊗, tv; on the west side of the football field, ☎766-6005, ⇌766-6132)* is the best hotel in the city of Puerto Viejo de Sarapiquí as far as appearance and layout are concerned. Free for children under twelve if they stay in their parents' room.

**West of Puerto Viejo de Sarapiquí**

**Islas del Río** *($$$$ bkfst incl.; hw, sb/pb, some rooms have bathtubs, ⊗, ℜ; 6 km west of Puerto Viejo, Bajos del Chilamate, ☎766-6898)* has 30 very comfortable rooms. Discounts for Youth Hostelling International members. They offer white-water rafting on the river, and there are hiking and horseback riding trails in the vicinity.

**Quinta de Sarapiquí Lodge** *($$$$; pb, hw, ⊗, ℜ; 5 km north of La Virgen on the main road between Puerto Viejo and La Virgen, then one km west; ☎761-1052)* is a country house with about 10 rooms, set in a beautiful garden on the banks of the Río Sardinal. It is a fun place to stay because of the many activities suggested by its friendly hosts, such as swimming in the river, mountain biking, birdwatching, horseback riding and sailing.

**La Selva Verde** *($$$$$; in Chilamate, a few kilometres west of Puerto Viejo; ☎766 6077, ⇌766-6011)* is a rustic hotel, set in its own 200-hectare reserve. Its lovely verandas, little library, restaurant, well-tended flowerbeds and trails in the reserve add to its charm. Whether you explore the trails alone or with a guide, you will come across birds, butterflies, mammals, reptiles, and all their friends. There are also outings on the Río Sarapiquí. Free for children under 12 if they stay in their parents' room.

**South of Sarapiquí**

**Ecolodge Sarapiquí** *($$$/person fb; sb, ⊗; just west of La Selva, ☎766-6122 or 253-2533, ⇌253-8645)* is a family-run affair on an 80-hectare dairy farm. The rooms are on the second floor of the main building and the bathrooms are on the ground floor. The place is as clean as can be and the home-cooked meals are good. You can go swimming in the Río Puerto Viejo, which runs through the property.

**El Plastico** *($$$/person fb; hw, sb; 12 km from Horqueta, Rara Avis)* in the Rara Avis ecological reserve was once a jungle penal colony. It is rustic (shared rooms and showers) but comfortable. Meals are vegetarian. Discounts for students and researchers.

**Waterfall Lodge** *($$$$/person fb; guided tours and transportation from Horquetas; hw, pb; 3 km from*

THE NORTH

*El Plastico, Rara Avis)* is next to a lovely waterfall; hence the name. Slightly less rustic than El Plastico, with a private bathroom and a balcony in each room, but no electricity.

### North of Sarapiquí

**El Gavilán Lodge** *($$$$ bkfst incl.; hw, sb/pb, wp; 4 km north-east of Puerto Viejo, ☎234-9507, ⇄253-6556)* is tucked away in a 100-hectare tropical rainforest reserve. It has fairly spacious rooms and *cabinas* with large, private bathrooms (a few of the rooms have shared baths). They organize horseback riding and excursions in the reserve and the surrounding area. You can birdwatch while enjoying meals made with freshly picked fruits from the jungle.

Much farther north, **Oro Verde Station** *($$$$ bkfst incl.; sb/pb; 40 km north of Puerto Viejo, ☎/⇄233-7479)* is a 2,500-hectare reserve located on the Río Sarapiquí, not far from the Nicaraguan border. It offers rustic *cabinas* with shared or private baths, but without hot water. There is also a dormitory *($)* for students, and others on tight budgets. Few of the staff in this remote place speak English, but if you understand Spanish they can tell you a lot about the surrounding environment.

## La Selva

You can stay at the ecological reserve, **La Selva** *($$$$$ fb; sb; 3 km south of Puerto Viejo de Sarapiquí, ☎740-1515, ⇄740-1414 or via OTS ☎240-6696, ⇄240-6783)*, by making reservations in advance. The bedrooms are in bungalows, with four beds per room. Everything is very clean. Meals are served in the dining hall where researchers and students also eat.

## Ciudad Quesada and Surroundings

**Hotel del Valle** *($; pb, hw, tv in main living room; 200 m north and 50 m west of the central park, Calle 3, Avenida 0, Ciudad Quesada, ☎460-0718)* is a typical small city hotel, ideal for people on a very tight budget who want to spend the night in Cuidad Quesada.

**La Central** *($$; hw, pb, tv; on the west side of the central park, Cuidad Quesada, ☎460-0766 or 460-0301, ⇄460-0391)* may be one of the best places to stay in town. With 48 clean rooms, it has the feel of a large hotel. It also houses a casino.

**DonGoyo** *($$; pb, hw in shower, 100 m south of the central park, Ciudad Quesada, ☎460-1780)* is newer than La Central, and has a more modern design. The13 rooms are clean, and there is a small restaurant on the main floor.

The herons that nest around **La Garza** *($$$; pb, hw, ⊛, ☎, laundry service, ≈; Platanar, between Florencia and La Muelle, northwest of Ciudad Quesada, ☎475-5222, ⇄475-5051)* can be seen from your hotel window in the evenings. The hotel was named after them: *garza* is Spanish for "heron." The hotel complex is near a ranch, a dairy farm and a 300-hectare forest where guests can participate in many activities. The wooden decor of the rooms is charming. The majestic Arenal Volcano is part of the landscape.

**Tilajari Resort** *($$$$; hw, pb, △, ≡, ☎, ≈, ℜ; Muelle de San Carlos, 22 km north of Ciudad Quesada, ☎469-9091, ⇄469-9095)* is a large hotel in the heart of the San Carlos Valley, 40 minutes from the Arenal Volcano. The 12-hectare property nurtures more than 150 species of tropical plants and trees that grow around the Río San Carlos. Hiking, horseback riding and butterfly "hunting" are some of the activities offered. The housekeeping meets high standards. The large hotel complex includes: a pool, a whirlpool, a sauna; tennis, racquetball and basketball courts; games and conference rooms; a bar, a nightclub and a souvenir shop.

**El Tucano** *($$$$; hw, pb, bathtubs, ≈, ⊛, ⌂, ℜ; 8 km northeast of San Carlos on the road to Aguas Zarcas, ☎460-6000 or 460-3152, ⇌460-1692, tucano@centralamerica.com)* is really a spa in the middle of a 182-hectare forest. It offers physiotherapy and therapeutic baths with water from the area's hot springs. This modern and attractively decorated hotel complex includes tennis courts and even minigolf. An Italian restaurant and vegetarian restaurant complete the facilities.

## The Arenal Region

### La Fortuna and Surroundings

La Fortuna hotel establishments often offer horseback riding excursions to the volcano and elsewhere. There are also so many little *cabinas* for rent that you should have no problem finding one, even during the high season. However, not all of them have swimming pools, a real disadvantage given how hot it can get in this part of the country.

Right in the city of La Fortuna, on the road along the Río Burío, is **Hotel La Fortuna** *($; hw, pb; ☎479-9197)*, a well-maintained, basic establishment whose outgoing owner organizes all kinds of excursions in the area. The restaurant serves simple *tica* and North American dishes in a friendly and sedate atmosphere.

**Cabinas Mayol** *($; pb, ⊗; ☎479-9110)* have eight sparsely furnished rooms (true of most of the cabinas in the area). There are plans for a restaurant and pool in the future. **Cabinas Jerry** *(☎479-9063)* offers the same level of accommodations as Cabinas Mayol.

Multilingual signs lead to **Cabinas Adriana** *($; pb)*, which boasts of having the least expensive rooms in town. This is hard to prove, since most of the cabinas in the city are similarly priced.

Just west of Cabinas Adriana, **Cabinas Sissy** *($; hw, pb; 100 m south and 100 m west of the church, La Fortuna, ☎479-9256)* is another good choice for anyone on a limited budget.

**Cabinas Carmela** *($$; hw, pb, laundry service; one street past the La Central hotel, near Avenida 0 and Calle 0, next to the church, La Fortuna, ☎479-9010)* offer the same type of accommodations as the other *cabinas* in the region (small bedrooms in small detached units on the property). But these *cabinas* also function as unofficial tourist information centres, since the owners can tell you all about the area and suggest all sorts of things to see and do.

There are three establishments that resemble each other in the downtown area of La Fortuna: **Cabinas La Amistad** *($$; hw, pb, P; on Principale, near the church, La Fortuna, ☎479-9364)*, **Grijalba** *($$; hw, pb, P; next to Cabinas La Amistad, on Principale, La Fortuna, ☎479-9129)* and **Oriuma** *($$; Calle 2; and Avenida 1, almost directly opposite Rancho La Cascada, La Fortuna)*. Each offers clean and simply furnished rooms.

**Cabinas Guacamaya** *($$; hw, pb, ≡, ℝ, laundry service; at the eastern edge of La Fortuna, ☎/⇄479-9393)* are two clean, modern *cabinas* set out in the owners' family garden. The little shaded porches are perfect for relaxing and admiring the volcano in hot weather. The friendly owner went even further to beat the heat: he personally installed the air-conditioning and refrigerators in the *cabinas*.

**Cabinas Villa Fortuna** *($$; pb, hw, ℝ, ≡; 500 m east of the Colegio Agropecuario, La Fortuna, ☎479-9139)* is immaculate. The lay-out of the rooms (in the small motel) or apartments makes it all the more pleasant to stay here, which is not the case for all the cabinas in the area. The only thing lacking is a pool, which is promised for the near future. The owners are hospitable, even to animals – they lovingly care for all the injured birds in the neighbourhood.

**Burio Inn** *($$$ bkfst incl.; hw, pb, ⊗; on Principale, between the El Jardin restaurant and the football field, La Fortuna, ☎/⇄479-9076)* offers attractively decorated rooms in the owners' home. The place is often full, even in the low season.

**Cabinas Monte Real** *($$$; hw, pb, ≡ or ⊗; 100 m west and 100 m south of Banco de Costa Rica, La Fortuna, ☎/⇄479-9243)* consist of three clean, simple rooms behind the house.

**San Bosco** *($$$; hw, pb, ≡, Calle 2, Avenida 1, 200 m north of the service station, La Fortuna, ☎479-9050, ⇄479-9109)* is a 29-room hotel with two *casitas* that are clean and comfortable, but simply decorated. There is even an observation tower. This is probably the one place among the town's establishments that deserves to call itself a hotel. There are plans for a swimming pool in the near future.

Between La Fortuna and El Tanque, **Las Cabañitas** *($$$; hw, ⊗, pb, ≈; ☎479-9400 or 479-9343, ⇄479-9408, gasguis@sol.racsa.co.cr)* offers very stylish wooden *cabinas* with pretty little verandas. There is a swimming pool (a blessing!) on the fair-sized grounds. The tropical landscaping includes lots of flowers.

**Rancho Corcovado** *($$$$; pb, hw, ≈; El Tanque de La Fortuna, ☎479-9300, ⇄479-9090)* has clean, functional motel rooms around a pool and restaurant. A little lake beautifies the spot, and is a great place for birdwatching. Taxiplane service is available. Like at most of the nearby hotels, excursions in the region can be arranged.

### Around the Arenal Volcano

The ecotourism inn **La Catarata Lodge** *($$; hw, pb; 1.5 km south of the main road to the volcano from La Fortuna, ☎479-9522)* has a butterfly garden, a little restaurant and very decent rooms. The main reason for staying here is to support the Associación Para el Ambiante y el Desarollo Sustenable, a local association that promotes sustainable development.

**Cabinas Rossi** *($$$ bkfst incl.; hw, pb, ⊗; 1 km outside La Fortuna towards the volcano, next to the La Vaca Muca restaurant, 479-9023, ⇄479-9414)* are a cut above the rest. The *cabinas* have refrigerators and breakfast is included.

**Montaña de Fuego** *($$$; pb, hw, ⊗; 8 km west of La Fortuna towards the Arenal Volcano, ☎382-0759)* has little wooden cottages with adorable solariums that look out to the volcano. The tropical landscaping is already pretty, and will improve as it fills out. You can have breakfast here.

There is nothing fancy about the accommodations at the **Arenal Observatory Lodge** *($$$; hw, pb, Lake Arenal, ☎257-9489, ⇄257-4220, arenalob@sol.racsa.co.cr)*, but it is the best place to observe the volcano. There are three bunk beds to a room, and meals are served in a communal dining hall. This establishment functions as a research centre for seismologists from the Smithsonian Institute and the Universidad Nacional de Costa Rica. There are organized visits to nearby points of interest.

Very close to the volcano, **Jungla y Senderos Los Lagos** *($$$; ℜ; between La Fortuna and the Tabacón Resort, ☎/⇄479-9126)* has very comfortable rooms and little *cabinas* in a complex that includes swimming pools with water slides, a lake for swimming and another for fishing. The hiking trails lead to the volcano's restricted zone, where you can touch hardened lava from the 1968 eruption. There are also a camping area and a restaurant. Plans have been made to add tennis courts, hot springs and whirlpools.

**Cabañas Arenal Paraíso** *($$$$; hw, pb, ⊛, ℝ, laundry service; 7 km west of La Fortuna towards the Arenal Volcano, very close to the Tabacon Resort, ☎/⇄479-9006)* rents clean, simply decorated little *cabinas* with private verandas from which you can admire the volcano up close. The landscaping has been recently done and will improve with time. There are hiking trails through the 60-hectare property.

The **Arenal Lodge** *($$$$; hw, sb, ℜ, ⊛; 2.5 km from the Lake Arenal dike, between La Fortuna and Nuevo Arenal, ☎228-3189 or 383-3957, ⇄289-6789, arenal@sol.racsa.co.cr)* has a "woodsy" decor, and so do its rooms in the main building and its little cottages. The library doubles as a billiards room, so you won't be bored! The view of the lake and of the volcano is lovely. Guided fishing trips on the lake are organized.

The new hotel **La Pradera** *($$$$; pb, hw, ⊗/≡, ⊛; on the road between La Fortuna and the Arenal Volcano, ☎/⇄479-9167)* offers modern, comfortable and very clean rooms in a motel-style building. Some rooms have whirlpool bathtubs. The restaurant that inspired the project is close by (see p 206).



**Around Lake Arenal**

Some 30 kilometres from La Fortuna, **Los Héroes** *($$$$ bkfst incl.; pb, hw, ≈, ℜ, ⊛, bar; ☎/⇄441-4193)* is a Swiss chalet-style hotel on a little hill above Lake Arenal. The common areas of the hotel are decorated with Swiss memorabilia, and the restaurant menu includes some Swiss dishes (see p 206). This is a fairly comfortable place to stay, with simple, sedate rooms.

**Villa Decary** *($$$$ bkfst incl.; 2 km east of Nuevo Arenal, on Lake Arenal, ⇄694-4330 or 694-4132)* is outstanding. The clean rooms are the utmost in comfort and beautifully decorated with wooden furnishings. They also have lovely little verandas with a view of the lake. This is a place to remember! The property also includes a separate cottage with kitchenette and a large porch. Tranquillity prevails here. The owners are eminently charming, and their breakfasts are divine. Don't hesitate to ask them anything about the region.

### Nuevo Arenal

**Cabinas Rodríguez** *($; sb/pb, hw; across from the football field, ☎694-4237)* has inexpensive rooms without much furnishing, besides the bed. Breakfast isn't available here, but the owner is very friendly.

**La Ceiba** *($$ bkfst incl.; pb, hw; 6 km from Nuevo Arenal going towards the volcano, ☎/⇒694-4297, scngrsp@sol.racsa.co.cr)* is a Bed & Breakfast with a lot to offer. First of all, it is located on a hill overlooking peaceful Lake Arenal. Secondly, it has been beautifully decorated by the owners, who are professional painters. Thirdly, the cuisine, made with ingredients from the hosts' organic garden, is excellent (you can even eat in the garden). Finally, you can commune with nature by hiking along the paths that lead through the surrounding forest, or by simply relaxing in a hammock between two trees. It is also possible to rent a sailboat.

**Aurora Inn B&B** *($$$ bkfst incl.; hw, ⊗, ☎694-4245 ⇒694-4262)* in downtown Nueve Arenal should be called a hotel in terms of cleanliness and comfort. There is no restaurant, but there is a bar open at night, with a view of the lake.

**Joya Sureña** *($$$; hw, pb, ℜ, ⌂, ⊘, ≈; ☎694-4057, ⇒694-4059, joysur@sol.racsa.co.cr)* is a small hotel complex on a coffee plantation with a lovely view of Lake Arenal. The rooms are soberly arranged. The main building is more Canadian in design, with sloping roofs and dormer windows (relatively rare in Costa Rica).

### Between Nuevo Arenal and Tilarán

**Rala de Arenal** *($$; hw, pb; close to the main road between Nuevo Arenal and Tilarán, the road that goes to Lago Coter Eco-Lodge and Telarán)* is a simple little hotel recommended for its small but clean rooms. The rooms are on the first floor; on the second are a restaurant with little tables, and a cozy, quiet bar. The building is set back from the road in the lush tropical vegetation that acts as a noise buffer. There are a small river and a fountain. The access road is in pretty good condition.

Located on a hill, **Chalet Nicholas** *($$$ bkfst incl.; pb, hw; 2 km west of Nuevo Arenal, ☎694-4041)* is actually a very attractive Bed & Breakfast where guests are really encouraged to feel at home. The owners are friendly, with a strong interest in ecology (organic gardening, reforestation, etc.) which has won them several awards. They will be more than pleased to tell you what there is to see and do in the area. Non-smokers only.

**Log Lagos** *($$$; hw, pb; 8 km west of Nuevo Arenal, on the road to Tlarán, ☎694-4271)* belongs to a very likable couple from the United States. The wife is the chef of the restaurant (see p 207). There is a magnificent view of the lake from here. The rooms in *cabinas* are clean and attractive.

Far from the main road, near the lovely little rushing river, **Puerto Lajas** *($$$ bkfst incl.; pb, hw; 200 m from the main road between Arenal and Tilarán, ☎694-4116 or 694-4169)* offers clean rooms in a home, as well as hiking, horseback and boat excursions.

**Villas Alpino** *($$$; hw, pb, K; 12 km west of Nuevo Arenal going towards Tilarán, ⇒284-3841)* consist of large *cabinas* with lots of rustic charm. They have bar-kitchenettes and large balconies with a view of the lake and the volcano in the distance. The well-tended landscaping will be beautiful once the plants are fully grown. Even the little road to the hotel is in good condition (which is unusual for this area).

**Cabinas Vista Lago Inn** *($$$; pb, hw; 17 km from Tilarán, towards Nuevo Arenal, near the municipality of Guadalajara, ☎661-1363)* has a few clean *cabinas* near the lake.

A little bit past the popular windsurfing spot, on the western side of Lake Arenal, **Xiloe Lodge** *($$$; pb, hw; ☎259-9806, ⇌259-9882)* has comfortable little *cabinas* and is sheltered from the noise of the road by some large trees. The management suggests places for going out, as well as horseback riding and boat rides.

**Lago Coter Eco-Lodge** *($$$$; hw, pb, balconies with some of the rooms, ℜ; near Lake Coter, northwest of Nuevo Arenal, ☎257-5075, ⇌257-7065)* is a real lodge for nature lovers, with an attractive rustic decor, which is very inviting, especially after making the arduous journey up the road to get there! You can participate in the many outdoor activities (hiking, horseback riding, mountain biking, birdwatching, water sports, excursions to different points of interest in the area, etc.), or stay indoors and just relax in front of the fireplace in the living room of the main building, play billiards, or watch television or videos in the game room. The lodge has private access to 260 hectares on Lake Coter and to the private biological reserve near the lake.

**Rock River Lodge** *($$$$; between Nuevo Arenal and Tilarán, on Lake Arenal, near the town of Guadalajara, ☎695-5644)* is owned by a dedicated sports lover. It reflects the great outdoors, with its wood construction and all the outdoor activities it offers. The rooms are quaint, and the cottages are charmingly rustic. The bar and restaurant (see p 207) are also very attractive. The view of Lake Arenal is breathtaking! Windsurfing boards and mountain bicycles can be rented here.

**Tilawa** *($$$$; hw, pb, ≈, ℜ, bar; between Nuevo Arenal and Tilarán, at the eastern end of Lake Arenal, ☎695-5050)* is an extraordinary little hotel complex, thanks to the owner's wife who decorated it like the palace of Cnossos, on the island of Crete. The rooms are modern and comfortable and have excellent views of this very windy part of Lake Arenal. There is a tennis court, and guided horseback and sailboat rides are offered. Mountain bicycles can also be rented. The wind makes the evenings quite chilly, and the fireplace in the hotel's living room provides welcomed warmth.

## The Monteverde Region

The village of **Santa Elena** is full of inexpensive little inns and *pensións*. Some of the roads leading to the hotels can be in bad condition due to the heavy rains. Because the region of Monteverde is one of the most popular tourist destinations in the country, it is best to make reservations in advance, particularly during the high season, from the end of December to April.

In Santa Elena, the Albergue Santa Elena (see below) also offers places for **camping** *($3/person; ☎645-5051)*.

Located behind the Banco Nacional de Santa Elena, **Hospedaje El Banco** *($; sb, hw)* rents single rooms, ideal if you are on a limited budget.

**Cabinas Marín** *($; sb, hw)* is located some 300 metres north of Santa Elena. The rooms are small, but decent enough for the price.

**Pension Colibrí** *($; sb, hw)* is somewhat far from the village. It has reasonably priced rooms and organizes horseback rides.

In the heart of Santa Elena, **Albergue Santa Elena** *($-$$; pb, hw, ℜ; ☎645-5051, ⇄645-5147)* offers small reasonably priced rooms. Students receive a discount. The restaurant serves a varied but tasty cuisine: the menu includes everything from traditional cooking to vegetarian dishes.

**Hotel El Tucán** *($-$$; sb/pb, hw, ℜ; ☎645-5017, ⇄645-5462*) is run by Señora Rosa Jiménez Venegas and her family. It is located 100 metres east of the Banco Nacional, in Santa Elena, and offers basic, clean rooms. The restaurant serves delicious home-style Costa Rican cooking that is sure to please tourists on tight budgets.

**Pensión El Sueño** *($-$$; sb/pb, hw; ☎645-3656 or 645-5021)* offers very simple and very inexpensive rooms in a family atmosphere.

At the northern end of Santa Elena, near the Reserva Bosque Nuboso Santa Elena, **Pensión La Flor de Monteverde** *($-$$; sb/pb, hw, ℜ; ☎/⇄645-5236)* provides immaculate rooms in a peaceful, family environment. The owner, Eduardo Venegas, is also an administrator at the *Reserva*. They offer transportation to the reserve and different guided activities.

Near the bank, **Albergue Marbella** *($$; pb, hw, ☎645-5153, ⇄645-5159)* has large, clean rooms and a relaxed atmosphere.

Perched on a hill above the village of Santa Elena, **Ecolodge Arco Iris** *($$-$$$; pb, hw, ℜ; ☎645-5067, ⇄645-5022, arcoiris@sol.racsa.co.cr)* has different rooms that range in price from $25 to $45. Campers can put up tents for $3 per person. The owners, Susanna Stoiber and Haymo Heyder, serve fresh produce from their organic garden during the tourist season.

**Cabinas Gulf View B&B** *($$$ bkfst incl.; pb, hw; ☎645-5263)* also rents simple rooms at a reasonable price. From here, you can see all the way to the Gulf of Nicoya.

**El Gran Mirador Lodge** *($$$; sb/pb, hw, ℜ, ☎/⇄645-5087)* is over eight kilometres from Santa Elena, in San Gerardo. Guests can rent *cabinas* with private bath *($50)*, or stay in a dorm with shared bath *($30)*. This establishment is peaceful and isolated, and has a superb view of the region with the imposing Arenal Volcano in the background.

About one kilometre from Santa Elena, **Sunset Hotel** *($$$ bkfst incl.; pb, hw, ℜ; ☎645-5048)* has attractive and very clean rooms. You can also see the Gulf of Nicoya from here.

**Cloud Forest Lodge** *($$$-$$$$; pb, hw, ℜ; ☎645-5058, ⇄645-5168)* is located northeast of Santa Elena, in a lush tropical forest. The wooden *cabinas* are comfortable and spacious. You can hike through the forest, end even explore it from the canopy (see p 194). There is an attractive view of the Gulf of Nicoya from the terrace in the garden and from the bar-restaurant.

#### Santa Elena to the Reserva Biológica Bosque Nuboso Monteverde

About four kilometres from the Monteverde reserve, **Pensión Manakin**

*($$; sb/pb, hw; ☎/⇄645-5080)* offers modest rooms with or without private bath.

Near the Butterfly Garden (see p 188), **Pensión Monteverde Inn** *($$; pb, hw; ☎645-5156)* has a friendly family atmosphere in a private and tranquil setting. A trail descends to the canyon in the valley. The rooms are modest and inexpensive *($10/person)*, while breakfast *($3.50)* is reputedly excellent. If you make reservations in advance, the owner can pick you up from the bus stop in Santa Elena.

Near La Lechería cheese factory (see p 189), **Pensión Flor Mar** *($$-$$$; sb/pb, hw; ☎/⇄645-5009)* has ordinary rooms in a warm family atmosphere. The meals are excellent. However, it was for sale when we went through the area.

**Cabañas Los Pinos** *($$$; pb, hw, K; ☎645-5252, ⇄645-5005)* are comfortable *cabinas* with kitchenettes. The owner, Señor Jovinos Arguedas, also runs a 140-hectare farm where he raises Brahma bulls.

Ruth Campbell and Arnoldo Beeche are the owners of **El Establo** *($$$; pb, hw; ☎645-5033, ⇄645-5041)*. They provide simple rooms in a relaxed atmosphere. Behind the establishment are 60 hectares of tropical rainforest just waiting to be explored. There is also a dining room that is only open to guests of the hotel.

The Vargas-Arguedas family runs **Hotel El Bosque** *($$$; pb, hw; ☎645-5221, ⇄645-5129)*, and the restaurant of the same name. They offer modest, but very clean rooms. The hotel also provides green spaces for campers *($2.50/person)*. There is a volleyball court on the premises. You can walk to the nearby Bajo del Tigre reserve, which is great for hiking and birdwatching.

Just at the end of the village of Santa Elena, near the road going to Monteverde, **Hotel Finca Valverde** *($$$; pb, hw, ℜ; ☎645-5157, ⇄645-5216)* rents wooden *cabinas* near the family farmhouse which has a balcony on the second floor.

**Hospedaje Mariposa** *($$$ bkfst incl.; pb, hw; ☎645-5013)* offers three clean, simple rooms. The owners, Luzmery Mata and Rafael Vargas, serve meals exclusively to their guests.

North of the main road to the Monteverde reserve, **El Sapo Dorado** *($$$$; pb, hw, ℜ, ℝ; ☎645-5010, ⇄645-5180, elsapo@sol.racsa.co.cr)* offers 20 luxurious mountain *cabinas* in two categories. The "Sunset Hill" *cabinas* have refrigerators and a spectacular view of the Gulf of Nicoya, while the "Classic" ones have fireplaces, and are more romantic. The restaurant (see p 208) is one of the best in the region.

High on a hilltop, **Hotel Belmar** *($$$$; pb, hw, ℜ; ☎645-5201, ⇄645-5135)* looks out over the Gulf of Nicoya. To get there, take the little road next to the service station. The spacious, comfortable bedrooms are in two charming mountain cottages, with very pleasant surroundings. The restaurant serves excellent international cuisine.

Charming and comfortable, **Hotel Heliconia** *($$$$; pb, hw, ℜ, ⊛; ☎645-5109, ⇄645-5007)* is just one kilometre outside Santa Elena, on the way to the Monteverde reserve. The rooms and *cabinas* are pleasant and clean. Some have rocking chairs on the terrace. There is a restaurant-bar, a whirlpool bath, and a fireplace that is fitting for a mountain cabin. Guests can wander through the large forest area that belongs to the owner of the hotel.

Right on the main road, **Hotel Montaña** *($$$$; pb, hw, ℜ, ⊛; ☎645-5046, ⇌645-5320, monteverde@sol.racsa.co.cr)* is one of the oldest hotel establishments in the area. Its 32 rooms and suites offer comfort and luxury. Guests have access to the mineral baths, whirlpool, sauna, restaurant, bar, conference room, hiking trails, evening slide presentation, etc.

**Hotel Fonda Vela** *($$$$-$$$$$; pb, hw, ℜ, ⊗, ℝ; ☎/⇌257-1413, fondavel@sol.racsa.co.cr)*, near the Monteverde reserve, is an elegant hotel. Its owners, the Smiths, have created a relaxing, country atmosphere. There are 28 spacious rooms and suites. You can explore the surrounding tropical rainforest on hiking trails.

Off the main road, about two kilometres from the Monteverde reserve, **Hotel Villa Verde** *($$$$-$$$$$ bkfst incl.; pb, hw, K, ℜ; ☎645-5025, ⇌645-5115, estefany@sol.racsa.co.cr)* offers total relaxation in standard, comfortable rooms, or suites with kitchenettes and fireplaces. The restaurant serves Costa Rican dishes and international cuisine. There is a free slide presentation in the evenings about the region's wealth of flora and fauna.

Staying at the **San Luis Ecolodge and Biological Station** *($$$-$$$$ fb; sb/pb, hw, ℜ; ☎/⇌645-5277, smithdp@ctrvax.vanderbilt.edu)* is a whole different kind of vacation experience thanks to the many activities offered by its owners, ecologists Diana and Milton Lieberman. The 70-hectare biological research station is geared towards ecotourism and education. There are two types of accommodations: dormitory with shared bath *($50/person, meals included)*, or room with private bath *($80/person, meals included)*.

The well-respected **Monteverde Lodge** *($$$$$; pb, hw, ℜ, ⊛, non-smoking; ☎257-0766 or 645-5057, ⇌257-1665, costaric@expeditions.co.cr)* is owned and operated by Costa Rica Expeditions and blends harmoniously with the tropical rainforest. This luxury hotel has been redesigned to emphasize the beauty of the natural treasures surrounding it. The Monteverde Lodge is particularly proud of its gardens: little paths run through them, along which you can discover indigenous plants of the region and the many different bird species. The 27 tasteful and elegantly decorated rooms are also very charming. A table for two in front of a large window looking out onto the forest is the perfect place to relax after a day of exploring in the Monteverde reserve. The spacious bathroom is fully functional. The meals in the restaurant are superb (see p 208). In the evening, guests gather around the circular fireplace in the bar next door to exchange stories about their day's adventures and sip some of the wonderful fruit punch. The 15-person hot-tub is also relaxing. Most of the activities take place in the Monteverde and Santa Elena reserves. The guided night tour is especially interesting, because it gives you the chance to observe nocturnal animals and plants. There is a 10-minute-long path from the hotel to the Finca Ecológica, where there are more trails and scenic views. In the evening, there is a slide presentation in the conference room about the region's flora and fauna. During the high season, the price for a double-occupancy room is $90.79; full board plus taxes costs $97.60 per person per day. A stay of three days and two nights, including transportation from San José, double-occupancy room, meals and a guided excursion in the Monteverde reserve, comes to $399 per person. Note that smoking is strictly forbidden inside the hotel.

## RESTAURANTS

### The Puerto Viejo de Sarapiquí Region

**El Bambu** *($$; 7am to 10pm; on the east side of the football field, Puerto Viejo, ☎766-6005, ⇌766-6132)* is one of the most modern and well-maintained restaurants in the city. It serves mainly Costa Rican food and a few international dishes.

We recommend the hotel restaurant at the **Mi Lindo Sarapiquí** *($$; 9am to 10pm; south side of the football field, Puerto Viejo, ☎766-6281 or 766-6074)* (see p 195) not only for the quality of the food, but also for the service.

### Ciudad Quesada and Surroundings

Cuidad Quesada has a whole series of little restaurants that are more like *sodas*, than real restaurants, particularly around the central park. **El Parque** *($; Avenida 0, Calle 0)* is one of them.

As its name implies, **Pizzería y Pollo Frito Pin Pollo** *($; Avenida 1, Calle 0, Cuidad Quesada, ☎460-1801)* serves pizza and fried chicken at reasonable prices.

**La Jarra** *($$; south side of the cathedral in Ciudad Quesada, ☎460-0985)* serves local cuisine and fast food (hamburgers). It is clean, and one of the few restaurants in the downtown area that isn't better described as a hole in the wall.

**Tonjibe** *($$; on the avenue alongside the park, between Calle Central and Calle 1, Cuidad Quesada)* serves a variety of dishes, and is cleaner than most of the other restaurants in the city. A dance club in the back gets going at night.

### The Arenal Region

**Near La Fortuna**

For pastry, go to the *panadería-repostería*-coffee shop **Los Antojitos** *($)*, next to the La Fortuna post office.

For ice-cream, there is a **Mönpik** *($)* in La Fortuna.

On the same road as the post office in La Fortuna, **Nene's** *($; ☎479-9192)* serves good, reasonably priced steak, among other dishes.

Just before leaving La Fortuna, towards El Tanque, **Pizzería Luygi's** *($; ☎479-9636)* serves good pizza.

The tiny, recently opened *soda*, **La Tía Ara** *($; every day 6am to 10pm; diagonally across from the La Fortuna Hotel, ☎479 9172)* is a great find! Aunt Ara serves wonderful little hamburgers and other fast food dishes with a smile.

**Choza de Laurel** *($$; Principale, on the west side of La Fortuna)* serves a *tico* buffet.

**El Jardín** *($$; on Principale, one block from the football field, in La Fortuna)* is a large restaurant with an outdoor terrace. Its *tica* dishes are good quality for the price.

On the opposite side of the park, **Rancho La Cascada** *($$; Calle 2, Avenida 1, La Fortuna)* is in a huge hut with a thatched-palm roof. The food is good and provided by the San Bosco hotel (see p 198).

At the outskirts of La Fortuna, towards the Arenal Volcano and near Cabinas Paraíso Tropical, is the **Restaurante Vegetariano** *($$)*, and inexpensive and very pleasant vegetarian restaurant.

Also at the limit of La Fortuna, towards the volcano, is **La Pradera** *($$; ☎479-9167)*, which serves *tico* dishes; steaks and seafood in an enormous, open-air hut. Service is courteous.

**Pizzería-Spaghettaría Vagabondo** *($$; Mon to Fri 5pm to 11pm, Sat and Sun 12pm to 12am; 1.5 km west of the church in La Fortuna, towards the Arenal Volcano, ☎479-9565)* is run by Italians. Excellent pizzas are served in an open, airy dining room. Relaxed atmosphere.

### Near the Arenal Volcano

International cuisine is served under the roof of a large hut at **El Novio** *($$; between La Fortuna and Arenal, not far from Tabacón Resort)*. This is *the* place for outdoor dining.

The two restaurants at the **Tabacón Resort** *($$; every day 10am to 10pm; 13 km west of La Fortuna, on the road to the Arenal Volcano, ☎222-1072 or 233-0780, ⇄221-3075)* really light up at night. They are pleasantly set up next to the hot spring swimming pools. One restaurant serves international, *tica* and even vegetarian dishes, and the other offers lighter, simpler meals in a less formal atmosphere.

**Vaca Muca** *($$; closed Mon; 3 km west of La Fortuna on the road to the Arenal Volcano, ☎479-9186)*, which means "cow without horns," serves Costa Rican cuisine on a terrace surrounded by gardens, or in a large indoor dining room with big wooden chairs. This is a very popular restaurant.

### Around Lake Arenal

At the Nuevo Arenal Unión, a few kilometres before the village of Nuevo Arenal, **Sabor Italiano** *($$)* serves home-cooked Italian food and also has a very lovely handicrafts shop.

The hotel-restaurant at **Los Héroes** *($$$; about 30 km from La Fortuna on Lake Arenal, ☎/⇄441-4193)* serves *tica*, international and Swiss specialties, such as fondues. The interior decor is very Swiss.

### Nuevo Arenal

On the second-largest street in the village of Nuevo Arenal, across from the park and very near the social welfare building, there are three little restaurants worth mentioning: the *panadería-cafetería* (coffee shop) **La Sabrosa** *($)*, **Pipo's Fast Foods** *($; every day 6am to 10pm)*, and the *restaurant-soda* **Picante** *($; ☎694-4132)*. All serve Costa Rican food and simple international fare. You can get some good tourist information (mostly verbal) and even take Spanish lessons here.

The bar-restaurant **Mirador Típico Arenal** *($$; Nuevo Arenal, ☎694-4159)* has a terrace facing the lake. The owners are friendly and serve simple, mostly *tica*, food.

Right in the middle of the village of Nuevo Arenal, **Pizzería Tramonti** *($$; 11:30am to 3pm, and 5pm to 10pm, closed Mon; Nuevo Arenal, ☎694-4282)* is known for its excellent pizza cooked in a wood-burning oven. Quebecker Luc and his wife Soledad own the **Concha del Mar** *($$$; every day 10am to 9pm, closed Tue; Nuevo Arenal, ☎694-4169)*, a seafood restaurant with a lovely decor. They can also give you some good tourist information.

**Between Nuevo Arenal and Tilarán**

At the base of the Xiloe Lodge, there is a very popular little barbecue restaurant, **Equus BBQ** *($$; 11am to midnight)*. Its outdoorsy, western ranch-style decor suits the setting. It is pleasantly surrounded by trees and faces the lake – the perfect place to relax outside in the evening with friends and discuss the day's events. The food is prepared on an outdoor grill.

The American owner and chef of the hotel-restaurant **Los Lagos** *($$; 6am to 10pm; 8 km west of Nuevo Arenal on the road to Tilarán, ☎694-4271)* is always cooking up something new. The view of the lake is worthwhile in itself. The restaurant also has complete bar service and a fireplace.

**Mystica** *($$; 300 m off the main road between Arenal and Tilarán, a few kilometres west of Equus BBQ)* is a popular restaurant-pizzeria.

The restaurant and bar of the **Rock River Lodge** *($$; between Nuevo Arenal and Tilarán, on Lake Arenal, ☎695-5644)* are very attractive with their stylish wood decor, magnificent fireplace, and splendid view of Lake Arenal. The menu is varied, and the owners claim that their breakfasts are the best in the area. The bar is open from 5pm until midnight.

## The Monteverde Region

The little village of **Santa Elena** has a few reasonably priced restaurants and *sodas*. There are also some restaurants and cafes on the road to the Monteverde reserve. Most hotels have restaurants for their clientele, and some of them are open to the public.

The **Panadería Jiménez** *($-$$; ☎645-5035)*, in the village of Santa Elena, is a bakery that serves light snacks as well as homemade bread and pastries. Upstairs, the **Rocky Road Soda** *($-$$)* serves sandwiches and gigantic hamburgers.

**El Daiquiri** *($-$$; ☎645-5133)* and **Soda Central** *($-$$)* are two *sodas* across the street are from the *panadería* in Santa Elena that serve very simple local dishes.

Across from the CASEM cooperative, **Stella's Bakery** *($-$$; Monteverde, ☎645-5560)* makes excellent homemade breads, doughnuts, cookies and other little treats, to eat in or take out.

In addition to renting rooms, the Arguedas family runs the popular **El Bosque** *($-$$; Monteverde, ☎645-5221)*. They serve simple Costa Rican dishes that win high praise.

**Pizzería Johnny** *($-$$; Monteverde, ☎645-5066)* serves excellent pizza and pasta at reasonable prices. Under the same roof, **Café Neotrópica** *($-$$)* has vegetarian food, and **Café Morphos** *($-$$)* is macrobiotic.

On the side street that goes to the Butterfly Garden, **Restaurante de Lucía** *($$; Monteverde, ☎645-5337)*, run by José and Lucía Belmar, serves beef, chicken and fish dishes that are extremely popular with customers.

**Arco Iris** *($$-$$$; Santa Elena, ☎645-5067)*, located in the hotel of the same name, is owned by Susanna Stoiber and Haymo Heyder. They serve international, vegetarian and Costa Rican cuisine. During the tourist season, the owners use fruits and vegetables from their own organic garden to prepare their famous meals. The restaurant is closed during the low season. It is best to make reservations in advance.

Among the hotel-restaurants that are open to the public, two of the best are at **Hotel Fonda Vela** *($$-$$$; ☎2571413)* and **Hotel Belmar** *($$-$$$; ☎645-5201)*. Their excellent meals are very popular with tourists.

**El Sapo Dorado** *($$-$$$$; ☎645-5010)* is in the luxury hotel of the same name (see p 203). There are international and Costa Rican dishes on the menu, including some that are vegetarian. It has a relaxing atmosphere and the terrace looks out over the Gulf of Nicoya.

The non-smoking, airy restaurant at the **Monteverde Lodge** *($$$-$$$$; ☎645-5057)* (see p 204) is unquestionably one of the best in the region. The mainly wooden decor and the many windows create a very attractive setting. The atmosphere and service are matched only by the quality and freshness of the food. International and regional dishes are served, and the portions are generous and tasty. The salads and the fish are particularly delicious.

## SHOPPING

### The Puerto Viejo de Sarapiquí Region

While in the region of Puerto Viejo de Sarapiquí, stop at the **MUSA** cooperative *(El Tigre, on the Horquetas road)* (see p 179), where natural products (shampoo, etc.) made from the herbs grown on this farm are for sale. Authenticity is guaranteed!

### The Arenal Region

**Around Lake Arenal**

**La Unión de Nuevo Arenal**, between Nuevo Arenal and La Fortuna, sells prints, ceramics and hand-crafted wooden items at **Sabor Italiano**, a restaurant that serves home-made Italian cuisine (see p 206).

### The Monteverde Region

In the Monteverde area, the local handicrafts co-op **CASEM** (see p 189), **Galería Colibrí** (see p 189) and **Galería Sarah Dowell** (near the cheese factory) are good places to pick up some souvenirs to bring home. The Monteverde and Santa Elena parks, and the **Butterfly Garden** (see p 188) also have interesting little souvenir shops.

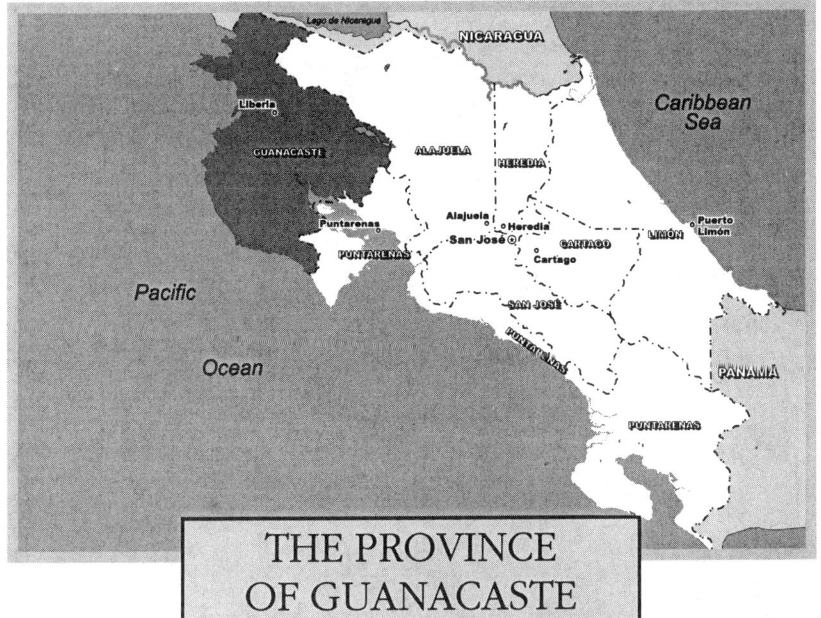


# THE PROVINCE OF GUANACASTE

Guanacaste is one big province! Thanks to the new international airport in Liberia, its 300 kilometres of shoreline and 70 beaches have become more accessible to travellers. A whole slew of activities awaits visitors to this coastal region: fishing, swimming, windsurfing, surfing, scuba diving and turtle- and bird-watching.

Guanacaste isn't all sand and surf, however; it also has many parks and wildlife reserves protecting lakes, volcanoes, forests and caves. In fact, more than a third of the country's parks are located in this province. Guanacaste also boasts the world's largest protected expanse of tropical dry forest, which once covered some 550,000 square kilometres from the southern Pacific coast of Mexico to Costa Rica. Only 2% of this huge forest has survived; the rest has been cut down for timber or cleared for farming and stock breeding.

Once part of Nicaragua, Guanacaste first allied itself with Costa Rica so that country would have a large enough population to elect a representative in Spain. Then, in 1825, the residents of Guanacaste chose to become part of Costa Rica. Guanacaste is a very lively place during the week of July 25, when locals commemorate the day the province joined Costa Rica. Though Guanacaste is the largest province in the country, it is home to less than 10% of the population.

Away from the coast, which is undergoing massive development, stock breeding has traditionally been the main activity in Guanacaste. It is not uncommon to see locals on horseback following their cattle through the fields; you might even encounter people riding their horses in town! Horses can be seen grazing right next to the Interamericana or roaming freely along secondary roads. It should be noted that you won't see a lot of luxuriant

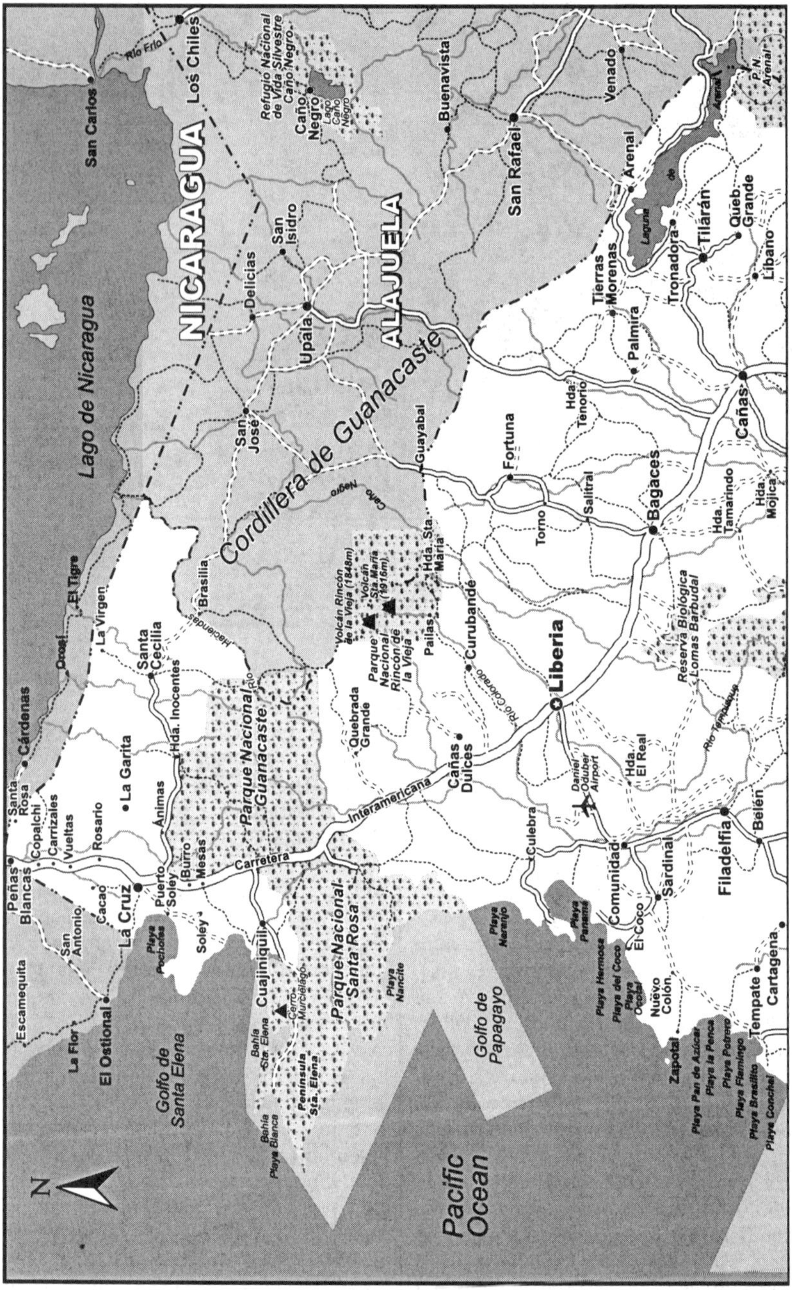
N
Lago de Nicaragua
NICARAGUA
ALAJUELA
Cordillera de Guanacaste
San Carlos
Río Frío
Los Chiles
Refugio Nacional de Vida Silvestre Caño Negro
Caño Negro
Lago Caño Negro
Buenavista
Venado
San Rafael
Arenal
Laguna de Arenal
P.N. Arenal
San Isidro
Delicias
Upala
San José
Guayabal
Caño Negro
Brasilia
El Tigre
La Virgen
Santa Cecilia
Haciendas
Río
Volcán Rincón de la Vieja (1848m)
Volcán Sta. María (1916m)
Parque Nacional Rincón de la Vieja
Hda. Sta. María
Pailas
Curubandé
Fortuna
Hda. Tenorio
Tierras Morenas
Palmira
Tronadora
Tilarán
Queb. Grande
Líbano
Cañas
Bagaces
Salitral
Torno
Hda. Tamarindo
Hda. Mojica
Reserva Biológica Lomas Barbudal
Río Tempisque
Liberia
Río Colorado
Cárdenas
Santa Rosa
Copalchí
Carrizales
Vueltas
Rosario
La Garita
Animas
Hda. Inocentes
Parque Nacional Guanacaste
Quebrada Grande
Cañas Dulces
Interamericana
Carretera
Peñas Blancas
San Antonio
Cacao
La Cruz
Puerto Soley
Burro
Mesas
Soley
Playa Pochotes
Cuajiniquil
Escamequita
La Flor
El Ostional
Golfo de Santa Elena
Bahía Sta. Elena
Cerro Murciélago
Parque Nacional Santa Rosa
Playa Nancite
Península Sta. Elena
Bahía Playa Blanca
Golfo de Papagayo
Pacific Ocean
Playa Naranjo
Playa Panamá
Culebra
Daniel Oduber Airport
Hda. El Real
Comunidad
Sardinal
El Coco
Playa Hermosa
Playa del Coco
Playa Ocotal
Nuevo Colón
Filadelfia
Belén
Cartagena
Tempate
Zapotal
Playa Pan de Azúcar
Playa la Penca
Playa Potrero
Playa Flamingo
Playa Brasilito
Playa Conchal

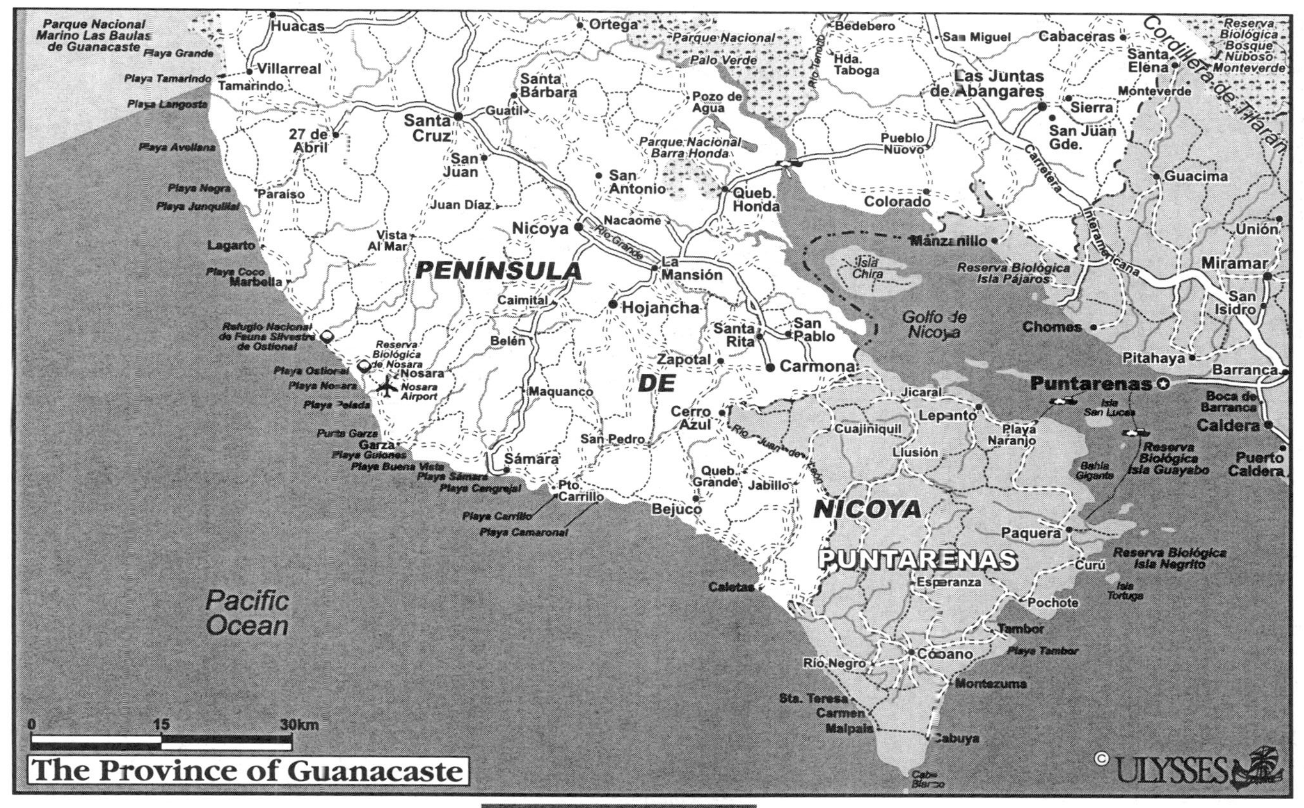
The Province of Guanacaste
Pacific Ocean
PENÍNSULA DE NICOYA
PUNTARENAS
Golfo de Nicoya
Cordillera de Tilarán
Carretera Interamericana
Parque Nacional Marino Las Baulas de Guanacaste
Playa Grande
Playa Tamarindo
Playa Langosta
Playa Avellana
Playa Negra
Playa Junquillal
Huacas
Villarreal
Tamarindo
Ortega
Parque Nacional Palo Verde
Bedebero
Hda. Taboga
San Miguel
Cabaceras
Las Juntas de Abangares
Santa Elena
Monteverde
Reserva Biológica Bosque Nuboso Monteverde
Sierra
San Juan Gde.
Santa Bárbara
Guatil
Santa Cruz
27 de Abril
San Juan
Pozo de Agua
Parque Nacional Barra Honda
Pueblo Nuovo
San Antonio
Queb. Honda
Colorado
Guacima
Paraíso
Juan Díaz
Nacaome
Nicoya
Río Grande
Vista Al Mar
Lagarto
Playa Coco
Marbella
Manzanillo
Unión
Isla Chira
Reserva Biológica Isla Pájaros
Miramar
La Mansión
Caimital
Hojancha
San Isidro
Chomes
Refugio Nacional de Fauna Silvestre de Ostional
Reserva Biológica de Nosara
Belén
Santa Rita
San Pablo
Pitahaya
Playa Ostional
Nosara
Nosara Airport
Playa Nosara
Zapotal
Carmona
Barranca
Puntarenas
Maquanco
Jicaral
Isla San Lucas
Boca de Barranca
Cerro Azul
Lepanto
Caldera
Cuajiniquil
Playa Naranjo
Punta Garza
Garza
Playa Guiones
Playa Buena Vista
Playa Sámara
Playa Cangrejal
San Pedro
Sámara
Río Juan de León
Llusión
Reserva Biológica Isla Guayabo
Bahía Gigante
Puerto Caldera
Pto. Carrillo
Queb. Grande
Jabillo
Bejuco
Playa Carrillo
Playa Camaronal
Paquera
Reserva Biológica Isla Negrito
Curú
Caletas
Esperanza
Isla Tortuga
Pochote
Tambor
Playa Tambor
Río Negro
Cóbano
Montezuma
Sta. Teresa
Carmen
Malpais
Cabuya
0 15 30km
© ULYSSES

tropical vegetation while exploring Guanacaste, but rather vast stretches of steppes and prairies, which might look very dry during the busy tourist season.

A country within a country, Guanacaste enjoys a hot but dry climate that helps to make it one of Costa Rica's most popular tourist destinations.

## FINDING YOUR WAY AROUND

### By Plane

Though Liberia's **Aeropuerto Daniel Oduber Quiros** *(open every day 6am to 9pm; ☎667-0199 or 667-0032, ⇒667-0000)* (see p 33) is technically an international airport, most of its traffic consists of charter flights for tourists arriving from North America.

**Sansa** *(☎221-9414)* and **Travelair** *(☎220-3054)* both offer daily flights from San José to **Tamarindo**, usually very early in the morning. Both airlines' schedules vary, so be sure to inquire beforehand. A return ticket costs between $110 and $140.

Sansa and Travelair both offer daily service from San José to **Nosara**; Sansa leaves early in the morning, Travelair around noon. A return ticket costs between $110 and $140.

Sansa and Travelair also offer daily flights from San José to the little airport at Playa Carillo, which serves the entire **Playa Sámara** region. The planes usually leave in the morning. Reservations are recommended during the tourist season.

### By Car

**Around Tilarán - Cañas - Bagaces**

**Tilarán** lies at the edge of the province, near Lake Arenal. To get there from the village of Nuevo Arenal, follow the west shore of the lake, then head inland toward Guanacaste for about 10 kilometres. The road is clearly indicated. If you are coming from Guanacaste, take the Interamericana to Cañas, where a lovely road leads 25 kilometres northeast to Tilarán.

**Cañas** and **Bagaces** are both located on the Interamericana, about 25 kilometres apart, and are thus easy to reach from either San José or Liberia.

**Parque Nacional Palo Verde and Reserva Biológica Lomas Barbudal**

From the town of Bagaces, located on the Interamericana, take the small, unpaved road leading southwest (on the left if you are coming from San José). The road is across from a gas station, and there is a small sign for the park. Turn right at the first intersection, left at the second, then follow the signs to the park, located 28 kilometres from the Interamericana. At one point, you'll come to a T-shaped intersection. Parque Nacional Palo Verde lies to the left, the Reserva Biológica Lomas Barbudal to the right.

**Parque Nacional Rincón de la Vieja**

To get to the **Las Pailas sector**, located 25 kilometres from Liberia, take the Interamericana northwards for five kilometres, then turn right on a small, unpaved road (there will be a sign). After about 200 metres, head to the left and continue to the village of

Curubandé (15 km). A few kilometres past the town, you'll have to stop at a gate and pay an entrance fee *($1.50/person)*, since the road runs over private property (the Hacienda Lodge Guachipelín). The last 1.5 km of the road leading to the park entrance is rough going; if you don't have four-wheel drive, you should leave your car by the side of the road and walk.

To get to the **Santa María sector**, also located 25 kilometres from Liberia, take Avenida 6 from the Barrio La Victoria, in the east part of town and follow the little road that leads to the park entrance by way of San Jorge (18 km). Depending on the season, the road might be impassable by car (call the park before setting out).

### Parque Nacional Guanacaste

To reach the **Maritza biological station**, located 60 kilometres from Liberia, take the Interamericana north for 43 kilometres, then turn right on the small, unpaved road that begins across from the road leading to the little town of Cuajiniquil. From there, it's a pretty bumpy 17 kilometres to the station, so you'll need a four-wheel drive vehicle.

To get to the **Cacao biological station**, about 40 kilometres from Liberia, take the Interamericana north for 23 kilometres, then turn right on the little road leading to the village of Quebrada Grande (7 km). From there, a small, unpaved road on the left leads north to the station. A four-wheel drive vehicle is a must for this last stretch of the trip (approx. 10 km).

### North of Liberia

**La Cruz** is located on the Interamericana, about 60 kilometres (an hour's drive) from Liberia.

### Parque Nacional Santa Rosa

La Casona, the park headquarters, the research station and the campsites are all located at the **main entrance of the park**, located 42 kilometres from Liberia. To get there, take the Interamericana north for 35 kilometres. The little road leading to the park entrance and facilities (7 km) will be on your left; look for the sign.

To reach the **Murciélago sector**, 62 kilometres from Liberia, drive north on the Interamericana for 43 kilometres, then turn left on the road leading to the little town of Cuajiniquil (8 km). From there, a small road leads west to the administrative office for this sector of the park (9 km).

### Refugio Nacional Bahía Junquillal

This park lies 57 kilometres from Liberia. Take the Interamericana north for 43 kilometres, then turn left on the road leading to the little town of Cuajiniquil (8 km). Continue for two kilometres then turn right on the little road leading to the park entrance (4 km).

### Around Liberia

**Liberia**, the capital of Guanacaste, lies in the heart of the province. It is the gateway to the northern part of the region and the beaches on the Nicoya Peninsula. It is located on the Interamericana, about 50 kilometres north of Cañas (45 min).

There are three gas stations at the intersection of the Interamericana and the main road to Liberia, all of which are open on holidays.

**Playa del Coco**, **Playa Hermosa** and **Playa Panamá** are all located about a half-hour's drive from Liberia. For the last two, follow the signs for Condovac La Costa from the intersection right before Playa del Coco. The first road to Playa Panamá is paved. After that, a dirt road leads to the hotels like the Sula Sula and the Blue Bay.

There is a gas station on the road to Playa del Coco, after the turn-off for Sardinal.

**Around Filadelfia**

About 10 kilometres south of Filadelfia (just south of Belén), on the road to Nicoya, there is a road leading to a string of beaches (**Playa Conchal, Playa Brasilito, Playa Flamingo, Playa Potrero, Playa Penca** and **Playa Pan de Azúcar**). When you get to Huacas, turn right; the first beach, Playa Brasilito, is less than 10 kilometres away. The last few kilometres to Playa Pan de Azúcar make for a pretty bumpy ride.

There are no real gas stations in this area. If you're running low on fuel, head to the *abastecedor* **Villamar** (at the corner of the road to Playa Brasilito and the road to the other beaches farther north), where an employee will pour a few litres into your tank from a can. A lifesaver in a pinch!

**Tamarindo**: To get to **Playa Grande** from Belén, you have to pass through Huacas and drive west, toward Matapalo. Playa Tamarindo lies nearly 15 kilometres south of the village of Huacas.

**Parque Nacional Marino Las Baulas**

From Liberia, take Highway 21 southwest to the little town of Filadelfia (31 km). Continue six kilometres to the village of Belén, then turn right toward famous Playa Tamarindo. Stay on this road until you reach Huacas (24 km), then take the unpaved road leading to Salinas, Playa Grande and the park entrance (8 km). The total distance is 69 kilometres, about a 90-minute drive.

**Around Santa Cruz**

**Santa Cruz** lies on the big road between Liberia and Nicoya, about 60 kilometres southwest of Liberia. The road is paved and generally in very good condition.

An alternative route is to take the ferry across the Río Tempisque to the town of Nicoya, south of Santa Cruz. To do so, follow the paved road that branches off the Interamericana just north of the exit for Las Juntas (there's a sign for the ferry).

**Playa Junquillal**: If you are coming from Liberia on the road to Nicoya, you'll see the road to the beach just before Santa Cruz; there is a sign showing the way. When you get to the village of Veintisiete de Abril, turn left and continue to Paraíso. Playa Junquillal lies 12 kilometres farther. The road could really use some repairs, especially near Santa Cruz.

You'll have a hard time finding a gas station in the Playa Junquillal area, but the first little village on the beach sells gas from a can.

**Playa Avellanas** lies about five kilometres north of Playa Junquillal. From Santa Cruz, go to the village of 27 de Abril, then follow the signs. It's likely to be a bumpy ride, especially during the rainy season. Inquire about the road conditions before setting out.

### Around Nicoya

**Nicoya**: As in the case of Santa Cruz, there are two routes to Nicoya. If you are coming from Liberia, simply take the Liberia-Nicoya highway (approx. 80 km). If you are coming from San José, join the road to the Río Tempisque from the Interamericana (a few kilometres north of the exit for Las Juntas; look for the sign), take the ferry across the river then continue to Nicoya.

**Playa Nosara and Playa Guiones**: From Nicoya, take the road that leads southwest out of town, toward Sámara. After 30 kilometres, you'll come to a fork in the road; Nosara is on the right. From that point on, the journey becomes a bit more of an adventure, as the dirt road is not always in the best condition; you'll even have to ford a few rivers! The Ostianal beach and the Nosara park are at the end of the road, which, after Nosara, becomes impassable if you don't have four-wheel drive.

**Playa Sámara, Playa Buena Vista, Playa Carrillo** and **Playa Camaronal**: Like Nosara, the beaches in the Sámara area are accessible via the road that leads southwest out of the town of Nicoya. When you reach the fork in the road 30 kilometres farther, turn left and head to Sámara. The road is in very good condition.

To reach Playa Buena Vista from the village of Sámara, head north on the street where the Isla Chora hotel is located. You'll know you're going the right way if you pass the Mágica Cantarana hotel. The beach is at the end of this stretch of road (which can be hard to negotiate during the rainy season), after a small lagoon that can fill up at high tide.

Just as you are entering the village of Sámara, you'll see a road on your left. This leads to Playa Carillo, located a few kilometres to the south. The road is pretty bad in places but gets much better near the beach. Playa Camaronal lies farther south on the same road.

### Parque Nacional Barra Honda

If you are coming from the Interamericana, you'll have to take the ferry across the Río Tempisque then follow the little highway about 15 kilometres until you reach a small road (on the right) leading to the village of Nacaome and the park entrance. If you are arriving from Nicoya (23 km from the park entrance), take the main road south and turn left on the road to the Río Tempisque ferry. Not far from the intersection, a small road on the left leads to the village of Nacaome and the park entrance.

## By Bus

### Around Tilarán-Cañas-Bagaces

**Tilarán**: The bus from Ciudad Quesada to Arenal passes through Tilarán. There are two daily departures, one at 6am and the other at 3pm. The buses heading in the opposite direction leave Tilarán at 7am and 1pm. The trip takes four hours. There is also daily bus service from Monteverde to Tilarán. The bus leaves Monteverde at 7am, with return service at 1pm.

### Parque Nacional Rincón de la Vieja

The youth hostel in Liberia offers a shuttle service to and from the park. During the high season, there are up to three departures, beginning at 7am.

### North of Liberia

**La Cruz**: There are four daily departures from San José to La Cruz; the buses continue on to Peñas Blancas, at the Nicaraguan border. The trip from San José to La Cruz takes about six hours; the bus stop in San José is on Calle 14, between Avenidas 3 and 5. There are five buses per day to Liberia, departing between 5:30am and 6pm, and nine buses in the opposite direction, leaving between 6am and 6pm. The bus stop is right in the centre of La Cruz; for more information, call ☎224-1960.

**Nicaragua**: The buses to La Cruz continue on to the Nicaraguan border, 14 kilometres farther north. At the border, you have to walk about 800 metres, then wait for a minibus to take you to customs, four kilometres farther.

### Around Liberia

**Liberia**: There is frequent bus service between San José and Liberia – nearly every two hours from 7am to 8pm for the trip to Liberia, and from 4:30am to 8pm for the trip back to San José. The ride takes four hours. There is bus service to Liberia from Santa Cruz and Puntarenas as well, once a day at around 5:30pm for the trip there, and around 8:30am for the trip back. It takes two and 2.5 hours to travel from Puntarenas to Liberia. Buses to and from San José depart from and arrive at the Palmitán bus station *(Av. 3, Calle 12)*. There is another station for local buses on Avenida 7, just east of the Interamericana.

**Playa del Coco**: There is daily bus service from San José to Playa del Coco at 8am and 2pm. The trip takes five hours. There are also four buses per day from Liberia to Playa del Coco between 5am and 5pm. You can catch a bus back to Liberia between 7am and 6pm.

**Playa Hermosa** and **Playa Panamá**: There is only one bus per day from San José to Playa Hermosa and Playa Panamá. It sets out at 3:20pm *(Calle 12, Av. 5/7)*, while the bus back leaves each morning at 5am. There is bus service between Liberia and these two beaches as well.

### Around Filadelfia

**Playa Conchal**, **Playa Brasilito**, **Playa Flamingo**, **Playa Potrero**: There is daily bus service from Santa Cruz to these beaches at 6:30am and 3pm. You can catch a bus back to Santa Cruz at 9am or 5pm. There are also two daily departures for Playa Brasilito and Playa Flamingo from San José at 6:30am and 3pm. The buses back leave at 9am and 5pm.

**Playa Tamarindo**: A bus sets out for Playa Tamarindo from San José every day at around 4pm. The trip takes a good six hours. The bus from Santa Cruz to Playa Tamarindo leaves every night at 8:30pm; the bus back, every morning at 6:45am.

### Around Santa Cruz

**Santa Cruz**: There are four buses per day from San José to Santa Cruz between 7:30am and 6pm; the trip takes over five hours. The main bus station is about 400 metres east of downtown. There is a stop on the north side of Plaza de Los Mangos for buses to Nicoya and Liberia.

**Playa Junquillal**: A bus sets out from San José for Playa Junquillal every day at 2pm *(Av. 3, Calle 20)*. The trip takes six hours. The bus back leaves at 5am. The bus from Santa Cruz to Playa

Junquillal leaves at 6:30pm and heads back at 5am.

**Around Nicoya**

**Nicoya**: There is frequent bus service from San José *(Calle 14, Av. 5)* between 6am and 5pm, with no fewer than eight departures (approximately one every two hours). The trip takes at least four hours. Buses set out for Nicoya from Liberia every hour from 5am to 7pm. The bus station is near the Río Chipanzo, on Calle 5, south of downtown.

**Nosara**: The bus to Nicoya leaves Nosara every day at 1pm and starts back at 6am. The trip takes 2.5 hours. There is direct bus service from San José to Nosara, with a daily 6am departure. There is also direct bus service from Nosara to Liberia (4am).

**Playa Sámara**, **Playa Buena Vista**, **Playa Carrillo** and **Playa Camaronal**: The Alfaro bus company offers direct service to Sámara from San José. The bus leaves every day at noon *(Av. 5, Calle 14/16, ☎222-2750, 223-8227 or 223-8361)*, with an estimated travel time of six hours. There are also daily departures from Nicoya at 8am, 3pm and 4pm, with return service at 5:30am and 6:30am. The buses from Nicoya stop at Playa Carrillo.

**Around Tilarán-Cañas-Bagaces**

**Cañas**: You'll find a Banco de Costa Rica near the south side of the central park and a Banco Nacional on the north side. There is a pharmacy (Farmacía Cañas) on the road that runs alongside the central park then continues northward. The bus stop is near Avenida 11 and Calle 1, north of downtown.

**North of Liberia**

**La Cruz**: There is a tourist information office in La Cafetería, a pleasant little restaurant on the street that heads out of town to Playa Pochote. A bank can be found on the Interamericana on the way into town.

**Around Liberia**

**Liberia**: There is a hospital in Liberia *(Av. 9, Calle 13)*.

You can find a Banco Popular with an automated teller machine on Avenida Central, near Calle 8, and a Banco Costa Rica immediately northeast of Parque Central.

The staff at the **Info-Cen-Tur** tourist information centre, in the Centro Commercial Bambú *(Calle 1, Av.3)*, will be glad to help you in any way they can. A few English-language papers are usually available here during the high season.

**Playa del Coco**: There is a Banco Nacional on the road to the village, just past the road leading to Playa Ocotal. You'll also find a supermarket on the road that runs alongside the beach and heads west after the football field.

**Around Filadelfia**

**Playa Tamarindo**: A few kilometres before Tamarindo, you'll pass a tourist information centre. Although it is only open during the high season, there is a sign outside indicating the local points of interest year-round. There is another tourist information centre in the village (at the edge of town, opposite the

El Milagro hotel), as well as a shopping centre (a little farther into town, across from the Tamarindo Diriá hotel) with a small grocery store and a gift shop. A larger grocery store, the Super Mercado El Pelicano, can be found on the road that runs around the traffic circle in the centre of the village. The local Banco Nacional is at the edge of town, on the beach side of the road.

### Around Nicoya

**Nicoya**: Nicoya has a hospital with all the basic facilities and services. It is located north of the downtown area, on Calle 3, the main street off the Nicoya-Liberia road. On the same street, just south of the hospital, you'll find a Banco Popular with an automated teller machine, right across from the local branch of the Banco Nacional.

**Playa Nosara**: The Supermercado Nosara is a big grocery store for this area – it even sells film. The village also has a gas station, another rarity in this part of the country. Outside of town, you'll find a community centre and a tourist information office on the road to the beaches (south of Nosara, near the restaurant La Dolce Vita).

**Playa Sámara**: There is a grocery store (Super Sámara) in the centre of the village, on the road that runs along the beach.

### Guided Tours

**Ecotours** *(Playa Hermosa, ☎/≠672-0175)* offers about 10 guided tours all over Guanacaste. Whether you want to climb Rincón de la Vieja Volcano, travel down the Río Corobicí for some fantastic birdwatching, go horseback riding around Orosí Volcano, watch a leatherback turtle lay its eggs on Playa Grande or explore Parque Nacional Santa Rosa, guide Marc Fournier, a native of Québec, will share his love of Costa Rican nature with you. Each tour costs $75 per person and includes transportation, lunch, park fees and the services of a guide. If you have a car, you only have to pay for the guide *($60/day plus expenses)*, no matter how large your group is.

## EXPLORING

### Around Tilarán-Cañas-Bagaces

A cathedral town, **Tilarán** lies in a part of Guanacaste that is fairly windy, because of its altitude, but nonetheless enjoys a pleasant temperature year-round. The area is also quite sunny, since it lies west of Lake Arenal, where it is much drier than east of the lake, which has more clouds and capricious temperatures. Tilarán itself is hilly but has little charm. Its **cathedral** is relatively modern, with an interior decorated with marquetry, lending it a distinctive character. All in all, Tilarán is a quiet place with few tourist attractions to speak of.

The town does have two points of interest, however. First, the area is home to the **largest tree in the country** ★ – according to local residents, at least. It is indeed a very impressive specimen: the base alone has a girth of more than 30 metres! However, it happens to stand on private property, about five kilometres southeast of town. After a good meal at La Carreta (see p 261) in downtown Tilarán, ask the owner, who knows everyone, if he can take you to see it.

The other attraction around Tilarán are the **waterfalls** ★, located near the little town of **Libano**. To get there from Tilarán, go through Libano, cross the

***Arbol de Guanacaste***



river, pass the church and the school, then follow the signs for the *cascadas*.

Located 80 metres above sea level, **Bagaces** is hot and doesn't qualify as a top-notch tourist resort. Like **Cañas**, however, it can be a practical place to stop during your tour of the province's hinterland, most notably to visit Parque Nacional Palo Verde or the Reserva Biológica Lomas Barbudal.

## Parque Nacional Palo Verde

Avid birders won't want to miss **Parque Nacional Palo Verde** ★ *($6; every day 8am to 4pm; ☎659-9039 or 284-6116, ⇌659-9039)*, where 279 avian species have been spotted. The diversity of the birds found here can be attributed to the fact that the park contains about a large variety of natural habitats – a low-altitude, tropical dry forest made up of wooded hills, salt- and freshwater lagoons, mangrove swamps, marshes and grasslands. Furthermore, a large part of the territory is flooded by heavy rains and overflow from the Tempisque and Bebedero rivers, which run along the edge of the park. Because the water drains slowly, the grasslands turn into swamps for months at a time, transforming the landscape of the park. Because these damp coastal areas are quite rare in Guanacaste and elsewhere in Costa Rica, Parque Nacional Palo Verde was included in the Ramsar Convention in 1992.

There is more in the park than wetlands and flood zones, however. Over 150 species of trees have been identified to date, including the *palo verde* (green wood), whose trunk, branches and leaves remain green year-round. Of course, the *palo verde* happens to be found mainly in the swampy parts of the park...

Parque Nacional Palo Verde, which covers an area of 16,804 hectares, was founded as an ecological reserve in April 1978 and became a national park on June 13, 1980. It lies about 30 kilometres southwest of the little town of Bagaces, where the Río Tempisque starts widening its way to the Gulf of Nicoya. It takes about an hour to drive from Bagaces to the middle of the park (see p 212), where the welcome centre and administrative offices are located. The OTS *(Organization of Tropical Studies, ☎240-6696)* research centre, located a little farther (7.5 km), has accommodations for visitors wishing to stay in the park for a few days, and gives guided tours *($17, lunch included)* that focus on the area's natural history. Camping is also permitted (see p 246) in the park.

It is generally best to visit the park during the dry season (December to March), and more specifically in January and February. During these months, most of the water has receded from the fields and the rivers are at their lowest point, so most of the animals are grouped in well-defined areas, making it easier to observe them. In the evening, scores of animals flock to the few watering places in the region. You're likely to spot some white-faced capuchin monkeys, as well as howler monkeys, coatis, iguanas and white-tailed deer. The **Río Tempisque** is home to many crocodiles, some of which are up to five metres long!

During the wet season, on the other hand, Parque Nacional Palo Verde is more interesting for its birdlife; its watering places, swamps and wetlands attract some 300 species of land and water birds, including toucans, parrots, wigeons, egrets, herons, white ibises and jabirus. The scarlet macaw, now very rare in Costa Rica, has been spotted here as well. Furthermore, **Isla Pájaros** (2.3 ha), located in the Río Tempisque, has one of the largest colonies of black-crowned night herons (*Nycticorax nycticorax*) in the country. Parque Nacional Palo Verde also boasts the largest concentration of water and wader birds in Central America.

Finally, the park is the only Costa Rican breeding ground of the endangered

***Jabiru***

jabiru, a huge wader bird with a large beak, and a close relative of the stork.

The park has a small network of hiking trails (6 km total), as well as a few forest roads. The heat can be truly suffocating during the dry season, so don't forget to bring along a large supply of fresh water. **Las Calizas** (300 m), **El Manigordo** (1.5 km), **El Mapache** (2 km) and **La Venada** (2 km) are short trails, but still give visitors a chance to see the many types of natural habitats that make up this region and view the magnificent surrounding hills and the plains that flood during the wet season.

However, before you head down one of these trails or pitch your tent, ask for the latest information about the ferocious **African bees** (*abejas africanizadas*) that have taken up residence in the park.

## Reserva Biológica Lomas Barbudal

The **Reserva Biológica Lomas Barbudal** *($6; every day)* covers 2,279 hectares just northwest of Parque Nacional Palo Verde. Here, too, the climate is oppressively hot during the dry season (December to March). Visitors to the reserve can go hiking, camping *($1.25/person/day; near the welcome centre)*, observe the local plant and animal life or cool down by a river that flows year-round. Depending on the season, there might not be anyone on duty at the welcome station, which means that you'll have to explore the park without first obtaining all the necessary information and advice to ensure that your visit is as safe and enjoyable as possible.

Before setting out to explore this stretch of tropical dry forest, take note that some 240 species of bees, including the aggressive African bee, are found in the reserve. Make sure that you understand all posted safety precautions (usually in Spanish only) and steer clear of the places that the bees have claimed as their territory. If you have the misfortune of being pursued by these winged psychopaths, run in a zigzag and cover your head with your arms. Of course, this is easier said than done, since the terrain or path you're on might not be well-suited to this unusual exercise!

Aside from bees, the reserve is home to 60 species of butterflies and over 200 species of birds, including scarlet macaws and jabirus. Mammals commonly spotted here include howlers, white-faced capuchins, coatis, raccoons and coyotes.

The Reserva Biológica Lomas Barbudal contains seven natural habitats, though about 70% of its territory is covered by deciduous forests. During the dry season, these trees lose their leaves, just like broad-leaved trees in North America do each autumn. Furthermore, in March, a beautiful but fleeting phenomenon occurs: the blossoming of the *Tabebuia ochracea*, referred to by Costa Ricans as the *corteza amarilla* (yellow bark). All at once and for only a few days, these trees are literally covered with thousands of yellow flowers, lending the landscape a surreal appearance.

In addition to this spectacular tree, the reserve contains magnificent rosewoods, which are a purplish hue mixed with black and yellow, and mahoganies, an American tree whose hard, reddish wood is still much coveted throughout the world. Of course, these trees are becoming rarer and rarer in Costa Rica and elsewhere in the Americas, and the parks and reserves deserve a great deal of credit for their tremendous efforts to preserve them.

Deforested regions like eastern Guanacaste can suffer greatly during the kind of drought caused by El Niño in 1997, which turned the landscape into vast, desolate yellow stretches. Canada and other countries are helping Costa Rica reforest this area. The results so far can be seen a few kilometres east of the Interamericana, between Bagaces and Cañas.



## North of Liberia

The area north of Liberia mainly consists of vast stretches of protected wilderness. The only sizeable town is **La Cruz** (not to be confused with Santa Cruz, on the Nicoya Peninsula), which has a population of a few thousand and is the last stop on the Interamericana before the Nicaraguan border. There is little to do in La Cruz, other than going to **Playa Pochote**, where Costa Ricans like to go swimming, and one of the last beaches in the country before Nicaragua. The other beaches in the area that are worth visiting are located in the parks.

In this region, you can also see the Guanacaste of the big *rancheros* (cattle and horse ranchers), and admire the majestic silhouettes of the volcanoes in the Cordillera de Guanacaste, such as Rincón de la Vieja and Orosí, rising up amidst the rather flat surroundings.

It should be noted that few people live between Liberia and La Cruz, so there aren't many places to eat.

## Parque Nacional Santa Rosa

It isn't often that you find sand, surf, plains, mountains, tourist facilities and a well-preserved historic site in one park. And yet that's exactly what awaits you at the impressive **Parque Nacional Santa Rosa ★★** *($6; every day 8am to 4:30pm; ☎/≠695-5598 or 695-5577)*, located in the northwestern most part of the province, just a few kilometres from the Nicaraguan border.

Covering an area of 37,117 hectares, the park was designated a national site in 1966, then became a national park on March 20, 1971. It occupies a large portion of the Santa Elena Peninsula and has been expanding continuously for years, absorbing the Murciélago sector, farther north, in 1980, and the Hacienda Santa Elena in 1987. It has not finished growing either: negotiations with area landowners are still underway.

Parque Nacional Santa Rosa is not only one of the largest parks in Costa Rica, but also the fourth most popular with tourists: over 54,000 people came here in 1996. There are a number of reasons for this. First, the park is located right near the Interamericana, at the end of a seven-kilometre-long paved road, making it easy to get to. Furthermore, **La Casona** *(free admission; near the park headquarters)*, a large and fascinating historic site, lies within its boundaries. La Casona is the main house of the Hacienda Santa Rosa, one of the largest ranches in Costa Rica, which has played an important role in the country's history since the 18th century. A symbol of Costa Rican independence and national pride, La Casona was the scene of three decisive battles, whose outcome helped preserve democracy in the country.

The first of these conflicts took place on March 20, 1856, when an American named William Walker (see p 23) came here from Nicaragua with a band of 200 mercenaries to stir up a revolution in Central America. Late one afternoon, while Walker and his men were quartered at the Hacienda Santa Rosa, they were attacked by 5,000 Costa Rican troops. Supposedly, the battle lasted only 14 minutes, with the Costa Ricans emerging victorious.

The second conflict, known as the Sapoá Revolución, occurred on May 8, 1919, when a group of 800 men tried to overthrow the government of President Federico Tinoco. While camped at the hacienda, these revolutionaries were defeated and forced to flee back to Nicaragua, where they had come from.

The third battle began in 1955, during the presidency of José Figueres, known as Don Pepe. Apparently, a large group of former Costa Rican president Dr. Rafael Ángel Calderón Guardia's supporters invaded the country from Nicaragua. Though Costa Rica had eliminated its army in 1948, the population rose up to defend their country's freedom. There was violent fighting around La Casona, and Figueres's troops managed to fight off the invaders. Two military vehicles (*tanquetas*) abandoned during the battle can be seen three kilometres from the park entrance.

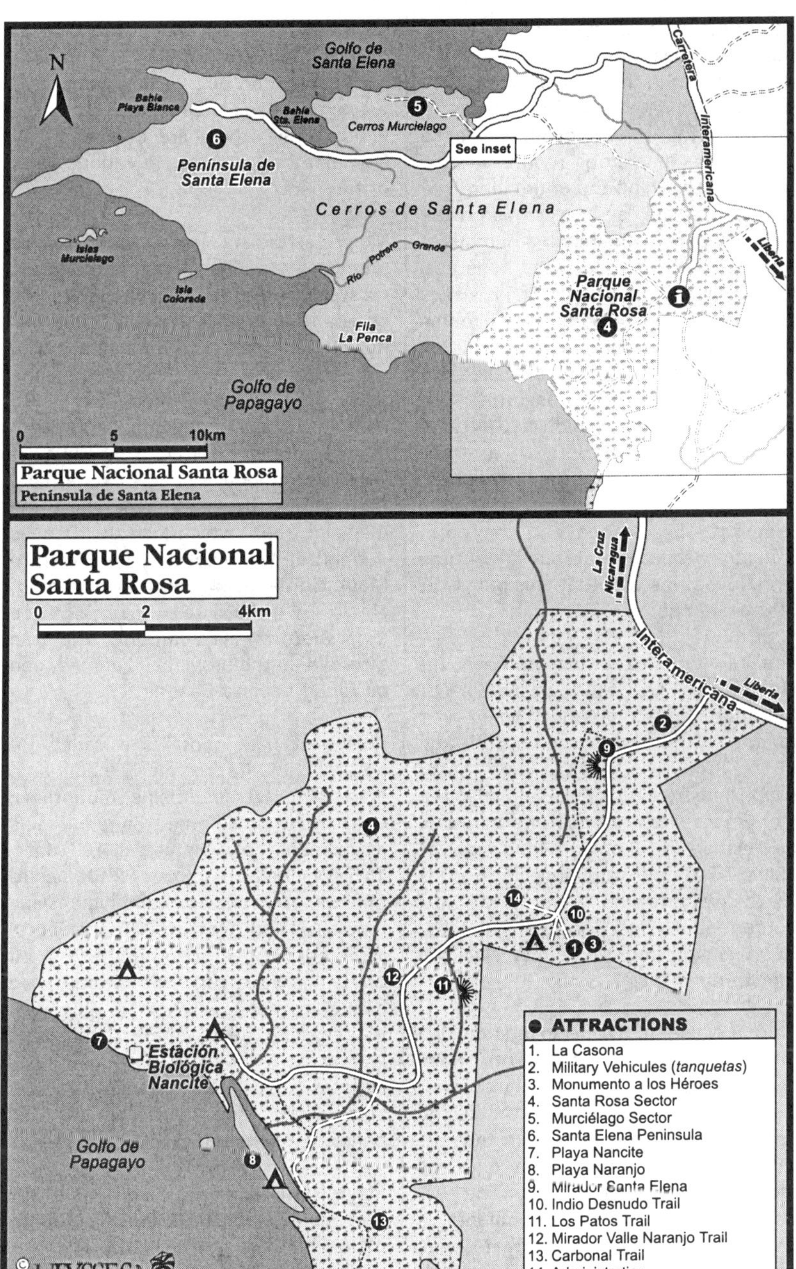
Golfo de Santa Elena
N
Bahía Playa Blanca
Bahía Sta. Elena
Cerros Murcielago
See inset
Península de Santa Elena
Cerros de Santa Elena
Carretera Interamericana
Liberia
Islas Murcielago
Isla Colorada
Río Potrero Grande
Fila La Penca
Parque Nacional Santa Rosa
Golfo de Papagayo
0 5 10km
Parque Nacional Santa Rosa
Península de Santa Elena
Parque Nacional Santa Rosa
0 2 4km
La Cruz Nicaragua
Interamericana
Liberia
Estación Biológica Nancite
Golfo de Papagayo
ATTRACTIONS
1. La Casona
2. Military Vehicules (tanquetas)
3. Monumento a los Héroes
4. Santa Rosa Sector
5. Murciélago Sector
6. Santa Elena Peninsula
7. Playa Nancite
8. Playa Naranjo
9. Mirador Santa Elena
10. Indio Desnudo Trail
11. Los Patos Trail
12. Mirador Valle Naranjo Trail
13. Carbonal Trail
14. Administration
© ULYSSES

Nowadays, La Casona is a quiet, peaceful place, invaded only by the blazing sun and the bats who rest here during the day. Made of big planks of wood and topped with ceramic tiles, La Casona has numerous rooms, a large veranda stretching the entire length of its main façade, and balconies on the second floor. At the back, a number of buildings have been joined together, forming a large courtyard. The house is open to the public. Some of the rooms are decorated with period furnishings, complete with mannequins decked out in vintage clothing. An assortment of riding equipment is also on display. One of the buildings contains a small souvenir shop that sells statuettes, handicrafts and various other objects related to La Casona and the park. Outside, near some stately trees, is a long, low stone wall that was built over 300 years ago.

The **Monumento a los Héroes** was erected near La Casona in memory of the courageous men and women who fought in the battles of 1856 and 1955. Consisting of a large beam supported by two brick columns, the monument sits on a hill, and can only be reached by climbing a long flight of stairs. The view from the hill extends all the way to the Cacao and Orosí volcanoes, in Parque Nacional Guanacaste, and to Parque Nacional Rincón de la Vieja.

Parque Nacional Santa Rosa is divided into two sectors: the **Santa Rosa sector**, which is most popular with visitors, and the smaller **Murciélago sector** farther north. Between them lie the Santa Elena Peninsula and the mountains of the same name. The park contains one of the last remnants of the tropical dry forest that once extended along the Pacific coast from Mexico to Panamá. It thus serves the dual purpose of protecting these woodlands and providing the proper environment for the surrounding pastures to be reforested. The process of regeneration occurs in a variety of ways: some seeds are scattered by the wind, while others are consumed by animals, then excreted in various parts of the park.

Many scientists are studying this process and making sure that the forest reestablishes itself in the area. To ensure the project's success, it has been necessary to educate local residents, who have been clearing the land continuously since the 16th century to sell the wood and create huge pastures; after all, Guanacaste is known as the Far West of Costa Rica. Fortunately, the park still has some majestic trees, which lose their leaves during the dry season (November to May). Some magnificent specimens of the impressive *guanacaste* (*Enterolobium cyclocarpum*), the tree after which the province is named, can be found near La Casona.

This vast park contains a variety of natural habitats (sea, beaches, mangrove swamps, plains, mountains, etc.) and is thus home to a remarkable assortment of animals. To date, 115 species of mammals, 250 species of birds, 100 species of amphibians and reptiles – and over 30,000 species of insects have been counted! With a bit of luck, you can see white-faced capuchin monkeys, howler monkeys, white-tailed deer, coatis and large iguanas (*Ctenousaura similis*). Pumas, coyotes and boa constrictors are among the less commonly spotted denizens of the park.

**Playa Nancite** is considered one of the two most important breeding grounds of **olive ridley turtles** (*Lepidochelys olivacea*, known to Costa Ricans as the *tortuga lora*) in the world, the other being Playa Ostional in the Refugio Nacional de Vida Silvestre de Ostional

***Iguana***

(see p 243). These turtles are not very big, weighing only 40 kilograms on average, but thousands of them come to the beach to lay their eggs. This spectacular phenomenon, which local residents refer to as *arribadas* (massive influxes), occurs frequently between the months of July and November and most often in August and September.

Of all the parks in Guanacaste, Parque Nacional Santa Rosa is best equipped to welcome visitors. It has eight rooms, campsites (see p 248) and a cafeteria that serves excellent food *(breakfast $3.50, lunch $5, dinner $4.25)*.

The Santa Rosa sector has a number of hiking trails, which lead past various natural attractions. Near the park entrance, a lookout known as the **Mirador Santa Elena** offers a view of the Santa Elena Mountains, which are about 85 million years old. Near La Casona, you can go on a half-hour hike along the **Indio Desnudo** trail *(0.8 km)*, from which you can observe the various plant and animal species that coexist harmoniously in the tropical dry forest. Near a small natural bridge, are some petroglyphs carved into the stone.

A small, unpaved road leads from the park headquarters to **Playa Naranjo**, 12 kilometres away. It is only passable during the dry season (November to May), and even then a four-wheel drive vehicle is required. In fact, the road is in such poor condition that motorists often run into problems, so be sure to ask for authorization before setting out.

If you want to camp at Playa Naranjo and decide to go by foot, it will take you between three and four hours to get there. Don't forget to bring along a good supply of food and drinking water. The other campground is located near Playa Nancite, five kilometres farther north. There are two small, pleasant secondary trails along the road from the park headquarters to Playa Naranjo. On the left, **Los Patos** (1.5 km each way) leads into the wooded valley of the Río Poza Salada. A little farther and on the right, the **Mirador Valle Naranjo** (1 km each way) leads to a lovely lookout from which you can admire the dry forest, the valley and part of Playa Naranjo and the Real estuary. South of the beach, the **Carbonal** trail (3 km each way) runs along the Limbo lagoon, where howl-

### Stuck in the Mud...

Believing that we had been given permission to drive to Playa Naranjo in mid-December, we ended up getting stuck in a metre of mud and water four kilometres into the journey and had to walk back for help. A park official tersely informed us that there was no way to retrieve our vehicle unless we called in a tow truck from Liberia ($145!). Finally, after much pleading, we found a good samaritan willing to give us a hand. We later learned that the park has had a lot of trouble with surfers, who go to the beach whenever they please and have no qualms about breaking park rules. So the park authorities decided not to do anything about the condition of the road to discourage surfers from coming. But there's a better solution to that problem, however: a good gate!

ers, white-faced capuchins and even spider monkeys can often be spotted.

To get to the **Murciélago sector**, leave the park and head north on the Interamericana (see p 213). This part of the park has campsites *($1.25/person/day, drinking water, showers, bathrooms)*, picnic areas and a network of hiking trails, as well as several small, unpaved roads (four-wheel drive required) leading to the bays of **El Hachal**, **Santa Elena** and **Playa Blanca**. The Murciélago sector has a lengthy history. A farm named El Murciélago (The Bat) was built here in 1663 and served its original function until the 1970s, when it was purchased by the family of Nicaraguan dictator Anastasio Somoza and converted into a military base. The Costa Rican government expropriated the Somozas in 1979 and made the farm part of the Área de Conservación Guanacaste (ACG) in November 1980.

## Refugio Nacional Bahía Junquillal

The **Refugio Nacional Bahía Junquillal** *($1.50; every day 8am to 5pm; ☎/⇄695-5598 or 695-5577)* lies about 20 kilometres south of La Cruz (by way of Puerto Soley), which is the last sizeable town before the Nicaraguan border. This small nature reserve, which covers an area of just over 500 hectares and is also part of the Área de Conservación Guanacaste (ACG). It has a magnificent beach that stretches about two kilometres and occasionally serves as a nesting ground for ridley, leatherback and green turtles.

In addition to lounging on the beach and observing the wide variety of aquatic birds, you can also go swimming and snorkelling here. A small trail known as **El Carao** leads about 600 metres through the dry coastal forest, where you can observe the process of regeneration. Twenty-five campsites *($1.25/person/day)* have been laid out here, and visitors have access to picnic tables, grills, drinking water, restrooms and showers.

## Parque Nacional Guanacaste

**Parque Nacional Guanacaste ★** *($6; every day 8am to 5pm; ☎/⇄695-5598 or 695-5577)* was created on July 25, 1989, the provincial holiday. Covering an area of 32,512 hectares, it is actually an extension of Parque Nacional Santa Rosa, which lies on the other (west) side of the Interamericana. This stretch of parkland forms a natural corridor that is crucial to the survival of all sorts of animals. Many of these require vast hunting grounds; depending on the season, they stalk their prey in the mountains, on the plains or along the shore. This park protects an assortment of natural habitats, all the way from the Pacific coast to the top of Cacao Volcano, 1,659 metres above sea level. Efforts are being made to create a similar natural corridor by joining Parque Nacional Guanacaste and Parque Nacional Rincón de la Vieja, just a few kilometres to the southeast. The project is going well, and only a small strip of land on either side of the highway remains to be protected between the two parks. However, as these pieces of land are privately owned, an agreement will probably require lengthy negotiations.

### *Conservación*

Parque Nacional Guanacaste is part of the **Área de Conservación Guanacaste** (ACG), whose headquarters are in Parque Nacional Santa Rosa. Located in the northwest part of the province of Guanacaste, the ACG includes three national parks, Guanacaste, Santa Rosa and Rincón de la Vieja, as well as the Refugio Nacional Bahía Junquillal and the Horizontes forestry station. It protects a total of over 120,000 hectares of land and 75,000 hectares of shoreline.

Authorities naturally want to keep Parque Nacional Guanacaste as pristine as possible, while still allowing visitors to admire the natural treasures contained within its boundaries. An emphasis has been placed on research, so that all the plant and animal species in the area can be identified. Scientists come here from all over the world to work, to help conduct research or to teach various techniques of biological cataloguing. Given that the park is home to 3,800 species of geometrids (large moths) alone, the project is quite complicated and labourious – not to mention time-consuming!

Three research stations, **Maritza**, **Cacao** and **Pitilla**, were built so that the scientists would not have to leave the park every evening after roaming the valleys and the mountains. Maritza stands at the foot of **Orosí Volcano** (1,487 m), while Cacao is at an altitude of 1,100 metres, near the volcano of the same name (1,659 m). Pitilla sits on the east side of Orosí, which receives more precipitation and is thus damper than the Pacific side of the volcano. The rivers on the volcano's east side flow eastward to the Caribbean Sea, just under 200 kilometres away.

When these three stations are not occupied by researchers, visitors and tourists passing through the area are welcome to stay in them. The accommodations are rustic – dormitory-style rooms with shared bathrooms and no hot water. Each station can house 20 to 30 people and costs $10 to $15 per person per night. Reservations are required, and visitors must bring their own food. Though there are no actual campsites, you can pitch your tent near the stations *($1.25/person/day)* if you ask permission beforehand.

There are several hiking trails around the stations. **El Pedregal** (3 km total), near Maritza, runs through pastures and a transitional forest (tropical dry to tropical rain). It leads to the foot of Orosí, where you can admire some of the 800 pre-Columbian petroglyphs carved onto boulders made of volcanic rock. The **Cacao-Maritza trail** (6 km

## Rincón de la Vieja

The name Rincón de la Vieja (Old Woman's Place) comes from a Native American legend. Long ago, the great chief Curubandé's daughter, Princess Curubanda, fell in love with Prince Mixcoac, the chief of a neighbouring enemy tribe. When Curubandé learned of this dangerous liaison, he had the prince captured and taken to the top of the volcano. With no further ado, poor Mixcoac was thrown into the crater. Curubanda was so distraught that she lost her mind. It is said that she went to live at the top of the fearsome volcano to be near her deceased lover. A baby was later born of this tragic union. Wanting the child to live with his father, the grief-stricken princess threw him into the mouth of the crater as a final offering to her beloved. According to the legend, after years of isolation, Curubanda became a great healer, using plants, mud and volcanic ash. When people climbed the volcano to consult the *curendera* (healer), they would say *"voy para el rincón de la Vieja"* (I'm going to the old woman's place).

each way) takes about two hours and links the two stations after which it is named, passing Casa Fran, a house used occasionally by park employees, along the way. If you want to climb to the **top of Cacao** (1,659 m), you are better off setting out from the Cacao station (2 km total) than the Maritza station (14 km total). From the Cacao station (1,100 m), the trail climbs continuously, winding its way through the tropical rain forest to the top of the volcano. It's a short (1 km each way) but steep hike (change in altitude: 559 m), requiring considerable effort. The top of the volcano is wooded, but there is a lookout that offers a sweeping view of the surrounding valleys.

## Parque Nacional Rincón de la Vieja

Quite simply one of the most beautiful parks in Costa Rica, **Parque Nacional Rincón de la Vieja** ★★★ *($6; every day 7am to 5pm; ☎/⇌659-5598 or 659-5577)* has everything a nature lover and hiking enthusiast could hope to find. Oddly enough, it is only the ninth most popular park in the country (22,173 visitors in 1996). So get out there and enjoy it while it's still a well-kept secret! The park boasts magnificent scenery, breathtaking views, a distinctive volcano, soothing rivers, spectacular waterfalls, relaxing hot springs, places to swim, picnic areas, campgrounds and well-marked trails, not to mention detailed documentation (brochures and maps) – something of a rarity in Costa Rica.

Parque Nacional Rincón de la Vieja covers an area of 14,084 hectares, and lies about 25 kilometres northeast of Liberia, the capital of the province of Guanacaste. It is divided into two sectors, **Las Pailas** and **Santa María**, which are about eight kilometres apart. For directions to these sectors, see p 212. The park was created on October 23, 1973 to protect the region's rich plant and animal life and the many water sources that supply some parts of the province.

Anyone who has been to the arid regions of Guanacaste will be amazed by all the rivers in the park! Because the watershed runs along the Cordillera de Guanacaste and the Continental Divide, past Rincón de

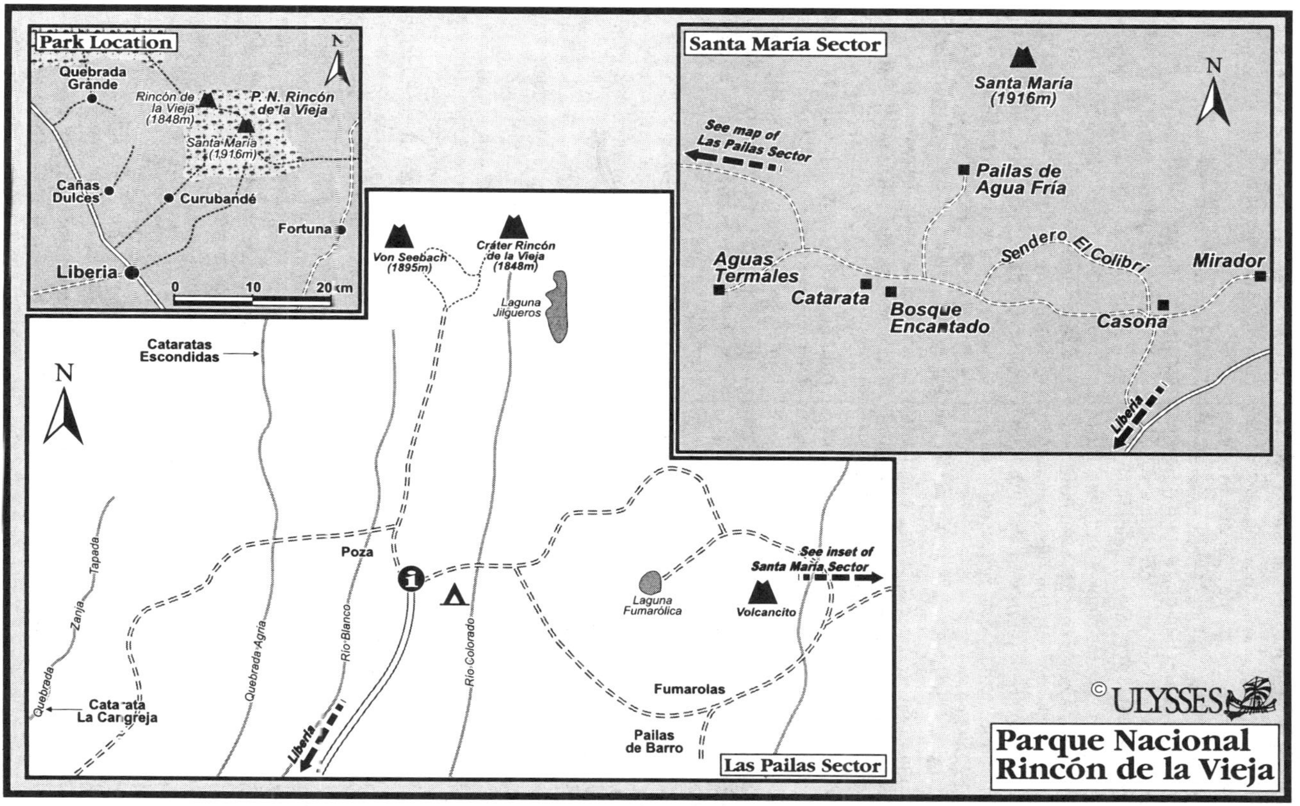
Park Location
N
Quebrada
Grande
Rincón de
la Vieja
(1848m)
P. N. Rincón
de la Vieja
Santa María
(1916m)
Cañas
Dulces
Curubandé
Fortuna
Liberia
0
10
20 km
Santa María Sector
Santa María
(1916m)
See map of
Las Pailas Sector
Pailas de
Agua Fría
Sendero El Colibrí
Aguas
Termales
Catarata
Bosque
Encantado
Casona
Mirador
Liberia
Von Seebach
(1895m)
Cráter Rincón
de la Vieja
(1848m)
Laguna
Jilgueros
Cataratas
Escondidas
Poza
Laguna
Fumarólica
Volcancito
See inset of
Santa María Sector
Tapada
Zanja
Quebrada
Quebrada Agria
Río Blanco
Río Colorado
Catarata
La Cangreja
Liberia
Fumarolas
Pailas
de Barro
Las Pailas Sector
© ULYSSES
Parque Nacional
Rincón de la Vieja

la Vieja (1,895 m) and Santa María (1,916 m), the rivers flowing north and east empty into the Caribbean Sea, while those flowing south and west empty into the Pacific, watering Liberia and various villages along the way. No fewer than 32 rivers originate in the park, and 16 additional streams form during the rainy season. Many of these rivers link up with the Río Tempisque, the largest waterway in the province and one of the most impressive in all of Costa Rica.

**Rincón de la Vieja Volcano**, which has nine craters, has always attracted lots of attention. It is said that in the past, the volcano erupted so often that sailors making their way along the Pacific coast would use it as a sort of lighthouse. However, the first observation reports dating from 1851, describing eruptions, ash and smoke, are more plausible. Numerous minor eruptions were reported over the following years. Then, around 1967, when the volcano started spewing out large stones (up to 2 kg), and local residents began to fear the worst. Several forests and meadows were destroyed, and a number of rivers were polluted by toxic gases.

Further activity in 1983, 1984, 1991 and again in 1995 confirmed that the volcano was erupting regularly, as if to show that it could unleash its fury at any moment. The most recent eruption took place in the spring of 1998, mainly affecting the nearly uninhabited north side of the volcano, which faces Nicaragua. Fortunately, this side of the volcano has borne the brunt of the eruptions so far, while the south and west sides, where most of the villages, hotels, park facilities, trails and tourist attractions are located, have been spared. Vulcanologists believe that the numerous geysers and mudpots, which emit sulfurous fumes, allow for a constant release of internal pressure, reducing the risk of a major eruption.

The park's varied elevation, which ranges from 600 to nearly 2,000 metres, allows for a very wide range of vegetation to grow here, a phenomenon which is enhanced by the frequent rainfall and fertile volcanic ash to which the region is exposed. A dry forest made up of species like the *guanacaste* (*Enterolobium cyclocarpum*), the laurel (*Cedrela odorata*) and the *cedro amargo* (*Cedrela odonta*) flourishes between 600 and 1,200 metres above sea level. Between 1,200 and 1,400 metres, where the rainfall is heaviest, is a rainforest characterized by the presence of numerous *copey* (*Clusia rosea*) trees, which thrive in this environment. Above 1,400 metres, the trees become stunted before giving way to shrubs and moss. Lilac-coloured cattleya orchids, which are the national flower of Costa Rica and known as the *guaria morada*, also abound in the park.

The park's animal life is as fascinating as it is varied. With a little luck, and if you're very quiet, you'll see iguanas, agoutis, coatis, howlers, white-faced capuchins and spider monkeys. Less commonly seen creatures include armadillos, Baird's tapirs, peccaries, ocelots, pumas and jaguars. Some 300 avian species make their home here as well, most notably parrots, toucans, trogons (including the odd quetzal), hummingbirds, doves, woodpeckers, owls and eagles. You'll also come across some magnificent butterflies.

**Las Pailas Sector**

This sector, located at the foot of Rincón de la Vieja, is named after the numerous "cauldrons" (*pailas*) – hot springs, geysers and mudpots – found here. At the information and welcome centre at the entrance to the sector, you can pick up documentation on the park (brochures and maps). A large model of the park is also on display. Nearby, on the Río Colorado, there are well-shaded campsites equipped with picnic tables *($1.25/person/day, drinking water, showers, restrooms)*.

If you only have a few hours, we strongly recommend taking the easy and fascinating **Pailas trail** (3 km), a loop that leads past a lovely waterfall, fumaroles, boiling mudpots and a miniature, newly formed volcano known as *volcancito*. You'll walk through fields and a luxuriant forest echoing with the cries of howler monkeys. **WARNING:** Many visitors have suffered serious burns by applying masks of volcanic mud. If you're interested in trying out this beauty treatment, ask an experienced guide from the park or a local hotel for advice.

If you want to go to the **Santa María sector**, take the Pailas trail to the halfway point, where you'll see a sign for the path to follow. The welcome centres of the two sectors are about eight kilometres apart.

About 800 metres from the Las Pailas welcome centre, you can take an invigorating dip in the cold waters of the **Río Blanco**. A short but steep little trail leads down to a swimming hole where hikers often come to cool off in the water or lounge about on the rocks.

In the same direction, but 4.3 kilometres (each way) from the welcome centre is a trail leading to the **Cataratas Escondidas** (Hidden Falls), three waterfalls located west of the Escondida and Agria streams. Two of the falls are visible from the canyon, but you have to walk a bit farther to see the third, where you'll also find a good spot to go swimming.

Even farther west and more to the south, you'll come to a magnificent waterfall known as **La Cangreja** (The Crab). At the foot of the falls, which plunge about 25 metres, a lovely pool with turquoise waters beckons visitors to go for a dip. La Cangreja is 5.1 kilometres (each way) from the welcome centre.

If you want to climb to the **top of Rincón de la Vieja** (1,895 m), it is best to set out around 7:00 or 8:00 in the morning, since the trail is about 16 kilometres (return) and takes between six and eight hours to hike (plus stops, picture taking, lunch, etc.). Furthermore, since there is a 900-metre change in altitude and the trail climbs continuously, only those in reasonably good physical condition will be able to fully enjoy this memorable outing. By leaving early (allow at least an hour for the drive from Liberia to the park), you will also avoid arriving at the top of the volcano in the late afternoon, when the clouds are more menacing, and finishing the hike in the dark (night falls at around 5:30pm), matches or flashlight in hand. Don't forget to bring along warm, waterproof clothing, a sufficient supply of food and lots of water.

The first part of the trail leads through a dense forest where spider monkeys and woodpeckers thrive. When we were there, a pair of spider monkeys put on a real show to intimidate us. One stood on the shoulders of the other, while they shook the branches of a big tree so hard that the wood cracked. Frightened by the sound, one of them went hurtling through the air like some sort of circus clown!

After four kilometres, the trees give way to shrubs and moss. The trail becomes more difficult, and you have to climb some big mud steps. From that point on, there is lots of wind, rain and fog. On the positive side, the trail is well marked with little flags, cairns and signs. At the top, it runs along the edge of the volcano and becomes very narrow – about a metre wide! If the wind is blowing hard, which is often the case, it is wise to rope yourselves together to avoid any disastrous falls. You can relax and enjoy the 360 degree view until you get a lungful of sulfur fumes, at which point you'll probably feel like heading back. Because the trail is so steep, the trip down takes almost as long as the climb up. Reward yourself with a swim, or at least dip your feet in the cool waters of the **Río Blanco**, near the welcome centre (see above).

### Santa María Sector

This sector lies about eight kilometres east of Las Pailas, but you'll have to take a different road from Liberia (see p 212) if you want to drive there. One of the largest haciendas in this mountainous region was in operation here until 1973. Cattle and dairy cows were kept on the farm, which also produced coffee and sugarcane. Visitors can tour the main house, known as La Casona, which has been converted into a welcome centre (see p 231). One of the rooms contains an exhibition of photographs of the volcano and an assortment of tools that were once used at the hacienda.

There are picnic areas and campsites *($1.25/person/day, drinking water, showers, restrooms)* near La Casona. Next to the campsites, the **Colibrí trail** (500 m) leads through a secondary forest and to the place where the sugarcane used to be pressed.

On the east side of La Casona, is a short trail (about 500 m each way) which leads to a ***mirador*** that offers a magnificent view of the park, the surrounding plains, the town of Liberia and Miravalles Volcano (2,028 m). On the west side, another trail leads to the **Pailas de Agua Fría** (1.6 km each way), or cold-water springs. Even closer to La Casona (1.1 km each way), on the Río Zopitote, you'll find the lovely waterfall known as the **Bosque Encantado** (Enchanted Forest). One of the sector's main attractions, however, are the **Aguas Termales** (hot springs), located 2.8 kilometres (each way) from La Casona. Produced by volcanic activity, these hot, sulfurous springs are believed to have medicinal powers. Whether or not that's true, it is wonderfully relaxing to soak in them, and that's got to be good for you! Be careful not to get the sulfurous water in your eyes, though, and take a few short dips (about five minutes at a time) rather than soaking for a long time.

## Around Liberia

### Liberia and Surroundings

The capital of the province of Guanacaste, **Liberia** ★ has a population of about 40,000. All in all, it is quite a pleasant town and has lots of shops and services, which can be helpful when you're heading off to the beaches or the local attractions. Liberia is bustling with activity during the day and remains lively at night. If it doesn't seem that way to you, go to the big **Parque Central**. Shaded by lovely old trees during the day, the park fills with people after dinner. Calle Central, which runs between the park and the church of the Immaculate Conception has been turned into a pedestrian street, making the park that much more popular. The shrubbery around the Parque Central is home to scores of birds, who make a quite a racket.

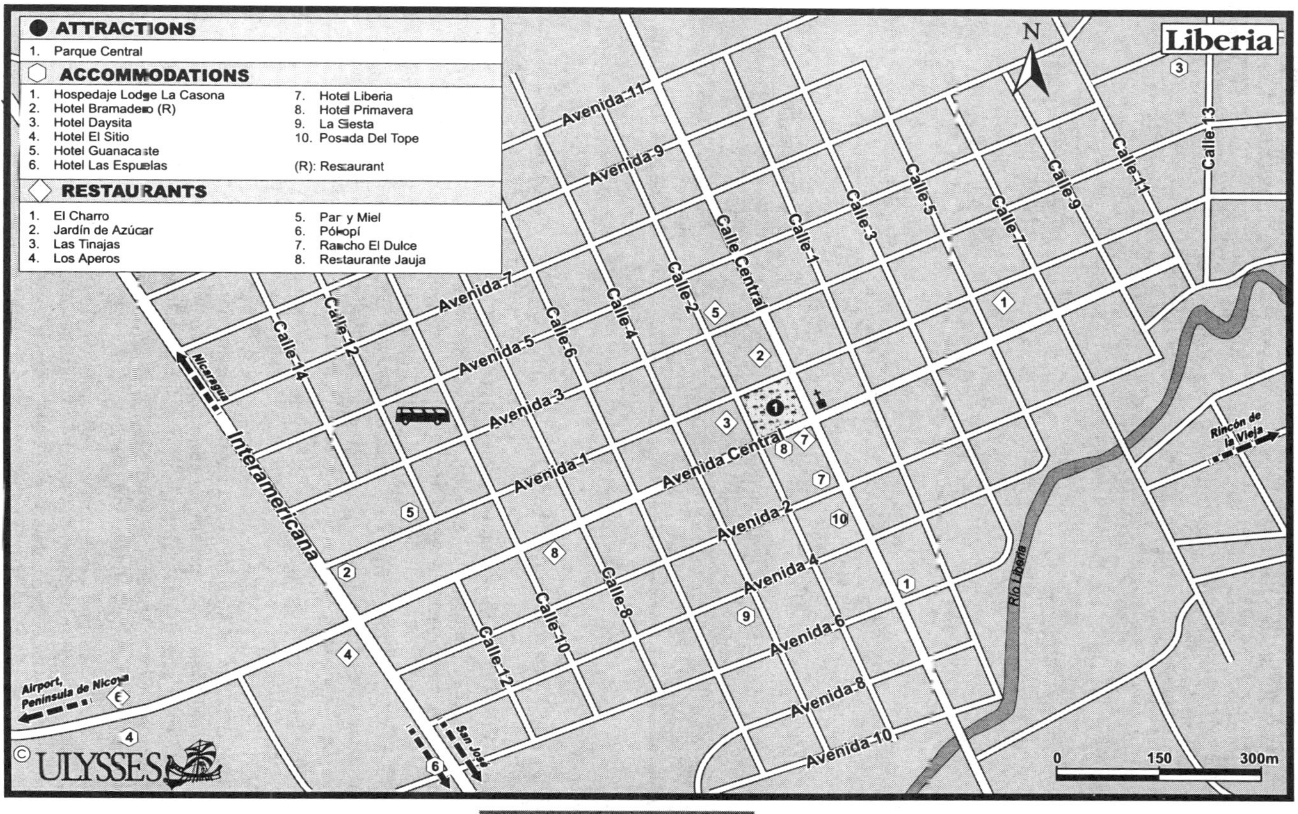
ATTRACTIONS
1. Parque Central
ACCOMMODATIONS
1. Hospedaje Lodge La Casona
2. Hotel Bramadero (R)
3. Hotel Daysita
4. Hotel El Sitio
5. Hotel Guanacaste
6. Hotel Las Espuelas
7. Hotel Liberia
8. Hotel Primavera
9. La Siesta
10. Posada Del Tope
(R): Restaurant
RESTAURANTS
1. El Charro
2. Jardín de Azúcar
3. Las Tinajas
4. Los Aperos
5. Pan y Miel
6. Pókopí
7. Rancho El Dulce
8. Restaurante Jauja
N
Liberia
Calle 13
Calle 11
Calle 9
Calle 7
Calle 5
Calle 3
Calle 1
Calle Central
Calle 2
Calle 4
Calle 6
Calle 8
Calle 10
Calle 12
Calle 14
Avenida 11
Avenida 9
Avenida 7
Avenida 5
Avenida 3
Avenida 1
Avenida Central
Avenida 2
Avenida 4
Avenida 6
Avenida 8
Avenida 10
Interamericana
Nicaragua
San José
Airport, Peninsula de Nicoya
Rincón de la Vieja
Río Liberia
0
150
300m
© ULYSSES

**Playa del Coco and Surroundings**

This is the first of the string of beaches that makes Guanacaste one of the country's major seaside resort areas.

**Playa del Coco** ★ lies about 35 kilometres from Liberia. One of the closest beaches to the capital, it was also one of the first in Guanacaste to attract tourists.

Playa del Coco is actually two beaches separated by a small stream, which is why it is sometimes referred to as Playas del Coco. Though they are right next to each other, each section has its own access road. Both are very popular, though the one to the south is more residential. People use all sorts of small boats to get around the little bay in which the beach is located, and these vessels are moored offshore. Playa del Coco has a pier and a small central park by the edge of the beach, and is surrounded by bars and inexpensive restaurants, many over 20 years old. All these factors make it a pleasant spot for visitors looking for an authentic Costa Rican experience. The farther you get from the centre of town, the newer the hotels become, as more are going up all the time. The area has been quite densely developed, and has a distinctly Costa Rican feel about it. Playa del Coco is also a bustling fishing port. The beach is fairly wide at low tide, but almost disappears at high tide.

**Playa Ocotal** lies a few kilometres farther south. If you're looking for peace and quiet but don't want to stray too far from town, you might want to try this magnificent little beach, which is nestled in a cove and flanked by steep slopes. For safety's sake, you should stick to the middle part of the beach if you want to go swimming.

Located to the north, **Playa Hermosa ★** ("Beautiful Beach" in Spanish) is also quieter (and cleaner) than Playa del Coco. It stretches a kilometre and a half, and is nice and wide. Partly sheltered by a bay, the water here is relatively calm and clear, and the sand is on the grey side. One of the best things about this beach is that it is fairly well shaded by the vegetation growing alongside it. It is also flanked by rocks, making it a good place to go surfing.

**Playa Panamá**, just north of Playa Hermosa, lies practically in the middle of the bay formed by the Punta Culebra, a spit of land a few kilometres farther north, so the water here is fairly calm. This beach has only been developed fairly recently, because it is hidden away in a magnificent wooded area. Still, large-scale residential and resort developments, complete with an 18-hole golf course, have already been built. All these projects are supposedly "ecological", meaning sizeable portions of the land is supposed to be kept in its natural state. Nevertheless, the presence of humans is evident throughout.

## Around Filadelfia

You have to go through **Filadelfia** and **Belén** to get to the beaches south of the Liberia area. The road from Belén leads to two groups of beaches (those around Flamingo and those around Tamarindo) that have been undergoing residential and tourist development for several years now.

### Playa Flamingo and Surroundings

There are actually six beaches along this part of the coast, but we have lumped them all together under the name of the swankiest of the group, Playa Flamingo, which is this area's hub.

**Playa Flamingo ★** is both a point that extends into a bay and a strip of white sand (it used to be called Playa Blanca, meaning "White Beach"). The only full-service marina on the northwest coast is located here. Playa Flamingo is a mecca for sport fishing and hosts an annual tournament. Many affluent people have a secondary residence on the shore here. There are a few restaurants and stores selling consumer goods (including a supermarket) at the base of the point, the rest of which is occupied by big hotels and upscale residential complexes. It is fashionable (and quite expensive) to stay at Playa Flamingo.

Not far to the south, **Playa Brasilito** is the exact opposite of Playa Flamingo. A little village made up mainly of middle-class homes (permanent and vacation), it doesn't have much to recommend it to foreign tourists and is still relatively undeveloped. The sand in this area is quite grey.

Immediately south of Playa Brasilito, gorgeous **Playa Conchal ★★** is aptly named (*concha* is the Castilian word for shell), since a large part of it is covered with shells. In fact, you'll even find shells in the strip of vegetation growing alongside it and in the water as well, blanketing the ocean floor immediately offshore. The beach is dominated by the famous Melia Playa Conchal hotel complex (see p 253).

North of Flamingo, the shore is interspersed with several other

## The Leatherback

Las Baulas is the plural of the Costa Rican name for the leatherback *(la baula)*. This giant turtle, which grows to a length of 1.5 to two metres and weighs around 500 kilograms (the record is about 900 kilograms), can dive to depths of over 1,300 metres. Researchers Karen and Scott Eckert calculated that it takes a leatherback turtle an average of 37 minutes to reach a depth of over 1,200 metres. Its size and diving feats aren't the only things that distinguish the leatherback from your average turtle, however; it also has an elongated shape and seven clearly visible, ridges along the length of its shell. Furthermore, the shell is not made of the same hard substance as that of other marine turtles but rather of thick, leathery skin; hence the turtle's name.

Leatherbacks feed almost exclusively on jellyfish. Sadly, many choke to death each year after ingesting plastic bags that litter the sea and can easily be mistaken for jellyfish. The leatherback makes one of the longest migratory voyages of any animal in the world. One tagged turtle was found nearly 6,000 kilometres from its usual breeding site! Female leatherbacks supposedly return to the same beach every two or three years to lay their eggs. On the Pacific coast, the laying season falls between October and March; on the Atlantic, between April and August.

During the egg-laying season, each female returns to the same beach four to 10 times to lay eggs. Using her front flippers, she digs a hole about 70 centimetres deep, in which she lays nearly 100 soft-shelled eggs, each about the size of a tennis ball. Once she has finished, she carefully covers the hole with sand and heads back into the water. The incubation period lasts about 68 days, after which the hatchlings make their way to the sea, guided by the moonlight reflected on the water. Unfortunately, they sometimes get confused by the lights of the houses and hotels along the beach and head inland, where they succumb to dehydration or exhaustion.

beaches, which are nearly undeveloped and thus feel more private.

The first of these, **Playa Potrero**, attracts few beach-goers. A four-kilometre-long, curving strip of brownish-grey sand, it is nonetheless perfect for swimming. A little farther, you'll come to **Playa Penca**, a white sandy beach. Still farther north lies another white-sand beach, **Playa Pan de Azúcar**.

**Playa Tamarindo and Surroundings**

We have named this part of the province after Tamarindo simply because the town is a populous centre. The road out of the village actually leads to a vast region encompassing Parque Nacional Marino Las Baulas and the two beaches at its edges (Playa Grande and Playa Tamarindo).

Primarily a surfer's hangout, **Playa Grande** ★★★ is a magnificent, uncrowded beach right near Parque Nacional Marino Las Baulas. Sheltered by the park, it is very clean and has lovely, light-coloured sand. The beach is accessed by a bumpy road that leads through the park. Developers are presently negotiating with park authorities so that they can start building hotels in this heavenly spot. Sites have already been cleared for residential development some distance from the beach, outside the park's boundaries. Since the roads still need some work, the few local inhabitants are living pretty much in the wild. At the same time, roads have been cleared through the forest and are simply waiting to be paved. A few houses and hotels have sprung up here and there. Nevertheless, there are barely a dozen oceanfront homes on the three-kilometre-long beach.

Though **Playa Tamarindo** ★ is under continuous development, most of the hotels built here are smaller than those at Playa Flamingo. Still, the place is attracting more and more people, particularly surfers. Several surf shops have opened up in town. The beach itself is a long strip of white sand with little vegetation growing along it, so the village is somewhat dusty. **Warning**: The surf can be quite heavy and there are lots of rocks jutting out of the water offshore. Keep your distance from the estuaries or you might find yourself carried out to sea by the currents.

**Playa Langosta** lies at the far end of Playa Tamarindo, nestled in a bend in the shoreline. In recent years, this beach has started to see some of the development that has been going on in Tamarindo. This is a great spot for surfing, especially near the little river that empties into the ocean.

## Parque Nacional Marino Las Baulas

If you're looking for a fascinating, moving and enriching experience, head to **Parque Nacional Marino Las Baulas** ★★ *($6, guided tour included; open year-round, ☎/≠680-0779)* to watch **leatherback turtles** (*Demochelys coriacea*) lay their eggs on **Playa Grande**. This spectacle can be observed nearly every night from October to March, particularly in December and January.

**Important notice**: The turtles only lay their eggs on the beach at night, during low tide. To avoid a long wait, we strongly recommend calling the El Mundo de la Tortuga museum (see further below) a few hours beforehand to get an update on the tides and find out the best time to go.

Parque Nacional Marino Las Baulas has a total area of 22,500 hectares, only 500 of which are on land. It was created on July 9, 1991 to protect this breeding site, one of the largest in the world. Over the years, the area had become overrun with tourists, some of whom were so careless that they would ride around on the turtles' backs! Nowadays, park officials keep a close watch over the beach during the laying season and visitors are only welcome in groups and must be accompanied by a guide. Unfortunately, the guides usually speak in Spanish and might not be able to explain the egg-laying process in English. If you aren't fluent in Spanish, stop by the El mundo de la tortuga museum (see below) before your outing to get a better understanding of what you are about to see. A number of rules should be followed. One of the most important is to keep quiet and stay behind the turtle so you don't frighten it. The use of cameras with flashes and video cameras with lighting is also strictly forbidden.

The **El Mundo de la Tortuga museum** ★★ *($5, children admitted free of charge; every day after 4pm, early Oct to mid-Mar; just before the* *park entrance, ☎/⇌653-0471)* is a must if you want to learn more about sea turtles in general and leatherbacks in particular. Furthermore, if you're planning a trip to Parque Nacional Marino Las Baulas to watch the leatherbacks lay their eggs, this is the perfect place to wait for the tide to go down, since it has a small outdoor café and a souvenir shop where you can while away the time (sometimes several hours).

When you enter the museum, you will be given a headset. The 30-minute recorded tour (available, in English, French, Spanish and German) takes you to 27 stops, where you'll see stunning photographs of these impressive but vulnerable creatures and gain insight into their reproductive cycle, how they live, the threats they face and the efforts being made to protect them. The tour ends at the souvenir shop, where the staff will gladly answer any questions you might have. This museum is sure to touch your heart and fill you with wonder. Those who know nothing about leatherback turtles will emerge half an hour later feeling that they understand the captivating world of the biggest sea turtles on Earth. For this reason, we strongly recommend visiting the museum before going to the park, not after.

The museum opened on October 1, 1996, thanks to the efforts of three Frenchmen and a Spaniard with a passion for marine turtles. In 1994, Corina Esteban, one of the museum's founders, came to the region and worked as a volunteer at Parque Nacional Marino Las Baulas. Shortly thereafter, she had the idea of opening a small museum so that tourists could learn about the turtles they would be observing. Park officials are thrilled with the museum. Furthermore, the park guides and museum staff talk to each other by walkie-talkie while waiting for the turtles to arrive at night, so that everyone knows when a turtle has made it to the beach and the tourists can be divided up into groups.

The museum offers a package rate to visitors staying in the Playa Grande and Tamarindo areas. At only $20, it is a real bargain as it covers transportation to and from your hotel, admission to the museum, a non-alcoholic beverage and a nighttime visit to the breeding site (park fees included).

## Around Santa Cruz

### Santa Cruz and Surroundings

Its *fiestas* (particularly those in January) and distinctive regional cuisine make **Santa Cruz** the national folklore capital of Costa Rica. There is nothing really special about the town itself, though it does have a lovely central park, an attractive modern church, an historic bell tower and a pretty little public square. On the east side of the square, is a small covered market that is open at night and sells good produce, among other things.

The little village of **Guaitil ★** is about a dozen kilometres east of Santa Cruz and known for its magnificent pottery (vases, plates, bowls, etc.). Most of the pieces are made according to Native American designs, using traditional Chorotega decorations and natural colours. The artisans sell their pottery themselves, and it is fun to go from one house to the next and chat with them. You will likely hear that some families of craftsmen are descendants of the Chorotegas, who lived in the region in pre-Columbian times. Though Guaitil attracts plenty of tourists (therefore try to go in the late afternoon), the prices are still very affordable. You'll find all sorts of small

***Zebu***

items that can easily fit in your suitcase. The small paved road leading to the village is absolutely lovely and makes for a delightful trip. You'll pass by tall trees, pastures and herds of zebus. If you don't have a car, you can take the bus from Santa Cruz.

**Playa Junquillal and Surroundings**

The town of Santa Cruz is the gateway to the Playa Junquillal area, which is relatively undeveloped in comparison to Playa Tamarindo and Playa Flamingo farther north. To get to this part of the coast, you have to take a bumpy road, which is particularly bad right near Santa Cruz. Four-wheel drive vehicles are recommended.

**Playa Avellanas** is fully exposed to the sea: unlike Sámara, farther south, it is not protected by coral reefs, which curb the power of the surf. It is thus perfect for surfing but unsuitable for swimming, particularly its central portion, where rocks can be seen jutting out of the water. Located some five kilometres from Playa Junquillal, Playa Avellanas is also relatively isolated.

**Playa Junquillal** is bounded by tall grass, which distinguishes it from most of the other beaches in the country. This place truly feels like the middle of nowhere, and what little activity there is centres entirely around the hotels. There are only eight little hotels scattered about in the forest and on the waterfront, which comprises a kilometre-long stretch of clean, dark sand. The water is not very deep and the surf is quite heavy.

**Playa Negra** is a nearly undeveloped beach just north of Playa Junquillal, and is perfect for surfing.

## Around Nicoya

**Nicoya and Surroundings**

The city of **Nicoya** ★ (named after an early 16th-century Native American chief) is the peninsula's commercial hub. It is also the centre of activity for

***Nicoya Church***

the local cattle industry and hosts a rodeo every July. Nicoya boasts the **second oldest colonial church in the country ★**, which stands at the northeast corner of its central park. The town serves mainly as a gateway for people exploring the region, particularly Parque Nacional Barra Honda and the beaches around Sámara. Many Chinese people immigrated to Nicoya in the past, and their descendants own a good number of the local businesses.

Nosara, Sámara and Carrillo are the seaside resorts in this part of the province. Sámara lies between the two others and is the most populous of the three. There are also two stretches of protected wilderness in the area, both immediately north of Nosara: the Refugio Nacional de Fauna Silvestre de Ostional and the Reserva Biológica de Nosara.

**Playa Sámara and Surroundings**

The area immediately surrounding **Playa Sámara ★★** can be divided into three sections. First, there is **Buena Vista**, a large, uninhabited (and thus quiet) beach a short distance north of crowded Sámara. To get there, take Isla Chora street north from the village of Sámara. Next is **Playa Congrejal**, which is more or less the northern extension of Playa Sámara and has a few hotels and restaurants. Finally, there is **Playa Sámara** itself, a pretty beach that is protected by coral reefs and thus has calm waters perfect for swimming. The village of Sámara, located alongside the beach, offers a fairly broad range of services for the region – it even has a few bars and nightclubs worth checking out (see p 269).

Located five kilometres south of Playa Sámara, **Playa Carrillo** is a long, wide stretch of white sand flanked by two spits of land covered with luxuriant vegetation. The airfield for the Sámara region lies right near this lovely, uninhabited beach, where you can go for a dip. Access to Playa Carrillo is gained by a shady urban boulevard with no hotels along it, creating a lovely perspective that lends a certain majesty

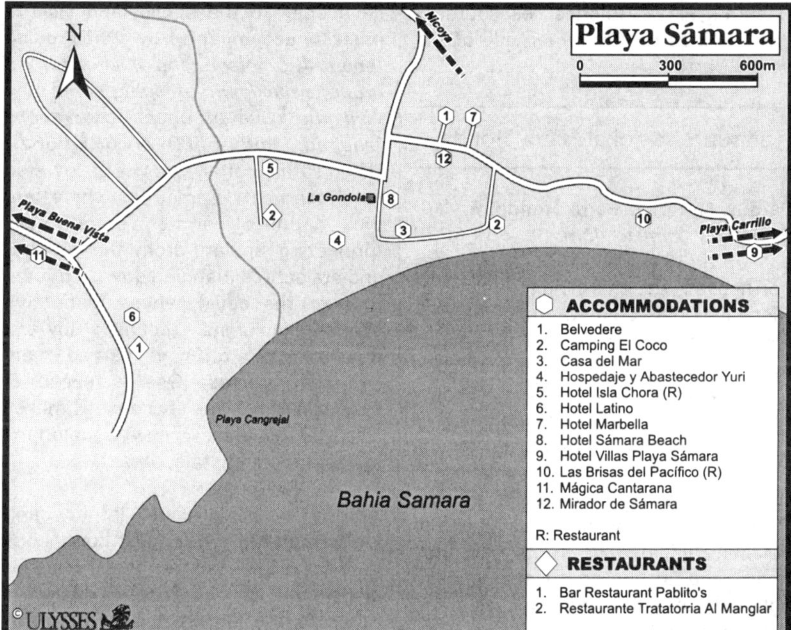




to the surroundings. It should be noted, however, that the road between Sámara and Carrillo is a bit rough and nowhere near the same quality as this broad street. **Punta Carrillo**, the nearby village, lies a little farther south.

The road to Playa Carrillo also leads to the other beaches south of Sámara, including **Playa Camaronal**.

### Playa Nosara and Surroundings

The **Reserva Biológica de Nosara**, which lies along the coast north of Nosara, is a private wildlife reserve with Swiss owners. Located along the **Río Nosara**, it contains mangrove swamps and rainforest and is home to over 170 species of birds, as well as monkeys, *jaguarundis*, crabs, reptiles and amphibians. If you want to visit the reserve, your best option is to stay at the owners' nearby hotel, the Lagarta Lodge (see p 260).

The village of **Nosara** is in the middle of the area immediately south of the reserve (5 km inland), but has no attractions per se. However, the regional airport, the **Aeropuerto de Nosara**, is located here, along with various services, including a gas station and a fairly well-stocked supermarket.

The **countryside around Playa Nosara** ★ (between Nosara and the beach) is scattered with a small number of restaurants and places to stay. The area is being developed but the process is still in its early stages, so visiting here will still give you a good feel for life in the Costa Rican jungle. Nosara's **Playa Pelada** is not suitable to swimming, particularly the section with the public entrance. Though pretty, the beach is pounded by heavy surf and hemmed in by large rocks on either side.

Nosara's **Playa Guiones** lies south of Playa Pelada, on the other side of the Punta Garza.

## Parque Nacional Barra Honda

**Parque Nacional Barra Honda** ★ *($6; every day 7am to 4pm; ☎/≠659-9039 or 659-9194)* lies 23 kilometres northeast of the charming little town of Nicoya. It was created on August 20, 1974 to protect the numerous caves, some very deep, that had just been found. Most local residents didn't know this network of caves existed before it was discovered by members of the Costa Rica's speology association in the early 1970s. They believed that these holes in the mountain were of volcanic origin. The rumblings they heard and attributed to the volcano actually came from huge cavities inside the mountain.

Barra Honda is the name of the big mountain that towers over the plain from an altitude of 423 metres. It is about 60 million years old and was forced from the depths of the sea by tectonic pressure. The mountain is composed mainly of limestone and, due to the effects of rain and carbon dioxide, has become riddled with caves where stalactites and stalagmites have formed over the centuries.

Since the 1970s, 42 caves have been discovered. To date, scientists have explored 19 of them, the longest being Santa Ana, which is 240 metres deep. Tourists can safely explore **Terciopelo**, a 62-metre-deep cave which got its name because a dead fer-de-lance, one of the most poisonous and dangerous snakes in the world, was found here when the cave was first being explored. Fortunately, no others, either alive or dead, have been seen here since. For now, Terciopelo is the only cave open to the public, and **visitors must be accompanied by a local guide** *(about $25/person, and much less for a group; a maximum of eight people may visit the cave at once; reservations required; ☎685-5580 or 685-5667)*. Using safety cords, you will be lowered to a depth of 20 metres, where you can admire some stalagmites (projecting upward from the ground) and stalactites (hanging down from the roof of the cave) whose distinctive shapes (columns, pearls, flowers, mushrooms, etc.) have earned them evocative names. One is called **El Organo** (The Organ) because it makes all sorts of sounds when you tap on the stalagmites and stalactites.

Among the other caves in the park, **La Trampa** has the longest continuous descent (52 m) and the largest galleries discovered so far. **Pozo Hediondo** is home to the largest concentration of bats in the park. From an historical point of view, however, **Nicoa** is the most interesting, since human skeletal remains were discovered inside it along with pre-Columbian objects, which would indicate that it was a burial place. Supposedly, explorers even found a stalagmite that had formed on a human skull!

Though Parque Nacional Barra Honda is not very big, visitors only have access to its southwestern part, where the welcome centre, park headquarters, picnic areas and campsites *($1.25/person/day)* are located. Campfires are not permitted due to the risk of forest fires. If you don't have food or a portable stove, you can eat at the park if you reserve your meal a day ahead.

The lovely hiking trail called **Los Laureles** is a 9.3-kilometre loop that leads past the park's most interesting sites. The outing takes three to five hours. Though the trail leads all the way to the top of the **Cerro Barra Honda** (423 m), 70% of it is flat, so it makes for an easy hike. The view from the hilltop is stunning, encompassing a large part of the Gulf of Nicoya, Chira Island and a vast plain covered with forests and little villages.

The trail also goes past the famous cave known as Terciopelo and offers hikers a chance to observe the local plant and animal life, which are perfectly adapted to the mountain rising up in the midst of the plains. The park is home to numerous species of trees, including the *matapalo*, the *javillo*, the laurel and the *tempisque*. Some of these bear fruit, providing a feast for many of the animals who inhabit the area (bats, parrots, macaws, agoutis, white-tailed deer, monkeys, etc.).

Since it can get incredibly hot in the park (over 35°C) in the afternoon, it is very important to bring along plenty of fresh water on your outings. Furthermore, the fact that two German tourists disappeared in 1992 after venturing onto a part of the mountain that was supposed to be off-limits to visitors should be enough to convince you to stick to the trails. This unfortunate incident, which made news all over the country and found its way into most travel guides, has unfortunately led to a drop in the number of tourists visiting the park (about 60% between 1994 and 1997).

## Refugio Nacional de Fauna Silvestre de Ostional

The **Refugio Nacional de Fauna Silvestre de Ostional** ★ *($6; open year-round; ☎/⇌659-9039 or 659-9194)* lies about 50 kilometres southwest of the town of Nicoya, by Playa Nosara and Playa Ostional. It is eight kilometres long but only a few hundred metres wide, covering a total area of 162 hectares of land and an additional 587 hectares of sea. The sanctuary was created in order to protect an area where thousands of marine turtles come to lay their eggs each year.

Playa Ostional and Playa Nancite, both in Parque Nacional Santa Rosa (see p 224), are considered the most important breeding sites in the world for the **olive ridley turtle** (*Lepidochelys olivacea*), which Costa Ricans refer to as the *tortuga lora*. These turtles are relatively small (40 kg on average) compared to leatherbacks (360 kg), but they come to this beach by the thousands to lay their eggs. This remarkable nocturnal phenomenon, known as *arribadas* (massive influxes), takes place frequently between July and November and most often in August and September. The touching and unique spectacle can thus be observed nearly every month, usually when the moon is in its third quarter. Even if there are no *arribadas* during your visit, you'll probably still see a few lone turtles.

In addition to the ridley, certain other kinds of turtles, including the **leatherback** (*Dermochelys coriacea*) and the **green turtle** (*Chelonia mydas*) sometimes lay their eggs at the Refugio Nacional de Fauna Silvestre de Ostional as well. Even if there are no turtles to be seen during your visit, you'll certainly have a chance to observe some capuchin monkeys and hear the loud calls of howler monkeys in the forest bordering the beach. You're also likely to see iguanas, coatis, crabs and some of the 100 species of birds that live in the area. There is a mangrove swamp southeast of the sanctuary, at the mouth of the Río Nosara, while Punta India, a rocky point strewn with numerous pools of water teeming with marine life, lies to the northwest.

## OUTDOOR ACTIVITIES

### Cycling

Small, unpaved trails (not the hiking paths) in **Guanacaste** and **Santa Rosa parks** are wonderful for mountain-biking. The trail from La Casona to Playa Naranjo (12 km) and Playa Nancite (5 km north of Naranjo) in Parque Nacional Santa Rosa is especially worth mentioning. To rent a bicycle, ask at your hotel reception or Liberia's tourist information office. At press time, the bicycle shop at the centre of town had closed down.

### Hiking

**Parque Nacional Rincón de la Vieja** (see p 228) has by far the best network of hiking trails in Guanacaste, and one of the best in the country in general. The climb to the top of the Rincón de la Vieja Volcano is very challenging, but is one of the most superb mountain hikes in Costa Rica, along with that of Cerro Chiripo.

**Parque Nacional Barra Honda** (see p 242) also has an enjoyable 10-kilometre-long trail. If you are looking for a shorter trek, go to **Parque Nacional Santa Rosa** (see p 222), which is easy to get to and has an interesting history.

### Rafting

The **Safaris Corobicí** *(Cañas, ☎/⇛669-1091)* agency specializes in rafting, particularly on the Río Corobicí, as its name indicates.

### Fishing

Guanacaste is one of the best places in Costa Rica for deep-sea fishing. Many hotels offer excursions during the fishing season, or can refer you to a local agency. If not, contact the **Americana Fishing Services** *(☎223-4331, ⇛221-0096)* to get the name of the nearest agency that offers such excursions.

### Surfing

Most beaches in Guanacaste are known for their good surfing conditions. The Protero Grande, Naranjo (Witch's Rock), Grande, Tamarindo, Langosta, Avellanas, Negra and Nosara beaches are considered excellent. **Basoa Surf Expeditions** *(☎257-1138)* and **Papagayo Surf Trips** *(☎670-0354)* organize surfing expeditions.

### Scuba Diving and Snorkelling

Scuba Diving and snorkelling are possible all along Guanacaste's coast, especially in the province's northwest. The Hermosa, Del Coco, Ocotal and Flamingo beaches are reputed to be excellent places to practice these sports. **Bill Beard's Diving Safari** *(☎/⇛670-0012)*, **Rich Coast Diving Company** *(☎/⇛670-0176)*, **El Ocotal Diving Safari** *(☎222-4259)* and **Resort Divers de Costa Rica** *(☎/⇛670-0421)* offer diving lessons and excursions.

### Horseback Riding

East of Santa Cruz, the **Los Inocentes** *(☎679-9190, ⇛265-6431)* farm is the best place for horseback riding in this part of Guanacaste. The horses are properly trained and well-treated. Various excursions into the mountains and through the countryside are organized.

## Birdwatching

**Parque Nacional Palo Verde** (see p 219) is well-known for the diversity and abundance of its bird species. Close to 300 types of birds have been spotted here.

**Parque Nacional Santa Rosa** (see p 222) is home to nearly 250 species of birds in its many different natural habitats (sea, beach, pastures, mountains, etc.).

## Golf

The **Ranchos Las Colinas** *(☎/⇌654-4089)* golf club at **Playa Grande** has an 18-hole course.

The **Melia Beach and Golf Resort** *(☎654-4123)* at **Playa Conchal** has an 18-hole course along the Pacific Ocean.

## Canopy Tours

Situated on the road that climbs to the national park of the same name, the **Rincón de la Vieja Volcano Mountain Lodge** *(☎/⇌695-5553)* offers **canopy tours** *($50 for 4 hours, or $77 for the day)*, which allow you to see the forest from 16 solid platforms high in the treetops.

## Water Sports

**Aquasport** *(on the road along the beach, ☎670-0450)* rents sports equipment on Playa Hermosa. For example, you can rent a pedal-boat for less than $5 an hour.

Flamingo has a **Marina** *(☎/⇌654-4203)* that offers all kinds of services.

# ACCOMMODATIONS

In addition to the hotels listed here, it is also possible to rent houses or condos in Costa Rica, particularly in Guanacaste, for longer stays, or if you come with a family or a large group.

## Around Tilarán-Cañas-Bagaces

For the region north of Tilarán, around Lake Arenal, see "The North" chapter.

THE PROVINCE OF GUANACASTE

### Tilarán

**Cabinas El Sueño** *($; hw, pb, ⊗; next to the cathedral, ☎695-5347)* rents basic clean rooms with a large balcony from which you can see what's happening on the street. You can also rent a television.

**Hotel Naralit** *($; hw, pb, ctv, ⊗; on the south side of the cathedral, ☎695-5393, ⇌695-6767)* is by far the best deal in Tilarán in terms of quality/price ratio. The lobby is nothing special, but the place is well-kept, and the rooms are comfortably furnished – they even have desks. The hotel has been laid out with green spaces. You can ask for a refrigerator for your room.

**Hotel Tilarán** *($-$$; sb/pb, hw, P, ℜ; west side of the cathedral park, ☎695-5043)* is behind the restaurant of the same name. The rooms are small and lacking in charm, but clean.

**Cañas**

**Hotel Guillen** and **Hotel El Parque** *($; sb/pb, ⊗; south side of the central park, ☎669-0070 for Guillen and ☎669-2213 for El Parque)* are perfect for travellers on a low budget who aren't fussy about room size and amenities.

One of the best places to stay in the area is **Hacienda La Pacífica** *($$$$; hw, pb, ⊗, ≡, ≈, ℜ, bar, conference rooms, library; 5 km north of Cañas, on the Interamericana, ☎669-0050 or 669-0266, ⇌669-0555)*, named for the wife of the former Costa Rican president, Bernardo Soto. The hotel started off as a ranch and is accessible by horse or car; the *casona* turned museum is on the northwest corner of the property. Horseback rides, mountain bike excursions and hikes are organized along the property's trails, most notably along Río Corobicí. Hacienda La Pacífica is more than a hotel – it is an example of sustainable development, combining cattle-raising, cultural tourism, reforestation and forest conservation. Guests stay in charming little well-ventilated *cabinas* with big windows that let in a lot of light. Each has a patio that leads onto the rest of the vast premises (most *cabinas* have two units).

**Bagaces**

**Albergue Bagaces** *($$; pb, ⊗, ℜ, on the Interamericana, east side of the gas station, ☎671-1267)* is the best place to stay in town. The rooms are simple, but the bathrooms are impeccable. The owners are British. Breakfast is served in the restaurant (see p 262).

## Parque Nacional Palo Verde

The Organization for Tropical Studies, which protects the park's natural environment, has dormitories *(45 beds)* for researchers, students and anyone interested in staying here *(40$/person, meals incl.; sb; ☎240-3671, ⇌240-6783, pverde@ns.ots.ac.cr)*. This place is very popular, so reservations should be made one month in advance. It takes 45 minutes to get to the park from Bagaces on a relatively well-maintained dirt road. Camping is also permitted *($1.25/person/day, bathrooms, showers and running water)* next to the park warden's residence.

## North of Liberia

**Cabinas Santa Rita** *($; pb; opposite the Tribunales de Justicia, La Cruz, ☎697-9062)* are worth keeping in mind for their good price.

**Amalia's Inn** *($$$ bkfst incl.; hw, pb, ≈; main street, La Cruz, ☎697-9181)* is a family-style inn (more like a Bed & Breakfast) run by a friendly elderly lady. The rooms are tastefully decorated and large – they even have a sofa to relax on! There is a magnificent view of Baia Salinas from here.

**Colinas del Norte** *($$$; pb, hw, ≈, ℜ, bar; 6 km north of La Cruz, on the Interamericana, ☎/⇌679-9132 or 284-3972)* is an interesting hotel north of La Cruz. Its guest rooms and common areas are tastefully decorated with wood furnishings. There is a beautiful view of the surrounding area from the rooms. The hotel has a weekend nightclub and an Italian restaurant called Marco Polo (see p ?), which also serves Costa Rican dishes.

**Hacienda Guachipelin** *($$$ bkfst incl., sb/pb, hw, 5 km from the Parque Nacional Rincón de la Vieja "Las Pailas" entrance via the road to Curubande, ☎442-2818 or 284-2049, ⇄442-1910, hacienda@intnet.co.cr)* is on a 100-year-old ranch. Though the rooms in the lodge are simple, the whole pleasure of staying here is in the experience of farm life. The hacienda is involved in a reforestation project on 40% of its 1,300 hectares. Various excursions to Parque Rincón and the surrounding area – the Azufrales hot springs, the Las Pailas sands, the volcano, the Jilgueros lagoon, the falls, etc. – are organized.

The **Santa Clara Lodge** *($$$; discounts for Hostelling International card holders; sb/pb, cw; 4 km southeast of Quebrada Grande, 7 km east of Potrerillos on the Interamericana, ☎223-7141, ⇄666-0475)* is a pleasant, family-style dairy farm at the foot of Guanacaste's volcanos, near a small river. The property is fairly shaded and has a pool of effervescent mineral water fed by a waterfall whose petroglyphic rocks are one of the sites to see in the area. Guided hiking and horseback riding excursions can be organized. The rooms are rather rustic and the meals are copious.

It's home on the range at **Los Inocentes** *($$$$; hw, sb, ≈, ℜ, bar; 14 km off the Interamericana on the road that leads to Upala and Santa Cecilia, several km before La Cruz, ☎/⇄265-5484 or 679-9190)*, a horse and cattle ranch. The place is off the beaten tourist track and has a relaxed atmosphere with its wooden lodge, spacious common rooms, hammocks and rocking chairs. The owners have become increasingly dedicated to conservation and sustainable development since they began their cattle-raising enterprise. People come from all over to participate in Los Inocentes' hiking and horseback riding excursions, which are just some of the goodies in store for you here. The hacienda borders Guanacaste national park to the north. The rooms are simple and comfortable, and the service is attentive. There is also a good view of the Orosí volcano from here.

The completely wood-built **Rincón de la Vieja Lodge** *($$$$; sb/pb, ≈, ℜ, bordering Parque Nacional Rincón de la Vieja on the road to Curubande, ☎/⇄695-5553 or 666-0473, rincon@sol.racsa.co.cr)* is affiliated with Hostelling International and has 27 somewhat dilapidated rooms. Nevertheless, US diplomats and their families stay here for the outstanding service and friendly ambiance. Furthermore, it is the closest lodge to Parque Rincón, and its 600 hectares contain a scientific library, an insect and butterfly collection – and even a serpentarium! A calm and inspiring place. The staff organizes all sorts of guided excursions.

Newly opened on a 200-hectare property that includes tropical dry forest, **Posada El Encuentro** *($$$$$ bkfst incl.; hw, pb, ≡, ≈; off the road to Parque Nacional Rincón de la Vieja, near Curubande, ☎/⇄382-0815)* offers beautifully furnished rooms of the highest comfort and cleanliness. The family atmosphere makes the service personalized. The *posada* has a telescope to view the surroundings and plenty of indoor games, such as pool and ping-pong, to entertain its guests. Breakfast and other meals are served in the establishment's charming little dining room.

## Parque Nacional Santa Rosa

The **Parque Nacional Santa Rosa** has the best accommodation setup with 8 rooms for 64 people, including students, researchers and tourists (if there's room). Lodging here costs $14.50 per person, and a little less *($10)* if you stay at the Nancite beach biological station. A **campsite** *($1.25/person/day)* with running water, bathrooms, showers, picnic tables, garbage cans, etc. has been set up between the administrative offices and La Casona. There are two more campgrounds north and south of Playa Naranjo (bring your own food and drinking water), about a dozen kilometres from the administrative offices. There is a cafeteria *(bkfst. $3.50, lunch $5, supper $4.25)*, but if you camp near the administration and want to eat there, you have to give them three hours notice.

## Around Liberia

### Liberia and Surroundings

There is **camping** on the grounds of Liberia's youth hostel.

**Hospedaje Lodge la Casona** *($; pb, ⊗; 300 m south of the central park, ☎/⇌666-2971)* is hospitable, but like **Posada del Tope** *($; sb, P; 150 m south of the central park, ☎385-2383 or 666-3876)*, is more like a youth hostel in terms of comfort.

**Hotel Guanacaste** *($, discounts for Hostelling International card holders; pb, ⊗, ≡, parking , 25 m west and 100 m south of Pulmitan's bus station, ☎666-0085, ⇌666-2287, htlguana@sol.racsa.co.cr)* is a youth hostel with simply furnished rooms. Like most establishments of its type, Hotel Guanacaste is appealing for its warm reception and personalized service. There is a friendly neighbourhood restaurant inside. The hotel is often full. Laundry service.

**Hotel Liberia** *($; sb/pb; 75 m south of the plaza on Calle 1, ☎/⇌666-0161)* has clean rooms which are usually booked. The staff is friendly and the place is furnished like a youth hostel. The hotel can do your laundry and serves breakfast. Souvenir shop.

**Hotel Daysita** *($$; hw, pb, ⊗, ≡, ≈, P, ℜ, bar, conference rooms; south side of the stadium, ☎666-0197, ⇌666-0927)*, in the centre of Liberia, provides clean rooms and free airport pick-up. There is a nightclub on the premises.

The very tidy **Hotel Primavera** *($$; pb, ⊗, tv, ≡, P; south side of the central park, ☎666-0464, ⇌666-2271)* offers very good value for your money, and therefore is often full to capacity, even in low season. The hotel is located at the end of a courtyard.

One of the oldest hotels in the area, the **Hotel Bramadero** *($$$; hw, pb, ≡, ≈, ℜ, bar; on the Interamericana, near Liberia's main thoroughfare, ☎666-0371, ⇌666-0203)*, whose name has something to do with bullfighting, offers motel-style rooms with a non-descript decor. Try to get a room as far away as possible from the noisy restaurant-bar and Interamericana.

**La Siesta** *($$$; hw, pb, ≡, ℜ, bar; 5 streets into Liberia, 250 m right of Farmacia Lux, ☎666-0678, ⇌666-2532)*, in the middle of Liberia, is more of a motel: it's long shape encloses a small garden and a swimming pool. Overall, a clean and friendly place.

**Hotel El Sitio** *($$$$ bkfst incl.; hw, pb, ctv, ☎, ⊗, ≡, ≈, ⊘, ♿, conference* *rooms; off the road to Santa Cruz, near Liberia, ☎257-0744 or 666-1211, ⇌666-2059)* looks like Hotel Las Espuelas with its large property, but is lower in quality and price. There are a pool, *rancho*-style restaurant, children's games and a whirlpool onsite, and a travel agency and souvenir shop in the hotel itself. The common rooms open out onto a spacious outdoor patio with elegant floor tiles. We found the service could have been a bit more refined, and the same can be said for the rooms, despite their being air conditioned and recently renovated (the bedding was worn, for example).

Modern and classy, **Hotel Las Espuelas** *($$$$$; hw, ctv, ≡, ≈, conference rooms; 2 km south of Liberia on the Interamericana, ☎293-4544 or 239-2000, ⇌293-4839)* is one of the better hotels in town. The one-floor establishment is surrounded by wide-open green spaces in the countryside, away from the highway. The rooms are fairly attractive and clean, as is the restaurant. The place is very cowboy-style: *Espuelas* is Spanish for "spurs". This is Guanacaste, after all!

### Playa del Coco and Surroundings

#### Playa Panamá

Hotel Malinche Real, formerly known as the **Blue Bay** *($$$$$; hw, pb, ctv, ☎, ≈, ⊗, ≡, ℝ, ≈, ⊛, ℜ, bar, ⊘; near Giardini di Papagayo, at the end of the road, ☎/⇌670-0033 or 670-0300, hmreal@sol.racsa.co.cr)* is a huge luxury hotel complex on a vast stretch of land sloping toward the ocean. There is plenty to do here (water and land sports). Souvenir shop. Treat your body and mind to a relaxing massage – a service you'll find in most high-end hotels.

**Costa Smeralda** *($$$$$; hw, pb, ≡, ≈; Bahía Culebra, on the Golfo Papagayo, north of Panamá, ☎670-0231)* is a large resort with lots of activities for its guests; everything from scuba diving to Spanish and dance lessons. The hotel is located on an inlet.

**Sula Sula Beach Resort** *($$$$$; hw, pb, ctv, ☎, ≡, ≈, ℜ, ℝ, ♿; ☎672-0116 or 672-0117)* was one of the first hotel complexes built in Playa Panamá. Everything has been done to make the place wheelchair accessible, and the resort is located on flat ground. Each double-occupancy two-room unit is tastefully decorated in subdued tones, and comes with a refrigerator and shared patio.

#### Playa Hermosa

**Villa Boni Mar** *($$$; ⊗, ≈, K; ☎670-0397 or 487-7640)* rents villas that can accommodate up to eight people. Very similar to Villa Huetares next door, but smaller and not as well maintained. Not much has been done with the outside either.

**Villa del Sueño** *($$$; pb, hw, ⊗, ≈, ℜ; ☎/⇌672-0026, delsueno@sol.racsa.co.cr)* is a place to check out. Owned by eight friendly Quebeckers, this hotel offers first-class comfort and service for this price range. The guest rooms and common areas are at once sunny and subdued, and tastefully decorated with wood and ceramics. Sit back and relax, read a magazine, chat with other guests, or linger over a coffee or fresh fruit juice on the shaded terrace in front of the hotel. The restaurant, also located on the terrace, is a real gem (see p 263). The hotel is about 100 metres from Playa Hermosa, providing total peace and tranquillity. The pool is a popular afternoon meeting place where guests recap their daily adventures. The owners organize different excursions in the area, and will be glad to suggest other activities you can do in Guanacaste.

**Villa Huetares** *($$$$; pb, ≈, 150 m from the beach, off the public road to Playa Hermosa, ☎/≈460-6592)* rents neat little villas with kitchens and dining rooms. Airconditioning should be in place by year's end. There is a volleyball court on the property and the landscaping complements the surrounding countryside.

**El Velero** *($$$$-$$$$$; hw, pb, ⊗ or ≡, ≈, ℜ, bar; ☎/⇌670-0310, ☎670-0330)* is a small, stylish beach-side hotel and a nice change from the surrounding mega-resorts. The second-floor rooms are a little simpler than those on the ground floor. Souvenir shop, water sports equipment rental.

**Cacique del Mar** *($$$$$; hw, pb, ≡, ≈; ☎296-5398 or 670-0345)* is actually two resort villages: **Los Altos del Cacique** is a residential complex currently under construction on the point that separates Playa Hermosa and Playa del Coca, and **La Costa del Cacique** is a hotel and villas just north of Playa Hermosa. It is part of a huge hotel development project in the area. Definitely worth looking into.

**Condovac la Costa** *($$$$$; hw, pb, ctv, ℜ, bar, nightclub; north end of the beach, next to the Sol Playa Hermosa hotel, ☎221-2264 or 233-1562, ⇌222-5637)* is located on a coastal inlet. This resort-style hotel offers its guests a number of services and activities, the latter including fishing, surfboarding, water-skiing, jet-skiing, scuba diving and tennis. The villas are spread over the property; there is a shuttle service to the beach.

**Sol Playa Hermosa** *($$$$$; pb, hw, ≡, ctv, ≈, ℜ, bar, conference rooms, convenience store; ☎290-0565, ⇌290-0566, hermosol@sol.racsa.co.cr)* is a huge resort complex that is part of the Sol chain. Surprisingly, the rooms are simply furnished for such an upscale hotel. However, the magnificent view of the ocean from the balcony makes up for the lack of decor. The villas come fully equipped – some even have their own pool! A souvenir and sports equipment rental shop, tennis courts and ping-pong tables are just some of the facilities you'll find here.

### Playa del Coco

The grounds of **Cabinas Sol y Mar** *($$; pb, 150 m north of the club Astilleros, off the road to Playa del Coco, ☎670-0368 or 551-3706)* could be better maintained. The large *cabinas* have a bedroom, living room, small kitchen and veranda. Everything is very clean. We hope they'll add a pool and *rancho* sometime in the near future.

**Hotel Anexo Luna Tica** *($$; pb, ⊗; ☎670-0127, ⇌670-0459)* is a small Tico hotel. The rooms are gloomily furnished but clean.

**Apartamentos Casa Lora** *($$$; hw, pb, tv, ≈; ☎670-0021)* can accommodate up to seven people.

**Cabinas del Coco** *($$$; right on the beach facing the public pier, ☎670-0110 or 670-0276, ⇌670-0167)* was built in the 1950s. The rooms are minimally furnished but clean. This hotel is right in the middle of Playa del Coco, and is the closest one to the beach. However, its central location means more noise, especially from the nightclub next door. There is a restaurant (see p 263).

**Coco Palms** *($$$; pb, ⊗, ≈; on the west side of the football field, ☎/⇌670-0117)* has rather dull rooms.

**Hotel Pato Loco Inn** *($$$; pb, ℜ; 800 m from the beach, off the road to Playa del Coco, ☎/⇄670-0145)* has simply furnished rooms with a small back yard. Very clean, but the only facility on its small grounds is a restaurant (see p 264).

**Villas Playa Nacazcol** *($$$; hw, pb, tv, K, ≡, ℜ; on the road to Playa del Coco, 4 km from the beach, ☎670-0416)* have everything you could ask for at a good price, but could be better maintained. Tennis court. Convenience store on site.

The brand-new **Puerta del Sol** *($$$; hw, pb, ≈, ⊘; 150 m from the beach, one street east of Playa del Coco's main street, ☎/⇄670-0195)* will catch your eye with its pretty yellow exterior; it is also very clean. The rooms are modern and comfortable with sofas. However, because the plants are still quite young, the outdoor common areas could be better shaded. The restaurant, El Sol y la Luna, is appealing (see p 264).

A few metres from the beach, **Villa del Sol** *($$$ bkfst incl., hw, pb/sb, ≈, ⊛; 1 km east of Playa del Coco's main street, on a perpendicular road that passes by San Francisco Treats, ☎/⇄670-0085)* is more like a Bed & Breakfast, but its owners from Québec also rent out two fully equipped houses for stays of several days or longer.

**Flor de Itabo** *($$$$; hw, pb, ≈, ≡, ctv, 1 km from the beach, on the way into Playa del Coco, ☎670-0011 or 670-0292, ⇄670-0003)* is a pretty little hotel. Its rooms are very well decorated and very clean. It is a bit far from the beach – but from the noise of the town, as well. The restaurant serves Italian cuisine. Bungalows and apartments for rent.

**Villa Casa Blanca** *($$$$ bkfst incl.; hw, pb, ≡; on the way to El Ocotal, ☎/⇄670-0448, vcblanca@sol.racsa.co.cr)* is a pretty little Bed & Breakfast a few minutes away from the beach. Its natural surroundings and romantic decor make it an enchanting place. The common areas are calm and cozy. The breakfast served is a combination of Costa Rican and North American, something other hotels in the area don't do. The Western Canadian owners know how to treat their guests well.

**Villa Flores** *($$$$; hw, pb, ≈, ≡, ⊘; 200 m east of Playa del Coco's main street, on a perpendicular road that passes by San Francisco Treats, ☎670-0269)* is well maintained and decorated, with elegant and relaxing gardens surrounding it. Since it is almost opposite Puerto del Sol, it's a few minutes walk to the beach. Friendly owners.

**Coco Verde** *($$$$; hw, pb, ≡, ≈, ℜ, bar; 200 metres from the beach, on the Playa del Coco's main street, ☎/⇄670-0494)* is a modern ensemble of lodgings in a large building that is stylish on the outside. Once inside, however, the rooms are clean but lack the charm of other hotels in the area, such as Puerto del Sol. They are minimally equipped, and strung out in a row along a shared balcony.

### Playa Ocotal

**El Ocotal Beach Resort** *($$$$$; hw, pb, ctv, ℝ, ☎, ⊗, ≡, ≈, ⊛; ☎670-0321 or 670-0323, ⇄670-0083)* is a classy hotel perched on a hill overlooking Playa Ocotal – and what a view! The rooms come with a kitchen table, desk and coffee machine. If you are not staying at the hotel, you can still dine in its restaurant (see p 264) just to see the place. Tennis court.

## Around Filadelfia

### Playa Flamingo and Surroundings

#### Playa Pan de Azúcar

At **Hotel Sugar Beach** *($$$$$; hw, pb, ⊗, ≡, ≈, ℜ, bar; 15 km from the turnoff to Huscas, ☎654-4242, ⇌654-4239)* you can get away from it all. It is the only hotel on the beach, at the end of the road leading there. There is a beautiful view of the ocean from the restaurant on the hillside. Monkeys, iguanas, toucans and parrots can be spotted here. The decor is nothing out of the ordinary. The hotel rents all kinds equipment for water-sports and land excursions.

#### Playa Penca

**El Sitio Cielomar** *($$$$ bkfst incl.; hw, pb, ⊗, ≡; ☎666-1211 or 654-4194, ⇌666-2059)* has the same owners as El Sitio de Liberia. It has no pool, which is surprising for a chain hotel. We also found the service a bit less refined than at El Sitio de Liberia. The rooms are standard in terms of decor and comfort. The lawn in front of the hotel sprawls out to the ocean. Water sports equipment rental.

#### Playa Potrero

**Bahía Potrero Beach Resort** *($$$$$ bkfst incl.; hw, pb, ⊗, ≡; ☎654-4183, ⇌654-4093)* is a small, comfortable hotel. The rooms are large enough to fit the table set in the corner. The front lawn sprawls out to the ocean. A very good place for rest and relaxation, the elements of a perfect vacation.

#### Playa Flamingo

It's not hard to find your way around the **Mariner Inn** *($$$$; hw, pb, ctv, ≡, ≈; ☎654-4081, ⇌654-4024)*, next to the marina. Everything, including the rooms, is found in the one building of this small hotel complex (the swimming pool is on the second floor, for example). The place is laid back, as you can tell by its restaurant (see p 265) and guests. Good view of the marina. The beach is 300 metres away.

**Fantasias Flamingo** *($$$$$; hw, pb, ≡, ≈, ℜ; ☎654-4350 or 222-9847, ⇌257-5002, flamingo@sol.racsa.co.cr)* is a brand-new Canadian-owned hotel, and is very North American indeed. The architecture's shape and colour is a bit cold, however. Some rooms access the pool directly, and all have a beautiful view of the ocean. A casino is in the works.

**Aurola Playa Flamingo** *($$$$$$; hw, pb, ctv, ⊗, ≡, ☎, ≈, ⊘, video, bar, casino; ☎233-9233 or 654-4010, ⇌654-4060)* is a huge luxury hotel complex. The very comfortable rooms and suites all have balconies. All the buildings face the ocean. A classic in the area along with the Flamingo Marina Resorts. Game room for kids.

**Flamingo Marina Resorts** *($$$$$$ bkfst incl.; hw, pb, ⊗, ≡, ℝ, ≈, ℜ, ⊛, ctv, bar; ☎290-1858 or 654-4141, ⇌231-1858 or 654-4035)* practically take up all of Flamingo Bay! There are actually three hotels in one: the Flamingo Marina Hotel, with rooms facing the marina; the Flamingo All-Suites, which has suites with kitchenettes (some even have jacuzzis!); and finally, Club Playa Flamingo, which has fully-equipped apartments. There are a tennis court and souvenir shop on the premises. All sorts of activities are offered at this huge complex.

The residents of the **Presidential Suites** *($$$$$$; hw, pb, ctv, ☎, ≈; ☎654-4485, ⇌654-4486)* rent their condos when they're away. Therefore, what you get is a fully equipped apartment that can have a somewhat lived-in feel. The magnificent view of the beach, only 10 minutes away, makes up for this, though. The place is enormous, but lacks the charm of smaller complexes. Maid service. The longer you stay, the more you save.

### Playa Brasilito

**Cabinas El Caracol** and **Cabinas Nany** *($$ bkfst incl.; pb, ⊗; 200 m south of and 75 m east of the village football field, ☎654-4320)* are clean, but basic and a bit overpriced. Friendly owners.

**Ojos Azulejos** *($$ bkfst incl.; hw, pb, ⊗; on Playa Brasilito's main street, ☎654-4346)* has friendly Swiss owners. The landscaping isn't finished because the place just opened. The rooms are simply furnished, clean and big enough for a family. There is no pool.

**Hotel Brasilito** *($$$; pb, ⊗, ℜ, bar; ☎654-4237, ⇄654-4247)* is somewhat outdated, but right near the ocean in the centre of Brasilito. It can get noisy because of its location. Basic, clean rooms.

### Playa Conchal

**Melia Playa Conchal** *($$$$$$; hw, pb, ⊗, ≡, ≈, ℜ, ctv, bar, conference room; ☎654-4123, ⇄654-4181)* is a beach and golf resort on Playa Conchal, south of Brasilito. Each suite comes with a balcony, bedroom and big living room. Kids under 12 can stay for free in their parent's room. Tennis courts, health and aqua club, casino, nightclub, and of course – golf! Impeccable service. The place has an original setup – just go to the rental office overlooking the hotel to see for yourself.

## Playa Tamarindo and Surroundings

### Playa Grande

**Centro Vacacional Playa Grande** *($$$; pb, ⊗, K, ℜ; 1.5 km from Playa Grande, at the entrance to Parque Nacional Marino Las Baulas, ☎237-2552 or 260-3991, ☎/⇄653-0467)* is almost like a vacation campground with its bungalows with bunk-beds and kitchenettes.

**El Bucanero** *($$$ bkfst incl.; hw, pb, ℜ; ☎653-0480)* is a small hotel with large, basic, clean rooms. A pool is in the works. There is a good view of the beach from its ground-floor restaurant.

If you haven't guessed by its name, you will by its laid-back atmosphere: **Rancho Diablo Surf Camp** *($$$; hw, pb, ⊗; on the beach road, ☎/⇄653-0490)* caters to a surfer clientele. Lodging is in huts on stilts; these are basic, large, clean and comfortable. The neighbouring restaurant, Grande Bob's, is a surfer hangout (see p 265).

The Brand-new **Cantarana** *($$$$ bkfst incl., ½b also available; hw, pb, ⊗, ≡, ≈; ☎653-0486, ⇄653-0491)* rents clean rooms with a table, chairs and a comfortable bed. The outside is very simply but tastefully set up. The beach is five minutes away, at the end of the property.

**Villa Baula** *($$$$; hw, pb, ⊗, ≈; ☎653-0493, ⇄653-0459)* is very peacefully isolated, as it is the last hotel on the beach strip before the river that separates Playa Grande from Playa Tamarindo. The rooms are large with wood furnishings. Bungalows on stilts with kitchens and large balconies can also be rented. A charming place! Everything is set up in close contact with nature: the hotel is right next to the beach – ideal for turtle-watching.

**Casa del Mar** *($$$$$ bkfst incl.; hw, pb; two blocks from Las Tortugas hotel, ☎653-0479)*, is a Bed & Breakfast in a luxurious Mediterranean-style house, directly on the beach. Rates are much lower in the off-season. You can even rent the whole house.

Chalet-style **Casa Linda Vista** *($$$$$; hw, pb, tv, ⊗; ☎653-0474)* is on a hill and has a beautiful view of its surroundings. It comes with a kitchenette and sleeps six. Peace and tranquillity assured, as this place is 500 metres from the beach. Very good value for your money.

Located on Playa Grande, **Hotel las Tortugas** *($$$$; hw, pb, ≡, ≈, ⊛, bar; ☎/⇌653-0458, mela@cool.co.cr)* was carefully set up to prevent light from reaching the beach and disrupting the egg-laying process of the many turtles who frequent it. The rooms have stone floors that have a cooling effect if you don't want to use airconditioning. The owners have done everything they can to protect the turtles and natural surroundings after their request to turn the area into a national park was turned down. Pretty view from the hotel restaurant.

### Playa Tamarindo

In addition to the hotels mentioned below, you can pitch your tent right beside the beach at **Tito's Camping**, opposite Cabinas 14 de Febrero, next to **Paniugua Camping**.

**Cabinas Coral Reef** *($; hw, pb; ☎653-0291)* are simple but clean and ideal for surfers. The beach is not far away.

**Cabinas Dolly** *($$; sb)* seems like a youth hostel with its young clientele and basic rooms. The bathrooms are clean, however. Directly on the beach. The grounds are small and simple, but the beach is like a front yard.

**Cabinas Marielos** *($$; pb, ⊗, K; ☎653-0141)* are small, basic, clean, and fairly bright. The owners are friendly and the gardens are lovely. Guests can use the kitchen.

**Cabinas Zully Mar** *($$; hw, pb, ⊗, ≡; near the loop of the first road along the beach, ☎653-0140)* are ideal for travellers on tight budgets. There are two kinds of rooms, built at different times: the oldest are smaller, whereas the newer ones have a better layout, but both are clean. Located in the middle of the village, right near the beach.

**Tamarindo Bay Resort Club** *($$; hw, pb; south end of the village, ☎653-0383, ⇌255-3785)* has cheap rates, and you'll understand why. The place is outdated, and the rooms have few windows and bare furnishings (some pieces are even broken!). Some rooms come with kitchenettes and/or *casitas* with a living room.

**Cabinas 14 de Febrero** *($$$; hw, pb)* are clean and charming. The place forms a square around a simply laid-out tropical garden. Since it was recently built, the rooms were made mostly out of plaster and wood. There is a laundry space behind the main building. You can have breakfast on the outdoor terrace.

**Cabinas Arco Iris** *($$$; pb, hw)* are small, colourful cottages next to the vegetarian restaurant of the same name (see p 265).

The friendly owners of **Cabinas Pozo Azul** *($$$; pb, ≡, K, ℜ, ≈; just after entering the village, ☎653-0280)* rent standard comfort rooms equipped with a small stove and refrigerator.

The rooms at **Pueblo Dorado** *($$$; hw, pb, ≈; ☎653-0008, ⇄653-0013)* are simply and modernly furnished with a table and chairs.

**Condominiums Nahua** *($$$$; pb, hw, K; ☎653-0776)* are almost opposite the Hotel Pasatiempo and are of good value.

**Hotel El Milagro** *($$$$ bkfst incl.; hw, pb, ⊗, ≡, ≈, wading ≈, ℜ, bar; on your left once in the village, ☎653-0042, ⇄653-0050, flokiro@sol.racsa.co.cr)* has two types of rooms: the first has fans and cold water only, while the other has airconditioning and hot water. The hotel's natural surroundings are well kept, and the *cabinas* have an original layout: the shaded terraces with big patio doors almost seem like an extra room. The *cabinas* face each other, with lots of vegetation between them. The beach is across the street. The restaurant has a good reputation (see p 266).

Located in Tamarindo, not far from the beach, **Hotel Pasatiempo** *($$$$; pb, hw, ≈; ☎653-0096, ⇄653-0275)* is shaded by lush vegetation. The small bungalows have two rooms with terraces. There is a pool in the middle of the grounds.

**Tropicana del Pacífico** *($$$$; hw, pb, ⊗ or ≡, ≈; ☎/⇄653-0261)* is set back from the road across from the beach, and is built around its swimming pool. The rooms are large, clean and decently furnished. Italian owners.

**Casa Banyan** *($$$$$ bkfst incl.; hw, pb, ≈; ☎653-0072)* is a Bed & Breakfast in a huge modern house right on the beach.

**Hotel Capitán Suizo** *($$$$$ bkfst incl.; hw, pb, ⊗, ≡, ℝ, ☎, ≈, radio, bar; south end of the village, ☎653-0353 or 653-0075, ⇄653-0292)* is a small luxury hotel that belongs to the same chain that owns Grano de Oro in San José and four other hotels in the country, so you can expect the utmost in comfort. The place is built on different levels, creating a lovely architectural effect. The rooms are in duplexes; those on the ground floor have a terrace and are airconditioned, while those on the second floor have a balcony and are cooled by breezes. The rooms are also spacious and furnished with a sofa bed, pretty chairs, a writing desk and a small refrigerator. The hotel has wonderful gardens, a swimming pool, and even a *rancho*. There are also bungalows for rent and obviously lots of organized activities and excursions.

**Residence Luna Llena** *($$$$$; hw, pb, K, ≈; 200 m east of Iguana Surf, ☎653-0082, ⇄653-0120, lunallena@yellowweb.co.cr)* is an intimate place with only seven rooms. It has a pretty interior decor (wood and ceramics) and a unique spiral staircase that leads to the rooms upstairs. It is just as lovely from the outside, and the beach is only 200 metres away.

The **Sueno del Mar** *($$$$$ bkfst incl.; hw, pb, ⊗, ≡, ℜ, bar; ☎/⇄653-0284)* reigns at the south end of the second beach road, where it forms a loop in the village of Tamarindo. The small rooms have an eclectic but tasteful decor. *Casita* rentals available.

**Tamarindo Vista Villas Hotel** *($$$$$; hw, pb, ≡; ☎653-0114, ⇄653-0115)* rents modern apartments with a kitchen, dining and living room, and a patio or balcony with a good view of the ocean.

**Tamarindo Diriá** *($$$$$$ bkfst incl.; hw, ctv, ⊗, ≡, ≈, ☎, radio alarm clock; ☎290-4340, ⇄290-4367, ☎/⇄653-0031 in Tamarindo, tnodiria@sol.racsa.co.cr)* looks pleasant but shows its age – it was one of the first hotels built in the area, over a decade ago. The rooms are charming in an outdated way, but rather confining, and all share a balcony. The hotel is tucked far away in the tropical vegetation, and the gardens make the place, and especially the restaurant, look even better. It's worth coming here just to see the natural surroundings. Souvenir shop and tennis court. There is a little shopping complex next to the hotel, as well as the beach.

**Casa Cook** *($$$$$$; hw, pb, ⊗, ≈, K; ☎/⇌653-0125)* is a private property with two lovely fully equipped *cabinas* (with living rooms) and a suite on the second floor of the main house. The suite comes with a large patio and two bedrooms and two bathrooms. You will find peace of mind and all the comforts at this modern and luxurious property by the ocean.

The Mediterranean style of **El Jardin del Edén** *($$$$$$ bkfst incl.; hw, pb, ≡, ≈, ⊛, bar; 200 m from the beach, ☎/⇌654-4111, ☎653-0137)* is expressed in its white stucco walls, russet-tiled roof and light flagstone floors. Rooms with a view from the large balconies. A very intimate place. Shortcut to the beach. Excellent service.

## Around Santa Cruz

### Santa Cruz and Surroundings

Motel-style **El Diriá** *($$$; pb, hw, tv, ☎, ≡, ≈; Santa Cruz, ☎650-0442)* is nestled in lush tropical vegetation. Bungalows are clean, share a big shaded terrace, and surround the garden. Friendly staff.

### Playa Junquillal and Surroundings

#### Playa Avellanas

**Cabinas Las Olas** *($$$; hw, pb, ⊗, ℜ; ☎233-4455, ⇌222-8685)* has 10 comfortably furnished rooms. It is surrounded by nature, including a mangrove swamp which you can visit via a raised path. The owners go to great lengths to protect the flora and fauna. There is also a beautiful surfer's beach on Playa Avellanas.

#### Playa Junquillal

**Camping Los Malinches** *($; ☎653-0429)* has extremely friendly owners, lots of trees, and faces the ocean.

**Hotel Junquillal** *($$; hw, ℜ; next to the public beach on Playa Junquillal, ☎653-0432)* is turning 30 soon! The small wooden *cabinas* are simply furnished. There are hammocks hung up everywhere. Very popular with travellers on a tight budget. You can camp on the grounds, as well.

**El Castillo Divertido** *($$$; pb, hw, no phone number)*, across the street from the beach, looks like a chateau with its rotundas and castellated border along the roof. The rooms of this German-owned establishment are not very large, but those on the ground floor have a balcony.

Perched atop a hill, **Guacamaya Lodge** *($$$; pb, hw, ≈, ℜ; ☎/⇌653-0431, alibern@sol.raacsa.co.cr)* is very clean and pretty. Each bungalow has two large rooms and a front terrace surrounded by somewhat sparse vegetation. There is also a large, fully-equipped *casita ($$$$$)* with a marvellous view from its balcony. The owners' parrot is amusing!

The small, family-style **Hibiscus** *($$$; pb,; right near the public entrance to Playa Junquillal, ☎680-0737)* is charming with its simply decorated but inviting *cabinas* in the middle of a garden; however, they are a little too close to each other.

**Villa Serena** *($$$$ fb; hw, pb, ⊗, ≈; ☎653-0430)* rents two-person *cabinas* spread over its large property. Their decor is slightly outdated, and their furnishings rather minimal, but they are clean nonetheless. Directly on the beach. Tennis court.

Even though Playa Junquillal has only been recently developed for tourism, **Hotel Anumalal** *($$$$$ bkfst incl.; hw, pb, ⊗, ℜ, ≈; at the end of the beach-side road, ☎/≠650-0506)* has been around the longest, about 20 years. The bungalows are well spaced out and have two rooms that share a terrace. The rooms are very bright, simply but tastefully decorated, and have comfortable beds. Directly on the beach. There is a nightclub on weekends.

The Canadian-owned **Iguana Azul** *($$$$$; hw, pb; one kilometre north of Playa Junquillal, ☎/≠653-0121, iguanazul@ticonet.co.cr)* would be greatly improved by making its grounds more lush, especially around the bungalows of the terrace. The rooms, however, are prettily decorated with pastel colours and ornaments. The hotel's real draw is its two beaches: one is rocky, and the other is sandy. All kinds of sports equipment rentals and outdoor excursions are offered. The outdoor restaurant brings you even closer to the beach.

### Playa Negra

The **Finca Los Pargos de Playa Negra** *($$$; ☎383-6343)* is made up of a series of two-room *cabinas* on stilts with palm-thatched roofs, in the middle of an open grasslands area. There are even some goats that live on the grounds! This natural and "grungy" establishment is found at the end of the road that leads to Playa Negra. There is an Italian restaurant on the premises.

During our stay, the owner of the restaurant-bar **Pablo Picasso** *(Easy Street)* was just putting the finishing touches on some new, clean, air-conditioned *cabinas ($$$$)* that are ideal for surfers. You can also stay in the dormitory-style loft *($)* which is a lot less expensive and is *the* place to meet hard-core surfers. The owner is himself a surfing enthusiast, and his establishment has a very relaxed atmosphere that is definitely welcoming after an exhausting day riding the waves.

Located on Playa Negra, the **Hotel Playa Negra** *($$$$ bkfst incl.; hw, pb, ≈; ☎382-1301, ≠382-1302, playanegra@paradise.co.cr)* is somewhat secluded, but it is a very pleasant hideaway! The round *cabinas* with palm-thatched roofs are pretty, bright and airy, with comfortable furnishings consisting of a table, chairs, sofa and a bed. If you come here during the rainy season, ask about the condition of the road leading to the hotel, since you often need a four-wheel drive vehicle to reach it. The restaurant (see p 266) serves French cuisine, and other food.

## Around Nicoya

### Nicoya and Surroundings

**Jenny** *($$; pb, tv, ≡, P; 100 m south of the southwest corner of the square,*

☎685-5050) is a small, simple urban hotel right in the centre of town.

The new **Cabinas Nicoya** *($$$; hw, pb, ≈; 500 m east of the Banco Nacional, ☎686-6331)* are also located right in downtown Nicoya. The owner is friendly and very attentive to his clients' needs. The small rooms have a certain charm, thanks to such details as the pretty bedspreads. The grounds could be better-kept, especially since they are not that large.

The **Complejo Turístico Curime** *($$$; hw, pb, ≈, ≡, ℜ; south of Nicoya, on the road to Playa Sémara, ☎685-5238, ⇌685-5530)* rents out small apartments, so you can do your own cooking here. The seventies furniture is a little outdated and drab. However, the building's rather old exterior blends in well with its location on an isolated road. The hotel has pool tables and tennis courts.

**Playa Sámara and its Surroundings**

**Camping El Coco** *($3 per person with lights, electricity and sb)* is a small "urban" campground in the middle of Sámara, right by the beach. The sites are on sand and very shady, which is a blessing given how hot it can get here. The grounds are clean, if somewhat crowded, since lots of people come here in the summer. The owners are very friendly.

The **Hospedaje y Abastecedorn Yuri** *($; northern section of the beach, ☎680-0022)* has amazingly clean and tidy rooms. The furnishings are minimal, but the beds are comfortable. Though the building's exterior is not exactly pretty, the quality/price ratio of the rooms is very good, and the owners are friendly.

The A-frame *cabinas* at the **Belvedere** *($$ bkfst incl.; hw, pb, ⊛; across from Hotel Marbella, ☎656-0213)* have a certain charm, even though the rooms are small. They have large and attractive private balconies.

The exterior and common areas of the **Hotel Marbella** *($$ bkfst incl.; pb, ≈, ℜ, ☎/⇌656-0122)* are enhanced by the tropical vegetation that surrounds it, but the rooms are small and uncomfortable.

In the middle of Sámara and just 75 metres from the beach is the **Casa del Mar** *($$$ bkfst incl.; hw, pb/sb, ⊛, ℜ, bar; on the main street, ☎656-0264, ⇌656-1029)*. Owned by Quebecers, this place has clean, bright rooms situated around a small, landscaped courtyard in the centre of which is a whirlpool. The white walls and floor (painted or tiled) make the rooms seem more spacious, but the sparse furnishings have a jarring effect. Very friendly staff.

The **Giada** *($$$ bkfst incl.; ☎656-1032, ⇌656-0131)* is an attractive hotel. Although the rooms are small, they each have a small desk and a balcony or patio. Most open onto a charming inner courtyard that is beautifully landscaped with tropical vegetation. Try to get one of these rooms, rather than one facing the street. The beach is only 150 metres away.

Like the Mágica Cantarana (see below), the **Hotel Latino** *($$$ bkfst incl.; pb, hw, ⊗, ℜ, bar; northern section of the Playa Cangrejal, ☎/⇌656-0043)* has comfortable rooms in a long, two-storey building. The grounds could be in better condition. The balconies are quite large and private. The beach is only 200 metres away.

The **Mágica Cantarana** *($$$ bkfst incl.; pb, hw, ⊗, ≈, bar; Playa Buena Vista,* several km north of Playa Sámara, ☎656-0071, ⇄656-0260) hotel is situated near the road from Sámara to Playa Buena Vista. It has clean and comfortable rooms in a two-storey building that faces the swimming pool. A balcony runs along the rooms in the front, but the one at the back has a view of the green pastures surrounding the hotel. You can also rent a fully equipped apartment and take diving courses here.

**Las Brisas del Pacifico** *($$$$; hw, pb, bidet, ⊗ or ≡, ≈; southern section of the beach, ☎656-0250, ⇄656-0067)* is an attractive hotel complex amidst tropical greenery. The rooms are very clean and situated on beach level or on the hill. The latter have a magnificent view of the surroundings. Each room has a private terrace. Direct access to the beach.

The recently built **Hotel Isla Chora** *($$$$ bkfst incl.; hw, pb, ≡, ⊗, ≈, ℜ, bar, laundry service; ☎656-0174, ⇄656-0173, hechombo@sol.racsa.co.cr)* is one of Sámara's premier little hotel complexes. Its delicious Italian restaurant (see p 267) even has an ice cream parlour that serves wonderful gelato! The buildings' attractive modern design and the scenic landscaping add to the tasteful colours, furniture and general comfort of the rooms. The service is also first class: in high season, international newspapers are available to guests, and useful information about the local attractions is always on hand. The hotel offers all sorts of excursions. There is also a nightclub

The area surrounding the buildings of the **Hotel Sámara Beach** *($$$$ with ⊗, $$$$$ with ≡; hw, pb, bidet, ≈, ℜ, bar; on the road to the beach's public entrance, ☎656-0218, ⇄656-0326)* is covered with dense vegetation. The rooms are pleasantly subdued, with French windows that open out onto individual terraces.

Thanks to the design of its buildings and its hilltop location, the **Mirador de Sámara** *($$$$$; hw, pb, K; ☎650-0044, ⇄656-0046)* hotel has a magnificent view of Sámara's surroundings. The panorama can be enjoyed from hotel's attractive apartments, its little private bar where you can have a glass of wine in the evenings, or from the restaurant over breakfast. The hotel has a beautiful garden, and is only a short distance from the beach.

The **Hotel Villas Playa Sámara** *($$$$$; hw, pb, ≈, ⊛, ℜ, bar; ☎256-8228 or 656-0101, ⇄221-7222 or 656-0102, htlvilla@sol.racsa.co.cr)* is a huge hotel and residential complex on the edge of Sámara, on the beach. The units consist of one-, two- or three-bedroom villas with sunny rooms and red-tiled floors. The buildings blend harmoniously with the surrounding landscape, and a small, pretty pathway winds through the grounds. There are tennis, volleyball and badminton courts on the premises, as well as a wading pool.



### Playa Carillo

**El Sueño Tropical** *($$$; hw, pb, ≈, ℜ, bar; just south of Playa Carillo, ☎656-0151, ⇄656-0152)* is set back from the bustle of the Sámara and Carillo beaches. The rooms are fitted out with tasteful, tropical furniture and open onto a patio and the gardens of the vast property.

**Guanamar** *($$$$$$; hw, pb, ctv, ≡, ☎, ≈, ℜ; ☎656-0054, ⇄656-0001)* hotel is a well-laid-out and shady hotel complex on a hillside overlooking Carillo beach. The large, airy, charming rooms have their own bathrooms and private terraces, with French windows that seem to bring the outdoors inside.

### Playa Nosara and its Surroundings

#### Playa Nosara and Playa Pelada

**Almost Paradise** *($$$ bkfst incl.; hw, pb; Playa Pelada de Nosara, ☎682-0172, ⇌682-0173)* is a "Swiss Family Robinson"-style establishment on a hillside. A little restaurant with a pretty view is also on the premises. The charming *cabinas* are made of wood, and each have their own terrace with a hammock. Very friendly owners at this laid-back hotel.

The **Estancia Nosara** *($$$ with ⊗, $$$$ with ≡; hw, pb, K, ≈, tennis court, ℜ, bar; 5 minutes from the beach, 4 km south of Nosara, ☎/⇌680-0378)* feels like a secluded place as it is situated in the middle of a tropical 10-hectare property. Its rooms, restaurants, and gardens are all impeccable and tranquil. Swiss owners.

**La Casa Las Huacas** *($$$$ bkfst incl.; hw, pb, ≈; 3.5 km from the Playa Nosara, ☎680-0556)* is a secluded Bed & Breakfast in the forest, just a few kilometres from the Nosara beach. Located on a hill, it commands an impressive view of the coast. It is comprised of several small, modern, whitewashed houses and *cabinas*.

Right beside the Playa Pelada, the **Hotel Rancho Suizo** *($$$$ bkfst incl.; hw, pb, ⊛, ℜ, bar; Nosara's Playa Pelada, ☎/⇌284-9669, aratur@sol.racsa.co.cr)* is in a relaxed setting surrounded by luxurious vegetation. The rooms are very clean and comfortable. Most people come here for birdwatching. Grilled dishes are featured on the menu of the hotel's Pirata's Bar (see p 268), which also has a dance floor at night.

The **Lagarta Lodge** *($$$$ bkfst incl.; hw, pb, ⊗, ≈, ℜ; Playa Nosara, ☎680-0763)* is located near Nosara's private ecological reserve, and belongs to the same Swiss owners. Perched on a hilltop, it affords magnificent views of the surrounding region. The rooms are comfortable, very clean, and have a certain charm. People come here to visit the reserve, which harbours Ostional turtles, or simply to feast their eyes on the natural surroundings. The hotel is also not far from the beach. Because of its loction, the establishment offers its guests some interesting excursions (watching the turtles on the beach, a trip up the Río Nosara, etc.).

#### Playa Guiones

The friendly Italian- and French-speaking owner of the **Giardino Tropicale** *($; ⇌680-0749)* rents out two rooms to surfers for a small sum.

The **Café de Paris** *($$-$$$; hw, pb, K, ⊗, ≈, ℜ; 500 m from Playa Guiones)* hotel has Swiss-French owners and five bungalows for rent, each consisting of a large room with a kitchenette including a refrigerator and a smaller room that can be rented separately. Numerous excursions into the surrounding countryside are possible, and you can rent sports equipment from the hotel. The place has some pretty gardens. Don't miss trying the restaurant's and pastry shop's delicious French treats, even if you don't stay here!

The **Hotel Villa Taype** *($$$ bkfst incl.; hw, pb, ≡, ≈, ℜ, bar; between Punta Pelada and Playa Guiones, ☎382-7715)* is one of the largest establishments in the area. The place is made up of a motel-style row of little houses, each containing two simple, clean rooms. There are lovely tropical gardens and large common areas, some of which are covered to shelter guests from the sun as well as the rain. There are tennis courts and ping-pong tables, and the beach is only a short distance away.

**Olas Grandes Gringo Grill & Surf Shack** *($$$; sb, ℜ, bar; no ☎)* is perfect for people who love to surf and party! Each little cabin has two large rooms with ordinary furnishings. The staff is quite "alternative."

Next to the Hotel Villa Taype, the **Casa Toucán** *($$$$; pb, ℜ; ☎680-0749)* has four large, somewhat run-down, rooms. You can cook your meals here.

Along with the Hotel Villa Taype (see above), **El Villaggio** *($$$$$ bkfst incl.; hw, pb, bidet, ≈, near Punta Garza, ☎680-0784 or 233-2476, ⇌222-4073)* is the largest hotel of its kind in this area, which is better known for its smaller establishments. The rooms are in large, airy huts, and have private terraces. The large French doors let in a lot of light and open onto the magnificent scenery outside. Because the hotel is situated on a little bay, guests have almost exclusive access to the beach. There is a souvenir shop.

Standing on Punta Pelada's headland, the **Hotel Playa de Nosara** *($$$$$; hw, pb, ⊗, ≈; on Punta Pelada, ☎680-0495)* is easy to spot because of its whitewashed, somewhat kitschy, turret in which the reception and restaurant are found. The rooms are well-ventilated and pleasantly shaded, but the price is a bit too high for their decor and level of comfort. Because the hotel is slightly elevated, it has a great view of the surrounding scenery. Direct access to Guiones beach.

## RESTAURANTS

### Around Tilarán-Cañas-Bagaces

#### Tilarán

A series of small, inexpensive eateries can be found in the street northwest of the cathedral. The *soda* **Stefani** cooks up country-style food, **Nuevo Fortuna** *(11am to midnight)* serves Chinese food, and **Mac Pato** sells hamburgers, fries and other McDonald's-type fare in a friendly setting.

The **Restaurant Tilarán** *($$; ☎695-5043)* serves seafood and Costa Rican meals. The linen table cloths lend this dining room a touch of elegance. Clean and well kept.

**La Carreta** *($$-$$$; every day from 7am to 9pm; on the road behind the church, ☎695-6654, ⇌695-6593)* prepares excellent Italian and other dishes such as hamburgers. This family-owned establishment is the best place to eat in Tilarán – just look at the enthusiastic comments in its guest book! Meals are served indoors or on the veranda. Furthermore, the friendly owners will be more than pleased to recommend local attractions.

#### Cañas

Although Cañas is not reputed for its restaurants, a stroll through its centre lets you choose from fried chicken at **Pollo Frito Mimi** *(north-east corner of the central park)*, Chinese food at **Tai Va Alicia Lo Ho** *(north side of park)* or at **El Primero** *(west side of the park, ☎669-0219)*, or a light snack at the town's **Mönpik**, close to the central park.

On the Interamericana, the restaurant of **Hotel El Corral** *($-$$; ☎669-0367)* serves hearty country-style meals.

Stop at the **Restaurant Rincón Corobicí** *($$; 8am to 10pm; on the Interamericana, 4 km north of Cañas, ☎669-1234)* near Cañas for its international and Costa Rican cuisine (fish, steak, sandwiches, etc.). The restaurant's unique vantage point over the Río Corobicí will delight your senses as you take a seat in this enjoyable setting. A great place to stop if you're on your way to Liberia, and best appreciated in daylight.

Surrounded by small ponds on all sides, **Miravalles** *($$-$$$; 6am to 10pm; 5 km north of Cañas, on the Interamericana, ☎669-0050 or 669-0266, ⇌669-0555)* of the Hacienda La Pacífica (see p 246) prepares international and Costa Rican dishes. It also provides a much appreciated shady refuge from Guanacaste's intense heat.

### Bagaces

The restaurant at the **Albergue Bagaces** *($-$$; on the Interamericana, east of the gas station, ☎671-1267)* serves tasty seafood dishes in a large airy dining room. Breakfast is also served.

## North of Liberia

**Dariri** *($; every day 7am to 10pm; on the main street, near the Cabinas Santa Rita, La Cruz)* is a clean and friendly restaurant that prepares Costa Rican meals and tasty seafood platters, including delicious garlic shrimps.

In La Cruz, **La Cafetería** *($-$$; 50 m east of the central park, La Cruz, ☎679-9276)* is a good spot for *bocadillos*, hamburgers, *emparedados* and, of course, excellent coffee. The English-speaking owner, Ricardo Bolaños, is also an excellent tour guide, and his restaurant doubles as a tourist information centre.

The restaurant of the Colinas del Norte Hotel (see p 246), **Marco Polo** *($$; 6 km north of La Cruz, on the Inter-American, ☎/⇌679-9132)* has an inexpensive Costa Rican and Italian menu. Thursdays, pizza is less than three dollars. The restaurant occupies the second floor of the hotel, so you have a lovely view of the scenery. Local bands perform at the hotel on weekends.

With a name that means "god of winds" in the language of the Chorotegas, **Ehecatl** is perched high above the lowlands surrounding Salinas bay, and thus provides a panoramic view of the bay and ocean *($$-$$$; 10am to 10pm; 150 m east of the central park, La Cruz, ☎679-9104)*. Best enjoyed at sunset. The restaurant itself unfortunately does not live up to its spectacular view: the ordinary service and standard Latin American food are not exactly what you call "fine dining." The second floor is a little more stylish, however, and serves a selection of seafood dishes.

## Around Liberia

### Liberia and Surroundings

The **Jardín de Azúcar** *($; one street north of the main square, Calle Central, Av. 3)* has an eclectic, affordable menu.

Sit down and enjoy delicious cakes and scrumptious enchiladas at the **Pan y Miel** *($; Calle 2, Av. 3)* bakery and pastry shop.

**Rancho El Dulce** *($; Av. Central, Calle Central)* is a small fast-food establishment that also sells an array of candies and chocolates. Try to control you sweet tooth!

**Las Tinajas** *($; on the north side of the central park)* is a busy "soda-restaurant" that serves popular food (hamburgers, fries, etc.).

Despite its modest exterior, the **Pókopí** *($-$$; every day 11am to 10pm; just outside Liberia, on the road to Santa Cruz, facing the El Sitio Hotel, ☎666-1036 or 666-0769)* has an elegant dining room and, unlike other restaurants outside of town, features a variety of tasty dishes (fish, steak, pizza, chicken, etc.). For a quiet meal, be sure to eat before 9pm as the dance club next door can get noisy!

The **Los Aperos** *($$; on the Interamericana, at the corner of the road to Santa Cruz, ☎666-0873, ⇛666-1972)* restaurant and bar serves Costa Rican and North American dishes at good prices. The bar fills up with locals in the evening.

Red meat from the Guanacaste region is the specialty at the restaurant of the **Bramadero Hotel** *($$; on the Interamericana, near the main boulevard in Liberia, ☎666-0371, ⇛666-0203)*. Although very popular, It is not a top-notch steak house.

The **El Charro** *($$; 275 m east of the Banco de Costa Rica, ☎666-2239) marisquería* and bar serves decent seafood dishes.

**Restaurante Jauja** *($$; every day, restaurant 9am to 10pm, bar 10am to 2:30am; on the main boulevard in Liberia, just off the Interamericana, ☎666-0917)* serves pizza and pasta. The place becomes a popular bar at night.

**Playa del Coco and Surroundings**

**Playa Panamá**

**Casa Del Mar** *($)* sells hamburgers, sandwiches and salads at low prices. Breakfast is also served.

**Costa Cangrejo** *($; Tue to Sat 10am to 10pm, Sunday 10am to 6pm; south of the Sano Sano centre, beside the public access to the beach, ☎670-0050)* features Costa Rican dishes and fast food.

**Playa Hermosa**

Next to a small supermarket and a sport equipment rental service, the **restaurant of the Aquasport centre** *($$$; every day 9am to 9pm; ☎670-0450)* cooks up a variety of dishes, with a special emphasis on seafood. Relaxed ambience and good food.

The restaurant of the **Villa del Sueño** *($$$; ☎672-0026)* (see p 249) is undoubtedly one of the better restaurants in the region. Situated on the magnificent terrace in front of the hotel, it has a cozy decor and soft, pleasant music. Sylvia, one of the owners, concocts four delicious and original dishes every night. Her filet mignon is particularly succulent.

**Playa del Coco**

**Los Almendrós** *($)* is a small clean *soda* run by a German who also teaches languages. Perfect for breakfast.

Popular Costa Rican dishes are on menu at the restaurant of the **Cabinas del Coco** *($-$$; on the beach, in front of the public pier, ☎670-0110 or 670-0276)*.

Right on the beach, **Las Olas** *($$; Thu to Tue; on the road along the* *beach, south of the central park)* serves Costa Rican and international dishes in a large, open dining room.

The **Bar, Marisquería y Pizzería Cocos** *($$; on the other side of the square that is right by the beach, ☎670-0113)* is a nice place for a meal or a drink. The restaurant is quite busy, as people come here for a light snack as well as an evening out. It becomes lively at night.

The spaghettería located in the **Pato Loco Inn** *($$; Fri to Wed, 6am to 9pm; 800 m from the beach on Playa del Coco road, ☎670-0145)* serves authentic Italian food at very good prices.

**San Francisco Treats** *($$; on Playa del Coco road)* caters to people who relish North American fast food.

The **Sambuka Papagayo** *($$$; in front of the central park, where the beach meets the main road leading downtown, ☎670-0272)* restaurant and bar stands out from most restaurants in the region because of its open setting and varied menu.

The French-owned **Bistrot-Oasis** *(Costa Rican cuisine $$, French cuisine $$$; Tue to Sun; on the road leading to the beach, ☎670-0463)* has a simple, pleasant decor. Living in Costa Rica for the past 15 years, the owners have not lost the culinary art and style of their homeland. Such a typical bistrot is quite a rarity in a Costa Rican resort town!

The restaurant located in the hotel **Coco Verde** *($$-$$$; 200 m from the beach, on Playa del Coco's main road, ☎670-0494)* offers a varied menu.

**El Sol y La Luna** *($$$; every day 7am to 10am, 11am to 1pm and 6pm to 11pm; 150 m from the beach, one street east of the main road in Playa del Coco, ☎670-0195)* is a handsome trattoria whose modern Mediterranean design matches that of Puerta del Sol, the hotel in which it is situated (see p 251). The young and friendly owner specializes in Italian cuisine and can also make all kinds of coffee. Breakfast is served.

The **Flor de Itabo Hotel** *($$$; approx. 1 km from the beach, at the entrance to Playa del Coco, ☎670-0011 or 670-0292)* has an excellent Italian restaurant with a good reputation.

#### Playa Ocotal

The **Father Rooster Bar** *($$)* is in a renovated ranch house that faces the El Ocotal Beach Resort, with which it is affiliated. This laid-back restaurant and bar is the perfect place to go for a bite to eat if you're on the beach – you can walk in simply wearing your bathing suit! Dancing in the evenings.

The restaurant of the **El Ocotal Beach Resort** *($$$-$$$$; ☎670-0321 or 670-0323)* proposes an international menu that features seafood dishes. The food is excellent, but the magnificent view of Papagayo Gulf steals the show!

## Around Filadelfia

### Playa Flamingo and Surroundings

#### Playa Pan de Azúcar

The **Hotel Sugar Beach** *($$-$$$; every day 6am to 11pm; 15 km from the turnoff to Huscas, ☎654-4242)* has a circular open-air restaurant. Enjoy the marvellous view as you watch monkeys, iguanas, toucans and parrots carousing on the hotel grounds. International menu, and lunch-time specials.

### Playa Potrero

Seafood, steak, and a nice ocean view are what you'll find at the restaurant of the **Bahía Potrero Beach Resort** *($$-$$$; ☎654-4183)*.

**El Grillo** *($$$; Thu to Tue 5pm "til you drop!")* is a brand new restaurant and bar that specializes in French cuisine. Happy hour from 5pm to 9pm.

### Playa Flamingo

Next to the marina, the restaurant of the **Mariner Inn** *($$-$$$; ☎654-4081)* serves seafood in a relaxing setting.

Crowning the tip of Playa Flamingo, **Marie's Restaurant** *($$-$$$; near the Flamingo Marina Hotel, ☎654-4136)* is a pleasant place, with an alluring decor and lovely landscaping. The spacious, airy interior combines lush greenery with wooden trim. Ideal for breakfast, lunch or a simple evening meal. This very popular restaurant does not accept reservations so arrive early.

**Amberes** *($$$-$$$$; every day 6:30am to 10pm; near the Flamingo Marina Hotel, ☎654-4001)* is a restaurant, night club and casino that is very popular because it isn't attached to a hotel. It specializes in seafood, but many other dishes are available.

### Playa Brasilito

**Las Playas** *($$; ☎654-4237)* is the restaurant of the large beachfront Hotel Brasilito, and offers basic and affordable food in an outdoor setting.

As you travel from Filadelfia to beaches such as Brasilito or Conchal, stop at the roadside **Restaurante Chulamate** *($$; ☎675-0246)* for a quick and inexpensive meal. The owners are friendly, and the dining room is spacious.

## Playa Tamarindo and Surroundings

### Playa Grande

One of the only restaurants in the remote region of the Parque Nacional Marino Las Baulas is located in the **Centro Vacacional Playa Grande** *($-$$; 1.5 km before Playa Grande, at the entrance to the Parque Nacional Marino Las Baulas, ☎237-2552 or 260-3991)*, where inexpensive Costa Rican and North American meals are served.

**Grande Bob's** *($-$$; ☎653-0490)* serves seafood and North American basics (roasted chicken, steak etc.) in a *rancho* setting. Vegetarian meals are also available. The satellite TV, pool table and surfing videos are sure to please surfers and others looking for a relaxed atmosphere.

### Playa Tamarindo

The number of restaurants in the small village of Tamarindo is growing rapidly. The following are worth mentioning.

The **Panadería Johann** *($-$$; every day 6am to 8pm; at the entrance of Tamarindo)* pastry shop and pizzeria bakes a wide selection of goodies to be savoured on the spot or on the go.

The popular **Zully Mar Restaurant** *($-$$; every day 7am to 11pm; at the end of the first street that borders the beach, in the bend, ☎653-0140)* offers savoury Costa Rican dishes (the *ceviche* is excellent!) along with a nice view.

**Arco Iris** *($$; Tue to Sun)* serves inventive vegetarian cuisine.

The tropical ambiance of the **Coconut Café** *($$-$$$; on the opposite side of the first street that borders the beach)* will put you in the mood for seafood.

Fondue and other goodies are also featured on the menu.

**Fiesta del Mar** *($$-$$$; every day 8am to 11pm; at the end of the first street that borders the beach, in the bend)* serves steak and seafood in a tropical decor.

Nestled in lush gardens and surrounded by wonderfully carved sculptures reminiscent of pre-Colombian times **El Milagro** *($$-$$$; every day 7am to 11pm; on the left as you enter the village of Tamarindo, ☎653-0042)* is an attractive place to dine on *tica* and continental cuisine.

The **Tamarindo Diriá** *($$-$$$; ☎290-4340)* is definitively worth a stop, if only to admire its picturesque landscape. The kitchen prepares tasty international dishes that vary from day to day.

**El Jardín del Edén** *($$$; ☎654-4111 or 220-2096)* is a Mediterranean-style outdoor restaurant that excels in French and Italian cuisine.

## Around Santa Cruz

### Playa Junquillal and Surroundings

#### Playa Negra

Surfing fanatics flock to the **Pablo Picasso Restaurant and Bar** *($$; Easy Street)*. Owned by an American who also thrives on the sport, this inexpensive, laid-back eatery serves up large portions of popular food like hamburgers.

The restaurant of the secluded **Playa Negra Hotel** *($$-$$$; ☎382-1301)* is worth the extra mile (see p 257). Its Basque chef prepares French culinary treats, and hotel employees speak French. During the rainy season, enquire about road conditions before you head out. Most clients use four-wheel drive vehicles.

#### Playa Junquillal

The restaurant at the **Guacamaya Lodge** *($-$$$; ☎653-0431)* specializes in Swiss and international cuisine. It has lunchtime specials and a more elaborate dinner menu.

The restaurant of the **Junquillal Hotel** *($$; beside the public access to Playa Junquillal beach, ☎653-0432)* is a simple but friendly establishment that serves Costa Rican and North American food.

## Around Nicoya

### Nicoya and Surroundings

Stop at **Café Daniela** *($; ☎686-6148)* on Nicoya's main street for a light snack (pizza, chicken) or a rich desert.

**Restaurante Nicoya** *($$$)* is an unassuming Chinese restaurant located on the main street.

### Playa Sámara and Surroundings

#### Playa Guiones

**Olas Grandes Gringo Grill** *($$)* serves Costa Rican and North American dishes, as well as grill specialities, in a relaxed setting. At sundown, young surfers liven up the bar.

The menu at **La Dolce Vita** *($$-$$$; Tue to Sun 5pm to 11pm)* is Italian, and Italian only. The place lives up to its name: life does seem to be at its sweetest as you quietly sup beneath the canopy of a hut nestled in the jungle.

The **Café de Paris** *($$-$$$; every day 7am to 11pm; 500 m from Playa Guiones)* is affiliated with the hotel of the same name and owned by a Franco-Swiss couple. Start your day with a French or American breakfast, or sample its Costa Rican and French dishes for lunch or dinner. The **Café de Paris bakery and pastry shop** *($-$$; every day 7am to 5pm)* concocts authentic-tasting croissants and eclairs in the middle of the tropical jungle! Souvenir are also sold.

**Giardino Tropicale** *($$$)* cooks Italian dishes in a wood-burning oven. The friendly owner is Italian and speaks French.

### Playa Sámara

**Pablito's** *($; 7am to 10pm; Playa Cangrejal, northern section of Playa Sámara)* is a friendly Costa Rican bar and restaurant that also serves *bocas*.

You can dine on pizza and other Italian dishes in the large hut of the **Restaurante Tratatorria Al Manglar** *($$; approx. 100 m from Isla Chora, on a street which runs parallel to the main road leading to the beach)*.

The French owners bring many years of experience, acquired in their homeland, to the brand new **El Delfin** *($$)* pizzeria, right by the beach. Their home-cooked meals can be enjoyed along with the vista.

When it comes to Italian food, the pizzeria of the **Hotel Isla Chora** *($$-$$$; ☎656-0174)* deserves high praise. It serves a variety of delicious pizzas and fantastic Italian ice cream in a lovely decor that opens to the outdoors.

The restaurant of the **Hotel Las Brisas del Pacifico** *($$$; southern section of Playa Sámara, ☎656-0250)* serves international, *tico* and German dishes in a beautiful natural setting.

### Playa Carillo

Hearty food such as steaks and hamburgers are found on the menu of the seaside **El Mirador** *($$; ☎656-0307)*. A good place to quell midday hunger pangs.

**El Yate de Marisco** *($$; ☎656-0179)* is a seafood restaurant perched high on the cliffs towering over Carillo beach. The view of the coastline and the sea is spectacular.

Owned by cool young Italians, the **Fuego Latino** *($$; every day 7am to 11pm; ☎656-0450)* restaurant and bar has a tropical atmosphere with its thatched-roof dining area that opens on three sides. It specializes in Italian and Costa Rican flavours. Located near the El Sueño Tropical restaurant.

The restaurant of the **Playa Laguna Beach Resort** *($$; ☎656-0005)* serves Spanish cuisine in a very charming decor. This establishment's eye-catching design is quite extraordinary in the surrounding wilderness, not to mention in Costa Rica. Decorative details like ceramic-topped tables, fashionably modern chairs, walls painted in warm southern colors, and a lovely green-stained wooden counter make it an aesthetic masterpiece. And the excellent food is no less exceptional. We particularly enjoyed the Andalusian gaspacho.

An international menu is available at the restaurant and bar of the **Guanamar Hotel** *($$-$$$; ☎656-0054)*, which also has an attractive setting and a superb view.

In a large hut on a hill, the brightly decorated **El Sueño Tropical** *($$$; every day 7am to 9:30pm; south of Playa Carillo, ☎656-0151)* caters to lovers of Italian food in the hotel of the same name (see p 259).

### Playa Nosara and Surroundings

#### Playa Nosara and Playa Pelada

Next to the beach, **Olga's Bar** *($-$$; every day 6:30am to 10pm; beside the public access to Pelada de Nosara beach)* serves light meals (sandwiches, *casados*) and cool drinks.

Not far from the football field in the centre of town, **Soda Nosara** *($-$$)* was undergoing renovations when we were there. Costa Rican cuisine.

Next to the Playa Pelada de Nosara, **Pirata's Bar** *($$; ☎284-9669)* of Hotel Rancho Suizo (see p 260) cooks fish and chicken on an open grill. Its lush setting makes it a very pleasant place to nurse a drink or enjoy a meal.

The **Luna Bar and Grill** *($$-$$$; Playa Pelada de Nosara, next to the public beach access)* has a unique design with its tasteful interior opening onto a stunning terrace facing the sea. Owned by the Playas de Nosara Hotel, this beachfront bar and grill is ideal for a meal or drinks. The kitchen prepares roast chicken, seafood, salads and traditional Costa Rican dishes.

The charming and spacious restaurant of the hotel **Estancia Nosara** *($$$; 4 km south of Nosara, ☎680-0378)* is surrounded by 10 hectares of tropical gardens. International menu.

The restaurant of the **Villa Taype Hotel** *($$$; between Punta Pelada and Playa Guiones, ☎382-7715)* proposes an international menu in a most relaxing environment.

## ENTERTAINMENT

### Bars and Nightclub

### Around Liberia

#### Liberia and Surroundings

There is lively dance music at **Kurú** *(at the edge of Liberia on the road to Santa Cruz, in front of the El Sitio Hotel, Liberia, ☎666-1036 or 666-0769)* every Wednesday through Sunday. A giant screen TV also provides entertainment. The club opens at 9pm and is situated next door to the Pókopí restaurant (see p 263).

A congenial dance club and bar occupies the basement of the **Daysita Hotel** *(on the south side of the stadium, Liberia, ☎666-0197)*.

#### Playa del Coco and Surroundings

Once the sun sets, a young crowd gathers at the trendy **Restaurant and Bar Sambuka Papagayo** *(in front of the central park, at the corner of the beach and the main road to Playa del Coco, ☎670-0272)*.

For several years now, the **Coco Mar** *(in front of the central park behind the Cabinas del Coco)* has been a lively dance club.

The **Astillero Disco Club** *(☎670-0120)* is located on the road leading to Playa del Coco.

**Around Nicoya**

**Playa Sámara and Surroundings**

Jamaican rhythms and intimate corners create the warm atmosphere of the bar **La Gondola** *(on the road leading to the public access to Sámara beach, in front of the Sámara Beach Hotel)*. You can also enjoy a game of ping-pong, pool or darts here.

Young people dance the night away in the chic decor of the nightclub in the **Isla Chora Hotel** *(☎656-0174)*.

**Playa Nosara and Surroundings**

**Olga's Bar** *(beside the public access to Pelada de Nosara beach)* is popular with Costa Ricans on Saturday nights, and opens out onto a spacious open-air dance floor.

At **Pirata's Bar** *(Nosara, ☎284-9669)*, which is part of the Rancho Suizo Hotel, you can slow dance in tropical surroundings next to the beach.

## SHOPPING

### Around Liberia

**Liberia and Surroundings**

In Liberia, **Tiffany** *(Mon to Sat; 100 m south of, and 50 m west of Coopeconpro, Plaza 25 de Julio, Liberia, ☎666-0440)* offers a wide choice of souvenirs and handcrafted items such as stained-glass windows, jewellery and leather goods.

Located in Liberia's Bambú shopping centre, **Info-Cen-Tur** *(Calle 1, Av. 3, Liberia, ☎666-1833)* sells North American newspapers (during high season) and has a wealth of information on regional tourist attractions.

**Kaltak** *(4.5 km west on the road to the airport, ☎/≠667-0076)* is a reputable handicraft and souvenir shop located on the road from Liberia to Santa Cruz.

**Playa del Coco and Surroundings**

**Playa Hermosa**

In the vicinity of Playa Hermosa, **Aquasport** *(☎670-0450)* has a small supermarket that sells *The Miami Herald*.

**Playa del Coco**

The handsome boutique **Comercial Porto Fino** *(southeast corner of the playground, Playa del Coco)* sells basic medications and cosmetics, as well as souvenirs and gift ideas.

You will find an attractive **souvenir shop** on the main street in Playa del Coco, approximately 200 metres from the beach, in front of the Coco Verde Hotel.

### Around Filadelfia

**Playa Tamarindo and Surroundings**

**Playa Grande**

The **El Mundo de la Tortuga** museum (see p 237), located at the entrance to the Parque Nacional Marino Las Baulas near Playa Tamarindo, has a pleasant souvenir shop whose products focus on the region's giant turtles (clothes, jewellery, books, photos, etc.).

## Around Santa Cruz

### Santa Cruz and Surroundings

Handcrafted terra cotta pieces are available at the **Guaitil Artesanía** *(☎686-6608, on the road between Santa Cruz and Nicoya)*.

**Guaitil**, a small village near Santa Cruz, produces the lovely ceramics that decorate many hotels and restaurants in the Guanacaste region.

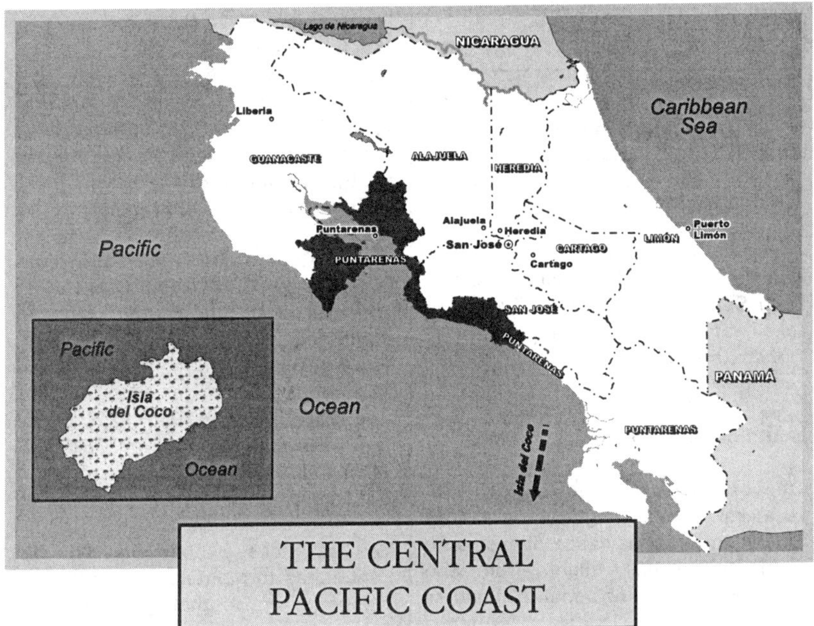


# THE CENTRAL PACIFIC COAST

Costa Rica's central Pacific coast is its most popular tourist destination, and is a favourite with Costa Ricans and foreigners alike. Countless hotels have sprung up along this stretch of the coast, which benefits from its proximity to the national capital and the country's international airport.

While the opening of the Liberia airport has brought an increasing number of tourists north to the province of Guanacaste, the central Pacific coast remains the destination of choice for many package tours and independent vacationers. The area's attractions include the untouched wilderness experiences to be had in the southern part of the Nicoya Peninsula, reached via Puntarenas, and the combination of stylish development and exquisite natural settings which makes the region between Quepos and Manuel Antonio ideal for vacations. Meanwhile, the Jacó region has all the facilities of a great resort area, and is less than two hours from the nation's capital!

Hidden pieces of unspoiled nature can be found in the less developed regions between these fashionable hot-spots, providing tranquil settings for leisurely strolls that leave you with a greater appreciation of Costa Rica's magnificent natural surroundings.

The climate is pleasantly temperate, in contrast to the exceptionally dry conditions in Guanacaste and the extreme humidity in the southern part pf the country. Vacationers, especially those escaping cold climates, bask in the sun during dry season, while the annual rains restore the lush plant life to its opulent splendour.

With all these splendours, the allure of the central Pacific coast of Costa Rica is hard to resist!

## FINDING YOUR WAY AROUND

### By Plane

**The Nicoya Peninsula**

**Tambor**: **Sansa** *(☎221-9414)* and **Travelair** *(☎220-3054)* offer daily flights from San José to Tambor. The flight takes about 30 minutes and the round-trip costs about $100.

**South of Puntarenas**

**Quepos**: has a small airfield that receives domestic flights. The airlines Sansa and Travelair (see above) both offer regular daily flights from San José. The trip takes about 20 minutes and costs approximately $75 for a round-trip. Once in the country, enquire about the flight schedule, as it is liable to change. The airport is about five kilometres north of Quepos.

### By Boat

**The Nicoya Peninsula**

**Puntarenas – Paquera Ferry**: visitors travelling by car should take the car ferry to Paquera rather than Playa Naranjo (see below), because the road between Playa Naranjo and Paquera is winding and poorly maintained. There are five departures every day in each direction (from both Puntarenas and Paquera) *(from 4:15am to 9:15pm)*. The fare is $1.25 for adults *($3.35 in first class)* and $8.75 per car. The crossing takes about 1.5 hours *(Naviera Tambor, ☎661-2084)*. There is also a passenger ferry *(3 departures daily, between 6am and 5pm; $1.25; ☎661-2830)*.

**Puntarenas – Playa Naranjo Ferry**: this car ferry is the best way to reach Carmona and Nicoya. There are five departures daily between 3:15am and 7pm. The crossing takes about an hour and the fares are comparable to those of the Puntarenas – Paquera ferry *(Ferry Conatramar, ☎661-1069)*.

**Isla del Coco**: there is no regular boat or ferry service to Isla del Coco. Most cruises depart from the city of Puntarenas and last one or two weeks. The crossing alone takes about 36 hours. The agencies **Okeanos Aggressor** *(☎290-6203, ⇄290-6205)* and **Undersea Hunter** *(☎228-6535, ⇄289-7334)* offer excursions of about 10 days.

You can take a boat directly from Puntarenas to **Montezuma**, which is a wonderful cruise that eliminates the bus trip between Paqueras and Montezuma. Also, you get to see Montezuma at its best if you arrive by sea. Ask around at the Puntarenas docks to find a reliable carrier who is setting out at a time that suits your schedule.

### By Car

**The Puntarenas Region**

**Puntarenas** can be reached from the Central Valley by taking the Interamericana Highway west to the Pacific coast. The Puntarenas exit is clearly indicated, about two hours into the trip.

**The Nicoya Peninsula**

**The Southern Nicoya Peninsula**: go to **Puntarenas** and take the ferry from there (see above). The road is unpaved between **Paquera** and **Cóbano** (35 km),

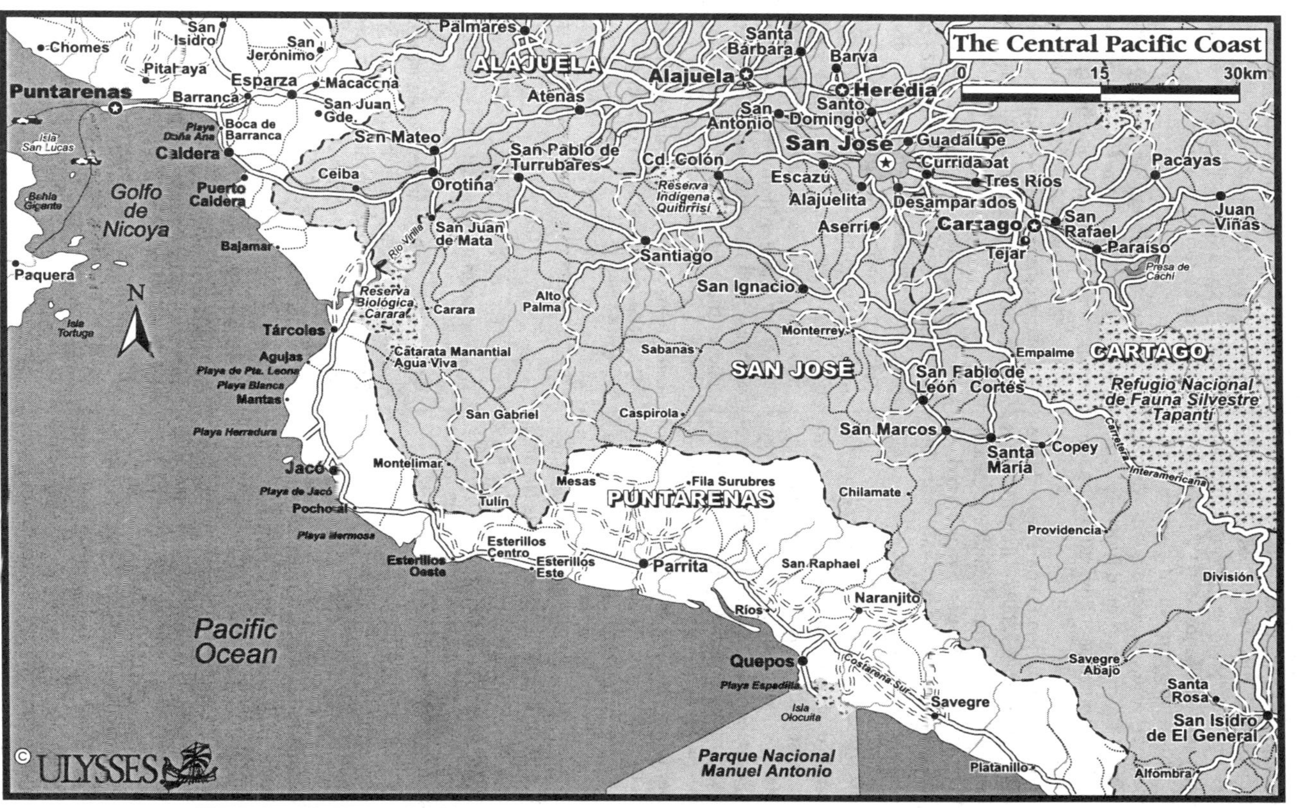


THE CENTRAL PACIFIC COAST

except for a short section near Tambor. However, the road is regularly maintained and in good condition between Cóbano and **Montezuma** (7 km). Depending on the season, the road between Cóbano and **Malpaís** (about 12 km) can be difficult for cars without four-wheel drive to negotiate.

If you arrive on the Puntarenas – Playa Naranjo ferry, be aware that the road that links Playa Naranjo and Paquera is very rough and poorly maintained. It can take over an hour to complete the 26-kilometre trip.

**Nicoya – Montezuma**: from Nicoya, in the province of Guanacaste, you can drive south to Tambor, Montezuma and Malpaís, instead of returning to the Interamericana Highway, driving to Puntarenas and taking the ferry. Head in the direction of the little town of **Carmona**, and about five kilometres before reaching it, take the little road on the left that leads to **Jicaral**, **Lepanto** and **Playa Naranjo**. The road is in good condition up to Playa Naranjo, but deteriorates between Playa Naranjo and Paquera. The trip from Nicoya to Montezuma is approximately 135 kilometres long and takes about six hours by car.

#### South of Puntarenas

**Playa Doña Ana**: the off-ramp that leads to this beach is found just before the highway bridge that is visible as you leave Puntarenas. The sign indicating the road is difficult to spot so be attentive.

**Reserva Biológica Carara, Playa Herradura and Play Jacó**: a two-hour drive from San José. Leave the Puntarenas highway at the Atenas exit. About 20 minutes before reaching Jacó, you will come to the entrance of Reserva Biológica Carara. The car entrance to Esterillos Oeste is 22 kilometres south of Jacó, and the entrance to Esterillos Este is about 5 kilometres further south.

A new section of highway now permits travellers coming from Puntarenas to reach these beaches in one hour. This road continues on to Quepos (70 kilometres further), Dominical and San Isidro de El General.

**Quepos** and **Manuel Antonio**: it takes 3.5 hours to get from San José to Manuel Antonio via the Atenas exit and the little, winding road that crosses the Aguacate mountains. In addition to beautiful panoramic views, this road provides glimpses of rural Costa Rican life. If you prefer highways, you can continue in the direction of Puntarenas, follow the directions for Jacó and continue on to Quepos. Although the latter route looks much longer on the map, it takes only a half hour longer to cover the distance.

### By Bus

#### The Puntarenas Region

**San José – Puntarenas**: departures every day, every half hour between 6am and 9pm. The trip takes two hours *($2.30; Calle 16, Av. 10/12; Empresarios Unidos, ☎221-5749)*.

#### The Nicoya Peninsula

**Paquera – Montezuma**: a bus waits for the ferry from Puntarenas at the dock in Paquera, and shuttles travellers to Cóbano and Montezuma. There are departures from Montezuma every day at 5:30am, 10am and 2pm.

**South of Puntarenas**

**Jacó**: there are three departures daily from San José. Plan for a two-and-a-half-hour trip.

**Quepos** and **Manuel Antonio**: three buses per day make the four-hour trip from San José. Buses travelling the **Puntarenas – Quepos** route leave three times a day, but this trip is only slightly shorter, taking 3.5 hours. There is frequent service on the short **Quepos – Manuel Antonio** hop, especially during the high season, for a minimal fare *($1)*. This bus stops at hotels on request.

## PRACTICAL INFORMATION

### The Puntarenas Region

**Puntarenas** is the capital of the Costa Rican province of the same name, and offers all of the basic services, which is very convenient for travellers headed to the sparsely populated tip of the Nicoya peninsula. The town's Mercado Central is on the north side of the spit *(Calle 2, Av. 3)*, right near where the ferry and fishing boats dock. Buses leave from the beach on the south side of Puntarenas, near Calle 2. The Banco Nacional and Banco de Costa Rica are located between the Museo Histórico Marino and the Mercado Central. Puntarenas also has a hospital at the corner of Paseo de los Turistas and Calle 9.

### South of Puntarenas

**Jacó** is the largest town on the pacific coast between Parrita and Puntarenas. It boasts *supermercados* (supermarkets), *farmacías* (pharmacies), a post office, bus stations, car rental offices and even a number of little shops that sell all sorts of merchandise. All of these services can be found on the main street that runs parallel to the beach. Jacó has a shopping mall, Centro Commercial Jacó Plaza, located north of the town on the main street, and also serves as a bus stop. There is a gas station at the edge of Jacó, on the road to Quepos.

**Quepos**

Quepos provides all the basic services. In addition to an airport and a recently built hospital a few kilometres north of the town, there is a *mercado central* in the heart of Quepos, as well as a bus station and a nearby taxi stand. There is a post office across from the football field, and the Banco Nacional, Banco Popular and Banco de Costa Rica are located on the quadrant of streets that make up the downtown, right near the entrance road into town (coming from San José and Jacó). Farmacía Quepos is a little south of downtown on this same street, near the park. There is a gas station on the road to the airport.

## EXPLORING

### The Puntarenas Region

People come to Puntarenas for two main reasons. The port of **Puntarenas** links the coast and the tip of the Nicoya Peninsula, so it is a convenient stopover for travellers on their way to the peninsula. But Puntarenas also has its own merits because of the historical role it played in the country's development.

For a long time, most of Costa Rica's export commodities were shipped to Europe from the coast of Puntarenas on the Pacific, because it was geographically the easiest to reach by mule or wagon, especially for the *cafeteros* of the Central Valley. Thus, Puntarenas was the gateway to Costa Rica's major markets in Europe during the 19th century. With foreign trade flourishing, Puntarenas grew continuously throughout this period.

The Pacific coast nonetheless had one major disadvantage as the centre of foreign trade: the European markets were across the Atlantic, so exporters had to send their merchandise on quite a trip to reach the "old world": goods were shipped down the entire coast of South America, around Cape Horn at the southern end of Chile, and then back up north to the European trade centres. Quite a journey! Going via Asia was even longer. (The Panama Canal was only inaugurated in the early 20th century.)

Though it was obvious that a port on the Caribbean could only facilitate trade, the hostile climate, geography and nature of the Pacific side of the country hindered such a project for a long time. The Central Valley was finally linked to the Caribbean coast by railroad in 1890.

This much more direct route to the European market took a little wind out of the sails in Puntarenas' port. The very recent inauguration of Puerto Caldera, a little to the south, put an end to the city's vocation as a commercial port once and for all.

Despite its decline, Puntarenas remains one of the largest cities in Costa Rica with its 100,000 residents. An important centre in the Costa Rican fishing industry, it is also the capital of the province of the same name, which extends to the southernmost part of the country along the coast.

The city's most interesting feature by far is the narrow spit of land that juts into the Gulf of Nicoya and gives the city its name, a corruption of *"punta de arena"*, which means "point of sand" in Spanish. The downtown and historic sections of the city are both located on this spit and draw a lot of visitors in the dry season. Meanwhile, the district is very quiet and peaceful during the rainy season.

**Paseo de los Turistas** (tourist road) runs alongside the town's beach on the southern shore of the spit. It can be very crowded with tourists who roam among the food stands and the various little shops. However, the Paseo is not completely without charm. Efforts have been made to clean up the beach, though the water is still not the most pristine in the country and is not ideal for swimming. Camping on the beach should also be avoided.

It is easy to get around Puntarenas because, although the city is a few kilometres long, it is only four streets (a few hundred metres at most) wide at most parts. The fishing docks, the ***mercado*** and the ferry landings overlook the shore opposite the beach (north side). A stroll through this area will give you a taste of daily life in this city.

The **Casa de la Cultura** *(Av. 1, Calle 3, Puntarenas, ☎661-1394)*, in the city centre, houses an art gallery and hosts concerts and plays. The **Museo Histórico Marino** *($1; Tue to Sun 9am to 5pm; Av. Central, Calle 3/5, Puntarenas)* presents the history of the city in a multimedia exhibition. The **Puntarenas church**, on Avenida Central west of the Museo Histórico Marino, is probably the most beautiful building in the city.

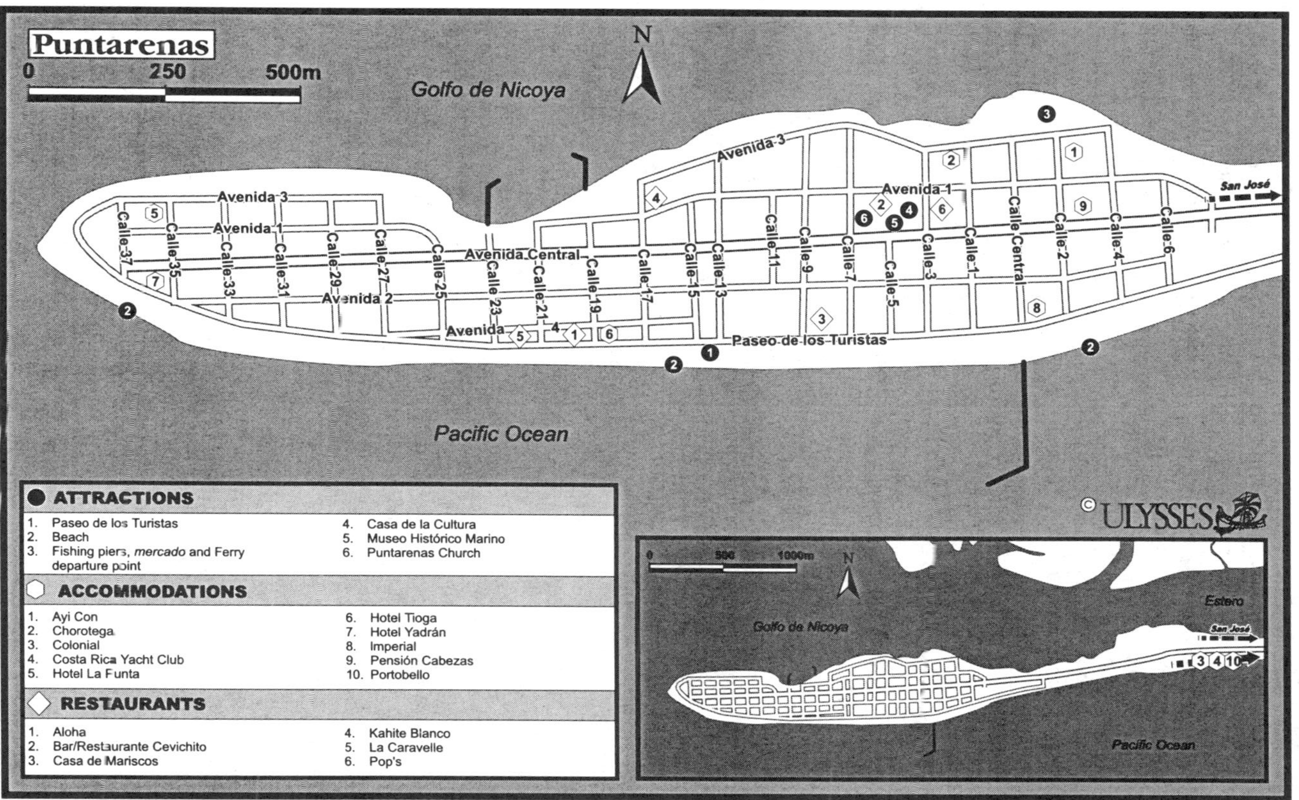

Puntarenas
0 250 500m
Golfo de Nicoya
Pacific Ocean
San José
Avenida 3
Avenida 1
Avenida Central
Avenida 2
Avenida 4
Paseo de los Turistas
Calle 37
Calle 35
Calle 33
Calle 31
Calle 29
Calle 27
Calle 25
Calle 23
Calle 21
Calle 19
Calle 17
Calle 15
Calle 13
Calle 11
Calle 9
Calle 7
Calle 5
Calle 3
Calle 1
Calle Central
Calle 2
Calle 4
Calle 6
© ULYSSES
0 500 1000m
Estero
ATTRACTIONS
1. Paseo de los Turistas
2. Beach
3. Fishing piers, *mercado* and Ferry departure point
4. Casa de la Cultura
5. Museo Histórico Marino
6. Puntarenas Church
ACCOMMODATIONS
1. Ayi Con
2. Chorotega
3. Colonial
4. Costa Rica Yacht Club
5. Hotel La Funta
6. Hotel Tioga
7. Hotel Yadrán
8. Imperial
9. Pensión Cabezas
10. Portobello
RESTAURANTS
1. Aloha
2. Bar/Restaurante Cevichito
3. Casa de Mariscos
4. Kahite Blanco
5. La Caravelle
6. Pop's

## The Southern Nicoya Peninsula

Unlike the rest of the peninsula, the southern Nicoya Peninsula is not part of Guanacaste province but rather belongs to the province of Puntarenas, which extends southward along the coast to Dominical. Because there was no well-maintained road to the area from Nicoya, and the ferry crossing takes an hour and a half, it was decided that this part of the peninsula would be annexed to the province of Puntarenas. The vast majority of tourists and residents still take the Puntarenas – Paquera ferry to reach this magnificent corner of the country.

### Paquera

The little village of Paquera is situated four kilometres from the ferry landing. It has a grocery store, a bank, and a campground, as well as a few places to stay and some small, moderately priced restaurants. Most tourists only stop in Paquera overnight if they want to make the first ferry the next day. Thus, the place has retained the peaceful atmosphere of a little out-of-the-way village, despite the heavy traffic that runs through it because of the ferry.

### North of Paquera

To the north, the **Playa Naranjo** area is seldom visited by tourists. Although there are a few hotels, useful for people planning to take the early morning ferry, this region has no pretty beaches or special attractions. Moreover, the road between Playa Naranjo and Paquera is in a deplorable state, ensuring an unpleasant start to any excursion you might want to make from here.

Further south, **Bahía Gigante** is an attractive bay in the Gulf of Nicoya, where visitors can discover **Isla Gitana** and its native burial ground. Once called Isla de los Muertos ("the island of the dead"), this island welcomes visitors for a day trip or a longer stay, as it has accommodations, campsites, a restaurant and a bar. There are trails, a pretty beach and many opportunities for water sports, as well as boat transportation to the island *(☎661-2994, ≠661-2833)*.

### Paquera to Montezuma

South of the Refugio Nacional de Fauna Silvestre Curú (see p 282), the road leads to the magnificent **Bahía Ballena** near the small village of **Pochote**. Pochote has preserved its picturesque quality and seems to be resisting the ongoing tourist development that is being undertaken in the surrounding area. Bahía Ballena is an immense bay, the largest in the southern Nicoya Peninsula, which stretches between Punta Tambor and Punta Piedra Amarilla. In the crux of the bay is a beautiful beach that is suitable for swimming and stretches over eight kilometres between the villages of Pochote and Tambor. The bay got its name because whales can sometimes be seen here (*ballena* means "whale" in Spanish), though it is more likely to be dotted with sailboats that come here for shelter from the great winds of the open sea.

**Tambor** is a tiny village with reasonably priced places to stay and small, inexpensive restaurants. However, the region has its share of tourists who stay in the large hotel complexes that have been built nearby. These resorts offer all-inclusive packages; pre-arranged vacations that include accommodation, meals, travel and numerous activities.

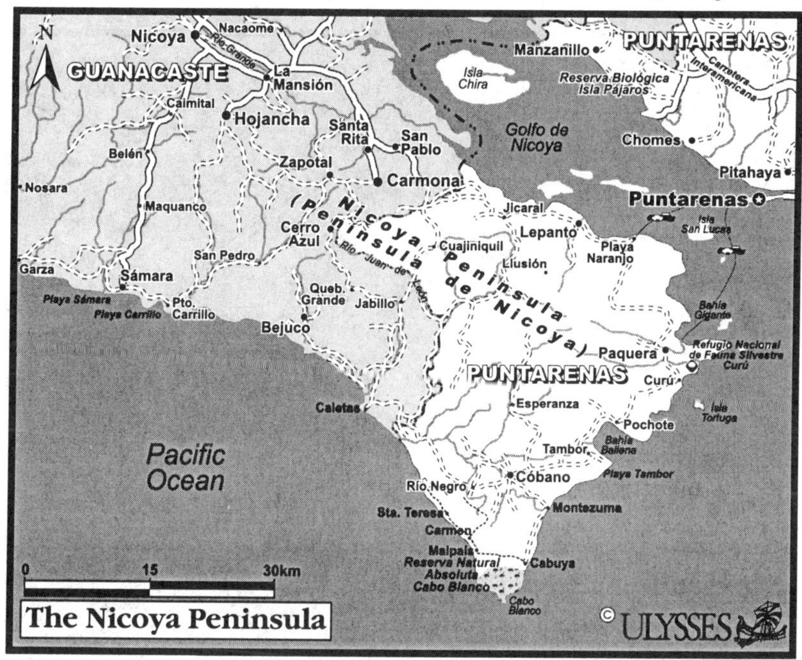


Past Tambor, the road veers back into the undulating farmland of the interior. Herds of zebus, large Indian bovids that have successfully adapted to the Costa Rican climate, can be spotted here – they are easily recognizable by their (most often) whitish colour, very long hanging ears and distinctive bump on the back near the head.

The village of **Cóbano** is 11 kilometres from Tambor, and has many services, such as a bank, post office, medical clinic, public telephones and a service station, as well as a few grocery stores, shops and little *sodas*. To reach Montezuma from here, take another little road on the left, heading south, from the village centre.

**Montezuma**

Just seven kilometres from Cóbano, **Montezuma** ★ is a pretty little seaside village with superb beaches and a vast selection of hotels, many of which are very affordable, as well as quite a few restaurants. It is reached via a small road that descends a very long, steep hill just before the village. Montezuma is small and has only a few streets, but many hotels are located at the edge of the village, on the roads to Cabuya and Cóbano.

Montezuma is overrun with young, free-spirited people from various countries (including Canada, Germany and the United States): hipsters, hippies, freaks and "granolas" stay here for weeks on end, and for very little money. Unfortunately, Montezuma was literally invaded by hordes of unscrupulous campers a few years ago. They polluted the area, and some didn't think twice about cutting down trees to fashion shelters, drink coconut milk or make bonfires on the beach. Because of these incidents, the village got a bad reputation as a haven for penniless drug users, youths and squatters who had been coming here since the early 1980s, making themselves unpopular

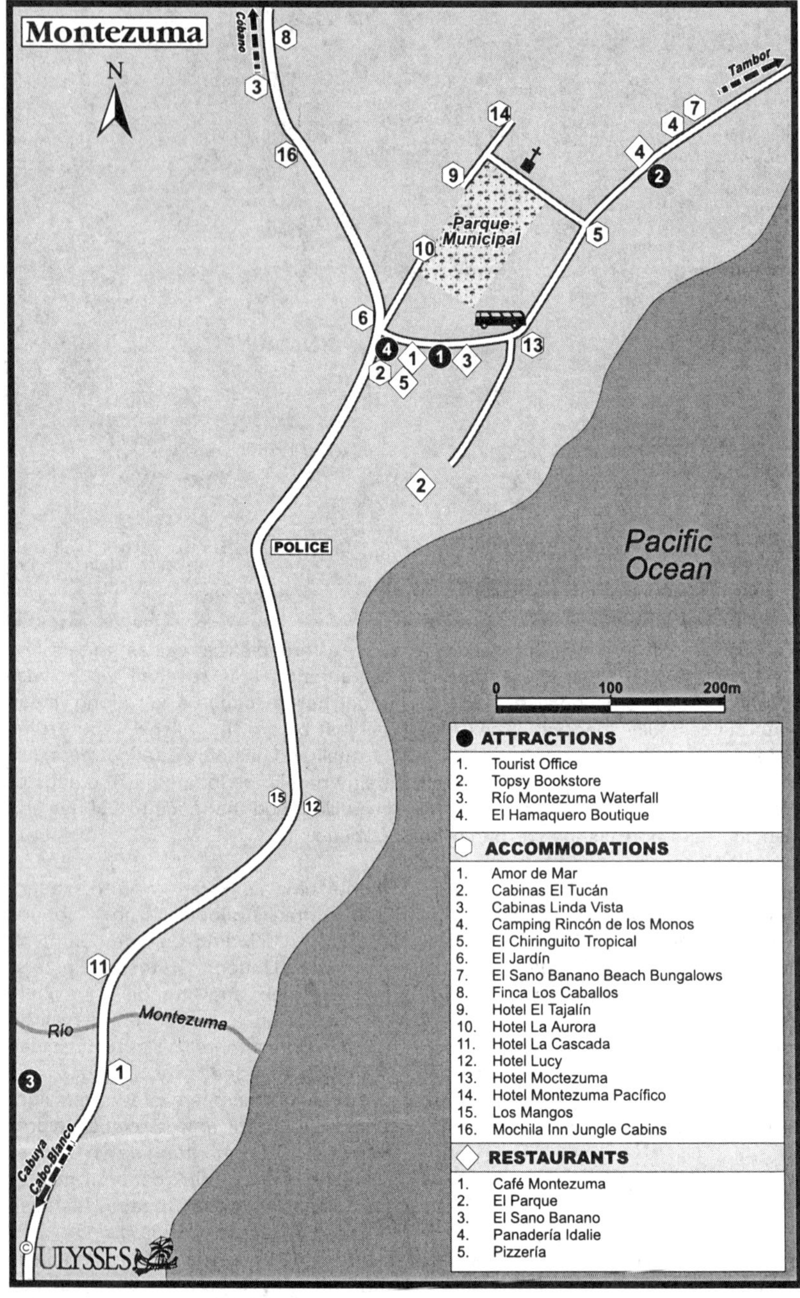
Montezuma
N
Cóbano
Tambor
Parque Municipal
POLICE
Pacific Ocean
0
100
200m
Río
Montezuma
Cabuya
Cabo Blanco
ULYSSES
ATTRACTIONS
1. Tourist Office
2. Topsy Bookstore
3. Río Montezuma Waterfall
4. El Hamaquero Boutique
ACCOMMODATIONS
1. Amor de Mar
2. Cabinas El Tucán
3. Cabinas Linda Vista
4. Camping Rincón de los Monos
5. El Chiringuito Tropical
6. El Jardín
7. El Sano Banano Beach Bungalows
8. Finca Los Caballos
9. Hotel El Tajalín
10. Hotel La Aurora
11. Hotel La Cascada
12. Hotel Lucy
13. Hotel Moctezuma
14. Hotel Montezuma Pacífico
15. Los Mangos
16. Mochila Inn Jungle Cabins
RESTAURANTS
1. Café Montezuma
2. El Parque
3. El Sano Banano
4. Panadería Idalie
5. Pizzería

with the region's locals by sunbathing nude.

Finally, the residents got together to improve the situation and protect Montezuma's natural beauty. Together with hotel-owners, they formed groups such as CATUMA (Cámara de Turismo de Montezuma), which organized cleanup and reforestation crews and led a campaign to sensitize other residents to the importance of preserving the region's environment. They also determined to keep Montezuma from becoming an overly developed tourist destination made up only of hotels or immense resort complexes like those around Quepos, Jacó and Tambor.

Their efforts were successful, and Montezuma has remained on a manageable scale where residents and tourists recognize and greet each other in passing. Of course, Montezuma is still a very popular tourist destination, so visitors looking for perfect tranquillity are better off near Malpaís or Cabuya. But if your budget is limited and you do not have a car, Montezuma is still an inviting, multifaceted region that abounds with all sorts of activities for all budgets.

Information about the region's many activities and natural attractions can be found at the **Montezuma tourist office** *(every day 8am to noon and 4pm to 8pm)*, located right in the centre of the village across from the municipal park. Among the most popular tours, we recommend those of the superb Reserva Natural Absoluta Cabo Blanco (see p 284) and the spellbinding **Isla Tortuga** ★. The excursion to Isla Tortuga *($30)* takes all day *(9am to 4pm)* and includes round-trip transportation by speedboat, breakfast, snorkelling equipment and a variety of fun activities. It is an unforgettable day on an idyllic island covered with white sand washed by turquoise water...

Montezuma can be visited on foot, and if you come by a car, parking can be difficult. Opt for the public parking lot *($2/day)* across from the tourist office, especially if you want to leave luggage in your car. To pick up reading material for a day on the beach, head to **Topsy** bookstore, where used books are bought and sold. On Wednesday evenings, **El Sano Banano** restaurant shows popular films, and visitors can enjoy that entertainment or just chat over one of their fabulous milkshakes.

A lovely stroll, as pleasant as it is refreshing, leads to the **Río Montezuma waterfall** ★★. Take the road to Cabuya for about 700 metres, until you reach hotel La Cascada on the north bank of Río Montezuma. Past the little bridge is a sign that indicates the path that climbs through the forest to the waterfall. After about 15 minutes of walking, you will arrive at the waterfall and its relaxing basin that is wonderful for swimming. Even if many tourists dive in from the top of the falls, this is quite dangerous. In fact, in 1990 one tourist lost his footing while attempting just such a plunge and died. This should be enough of a warning to discourage any would-be Tarzans.

### South of Montezuma

**Cabuya** is a tiny village located about eight kilometres south of Montezuma, and constitutes the entrance to Reserva Natural Absoluta Cabo Blanco, two kilometres to the south. It is quieter than Montezuma, and has a good selection of hotels, *cabinas*, and campsites nearby. The cemetery is unique in that it is located on an island, Isla Cabuya. The island can be reached on foot when the tide is at its lowest point.

**Northwest of Cabo Blanco**

Situated northwest of the Reserva Natural Absoluta Cabo Blanco (see p 284), the region of **Malpaís ★** and **Santa Teresa ★** is one of the best-kept secrets of the southern Nicoya Peninsula. First discovered by surfers attracted by its excellent waves, this region offers idyllic, semi-deserted (depending on the season) beaches as well as a good selection of hotels and restaurants in every price range. There is no commercial hub, but rather a small road lined with houses, hotels and restaurants that skirts the ocean for about six kilometres.

If you are looking for a quiet, peaceful spot and are not sure that Montezuma fits the bill, opt for this area – you will not be disappointed! Mountain biking and horseback riding, surfing classes, and full days of sunbathing or hours of swimming in the sea are among the activities to enjoy here. Here, the days end with a spectacular sunsets that are best enjoyed from a hammock, drink in hand!

## Refugio Nacional Fauna Silvestre Curú

**Refugio Nacional de Fauna Silvestre Curú ★** *($5; every day; reservations required; ☎661-2392, ⇒641-0060)* is located seven kilometres south of Paquera. This private 84-hectare park is part of the Curú hacienda (1,496 hectares), owned by the Schutt family since 1933. Its name comes from the *guanacaste* tree, which area natives called *curú*. Part of the hacienda was declared a national wildlife preserve in 1983 in order to protect the fragile marine habitat on the coast and the beach that borders it. The reserve also shelters a tropical dry forest, a tropical rainforest, mangroves, pastures and fruit-tree orchards.

The Schutt family worked hard to have this area, whose biodiversity is representative of the region as it was several decades ago. The place is now recognized at once as a site for scientific research, agriculture and tourism and attracts different groups of visitors who come to discover or study this complex environment whose abundant fauna and flora are remarkably concentrated on only a few hectares of land.

Refugio Nacional de Fauna Silvestre Curú is relatively unknown and little visited by tourists passing through the area. This is unfortunate, because they miss out on a fascinating new experience – the reserve is a wild, enchanting place that holds many surprises! The entrance to the wardens' house is at the edge of the main road from Paquera to Tambor. A few hundred metres further, a barrier marks the park gate, which visitors must open themselves. One of the functions of this barrier is to keep the livestock away from the main road. When we arrived, a fairly large spider monkey was relaxing on the barrier. Realizing that nobody dared leave their car, the monkey bounced onto the windshield and started examining us scrupulously. The roles were reversed and we felt caged, and observed from all sides! A few minutes later, the warden arrived by bicycle and the monkey fled at top speed.

Past the barrier, a small 2.5-kilometre-long road leads to the main buildings, the administrative offices and the visitor's centre. These building are set near the pretty beach nestled in the bend of the bay's shoreline. The Río Curú flows south of the beach, and empties into the waters of the Gulf of Nicoya. Northeast of the bay, Punta Quesera juts into the Gulf, while to the south, the Tortuga islands, veritable

*Coati*

paradises for snorkellers, kayakers and swimmers, protrude from the sea.

Because we arrived around noon, there was no one to greet us at the visitor's centre and the area seemed deserted. But a curious baby howler monkey, no more than 25 centimetres tall, came to meet us enthusiastically, happy to make new friends. Realizing that we were waiting for the warden's return, the little monkeys carefully climbed onto one person in our group and sat on his shoulder, wrapping its tail around his neck to keep its balance. Then, a brown coati (a sort of raccoon that Costa Ricans called *pizote*) appeared and began affectionately licking our toes! When the warden arrived, she did not seem at all surprised by this spectacle, and explained how the park functioned in a completely casual manner.

The park shelters truly exceptional flora and fauna. There are 500 species of plants, and part of the hacienda (200 hectares) has been reforested with about 10 types of indigenous trees. There are also 232 bird species, 78 mammal species, 87 reptiles species and 26 amphibian species. Depending on the day, you can observe sea turtles (Hawksbill and Ridley), iguanas, crocodiles, boa constrictors, peccaries, armadillos, agoutis, pumas, monkeys, etc., whether you are accompanied by a guide or not. The park is home to three species of monkeys; howler monkeys, white-faced capuchins and spider monkeys. The spider monkey, which is now extremely rare in Costa Rica, was completely exterminated in the region of Curú between 1960 and 1965. It was reintroduced to the reserve about 10 years ago, and in 1993 "Francisco" became the first spider monkey to be born in the region since the species' near extinction 30 years earlier.

You can snorkel, swim and walk in the park, which also has a picnic area. We suggest spending an entire day here in order to have enough time to see all the animals and different types of natural habitat. The network of walking trails includes 17 short paths whose lengths vary from a few hundred metres to four kilometres. The trails run through tropical forest, mangroves, pastures and orchards and lead to Punta Georgia in the south and Punta Quesera north of the park. Some trails reach the shore of the Gulf of Nicoya, while others climb to lookouts over the region. The great majority of hotels in the area offer guided tours of the park, as does the Montezuma tourist office.

## Reserva Natural Absoluta Cabo Blanco

**Reserva Natural Absoluta Cabo Blanco** ★★ *($6; Wed to Sun 8am to 4pm; ☎/≠642-0093)* is a haven of natural riches only 11 kilometres from Montezuma. The small road that leads to the reserve runs through Cabuya, is in good condition and passable for most cars. If you come from Malpaís by four-wheel drive vehicle, on horseback, or by mountain bicycle, you can take the small seven-kilometre-long forest road that links Malpaís and Cabuya. Its entrance is well marked by a small sign, and the road itself passes the Star Mountain Eco Resort after two kilometres. If you take this route, the trip to the reserve is only nine kilometres long, instead of the 30 kilometres if you go via Cóbano, Montezuma and Cabuya.

The reserve was created October 21, 1963 for the sole purpose of protecting the wildlife and vegetation of this magnificent point situated at the southern tip of the Nicoya Peninsula. It got its name because, until the end of the 1980s, it was *absoluta*, meaning access was restricted to authorized researchers, and visitors were not permitted at all. Since then, two hiking trails have been laid out and visitors are welcome to use them. However, a large proportion of the reserve is still off-limits to visitors, who must stay on the paths.

The reserve's short history dates back to 1955, when the Swedish couple Nils Olof Wessberg and Karen Morgenson settled on a farm in the area. Witnessing the rapid deforestation caused by the lumber industry, and realizing that the virgin forest of Cabo Blanco would disappear in a few years if logging continued to proceed at this rate, they went to great lengths to protect this wild region, which was home to jaguars, ocelots, coyotes, white-tailed deer, and other animals. After taking three years to convince skeptics, they succeeded in amassing enough money (about $30,000) to buy the 1,250 hectares of forest that make up the point of Cabo Blanco. Thus, the point became a nature reserve, and since then Nils Olof Wessberg is recognized as the father of national parks in Costa Rica. Continuing his work as a naturalist and forest protector, Wessberg travelled to the Osa Peninsula in the southwest of the country, in the summer of 1975 to promote the creation of a new park. Unfortunately, he was assassinated there and thus did not live to see the creation of Parque Nacional Corcovado in October of that same year. There is a commemorative plaque in his honour near the reserve's visitor's centre.

The visitor's centre is about 400 metres from the parking lot by foot. The staff is very friendly, and many volunteers work here. The visitor's centre is right by the sea, and is an excellent spot for picnicking; tables have even been set up for this very purpose. There are also washrooms, potable water, a shower and a little *soda* run by local women.

The rules of the reserve, the paths and attractions are explained at the visitor's centre. Lists of the various mammals and birds, with a map of the reserve on the back, and a flier describing a dozen of these mammals *(42¢)* can be obtained here. Rain boots and ponchos *($1/day each)* can be rented, as can binoculars *($3/day)* for watching some of the 133 bird species that come to the reserve.

The reserve is crisscrossed by many trails, but only two of these are open to the public, the others are reserved for researchers. The **Danés** trail forms a 2.3-kilometre loop and runs through a replanted forest that shows the different stages of the flora's regeneration. The reserve is made up of 85% secondary forest, and 15% primary forest that has not been cut by area residents before or after the creation of the reserve. The trail also crosses Río Cabo Blanco, with its trickle of crystalline water. It takes about 1.5 to complete the loop.

The other path is called **Sueco** and is 4.2 kilometres long (8.4 km round trip). It leads to the beach south of the reserve where there are potable water, picnic tables and showers. It is a pleasant spot for swimming, which is permitted. In addition to the 1,250 hectares of forest, the reserve comprises 1,700 hectares of protected waters, extending about one kilometre offshore. Three kilometres from the visitor's centre, the trail comes to a lookout (*mirador*) over the point, the sea and Cabo Blanco island, one kilometre from shore. The interpretive panels about the plant and animal life in the reserve were created by Colombian students. The round trip takes about four and a half hours to complete.

## Parque Nacional Isla del Coco

**Parque Nacional Isla del Coco** *($6; every day; ☎256-0365 or 233-4533, ⇒256-0365)* is a true national treasure because of its rich vegetation and, above all, the clear, lively waters of the Pacific Ocean that surround it. Because the park is an island situated about 540 kilometres off Cabo Blanco (Nicoya Peninsula), it remains much less frequented than the other national parks in Costa Rica.

Its offshore location has had the positive effect of preserving the place's natural beauty and wealth. With an area of 2,400 hectares, Isla del Coco is situated at 5°30'34" latitude North and 87°18'6" longitude West. The marine section of the park alone covers about 73,000 hectares. The island is named for the many coconut trees that were found here originally, though over the years they have given way to low altitude tropical rainforest, which receive an average of close to seven metres of rain annually. The vegetation here is very dense, and three plant species that are unique to the island have been discovered. Because the island is made up of many mountains, the tallest of which is 634-metre mount **Iglesias**, there are dozens of spectacular waterfalls, some of which cascade directly into the sea.

According to Mario A. Boza, author of the book *Parques Nacionales de Costa Rica*, Isla del Coco was discovered by the Spaniard Joan Cabezas, who navigated along the island's shores in 1526. Over the centuries, sailors would stop here to stock up on potable water. Some even left livestock (pigs, goats, dogs) on the island to be picked up on a later voyage or if they ran out of food. Over the years, the pigs adapted to the island particularly well, and became numerous enough to damage the environment, since hoofed animals cause excessive erosion by digging in the ground, especially during periods of heavy rain. Some even say that their presence here affected the coral reefs!

Even more fascinating is the legend that the island shelters three well-hidden treasure-troves. Between the end of the 17th century and the beginning of the 19th, pirates William Davies, Benito Bonito and William Thompson visited the island successively to hide money and valuables, including a life-size solid gold statue of the Virgin Mary! However, close to 500 expeditions undertaken so far have not found anything. The only treasure to have been discovered to date is the island itself!

Isla del Coco is renowned for its interesting ornithological site where 87 species of birds have been counted, including three that are specific to the island: its cuckoo (*Coccyzus ferrugineus*), flycatcher (*Nesotriccus ridgwayi*) and passerine (*Pinaroloxias inornata*). This last one is actually a descendant of those found on the Galapagos Islands.

However, the main attraction on Isla del Coco is unquestionably the marine setting that surrounds it. Several years ago, the island acquired an international scuba diving reputation. Most of the 2,800 visitors who come here each year are experienced divers who stay for about ten days to discover a fabulous world of 18 coral species and over 300 fish species. They encounter various species of sharks, including hammerheads (*Sphyrna Lewin*) and white sharks (*Triaenodon obesus*). Reports even say that it is not uncommon to observe up to 500 sharks in the course of a single dive!

Since there are no services on the island and camping is prohibited, visitors must sleep on boats. Most of the cruises leave from the town of Puntarenas and last between one and two weeks. The crossing alone requires about 36 hours. The agencies **Okeanos Aggressor** *(☎290-6203, ⇒290-6205)* and **Undersea Hunter** *(☎228-6535, ⇒289-7334)* offer 10-day, all-inclusive (transportation, cabin, meals, diving gear, guide, etc.) scuba-diving excursions *(about $2,500/person)*.

## South of Puntarenas

### Puntarenas to Jacó

**Playa Doña Ana** and **Boca Barranca** are two little beaches situated a little over

**● ATTRACTIONS**

1. Zoo
2. Minigolf

**⬡ ACCOMMODATIONS**

1. Amapola (R)
2. Aparthotel Flamboyant
3. Aparthotel Gaviotas
4. Aparthotel Sole d'Oro
5. Balcón del Mar
6. Best Western Jacó Beach Resort
7. Cabinas Alice (R)
8. Cabinas Antonio
9. Cabinas Cindy
10. Cabinas Clarita (R)
11. Cabinas El Coral
12. Cabinas Jacó Colonial
13. Cabinas Kalu
14. Cabinas Mar de Plata
15. Cabinas Zabamar
16. Chalets Santa Ana
17. Club del Mar (R)
18. El Mar
19. Hotel Cocal
20. Hotel Colibrí
21. Hotel Copacabana
22. Hotel Jacó Fiesta
23. Hotel Pochote Grande
24. Hotel Tangeri
25. La Cometa
26. Los Ranchos
27. Mango Mar
28. Mar de Luz
29. Marparaíso
30. Paraíso del Sol
31. Santimar (R)
32. Tropical Paradise
33. Villas Estrellamar
34. Villas Jacó Princess
35. Villas Miramar

(R): Restaurant

**◇ RESTAURANTS**

1. Banana Café
2. Buena Nota
3. Dountoun Jungle Bar
4. El Recreo
5. El Riconcito Peruano
6. Killer Munchies
7. La Bruja
8. La Hacienda
9. La Ostra
10. Los Faroles
11. Pollo Happy Land
12. Poncho Villa
13. Restaurante, Pizzería y Heladería Esperanza

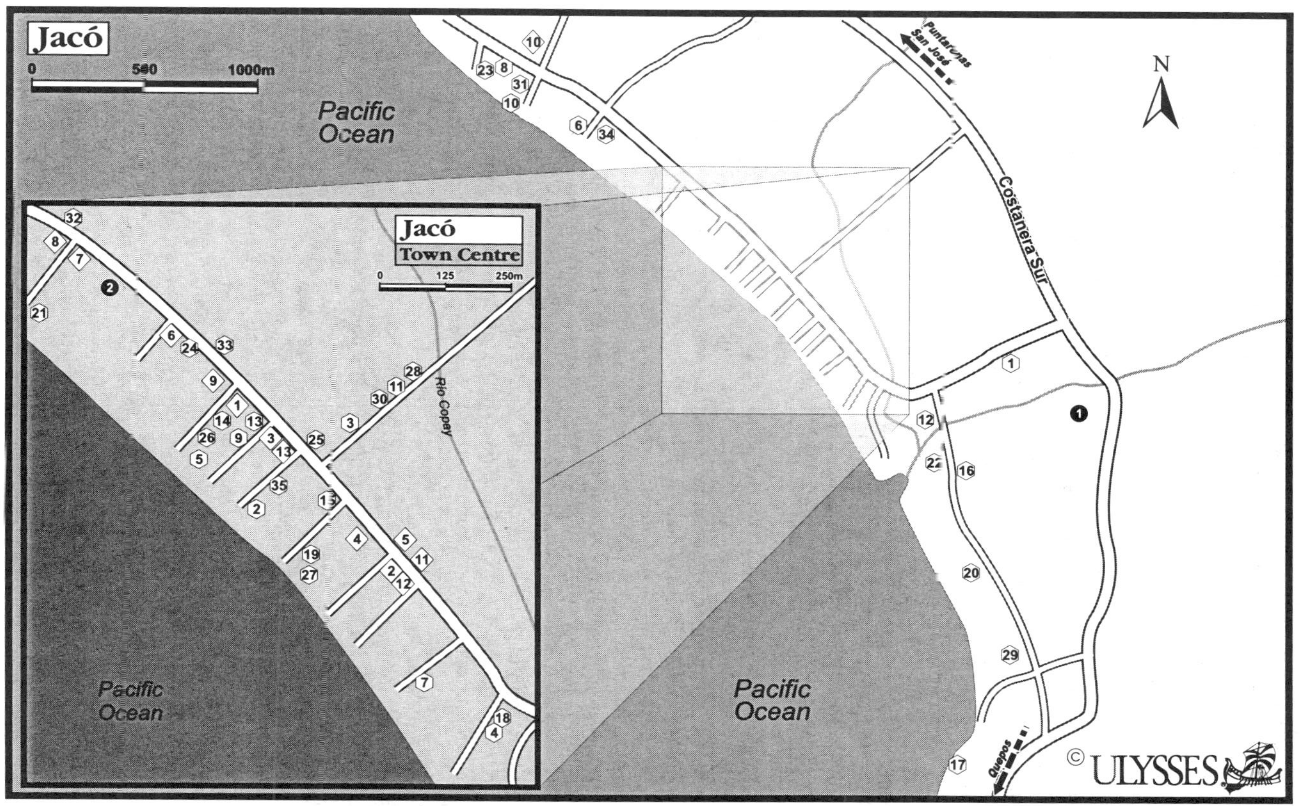
Jacó
0 500 1000m
Pacific Ocean
Puntarenas
San José
N
Costanera Sur
Jacó
Town Centre
0 125 250m
Río Copay
Pacific Ocean
Pacific Ocean
Quepos
© ULYSSES

10 kilometres southeast of Puntarenas. Because they are the first really clean beaches in the area, they can get very busy on weekends and during any Costa Rican holiday. Picnic tables, small food stands and a changing area are found on the edge of Playa Doña Ana. Surfing is pretty good at both of these beaches. There are relatively few places to stay around here, given the area's proximity to the Central Valley, which is where most of the visitors are from.

Two kilometres south of Reserva Biológica Carara (see p 291) is a little road that climbs up into the hills surrounding the **Catarata Manantial Agua Viva** ★, apparently the tallest waterfall in the country. The road winds around hairpin turns for several kilometres before it reaches the hills' summit, providing a spectacular and beautiful view. (Be especially careful when descending this road as you head back; in addition to being very steep, it is covered with gravel that are like little marbles under the tires and can easily make the car slip.) The waterfall can be reached from the first entrance, run by a private entrepreneur (a little cabin on the right), but we recommend continuing four kilometres to the "official" entrance run by the La Catarata Manantial Agua Viva *(☎661-1787)* ecological complex, which offers guided walks. There is a picnic area adjoining this entrance. Bring along lots of drinking water for this hike, which can be pleasant if you are well-prepared, as it passes rivers suited to swimming.

Across from the road to the waterfall (on the national highway San José – Jacó), there is an access road to the little village of **Tárcoles**. Tárcoles is of interest only because it has a nearby river that is inhabited by crocodiles (they sometimes carry birds as "accessories"!). Mario Fernando offers trips on the river to see this sight *($30; Jungle Crocodile Safari; ☎292-2316 or 383-4612, ⇌292-3808)*.

**Playa de Punta Leona** is a pretty little gray-sand beach nestled in a small, calm bay. **Playa Blanca** is situated a few hundred metres south of Punta Leona and has larger waves. The Ridley Scott movie *1492 – Conquest of Paradise*, starring Gérard Depardieu, was filmed here. Although all Costa Rica's beaches are public, the edges of Punta Leona and Playa Blanca are owned by the Punta Leona resort. Buses travel to Playa Blanca from the centre of the Punta Leona resort every half-hour from 8am to 5pm daily.

**Herradura** is the largest public beach closest to San José . Situated seven kilometres north of Jacó, it is shaded by vegetation, which is a blessing in the region's heat, and partly covered by rocks. It is not particularly charming, but it is clean and the water is calm. This beach is divided into two sections: the one to the north is more public, while the one to the south is more residential, and next to the old village. The beach is completely overrun on the weekend. Like Playa Doña Ana, this area has few hotels.

### The Jacó Region

**Playa Jacó** ★★ is a beautiful, wide, dark sand beach with giant waves that attracts surfers and sunbathers alike. Jacó started being developed long before Tamarindo in Guanacaste, and is therefore larger. Hotels are abundant and almost all the amenities of urban life are available. City officials decided to make the beach look like a vacation resort with a large access boulevard from the national highway and a main street parallel to the beach. The latter is broad and well landscaped with sidewalks separated from the road by

The pretty church in Sarchí's central park. The town is also known for its woodcrafts.
*- D. R.*

Taking a break from herding the cattle in Guanacaste.
*- R. M.*

Costa Rica's exceptional flora. The country contains 5% of the earth's plant and animal species. - *D.R.*

Frogs are among the most commonly seen animals in Costa Rica. - *D. R.*

decorative shrubbery. The street is lined by shops and restaurants of all sorts. With the cross streets that branch off from this main strip, there is enough room here for a whole armada of tourists! Many foreign travel agencies offer all sorts of package deals for vacations in Jacó.

Jacó is also an ideal place to "see and be seen." The spot attracts very trendy surfers, which has led to the development of a series of hip businesses. Jacó is a popular and lively place, even more so because it is so easily accessible for a weekend or even for a day trip for most Costa Ricans who live in the Central Valley. The streets that lead to the beach in the centre of town are especially lively, both during the day and at night.

Jacó has a **zoo** *($6; just south of Jacó, on the Jacó-Quepos national highway)* where visitors can have their pictures taken with small animals indigenous to the country (monkeys, toucans, parrots, etc.). In addition to the admission fee, donations are welcomed for the animals' upkeep. The zoo is at the foot of a mountain that can be explored on marked trails of various levels of difficulty. There is also a **miniature golf course** in Jacó, on the main street along the river.

### Jacó to Quepos

Because there are still only a few hotels around **Playa Hermosa**, it is a quiet spot, although it is popular with surfers.

Driving on the national highway toward Quepos provides some excellent opportunities for admiring the sea since the road often runs quite high above the ocean, especially between Playa Hermosa and Jacó. Some lookouts have been laid out along the way specifically for this purpose.

A little over 20 kilometres south of Jacó, **Esterillos Este**, **Esterillos Centro** and **Esterillos Oeste** are little neighbouring communities separated by small rivers. Their beaches have some pretty heavy surf (the waves can even be violent at times), and are covered with dark sand that is even finer than at the beach in Jacó. Laid out side by side, the Esterillos beaches are very long – several kilometres in fact – and are mostly bordered by residential areas. The few hotels that have opened here thus offer their guests a very tranquil setting, especially compared to the urban bustle of nearby Jacó.

The only sizeable town between Jacó and Quepos is **Parrita**. The city itself is of little interest, but the nearby beaches are attracting an increasing number of hotels and, therefore, vacationers.

### The Quepos Region

**Quepos ★** is quite pretty overall. Many different bars, restaurants and other businesses are concentrated in the centre of town. It is the last large town in the area. However, visitors should avoid swimming in Quepos because the water is polluted here.

### Quepos to Manuel Antonio

**Playa Espadilla** is the main beach between Quepos and Manuel Antonio park. It is a very beautiful beach that is popular with surfers for its waves: swimmers should be prudent, however. Hotels are spread along the long strip of forested coastal land above the beach. The landscape is hilly, and thus provides magnificent views of the ocean. Hotels have taken advantage of

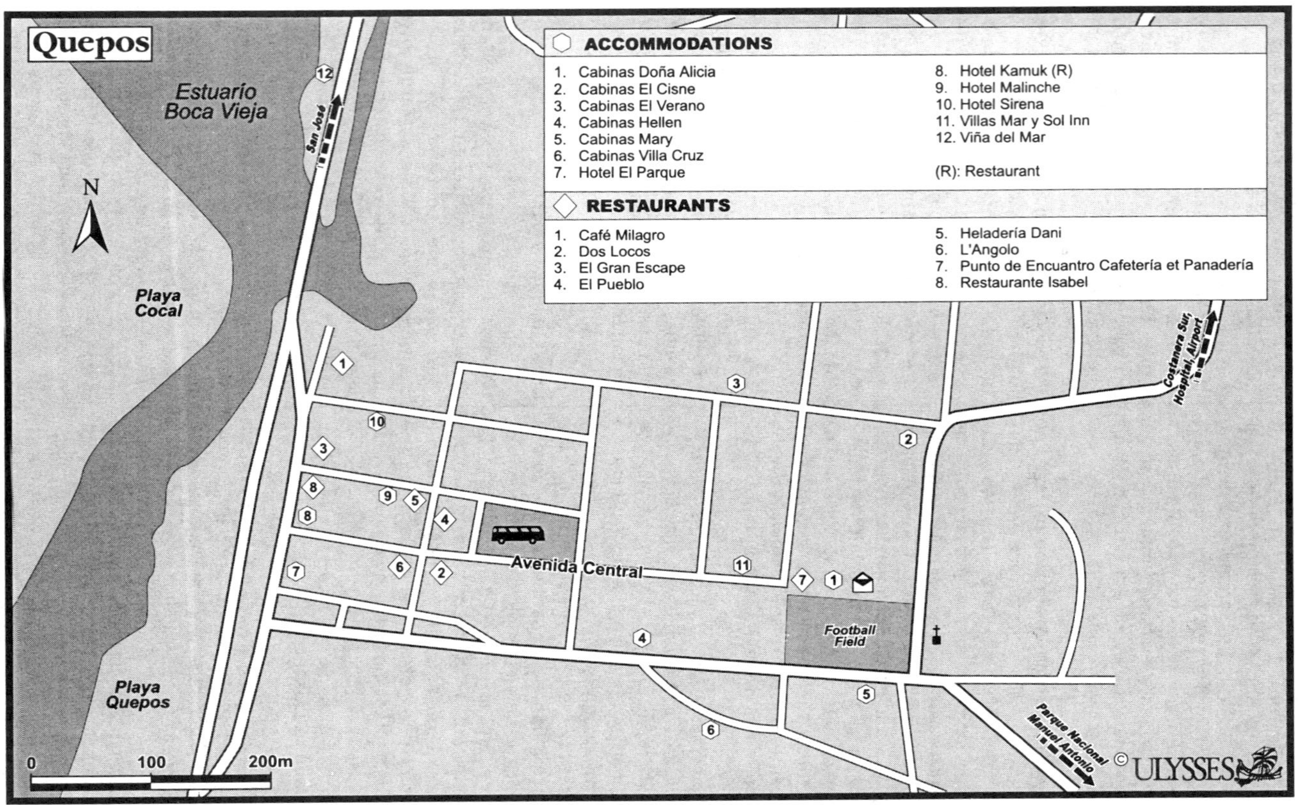
Quepos
ACCOMMODATIONS
1. Cabinas Doña Alicia
2. Cabinas El Cisne
3. Cabinas El Verano
4. Cabinas Hellen
5. Cabinas Mary
6. Cabinas Villa Cruz
7. Hotel El Parque
8. Hotel Kamuk (R)
9. Hotel Malinche
10. Hotel Sirena
11. Villas Mar y Sol Inn
12. Viña del Mar
(R): Restaurant
RESTAURANTS
1. Café Milagro
2. Dos Locos
3. El Gran Escape
4. El Pueblo
5. Heladería Dani
6. L'Angolo
7. Punto de Encuentro Cafetería et Panadería
8. Restaurante Isabel
Estuario Boca Vieja
San José
N
Playa Cocal
Playa Quepos
Avenida Central
Football Field
Costanera Sur, Hospital, Airport
Parque Nacional Manuel Antonio
0
100
200m
© ULYSSES

this topography and are built in such a way as to give guests fabulous views of the beautiful blue and green expanses of the surrounding ocean and countryside.

A series of small *sodas* and little shops line the last kilometre of Espadilla beach before Manuel Antonio park, which was established to preserve at least a part of this superb natural setting.

## Reserva Biológica Carara

A birdwatcher's paradise, the **Reserva Biológica Carara** ★ *($6; every day 7am to 5pm; ☎416-6576, ⇄416-7402)* was created in April 1978 to protect this part of the province of Puntarenas. Situated only 17 kilometres from Jacó, one of the country's tourist hot spots, the reserve encompasses some 4,700 hectares of forest, the preservation of which remains a priority especially since many animal species depend on it. The Carara reserve, which is part of the national parks system, ranks fifth among the most frequented parks in the country, with an average of close to 30,000 visitors annually (1996).

The reserve comprises two types of forest: tropical rainforest, which predominates in the southwest of the country, and tropical dry forest, which is found in the northwest of Costa Rica, mainly in the province of Guanacaste. The reserve is situated in the transition zone between these forests. With altitudes varying from around sea-level to just over 1,000 metres, it contains five different Holdridge Life Zones, or natural habitats.

Carara's lush forest is made up of 750 species of plants and trees, which sometimes reach gigantic heights of over 50 metres. Among the plants most characteristic of the region, are the *espavel* (*Anacardium exelsum*), *ceiba*, *higuerón*, *gallinazo*, *javillo* (*Hura crepitans*) and *guácimo colorado* (*Guazuma ulmifolia*).

If you are arriving from San José (90 kilometres, about two hours driving), you should definitely stop at the **Río Tárcoles bridge** to see the **crocodiles**. This river is the reserve's northwestern border, and it is easy to park on the south side of the bridge since many cars and buses stop here regularly. The last time we were here we were treated to the sight of a dozen crocodiles wading under the bridge, some of which were at least five metres long! Unfortunately, the Río Tárcoles is not very clean, and along with the crocodiles, you will spot some old discarded tires that tarnish the charm of the surrounding landscape.

It is a happy realization that the reserve's varied fauna have adapted and thrived within the limits of this wild territory surrounded by farm- and pastureland. The most commonly seen animals are monkeys (white-faced capuchins, howler and spider monkeys), sloths, agoutis, coatis and Virginia white-tailed deer. Mammals such as coyotes, anteaters and big cats (jaguars, pumas, ocelots) are very rarely spotted, though you might occasionally see tracks. Going around a bend in a path may result in a surprise encounter with an iguana, a lizard, a toad or a little black-and-green venomous frog. However the reserve also has several species of snakes, including the fearsome "fer-de-lance" (spearhead), which Costa Ricans call *terciopelo*.

Despite all these attractions, it is the winged fauna that attracts most visitors. In fact, with its high number of bird species per square kilometre, Reserva Biológica Carara is classed as one of the best birding spots in Costa Rica. Aside from the overwhelming quantity – the total number of species has yet to be determined – Carara has some truly unique kinds of birds. Visitors can see the superb and impressive **scarlet macaw** (*Ara macao*), which Costa Ricans call *lapa roja*. These huge multicoloured parrots are now very rare outside of Parque Nacional de Corcovado, in the southwest, and Reserva Biológica Carara. One of the best spots for observing scarlet macaws is the Río Tárcoles bridge where they make their nocturnal migration at about 5pm, flying from the reserve's tropical forest to the mangroves at the mouth of the river. The number of scarlet macaws in the region is estimated at around 300. Among the other birds likely to be spotted are toucans, trogons, hawks and hummingbirds.

Reserva Biológica Carara also has 15 archeological sites, dating back to the area's two main eras of settlement; the Pavas era (from 300 BC to the 4th century AD), and the Cartago period (from the 9th century to the 16th century AD). These sites mainly attract archeology students, though visitors can reach them with the help of a guide.

The reserve has two official hiking trails. The **Las Aráceas** (one km) trail forms a loop that can be walked in under an hour. It penetrates the primary forest and runs through four Life Zones where many species of flora and birds can be seen. The **Laguna Meándrica** trail (4 km each way) winds through a secondary forest to a spot near Río Tárcoles. Monkeys and brown coatis, called *pizotes* in Costa Rica, are frequently encountered along this path. Leave yourself about three hours to make the eight-kilometre round trip with enough time to appreciate the reserve's wildlife and vegetation.

To see a large variety of animals and identify the many plants and trees in the reserve, we strongly recommend that you go with a naturalist guide who knows the area. Most hotels around Jacó and Quepos, and in San José, offer guided tours of the Carara reserve. As well, many agencies that specialize in outdoor activities, such as **Geotour** *(☎534-1867, ⇌227-4029)*, **Costa Rica Expeditions** *(☎257-0766, ⇌257-1665)* and **Expediciones Tropicales** *(☎257-4171, ⇌257-4124)* (all three of which are based in San José) organize guided tours of the reserve. These tours cost about $70 per person, including round-trip transportation from San José, breakfast, lunch, admission and a naturalist guide. Sometimes the day is topped off by a trip to the beach in Jacó, for a relaxing swim before returning to the hotel.

## Parque Nacional Manuel Antonio

The Quepos region has quickly become one of Costa Rica's most developed tourist destinations. Within just a few years, hotels have sprouted up like mushrooms, considerably reducing the amount of lush vegetation found in the area. Fortunately, it was decided early on to protect a portion of this territory by creating the Manuel Antonio national recreational park on November 15, 1972, which became **Parque Nacional Manuel Antonio ★★** *($6; Tue to Sun 7am to 5pm; ☎777-0644, ⇌777-0654)* in August 1982.

Situated only seven kilometres from the village of Quepos, and 157 kilometres from San José, Parque Nacional Manuel Antonio is one of the smallest parks in Costa Rica, with an area of

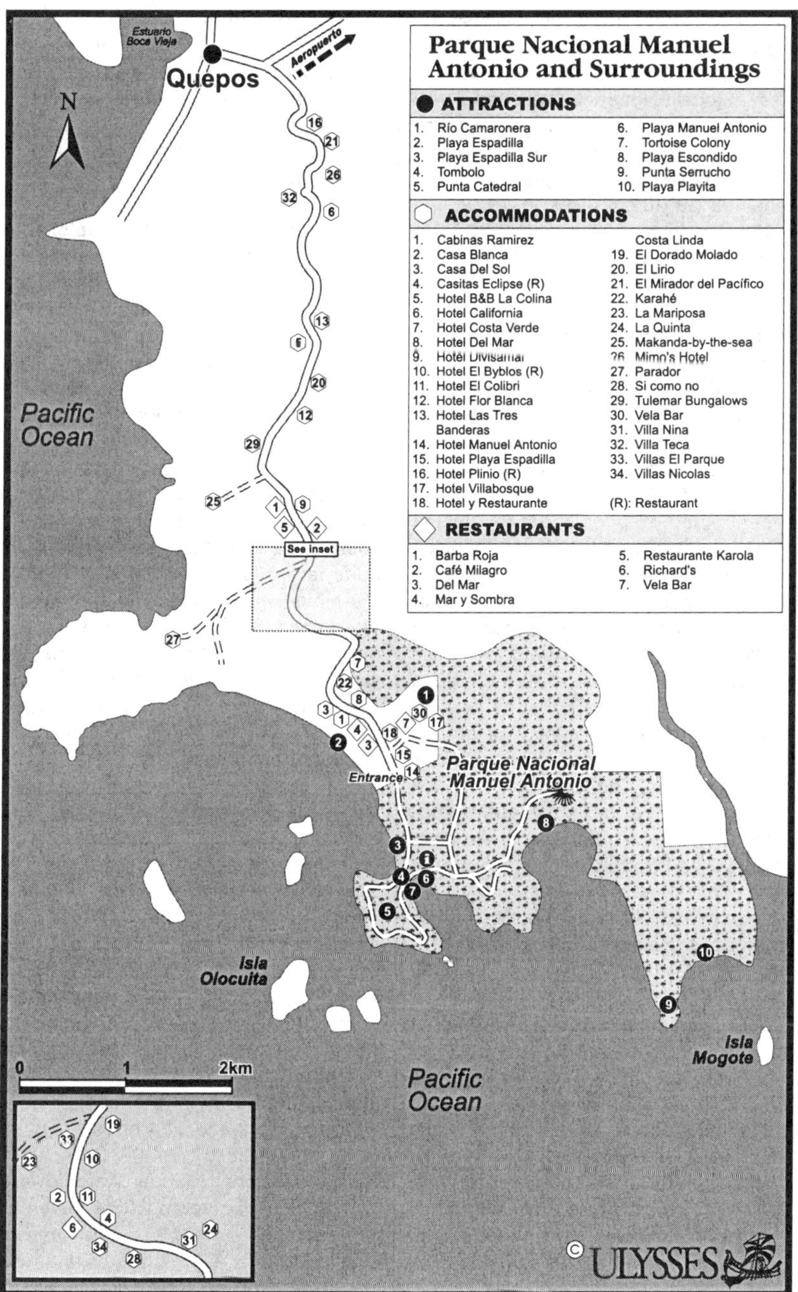
Parque Nacional Manuel Antonio and Surroundings
ATTRACTIONS
1. Río Camaronera
2. Playa Espadilla
3. Playa Espadilla Sur
4. Tombolo
5. Punta Catedral
6. Playa Manuel Antonio
7. Tortoise Colony
8. Playa Escondido
9. Punta Serrucho
10. Playa Playita
ACCOMMODATIONS
1. Cabinas Ramirez
2. Casa Blanca
3. Casa Del Sol
4. Casitas Eclipse (R)
5. Hotel B&B La Colina
6. Hotel California
7. Hotel Costa Verde
8. Hotel Del Mar
9. Hotel Divisamar
10. Hotel El Byblos (R)
11. Hotel El Colibri
12. Hotel Flor Blanca
13. Hotel Las Tres Banderas
14. Hotel Manuel Antonio
15. Hotel Playa Espadilla
16. Hotel Plinio (R)
17. Hotel Villabosque
18. Hotel y Restaurante Costa Linda
19. El Dorado Molado
20. El Lirio
21. El Mirador del Pacífico
22. Karahé
23. La Mariposa
24. La Quinta
25. Makanda-by-the-sea
26. Mimo's Hotel
27. Parador
28. Si como no
29. Tulemar Bungalows
30. Vela Bar
31. Villa Nina
32. Villa Teca
33. Villas El Parque
34. Villas Nicolas
(R): Restaurant
RESTAURANTS
1. Barba Roja
2. Café Milagro
3. Del Mar
4. Mar y Sombra
5. Restaurante Karola
6. Richard's
7. Vela Bar
Estuario Boca Vieja
Quepos
Aeropuerto
N
Pacific Ocean
See inset
Entrance
Parque Nacional Manuel Antonio
Isla Olocuita
Isla Mogote
Pacific Ocean
0
1
2km
© ULYSSES

682.7 hectares. However, it is also the second most visited park in the country, after Parque Nacional Volcán Poás. Since its inception, the popularity of this park has skyrocketed, as evidenced by the number of visitors surveyed over the years: while the park received 29,087 visitors in 1979, the number rose to 191,493 in 1992, an increase of 558%, or an average of 445 more visitors per day!

Park authorities were forced to limit the number of visitors to better manage the area and protect the fauna and flora before it could be subjected to irreparable damage. Today, the number of tourists is limited to 600 during the week and 800 on weekends. As well, the number of people on the hiking trails is restricted to 400 at any given time, and no more than 300 people are allowed on the beaches at one time. The number of hikers per group is also limited and the departures of these groups are spaced out so that there are not too many walkers in one area at once. Camping in the park is strictly prohibited. On Mondays, the park is closed to the public. One of the decisions made by park authorities, which halved the number of visitors per year (90,741 in 1995), was to increase park admission fees from $2 to $15 per person in 1994! Much to our relief, the price of admission was decreased to $6 in April 1996.

Parque Nacional Manuel Antonio is overflowing with natural beauty that will enrapture any visitor. Tropical dry forest meets rainforest in this transitional forest where primary and secondary forests stand side by side, and lagoons can be found along with vegetation that grows only along the beaches. However, the park's old-growth forest was hard-hit by Hurricane Gert on September 14, 1993. Many thousands of trees were knocked down, and flora that had taken decades to grow to maturity were destroyed in one fell swoop. Fortunately, the hurricane did not hit the seaside and the beach regions with as much ferocity, leaving these paradisiac settings relatively intact, compared to the wooded hills.

One of the most deplorable consequences of this hurricane was the disappearance of about half the population of marmosets (*Saimiri oerstedii*), which Costa Ricans call *mono tití*. The marmoset is the smallest of the four monkey species found in Costa Rica, but, more importantly, it is the rarest of the four. The Parque Nacional Manuel Antonio shelters a few families, as does the Parque Nacional Corcovado in the southwest of the country. Incidentally, although it is quite rare to spot a marmoset, visitors are almost guaranteed a sighting of a white-faced capuchin or to hear the powerful cries of the howler monkeys, which are much smaller than one would expect (they are 50 to 60 centimetres tall, and usually weigh between five and eight kilograms).

Other animals that populate the park include coatis, agoutis, iguanas, sloths, racoons, lizards and many species of snakes. Of these last, a few are venomous, so visitors must be constantly alert on the trails or when taking breaks. **Always** look down when you walk, and carefully examine leaves, plants and trees before touching any of them. These simple safety rules apply to every region of Costa Rica. Other species that live in the park include 109 mammals and 184 birds.

Parque Nacional Manuel Antonio also has a pleasant climate with an average temperature of 27°C. The annual precipitation is 3.8 metres of rain, and the dry season extends from December to April. The park is criss-crossed by a small network of hiking trails that total about five kilometres, and permit visitors to admire all of its natural attractions, including four magnificent beaches, as well as pretty points that jut into the ocean and a lush forest bustling with life.

To reach the park, cross the mouth of the Camaronera stream, south of the village of Manuel Antonio. Now, you are near **Playa Espadilla**, which most locals call "first beach." The path then runs along the second beach, **Playa Espadilla Sur**, which leads to a small bay. This 800-metre-long beach is not recommended for swimming because the waves are especially powerful here.

At the end of the beach stands a geomorphological formation that is unique in the world, the **tombolo of Punta Catedral**. The tombolo is a strip of land that formed over the millennia between what was once Catedral island and the mainland. This spectacular formation was created by a sand bar on which vegetation flourished until it finally became a natural path of grasses and trees. Researchers estimate that it took 100,000 years to create this geomorphological phenomena, which is one of the most beautiful of its kind on the planet. It takes about an hour to hike around Punta Catedral, a distance of 1.5 kilometres. Along the way are majestic trees, among the oldest in the park, and a superb lookout over the Pacific Ocean.

The third beach, called **Playa Manuel Antonio**, lies near Punta Catedral. This is the most popular beach in the park because it consists of beautiful white sand and is safe to swim at. The spot is also renowned for snorkelling, especially during the dry season from December to April when the water is incredibly clear. There are 19 species of coral, 17 species of algae, 10 species of sponge, 24 species of crustaceans, and 78 species of fish that live in the area, many of them very colourful.

Manuel Antonio beach also served as a sea turtle hunting ground about 1,000 years ago. The natives who lived in the area lined up a series of stones in a semi-circle, creating a natural dam to prevent the turtles from returning to sea when the tide went out. When the tide is at its lowest, it is possible to see these turtle traps at the western end of the beach.

Further east is **Playa Escondido** (the fourth beach), which is less frequented and quieter because it is partly covered by water at high tide. Not far from here, a trail climbs to a lookout from which there is a view of **Punta Serrucho**, which jauntily juts into the sea. The fifth and last beach, **Playita**, is hidden on the other side of this point.

## OUTDOOR ACTIVITIES

### Cycling

The area around the villages of **Montezuma**, **Cabuya** and **Malpaís** is perfect for cycling trips since the unpaved roads are not very busy. Many hotels in the area rent bicycles, as does the **Surf & Sport Camp** *($10/day, ☎642-0047)* in Malpaís.

### Hiking

The **Refugio Nacional de Fauna Silvestre Curú** (see p 282) has a pleasant network of trails from which the abundant and diverse wildlife can be observed.

In the **Reserva Natural Absoluta Cabo Blanco** (see p 284), you can meander through the secondary forest to a superb beach along the two trails open to visitors.

Walking is the best way to discover the **Reserva Biológica Carara** (see p 291), where you can admire scarlet macaws and crocodiles among other animals.

The hiking trails in **Parque Nacional Manuel Antonio** (see p 292) lead to superb beaches, to points of land that jut into the ocean and to lookouts over the surrounding area.

## Surfing

The villages of **Malpaís** and **Santa Teresa** are becoming more and more recognized as good surfing destinations. To take an introductory course, rent a board, watch videos or get tips from the surfing fanatics, head to the **Surf & Sport Camp** in Malpaís (see p 302).

You can rent *($10/day)* or buy *($200 to $500)* surfboards in Jacó. Around Jacó, the best beaches for surfing are **Playa Doña Ana** and its neighbour **Boca Barranca; Playa Hermosa**, the **Esterillos** beaches as well as **Espadilla** beach, between Punta Quepos and Manuel Antonio park, where some of the classiest hotels in the region are located.

David Klostermann *(☎643-1569)* gives surfing lessons *($25/hour)* in the **Jacó** area.

## Scuba Diving and Snorkelling

Located over 500 kilometres offshore in the Pacific, **Parque Nacional Isla del Coco** (see p 285), is unquestionably the most spectacular destination for scuba diving.

**Isla Tortuga** is a natural paradise of beaches and crystalline waters off the coast of Curú and the Nicoya Peninsula. Snorkelling here is easy, pleasant and safe. The vast majority of hotels around Montezuma and Tambor, as well as the **Montezuma tourist office** (see p 281), organize daytrips with snorkelling equipment included. From San José, **Calypso Tours** *(☎256-2727, ≠256-6767)* and **Bay Island Cruises** *(☎258-3536, ≠258-1189)* also offer unforgettable day trips to Isla Tortuga. Budget about $100 per person for the day, which includes transportation by bus, the ferry crossing, activities, food, snorkelling equipment, etc.

At **Parque Nacional Manuel Antonio** (see p 292), snorkelling is reportedly excellent near Playa Manuel Antonio, which can only be reached by foot.

## Horseback Riding

The southern section of the Nicoya Peninsula is marvellous for horseback riding, and the long beaches and hills around **Montezuma**, **Cabuya** and **Malpaís** offer breathtaking scenery. While you can rent horses and hire a guide almost anywhere (ask at your hotel), the excursions organized by Barbara MacGregor, a Canadian, at the "ranch-hotel" **Finca Los Caballos** (see p 300) near Montezuma, have an excellent reputation in the area.

David Klostermann *(☎643-1569)* leads very worthwhile outings on horseback in the area surrounding **Jacó**. The horses are well-treated and are gentle, and David, who used to own horses in California, is very friendly. He also gives riding lessons.

**Playa Hermosa Stables** *(☎643-3808)* organizes horseback riding excursions

*($35/person for 4 hrs.)*; inquire at the David hotel in Playa Hermosa.

### Birdwatching

If you are a birding buff, you will certainly want to see the superb **scarlet macaws** that brighten the skies of **Reserva Biológica Carara** (see p 291).

### Golf

Golfers can indulge in their favourite sport at the **La Roca Beach Resort and Country Club** in **Caldera**, south of the town of Puntarenas.

A very pretty nine-hole course awaits golfers at the **Tango Mar Resort and Country Club** *(☎289-9328 or 683-0001)* in **Playa Tambor**.

### Water Sports

Punta Leona has an organization that specializes in all sorts of water activities at sea and on the nearby Río Tárcoles: **J.D.'s Watersports** *(☎257-3857, 256-8268 or 669-0511 ext. 34, ⇄256-6391, jdwater@sol.racsa.co.cr)*. Deep-sea fishing, sea kayaking, snorkelling, windsurfing and river cruises are offered – and more!

## ACCOMMODATIONS

### The Puntarenas Region

Be sure that your room is equipped at least with a fan, because the city is hot, especially in the dry season.

**Pensión Cabezas** *($; sb, ⊗; Av. 1, Calle 2/4, Puntarenas, ☎661-1045)* is friendly, clean and very reasonable. The rooms are rather small.

Located near the market, **Ayi Con** *($-$$; sb/pb, ⊗/≡; Calle 2 Av. 1/3, Puntarenas, ☎661-0164 or 661-1477)* is clean, but has some rather dark rooms.

The cleanliness of the rooms at **Chorotega** *($$; sb/pb; Calle 1, Av. 3, Puntarenas, ☎661-0998)* makes this hotel an excellent value for travellers with limited budgets. Also, it is located near the downtown bus terminal.

About three kilometres east of downtown, but still on the peninsula, the **Costa Rica Yacht Club** *($$$; hw, ≈; Puntarenas, ☎661-0784, ⇄661-2518)* offers plain, but comfortable rooms. However, it is mainly reserved for club members. Free mooring for sailboats.

The old wood building of the **Imperial** *($$$; sb/pb, ⊗; near Calle Central and Paseo de los Turistas, Puntarenas, ☎661-0579)* charms almost anyone who sees it. It has a good location, right by the beach and near the bus stops. The upper rooms have balconies and a view of the ocean. The ground-floor rooms, however, are darker.

West of the city and near the ferries, the little **Hotel La Punta** *($$$; hw, ⊗/≡, ≈, ℜ; Calle 35, Av. 1, Puntarenas, ☎661-1900, ⇄661-0690)* is clean and quiet. The rooms have balconies.

After 35 years, **Hotel Tioga** *($$$-$$$$ bkfst incl.; hw, pb, ≡, ≈, cafeteria; Paseo de los Turistas, Calle 17/19, Puntarenas, ☎661-0271, ⇄661-0127)* is still popular. The clean rooms have views of the ocean or the pool. The upstairs dining room has a beautiful view of the open sea.

**Las Brisas** *($$$$; hw, pb, ≡, ≈; Paseo de los Turistas, Calle 31, Puntarenas, ☎661-4040, ⇄661-2120)* has large, clean rooms.

Next to the Yacht Club, the **Colonial** *($$$$$ bkfst incl.; hw, ≈, ℜ; Puntarenas, ☎661-1833, ⇄661-2969)* and the **Portobello** *($$$$; hw, ≈, ≡, ℜ; Puntarenas, ☎661-2122 or 661-1322, ⇄661-0036)* are two excellent hotels that have pleasant rooms and good restaurants. The grounds of the latter are ravishing. Free yacht mooring.

**Hotel Yadrán** *($$$$$; hw, pb, tv, ≡, ≈; Paseo de los Turistas, Calle 35, Puntarenas, ☎661-2662, ⇄661-1944)* is a large, beautiful hotel complex (bar, casino, nightclub), pleasantly located near the end of the sand spit on which the city is built.

## The Southern Nicoya Peninsula

### Paquera

There are rudimentary **campsites** *($2/person)* on the road that leads to the ferry landing. Inquire with the shopkeeper at the little grocery store next to the sites.

The little village of Paquera also has a few modestly priced lodgings. **Cabinas y Restaurante Ginana** *($; pb, ⊗, ℜ; ☎641-0119)* is one of the most popular in the area. It has about 20 clean, simple rooms.

### North of Paquera

#### Playa Naranjo

Near the ferry landing are a service station, a grocery store and the hotel and restaurant **El Ancla** *($$$; pb, ≡, ≈ℜ; ☎/⇄661-4148)*. The hotel has 10 airconditioned rooms with small terraces and hammocks. The open-air restaurant, which has a public telephone, is a pleasant place to wait for the ferry and munch on a sandwich and tasty home-made french fries.

Near the dock for the ferry from Puntarenas, the **Oasis del Pacífico** *($$$ bkfst incl.; pb, hw, ⊗, ≈, ℜ; ☎/⇄661-1555)* hotel has 36 rooms with private washrooms and hot water. The hotel's advertisement promises free lodgings for one night if the sun does not shine during the day! It has a pool, a tennis court, a volleyball court, a restaurant and a bar.

**Hotel Bahía Luminosa** *($$$$ bkfst incl.; pb, hw, ≡, ⊗, ≈, ℜ; ☎381-2296)* is on a hillside about 10 kilometres south of Playa Naranjo. It has 14 clean rooms for $75 a night. The many water sports include fishing, scuba diving, sailing, etc.

#### Bahía Gigante

Activities centre around sport fishing at the **Bahía el Gigante** *($$$-$$$$; pb, hw, ⊗, ≈, ℜ; ☎/⇄661-2442)* hotel. There are rooms or condos for rent, both of which are very comfortable. The restaurant serves Costa Rican and international cuisine.

#### Isla Gitana

Right in the middle of Bahía Gigante, a few minutes by boat from the shore, **Isla Gitana** *($$-$$$ fb; pb/sb; ☎661-2994, ⇄661-2833)* was once called "Isla de los Muertos" because a native burial ground was discovered on the island. Three types of accommodation are offered: basic rooms with private washrooms and cold water, rooms with shared bathrooms, and camping. The island has hiking trails that lead through the forest, as well as a white sand beach.

You can participate in various water sports including kayaking, windsurfing, scuba diving, etc.

**Paquera to Montezuma**

**Pochote**

Nestled in the magnificent hills near the little village of Vainilla, three kilometres from the beach of Pochote, is the **Hotel y Restaurante La Paillote** *($$$; pb, hw, ℜ; ☎/⇌683-0190)*. Franck, Aline, Alain and Christine, all from France, run the hotel and are very welcoming and friendly. Six pretty, comfortable rooms are found in three small *cabinas* with terraces. Perched a little higher, the restaurant (see p 317) has a panoramic view of the valley. Many excursions are organized, especially the spectacular horseback riding outings in the back country. A room for two costs $35 per night, and full board is available for $40 per person, per day *($250/week)*.

**Tambor**

If you prefer **camping**, head to the restaurant-bar **Los Gitanos** or to **Camping y Soda Albergue Río Mar**.

**Cabinas y Restaurante Cristina** *($-$$; cb/pb, ⊗, ℜ)* has six modestly priced rooms, three of which have private bathrooms. The restaurant serves excellent food at reasonable prices. When we were there, renovations were well underway and the terrace was almost finished.

Next door to Tambor Tropical (see further below) is **Hotel Dos Lagartos** *($$; sb/pb, ⊗, ℜ; ☎683-0236)*, which faces the ocean and rents out very simple, clean rooms with private or shared bathrooms. Ideal if you are travelling on a limited budget in this part of the Peninsula, where hotel rates are often exorbitant.

Located near the river, **Cabinas y Restaurante Tambor Beach** *($$; pb, ℜ)* has simple rooms at affordable rates.

The huge **Barceló Playa Tambor** *($$$$$ fb; pb, hw, ≡, ⊗, ctv, ☎, ℝ, ℜ; ☎683-0303, ⇌683-0304, tambor@sol.racsa.co.cr)* hotel complex offers an all-inclusive package with a multitude of activities. In addition to its 402 rooms, the hotel has restaurants, pools, three bars, a disco, etc. However, it has been accused of violating environmental laws to build the resort.

Pleasantly located next to a beautiful white sand beach, **Tango Mar** *($$$$$ bkfst incl.; pb, hw, ⊗, ≡, ⊛, ≈, ctv, ℜ; ☎289-9328 or 683-0001, ⇌289-8218)* is a luxurious vacation resort. It offers different types of lodging including large, comfortable rooms with views of the ocean, spacious palm-thatched *cabinas* on stilts, and sumptuous villas that can house up to six people. Prices vary from $145 to $320 per night, including breakfast. There are a nine-hole golf course, a pool, trails, a 12-metre waterfall, tennis courts, a volleyball court, etc. on the grounds. Among the organized activities are horseback riding, sport fishing, sailing and sea outings.

Facing the ocean on a property enhanced by lush vegetation, are the 10 spacious, attractively designed *cabinas* of **Tambor Tropical** *($$$$$ bkfst incl.; pb, hw, ⊗, K, ≈, ℜ; ☎683-0011, ⇌683-0013, tambort@aol.com)*. Each *cabina* is comprised of two rooms on two stories, both equipped with kitchenettes. The upper room, which has the better view, costs $150 per night, including breakfast, which is $25 more than the downstairs room. The rates here are the same year round. This spot is a true oasis of calm and relaxation if you want to escape from the pressures of work, which is why the owners from the United States decided not to put televisions, fax machines or telephones in the rooms. As well, children are not encouraged as guests. In addition to the swimming pool with whirlpool right next to the beach, various activities are organized in the area.

**Montezuma**

Montezuma has suffered from the effects of careless campers who have installed themselves haphazardly on the beach and around the village for some time now. It is recommended, and safer, to set up camp at **Rincón de los Monos** *($3)*, near the beach, 400 metres north of the village. There are toilets, showers, a *soda* and various equipment for rent (tents, hammocks, windsurfers, bicycles, etc.) here.

**Cabinas el Tucán** *($; sb, ⊗; ☎642-0284)*, which has been owned by a very friendly local woman, Marta Rodríguez, since 1990, comprises nine small, tidy rooms that are rented at affordable rates. However, the owner's dogs are quite noisy.

Across from Hotel Los Mangos, **Hotel Lucy** *($; sb, hw, ℜ; ☎642-0273)* has very simple rooms at modest rates. This small, rustic wooden hotel was built on the seaside. The restaurant serves typical Costa Rican cuisine. There is also a souvenir shop on the premises.

**Hotel Montezuma** *($; sb/pb, ⊗, ℜ; ☎642-0258, ⇌642-0058)* is located in the centre of the village, near the beach. It rents out 32 reasonably priced rooms, some with private bath. The site is quite noisy, however. The restaurant and the bar have a beautiful view of the ocean, and are very busy.

On the main street, adjacent to the municipal park, **Hotel La Aurora** *($$; pb, ⊗, #, ℝ; ☎/⇌642-0051)* rents out nine rooms, including an apartment that can accommodate up to five people and has a private terrace. This wooden building exudes an antiquated charm with its many hammocks and its library. Breakfast *($2-$3)* is served from 7am to 11am, while coffee, tea and purified water are available free of charge throughout the day.

Near Topsy bookstore, **El Chiringuito Tropical** *($$; pb, ⊗, ℜ; ☎642-0065)* has clean, simple rooms and a restaurant.

**Cabinas Linda Vista** *($$-$$$; pb, hw, ⊗, ℝ; ☎642-0274, ⇌642-0104)*, less than two kilometres from Montezuma, are four very clean *cabinas* that can accommodate up to four people each. Each *cabina* has its own refrigerator, terrace and hammocks, and an excellent view of the ocean below. The owner, Arnoldo Rojas, lives in a house near the *cabinas*.

Just before the village, on the right hand side, **Mochila Inn Jungle Cabins** *($$-$$$; sb; ☎642-0030)* rents rooms with shared bathrooms.

**Hotel La Cascada** *($$$; pb, ⊗, ℜ; ☎/⇌642-0057)* got its name because of its proximity to the imposing Río Montezuma waterfall. The 14 rooms are simple and clean *($30)*. The owners, William and Viky Sánchez, also run the restaurant next door to the hotel, which serves a regional cuisine that often includes fresh seafood.

Up in the mountains, 3 kilometres from Montezuma, **Finca Los Caballos**

*($$$; pb, hw, ⊗, ≈, ℜ; ☎/⇌642-0124, naturelc@sol.racsa.co.cr)* has a magnificent view of the forest and the sea. Conceived and built by a Canadian, Barbara MacGregor, this small farm resembles a Spanish ranch and includes eight pretty, comfortable rooms with terraces. It is the perfect place for relaxation, especially around the blue-tiled pool surrounded by a tropical garden. The open-air restaurant serves high quality international cuisine. Mrs. MacGregor is passionate about horseback riding and organizes various excursions in the area.

The nine superb wood-panelled rooms at **El Jardín** *($$$; pb, hw, ⊗, ℜ, ℝ; ☎/⇌642-0074)* provide perfect comfort and relaxation. Every room has its own terrace with a view of the sea. The hotel is slightly set back and is surrounded by beautiful, lush gardens. The restaurant serves Italian cuisine. There are also an information booth and a small souvenir shop on the premises.

Located near the church, at the end of the little street that runs behind the municipal park, the **Hotel Montezuma Pacífico** *($$$; pb, ≡, ⊗; ☎642-0204, in San José ☎222-7746)* rents single rooms *($30)*, some of which are airconditioned *($40)*. There is free coffee from 8am to 11am.

Next door, the **Hotel El Tajalín** *($$$ bkfst incl.; pb, hw, ≡, ⊗; ☎642-0061, ⇌642-0527)*, run by Italians, comprises 13 clean, comfortable rooms *($35)*, some of which are airconditioned *($50)*. When we were there, major renovations were under way. A cafeteria on the top floor provides a view of the ocean.

**Amor de Mar** *($$$-$$$$; sb/pb, hw, ⊗, ℜ; ☎/⇌642-0262, shoebox@sol.racsa.co.cr)*, owned by Richard and Ori Stocker, is just across the Río Montezuma bridge. The hotel was built on a magnificent plot along the Río Montezuma that faces the sea. The ground floor and upstairs rooms are prettily decorated and comfortable. Some of them have private terraces and ocean views. The site is dotted with palm trees between which many hammocks have been suspended. Homemade bread and yogurt are served at breakfast and lunch, among other treats.

About 400 metres from the village, toward Cabuya, **Los Mangos** *($$$-$$$$; pb, hw, ⊗, ≈, ℜ; ☎642-0076 or 642-0259, ⇌642-0050)* comprises 10 rooms and 10 bungalows, in addition to a charming pool. Some rooms in the main building have private bathrooms. The prettily decorated wooden bungalows have private washrooms with hot water, terraces and hammocks. The restaurant serves tasty Italian cuisine.

Magnificently located at the edge of the beach, and only a fifteen-minute walk from the village, the *cabinas* at **El Sano Banano Beach Bungalows** *($$$$; pb, ⊗, ℜ, ℝ; ☎/⇌642-0068, elbanano@sol.racsa.co.cr)* are owned by Lenny and Patricia Iacono. They also own the restaurant of the same name in the centre of the village. The very pretty and clean white *cabinas* look like igloos spread out in the lush forest two steps from the ocean. Some come with kitchenettes, and all of them are equipped with refrigerators, water purifiers, coffee machines and coffee. In addition to the *cabinas*, three rooms and a large apartment, which can accommodate up to eight guests and has a kitchen, are available. Because the site is not accessible by car, guests' luggage is transported by all-terrain vehicle (public parking in the village costs $2/day).

**South of Montezuma**

In Cabuya, the seaside **Cabinas El Yugo** *($$; pb, ⊗, K; ☎642-0303 or 453-1824)* include five pretty *cabinas* that can accommodate up to eight people each. They are equipped with kitchenettes and private bathrooms and are very affordable. Guests have free use of a washing machine.

Located seven kilometres from Montezuma and two kilometres from Cabo Blanco, the restaurant (see p 317) and *rancho* **El Ancla de Oro** *($$; sb/pb, ⊗, #, K, ℜ; ☎/⇉642-0369, ancladeoro@multicr.com)* offers vacationers a real wilderness experience in traditional *cabinas*, some of which have kitchenettes. Three small rooms can be rented in the main building. Various activities, including horseback riding and sea excursions, are organized.

Facing the sea, and 2.5 kilometres from Montezuma, **Cabinas Las Rocas** *($$-$$$; sb/pb, ⊗, K, ℜ; ☎/⇉642-0393)* offer several types of accommodation. These include four simple, clean rooms *($20)* with a shared bathroom in the family home of Reto Müller and Gisella Di Falco. In a nearby building there are two rooms with private bathrooms and fully equipped kitchens. The room on the ground floor can house two people *($30)*, and the upstairs room is large enough for three guests *($40)*. The small open-air restaurant serves healthy cuisine made with fresh ingredients.

At the time of our visit, the new owners of the **Cabo Blanco Hotel** *($$-$$$; pb, hw, ≡, ⊗, tv, ≈, ℜ)* were busy sprucing it up. The hotel is has nine simple rooms, with or without airconditioning. The open-air restaurant-bar, the pool and the magnificent beach complete the scene. Kayaks are available for guests free of charge.

**Hotel Celaje** *($$$; pb, hw, ⊗, ≈, ⊛, ℜ; ☎/⇉642-0374)* has seven superb two-story thatch-roofed *cabinas*, magnificently located at the edge of the white-sand beach. The pool, surrounded by palm trees, is one of the prettiest in the area. The open-air restaurant-bar serves international cuisine. Many water sports and other activities are organized.

**Northwest of Cabo Blanco**

**Malpaís**

With its wonderful seaside location, **Cabinas Mar Azul** *($-$$; pb, ⊗, ℜ; ☎/⇉640-0098)* also serves as a local meeting place where locals come to play pool and chat at the bar. The 11 *cabinas* are somewhat neglected but are modestly priced. You can also pitch a tent here for less than two dollars per person, with access to the showers and toilets.

**Cabinas Bosque Mar** *($$; pb, hw, ⊗, ℝ; ☎226-0475)* rents clean, comfortable *cabinas* that can accommodate up to four people each for $25. Gas stoves may be rented for three dollars per day.

The 10 rooms at the **Hotel Lauramar** *($$; pb, ⊗; ☎382-8876)*, lined up motel-style, are clean and well kept, although they don't seem to be too popular.

As its name indicates, the brand-new **Surf & Sport Camp** *($-$$$; sb/pb, hw, ⊗, ≈, ℜ; ⇉642-0047)* caters to people who come to the area to ride its famous waves. You can stay in simple but pretty shelters, in *cabinas* or in a superb, spacious, comfortable house. The landscaping is very pretty, and the large pool is inviting. Introductory surfing lessons are available *($15 to $20/hour)*, and surfboards and mountain bikes can be rented by the day *($10)*. The establishment also includes a restaurant (see p 317), a bar and pool tables.

Located two kilometres from Malpaís, on the little road that links Malpaís and Cabuya, the **Star Mountain Eco Resort** *($$$$ bkfst incl.; pb, hw, ⊗, ≈, ℜ: ☎296-2626, ext. 125000, info@starmountaineco.com)* provides rest and relaxation in the mountains on a vast 87-hectare estate. The long, covered terrace furnished with rocking chairs is the perfect place to unwind. Next door, an old wood house (*bancos*) is available to families and groups. The open-air restaurant-bar (see p 318) serves excellent food. The pool has a whirlpool and is surrounded by rich, dense forest teeming with life.

At the southern tip of Malpaís, almost at the border of the Cabo Blanco reserve, the **Sunset Reef Marine Lodge** *($$$$$; pb, hw, ≡, ⊗, ≈, ℜ, ⊛; ☎/⇌640-0012, sunreef@sol.racsa.co.cr)* is magnificently situated on a rocky point of land in the sea. This point is embellished by marvellous gardens, from which fantastic sunsets can be seen. Enjoy the sight from a hammock for the most idyllic experience! There is a pool with a whirlpool and a small waterfall, surrounded by greenery and tropical plants. The 14 wood-panelled rooms are large, comfortable and very clean. The meals are excellent. A friendly Belgian couple, Nathalie and Eric, make sure that guests have a pleasant, relaxing stay. Among the many activities offered (fishing, scuba diving, kayaking, horseback riding, etc.), there is one that is as educational as it is pleasant: early in the morning, the hotel manager, William Granados, leads a short nature walk in the surrounding area. A true bird lover, William can tell you all about the 83 bird species spotted here to date, and about the flora and various animal species that inhabit the area.

## Santa Teresa

**Cabinas Camping Zeneida's** *($; sb, ℜ)* has simple, rustic, inexpensive rooms overlooking the beach. You can also camp here for a small fee. The manager, Zeneida, prepares succulent meals if you ask in advance. You can even negociate the prices for the rooms, campsites and meals with this friendly woman.

Managed by a very laid-back man, the **Cabinas Santa Teresa** *($-$$; pb, ⊗, K)* are located across from the Saloon Laura Amarilla, about 200 metres from the ocean. Of the eight *cabinas*, two come with kitchenettes. The rooms are large, clean and inexpensive.

Set in the forest, about a hundred metres from the road, the three **Cabinas El Bosque** *($$; pb, K)* can accommodate up to four guests each. The A-frame *cabinas* are simple but clean, with the bedrooms upstairs. The friendly Costa Rican owner, Gladio Montoza Villagas, lives in the pretty house on the edge of the road.

Located between Malpaís and Santa Teresa, where the road climbs toward Cóbano, **Frank's Place** *($$; pb; ⇌642-0296)* is a popular restaurant (see p 317) that also rents out four rooms and three clean, comfortable *cabinas*.

**Casa Cecilia** *($$$ bkfst incl.; pb; in Québec ☎418-775-2898 or 418-775-3209, ⇌418-775-9793)* is a pretty, comfortable Bed & Breakfast owned by friendly Quebeckers, Cécile Wedge and Jean-Pierre Pineault. From

June to October, they manage another Bed & Breakfast in Sainte-Flavie, Québec, called La Québécoise. Built at the edge of a superb white sand beach, the inn has four impeccable rooms with ocean views. Breakfast and lunch are served in an open-air dining room. Transportation and company (optional) are provided for guests to the restaurants of the area. Cécile and Jean-Pierre have created a package that is very popular with vacationers, which includes shuttle service from the airport in San José, ferry crossings, 14 nights accommodation, breakfast and transportation to restaurants for supper *($420/person, double occupancy)*.

Austrian Peter Ottinger and his Brazilian partner, Fatima, named their brand-new hotel **Ranchos Itaúna** *($$$; pb, ⊗, ℜ, K; ☎642-0047)* in honour of one of the most famous surfing beaches in Brazil. The hotel comprises four spacious, comfortable *cabinas*, two of which have kitchenettes. When we were there, a restaurant-bar was under construction, which will serve Brazilian meals concocted by Fatima. The beachside location is perfect for relaxation, and there is an outdoor ping-pong table.

The **Tropico Latino Lodge** *($$$$; pb, hw, ⊗, #, ≈, , ℜ; ☎/⇌640-0062, tropico@centralamerica.com)* is directly overlooking the magnificent white sand beach and consists of six charming, comfortable Italian-style bungalows constructed in 1995. Spacious and prettily decorated, they have a large terrace that is perfect for unwinding in a hammock. The managers, Steve and Florencia, strive to maintain the place's natural peace and tranquillity. The pool is worth the trip in itself: it has a whirlpool and a fabulous setting, almost right on the beach!. There is also a restaurant (see p 318) on the premises.

## South of Puntarenas

### Puntarenas to Jacó

A little north of Punta Leona, **Cabinas Paradise** *($$$; hw, ≈; on the San José-Jacó road, ☎267-0157 or 228-9430)* is slightly set back from the road in a small residential neighbourhood between the road and the ocean. The A-frame *cabinas* are too close to each other. Some of them have two stories, with bedrooms upstairs. The site as a whole is not very attractive, but the cottages offer an acceptable level of comfort.

If staying on the beach is not a priority, **Villa Lapas** *($$$$; hw, pb, ≈, ℜ, miniature golf course; at the beginning of the road to Catarata Manantial Agua Viva, from the San José-Jacó road, ☎663-0811, ⇌663-1516)* is enticing. The hotel is actually set on the banks of a river in the forest, and is thus surrounded by pleasant background sounds. Dinner in the very pretty restaurant is an excellent opportunity to enjoy this natural music to its fullest (see p 319). The rooms, all in a row in one building, have a standard modern wood decor, but are very clean.

Near Playa Doña Ana, **Hotel Fiesta** *($$$$$; pb, hw, ctv, ≡, ≈, ⊘, ℜ; 11 km southeast of Puntarenas, ☎663-0808, ⇌663-1516)* is a luxurious establishment. In fact, it is really more of a resort: in addition to its hundreds of rooms, the Fiesta also has suites and condominiums. Guests have access to a private beach and many restaurants. There are several pools, as well as tennis and volleyball courts. A casino, conference rooms and a gym complete the facilities. Sea outings are possible.

The **Leona Mar** *($$$$$; hw, pb, ≈, ℜ, bar: near Punta Leona Mar, on Play*

*Blanca, ☎231-3131, ⇌232-0791)* is a very pretty condominium complex hidden away in the wilderness on a hill overlooking Playa Blanca, not far from the Punta Leona Resort, with which it is affiliated. The condos are fully equipped: microwave ovens, dishwashers, washers and dryers, etc. The buildings are painted in bright pastel colours that reflect the region's eternal summer. There is a minimum stay of three nights. Guests of the Leona Mar have access to the services of the Punta Leona Resort.

The **Punta Leona Beach and Resort** *($$$$$; hw, pb, ctv, ≡, ≈, ℝ or K, ℜ; a few km north of Herradura, ☎231-3131, ⇌232-0791)* is set on the edge of the beaches of Punta Leona and Blanca. This large resort deserves its reputation: it covers a huge area of land, parts of which have been left untouched, and provides all sorts of services and facilities (football, basketball, volleyball, conference rooms, nightclub, wading pool, souvenir shop, etc.) and many styles of lodging (standard rooms, one- or two-bedroom cottages with living rooms and kitchenettes, or apartments). The general layout is very pretty, and is an ideal setting for a family vacation. Guests of the hotel have exclusive access to Punta Leona beach. There is a shuttle to neighbouring Playa Blanca

Ah, the **Villa Caletas** *($$$$$$; pb, hw, ⊗ or ≡; ☎257-3653, ⇌222-2059)*! This place is nothing short of an idyllic dream, far away from its neighbours, perched on a rocky peak that dominates the surrounding landscape. This airy Victorian building blends perfectly with its natural surroundings. The attractive design of its rooms and its first-class service combine to make it one of the best establishments in the area. To give you an idea of how much care went into its design; the hotel pool is built on one of the mountain's cliffs, so it has a view that extends to the ocean. The colour of the water matches the ocean in the distance, so it seems like one continuous expanse! Also, the hotel's magnificent open-air amphitheatre is one of the stages of the Festival Internacional de Música de Costa Rica. Just imagine listening to a concert with a breathtaking view over the gulf of Nicoya as the backdrop! To ensure absolute peace and quiet, there are no televisions in the rooms. Even if you cannot afford to stay at Villa Caletas, at least stop in for a meal (see p 320) or a drink at the bar. Guests have exclusive access to the beach below.

### The Jacó Region

**Cabinas Antonio** *($; pb, hw; 300 m north of Hotel Jacó Beach, at the corner of the street that runs along the beach at the northern end of Playa Jacó, ☎643-3043)* is a small family establishment that offers rather plain, but clean rooms.

**Cabinas Clarita** *($; pb, ⊗; 50 m west of the restaurant Santimar, Playa Jacó, ☎643-3013)* has simple rooms that provide minimal comfort, and is right on the beach, though it has no outdoor facilities. Ideal for surfers who just want the beach, the sun and the sea.

The **Santimar** *($; pb, ⊗; 200 m north and 200 m west of Hotel Jacó Beach, ☎643-3605)* restaurant has a few tiny rooms for rent. They have no particular charm, but are clean.

The Québec-owned **La Cometa** *($ sb, $$ pb; ⊗; on the main street, Playa Jacó, ☎643-3615)* has clean, simple rooms for rent.

**Aparthotel Gaviotas** *($$; hw, pb, ctv, ⊗, K, ≈; 25 m north and 50 m east of*

*Banco Nacional de Costa Rica, Playa Jacó, ☎643-3092, ⇌643-3054)* rents apartments with fully equipped kitchenettes, small living rooms, separate bedrooms and terraces by the pool – all this at relatively modest rates! Unfortunately, the buildings look like concrete boxes and are somewhat too crowded around the pool.

The **Cabinas Alice** *($$; ≈, ℜ; 100 m south of the Red Cross, on one of the streets to the beach, Jacó, ☎/⇌643-3061)* are simply decorated, and have an almost private terrace. The grounds are right next to the beach. An apartment with a fully equipped kitchenette can also be rented.

**Cabinas Jacó Colonial** *($$; hw, pb, ≈; diagonally across from Cabinas Naranjas, on the road to the hotel Club del Mar, Playa Jacó, ☎643-3359)* is similar to most of the motels on Jacó's little side streets and has about 10 rooms laid out on two stories of a building on a small lot. The foliage surrounding it separates it from its neighbours, and the building is well designed and blends in quite well with its surroundings.

Next door to Cabinas Cindy (see further below), the rooms at the Canadian-owned **Cabinas Kalu** *($$; ☎643-1107)* are slightly cleaner and more modern than those at the neighbouring establishment. However, all of the rooms share one terrace.

**Cabinas Mar de Plata** *($$; Jacó, ☎643-3580)* is a good place for people on a tight budget and is popular with surfers.

**Cabinas Roble Mar** *($$; on one of the streets to the beach, Jacó, ☎643-3173)* is a series of small *cabinas* housed in a building that sits on one of the long, narrow plots of land typical in this area. Relatively clean and very popular with surfers because of its proximity to the beach.

On the streets that run from Jacó's main boulevard to the beach, you can find a whole series of small hotels set up on this neighbourhood's long, narrow lots that run down to the sea. The unpretentious little *cabinas* at **Cabinas Sol y Palmeras** *($$)* and **Cabinas Cindy** *($$; pb; ☎450-0532)* are found on one of the liveliest streets in the heart of the town.

**Chalets Santa Ana** *($$-$$$ for up to 5 people; hw, pb, ⊗; Playa Jacó, ☎643-3233)* have a rather simple decor, but are clean and comfortable. They are not on the beach, and are also quite far from the centre of the town. Rooms and *cabinas* are available.

**Apartamentos El Mar** *($$$; hw, pb, ⊗, K; Playa Jacó, ☎643-3165)* are clean and quiet, with pretty landscaping around a beautiful large pool. The apartments are in a building that surrounds the pool, and have fully equipped kitchens and private terraces.

**Aparthotel Flamboyant** *($$$; hw, pb, ⊗, K; Playa Jacó, ☎643-3146, ⇌643-1068)* is pleasantly calm. The *villas-cabinas* are very well designed with beautiful, large and very private terraces in the front, and small but pretty kitchens and bathrooms, both completely decorated in clean white ceramic tiles. The beautiful tropical garden isolates the establishment from its noisy surroundings in the centre of town. There is direct access to the beach.

**Apartamentos Nicole** *($$$; hw, pb, K; on the main street, Jacó, ☎/⇌643-3384)* are found behind the stores of the same name. They offer rooms with fully equipped kitchens in a relatively large but rather dark space.

The buildings are on a small, unadorned lot.

The hotel **Balcón del Mar** *($$$; hw, pb, ≡, ℝ; next to the police station on the beach, Playa Jacó, ☎/⇌229-2222 or 643-3251)* lives up to its name. Its rooms are spread over three stories, and each has a little balcony with a view of the establishment's pool and the nearby beach. The balconies are slightly recessed to increase their privacy.

A small stream runs through he grounds of the **Hotel Colibri** *($$$; hw, ⊗; on the beach, Playa Jacó, ☎643-3419 or 643-3770, ⇌643-3730)*, adding to the establishment's special charm. The rooms are simple and pretty, but do not have outdoor terraces.

Despite its name, **Hotel Mango Mar** *($$$; hw, pb, ≡, K; Playa Jacó, ☎643-3670)* rents out small apartments with kitchens rather than hotel rooms. The exterior is quite attractive, given the site's limited space. The pool and the beach are just next to the hotel, and very inviting!

The **Marparaíso** *($$$; pb, ⊗, ⊛, ≈, ℜ; near the southern end of the beach, Playa Jacó, ☎221-6544, ⇌221-6601)* is essentially geared toward groups. The patios are quite spacious, but the service and decor is rather indifferent. Especially popular with Costa Ricans.

**Mar de Luz** *($$$; hw, pb, ≡, K, ≈; on one of the streets that runs from the main street toward the interior, Jacó, ☎643-3259)* belongs to a very friendly man from the Netherlands. The hotel is very clean and is elegantly decorated with beautiful use of wood and stone, pleasant kitchenette-dining areas in the rooms, and tasteful furniture on the rooms' private patios. It is a bit of a walk to the beach.

**Paradíso del Sol** *($$$; pb, hw, ⊗, ≡, K, ≈, laundry service; 100 m from the ice factory, Playa Jacó, ☎643-3250, ⇌643-3137)* is a small complex whose buildings are tightly clustered around a pool. It can get noisy when the pool area is busy, especially since the rooms' terraces are quite close together and all surround the pool. The slightly crowded grounds leave little room for greenery.

You'll easily recognize the **Hotel Pochote Grande** *($$$; hw, pb, ≈; Playa Jacó, ☎643-3236), ⇌220-4979, pochote@sol.racsa.co.cr)* by the immense tree (*pochote*) that towers over its grounds. The rooms are clean, simple and quite spacious, with large terraces and windows. The setting is very pretty, covered with beautiful tropical vegetation, right next to the beach. Ideal for relaxation.

**Villas Estrellamar** *($$$; hw, pb, ⊗/≡, ≈, bar; Jacó, ☎643-3102, ⇌643-3453, brunot@sol.racsa.co.cr)* are beautiful, large villas that can accommodate up to five people each. They are well spaced out in attractively landscaped surroundings, and have good-sized terraces as well as all the necessary amenities, including well-equipped kitchenettes, to make for a pleasant stay of more than one night. The Estrellamar is very popular, so reservations are a good idea. A short walk from the beach.

The **Villas el Cisne** *($$$; pb, hw, ⊗, K; Playa Jacó, ☎643-1076)* complex has a pretty colourful green and yellow exterior, but the rooms lack charm, though they have large windows. A bit of vegetation outside would be an improvement.

The bungalows at **Los Ranchos** *($$$-$$$$; hw, pb, laundry service, ⊗, ≈; next to Cabinas Mar de Platas, 50 m west of the Banco de Costa Rica and* *the main street, Playa Jacó, ☎/⇄643-3070)* are located on a beautiful, well-landscaped property that includes a playground for children, a pool and even a little waterfall! The owners are surfers themselves, so they can offer plenty of advice if you want to take up this popular sport in the region. Thus, Los Ranchos is very popular with young, sporty travellers. Two-story apartments with patios and hammocks, and smaller accommodations are for rent.

Squeezed onto a tiny lot, **Cabinas Zabamar** *(**$$$** ⊗, **$$$$** ≡; hw, pb, ≈, ℝ, ℜ; Playa Jacó, ☎/⇄643-3174)* are clean, and simply but adequately furnished.

**Hotel Copacabana** *(**$$$-$$$$** ≡, **$$$$$** ≡ and K; pb, hw; Playa Jacó, ☎/⇄643-3131)* is the place for active – and passive – sports enthusiasts. Various equipment for athletic activities (kayaks, for example), or for relaxation (lounge chairs, etc.) can be rented, or you can simply watch sports on the hotel's satellite television. Apartments with kitchenettes and living rooms are also available. The hotel is aging a bit, and its rooms are a little worn. The owner is friendly, and strives to make the place welcoming for surfers.

The condominiums at **Tropical Paradise** *(**$$$$**; hw, pb, ≡, ctv, K, ≈; Playa Jacó, ☎256-0091, ⇄256-0027)* make up a semi-autonomous little village in the town of Jacó, with streets and a "business" centre in the heart of the agglomeration! They are for sale (fully equipped), but it is also possible to rent them.

**Amapola** *(**$$$$**; hw, pb, ≡, ctv, ⊗, ≈, wading pool, ℜ; near the southern exit of the town, Jacó, ☎/⇄643-3668 or 643-3337)* opened quite recently, and rents out rooms as well as three beautifully decorated, uncompromisingly comfortable cottages. The establishment was carefully designed, both inside (common day rooms, restaurant, etc.) and out. Of course, the landscaping will be even more attractive when the vegetation is fully grown. The room's terraces are well isolated. Amapola has an Italian restaurant (see p 319), but is somewhat far from the beach (500 m) and from the centre of the town (2 km).

**Aparthotel Sole d'Oro** *(**$$$$**; pb, hw, ≡, ≈; Playa Jacó, ☎/⇄643-3172)* shares a very cramped lot with its small swimming pool, so its layout leaves something to be desired. The interior is simple and clean.

The **Cabinas El Coral** *(**$$$$**; pb, ≡, K, ctv; 100 m north and 75 m east of Supermercado Rayo Azul, Playa Jacó, ☎643-3133)* are pretty and spacious, and have kitchenettes and living rooms. The establishment's overall decor is rather plain, but clean. It can get a bit noisy since the concrete units are set quite closely around the pool.

People come to the **Hotel Jacó Fiesta** *(**$$$$**; pb, hw, ≡, ctv, K, ☎, ℝ, ≈, ℜ, conference rooms; Playa Jacó, ☎643-3147, ⇄643-3148)* because of its, in our opinion overrated, reputation. The rooms are rather ordinary, and it is hard to believe that this hotel has won prizes for ecological distinction, as advertized in its brochures. The outdoor layout is certainly pleasant enough, but does not reveal any particular preoccupation with integrating the establishment into its natural surroundings.

**Hotel Tangeri** *(**$$$$**; hw, pb, ≈; on the main street, Playa Jacó, ☎643-3001)* is extremely well designed. About 10 small, clean, pretty villas can accommodate up to eight people each. Located along a beautiful little path that leads to the pool, they are idyllic little summer cottages with large terraces. There are even a volleyball court and a children's wading pool on the premisses.

**Villas Miramar** *($$$$ bkfst incl.; hw, pb, ⊗, K, ≈; Playa Jacó, ☎643-3003)* are clean, tastefully decorated and provide plenty of privacy on their relatively small lot in the centre of the town. The landscaping is exquisite and the area as a whole is very quiet, although it is just two steps from the beach. Good value.

As a large hotel complex that is part of a chain, the **Best Western Jacó Beach Resort** *($$$$$ bkfst incl. off-season; hw, pb, ≈, disco, conference rooms; Playa Jacó, ☎220-1772 or 220-1725, ⇌232-3159, jacohote@sol.racsa.co.cr)* is very popular with tourists, especially Canadians. This hotel is often included in vacation packages, so it is very busy. The clientele mostly consists of families, which the hotel's services cater to, with facilities that include ping-pong tables, pinball, tennis and volleyball courts, bicycles, etc. Disco music is played in the reception area. The hotel grounds are vast and well-landscaped, and directly on the beach. The hotel is a short walk from the centre of the town.

**Club del Mar** *($$$-$$$$$; hw, pb, ≈, ℜ; Playa Jacó, ☎/⇌643-3194)* is a very attractive resort in a beautiful setting, set back from the bustle of the town, at the very southern end of Jacó's beach. The owners have perfectly integrated their establishment with the natural environment on a large property right on the beach. The four types of rooms (with or without airconditioning, kitchen equipment, living rooms, etc.) are tastefully decorated, and most have private balconies. There is a beautiful, large common reading area for guests. Its main attraction, however, are the friendly and attentive owners who take pleasure in organizing outings in the area for guests. The restaurant specializes in seafood and Chateaubriand (see p 319).

The rooms at **Hotel Cocal** *($$$$$ bkfst incl.; hw, pb, ≡, ≈; Playa Jacó, ☎643-3067, ⇌643-3082)* are arranged single file along a shared terrace. Those facing the ocean are not airconditioned. The layout of the exterior is quite polished, despite the fact that it is somewhat crowded around the pool.

The condominiums at **Villas Jacó Princess** *($$$$$; hw, pb, ctv, ☎, K, ≡, ≈; Playa Jacó, ☎220-1441, ⇌232-3159)* can accommodate five guests each. In addition to kitchenettes, they come with living rooms and private patios. Guests have free use of bicycles and the facilities at the Best Western Jacó Beach Resort (see further above).

### Jacó to Quepos

Run by friendly Quebeckers Mariette Daignault and Pierre Perron, the **Auberge du Pélican** *($$$; sb/pb, hw, ⊗, ≈, ℜ, ♿; playa Esterillos Este, ⇌779-9236)* is an excellent value, with its 10 rooms starting at only $35 per night. The grounds are pretty and the patios and balconies are relatively private. The rooms are clean and comfortable, and guests are lulled to sleep by the sound of the ocean waves. The inn is situated directly on the magnificent and very calm Playa Esterillos Este, one of the most beautiful beaches on the Pacific, where the sunsets are absolutely heavenly! The owners have made two rooms wheelchair accessible. The grounds include a pretty pool, a hopscotch game that is lit up at night, lounge chairs, parasols and plenty of hammocks that are perfect for relaxing! The hosts can organize deep-sea fishing excursions *($30/half day for two people)*, horseback rides or outings into the mountains of the back country in an all-terrain vehicle. The only drawback of this place is that the charming restaurant's delicious food is only available for guests.

There are still very few hotels around Parrita. However, five kilometres from the town on Playa Palo Seco is the Québec-owned Bed & Breakfast **Beso del Viento** *($$$ bkfst incl.; pb, hw, ≈; ⇌779-9108)* where you can stay in a family atmosphere near a beautiful, little-known beach. You can also rent an apartment and have lunch and dinner at the inn.

**Cabinas Vista Hermosa** *($$$; pb, K; Playa Hermosa, ☎643-3422, ⇌224-3687)* are similar to Cabinas Las Olas (see below). There is a small pool table used by local young people and guests.

Québec-owned **La Felicidad** *($$$; hw, pb/sb, ⊗, ≈, ℜ, ♿; Esterillos Centro, ☎/⇌779-9003)* is set in a perfectly tranquil location. Some of its rooms have kitchenettes, and two have been adapted for wheelchair access. The restaurant serves local and international dishes. Weekly and monthly packages are available. Direct access to the beach.

**Las Olas** *($$$; pb, hw, K; Playa Hermosa, ☎/⇌643-3687)* has several bunk beds or single beds on the upper floors of A-frame *cabinas*. This establishment is perfect for surfers. Rates are negotiable, especially for stays of more than one week.

**Villa Ballena** *($$$; hw, pb, ≈; Playa Hermosa, ☎643-3373, ⇌643-3506)* has a lovely exterior and offers *cabinas* with fully equipped kitchens surrounded by beautiful tropical vegetation. Directly on the beach. Guests have free access to the gym at the Plaza Jacó (see p 322).

Like the Pélican and La Felicidad, **Cabinas Flor de Esterillos** *($$$-$$$$, pb, hw, K, ≈, ℜ; a bit east of Auberge du Pélican, Esterillos Este, ⇌779-9141 or 779-9108)* are also Québec-managed. The *cabinas* are now fully equipped with kitchenettes. The entire site is surrounded by greenery and there is direct access to the beach. The owners offer reduced rates to guests who stay for several nights.

The **David** *($$$$ bkfst incl.; hw, pb, ≡, ☎, ≈, ℜ, bar, ⊘; Playa Hermosa, ☎643-3737, ⇌643-3736)* hotel is relatively new and sparkling clean. It is owned by a charming retired Swiss-Italian couple. Each room has a private terrace. Though its vegetation is not yet completely grown, the property adjoins the beach. Tranquillity guaranteed.

**Terraza del Pacífico** *($$$$; hw, pb with bath, ctv, ≡, ≈, ℜ, bar; on the national highway, Playa Hermosa, ☎643-3222, ⇌643-3424)* has about 50 rooms spread over a two-story complex surrounded by rather pretty landscaping. Each room has a patio or a balcony. A band plays here twice a week, and there is a children's wading pool. Direct access to the beach.

### The Quepos Region

Apart from a few moderately-priced hotels near the entrance to Parque Nacional Manuel Antonio or in the town of Quepos itself, the region between Quepos and Manuel Antonio is generally frequented by a relatively well-off clientele. This is reflected in the quality of the hotels in the area, many of which have breathtaking settings in the hills overlooking the sea.

Bus service between Quepos and Manuel Antonio is frequent, making travel easy for tourists without cars.

**Cabinas Cali** *($$)* are set at the end of a small street that leads into a hilly region north of downtown Quepos. It has minimal comfort, but very good rates. At the corner of the street, the **Las Palmas** *($$)* restaurant rents *cabinas* of similar quality.

**Cabinas Doña Alicia** *($$; pb; near the northeast corner of the football field, ☎777-0419)* are absolutely utilitarian, and nothing more. For tight budgets.

**Cabinas El Verano** *($$; pb, ⊗, ℝ in some rooms; ☎777-1495)* and **Cabinas El Cisne** *($$; pb, ⊗; ☎777-0590)* are somewhat similar to Cabinas Ramace (see further below) but a bit larger. The building that encloses the rooms surrounds a central court in which there are only a few trees. The furnishing of the rooms is minimal. It is often noisy, as the place is quite cramped.

Unlike the nearby Cabinas Quepos (an establishment we decided not to include), the rooms at **Cabinas Hellen** *($$; hw, pb, P; one street south of the Sansa offices, ☎777-0504)* provide a decent level of comfort, and lead directly out onto the small, plain property. Guests have access to the parking lot.

**Cabinas Mary** *($$; pb; across from the football field, ☎777-0128)* have very clean *cabinas* for the price. Travellers with limited budgets know this and flock here in great numbers.

**Cabinas Ramace** *($$; hw, pb, ⊗, ℝ; ☎777-0590)* are very clean. The friendly owners rent out three rooms on their small, simple but pleasantly arranged property.

**Cabinas Villa Cruz** *($$; ☎777-0271, ⇄777-1081)* are also very clean. The *cabinas* are lined up in one building and share a terrace that looks out over a small, cramped, but tranquil courtyard.

**Hotel El Parque** *($$; across from the park along the lagoon)* is superior to Cabinas Quepos, an establishment we chose not to include. On its upper floor are a string of very pretty little dormitory-style rooms that open onto a central corridor. Windows look out over the street. The view of the park and the water is one of its advantages over the Cabinas Quepos.

**Hotel Malinche** *($ ⊗, $$$ ≡; pb; 75 m west of the bus terminal, ☎777-0093)* has two types of rooms: the older rooms are equipped with fans and are rather antiquated, while the newer, prettier rooms have airconditioning.

**Viña del mar** *($$$; pb, ≈; ☎777-0070)* has some rather rundown rooms, but is an interesting place to stay because of its location slightly outside of the town on the lagoon.

**Villas Mar y Sol Inn** *($$$; hw, pb, ≡, P; ☎777-0307, ⇄777-0562)* has eight rooms decorated in South American style. Stone surfaces make up much of the property, but these go well with the site's vegetation, and the effect is quite charming. The welcome could be more friendly.

**Hotel Kamuk** *($$$$; hw, pb, ≡, ☎, ≈, ℜ, casino; on the main street facing the ocean, ☎777-0379, ⇄777-0258)* is a very urban little hotel. Its rooms are spread over three stories of a building right in the middle of town, are clean and comfortable, and have the decor you would expect of this type of establishment. Some have balconies overlooking the ocean. The pool is refreshing, especially after spending a day walking around in the heat.

The **Hotel Sirena** *($$$$ bkfst incl.; pb, hw, ≡, ≈; 50 m east of Costa Rican Sportsfishing, one block from the bridge, at the centre of Quepos, ☎7777-0528)* can get noisy when people are using the pool in the middle of the building. The rooms are nothing special, but they are clean and their windows open onto the pool.

**Hotel Villa Romántica** *($$$$ bkfst incl.; pb, hw, ≈; at the exit from the town, Quepos, ☎/⇌777-0037)* has beautiful rooms and is tucked away in natural surroundings that create welcome shade in this hot region.

### Quepos to Manuel Antonio

**Cabinas Ramírez** *($; pb; near the entrance to the park on the beach side, Manuel Antonio, ☎777-0003)* have two new owners; a friendly Quebecker-Costa Rican couple. This clean establishment is especially recommended to young backpackers. The *cabinas* have a minimal level of comfort, but are very close to Manuel Antonio park! The new owners have many projects on the go, including a *rancho* for breakfast al fresco, a swimming pool and a garden, which will definitely improve the establishment's overall appeal.

**Hotel y Restaurante Costa Linda** *($; sb/pb, K; on the last cross street before the park, ☎777-0304)* is a small, plain youth hostel with no particular charm. The establishment is perfectly suitable for young backpackers.

**Hotel Del Mar** *($$$; hw, pb; on the Quepos-Manuel Antonio road, on the inland side 1 km before the park, ☎777-0543)* is made up of two buildings. The small, colourful rooms are very bright and comfortable, with large windows in the front. The patios are shared, though. Very clean. Many additions to the establishment are planned.

The Costa Rican-style **Hotel Flor Blanca** *($$$ bkfst incl.; pb, hw, ≡; on the Quepos-Manuel Antonio road, ☎777-1620, ☎/⇌777-1633)* is clean, but shows its age.

**Hotel B&B La Colina** *($$$ bkfst incl.; hw, pb; about 3 km from Quepos toward Manuel Antonio, ☎/⇌777-0231)* is very warm and friendly and comprises two buildings perched on a steep slope. The establishment as a whole is very compact, but the hill and the vegetation makes it seem more private. When we were there, expansion was underway and refrigerators were available in some suites. The breakfast has a lot of variety and includes pancakes with syrup!

**Hotel Manuel Antonio** *($$$; pb, ⊗; next to the park, Manuel Antonio, ☎777-1237)* is a small, fairly clean hotel with small rooms on the building's upper floor. Its main advantage is its proximity to the park, the beach and the surrounding natural environment. Obviously, these assets attract young travellers. There is a restaurant on the ground floor.

**Karahé** *(on the Quepos-Manuel Antonio road, ☎777-0170, ⇌777-1075)* has three types of *cabinas*. The oldest *($$$; hw, pb, ⊗, ℝ, ℜ, ≈)* are also the least expensive. Set on a hill, they have beautiful views – but guests must climb quite a slope to reach them! More cottages are located across the road *($$$$; hw, pb, ≡, patios)*, and the most expensive are near the beach *($$$$$; hw, pb, ≡, patios)*. In addition to the upstairs restaurant, lunch is served downstairs, near the pool.

**Vela Bar** *($$$; hw, pb, ⊗, K, ℜ; on the Quepos-Manuel Antonio road, near the park entrance, 100 m from the main road, ☎777-0413, ⇄777-1071)* rents out small, worn and not very comfortable rooms whose charm is somewhat faded. However, the owner is very friendly.

**El Dorado Mojado** *($$$-$$$$ bkfst incl.; hw, pb, ≡, K; on the Quepos-Manuel Antonio road, ☎777-0368, ⇄777-1248)* has rooms decorated in subdued tones, with large windows that open onto the surrounding scenery.

The Canadian-owned **Casa Del Sol** *($$$$; hw, pb, with or without K; on the Quepos-Manuel Antonio road, near Cabinas Ramírez, ☎777-1805, ⇄777-1311, verdemar@sol.racsa.co.cr)* is brand new and beautiful! The spacious rooms are decorated with warm shades of ochre in Mexican-Californian style, and easily meet North-American standards of comfort. Also, the owner is ecologically minded – the beach is accessed via a raised boardwalk to protect the marshy vegetation between the hotel from the seaside.

**Casitas Eclipse** *($$$$, $$$$$ with K; pb, hw, ⊗, ≈; on the Quepos-Manuel Antonio road, ☎/⇄777-0408 or 777-1738)* has standard rooms, as well as very bright, clean, airy cottages whose beautiful, multi-pane windows and living rooms (equipped with full kitchens) add to their appeal. The establishment is situated on a huge property with a gorgeous view.

The rooms at the Québec-owned **Hotel California** *($$$$; hw, pb, ⊗, tv, ≈; a bit set back on a road that intersects the Quepos-Manuel Antonio road, ☎777-1234, ☎/⇄777-1062)* are pretty and clean. The decor is interesting, with figurative paintings on the walls. The building that houses the rooms has a rather original and unique exterior design.

The Québec-owned **Hotel El Colibri** *($$$$; pb, hw, ⊗, K, ≈; on the Quepos-Manuel Antonio road, ☎777-0432)* is a modern building similar to that of La Quinta (see further below), but is a bit more refined. The rooms are decorated with beautiful colours, and there is a path that leads to a pretty little waterfall. El Colibri is closer to the road than La Quinta, however.

**El Lirio** *($$$$ bkfst incl.; hw, pb; on the Quepos-Manuel Antonio road, ☎777-0403, ⇄777-1182)* is certainly very clean! The landscaping beautifully integrates the natural surroundings. The rooms share outdoor patios, and have a simple, but pleasant, decor. The service is just a touch amateurish.

**Mimo's Hotel** *($$$$; hw, pb, K in the suites, ≈, ♿; on the Quepos-Manuel Antonio road, 4 km from the park, ☎/⇄777-0054)* is proudly Italian. Its rooms and suites are tastefully decorated and very spacious. The grounds have lots of lovely greenery. The hotel also has rooms that are wheelchair- accessible.

**El Mirador del Pacífico** *($$$$; hw, pb, ≈, ℜ; on the Quepos-Manuel Antonio road, Quepos, ☎/⇄777-0119)* is largely made of wood. The rooms are very pleasant, with attractive furnishings and white walls. They are also large and bright. However, they all share one terrace. Guests can have their meals on the *mirador* (hence the name), while enjoying a superb view of the surroundings.

**Hotel Playa Espadilla** *($$$$; pb, hw, ≡, ≈; Playa Espadilla, ☎/⇌777-0903)* has small, very clean apartments with fully equipped kitchens. Their decor is simple but pleasant. The landscaping will improve when the vegetation matures.

**La Quinta** *($$$$; hw, pb, ⊗, ≈; a little higher than villa Niña, on a road that leaves the Quepos-Manuel Antonio road toward the hills, ☎/⇌777-0434)* is about 20 years old, and its charm has faded quite a bit. Located at the end of a lane, it even looks a little neglected, which makes it seem slightly gloomy. It is made up of small villas (some have kitchens) tucked away in the greenery. They offer magnificent views.

**Hotel Las Tres Banderas** *($$$$; pb, hw, ≡, ≈, ⊛, ℜ, bar; on the Quepos-Manuel Antonio road, ☎777-1284 or 777-1871, ⇌777-1478, info@hotel-tres-banderas.com)* rents about 10 rooms in one villa, with a shared patio. The rooms are tastefully decorated with wood and ceramic tiles.

**Hotel Villabosque** *($$$$; hw, pb, ⊗, ≡, ≈, ℜ, bar; on the Quepos-Manuel Antonio road, a few hundred m before the park entrance and 125 m from the beach, ☎777-1152 or 777-0473, ⇌777-0401)* is very charming. The building itself is beautiful, the ornamental landscaping is accomplished, and the well-proportioned rooms have a Spanish flavour. The rooftop pool is rather original.

**Villa Nina** *($$$$ bkfst incl.; hw, pb, ≡, ℝ, ≈, ℜ; on the road that branches off on the Quepos-Manuel Antonio road near Casitas Eclipse, ☎777-1628, ⇌777-1497)* has pretty rooms in a Florida Art Deco-style building that has lots of character.

**Villa Teca** *($$$$ bkfst incl.; pb, hw, ≡, ≈, ℜ; on the Quepos-Manuel Antonio road, ☎777-1117, ⇌777-1578)* has two simple, pleasant rooms per building or villa, each of which has a small patio. It is very clean, and the large property that surrounds it is pleasantly natural.

**Casa Blanca** *($$$$-$$$$$; pb, hw, ≡, ℝ, ≈, ℜ; on the Quepos-Manuel Antonio road, ☎/⇌777-0253, cblanca@sol.racsa.co.cr)* is restricted to a gay and lesbian clientele and their friends. The rooms, suites and apartments are very prettily decorated, and the grounds are very relaxing and enjoyable. There is also a fully equipped cottage that is perfect for honeymoons. The beach is a 20-minute walk from the hotel.

**Hotel Costa Verde** *($$$$-$$$$$; hw, pb, ≈, ℜ; on the Quepos-Manuel Antonio road, ☎777-0584, ⇌777-0560, costaver@sol.racsa.co.cr)* has a magnificent view of the ocean. It is difficult to find airier lodgings than those at Costa Verde – large sections of the rooms are actually open to the outdoors, thanks to large screened windows and glass doors. The spacious terraces are quite private. The hotel is set on a slope, which keeps it somewhat isolated and adds to the design.

**Hotel Plinio** *($$$$-$$$$$ bkfst incl.; hw, pb; set back about 100 m from the road, 1 km from Quepos, ☎777-0055, ⇌777-0558, plinio@sol.racsa.co.cr)* is very charming with its wooden building that creates a tastefully rustic atmosphere. It has managed to preserve its idyllic character for decades now. The dark wood-panelled rooms are very stylish, and are located on two floors, with large terraces along the front. Very clean.

**Villas Nicolas** *($$$$-$$$$$; hw, pb, ⊗, with or without K, ≈; next to Si Como No, on the Quepos-Manuel Antonio road, ☎777-0481,*

*☎/⇌777-0451)* is a 10-year-old condominium complex whose units are rented out by the owners when they are not there. Some of the living quarters are rather faded, though the general design of these condos is far from lacking in charm. They have magnificent views of the jungle and the sea below from the private veranda. The most expensive condos have two stories, two balconies with hammocks, two bedrooms and two bathrooms, as well as fully equipped kitchens.

**Hotel El Byblos** *($$$$$; hw, pb, ℝ, ☎, ctv, ≡, ≈; on the Quepos-Manuel Antonio road, ☎777-0411, ⇌777-0009)* is French owned. Bungalows and suites are available; all of them have balconies, are spacious, and are decorated in a refreshing style with tile, rattan, pastel tones, etc. The hotel restaurant is worth a stop (see p 321).

**Hotel Divisamar** *($$$$$; hw, pb, ≈, ≡, ℜ; on the Quepos-Manuel Antonio road, Quepos, ☎777-0371, ⇌777-0525)* is owned by a Costa Rican family. The rooms share the veranda in the middle of the multi-story buildings. The rooms are clean and have large windows. The light colours of their decor makes them even brighter.

The **Villas El Parque** *($$$$$; hw, pb, ⊗, ℜ, bar; on the Quepos-Manuel Antonio road, 2 km from the park, ☎777-0096, ⇌777-0538, vparque@sol.racsa.co.cr)* are simply beautiful! They are airy, attractively designed, and reminiscent of southern Europe. Some have fully equipped kitchens. The terrace has a splendid view of the surrounding forests and the ocean. Airconditioning is available if requested at the time of the reservation.

**Villas de La Selva** *($$$$$; hw, pb, ≈, ⊛; on the Quepos-Manuel Antonio road, ☎/⇌777-1137, San José ☎253-4890)* are apartments and *cabinas* with private terraces and fully equipped kitchens. They are somewhat rustic, but quite pleasant. The whole the complex is very pretty overall, and has a breathtaking view of the bay of Manuel Antonio. The villas are a bit of a walk from the beach, which is reached by a path. The villas are on a road that branches off the main road. A childcare service is available. Groups can rent a villa and an adjoining apartment.

**Makanda-by-the-Sea** *($$$$$$ bkfst incl.; hw, pb, K, ≈; 1 km down a road that branches off from the Quepos-Manuel Antonio road toward the sea, near the restaurant Barba Roja, ☎777-0442, ⇌777-1032, makanda@sol.racsa.co.cr)* definitely knows how to make a good first impression, and extends an absolutely perfect welcome to guests when they arrive. The emphasis is on attentive service – with a smile! The fully equipped villas have to be seen to be believed: they overlook the sea, providing natural ventilation and contact with the outdoors that are hard to beat. The "cathedral ceilings" and the combination of wood and tile in the decor add to their charm. They are scattered on a hillside in such a way as to guarantee privacy. There is access to a private beach at low tide, when the famous pre-Columbian turtle traps are visible.

**La Mariposa** *($$$$$$ bkfst incl.; hw, pb, ≡, ⊛, ≈, ℜ; at the intersection of a marked road that also leads to the El Parador hotel and the Quepos-Manuel Antonio road, ☎777-0355 or 777-0456, ⇌777-0050, mariposa@sol.racsa.co.cr)* has beautiful two-story villas with a magnificent view that can be appreciated from the rooms' whirlpools! The bamboo, tile and wood, interiors are also very pretty.

The **Parador** *($$$$$$; pb, hw, ctv, ≡, hair dryers, ≈; at the end of the marked road that also leads to La Mariposa and the Quepos-Manuel Antonio road, ☎777-1411, ⇄777-1437)* is luxury itself! On top of a rocky peak, it offers first-class accommodations in a natural environment. Its rooms and villas are extremely comfortable, and each has its own terrace. The common living areas are elegantly furnished and very pleasant. There is an absolutely breathtaking view of the surroundings from the dining room! The impeccable service is extremely courteous and attentive.

With its terraced architectural design on a mountainside, the **Si Como No** *($$$$$$ ; hw, pb, ⊗, ≡, ≈, ⊛, ℜ, bar conference room; 4 km from Quepos, on the Quepos-Manuel Antonio road, ☎777-0777, ⇄777-1093, sicomono@sol.racsa.co.cr)* hotel complex is absolutely gorgeous! Its views are magnificent, and the ecologically minded owner uses solar energy, recycled water, and cultivated wood instead of the country's rare natural wood in running his hotel. This takes absolutely nothing away from the establishment's uncompromising beauty and comfort. A shuttle takes guests to the beach. Films can be screened in a small private movie theatre!

**Tulemar Bungalows** *($$$$$$ bkfst incl.; hw, pb, ≡, ≈; on the Quepos-Manuel Antonio road, ☎777-0580, ⇄777-1759, tulemar@sol.racsa.co.cr)* are located on a large property, most of which has been left in its natural state, so you can go on instructive forest hikes. The bungalows' octagonal form gives them multiple points of access to the outdoors. They are comfortable and pleasantly decorated. Guests can use the sea kayaks with no additional charge. Children under 12 stay for free. The hotel has its own access to Tulemar beach, below the complex, where you can see the pre-Columbian turtle traps at low tide.

## RESTAURANTS

### The Puntarenas Region

There are many little restaurants in the city of Puntarenas, including those found in most of the better hotels. There is also a Pop's that serves ice cream in the heart of the city.

You can enjoy good seafood for prices that are more than reasonable at **Casa de Mariscos** *($-$$; Puntarenas)* and **Bar-Restaurante Cevichito** *($-$$; Puntarenas)*.

**Kahite Blanco** *($-$$; Av. 1, Calle 15/17, Puntarenas, ☎661-2093)* Is very popular, especially with Costa Ricans, as it serves generous portions of seafood and hearty *bocas*.

**Aloha** *($$-$$$; west of the Tioga hotel, Puntarenas, ☎661-0773)* is considered one of the better restaurants in the city, especially for seafoood.

Finally, the French restaurant **La Caravelle** *($$$; Tue to Sun; on the ocean side, Puntarenas)* is renowned for its entrées. It can be very busy, especially during the high season.

### The Southern Nicoya Peninsula

#### Paquera to Montezuma

##### Tambor

Located next to the dock, the restaurant-bar **Bahía Ballena Yacht Club** *($$-$$$; 10am to midnight)* has a varied menu of dishes with Mexican, Cajun and Caribbean flavours.

Located in the mountains near Tambor and Pochote, **La Paillote** *($$-$$$; ☎683-0190)* serves excellent food. This French restaurant is perched just high enough to offer a panoramic view of the lush, green valley and the hills. The menu is made up of excellent and affordable French cuisine, made with fresh ingredients. The kitchen can cook up your very own "catch of the day" on request. This establishment also provides accommodations (see p 299).

A Swiss flag hangs at the seaside location of the restaurant-bar **Perla Tambor** *($$-$$$)*, which prepares international cuisine.

**Ristorante Italiano** *($$-$$$; 11am to 11pm; ☎683-0148)* has a view of the ocean, and serves pizza, pasta and seafood.

### Montezuma

Many of the hotels in Montezuma have restaurants that are open to the public.

Across from Topsy bookstore is **Panadería Idalie**, a bakery that makes fresh bread and pastries and has a tiny terrace.

**Café Montezuma** *($-$$)* serves excellent breakfasts and lunches, as well as tasty fruit juices, at modest prices. A small **pizzeria** next door is open in the evening.

On the beach near Hotel Montezuma, the menu at **El Parque** *($$-$$$)* features fresh fish.

**El Sano Banano** *($$-$$$; ☎642-0068)* makes delicious vegetarian dishes with fresh ingredients, including excellent soups and salads. The banana, chocolate, and mocha milkshakes are especially tasty, although they are a bit expensive. On Wednesday nights films are shown.

### South of Montezuma

#### Cabuya

**El Ancla De Oro** *($$-$$$; ☎642-0369)* is still one of the best restaurants in Cabuya. The owner, Alex Villalobos, is a first-class chef who has an excellent reputation in the region. The menu features simple, original cuisine that emphasizes seafood, fish and vegetarian dishes at reasonable prices. The establishment also rents out *cabinas* (see p 302).

### Northwest of Cabo Blanco

The vast majority of the hotels in this area have restaurants that are open to the public.

Across from the *cabinas* at Zaneida's campground is the brand-new *soda* **Break Point** *($-$$; Santa Teresa)*, which serves French-style fast food.

Certainly the best value in the region, **Frank's Place** *($-$$; between Malpaís and Santa Teresa, ☎642-0296)* is a very friendly meeting place where people flock after a day of outdoor adventures. A variety of local and international dishes can be had here, including excellent and inexpensive scampi.

The **Surf & Sport Camp** *($-$$; Malpaís, ☎642-0047)* (see p 302) has a restaurant that serves affordable international cuisine. People come here to play pool or sip a beer at the bar while watching surfing videos or satellite television.

For tasty pasta, pizza and seafood, or simply to sip a rich espresso, the open-air restaurant **Albimat Dulce Magia** *($$-$$$; Malpaís)* is the place to go. The Neapolitan owners are especially proud of their fish fondue and *ceviche*. The restaurant also has a very busy bar that is popular with tourists and Costa Ricans alike.

The **Star Mountain Eco Resort** *($$$; Malpaís, ☎296-2626, ext. 125080)* is located in the mountains, two kilometres from the sea. The open-air restaurant-bar serves excellent international cuisine in a friendly atmosphere. Restaurant guests can also spend the afternoon at the hotel's superb pool (see p 303).

The restaurant at the **Sunset Reef Marine lodge** *($$$; Malpaís; ☎640-0012)* (see p 303) serves excellent food. The Belgian chef, Nathalie, prepares tasty international, European and local dishes. Since fishermen dock at the village just a few metres from the hotel, the fish here is always remarkably fresh.

The **Tropico Latino Lodge** *($$$; ☎640-0062)* in Santa Teresa has an open-air restaurant that serves Italian and local cuisine. The curried chicken is especially delicious.

## Reserva Natural Absoluta Cabo Blanco

Just before the entrance to the Cabo Blanco reserve, on the right, the restaurant **Limón Dulce** *($$-$$$)* is a good choice.

## South of Puntarenas

**The Jacó region**

The restaurant at **Cabinas Alice** *($; 100 m south of the Red Cross, Playa Jacó, ☎643-3061)* serves Costa Rican dishes in a shady area.

**El Recreo** *($; Jacó, ☎643-3012)* serves excellent, inexpensive food (the price of the shrimp is unbeatable). The restaurant is quiet and the Latin American background music is very pleasant.

**Restaurante Clarita** *($; 50 m west of the Santimar restaurant, Playa Jacó, ☎643-3013)*, adjoining the *cabinas* of the same name, is clean and serves mainly Costa Rican cuisine in a very simple dining room. Its main advantage is its location right on the beach.

The **Sunrise Grill** *($; Thu to Tue 7am to noon; on the main street, Jacó)* is known as "the breakfast place" because of its reasonably priced American style morning repast: waffles, pancakes, toast and eggs.

At he corner of the main street and the street that leads to the beach and to the La Central nightclub is the **Buena Nota** *($-$$; every day; Jacó)*, which serves kebab sandwiches and even light fast-food type meals for under five dollars.

A bit further along the main street, **Downtown Jungle Bar** *($$; across from Supermercado Paola, Jacó)* specializes in light, simple meals similar to those served at Pollo Happy Land and Buena Nota.

**Restaurante, Pizzería y Heladería Esperanza** *($$; Playa Jacó, ☎/≠643-3332)* is *the* place for Italian cuisine (they make a good *calzone*) at reasonable prices.

**Los Faroles** *($$; every day; at the corner of the main street and the northern entrance to Jacó from the San José-Jacó highway)* is a seafood restaurant with reasonable prices.

The *pescadería* **La Fiesta del Marisco** and **Tico Tico** *($$; just south of Steve & Lisa's restaurant on the San José-Jacó road, Punta Leona, on the seaside)* both specialize in seafood served in a generally attractive decor.

The restaurant-bar *marisquería* **La Hacienda** *($$; on the main street, Jacó)* is where Jacó's young people go to see and be seen, especially on the front terrace.

**Killer Munchies** *($$; lunch and dinner; 300 m south of the Jacó Beach hotel, Jacó, ☎643-3354)* is the place to go for pizza. The atmosphere is very lively.

Similar to and diagonally across from the Buena Nota, **Pollo Happy Land** is a small beach restaurant with an appealing decor that serves... chicken, of course!

On the main street, across from the road to Discoteca La Central and next to the Rayo Azul supermarket, **El Riconcito Peruano** *($$; Jacó)* serves tasty Peruvian dishes.

**Santimar** *($$; Fri to Tue 11am to 9pm; 200 m north and 200 m west of the Jacó Beach hotel, next to the Clarita, Playa Jacó, ☎643-3605)* is a pretty and good little restaurant with a refined decor that serves Costa Rican cuisine.

**Steve & Lisa's** *($$; on the seaside on the San José-Jacó road, Punta Leona)* serves Costa Rican specialties. You can recognize this attractive restaurant by its small *mirador* (belvedere) near the ocean where you can dine a fresco.

Not far from Munchies, the **Banana Café** *($$-$$$; playa Jacó)* is a North American-style restaurant that serves seafood, sandwiches, Chinese food and, according to some, the best steaks in town.

The restaurant at the hotel **Amapola** *($$$; near the southern exit from town, Jacó, ☎/≠643-3668 or 643-3337)* prepares pizza from a wood burning oven. Like the rest of the building, the brand-new dining room has a refined decor.

The restaurant at the **Club del Mar** *($$$; at the very southern end of Jacó, ☎/≠643-3194)* serves great seafood and excellent chateaubriands in a peaceful environment surrounded by beautiful greenery.

Three houses south of La Hacienda, the very clean Swiss-run restaurant-bar **La Bruja** *($$$)* comes highly recommended. Swiss and international specialties are served.

**La Ostra** *($$$; at the corner of Jacó's main street and the road to Los Ranchos, Jacó)* serves very good meals of various types (seafood, steaks, hamburgers). The decor and service are quite pleasant.

The **Poncho Villa** *($$$; on the main street at the corner of the road to Discoteca Los Tucanes, Jacó)*, has an attractive decor and good food.

Looking for a special atmosphere and a good meal? The restaurant at **Villa Lapas** *($$$; at the beginning of the road to Catarata Manantial Agua Viva, where it branches off the San José-Jacó road, ☎663-0811, ≠663-1516)* fits the bill. The hotel's location (see p 304) in a very sonorous forest next to a river lets you take in all the seductive sounds of Costa Rica's wilderness while dining in its very pretty restaurant. The natural surroundings and pleasant decor add to the enjoyment the restaurant's international cuisine.

The restaurant at **Villa Caletas** *($$$$; between Punta Leona and Jacó, on a secondary road that branches off the national highway, ☎257-3653, ≠222-2059)* is as exceptional for its beauty as for its service. Perched on a hill, it offers a breathtaking view of the surroundings. The classic interior decor exudes tastefully subdued elegance. You can enjoy the international cuisine served here, or just come to have a drink at the bar.

### Jacó to Quepos

#### Parrita

Parrita is the place to stop for a bite to eat between Jacó and Quepos. **Los Tucanes** *($; across from Supermercado La Julieta, on the main street, Parrita, ☎779-9129)* is an unpretentious restaurant that serves simple Costa Rican dishes. **Café Yoli** *($$; every day 7am to 11pm; near the exit from the town toward Jacó, on the main street, Parrita)* is the best place for a meal. Although its Québécoise owner has put together a menu of mainly pizza, you can also have good hamburgers, breakfasts and Costa Rican meals in its inviting, beautiful, recently renovated surroundings.

### The Quepos Region

**Heladería Dani** *(Av. Central, next to the Malinche hotel)* offers 28 flavours of ice cream and sherbet as well as banana splits, sundaes, milkshakes, etc.

On Avenida Central, past Twisted Lemon, heading toward the lagoon, **Angolo** is a small shop that sells fresh bread and pasta, and also prepares sandwiches.

The market adjacent to the bus station is a good spot for a light lunch.

**Café Milagro** *($; along the road parallel to the estuary, ☎777-1707)* is everything you could ask for in a café. The desserts are excellent (chocolate and cheese brownies, what a treat!), and there is an extensive selection of coffees, jams, syrups, coffee cups and cigars. The atmosphere is pleasant and friendly, with the enticing aroma of coffee wafting through the air. Some popular North American magazines, such as *Mademoiselle*, *The Enquirer* and *Billboard*, as well as dailies like *USA Today*, are available.

**Punto de Encuantro Cafetería y Panadería** *($; Av. Central, next to Cabinas Doña Alicia)* is a very friendly spot for breakfast, hot chocolate, tea, coffee and fresh juice.

Head to the very popular **El Pueblo** *($)* restaurant for a drink or a late-night bite to eat.

**Dos Locos** *($$; ever day 7:30am to 11pm; Av. Central, Calle Central, across from Angolo)* has a pretty decor and is very clean. There is a small bar adjacent to the restaurant.

On the ground floor of **Hotel Kamuk** *($$; on the main street across from the ocean, ☎777-0379)*, is a beautiful little restaurant with a refined, attractive decor. The Kamuk has another **restaurant** *($$$)* on the third floor, which is isolated from the town traffic and has a lovely view of the surroundings. International menu.

Quiet and yet very popular, **Restaurante Isabel** *($$; near Buena Nota)* is the perfect place for a tasty light seafood meal right in the heart of Quepos.

**El Gran Escape** *($$$; Wed to Mon)* is one of Quepos's many seafood and fish restaurants. A sign in front of the restaurant reads, "You hook 'em, we cook 'em." The interior has an attractive decor and is very clean. Serves good breakfasts.

**Quepos to Manuel Antonio**

Most of the restaurants of the hotels in this area are open to the public, but here is a list of places worth remembering.

There is a **Café Milagro** on the road from Quepos to Manuel Antonio, diagonally across from the entrance to the Mariposa hotel. Like the café in Quepos, it sells souvenirs, muffins, cakes, cigars and excellent coffees. It occasionally doubles as an art gallery.

Diagonally across from Café Milagro, **Barba Roja** *($-$$; Tue to Sun 7:30am to midnight)* is simultaneously a very popular restaurant and an art gallery. It serves North American cuisine (hamburgers, sandwiches, steaks, some seafood, etc.), which is popular with people who like this type of food, particularly at breakfast.

The restaurant-bar **Del Mar** *($$; on the beach just before Manuel Antonio park)* has a lively Costa Rican atmosphere and menu. The background music caters to the rather young, dynamic clientele that frequents the place in the late afternoon and evenings. *Tico* menu.

**Mar y Sombra** *($$; 500 m from the entrance to Manuel Antonio park)* is a popular restaurant that is also right on the beach, but is a bit larger than the Del Mar. Its decor, including the landscaping, is sightly better. Costa Rican cuisine.

Part of the Casitas Eclipse complex (see p 313), the restaurant and bar **Jardin Gourmet** *($$-$$$)* serves Mediterranean cuisine in a decor to match. Breakfast, lunch and dinner are served.

**Restaurante Karola** *($$$; Thu to Tue; between Barba Roja and the road to Mariposa, on the Quepos-Manuel Antonio road, ☎777-0424)* opens for breakfast at 7am. Specialties include macadamia nut pies, eggs *ranchero*, steaks, enchiladas, etc.

The restaurant at the **Hotel Plinio** *($$$; set back a few hundred m from the road, 1 km from Quepos, ☎777-0055, ⇌777-0558)* is good and recommended. The atmosphere is very pleasant, and the homemade bread and daily specials are delicious. The Plinio makes a delicious *tiramisu*, which might well be the best in the country. It is a good idea to make advance reservations.

The restaurant at the hotel **Vela Bar** *($$$; 100 m from the main Quepos-Manuel Antonio road, near the park entrance, ☎777-0413, ⇌777-7071)* is pleasantly nestled in greenery and serves vegetarian cuisine.

The French-managed restaurant at **Hotel El Byblos** *($$$$; on the Quepos-Manuel Antonio road)* offers authentic French cuisine in a subdued, distinguished environment. This is the place for shrimp Provençale and succulent *profiteroles*!

Across from El Byblos, **Richard's** *($$$$; on the Quepos-Manuel Antonio road)* is a classy pasta and seafood restaurant.

## ENTERTAINMENT

### South of Puntarenas

#### The Jacó Region

**Bar El Zarpe** *(in the Jacó shopping centre)* really livens up at night. It is always busy and the staff is very friendly.

There are two nightclubs in Jacó; **La Discoteca los Toucanes** and **La Central**, at the ends of the streets from downtown to the beach. La Central is perhaps more of a typical nightclub than the other, and offers parking.

#### The Quepos Region

**Pub Kamuk** *(on the main street, facing the ocean, Quepos, ☎777-0379)*, at the hotel of the same name, is a live music venue that is quite busy.

**Bahía Azul** *(next door to the Quepos marina)* is a restaurant and dance bar that has pretty views of the port and the sea. An excellent spot for a cool cocktail and a breath of fresh air, since it is a bit cooler here than in the rest of the town.

**Arco Iris** *(next to Bahía Azul, in the Quepos marina)* is a nightclub that attracts twenty-somethings.

**Twisted Lemon** *(next door to Banco de Costa Rica, at the centre of Quepos on Avenida Central)* is a place to have a drink, listen to music and play pool.

**La Boquita** *(on the second floor, across from the restaurant El Pueblo)* is also very popular.

**El Banco Bar** *(across from the Ramus hotel in Quepos)* is a very friendly, attractive bar covered with souvenir photos and frequented by a laid-back clientele.

## SHOPPING

### The Southern Nicoya Peninsula

#### Montezuma

Montezuma has many little shops that sell clothing, jewellery and souvenirs of Costa Rica. Whether you are looking for a hammock, sandals, a hat or a wet suit for surfing, you have a large selection. **El Hamaquero** *(next door to Café Montezuma)* as well as the shop upstairs from the tourist office, offers a large selection of clothing, some of which is made in Costa Rica. As in the rest of the country, you can also find clothing and jewellery from Indonesia, India and Guatemala.

### South of Puntarenas

#### The Jacó Region

Jacó has a full-fledged shopping mall, **Plaza Jacó**, located across from the Jacó Best Western. Inside there is a branch of Banco de Costa Rica, of course.

Wine and spirits are available at **Licorería del Mar**, a short distance south of the restaurant Killer Munchies, in Jacó.

The **Garden Café Jacó Beach Gift Shop** *(☎643-3404)* sells cigars and souvenirs of all sorts. Surfing and fishing and snorkelling equipment are also available here.

### The Quepos Region

You can buy some magazines at the **Botica Quepos** pharmacy, in Quepos, at the corner of Avenida 2 and Calle 2, across from the lagoon.

Beside the playground in Quepos is **Galería Costa Rica**, a shop that sells crafts and colourful summer clothing. Very attractive and friendly.

Not far from here, **Galería Del Sol Gift Shop**, next to Cabinas Hellen, also sells souvenirs and colourful clothing.

**Uluwatu** is a shop similar to those above, and is next door to Twisted Lemon.

**Motmot**, next door to the Malinche hotel, is a very appealing shop that sells crafts, beautiful agendas, original clothing, charm bracelets, jewellery, tinted glasses and pretty greeting cards, as well as lovely postcards, which are not very common in Costa Rica.

The "multi-boutique" **Aventura** *(Calle Central, Av. Central/1, Quepos, ☎777-1019 or 777-0429, ⇌777-0279)* is Québec-owned and sells high-quality crafts.

### Quepos to Manuel Antonio

Located one kilometres before the park, the little shop **La Buena Nota** *(every day 8am to 7pm)* sells newspapers, magazines, postcards and some summer and beach clothing in bright colours with appealing prints.

At the friendly **Café Milagro** *(two locations: on the street that runs parallel to the estuary in Quepos proper, ☎777-1707; and on the Quepos-Manuel Antonio road)* you can buy coffee, jam, syrup, coffee cups, cigars, etc., and pick up some popular North American magazines (*Mademoiselle*, *The Enquirer* and *Billboard*) and newspapers such as *USA Today*.

The South
0
15
30km
Caribbean Sea
LIMÓN
CARTAGO
SAN JOSÉ
PANAMÁ
PUNTARENAS
Pacific Ocean
Reserva Indígena Alto Y Bajo Chirripó
Reserva Indígena Tayni
Reserva Biológica Hitoy-Cerere
Refugio Nacional de Fauna Silvestre Tapantí
Parque Nacional Chirripó
Reserva Indígena Telire
Reserva Indígena Talamanca-Bribri
Cordillera de Talamanca
Parque Internacional La Amistad
Reserva Indígena Ujarras-Salitre
Reserva Indígena Cabagra
Reserva Indígena Boruca
Valle de El General
Cahuita
Bribri
Copey
S.Gerardo de Dota
S.Gerardo de Rivas
Quebradas
Santa Rosa
Rivas
Gral.Viejo
San Isidro de El General
Palmares
Platanillo
Barú
Cajón
San Pedro
Dominical
Dominicalito
Ceibo
San Rafael
Volcán
Buenos Aires
Pejibaye
Ojochal
Las Pilas
Potrero Grande
Palmar Norte
Ciudad Cortés
Palmar Sur
Sierpe
Limoncito
Sabalito
San Vito
Chacarita
Wilson Botanical Gardens
Agua Buena
Río Claro
Ciudad Neily
Golfito
Canoas
La Cuesta
Progreso
Puerto Armuelles
Bahía de Charco Azul
Bahía de Coronado
Mangrove
Drake
Bahía Drake
Agujitas
Ranchito Quemado
Rincón
Pto. Escondido
Charcos
Los Planes
La Palma
Los Patos
Barrigones
Agujas
Sándalo
Lajitas
Tigre
Dos Brazos
Río Nuevo
Puerto Jiménez
Golfo Dulce
Finca Catalina
Finca Ojo de Agua
Carate
Agua Buena
Madrigal
La Leona
La Sirena
Pavo
Parque Nacional Corcovado
Península de Osa
Cabo Matapalo
Playa Zancudo
Playa Pavones
Playa Gallardo
Playa San Josecito
Parque Nacional Corcovado
Marenco
Playa San Josecito
San Pedrillo
Punta Llorona
Playa Llorona
Playa Corcovado
Punta Burica
Río Sereno
Pta. Dominical
Playa Hermosa
Reserva Biológica Oro Verde
Playa Ballena
P.N. Marino Ballena
Playa Piñuela
Playa Tortuga
Cataratas Mauyaca
Costanera Sur
Carretera Interamericana
Cerro Blanco (3800m)
Cerro Chirripó (3819m)
Cerro Terbi (3760m)
Río General
Río Grande de Térraba
Río Sierpe
Río Colorado
Río Telivé
Río Sixaola
Río Carbón
© ULYSSES

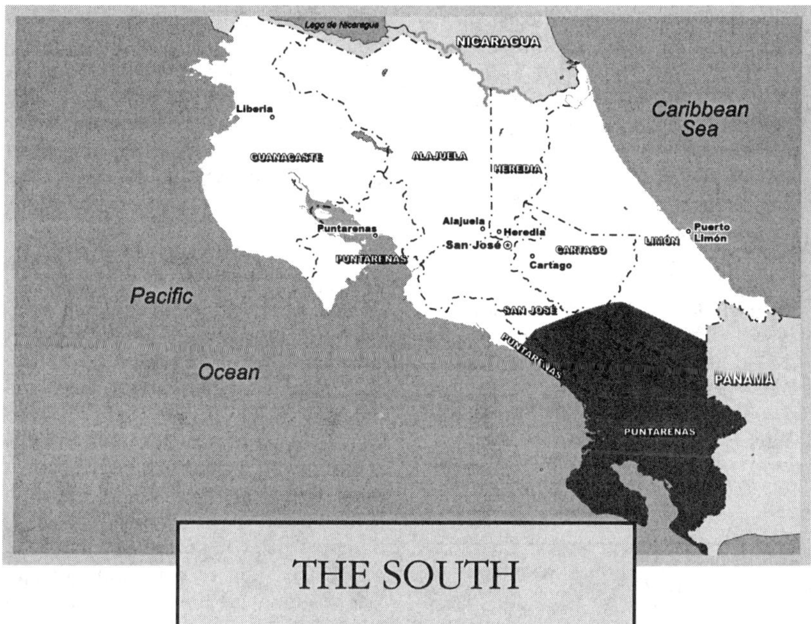


# THE SOUTH

Not many vacationers venture to the southern parts of Costa Rica, though it has more pristine areas than any of the other regions, providing ample opportunities to commune with nature.

This chapter covers the region that extends from the Talamanca mountain range (in the middle of the country) to the Panamanian border in the south and the Pacific coast in the west. Many roads, including the Interamericana cross this region of striking contrasts. It has the country's highest peak (Mount Chirripó), largest park (La Amistad), the Pacific coast's extreme heat and humidity and the country's coldest climatic zones! These factors have contributed to the diversity of the landscape: tundra vegetation caps the summits of the central mountains, whereas humid tropical forests flourish along the coast. The region's many charms include crystal-clear waterfalls, beaches ideal for surfing, rivers made for whitewater rafting, and tropical forests sheltering the exotic quetzal bird.

Southern Costa Rica also has a unique cultural and archeological heritage. Native people descended from Pre-Columbian tribes are reminders of the country's pre-colonial past.

In brief, southern Costa Rica offers many opportunities for discovery, relaxation, recreation, and learning.

## FINDING YOUR WAY AROUND

### By Plane

**Osa Peninsula**

**Puerto Jiménez**: **Sansa** *(☎221-9414)* and **Travelair** *(☎220-3054)* airlines offer daily service from San José to Puerto

Jiménez. The flight takes nearly 1.5 hours, for about $150 return fare.

**The Region's North**

**Palmar:**The airport is located in Palmar Sur, south of the Río Grande de Térraba. Most arrivals are greeted by a fleet of taxis.

**Golfito**: **Sansa** *(Mon to Sat; $51 one way; ☎233-0397, 233-3258, 233-5330 or 255-2176)* and **Travelair** *(every day; $66 one way; ☎232-7883, 220-3054 or 220-0413*) offer regular service between Golfito and San José

## By Car

**The Region's North**

A completed section of the Costarena Sur highway now runs between Dominical and Palmar on the northern portion of the Pacific coastline. More and more motorists, as well as transport trucks from Golfito or Panama, prefer the Costarena Sur to the more central Interamericana, which has less favourable conditions. Beautiful wilderness borders the Costarena Sur. However, the arrival of this road will probably lead to the economic development of the area, with all the potential benefits and drawbacks this entails.

**San Isidro de El General**: Take the southbound Interamericana.

**San Gerardo de Dota**: Take the exit at kilometre 80 on the Interamericana.

**Dominical**: An asphalt road in fairly good condition runs from San Isidro de El General to Dominical in less than an hour. Drive cautiously, as this road snakes through the multitude of hills separating the two regions. You can also drive to Dominical from Quepos in 45 minutes on a fairly decent road that travels inland via Savegre. This road joins a section of the Costarena Sur that is under repair (but is passable) between Dominical and Palmar.

**Parque Nacional Chirripó**

The 22 kilometres between San Isidro and San Gerardo de Rivas take nearly 1.5 hours. From San Isidro, take the south-bound Interamericana. Cross the Río San Isidro bridge, then the Río Jilguero bridge, and turn left after a few hundred meters on an unmarked road. This small road is paved up until Rivas, where it becomes narrow and bumpy. Once you pass the small village of Canán, keep to your right for San Gerardo de Rivas (the left will take you to Herradura).

**Osa Peninsula**

**Puerto Jiménez**: To reach the Osa Peninsula, you can take the Interamericana or the southbound coastal road to Palmar Norte. In the latter case, once you reach Chacarita (33 km south of Palmar Norte), keep your eyes open for a small sign (on the right, near the gas station) indicating the road that leads to the tip of the Osa peninsula. It takes about two hours to drive the 78 kilometres to Puerto Jiménez on the Interamericana. The road is paved and in fairly good condition to Rincón (45 km), after which it deteriorates somewhat before arriving in Puerto Jiménez.

**Parque Nacional Corcovado (Carate)**

Most visitors access the park via the La Leona entrance near Carate. From Puerto Jiménez, a small road leads to

Carate (43 km, approx. 2 hours). All types of cars can make it to Cabo Matapalo (approx. 20 km), but you need a four-wheel drive to reach Carate. During our visit, we crossed 13 streams, three of which were fairly large. In Carate, which is less of a town than a stopping place, the road ends near a small landing strip and a *pulpería.* Park your vehicle at the *pulpería* ($2/day) and walk 2 kilometres along the beach to reach the park entrance.

**The Region's South**

**Palmar**: From San José or San Isidro de El General, follow the Interamericana to Palmar. Alternately, drive along the Pacific coast by way of the Costarena Sur, which passes through Dominical.

**Sierpe**: There is an access route to Sierpe on the Interamericana, close to Palma Sur. This road is poorly signed out so ask locals for directions.

**Boruca**: This reserve is set back from the Interamericana, reached via the road joining the Interamericana and Boruca, a few kilometers south of Curré. This road is quite rough and a four-wheel drive is probably necessary during the rainy season.

**Golfito**: Take the Interamericana from San José or San Isidro de El General. The exit for Golfito appears in Río Claro. Turn off the Interarmericana, onto a road that leads to the coast. From San José, it is about a seven-hour drive.

**Zancudo**: The road from the Interamericana to Golfito branches to Zancudo. You will have to cross the Río Coto Colorado by ferry before continuing on to Zancudo. The road is not well signed out, so ask locals for directions.

**Pavones**: Situated some 10 kilometres south of Zancudo.

**San Vito**: From San Isidro de El General, take the Interamericana to Paso Real. to get to the Coto Brus road (asphalted and in fairly good condition), turn left onto the bridge crossing the Río Grande de Térraba. It should take you just over two hours to get to San Vito. If you are coming from Golfito, head to Ciudad Neily and drive up the steep road located north of the city. The views of the mountains and coast are beautiful, but stay focussed on the road which, though mostly asphalted, is quite narrow and steep, with many hairpin turns. There are many potholes and thick fog is frequent at certain times of the year.

**Wilson Botanical Garden**: The Wilson Botanical Garden is 15 minutes south of San Vito, on the road to Ciudad Neily.

## By Bus

**The Region's North**

**San Isidro de El General**: The bus station for San José is situated on the Interamericana, between Calles 2 and 4. The Vargas Rojas bus company *(☎222-9763 in San José or 771-0419 in San Isidro)* offers four departures to San Isidro from San José (*$2; 6:30am, 9:30am, 12:30pm and 3:30pm)*. The schedule is the same for the return trip.

**San Gerardo de Dota**: From San José, take the bus to San Isidro and ask the driver to let you off at the *Entrada* in San Gerardo, at kilometre 80 on the Interamericana.

**Parque Nacional Chirripó**

A bus from San Isidro (daily departures at 5am and 2pm) stops right in front of the park's administrative offices in San Gerardo de Rivas. The trip takes approximately 1.5 hours. Buses leave for San Isidro at 7am and 4pm.

**Osa Peninsula**

**Puerto Jiménez**: From San José, a bus *(daily departures at 6am and 12pm; corner of Calle 12 and Av. 7)* goes directly to Puerto Jiménez, which is the main village on the Osa peninsula. The nine-hour trip costs $6 *(Transportes Blanco-Lobo, ☎257-4121)*.

**The Region's South**

**Boruca**: Buses depart for Boruca twice a day from the Mercado Central in Buenos Aires. The trip takes 1.5 hours and costs a few dollars.

## By Boat

**Osa Peninsula**

**Golfito – Puerto Jiménez**: A passenger ferry *(☎735-5017)* commutes between Golfito (daily departures at 11am) and Puerto Jiménez (daily departures at 6am). The crossing takes about 1 hour and 15 minutes and costs $3. Depending on your destination, you can also take a taxi-boat *(Abocap, ☎775-0357)*.

**Bahía Drake – Sierpe**: It takes approximately 30 minutes to drive from Palmar Norte to Sierpe (car, bus or taxi). If you have a reservation, most of the region's hotels provide boat transportation to and from Sierpe. Otherwise, taxi-boats can be hired at the dock. The Pulpería Fenix or the Pargo Hotel *(☎788-8111)* can assist you in finding a taxi-boat. The crossing takes about 1.5 hours and costs approximately $15 per person (each way).

**The Region's South**

**Sierpe**: (See above.)

**Zancudo**: Departures to Zancudo, from Muellecito de Golfito, twice a day. Departure times are likely to change so enquire first.

## PRACTICAL INFORMATION

In southern Costa Rica, the towns of San Isidro de El General, Golfito, Palmar Norte, Ciudad Neily, and San Vito provide basic services, such as banking (branch offices and ATM). Such services are rare in the Osa Peninsula, especially outside of Puerto Jiménez.

**San Isidro de El General**: The Banco del Commercio is located on the Avenida Central, between Calles 2 and 4. The Banco Popular (for cash advances using Visa cards) is on the corner of Avenida 2 and Calle 1. The Banco Nacional de Costa Rica is situated on the corner of Avenida 1 and Calle Central. The tourist information center is situated on Calle 4, between Avenidas 1 and 3. The Selvamar tourist reservations center is situated on the Calle Central, a little outside the downtown core, south of Avenida 10.

**Palmar Norte**: There is a branch office of the Banco Popular in a small shopping center, north of the Interamericana. The Banco Nacional is situated on the other side of the Interamericana, slightly to the east.

**Ciudad Neily**: Ciudad Neily centre has a modern and well-stocked Supermercado Loaiza, a *mercado*, a bus station, and a Banco Popular, Banco Nacional and Banco de Costa Rica.

**San Vito**: The Licorería La Cruz, in the northwest section of the town centre, sells English magazines. The Supermercado B&M is located close to the main intersection of the town centre. The Bancrecen, Popular, Nacional and Costa Rica banks all have branch offices in San Vito.

**Golfito**: The Banco de Costa Rica has a branch office in Golfito, close to the Muellecito. There is also a Banco Popular ATM at the Deposito Libre. Two reputable *supermercados*, Granados and Consucoop, are located side by side in the Pueblo Civil on Golfito's main boulevard.

## EXPLORING

### The Region's North

**The San Isidro de El General Region**

The northern part of the region includes the alpine zone of the Talamanca mountain range, which you have to cross to get to San Isidro. The change of climate and vegetation will become apparent as you drive along the Interamericana. As the road rises to the **Cerro de la Muerte ★★**, the highest point before the descent to San Isidro, the lush forests that are common in other regions gradually give way to stunted tundra-like vegetation. The stunning panorama of green slopes plunging vertically into gorges far below can be admired from the *miradores*, or lookouts, along the way. The covered **Mirador Vista del Valle** is especially scenic.

Set out early in the morning to avoid the heavy fog that tends to encase these high-lying regions later in the day. And avoid driving night! This narrow stretch of road, often devoid of a shoulder and protective railing, is made hazardous by fog (or rain), poor lighting, a heavy flow of trucks, and aggressive, erratic drivers.

Nestled in the Talamanca mountain range, Copey de Dota and San Gerardo de Dota are two lovely places from which to savor the landscape. The unique climate and topography of both moutainside towns will undoubtedly leave a lasting impression on you.

At an altitude of 2 000 metres, **Copey** (7 km below the Interamericana, at km 58) grows apples, avocados, peaches, and prunes. Lush forests, green pastures and a flowing river hemmed in by steep banks constitute the pastoral scenery of **San Gerardo de Dota ★** (9 km below the Interamericana, at km 85), a small town tucked into a valley. Myriad plant species flourish in the forest, including several types of colorful mushrooms. Oaks are over a hundred years old. The area looks lovely, even when it rains (just remember that at this altitude, the rain can be quite cold). However, to get there, you must drive down a very steep and narrow road (partially asphalt) that meanders down 9 kilometres of mountainside. Four-wheel drives are highly recommended in this region.

The **view ★★** of San Isidro de El General and its valley from Dominical or the Cerro de la Muerte is gorgeous. As you drive through the area, you will catch glimpses of the vast expanse of green landscape surrounded by majestic mountains.

With a population 40,000, **San Isidro de El General**, is the southern region's capital and largest city. Although the city itself has no spectacular sights to offer, you can enjoy people-watching in the central park or explore the busy marketplace, which is always in full swing since San Isidro is a major centre for agricultural and other produce. The **Museo Regional del Sur** *(Mon to Fri 9am to noon and 1pm to 5pm; inside the cultural centre that formerly housed the municipal market, San Isidro, ☎/≠771-5273)* has several exhibits on Costa Rica's cultural and environmental issues.

San Isidro de El General is also the southern region's main point of departure for any destination. The city is an important stop between San José and the neighbouring country further south, Panama. Thus, you have to pass through San Isidro to get to the Quebradas region, Mount Chirripó, Dominical on the Pacific coast, and the southern sector of the region, which lies along the Interamericana.

Seven kilometres north of San Isidro, the **Las Quebradas centre for biology ★** *(Tue to Thu 8am to 14pm, Sat to Sun 8am to 3pm, closed in Oct; Quebradas, ☎/≠771-4131)* is a protected nature reserve that promotes the conservation of the Río Quebradas basin, which is the principal source of drinking water for the El General region. Various nature-related activities are offered in this sector located at an altitude of 1,000 metres. Many varieties of plants and animals can be observed along the 2.5 kilometres of paths. Picnicking and camping are permitted on site. During the rainy season (September and October), it is best to come here with a four-wheel drive.

### The Rivas Region

The region of Rivas is located 10 kilometres northeast of San Isidro de El General. Not only is this region the gateway to Mount Chirripó, but it is also one of the country's most important archeological sites, where ongoing excavations are providing new insights into pre-Columbian societies. Eventually, when more objects will be uncovered, Rivas will become as archeologically significant as Turrialba and Guayabo (see p 116 and 119).

Take a day to visit the **Rancho La Botija** *(adults $5, children $3; Tue to Sun 7am to 8pm; 6 km from San Isidro, on the road to Rivas, ☎382-3052, ≠771-1401)*, a small recreation center (playgrounds, game rooms, pool, etc.), located in what used to be a sugarcane refinery. The owners will give you a short tour of the property, stopping to examine objects from the past, such as an old *trapiche* (sugar mill), and a series of stones etched with glyphs (found all over Rivas) dating from the Pre-Columbian period. You can also enjoy a light meal on site.

Like La Botija, **La Pradera** *(on the San Isidro – Rivas road, before reaching Albergue Talari, Rivas)* is a recreation centre where you can take part in all kinds of outdoor and sports activities (football, etc.). Or, stroll through the picturesque rolling countryside of Rivas, where you will come across many stones inscribed with glyphs.

A little farther down the road, just before the entrance to Mount Chirripó park, is **San Gerardo de Rivas ★**. Although most people drive straight through this little village on their way to the park, you might want to stop to better enjoy the beauty of the surroundings. Bird lovers will be particularly appreciative. What's more, just a kilometre from San Gerardo, on the road to **Herradura** (follow the one-km path to the right of the road), you can take a dip in a hilltop **hot spring**. It costs $1, which you pay to the owner who lives beside the spring.

**The Dominical Region**

If you are heading towards Dominical from San Isidro de El General, stop at the magnificent waterfalls **Cataratas Nauyaca** ★ or Santo Cristo *(midway between San Isidro and Dominical, ☎771-3187, ⇌787-0006)*. Situated in the mountains that separate the coastal region of Dominical and the San Isidro valley, the falls are 20 metres and 45 metres high, respectively, and feed a basin that is 6 metres deep and has a surface of 1,000 square meters. A truly superb spot! Because there is no road to the falls, you have to get there on horseback. The owners of the property organize daily tours that include the ride to and from the falls on forest paths, meals before and after the expedition, a visit to a small zoo and, of course, the falls themselves. It is possible to swim in the crystal-clear water. The Centro Turístico Nauyaca has a small inn and a campground.

Begin exploring the coastal region of Dominical by visiting the Hacienda Barú (see p 336), which is on the coast, one kilometre north of the village of Dominical.

The **Cataratas Terciopelo** ★ *(access on horseback; make reservations with Selva Mar, ☎771-4582, ⇌771-8841)* is located inland from Dominical, north of the Hacienda Barú . With the surrounding jungle as its backdrop, this lovely three-tiered waterfall cascades into emerald green waters 40 metres below. Paradise can't be much better than this!

The beach and surf attract throngs of young people to **Dominical.** In fact, many of the town's hotels and restaurants are owned by these surf lovers who have left their country, for a time, or perhaps forever, to live out their dream. In Dominical, the best surf is on the village beach at the mouth of the Río Barú, or a little further south in **Punta Dominical**. The **Escuelita Dominical** even offers Spanish courses right on the beach.

**Hermosa** and **Ballena** are among the best swimming beaches in Costa Rica's southern region. They are 20 kilometres south of Dominical, along the Costarena Sur, towards Palmar and Ciudad Cortés.

The drive along the Costarena Sur from Dominical to other picturesque coastal sites is very pleasant in itself. This new route crosses undulating valleys, with little or no inhabitants and very few hotels or restaurants. A few kilometers south of Dominical, **Las Escaleras** (The Stairs) is a new sector slowly developing in the hills above the seashore. The view is certainly worth the steep drive up to the neighbourhood's few hotels.

Close to Dominicalito, south of the Dominical, **Poza Azul** is an enjoyable place to visit. Set in the forest, it features a natural deep blue pool (*poza* is loosely translated as "swimming basin") fed by a waterfall. Accessible by car.

The Costarena Sur separates the coast from the hinterland. Here, you must decide whether to drive along the coast or turn inland into wooded areas. In San Josecito de Uvita, the **Reserva Biológica Oro Verde** *(20$/person; guided visit and light meal; a few kilometers from Uvita; make reservations with Selva Mar, ☎771-4582, ⇌771-8841)* is situated in the mountains, three kilometres from the Costerana Sur. Having owned the land for over 35 years, "Macho" Duarte has turned to tourism as a means of preserving the humid tropical forest covering his property. This very remote terrain is perched high in the mountains overlooking the Pacific coast, and is accessible on foot or horseback. Needless to say, the view at this altitude (600 m) is breathtaking! Selva Mar can arrange for you to meet members of the Duarte family, and possibly even share a meal with them. You can also learn the art of sugar making. Overnight stays are possible in one of two small ***cabinas*** *($$; bp)*.

Between the ocean and the Costarena Sur, a little south of the road to Oro Verde, the **Rancho La Merced** *($10 to 55$/person; make reservations with Selva Mar, ☎771-4582, ⇌771-8841)* is a sanctuary for wild animals as well as a livestock ranch. You can visit for the day or spend the night in a rustic setting dining on *campesino* fare (see p 359). Activities include horseback riding, mountain climbing, and local tours. A new addition to the ranch, the **Profelis Center** reintroduces endangered feline species to the wilderness. Reserve in advance as this site is very popular, even in low season.

A little farther south is **Uvita**, an unremarkable town on the route to the Parque Nacional Marino Ballena (see p 337).

## Parque Nacional Chirripó

With mountains over 3,000 metres high, immense creased rock faces and a glacial lake, as well as shelters and marked trails for visitors, **Parque Nacional Chirripó** ★★★ *($6; every day 5am to 12pm; ☎771-3297 or 771-3155, ⇌771-3155)* has something for everyone. Cerro Chirripó (3,819 m) is the highest mountain in Costa Rica – and second highest in Central America. Thus, hikers will be impressed by the challenging trails through this alpine paradise amidst the tropical rainforest.

Covering 50,150 hectares, Chirripó National Park is located 26 kilometres northeast of San Isidro de El General and 150 kilometres from San José. The park entrance is in the small village of San Gerardo de Rivas, at an altitude of 1,350 metres. The summit of Cerro Chirripó is some 2,500 higher up – quite an exhausting climb! This hike takes at least three days (two nights). There are also other trails to the neighbouring mountaintops, which have wonderful views in good weather.

The park receives approximately 3.5 metres of rain annually, and temperatures range between - 9°C and 20°C. Since the weather is unpredictable, it is best to bring warm, sturdy, waterproof clothing. Also, since some 3,000 people visit this park every year, you should make advance reservations if you want to stay here overnight, especially on weekends, and above all during Easter when Costa Ricans flock here *en masse*. However, during the rainy season, you might well have the trails to yourself and have no problem finding a place to stay. It is best to come between January and April, during the Costa Rican summer, when it rains less.

Although most people spend at least a few days in the park, it is also makes for a pleasant day-trip *($6, no reservations, arrive as early as possible in the morning)*. You can stroll through the lovely pastures and the dense tropical rainforest with its epiphytic plants and majestic trees, and see some of the smaller animals or tracks of the larger, more elusive ones (Baird tapirs, pumas, etc.) as well as several species of birds, including the resplendent quetzal. If you only have a day, it is not recommend to climb higher than the first shelter, known as **Llano Bonito**,

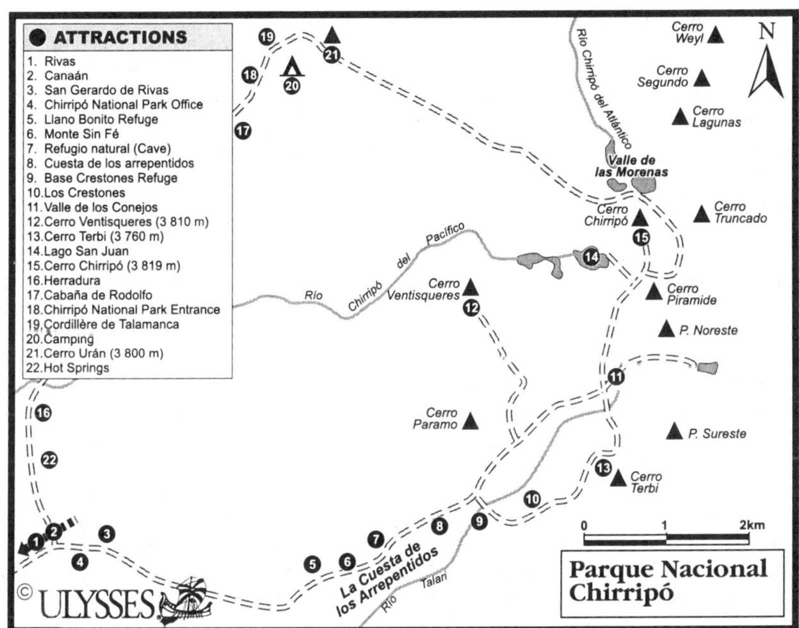


located about halfway between San Gerardo de Rivas and the main shelter.

The park is includes several distinct life zones. Thus, after passing through the tropical rainforest, you will come to a vast area of barren land swept by strong winds. The flora has adapted to this cold, wet habitat called the *páramo*, where there are many twisted trees whose growth has been stunted by the harsh climatic conditions. The Andean *páramo* stretches north to the Cerro Chirripó and the Cerro de la Muerte (along the Interamericana), a little further west.

The Cerro Chirripó rises over the Talamanca mountain range, which extends to the south. At the foot of the mountain lies a lovely, tranquil cold-water lake, **Lago San Juan**, which is a pleasant place to take a break. Closer to the shelter is the magnificent mass of creased limestone and igneous rock, known as **Los Crestones.** Both sites are picture-postcard perfect and easily accessible from the **Base Crestones** shelter at the summit.

If you only come to Costa Rica for two or three weeks, you might not be able to arrange for all the equipment (parka, backpack, sleeping bag, camping stove, etc.) or make the necessary reservations (transportation, shelters, guides, horses, etc.) yourself. However, if you stay at the **Talari** (see p 357) mountain inn in Rivas, the owners can make all the arrangements required for your stay in the Parque Nacional Chirripó if you notify them a few days or weeks in advance. This way, you can enjoy your mountain hike without any last-minute hassles.

Horses can be rented to carry your belongings on treks during the dry season (usually from December to May). One horse can transport the baggage of three or four hikers, and costs about $10 per day. Outside the dry season, you can hire porters *($20/day)*. In addition, you usually have to hire one of the local guides *(approx. $20/day)*, many of whom speak English. A small guiding association was established in the San Gerardo de Rivas and Herradura regions. The guides are reliable and friendly, and know the park trails like the backs of their hands.

You must register at the park office *(every day 5am to 5pm)* when you arrive in San Gerardo de Rivas, whether you have a reservation or not. You can leave your car and extra luggage near the office for a few extra *colones*. The park warden will give you a very basic map of the park and inform you about the condition of the trails and the latest weather reports. There is a park admission fee, and additional charges to stay at the shelters *($3/person/night)* or camp *($1.25/person/night)* near the Mount Uran summit, the only place in the park where it is permitted.

### Climbing Cerro Chirripó

The first day is a long and steady (16 km) climb from San Gerardo de Rivas to the Base Crestones shelter, at about 2,200 metres. It is best to set out as early as possible, around 5am and 6am. Park wardens usually do not allow you to start this trek after 11am, since night falls around 6pm. Depending on your fitness level, your hiking experience, the weight of your backpack and the weather, leave yourself 7 to 12 hours to cover this distance.

The trail is well marked out and easy to follow. There are signs indicating the altitude reached and the number of kilometres remaining to the summit of Cerro Chirripó approximately every two kilometres. Remember to bring enough water, since the first source of drinkable water is almost halfway to the Base Crestones, at the Llano Bonito shelter. The trail passes through pastures, the lowland tropical rainforest and the dense upper rainforest. You will see and especially hear many birds along the way, and there are often monkeys around the first shelter.

**Llano Bonito** is the first shelter, but is really more of a rest station and emergency stop in case hikers experience serious difficulties (exhaustion, injuries, suddenly bad weather, etc.), than a place to sleep. After this station, the trail climbs steadily to a small mountain known as **Monte Sin Fé**. The trees become smaller and the type of vegetation changes as the climate becomes drier. The Cerro Chirripó region has experienced a number of forest fires over the years (notably 1976, 1985, 1991 and 1992), destroying thousands of hectares of forest, plain and savannah. Many were caused by careless hikers.

A little farther on is a small cave known as a ***refugio natural*** that can accommodate about dozen hikers for the night, should you run into major difficulties. From here, it is only a one-to-two hour climb to the main shelter, after scaling the "Repentants' Hill" (*cuesta de los arrepentidos*). Finally, you will reach a huge rock face, pleated like an accordion: **Los Crestones**. The main shelter, **Base Crestones**, is so named because it is at the base of this cliff. Note that camping is prohibited in this region. When we visited the park, a new shelter was being built to replace the other shelters. It should be able to house sixty hikers and provide all the basic amenities.

The summit of Cerro Chirripó (3,819 m) is only four kilometres from the shelter. It takes 1.5 to 2 hours to reach, and is 300 metres higher up. Along the way, you will see the "Rabbits' Valley" (Valle de los Conejos), which was abandoned by these small creatures after a terrible fire in 1976. From the top of Cerro Chirripó, you will be able to see the Atlantic Ocean to the east and the Pacific Ocean to the west – if the sky is clear. Since it is often covered in clouds by early afternoon, we suggest that you wait for a clear morning before making this trek. If the weather is uncertain, you can hike along some of the other trails around the shelter, such as the **Valle de los Conejos**, **Cerro Ventisqueres** or **Cerro Terbi**.

### Climbing Cerro Urán

**Cerro Urán** is located approximately 12 kilometres northwest of the Cerro Chirripó. When the new shelter at Los Crestones was being built and access to Cerro Chirripó was closed, hikers had no choice but to take the path up the Cerro Urán. This trail starts in the tiny village of Herradura and passes through pastures before reaching the summit.

This climb leads you through exquisite valleys and a magnificent forest. You need a guide for this three-day hike, since the trails are not marked and cross privately owned farmland. You can either camp *($1.25/person/night)* on the mountain range (over 3,000 m in altitude) or sleep in the small shelter *($2/person/night)* known as **Cabaña de Rodolfo**, near the **Finca San Carlos**, about a four-hour walk from Herradura. We strongly recommend that you stay in the shelter, since the camp site is farther away and you will have to climb to it carrying all your equipment. Also, the area receives a lot of rain so camping is not always the most pleasant option.

The first day takes you along small trails through pastures from Herradura to the shelter. You will have spectacular views of the landscape, including the neighbouring valleys with their peacefully grazing cows. The view from the top of Cerro Urán is also incredible. However, protect yourself from the blazing sun, since the trail rarely ventures into the forest.

The next day is the steep climb to the summit. You should only take a small backpack on the trail that runs through superb tropical rainforest where moss, ferns and bromeliads abound. Farther on, the trail joins the Talamanca range. At this point, the lush vegetation gives way to small, sturdy trees that endure the strong winds that blow almost continuously. Since the cordillera is bordered by the mountain range, it also gets many clouds that bring fog and rain from the Atlantic. Thus, the weather can change quickly and with little warning. We were taken by surprise by bad weather, even though it had been fair at the shelter, and were forced to turn back just before reaching the top of Cerro Urán. Cerro Urán's exact altitude is disputed: books and maps indicate it to be anywhere between 3,600 and 3,800 metres high, thus slightly lower than Cerro Chirripó (3,819 m).

The third day takes you back to Herradura, a small town where horseback is still the main means of transportation. It is a perfect place to go horseback riding in the area (make reservations with your guide ahead of time) and discover the daily life of these proud and generous farmers. Our guide, René Robles Santamaría, cordially invited us to have dinner with him and his family, in a quaint house that is only accessible on horseback or on foot.

If you have any energy left, you can take a looping trail approximately 35 kilometres long that passes through Herradura, Cerro Urán, Cerro Chirripó and San Gerardo de Rivas. This hike takes four to five days and is very

***Cayman***

difficult, especially since you have to carry your heavy backpack. You can also hire a guide to take you from Herradura to the entrance of the Chirripó National Park, located between the shelter (Cabaña de Rodolfo) and the cordillera. You must reserve in advance (at the San Gerardo de Rivas park office) for the Base Crestones shelter, and pay admission to the park.

After hiking a few days, nothing beats spending some time in the soothing waters of the **hot springs** near Herradura. There are signs for the springs are along the right side of the road, and parking is available. A one-kilometre trail leads to a house from which you can access this site *($1/person)*.

## Hacienda Barú

The **Hacienda Barú** ★★ *($2; every day; ☎787-0003, ⇄787-0004)* is a magnificent 336-hectare private wildlife reserve, stretching west and northwest of Dominical. It encompasses many different habitats, including primary and secondary forest, pastures, mangroves, a former cocoa plantation and a superb beach on the Pacific with numerous trees and different types of vegetation

For the past twenty years, Jack and Diane Ewing have owned the park. Jack first came here in 1972 to run a 150-head cattle farm. Then, in 1978, he moved here permanently with Diane and their two children. At the time, the farm had no electricity, and the road was nothing but a small path. The Ewing family tried to grow rice, beans, soya beans and cocoa, but without any commercial success. In the late 1980s, the farm's main activity changed from farming to preserving the surrounding environment, and educating visitors about these natural riches. Now, the area is a park where you can stay one or more days in *cabinas* and tents in the jungle.

Steve Stroud teamed up with the Ewings in 1992 to help turn the area into a real ecotourist site with six *cabinas* (see p 360), a restaurant and many possible activities. You can spend a few hours or a whole day on the trails, learning about the plant and animal life and the history of this model park.

A waterfall in verdant surroundings: typical of Costa Rican scenery.
*- Didier Raffin*

Plants somehow manage to survive on the desolate rim of the Irazú volcano.
*- Claude Hervé-Bazin*

The park has a total of six kilometres of hiking trails. Admission is 500 colons *($2)*, which is divided between trail maintenance (300 colons) and the Department of the Environment (200 colons). You will receive a small leaflet outlining the trails, which lead to a teak plantation, a canal, the mangrove, the beach and the mouth of the Río Barú. For a more detailed description of the park (history, flora, fauna, etc.), we recommend buying the small book entitled *Trails & Tales* ($4.25; published by the Hacienda Barú, 1997, 74 pages), written by Jack Ewing and illustrated by his wife Diane.

You can also hire one of the six guides *($15 to $25/person, depending on the trail)* to explore the park's rich variety of animals and plants. There are an estimated 311 species of birds, 62 species of mammals, 50 species of amphibians and reptiles and hundreds of species of plants, including 75 types of orchids. This area is home to white-faced capuchin monkeys, sloths, coyotes, pumas, ocelots, caimans, crocodiles and 22 species of bats.

Some of the activities available in the area include the popular canopy tour *($35)*, where visitors (3 people at a time) are hoisted up to an observation platform suspended from a tree 34 metres in the air. You can also spend the night camping out in the jungle *($60)*, where you will wake up to the typical noises of the rainforest. There are also horseback riding excursions along the beach and through the mangrove *($25/3 hours)*, and kayaking through the mangrove at high tide *($35/3 hours)*.

The Ewings plan to finish building about 30 new *cabinas* by the sea by the end of 1999. The national Hacienda Barú wildlife reserve is bound to become one of the most popular ecotourist destinations in Costa Rica.

## Parque Nacional Marino Ballena

Just twenty kilometres south of Dominical, the **Parque Nacional Marino Ballena** ★ *($6; every day 8am to 4pm; ☎735-5036, ≠735-5282)* was created in 1990 to protect the largest coral reef on the country's Pacific coast. This 4,500-hectare park lies between Punta Uvita and Punta Piñuela, stretching along 13 kilometres of beach, rocks and mangroves.

This ocean park takes its name from the many humpback whales (rorquals) who come to the area between December and April. The humpback whale (*Megaptera novaeangliae*) is unquestionably the most spectacular of all the whales, since its tail emerges each time it dives, and it can jump quite high out of the water. Also, this whale will often dramatically slap the water with its flippers, as though in a fit of anger. It can grow up to 16 metres long and weigh as much as 36,000 kilograms. With an average life span of around forty years, it sometimes lives alone, but is often found in groups or pairs.

The **Isla Ballena** is found in the middle of the park and is the perfect spot for observing frigates, brown boobies and ibises, as well as green iguanas and basilisks. Ridley (*Lepidochelys olivacea*) and Hawksbill (*Eretmochelys imbricata*) turtles come to the beach to lay their eggs between May and November, especially in September and October.

The park currently has few visitor services (the information centre is in Bahía, beside Uvita). However, it will probably become more popular with the construction of the road along the coast, which now links Dominical and Palmar Norte. Camping is permitted, and the park's waters and coral reefs are great places for scuba diving and snorkelling. You can also go scuba diving around Isla Ballena and Rocas Las Tres Hermanas (The Three Sisters' rocks), off Playa Ballena. You can swim in the natural pools that form in the rocks at low tide.

## The Osa Peninsula

The **Osa Peninsula ★★** juts out into the Pacific Ocean from Costa Rica's southwest. This region has been largely ignored by tourists, who tend to stay close to San José and thus prefer the Central Pacific and Guanacaste regions. However, the number of visitors who come to explore the Osa Peninsula looking for adventure grows every year, especially since the region has become easier to access by car or bus (about 8 hours from San José), and is only 1.5 hours away by plane.

This beautiful, isolated peninsula has one of the only tropical rainforests along the Pacific Coast, and became home to an incredible variety of plants and animals over the centuries. However, because this area was unprotected, a large logging company bought it for next to nothing and set up shop here, along with dozens of settlers. Hunting and logging threatened the survival of much of the wildlife, which had already become extinct in other parts of the country. The government did not want the Osa Peninsula to undergo the same environmental degradation as Guanacaste, where deforestation caused the wildlife to disappear and even led to a dramatic change in temperature that turned the region into a desert. Thus, the Corcovado region (41,788 ha) of the peninsula was made a protected national park on October 24, 1975.

The Parque Nacional Corcovado has remained wild and difficult to access, and is thus a favourite destination for adventure-seeking tourists. In fact, most tourists come to Puerto Jiménez, Cabo Matapalo, Carate and Bahía Drake to visit this extraordinary national park, with its tropical forest and paradisiac beaches, where you might spot a jaguar, a majestic scarlet macaw (*Ara macao*) or a keel-billed toucan (*Ramphastos sulfuratus*). The scarcely populated peninsula is a wonderful place to observe wildlife, with over 125 species of mammals and 367 species of birds.

Although it is wild and isolated, different tour packages of the Osa Peninsula are available to fit all tastes and budgets. The small village of Puerto Jiménez and the Parque Nacional Corcovado are ideal for visitors on a tight budget, while the more comfortable luxury hotels between Puerto Jiménez and Carate or in the superb Bahía Drake cater to travellers prepared to splurge a little.

### The Puerto Jiménez Region

**Puerto Jiménez ★** is the only real town on the peninsula, with many hotels and restaurants, public phones, transportation networks (buses, ferries, taxis, airplanes), grocery stores, a post office, tourist information offices, tour operators, a medical clinic, a national bank, a gas station and the administrative offices of the Parque Nacional Corcovado (near the airport).

With quiet roads, and tranquil way of life, Puerto Jiménez has a certain charm, and seems far removed from San José – which it is! Even the dogs are happy and content, playing in the streets, sleeping on the sidewalks, or sometimes right in the middle of the road. Tourists wander through the

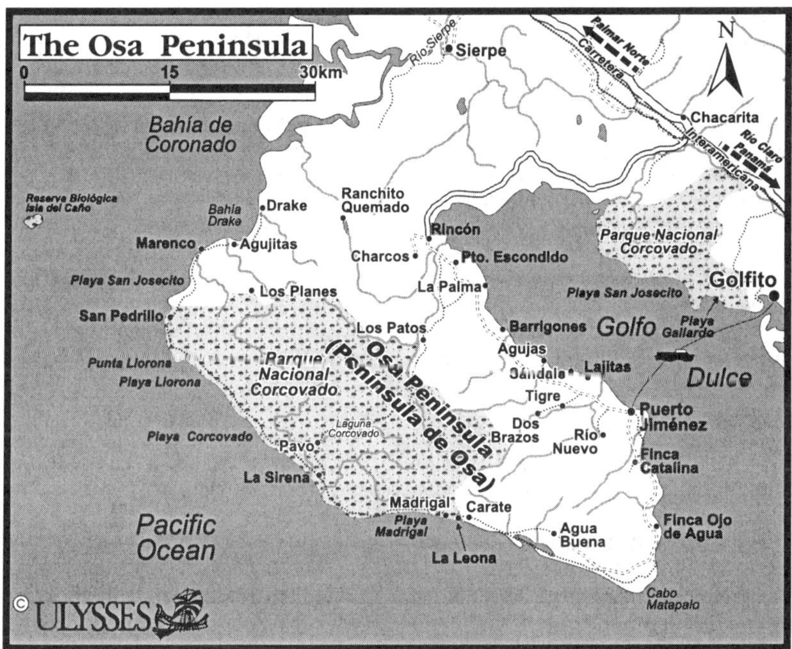


streets, despite the oppressive heat, planning their activities for the next day (fishing, kayaking, scuba diving, hiking, visiting the gold mine, horseback riding, mountain biking, etc.) or making inquiries about how to get to the national park. The **municipal beach** northeast of the city is the perfect place to take a late-afternoon dip in the **Golfo Dulce**.

Early one morning (around 6am), we were treated to an amazing spectacle: dozens of scarlet macaws, some large, brightly coloured parakeets (red, blue and yellow and 80 cm long), and hundreds of green parakeets flew overhead, each uttering their loud and distinctive cries – like the squeaking wheels of an old cart – before settling in the treetops!

The tourist information office at **Proyecto Osa Natural** *(Main Street ☎/⇌735-5440)* lists the region's many tourist agencies, most of which are local and specalize in tours of the peninsula's natural riches. Across the road, in the Carolina Restaurant, **Escondido Trex** *(☎/⇌735-5210)* is a good place to get information about excursions, hotels, restaurants, beaches and other activities around Puerto Jiménez. The friendly and helpful staff speaks English.

If you want to visit the Parque Nacional Corcovado but do not have a four-wheel drive vehicle, go to the *minimercado* **El Tigre** *(every day 6am to 7pm; Main Street; ☎735-5075)*, where one or more all-terrain taxis shuttle people between Puerto Jiménez and Carate every day at 6am. The trip takes approximately two hours and costs $6 (one way). Return trips leave from Carate every morning at 8:30am. The trip to Cabo Matapalo costs about half the price. You can take a taxi to the park at other times of the day, but be prepared to pay about $40 (a good price for groups).

### The Cabo Matalpo Region

South of Puerto Jiménez, the magnificent **Cabo Matapalo** region covers the southeastern part of the peninsula. This area has a beautiful beach lined with dense tropical forest. There is a pretty 25-metre waterfall – a great place for watching monkeys, coatis, sloth, toucans, macaws and many other exotic birds. Cabo Matapalo also has some of the most luxurious hotels, each beautifully landscaped to blend in with the surrounding environment.

After Cabo Matapalo, the road narrows and climbs up the mountain. You need a four-wheel drive vehicle to travel along it, since it is usually muddy and crossed by twelve rivers, some of which are several metres wide. Along the way (approx. 2 hours from Puerto Jiménez), there are pastures and a few houses and small farms. The road finally ends in **Carate**, on the Pacific Ocean. Carate basically consists of a *pulpería* and a landing strip, but is the entrance to the trail to the **Corcovado Lodge Tent Camp** (1.5 km; managed by the Costa Rica Expeditions agency), and La Leona du Parque Nacional Corcovado (2 km).

### Bahía Drake

**Bahía Drake** ★★ is wonderfully removed from the rest of the Osa Peninsula, which is itself far from the big cities of Costa Rica. You can thus imagine the tranquil solitude that permeates this area, which nevertheless has many comfortable hotels offering a wide range of activities. We strongly recommend that you stay here for at least three nights (four days) to allow enough time to leisurely explore the bay's surroundings or take a break and relax in a hammock by the Pacific Ocean, listening to the birds and the crashing of the waves.

The bay is very large, and bathed by the warm, tranquil Pacific Ocean. The coast has sections of rich tropical rainforest that extend right to the waters's edge. Offshore, the Isla del Caño biological reserve harbours natural and historical treasures, and is a favourite spot for scuba divers. On the bay itself, the small village of **Agujitas** has a *pulpería*, a public telephone, a school and reasonably priced accommodations (see p 364).

The hotels dotting Bahía Drake coast all have boats, which can take you to Sierpe and on other excursions, like to the Parque Nacional Corcovado and the Reserva Biológica Isla del Caño, situated ten kilometres south of the Río Sierpe. You can also go hiking, horseback riding, birdwatching, scuba diving, snorkelling, kayaking, fishing, swimming, etc. In short, there are plenty of ways to fill up those sunny days!

Apparently, a small unpaved road has recently been opened to Bahía Drake. According to local sources, it starts just south of the small city of **Rincón**, located almost halfway between the Interamericana and Puerto Jiménez. It takes approximately 1.5 hours to travel the 25-kilometre road that runs east to west through the tropical rainforest, and ends up at the Bahía Drake beach. However, you must leave your car in the village of Agujitas and either continue on foot, on horseback or by boat.

If you travel over land, however, you will miss the pleasure of travelling down the Río Sierpe. The number of flowers in the mangroves along this very wide, boggy river are dazzling, and the entire journey from Sierpe to Bahía Drake is very scenic. You might even

## Sir Francis Drake

Bahía Drake is named after the well-known English navigator Sir Francis Drake (1540-1596) who dropped anchor in the bay in 1579. Drake also visited the coasts of Chile and Peru during his travels in the South from 1577 to 1580. He fought several battles against Spain, and is credited with having played a major role in dispersing the "Invincible Spanish Armada," a fleet of 130 ships that Philippe II of Spain sent to England in 1588 to avenge the execution of Marie Stuart and re-establish Catholic rule.

spot caimans, monkeys, sloths, herons, trogons, egrets and parakeets. Upon arriving in Bahía Drake on the Pacific, you will be greeted by pelicans and sometimes even dolphins. Most tourists travelling to Bahía Drake go via the small village of **Sierpe**, on the Sierpe River. It has a park, a general store, public phones, a few hotels (many are on the outskirts of the village) and piers. The Sierpe region is becoming increasingly popular with birdwatchers and sports fishing enthusiasts, because of its location near many rivers and the Pacific Ocean.

The **Marenco** biological reserve *(☎221-1594, ⇌255-1346)* is located southwest of Bahía Drake, and 5 kilometres north of the Parque Nacional Corcovado. This 500-hectare private reserve can only be reached by boat (about 10 min. from the bay). Since the reserve is right next to the national park, its flora and fauna is very similar. Many kilometres of trails criss-cross the area, and biologists come here to study the complex and fascinating eco-diversity. The plant and animal life varies dramatically in this relatively small area as you go from the tropical forest to the rivers and their mouths and to the shores of the Pacific Ocean. The reserve provides its own accommodations (see p 364) and offers various excursions, including outings to the Parque Nacional Corcovado and the Isla del Caño.

## Parque Nacional Corcovado

The **Parque Nacional Corcovado ★★★** *($6; every day 8am to 4pm; ☎735-5036, ⇌735-5282)* is unquestionably one of the most captivating in Costa Rica. Its 41,788 hectares protect a large part of the Osa Peninsula's tropical rainforest, and boasts eight different natural habitats. There are an additional 12,751 hectares of forest on the other side of the Golfo Dulce (Piedras Blancas sector), just west of Golfito. The park is a birdwatchers' paradise, with 367 species of birds including the magnificent scarlet macaw and the keel-billed toucan. Moreover, 140 species of mammals, 117 species of amphibians and reptiles, 40 species of freshwater fish and 6,000 species of insects have been identified here!

With an annual rainfall of 5.5 metres a year, this tropical rainforest has an incredibly rich plant life that includes nearly 500 kinds of trees, some of which can grow from 40 to 50 metres tall! The largest is the *ceiba pentandra*, which can even reach heights of 70 metres. You can completely lose your sense of reality in the stifling heat among these giant trees covered in moss, epiphytic plants and vines.

We should point out, however, that this park is not to everyone's liking. We met several visitors (especially older travellers) who had visited the park on their own and complained about the heat and humidity, and especially the long distances between the park's different points of interest. Thus, you might want to take one of the many guided boat tours with numerous stops as well as hikes lasting from a few minutes to several hours. These are available from Puerto Jiménez, Cabo Matapalo or Bahía Drake.

On the other hand, if you like long hikes and sleeping under the stars or in rustic shelters, you will probably enjoy the Parque Nacional Corcovado. It is one of the only parks to offer a large network of trails, as well as some tourist infrastructure (campsites, shelters, meals, etc.). However, you should first visit the administrative office in Puerto Jiménez (near the airport) before venturing into the park, to obtain the latest information and reserve a spot in one of the shelters (also called "stations" or "watch houses") and plan out your meals. Note that you can make these reservations over the phone well in advance, as long as you know your schedule.

There are five shelters in the park, four of which are very popular with hikers (La Leona, La Sirena, San Pedrillo and Los Patos). However, during the dry season (from December to April), the trails are especially busy and it is quite common for up to thirty hikers to converge in one spot, especially at the busy La Sirena shelter. All shelters have very basic accommodations, but cost only $2 per person per night. You have to bring your own sleeping bag, and should also bring a mosquito net. If you plan on camping instead *($1.25/person/night)*, make sure you have all the equipment you need (tents and other camping gear can be rented from the tourist information office in Puerto Jiménez). Meals are available it you reserve in advance: breakfast costs $4 (served at 6am), and lunch (11am) and dinner (5:30pm) cost $6.25 each. If you plan on preparing your own meals, you must bring your own equipment (stove, dishes and utensils).

**Various Itineraries**

The Parque Nacional Corcovado has numerous hiking trails and three main entrances (**La Leona**, **Los Patos** and **San Pedrillo**), the busiest being La Leona. Over 60 kilometres of trails, most of which run along the beach, link the different shelters or stations. There are also other trails leading to the forest, beaches or vistas around the shelters. You can map out your own itinerary, depending on how many days you plan on staying and the number of kilometres you are ready to walk in the heat and humidity while carrying your backpack.

Getting to the park is not a problem, since all kinds of transportation is available. All-terrain taxis run from Puerto Jiménez *($6; depart at 6am from Minimercado El Tigre; 2 hours travel time; ☎735-5075)* to Carate, two kilometres from La Leona station. There is also a small plane from Puerto Jiménez that can drop you off or pick you up from La Sirena station *(approx. $200 for 5 passengers; ☎735-5178)*. From La Palma, all-terrain taxis can take you the three kilometres to Los Patos station. From Bahía Drake (Agujitas), it is relatively easy to find a boat that goes to San Pedrillo station.

Although most hikers spend three or four nights in the park, some decide to spend only the day (generally around La Leona), whereas others stay on over a week, to leisurely discover the park's plant and wildlife. If you are planning a long hike in the park, we strongly recommend that you join a group (see p 353) for safety reasons and also to benefit from the knowledge of an experienced guide. We don't want to alarm you, but the park is very big it is easy to get lost. Moreover, there are many poisonous snakes, including the formidable "fer-de-lance." Not to mention the roaming packs of peccaries, a type of boar, which sometimes charge at hikers (if this happens, climb a tree quickly!) and , of course, the voracious insects (remember your insecticide).

The **La Sirena** sector is by far the most popular place for hikers, since the trails from the other sectors meet here. It also has a biological station where scientists study the tropical rainforest's flora and fauna. The itineraries described later in this chapter all lead to this sector, so you can easily compare the relative distances. For instance, you can choose either a round trip (i.e.: Carate – La Sirena – Carate; 36 km) or a one-way excursion (i.e.: Los Patos – La Sirena – Carate; 41 km). Small brooks provide drinking water along the trails, but everyone should also have two litres of water on hand, since it can get very hot and humid.

To get to the park's entrance, you must travel two kilometres along the beach, from Carate to La Leona station. If you spend the night at this station, or even if you're just there for the day, we recommend taking a brand-new trail called the **Río Madrigal**. This very narrow path starts near the station, climbs into the tropical forest, and then descends to the Río Madrigal. From there, you can kick off your shoes and walk down to the water, follow this incredible river to the mouth of the Pacific, and return to the beach. If you walk quietly along the refreshing waters of the Río Madrigal, you can observe a number of birds, and perhaps even some animals.

Thanks to our observant guide, Paul Ruiz from Costa Rica Expeditions, we were even able to spot a superb jaguarundi by the river! A jaguarundi (*Felis yagouaroundi*) is a small jaguar (approximately 70 cm long) with thick, dark fur. It is quite short, and has a long, slender body, small rounded ears and brown eyes. Feeding on birds, hares, rodents, frogs and fish, it usually appear at dusk. It is extremely rare to encounter this animal, but you will increase your chances of seeing one by hiring a guide.

**La Leona to La Sirena** (16 km): The trail from La Leona (information, shelter, camping, meals, etc.) to La Sirena is 16 kilometres long and follows the shoreline along the beach. At some points, you will have to cross shallow sections of rivers, or turn off into the forest when rocks make it difficult to walk along the ocean. Five secondary trails also run along the beach, but go through the forest. You should also be wary of the tide (ask the park warden at the La Leona station), since certain portions of the trails, especially between Chancha and Salsiquedes, are impassable at high tide. About two kilometres before La Sirena, the Río Claro can be difficult to cross at high tide. If you find the water too high, head up the river about 200 metres. The river is shallower there (one metre at most), and you can cross it safely.

**Los Patos to La Sirena** (20 km): if you decide to drive to Los Patos with a four-wheel drive vehicle, be warned that the narrow road is difficult to manoeuvre, and you will have to ford several waterways. The **Los Patos** station is about 13 kilometres from **La Palma**. After a 30-minute drive, you will have to walk another 45 minutes to get to the station. Outside of the dry season (December to April), rivers and the numerous other waterways can become major obstacles.

The area around the Los Patos station once saw a number of *oreros*, or gold-diggers, who searched the peninsula's rivers for this precious yellow metal. Only a few of these prospectors struck it rich, although many did manage to make a modest living from their finds. Apparently, the region was so overrun with *oreros* in the mid-1980s that the park's rivers and *laguna* were in danger of silting up. Two kilometres from the Los Patos entrance, the **Cerro de Oro** saw intense mining activity, which was very common in this area of the park before it was prohibited. The abandoned machinery of the **Coope Unioro** mining cooperative, which used to mine gold from this mountain, can still be seen, along with the hills of gravel by the river. With their detailed knowledge of the tropical rainforest, these *oreros* make excellent guides. Puerto Jiménez offers a variety of guided tours that centre around the gold mining that took place in the area (see p 355).

From the Los Patos station, the **El Mirador** trail (14 km round trip) leads to a wonderful view of the Parque Nacional Corcovado plains. This path cuts through virgin forest, and climbs to a maximum altitude of 225 metres. Expect to spend more than one night at this station if you choose this trail, since distances are quite long and the hike to the La Sirena station takes a whole day.

The trail to La Sirena station is 20 kilometres (one way) and takes 6 hours to complete, not including stops to watch animals and plants, or simply to rest. The trail first goes through virgin forest, followed by a less dense secondary forest. Most of the trail is flat, and it never goes higher than 140 metres. The trail is well marked and easy to follow, and is not particularly difficult, except where it crosses two rivers. Depending on the season, you might encounter swarms of mosquitoes, so insecticide is a definite must. You can spot many species of birds, butterflies, frogs and monkeys along the trail, and it is not unusual to see the tracks of a Baird's tapir or ocelot.

**San Pedrillo to La Sirena** (24 km): San Pedrillo station is located northwest of the Parque Nacional Corcovado, and is only ten kilometres or so from Bahía Drake. Therefore, you cen get there on foot, although most people take a boat to the station or to Playa Llorona. This trail, which links San Pedrillo to La Sirena, is closed during the rainy season (May to December).

The 24-kilometre trail (one way) takes over seven hours to complete, not including stops for swimming, eating, or resting. Set aside an entire day for this trek, and leave as early as possible so that you can proceed at a leisurely pace, enjoying the stops along the way. You will have to cross three rivers, so be wary of the tide (ask the park warden about the tide schedule). The first seven kilometres go through the forest along the shore, culminating at the beach. There is a magnificent 30-metre waterfall at **Playa Llorona**, right on the beach. Farther south, a small trail branches off to a river where you can go for a refreshing swim. Further along, you will have to cross the Llorona, Corcovado and Sirena rivers. The Río Sirena, about two hours from the Río Corcovado, is the deepest of these. Since the current tends to be quite strong, and there are sometimes sharks and crocodiles at the mouth of the river, it is best to cross as far inland as possible. After the Río Sirena, it is only about one kilometre to the La Sirena station.

## Reserva Biológica Isla del Caño

You can spend a very pleasant day making all sorts of discoveries at the **Reserva Biológica Isla del Caño ★★** *($6; every day 8am to 4pm; ☎735-5036, ≠735-5282)*, near Bahía Drake, less than 20 kilometres from the Osa Peninsula. This 300-hectare island is a real paradise, bordered by lush vegetation and small beaches, no more than 100 metres long, and surrounded by rocks, coral reefs and warm, relaxing waters. It is thus not surprising that the Isla del Caño has quickly become a major tourist site! Fortunately, no large luxury resorts have been built on the island to date – so you can still visit this biological reserve without having a major impact on its ecosystem.

Following the creation of the Reserva Biológica Isla del Caño in March 1978, 2,700 hectares of ocean around the island were also protected. The 15 species of coral and other interesting underwater features make this a perfect place for scuba diving – and especially for snorkelling, since the turquoise water is so incredibly clear that the ocean's splendours can be admired without even going deep underwater! Most hotels on the Osa Peninsula, and especially around Bahía Drake, offer excursions to the Isla del Caño, which are not to be missed! Not only will you have the chance to do some snorkelling and swimming, but you can also discover the entrancing wonders of the island itself.

The Reserva Biológica Isla del Caño (3 by 1.5 km) is part of the Department of National Parks and has coasts rising almost 70 metres out of the ocean. Although the highest point of the island lies at 110 metres, most of it is an immense plateau covered by dense tropical rainforest, which lies at an altitude of approximately 90 metres and receives an annual rainfall of four to five metres. Trees grow to great heights, generally over 50 metres, and include the *vaco*, or "milk tree", which gets its name from its milky and edible liquid (latex). Other trees in the area include figs, wild coconuts and rubber trees, as well as fruit trees such as mango, orange, and banana trees, which are not indigenous to the island and were most likely introduced by early settlers. There are also 158 species of plants and ferns.

The island's forest is home to ten species of birds, including cattle herons (*Bubulcus ibis*), black falcons (*Buteogallus anthracinus*) and ospreys (*Pandion haliaetus*). There is not much animal life, but small rodents, bats, lizards, frogs, and small snakes, such as boa constrictors, have been sighted.

The Isla del Caño is known for its pre-Columbian cemetery and stones carved into perfect spheres. Apparently, these round stones, which range from 10 centimetres to 2 metres in diameter, were used to indicate the social status of the dead, although their exact significance is unknown. Archeologists believe that these rocks were made in the communities of the Osa Peninsula, and then transported to the island by boat before finally being rolled to the cemetery. Many pieces of pottery from the Aguas Buenas (3rd to 9th centuries) and Chiriquí (9th to 16th centuries) have been excavated.

A reserve warden station, which also serves as the reception and information office, is located on the northwest part of the island and has washrooms, showers, drinking water and picnic areas on the beach. There are two trails running through the forest on the island: **Sitio Arqueológico** (2 km round trip), leads to the pre-Columbian cemetery and the rock spheres, and **El Mirador** (3 km round trip) takes you to a beautiful area from which you can admire the sea, the towering trees and the different species of birds.

## The Region's South

To get to this sector, simply follow the Interamericana south from San Isidro de El General. This highway goes through most areas of interest, crossing the entire length of the Valle del General before turning off toward the lowlands along the coast to Panama. The Interamericana has turnoffs for two regional roads which lead to Playa Tortuga and Coto Brus (San Vito) respectively, completing the tour of the region.

### North of Palmar

While driving along the Interamericana towards Palmar, you will have the opportunity to admire the spectacle of the **Río Ceibo** between Buenos Aires and San Isidro de El General which blends two differently coloured kinds of water: the water near the surface carries volcanic earth, while the deeper water is more clear.

A bit further downstream, as you pass the Paso Real, eight kilometres in the mountains, you can visit the reserve of the **Borucas** Indians who are well-known for their handicrafts (wooden masks, cotton place mats and belts, gourds). Visitors are welcome to explore the surroundings (which is not always the case on reserves). The Borucas subsist on agriculture. There is a **museum** on the reserve has several displays, including native architecture, crafts and plants used to make textiles and medicine.

Around New Year's Day, the Borucas celebrate the three-day **Fiesta de los Diablitos** (The Festival of the Little Devils), which includes a dramatic re-enactment of a battle between the Spanish conquistadors and the native people, in which the natives emerged victorious. The actors wear flamboyant costumes and masks.

### The Palmar Region

Although the Diquis Valley region's only airport is located in Palmar Sur, **Palmar**'s immediate surroundings are quite uninteresting, except for its many large, mysterious **rock spheres ★**. These boulders date back to pre-Columbian times, and their perfectly round shape has yet to be satisfactorily explained. The rocks are similar to those found on the Isla del Caño and vary in size, some measuring over a metre in diameter! Palmar spheres are found in different parts of the city, and even in the courtyards of some houses. Ask around to see a few of them.

Palmar is where the new road, the Costarena Sur, begins. This route borders the Pacific Coast to the northwest and crosses the Playa Tortuga region before reaching Dominical. Thus, you can visit the entire area by starting your tour in Dominical.

On the road to Playa Tortuga, take a few minutes to stop in **Ciudad Cortés ★**. In our view, this city is far prettier than Palmar. Part of it was built all at once at the beginning of the 20th century, so its rather simple architecture is quite unified, and gives the city a definite character. Many of the buildings are made of wood and are painted in colours that blend in wonderfully with the vegetation, as colonial architecture of the late 19th and early 20th century often does.

Even the roads are picturesque (which is quite rare in this country). If this tiny village were developed, it would definitely have a lot to offer tourists who want to experience a different way of life for a short time.

The **Playa Tortuga** ★ region is about 25 kilometres west of Palmar and has only recently begun to be developed, since the Costarena Sur made it easier to reach. The Playa Tortuga meets up with the Pacific Coast, which is not possible farther east because of the Río Grande de Térraba delta. **Ojochal** is located near Playa Tortuga, nestled in the hills of the back country a few kilometres from the beach. Every year, new inns and restaurants open in the region. However, to preserve the environment, there are no establishments directly on the beach, which the country's first lady declared the cleanest beach in 1993. Many Canadians have settled in this area and own several of the local hotels and restaurants, making it easy to get by in English or French. For the next several years at least, you will still be able to experience Playa Tortuga's natural beauty, surrounded by nature and the sea, since no major development projects have been proposed as yet. We hope it remains that way, though hotels are cropping up here and there as more people discover the area. A small business complex is even being built at the corner of the Costarena Sur and the road to Ojochal. Moreover, there is talk of putting up a small shopping centre soon, which would allow an increased number of services as well as businesses that sell North American items and foodstuffs to open up.

If you go just a bit further west on the Costarena Sur, you will come to **Playa Piñuela**. This is where the Parque Nacional Maritimo Ballena begins (see p 337). The Piñuela Beach is not especially attractive, since it is quite stony, particularly at its northern end, but it is the best place in the area for swimming, along with Ballena and Uvita further north.

South of Palmar, the Interamericana runs through the hot, humid region of the Diquis Valley, to reach the Osa Peninsula, Golfito, Ciudad Neily, and finally the Panamanian border. Although you can get to San Vito via the Coto Brus Valley and Palmar, it can also be reached from Ciudad Neily in the north. We recommend taking the latter route.

The Diquis Valley illustrates the damaging impact that intensive agricultural exploitation can have on the landscape. Many of the large tracts of deforested land along the Interamericana are used for farming and grazing. In the summer, they are yellow and dry (sometimes even during the rainy season), and it is hard to imagine the lush jungle that used to cover the area. We can only rejoice that the authorities have decided to protect the remaining land in the region by creating the Parque Nacional Corcovado, on the Osa Peninsula

**Sierpe** (see p 341) is a particularly interesting region if you are interested in plant and animal life, with its **mangroves** *(Selva Mar offers hiking tours, ☎771-4582, ≠771-8841)* at the mouth of the Río Sierpe on the Pacific Ocean, just south of Palmar.

Just before Piedras Blancas, a trail leading to the Osa Peninsula branches off the Interamericana, to the right.

### The Golfito Region

The city of Golfito is also located at the end of a road, which splits off to the right from the Interamericana, but which starts in Río Claro. The road is well indicated, and you will know you are definitely on the right track when you pass the numerous palm tree plantations and the many billboards advertising the merchandise available at the Depósito Libre de Golfito (see further below).

**Golfito** ★ can be described as a "gulf within a gulf". The city lies at the end of a small gulf which opens into the larger Golfo Dulce, separated from the ocean by the Osa Peninsula. Thus, the waters in the two gulfs are very calm, making this area a good location for a port. Thus, Golfito is a seaport more than anything else. During the boom period of the United Fruit company, it was the main shipping centre for the company's fruit, especially for bananas exported from Costa Rica. However, the company shut down in the mid-1980s due to production-related problems that had developed over the years (increased export taxes, union problems, price drops, plant diseases, etc.). The city is still feeling the effects of the company's demise, which put an end to its period of prosperity.

The city's problems were partially solved with the establishment of a "free trade zone" (Depósito Libre) at the outskirts of the city and the growing tourist industry with people coming from Costa Rica and abroad to visit Corcovado, the Wilson Botanical Gardens, etc. In fact, tourism has increased to the point where you will have to reserve your accommodations in advance – especially during the high season and on weekends.

Despite its decline, Golfito remains an important city in the region. Its airport is convenient for anyone travelling to the southern part of the country.

The city is built on a relatively narrow strip of land between the bay and the green forested mountains, and contains three main sectors: The **Zona Americana** (American Zone) in the north was home to the heads of the United Fruit company; the Pueblo Civil in the centre boasts Golfito's main pier (*muelle*); and the *muellecito* sector (with a small pier) is a bit farther on. All in all, the city is almost seven kilometres long, and is divided by a main street that links all of its neighbourhoods. There a large taxi fleet in addition to the regular bus service that runs every 15 minutes during the day.

It is no surprise that the Zona Americana is the most elegant part of Golfito, since the United Fruit company's executives used to live here. The houses look sophisticated and are beautifully landscaped, bestowing a certain elegance on the entire sector, even if they are no longer as well maintained now that their original owners have left. The Zona Americana also encompasses the airport and the **Depósito Libre**. Since 1990, the Depósito Libre has been a free trade zone where consumer goods (from jeans to appliances) cost a little less than in other regions of Costa Rica. This Depósito Libre is very lively, especially on weekends. However, it is better to go there during the week when it is less crowded with Costa Ricans looking for discount prices. There is an entrance fee of a few dollars.

If the Zona American is where the upper classes lived, **Pueblo Civil** is for the working class. The architecture is less impressive, but the neighbourhood and the abundant restaurants are still very appealing. Many houses are made of wood.

The *muellecito* sector is not quite as frequented, but you can still find quaint little hotels and places to eat. The

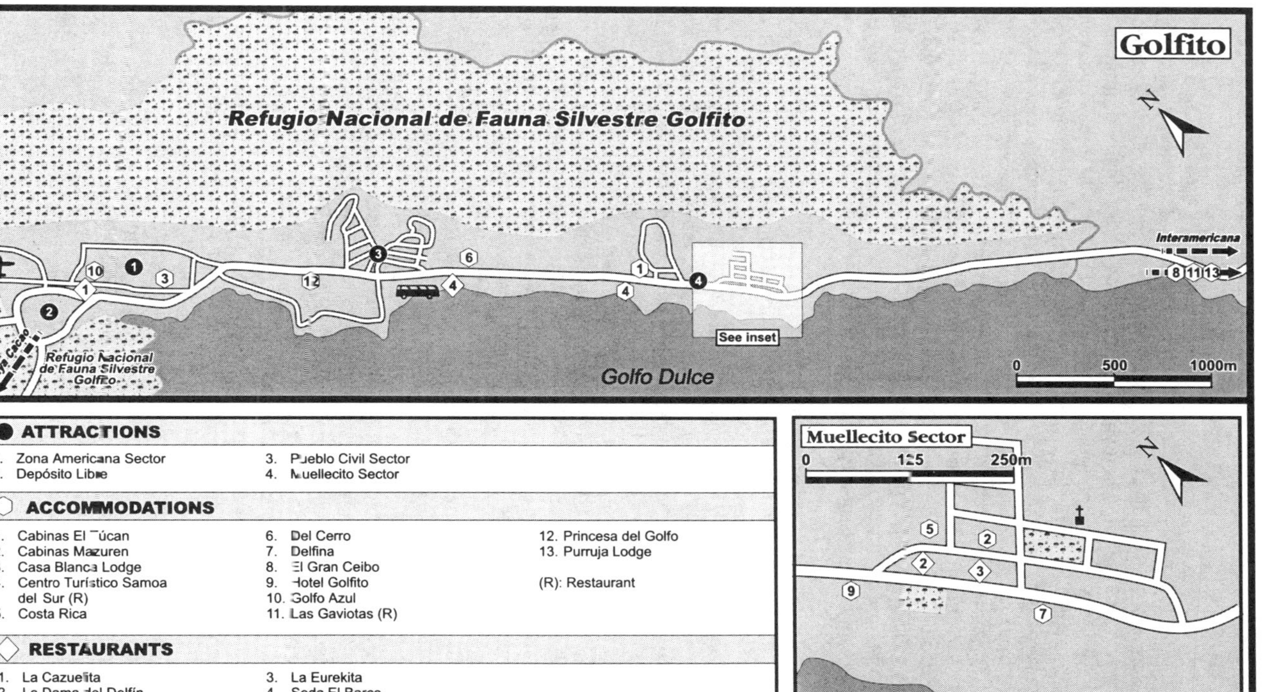
Golfito
Refugio Nacional de Fauna Silvestre Golfito
Interamericana
Playa Cacao
Refugio Nacional de Fauna Silvestre Golfito
See inset
Golfo Dulce
0 500 1000m
ATTRACTIONS
1. Zona Americana Sector
2. Depósito Libre
3. Pueblo Civil Sector
4. Muellecito Sector
ACCOMMODATIONS
1. Cabinas El Tucan
2. Cabinas Mazuren
3. Casa Blanca Lodge
4. Centro Turístico Samoa del Sur (R)
5. Costa Rica
6. Del Cerro
7. Delfina
8. El Gran Ceibo
9. Hotel Golfito
10. Golfo Azul
11. Las Gaviotas (R)
12. Princesa del Golfo
13. Purruja Lodge
(R): Restaurant
RESTAURANTS
1. La Cazuelita
2. La Dama del Delfín
3. La Eurekita
4. Soda El Barco
© ULYSSES
Muellecito Sector
0 125 250m
Golfo Dulce

owners of the Hotel Samoa del Sur plan to build a Maritime museum on their premises.

Most of Golfito's surroundings now belong to a wildlife reserve which you can access via several paths (many from the Zona Americana) which lead to hiking trails of varying lengths.

If you want to go out on the bay or the ocean, you can rent a boat from the *muelle* in Pueblo Civil or near the old United Fruit pier, or go with one of the tourist expeditions organized by local companies. You can also get to the beaches of Pavones, Zancudo and Cacao with boats that leave from Golfito's piers. Lastly, Golfito is a popular place for pleasure boats coming from other areas.

There are also some beaches where you can enjoy the bay waters along the edge of the peninsula across from Golfito. The best of these is **Cacao** beach, which has a great view of Golfito. **Gallardo** and **San Josecito** beaches to the west are also lovely.

**Zancudo** is a black-sand beach that stretches over many kilometres southwest of Golfito. Located on the point formed by the Río Coto Colorado, a river that flows into the Pacific Ocean, it is a very popular beach during the high season, but calm during the rainy season. It's a good place for swimmers and novice surfers, and even seems popular among the local fishers.

Also southeast of Golfito, **Pavones Beach** is one of the favourites with serious surfers, and most of its visitors come for the waves. Thus, you will rub shoulders with surf experts and fanatics, whether you like it or not – there can be a lot of them around, especially during the rainy season when the waves are at their highest.

### The Ciudad Neily Region

Though it is the last big city before Panama, **Ciudad Neily** is not that popular with tourists. Rather, people visit because it lies on the alternative to the Coto Brus route (located east of Palmar) to San Vito. However, the city is quite attractive, particularly along the two lively main thoroughfares in the downtown area. The Ricardo Neilly Park, in the heart of the city, is a perfect refuge from the heat that is prevalent in the area. There are many benches where you can socialize and get to know the locals a little.

### The San Vito Region

To drink in a magnificent panorama before you leave the Pacific coast region, don't miss the **view ★★** from the road just outside of Ciudad Neily, towards San Vito. The road climbs more than 1,000 metres, and the hot and humid temperature of Ciudad Neily rapidly gives way to the cooler and foggy climate of the San Vito region. However the road is winding and has some very sharp 90-degree turns! And although it is paved, the road is very narrow, has no shoulder, and has a few potholes that you won't see until the last minute. These conditions make it difficult to admire the scenery while driving!

The **Wilson Botanical Garden ★★★** *($5 half day, $8 full day, children 6 to 12 years half price; 2-hour guided tours $35; closed Mon; 5 km from San Vito on the Ciudad Neily-San Vito road, ☎240-6696, ⇌240-6783)* at the Las Cruces biological station is owned by the Organization for Tropical Studies (OTS). Its mission is to teach people about the tropical vegetation (particularly that of the mountain forest) found in the garden, which has the largest botanical collection in Central America. The station preserves endangered plant species from being destroyed in their natural habitat, and studies new plant species, especially for horticultural purposes. This site was created by two Americans, Robert and Catherine Wilson, in the early 1960s, and was taken over by OTS ten years later. As one of the three sites belonging to this organization, the Wilson Botanical Garden is a centre for research and education. At the beginning of the 1980s it was even recognized by UNESCO as part of the vast protected spaces that make up the Parque Internacional La Amistad and its appendages (472,000 ha of land!). You can learn about the several thousand plant species (including 700 types of palm trees), as well as the hundreds of birds, reptiles and mammals at the garden. It is said that over 3,000 species of butterfly live here.

Using the literature sold at the centre, you can plan out your visit around one of the many thematic itineraries (the Wilson Botanical Garden, the trees of the Wilson Botanical Garden, a tour of the palm trees, the birds of Las Cruces, the orchid trail, the hummingbird gardens, medicinal plants, etc.), or take a guided tour. Some guides speak English and the staff is very friendly and helpful. Some of the literature is available in English. A guided tour can be organized for handicapped visitors. You can also spend the night at the Wilson Botanical Garden (see p 351).

A few kilometres northeast of the Wilson Botanical Garden, towards San Vito, is the **Finca Cántaros**, bought and developed by the management of the Wilson Garden in 1994. This site is open to the public and will soon operate as an educational reforestation centre. With its splendid, peaceful rolling hills, the area is also being developed for recreational use (picnic tables, lake, and observation tower).

A few kilometres north of the Wilson Garden and Finca Cántaros is **San Vito ★**, a small town founded in the 1950s by Italian immigrants wanting to improve your lot. Today, the town has close to 40,000 inhabitants and is slowly losing its strictly Italian character with the influx of Spanish-speaking people from the rest of the country. Pictures and text about San Vito's settlement are on display at Catubrus *(☎/≠773-3570)*, the Cámara de Turismo (the tourist office) of Coto Brus, located in the centre of the city at the main intersection. You can have a good Italian meal at some of the restaurants in the area.

The city itself is beautiful and cool, which is a welcome change after the heat along the coast. San Vito is often shrouded in very distinctive fog, thick as pea soup, and should thus, in our view, be renamed San Vito-of-the-clouds. Lastly, the Parque Internacional La Amistad can be accessed from San Vito via Las Mellizas, on the Panamanian border.

## Parque Internacional La Amistad

The **Parque Internacional La Amistad** *($6; every day 6am to 5pm; ☎771-3297, ≠771-3155)* is more of an immense protected zone than a park. There is no infrastructure for receiving visitors or for outdoor activities. With 193,929 hectares, this is the largest park in Costa Rica, extending from Chirripó National Park to the Panamanian border. It protects much of the Cordillera de Talamanca, where mountains soar to heights of over 3,000 metres, as well as the forest of south-central Costa Rica. Since it extends into Panama (more than

***Puma***

400,000 ha), it is considered an international park and one of the largest protected areas in Central America.

Parque Internacional La Amistad (Friendship) belongs to the **La Amistad Biosphere Reserve**, whose total area of 248,337 hectares also comprises the Tapantí and Chirripó national parks, Reserva Biológica Hitoy Cerere, and several forest reserves and indigenous communities. This immense expanse of wilderness contains eight life zones, has one of the most impressive ecosystems in Central America, and was declared a biosphere reserve by UNESCO in 1982.

The Parque Internacional La Amistad is also home to diverse wildlife that includes over 400 species of birds and 263 species of amphibians and reptiles. It is estimated that 60% of all the vertebrate and invertebrate life found in Costa Rica lives in the park. This immense territory is one of the only in the country that is big enough for big cats such as jaguars, pumas and ocelots to hunt and reproduce. Jaguars, for examples, can weigh about 150 kilograms, and need hundreds of hectares to roam for hunting agoutis, pecari and deer.

The park currently has very little in the way of hiking trails and other visitor facilities. It is nevertheless a magical place where the most adventurous tourists (accompanied by local guides) used to long treks in dense tropical rainforest can scale the 3,000-metre-high mountains to observe animals that are rarely seen anywhere else in the country. Birdwatchers stand a good chance of spotting a quetzal in this pristine environment. The protected region of **Las Tablas**, northeast of San Vito next to the Panamanian border, is a favourite with many visitors, especially since there are hotels and guide services nearby.

Before visiting any of the park's three sectors (Tres Colinas, Estación Pittier and Altamira), we strongly recommended that you contact the National Park Service *(☎283-8004, ⇌283-7343)* or the Fundación de Parques Nacionales *(☎257-2239, ⇌222-4732)*, both located in San José, to get the most current information. When we visited were there, no detailed maps of the parks' regions or other information brochures were available yet.

## OUTDOOR ACTIVITIES

### Hiking

**Hacienda Barú** (see p 336) has six kilometres of trails that run through the tropical forest and along a magnificent beach.

**Parque Nacional Corcovado** (see p 341) has more than 80 kilometres of paths, most of which are along the beach and connect the park's various shelters. Only experienced hikers who are knowledgeable about tropical wet forest should tackle the long hikes (overnighting in the shelters) in this isolated region with dense vegetation and extreme heat. You can easily hire a guide through an agency: **Escondido Trex** *(☎/≠735-5210)*; **Proyecto Osa Natural** *(☎/≠735-5440)*; **Corcovado Tours** (☎735-5062, ≠735-5043); **The True Local Guide Organizer** *(Fernando and Carlos Quintero, ☎735-5216, ≠735-5414)*.

Situated less than 20 kilometres from the Osa Peninsula, near Bahía Drake, the **Reserva Biológica Isla del Caño** (see p 345) has two short paths through the forest.

The hike to the top of Cerro Chirripó (3,819 m), the highest peak in Costa Rica, is spectacular. The mountain is in the magnificent **Parque Nacional Chirripó** (see p 332), just north of San Isidro de El General. A brand-new shelter that has been built on the mountain can accommodate some 60 hikers overnight. In addition to the one to the main summit, there are several other trails for experienced hikers who have the necessary equipment for camping in high mountains.

### Scuba Diving and Snorkelling

There are excellent places for scuba diving and snorkelling in and around **Parque Nacional Marino Ballena** (see p 337). The **FDW Tres Marinos** *(☎771-1903)* agency offers snorkelling expeditions from a boat, and **Gino Salotti** *(☎256-9996, ≠788-8210)* in Ojochal has a course in scuba diving.

The **Osa Peninsula** in general, and the Golfo Dulce in particular, are magnificent places to scuba dive and snorkel. All tours in this region are organized by the following agencies: **Osatours** *(☎786-6534, ≠786-6335)*, **Osa Tropical** *(☎735-5063, ≠735-5043)*, **Aquatic Tours** *(☎735-5262, ≠735-5121)* and **Proyecto Osa Natural** *(☎/≠735-5440)*.

**Bahía Drake** (see p 340) and the **Reserva Biológica Isla del Caño** (see p 345) northwest of the Osa Peninsula are known for their scuba diving and snorkelling. The reserve's turquoise water is remarkably clear, and contains 15 different species of coral. Most hotels in Bahía Drake arrange scuba diving and snorkelling excursions.

### Sports Fishing

Some of the fishermen in **Uvita** *(☎771-1903)* will take you deep-sea fishing around Parque Nacional Marino Ballena.

Jeff Lantz and Stig Hanson from **Iguana Lodge** *(Puerto Jiménez, ☎/≠735-5205)* have an international reputation for organizing sports fishing excursions around the Osa Peninsula. Bob Baker and Jerry Cooper of **Golfito Sportfishing**

*(☎/⇄382-2716)* are just as well-known. Other agencies such as **Osatours** *(☎786-6534, ⇄786-6335)*, **Osa Tropical** *(☎735-5062, ⇄735-5043)*, **Aquatic Tours** *(☎735-5262, ⇄735-5121)* and **Proyecto Osa Natural** *(☎/⇄735-5440)* also organize fishing trips.

## Kayaking

**Hacienda Barú** (see p 336) offers kayak excursions through the mangroves.

South of Parque Nacional Marino Ballena, **Kayak Joe** *(⇄788-8210)* will take you on a tour of the coast and its numerous caves in a sea kayak.

For an excursion of one or more days around the Osa Peninsula, contact **Escondido Trex** *(Puerto Viejo, ☎/⇄735-5210)*. **Osa Tropical** *(☎735-5062, ⇄735-5043)* and **Iguana Lodge** *(Puerto Jiménez, ☎/⇄735-5205)* also organize trips on the river or ocean.

## Surfing

**Dominical** is considered one of the best places on the Pacific coast for surfing: the waves here are incredible and break very close to the beach. Unfortunately, however, the current has a very strong undertow, and several people drown here each year. The bar-restaurant San Clement is the place to go to find out about surfing conditions in the area and to meet other surfers from around the world.

Surfers should not miss **Pavones Beach**, south of Golfito. It is renowned for its "left-brake" waves, which are considered among the longest in the world.

**Bahía Drake** and **Cabo Matapalo**, the southeastern tip of the Osa Peninsula, also have superb waves for surfing.

## Horseback Riding

In the **Uvita** region, the **Duarte family** organizes guided tours in the Oro Verde private reserve and the neighbouring areas. The nearby **Rancho La Merced** also arranges rides, and lets you play "cowboy for a day" by helping out with some of the different chores around the farm. For information or to reserve, call the **Selva Mar** *(☎/⇄771-1903)* agency in Dominical.

On the Osa Peninsula, **Osatours** *(☎78-6534, ⇄786-6335)*, **Corcovado Tours** *(☎735-5062, ⇄735-5043)* and **True Local Guide Organizer** *(☎735-5216, ⇄735-5414)* arrange guided trips of one or more days. You can also rent horses by the hour or by the day at many other places. The **Proyecto Osa Natural** *(☎/⇄735-5440)* tourist information bureau in the centre of Puerto Jiménez can give you more information.

## Mountain Biking

The Osa Peninsula is a marvellous place for mountain biking! From Puerto Jiménez, you can go south as far as Carate and Parque Nacional Corcovado (43 km). Heading north, the road is narrow, unpaved and quiet as far as Rincón (35 km), where some smaller roads lead inland to the regions of Dos Brazos and Los Patos, among others. **La Llanta Picante** *(☎/⇄735-5414)* organizes mountain biking trips around the Río Tigre (Puerto Jiménez), and also rents high-quality, well-maintained mountain bikes.

## Water Sports

In Golfito, boats can be moored at **Eagle's Roost Marina** *(☎775-0838, or by radio VHF 12)* or **Sanbar Marina** *(☎775-0735 or 775-0874, ⇌775-0321)*.

## Rafting and Excursions

**Selva Mar** *(San Isidro de El General, ☎771-4582, ⇌771-8841)* is a major organization that arranges all kinds of outdoor activities in the south, and specializes in guided rafting trips for all levels. The agency can also help you plan horseback rides, boat trips and birdwatching excursions and, to top it off, is a reservation service that can help you arrange for accommodations or car rentals. Some hotels on the coast between Uvita and Dominical will refer you to this organization to make reservations.

## Canopy Tours

**Hacienda Barú** (see p 336) offers tours of the canopy from high observation platforms in the jungle.

## Visits to Gold Mines

For many years, and until quite recently, the **Osa Peninsula** attracted gold prospectors, called *oreros*, who came and settled there. You can visit the areas around Puerto Jiménez and **Dos Brazos**, and even become something of a prospector yourself, by learning all about this business. Guided tours are arranged in Puerto Jiménez: **Escondido Trex** *(☎/⇌735-5210)*; **Proyecto Osa Natural** *(☎/⇌735-5440)*; **Corcovado Tours** *(☎735-5062, ⇌735-5043)*; **The True Local Guide Organizer** *(Fernando and Carlos Quintero, ☎735-5216, ⇌735-5414)*.

# ACCOMMODATIONS

## The Region's North

The northern region consist mainly of the area around the beach near Domincal, but also includes the mountains of Cerro de la Muerte and the valley of San Isidro de El General. The temperatures in these sub-regions are much cooler than on the coast, so it is important to bring warm clothing, especially if you are staying at the higher altitudes (in the San Gerardo de Dota area, for example).

### San Isidro de El General

### Cerro de la Muerte and San Gerardo de Dota

Just past Albergue de Montaña Savegre (see further below), in San Gerardo de Dota, is **Paradero Lacustre Los Ranchos** *($; San Gerardo de Dota, ☎771-2376)*, a campground with electricity and hot water in the bathrooms. Some sites have cooking facilities. This waterside property has rowboats for boating and fishing, hiking trails, barbecue areas and a *mirador* for birdwatching.

**Georgina** *($$; hw, ⊛, ℜ; Cerro La Muerte, ☎771-1299 or 284-2760)* is a highway restaurant-hotel on the Interamericana, in the mountains of La Muerte. The hotel provides electric blankets because the climate is relatively cool. The rooms above the restaurant are comfortable and very clean. The place is pleasant overall, with two common living rooms that add to its charm. The owners also rent a *cabina* that houses six people.

For peace and tranquillity in refreshingly cool surroundings, **Avalon Lodge** *($$$; hw, pb/sb; north of Cerro de la Muerte, 3 km off the Interamericana, ☎380-2107, ⇄771-7226)* is highly recommended. Hidden away in the mountains in a newly created private forest reserve, Avalon Lodge has two *cabinas* (private bathroom) and four rooms (shared bathroom) that are comfortable, heated and made entirely out of wood. This place is perfect if you want to commune with nature. However, when mountain mists and a chilly breeze float in through the trees, you might find it hard to believe that this is really Costa Rica!

As you enter the more alpine atmosphere on the way to Cerro de la Muerte from the Central Valley, **El Toucanet Lodge** *($$$ bkfst incl.; hw, pb, ℜ; exit at km 58 from the Interamericana, near El Cañon de Guarco, then go 7 km to Copey de Dota)* is one of the first places that offers accommodations. This family-style lodge on a mountainside in the village of Copey de Dota has six rooms built completely of wood, with private terraces. There is also a little restaurant with a fireplace that serves country-style food.

Situated on the banks of a river, the very attractive **Trogón Lodge** *($$$$; pb, hw, heated; San Gerardo de Dota, ☎771-1266)* belongs to the Mawamba group, which has most of its hotels on the Caribbean coast. The wooden buildings blend well with this pastoral setting. The lodge is somewhat removed from the area's other hotel establishments, and is located at the beginning of the road that runs from San Gerardo to the Interamericana Highway. It is ideal if you want some privacy in a natural setting that has retained some aspects of wilderness. The restaurant is open for breakfast, lunch and dinner.

On a lovely hillside next to a mountain stream, with landscaping well-suited to its surroundings, **Albergue de Montaña Savegre** *($$$$$ fb; hw, pb; exit at km 80 on the Interamericana, then descend 9 km to San Gerardo de Dota, ☎/⇄771-1732)* has very clean, large, simple rooms with extra heaters and a shared terrace. Three meals per day are included in the rate, and are served in the warm and inviting dining room. With all the activities offered at the *albergue* (birdwatching, fishing, hiking, boating and horseback riding), and San Gerardo de Dota's cool, green valley, who could ask for more?

### San Isidro de El General

Small provincial hotels, **Chirripó** *($; hw, pb; ☎771-0529)* and **Amaneli** *($; hw, pb, ⊗, tv, P; ☎771-0352)* rent simple, clean rooms. Amaneli has a restaurant on the main floor.

The most inexpensive hotel in San Isidro, **El Jardin** *($; ☎771-0349)* rents clean little rustic rooms on a large wooden platform. They seem somewhat closed-in.

**El Valle** *($; pb/sb, P; above the Núñez hardware store, ☎771-0246)* is a new hotel with clean, simple rooms with televisions.

The small-town **Iguazu** *($$; pb/sb, ctv; above the Super Lido store, ☎771-2571)* hotel rents plain, but tasteful little rooms. Its cleanliness makes it a good choice if you are staying in San Isidro. The disadvantage is its noisy location right next to the Interamericana.

**Hotelera del Sur** *($$$; pb, hw, tv, ⊗ or ≡, ☎ ℜ, ≈; 6 km south of San Isidro on the Interamericana, ☎771-3033, ⇌771-0527)* is a better quality hotel than those available in San Isidro proper. The rooms and cottages with living- and dining-rooms are modern, and there are conference rooms, gardens, a pool and sports facilities (volleyball, basketball and tennis courts). The extensive grounds isolate the hotel from traffic noise fairly well.

### The Rivas Region

**Albergue de Montaña Río Chirripó Pacifico** *($$$ bkfst incl.; hw, pb, ℜ, bar; Canaán de Rivas, 18 km northeast of San Isidro, ☎771-4582, ⇌771-1903)* is situated on the road to Mount Chirripó, on the banks of the Río Chirripó, at an altitude of 1,000 metres. The inn has a rustic decor, featuring cypress wood, and a natural swimming pool. The establishment also organizes guided tours in the area. Hiking and horseback riding are available.

On a lovely eight-hectare estate beside the Río El General, 30 minutes from Parque Nacional Chirripó, **Talari Albergue de Montaña** *($$$; pb,hw, ⊗, ℝ, ≈, ℜ; ☎/⇌771-0341)* is a great place for peace and quiet. The eight rooms (*cabinas*) are clean, comfortable and subdued. Around the inn are the pool, the forest (partly new growth) and paths that go through dozens of varieties of fruit trees, plants and flowers. The natural surroundings have also attracted a multitude of birds: 143 different species have been spotted to date. The charming owners, Pilar and Jan, prepare the meals: delicious dishes made with fresh ingredients and served in the cozy dining room. Jan also takes pleasure in entertaining the guests by playing piano at dinner. A souvenir shop sells items made by the Boruca Indians, among other things. The inn is helpful in organizing visits to Parque Nacional Chirripó for their guests (reservations, transportation, guide, food, equipment, advice, etc.). The owners have some amazing stories to share about the region's pre-Columbian history.

### Dominical Region

#### Dominical

The rooms at **Cabinas Coco** *($$; sb, hw, ⊗; Dominical, ☎771-2555)* are very small, but clean. Be aware, though, that the place turns into a nightclub in the evening.

Like those at the San Clemente Bar & Grill (see p 372), **Cabinas San Clemente** *($$; pb, hw, ≡, laundry service; on the beach at Dominical, ☎787-0026, ⇌787-0055)* are perfect for hip tourists who come here for surfing and relaxation. The owner is from the United States and also has several beach houses for rent.

**Albergue Willdale** *($$$; hw, pb, ⊗; at the entrance of Dominical, reservations through Selva Mar, ☎771-4582, ⇌771-8841)* stands out for the friendliness of the hosts, who are long-time residents of Costa Rica. The six pretty *cabinas* are clean and airy and their hammocks are a real treat in this hot climate! The location, by the Río Barú estuary, is peaceful and shady. A wharf gives direct access to water sports and other interesting activities on the ocean.

Also near the beach, **Cabinas Nayarit** *($$$; pb, ⊗, ≡; Dominical, ☎787-0033 or 771-1878)* offers above average rooms that are simple and clean.

The **Cabinas Escondidas** *($$$ bkfst incl.; pb, hw; 3.5 km south of Punta Dominical on Costarena Sur)* are a lovely retreat and study centre in a private natural park setting. The *cabinas* are airy and situated quite far apart to insure privacy. The jungle, with its many delights (streams, fauna and flora), has been preserved for guests to enjoy. Therapeutic massage is only one of the numerous activities offered. The beach has some secluded areas for swimmers. The restaurant serves Asian vegetarian cuisine. Kayaking and horseback riding are available.

**Cabinas Punta Dominical** *($$$; hw, pb, ⊛, ℜ; 4 km south of Dominical, ☎787-0016)* is a warm, welcoming place on a spit of land jutting into the sea. The rustic and very clean cottages open to the outdoors on all four sides. This location has a wonderful view of the sea on two sides, with panoramic vistas and the impressive sound of the surf. The hotel is located some distance from Dominical, which is an advantage if you prefer tranquillity to the lively surfer crowd. The Punta Dominical restaurant (see p 372) is next to the cabinas.

**Casitas de Puertocito** *($$$; hw, pb, ⊗; 9 km south of Dominical; reservations through Selva Mar, ☎771-4582, ⇄771-8841)* is where movie makers have come to film tropical paradise. Thatched-palm roofs cover "tropics-style" *cabinas* that are tucked away in the foliage along 1,200 metres of oceanfront property. The *cabinas* are spacious, clean and charming, with large porches. The grounds have been kept in a natural state, and they are replete with streams, waterfalls, and luxuriant vegetation. A few lots are available for sale or construction here – very tempting!

**Villas Río Mar** *($$$$$; hw, pb, ⊗, ≈, ⌂; on a road signed out at the entrance of Dominical, look for the sign just after the Río Barú bridge, ☎787-0052 or 787-0053, ⇄787-0054, reservations in Selva Mar, ☎ 771-4582, ⇄771-8841)* has 40 attractive bungalows with lovely roomy terraces for rent on a large, beautifully landscaped property. There are tennis courts, a restaurant (local and international cuisine) and both a regular bar and one right in the swimming pool!

### Las Escaleras

The following hotels are located in Las Escaleras, a small mountainous region just south of Dominical. The region has wonderful views of the surrounding countryside and pleasantly cool evenings. However, the roads to its high-lying hotels are often so bad that you should only attempt them with a four-wheel drive vehicle. The road conditions change according to the season, and they can deteriorate completely in a day

**Pacific Edge** *($$$; hw, pb, K; Dominicalito, reservations in Selva Mar, ☎771-4582, ⇄771-8841)* is a great place for a picture-perfect vacation. The sea lies 200 metres below the property, and the tropical rainforest with its bird and animal calls is behind the comfortable wood *cabinas.* Each cottage has a living room, kitchenette, bedroom and balcony (hammock included, of course!). Take the road indicated by a sign, 100 metres south of the bridge in Dominical.

**Villa Cabeza de Mono** *($$$$$; hw, pb, K, ≈; reservations through Selva Mar, ☎771,4582, ⇄771-8841)* is a luxurious villa surrounded by jungle. It has a living-room and a dining-room in addition to the kitchen and two large, attractive bedrooms. It can accommodate a party of five in the privacy afforded by the lush vegetation all around it.

The former Escaleras Inn has been transformed into **Villas Escaleras** *(☎/⇄771-5247)*, which rents fully equipped villas. The main villa, which used to be the inn, costs $300 per night, and houses up to eight people. It has three bedrooms, five (!) bathrooms, a living room, library, pool, porch and terrace with a panoramic view. The friends' villa, a small cottage in its own garden, has a bedroom, living room, bathroom, balcony and terrace *($125 for two people)*. The newer two-storey stone-and-wood Villa II *($200/night, max. four people)* has two bedrooms, two bathrooms, a sitting room and a private swimming pool. The owners, originally from the United States, provide cleaning service, coffee and bed linen.

### Uvita

South of Uvita, in a completely natural setting on Costarena Sur, **Cabinas Flamingo** *($$; pb, hw; on the coast opposite Parque Nacional Marino Ballena, ☎771-8078 or 380-5948)* is a little restaurant with a separate, two-storey building containing two large bedrooms that can sleep six. They are furnished only with beds, but are comfortable and clean. Flamingo has direct access to the beach at Parque Nacional Marino Ballena.

Uvita itself has very few comfortable places to stay. **Cocotico Lodge** and **Cabinas Los Laureles** *($$; sb/pb, ≈; on a road that leads into farmland from the Uvita-Dominical national hwy.)* are located at the limits of Uvita's residential area. The rooms are very simply furnished. The owner of Cabinas Los Laureles prepares home-cooked meals. Horseback rides in the nearby tropical rainforest go to waterfalls and are great opportunities for birdwatching.

Between the sea and Costarena Sur, slightly south of the road to Oro Verde, **Rancho La Merced** *($$$; Uvita, reservations through Selva Mar, ☎771-4582, ⇄771-8841)* operates both as a wildlife refuge and cattle ranch (see p 332). It offers rustic accommodations and country-style meals *($$$)*.

The very friendly German-Swiss owners of **El Chamán** *($$$; sb/pb; on the coast opposite Parque Nacional Marino Ballena, a few km south of Uvita and 22 km south of Dominical, on Costarena Sur)* rent rooms in simple A-frame cottages scattered over their large property. The dining room-bar in the middle of the grounds serves three meals a day (hotel guests only), with so much warmth and gaiety that you'll feel like part of the family. There are no televisions or telephones on the premises, so you will have to go there in person to rent a room. Except on holidays, there is almost always something available. If not, the hosts will suggest camping on the beach! There is a higher rate for rooms with private showers. You can swim at the beach just across from the hotel.

Diagonally across from El Chamán, **El Bejuco** *($$$; hw, ≈; Uvita, 22 km south of Dominical, along the coast, ☎/⇄771-1855)* comprises a series of modern two-room bungalows perched on a lovely hill. The rooms have bathtubs rather than showers (which is unusual) and share the terrace. It would be better if there were more mature trees to provide shade in this hot climate, but the view of the ocean is wonderful. Members of the owner's family will give guided tours of the area.

## Hacienda Barú

On the pacific Coast, **Hacienda Barú** *($$$ bkfst incl.; hw, pb, ⊗, K; on the right, just before the village of Dominical, coming from Quepos, ☎787-0003, ⇌787-0004, reservations through Selva Mar, ☎771-4582, ⇌771-8841, sstroud@rasca.co.cr)* lets you visit a noteworthy private reserve and stay in one of the fine cottages not too far from the beach. Rental units closer to the beach are planned for the future. The cottages have living rooms and kitchenettes, with a small, secluded porch. There are guided tours, and self-guided trails crisscross the area between the cottages and the ocean.

## The Osa Peninsula

**The Puerto Jiménez Region**

**La Palma**

**Centro Turístico Playa Blanca** rents campsites *($2/tent)* with shared bathroom and shower facilities, as well as *cabinas* near the beach with an unbeatable view of the Golfo Dulce. There are also a bar, and a restaurant *(open at 11am)* that serves mainly fish and seafood. Different kinds of boats can be rented for fishing or boat rides.

In the centre of the village of La Palma, **Cabinas El Tucán** *($; pb)* rents simple rooms at a modest price.

Five kilometres from La Palma, and 500 metres from the entrance to Parque Nacional Corcovado, **Cabinas Corcovado** *($; sb/pb, ℜ; ☎775-0433, ⇌775-0033)* also has campsites *($4 for 2 people)*. The restaurant serves guests three typical Costa Rican meals for only $10 per day. The owner, Luis Angulo, is an experienced guide who can take you to visit the Guyami community.

**Cooperativa CoopeUnioro** *($$ fb; sb, #; ☎/⇌775-0033)* is an interesting place, created some years ago by gold prospectors settled refuge in what is now Parque Nacional Corcovado. Members of the cooperative take part in the conservation and reforestation of their 30-hectare property. It is a good place to learn all about tropical biology: over 80 species of medicinal plants are cultivated here! A rustic little house with two bedrooms is available for groups. Another building has six very simple rooms for rent. Full board, which includes three meals, drinks and various activities, costs between $20 and $30 per person per day, depending on the activities chosen.

**Dos Brazos**

Near the Río Tigre, **Bosque de Río Tigre Sanctuary & Lodge** *($$; sb/pb; ⇌735-5045)* is a paradise for birders. The hiking trails in the area allow for tranquil exploration of the surroundings, and lead to a 15-metre-high waterfall. The property has several different buildings set up to accommodate visitors, including the main building where there are four rooms for rent on the second floor

**Ecological Corcovado Guest House** *($$ bkfst incl.; ☎775-1422, ⇌735-5045)* is a Bed & Breakfast at the edge of the village of Dos Brazos. It has well-ventilated, comfortable, simple rooms, and the owner, Tali Cantena, can suggest various outdoor activities in the area.

Near Río Tigre, **La Llanta Picante** *($$$ fb; pb, hw; ☎/⇌735-5414)* specializes in mountain bike excursions. It rents comfortable *cabinas*, mountain bikes and kayaks.

### Puerto Jiménez

You can camp at **El Bambú**, one kilometre north of Puerto Jiménez, and at **Bosque Mar**, a few kilometres south of the village. However, the friendly Costa Rican owners of the latter were still waiting for their hotel license when we were there. Guests can roam in the magnificent gardens and admire the fruit trees. A short path leads to the beach.

Also in the centre of the village, **Cabinas Carolina** *($; pb; ☎735-5185)* rents five clean, fairly spacious rooms for only $5 per person. Right next door is its namesake, a very popular restaurant which is a good place to find out about the area.

Slightly outside the village, about 300 metres south of the service station, **Cabinas Eylin** *($; pb, tv; ☎735-5011)* rents three lovely, inexpensive rooms. Two of them can accommodate up to four people, while the third is large enough for one or two. The atmosphere is very familial and cordial. You can have coffee or meals with the owner, William, and his family.

In the village centre, **Cabinas Marcelina** *($; pb, ⊗; ☎735-5007, ⇄735-5045)* rents plain, but clean rooms. The owner, Lidiette Franceschi, organizes horseback riding and walking excursions.

Near the bar-restaurant El Rancho, **Cabinas Puerto Jiménez** *($; pb, ⊗; ☎735-5090)* has inexpensive, clean rooms, but gets noisy on weekends.

In the village centre, the brand-new **Cabinas Oro Verde** *($$; pb, hw, ⊗; ☎/⇄735-5241)* has 10 large, clean, inviting rooms. Located on the second floor, they catch whatever breeze there is.

One of the more luxurious places in Puerto Jiménez, **Hotel Agua Luna** *($$-$$$; pb, hw, ≡, ℝ, tv, ℜ; ☎/⇄735-5034)* is the only one to provide air-conditioning. It is right next to the landing for the ferry from Golfito, and faces the ocean. The rooms are clean and inviting. Its restaurant is 100 metres towards the village centre.

**Doña Leta's Bungalows** *($$$; pb, hw, ⊗, K, ℜ; ☎/⇄735-5180)* are near the airport, a few minutes from the village on foot. These *cabinas* are right on the beach, near mangroves that are teeming with life. Spacious and clean, they are also equipped for cooking. A bar-restaurant, volleyball court and kayaks round out the ensemble. The guide Juan Carlos can suggest several nature discovery activities.

**Iguana Lodge** *($$$; pb, ⊗, ℜ; ☎/⇄735-5205)* rents comfortable *cabinas* near the superb Platanares beach. They are just far enough away from the bustle of Puerto Jiménez to ensure peace and quiet. The wood *cabinas* are elevated to catch the ocean breeze and have a lovely view of the seascape. The water pump, lights and fans run on solar energy. The owners, Jeff Lantz and Stig Hanson, came here from southern California to set up a hotel for fishing and nature discovery activities. Fishing is their passion, and they will be glad to lead excursions to all the beautiful spots around the Osa Peninsula and the Golfo Dulce on their luxurious, modern, and well-equipped boat. Full board, with excellent buffet-style meals, costs $45 per person per day.

There is a new owner at the hotel and restaurant **Manglares** *($$$; ⊗, #, ℜ;*

*☎735-5002)*, near the airport. Rooms are spacious.

Six kilometres east of the airport, **Playa Preciosa Lodge** *($$$$; pb, ⊗, ℜ; ☎735-5062, ⇌735-5043)* rents eight attractive *cabinas* that have terraces with hammocks. There are a restaurant, an orchard and a hiking trail right outside the door. The lodge organizes several types of excursions.

**Cabo Matapalo**

In the rich, dense forest of the Osa Peninsula, hotels and inns are often far apart and hard to find south of Puerto Jiménez. We strongly suggest you make advance reservations by fax or phone, and ask for detailed directions. Unless you have a four-wheel drive vehicle, ask about the road condition.

About 20 kilometres from Puerto Jiménez, **Tierra de Milagros** *($$; sb; ☎233-0233, ⇌735-5045)* is a place where all sorts of "new age" activities are practiced (yoga, tai chi, etc.). The facilities are very rudimentary, which suits the owners' lifestyle. Everyone helps to prepare the vegetarian meals.

At the southern end of the peninsula, where the Pacific Ocean and the Golfo Dulce meet, **Bosque del Cabo** *($$$$ fb; pb, ≈. ℜ, #; ☎/⇌735-5206, 735-5043, boscabo@sol.racsa.co.cr)* has one of the region's most beautiful natural settings: it is lush and tranquil, and the vast grounds are superbly maintained. Lots of grass, and many flowers, plants and trees beautify the area. Hiking trails in the forest lead to a waterfall, and to the Pacific and gulf coasts. The Bosque del Cabo is well-known as a place where you can see various mammals, birds and reptiles. The seven *cabinas* are tastefully arranged, comfortable and airy. The most luxurious have solar-generated electricity and extra-large beds. The standard *cabinas* have double beds and are candle lit. All of them have views of the ocean. There is also a charming house for rent; the Casa Blanca has two bedrooms and a fully equipped kitchen. The restaurant serves local and international cuisine. Full board, including the room and three meals, costs $94 (standard) or $104 (luxury) per person per day (double occupancy).

When we went to **Hacienda Bahía Esmeralda** *($$$$$ fb; pb, ⊗, ≈, ℜ; ☎381-8521, ⇌735-5045, francisx@sol.racsa.co.cr)*, we were greeted by the loud screams of howler monkeys. This establishment is hidden away in the tropical rainforest, on a site that looks out over the Golfo Dulce. Behind the hacienda is a stone swimming pool filled with cool water from a mountain stream. The main building has three luxurious, large bedrooms with private bathrooms and big, orthopaedic beds. Right beside it are three comfortable *cabinas* with terraces from which you can take in the magnificent view. The cuisine is reputedly excellent and varied: Italian, Spanish, Thai, Indian, Mexican, Chinese and French dishes are on the menu, along with foods cooked on the restaurant's grill. Full board, including room, three meals, drinks, and transportation to and from Puerto Jiménez, is $117 per person per day.

Perched more than 100 metres above sea level, the 14 bungalows at **Lapa Ríos** *($$$$$ fb; pb, hw, ⊗, ≈, ℜ, #; ☎735-5179, ⇌735-5130, laparios@sol.racsa.cocr)* provide a worry-free vacation in the middle of primary and secondary tropical rainforest. The Minnesotan couple, John and Karen Lewis, came up with the idea of Lapa Ríos, and demonstrated that ecotourism and luxury could sometimes go together! Each bungalow has a romantic atmosphere, with its thatched roof and ocean view. The main building has a circular staircase that provides a magnificent view of the Golfo Dulce. Paths going though the surrounding forest allow you to experience the flora and fauna up close. Many guided tours are available. Full board, including room and three meals, costs $164 per person per day (double occupancy).

### The Carate Region

**Cabins Carate Jungle Camp** *($-$$; sb, #; ☎735-5211)* is located in the forest near Carate. This establishment rents a *cabina* with an outdoor shower and three very modest rooms that consist of double beds surrounded by mosquito netting. Full board, including the room and three meals, costs $30 per person per day. Guests are permitted to bring their own food if they wish.

Owned by Costa Rica Expeditions, **Corcovado Lodge Tent Camp** *($$$; sb, ℜ; ☎257-0766, ⇒257-1655, costaric@expeditions.co.cr)* is only a few minutes from Parque Nacional Corcovado on foot. Staying here is a unique experience that permits you to enter into the pristine protected natural surroundings. Significant efforts are being made to respect the environment, and the establishment in no way intrudes on its surroundings. Arriving in Carate by plane or all-terrain vehicle, guests walk along the beach for 30 or 40 minutes to get to the camp (while a horse-drawn cart carries the luggage). Corcovado Lodge has 20 large tents (3 m by 3 m) mounted on wooden platforms within sight of the ocean. Each airy tent contains two single beds and a small table. The platform extends into a terrace with two chairs. Only candles are used at night, so campers are encouraged to bring flashlights for getting around after sundown. The bathrooms are a short distance away. There is no hot water for the showers, but it is hardly missed, given the stifling heat in the area. The outdoor dining room has long tables where everyone gets together to share their day's adventures. The food is excellent, healthy and varied, although there is no menu. Meals are served at fixed hours (7am, 12:30pm and 6:30pm). In the recreation hall, you can relax in hammocks, chat at the bar, or simply enjoy the view from the terrace. There are slide shows featuring the region's flora and fauna on some nights. Behind the recreation hall, a trail climbs up into the rich, dense tropical rainforest, where it is quite common to see howler monkeys, agoutis, coatis, butterflies and numerous species of birds. You can have the experience of a lifetime in this forest: to be raised up to the top of a 40-metre-high tree *(Platform Experience, $69/person, half day)*! Well secured to the platform, and following the directions of an experienced guide, you can observe life in the forest canopy. When we were there, we saw two different species of toucans feeding in the treetops. You can also experience the canopy at night *($125/person)*. The guided tour *($25/person, half day)* in the tropical rainforest at Corcovado park follows a narrow trail that goes to Río Madrigal. Experienced riders can also go horseback riding in the park *($35/person for 2.5 hours)*. A tent for two costs $30 per day. Breakfast, lunch and dinner cost $13.05, $18.75 and $21.25, respectively. Full board, including the tent and three generous meals, costs $68 per person per day. A package of three days/two nights with round trip airfare from San José, shuttle service, meals, the canopy tour and entrance fee to the national park costs $649 per person.

In the mountains, just a few minutes from the Carate airport by car, **The Lookout Inn** *($$$ fb; pb, hw, ℜ; ☎735-5205, the office is next to the Puerto Jiménez bakery)* rents three rooms with private bathrooms and hot water. Each room has its own balcony with a view of the Pacific, and is furnished with a large bed, a dresser and table and chairs. There is a common living room upstairs with a stereo, cassette player, tv and library. Guests have free use of kayaks, canoes, fishing gear, mountain bikes and exercise equipment. Full board, including room and three meals, costs $65 per person per day.

### Bahía Drake

Because Bahía Drake is isolated from the rest of the country, it is usually accessible only by boat or by plane. It is more expensive to stay here than in other parts of the country, and reasonably priced accommodations are hard to come by. However, you can find inexpensive lodgings in and around the village of Agujitas.

For anyone travelling on a tight budget, **Cabinas Cecilia** *($$ fb; sb; leave a message at ☎771-2336)*, **Cabinas y Restaurante Jade Mar** *($$$ fb; ☎284-6681, ⇄786-6358)* and **Mirador Lodge** *($$$ fb; pb; ☎494-4337)* are among the least expensive. **Rancho Corcovado** *($$-$$$ fb; pb, ℜ; ☎788-8111)* rents very simple rooms near the beach. Campsites are also available for $6 per person per day, dinner included. Full board costs $35 per person per day.

**Cabinas Las Caletas** *($$-$$$; sb/pb, ℜ; ☎381-4052, ⇄786-6291)* has such a calm atmosphere that it will make you forget about the stress of daily life. Owners David and Yolanda only accept a few visitors at a time. Guests can stay in a room in the owners' house or in a *cabina* with a private bathroom and a little terrace. The menu includes Costa Rican and European specialties, and the food is prepared using fresh, homegrown ingredients. Full board, including meals and drinks, costs $35 (room) or $50 *(cabina)* per person per day.

Forty-five minutes on foot from Bahía Drake, **Corcovado Adventures Tent Camp** *($$$ fb; sb, ℜ; ☎223-2770, ⇄257-4201)* rents tents that have thatched roofs and are mounted on wooden platforms. Each contains a small bed, a large bed, and a small terrace. The shared bathrooms are in a separate building. Swimming, fishing, sea kayaking and surfing are some of the activities. There is also a short trail about 30 minutes long that goes to Río Claro close to the Marenco Lodge and Parque Nacional Corcovado.

Almost mid-way between Bahía Drake and Parqe Nacional Corcovado, **Marenco Lodge** *($$$ fb; bp, ℜ; ☎221-1594, ⇄255-1346, marenco@sol.racsa.co.cr)* has been turned into a private reserve dedicated to the preservation of the tropical rainforest. It rents rustic *cabinas* and bungalows, and has a dining room and a small library. Many excursions are organized from here, which are mostly nature-oriented.

**Albergue Jinetes de Osa** *($$$-$$$$; sb/pb, ℜ; ☎788-8111, 253-6909)* is located on the west coast of the bay, above the black sand beach. The inn is surrounded by fruit trees and many different flowers that attract parrots. It has nine rooms with shared or private bathrooms. Costa Rica Adventure Divers organizes various scuba diving excursions for guests here. Full board costs between $25 and $50 per person per day, depending on the season.

**Cocalito Lodge** *($$-$$$$; sb/pb, ℜ; ☎/⇌786-6150, in Canada ☎519-782-3978)* is owned by Canadians Marna and Mike Berry. They have set up their establishment to live in harmony with nature. One example of this is their organic garden, where herbs and all sorts of vegetables are grown and attract many different animals. Simple, but very clean, rooms and *cabinas* are available for guests, which are lit by candles at night. There are also three fully equipped tents, and campsites *($)*. The nearby beach is completely safe for swimming. The restaurant (5:30pm to 9pm) has a varied menu featuring grilled foods, seafood and organic vegetables, seasoned with fresh herbs from the garden.

**Casa Corcovado Jungle Lodge** *($$$-$$$$ fb; sb/pb, hw, ⊗, ℜ, #; ☎256-3181, ⇌256-7409, corcovdo@sol.racsa.co.cr)*, perched high above the beach, was built by a naturalist from the United States and is close to Parque Nacional Corcovado. The rooms are attractive and comfortable for a thoroughly enjoyable stay in the tropical rainforest. There are many trails throughout the area: one of them goes to the San Pedrillo entrance of Parque Nacional Corcovado, a half-hour away. This is a wonderful place for birdwatching, photography, fishing, kayaking and scuba diving. There are organized guided tours of the national park on Isla del Caño. Full board costs $50 to $80 per person per day.

**Drake Bay Wilderness Camp** *($$$-$$$$ fb; sb/pb, hw, ⊗, ℜ; ☎/⇌771-2436 or 256-7394, hdrake@ticonet.co.cr)* is on the Pacific Ocean and borders on Río Agujitas. Guests can enjoy the treasures of Bahía Drake here in a convivial family atmosphere. The site has 20 attractively decorated *cabinas* with double beds, private bathrooms, and terraces overlooking the bay and the tropical rainforest. Also available are four large tents with single beds, electricity, fans and shared bathrooms. By the Pacific, the restaurant serves excellent seafood, as well as homemade breads and desserts. Many guided tours are available: forest hiking, canoeing, kayaking, scuba diving, birdwatching and fishing. The swimming pool is in a natural rock formation. Full board is $55 (tent) and $75 (*cabina)* per person per day.

There is a spectacular view at **La Poloma Lodge** *($$$$ fb; pb, hw, ≈, ℜ, #; ☎239-2801, ☎/⇌239-0954, gladys@lapalomalodge.com)*. Each *cabina* with thatched roof, balcony and hammocks overlooks the ocean and enjoys the sea breezes. Larger *ranchos* that can accommodate up to five guests are also available. The hosts Sue and Mike Kalmbach offer personalized service to their clientele. Naturalist guides are pleased to share their knowledge on organized tours. Snorkelling and scuba diving are just some of the favourite activities.

**L' Aguila de Osa Inn** *($$$$ fb; pb, hw, ⊗, ℜ; ☎296-2190, ☎/⇌232-7722, aguilacr@sol.racsa.co.cr)* claims to be the most luxurious inn on Bahía Drake. The rooms are spacious, tastefully decorated and comfortable. The restaurant is reputed for its fine international cuisine thanks to the talents of chef Edgar Coolson, nicknamed *Cookie.* Snorkeling, fishing and other organized aquatic activities are available.

### Sierpe

**Hotel Pargo** *($$; pb, hw, ⊗, ≡, ℜ; ☎788-8111, ⇌788-8251)* in Sierpe is a good place to stay near Bahía Drake. Parking is free for guests who are spending a few days at the bay, and $1.50 per day for everyone else. All the rooms at the hotel have a single bed and a double bed. Those on the second floor have a view of the village and the river. The hotel has boats for all sorts of aquatic activities, as well as for transportation.

Like Mapache Lodge, **Río Sierpe Lodge** *($$$ fb; pb, hw, ⊗, ℜ; ☎284-5595)* is only accessible by boat. This place is also situated right in the middle of the area's hiking trails. There are some 20 large, plain rooms, and lots of organized activities, including everything from fishing and scuba diving to hiking in Parque Nacional Corcovado and horseback riding. The birdwatching excursions to the Caño and Violines Islands are especially popular. Full board costs $75 per person per day and includes transportation to and from Sierpe.

Two kilometres before the village of Sierpe, on the banks of Río Estero Azul, **Eco-Manglares Lodge** *($$$$ bkfst incl.; pb, hw, ℜ; ☎773-3192 or 778-8111)* rents truly charming rustic *cabinas*. They are well ventilated, comfortable and have little terraces. The restaurant serves Italian food. There are hiking trails throughout the neighbouring forest. The lodge also organizes river excursions.

Very close to Eco-Manglares Lodge, **Estero Azul Lodge** *($$$$; pb, hw, ⊗, ℜ; ☎788-8111, ⇌788-8251)* also rents attractive wooden *cabinas* that are well set up and can accommodate up to four people. The restaurant near the *cabinas* serves local fish and seafood dishes. Full board, including room, three meals and drinks, costs $65 per person per day. A six-metre-long boat takes guests on excursions on the river and to the Pacific Coast.

Located about 12 kilometres from Sierpe and only accessible by boat, **Mapache Lodge** *($$$-$$$$$, sb/pb; tv, ≈, ℜ; ☎786-6565 or 788-8111, ⇌768-6358, mapache@greenarrow.com)* is on 45 hectares of unspoiled land at the mouth of Río Toboga. Three types of lodging are available: two rooms with private bathroom in the owners', Guilio and Giuseppina's, house; three rooms with shared bath; and large tents on wooden platforms. The restaurant serves Italian dishes, including pasta and seafood. Guests can stroll on the little trails and observe some of the 160 identified bird species. Among the suggested activities are horseback riding, kayaking and hiking. Full board varies from $45 to $75 per person per day, depending on the type of accommodation chosen, and includes transportation to and from Sierpe.

## The Region's South

### Palmar

The best bet in Palmar is **Casa Amarilla** *($$; pb, ⊗; Palmar Norte, in front of the football field, ☎786-6251)* in the middle of the village. The upstairs rooms have balconies. Because it is the best place to stay in the village, it is often full. Even in low season, reservations are a good idea.

### Ojochal

**Casa Papagayos** *($$$; pb, hw, ⊗, ≈; Ojochal)* is run by Canadians who rent a few rooms. Clean, bright and very well ventilated (a *must* in this weather), they are arranged around a swimming pool, and tennis and basketball courts. Hats off to anyone who can do these sports in the intense heat that is normal for this area! The owners organize all sorts of excursions, including a trip through the mangroves.

**El Parozoso** *($$$ bkfst incl.; pb, hw, Ojochal, ☎786-6358)* is a Québec-owned inn. To get there, take the road off the Costarena Sur to Ojochal, and a little before Cabinas Papagayo to the right is the road that leads to the inn. Be careful fording the little river!

**Paraíso del Pacífico** *($$$; pb, hw, ℜ, ≈; Ojochal)* is another Québec-owned hotel in the Ojochal hills. Little buildings that are fairly close together each have two bedrooms with a living room area (good for long stays) and a semi-private terrace. It is relatively basic, but there is a pleasant view of the surroundings from the complex's hilltop location. A shuttle transports vacationers to the beach. Full board is available.

**Rancho Soluna** *($$$; ≠788-8210)* is like a family-style inn, owned by Leo and Michele from Québec. They rent two pleasant rooms with shared terrace. They are planning to build a room with kitchenette. Campsites are available with water and electricity, *($7/person under a thatched hut, $2.50/person without thatched hut)*. Michele runs the warm, intimate restaurant on the premises (see p 373).

**Ultimo Refugio** *($$$; 500 m south of the Ojochal village primary school, ≠786-6358)* is simultaneously a restaurant, a souvenir shop and a place to stay. While the grounds are relatively small, foliage hides the building from the street and improves the appearance of the setting. The owners, from Québec, have created a friendly atmosphere and the building is tastefully decorated.

### Playa Tortuga

We fell in love with **Villas Gaia** *($$$$; hw, pb, ⊗, ℜ; Playa Tortuga, ☎256-9956)*, and with good reason! The individual *cabinas* are tastefully decorated in warm, tropical colours and have private terraces. The raised pool has a splendid view of the ocean. The look of the place in general, the style and comfort of the *cabinas*, the resaurant's cuisine, the quality of the service: all are impeccable (the place settings alone is worth the trip!). There are all sorts of organized guided tours in the area.

### Playa Piñuela

In front of Parque Nacional Marino Ballena, on little Piñuela beach, **Cabinas Piñuela** *($$$; pb, hw, ≈, ℜ; ☎/≠788-8210)* rents two-storey, A-frame *cabinas* with one apartment on the ground floor and another upstairs. Each has a kitchenette and a living room with a view. The landscaping is somewhat uninspired and lacks mature greenery, but the place itself is practically right on the ocean, unlike most of the hotel establishments in the area. The owner's residence, a castle, is a recent addition and rather incongruous in this setting. Among the available activities are sea-kayaking lessons with an enthusiastic teacher, and volleyball. There is a rancho-style restaurant on the property.

## The Golfito Region

**Casa Blanca Lodge** *($; pb, P; 300 m south of Depósito Libre, Golfito, ☎775-0124)* rents little rooms that are only furnished with a bed, on the second floor of a house that is set back from the road by its grounds, somewhat like the Princesa del Golfo (see further below). There are also some rental units in a motel-style building on the property, which are more modern and more expensive. This is a peaceful, shady place.

**Cabinas Isabel** *($; pb, ⊗, P; downtown Golfito, ☎775-1774)* rents small rooms with nothing more than beds in them, but the little building itself has charm.

There is a cozy common living room on the second floor. The rooms are on both floors of the building, but all the windows open onto an indoor hallway.

**Cabinas y Restaurante Mar y Luna** *($; where Golfito begins, ☎775-0192, ⇄775-1049)* rents little rooms that only have beds in them and a common terrace, in a building on the gulf. A wharf was under construction when we were there.

In a wooden house that gives the place the look of a small-town hotel, **Cabinas Mazuren** *($; ⊗; Pueblo Civil, Golfito, ☎775-0058)* is inexpensive, but the small rooms open onto a hallway and there is no decor in them, except for the bed, if you can call it that.

**Cabinas El Tucán** *($; pb, ⊗ P; across from the Los Bruncas stadium, Golfito, ☎775-0553)* rents small rooms with a bathroom and a window with a view. They are pretty basic, but clean. In fact, the place prides itself on the cleanliness of its rooms!

**Delfina** *($; 200 m south of the quay, Pueblo Civil, Golfito)* is another of the many little small-town hotels in the Golfito region. It has small rooms on the upper floor of a wooden building. The hotel looks out onto the gulf, but some of the buildings crowded around it block the view from some of the rooms.

The rooms at **Hotel Golfito** *($; pb, ⊗; 25 m south of the municipal dock, Golfito)* are on the perimeter of a wooden building on the gulf, but you can't see much through the frosted glass windows. Only the bathroom window has a view! Also, the bedrooms contain nothing more than a bed and the reception is lukewarm.

The rooms at **Princesa del Golfo** *($; pb, ⊗; diagonally across from the Banco Nacional building, Golfito)* are in the home of the owners, former residents of the United States. What makes this place so special is that it is located on extensive grounds that remove it from the rest of town. Rooms on the main floor have private entrances. The furnishings are minimal: a bed and a bathroom.

Next to the bay, opposite the cemetery, **Villa Casanova** *($; pb; Golfito, ☎775-0730)* rents really inexpensive rooms that can accommodate four people – for $4 per person! The rooms are clean, but contain only four beds. There is no fan, but the gulf breezes supposedly cool the place down. The building is quite attractive, built on pilings in the water. An older lady lives on the main floor and takes care of rentals. The rooms are on the second floor.

**Cabinas Alamedas** *($$; Zona Americana de Golfito, close to Depósito Libre, ☎775-0126)* has lovely, large rooms and a restaurant (see p 373). Because it is in the Zona Americana, it is fairly shady, which is a blessing given the heat that plagues the region.

**Purruja Lodge** *($$; Golfito, ☎/⇄775-1054)* has a family-like atmosphere. The two small rooms are nothing spectacular, but they are in a separate *casita* with shared terrace. The landscaping is attractive, and there is a restaurant on the premises.

**Costa Rica** *($$; hw, sb/pb, ⊗; Pueblo Civil, Golfito, ☎/⇄775-0034)* is another of those small-town hotels where rooms open onto an inside corridor. However, some of the rooms have air-conditioning, which is something to keep in mind in Golfito's heat.

Another small-town hotel, **Del Cerro** *($$; hw, sb/pb, ⊗, P; across from the main wharf, Golfito, ☎775-0006,*

*⇌775-0551)* rents rooms by the week. They are simply furnished and the windows face the hallway, instead of the beautiful view of the bay. The restaurant specializes in seafood.

**El Gran Ceibo** *($$; pb, hw, ≡, ⊗, ℜ, bar, ≈, P; on the way into Golfito, ☎/⇌775-0403)* is one of the few hotels in the city of Golfito that has a swimming pool and other modern comforts that make it appropriate for a stay of more than one day. The rooms are clean and reasonably well arranged.

**Cabinas Los Cocos** *($$$; hw, pb, K; Playa Zancudo, ☎/⇌776-0012)* rents four *cabinas* with small gardens that have the ocean as a front yard. These cottages have covered verandas with hammocks. They offer many guided tours in the region. A taxi-boat picks up guests in Golfito.

**Cabinas Sol y Mar** *($$$; pb, hw, ⊗; 25 min on foot south of Playa Zancudo, ☎776-0014, ⇌776-0015)* consists of four seaside *cabinas*. There is also a little three-storey house, with a kitchen that can accommodate six people.

**Golfo Azul** *($$$; hw, pb; Depósito Libre, Golfito, ☎775-0871, ⇌775-1849)* is a hotel-restaurant. The rooms are in a modern, motel-style building behind the large restaurant. The landscaping looks like a parking lot. The rooms are standard in size and share a common porch along the front of the building.

The French-owned **Centro Turístico Samoa del Sur** *($$$; pb, tv, ℜ; Golfito, ☎775-0233 or 775-0573)* is a tourist centre and hotel, located on the banks of the gulf. The rooms share terraces and are in a motel-style building that extends out over the water. The building is above average in quality for this area: it is very clean, and the furniture is modern. There are plans for a pool and a maritime museum. The grounds are quite large (considering that this is the most urbanized area of Golfito). The buildings are set back from the street and are well spaced amid tasteful landscaping. This is a good place to stay compared to others in the area, and its restaurant adds a lot to its value (see p 374).

**Las Gaviotas** *($$$; hw, pb, tv, ≡, ≈, K, ℜ, bar; at the beginning of Golfito, ☎775-0062, ⇌775-0544)* is one of the best places to stay in Golfito. There are three bungalows (with kitchenettes) and 18 rooms on a well-landscaped, shady lot. While the rooms are in a long, motel-style building, each has a large, private terrace, which is a plus. Need we say how much the swimming pools were appreciated? The restaurant is also one of the best in town (see p 374).

Formerly Cabinas Las Palmas, **Isa's Place** *($$$; pb, ⊗, ℝ, ≈, ⊛; Playa Cacao, Golfito, ☎385-9622, ⇌775-0373)* gives you the chance to stay on the beach and still be just across from Golfito. When the renovations, taking place while we were there, are completed, eight huts (including one with kitchenette) will accommodate small groups on beautiful, shady grounds. There is shuttle service to Golfito and back, and to other beaches in the area, including a nude beach. The owners are friendly and laid back.

**Esquinas Lodge** *($$$$$ fb; pb, hw, ⊗, ℜ; La Gamba, 4 km from km 37 on the Interamericana, near Golfito, ☎775-0631, ⇌775-0131)* is a genuine ecotourism resort. The lodge was developed by the Austrian government as an experiment combining research, nature conservation and sustainable development. All profits from the resort go towards environmental conservation and back into the community. It is in a beautiful setting, with wood architecture and landscaping that blends perfectly into the natural surroundings. The main building is open to all sides, and the restaurant and common areas are very relaxing. The *cabinas* access a veranda with a bamboo rocking chair. The menu is international with a slight emphasis on Viennese cuisine. The swimming pool is fed by a clear, natural pond and a stream, and there are also some orchards on the property. A network of trails leads to caves and waterfalls hidden away in the tropical rainforest. There is free airport pick-up for guests, but reservations must be made for this in advance. If you are driving, note that the road is not always in good condition, but a four-wheel drive vehicle is not necessary. The room rate includes an excursion to Piedras Blancas.

**Ciudad Neily**

If it weren't for the lack of a swimming pool (a necessity in this region), **Andrea** *($$; Ciudad Neily, ☎/⇌783-3784 or 783-5240)* would be the best hotel in Ciudad Neily. The rooms are clean and pretty, with a bright, fresh look, in a building with front porches that extend along the entire length of both floors. The grounds are spacious and well maintained. There is one other disadvantage, however: only two of the rooms have hot water (a slight problem) and air-conditioning (disastrous!).

**Centro Turístico Neily** *($$; some rooms have air-conditioning; Ciudad Neily, ☎783-3301)* in Ciudad Neily rents 20 motel-style units in a rather ordinary building: average-sized rooms, view of the back of the property, not much of a terrace. However, the well landscaped, shady grounds include two swimming pools (a blessing!), a restaurant and a night club.

**San Vito**

**Centro Turístico Las Huacas** *($; hw, pb, on the way into San Vito, on the Coto Brus road, ☎773-3115)* is a community centre that functions as a bar and night club on weekends and has rooms for rent as well. The typically Costa Rican-style rooms are relatively clean; but the only furniture in the bedrooms is the bed.

**Rino** *($; hw, pb; Al Pizar commercial centre, downtown, San Vito, ☎773-3071)* is a tiny hotel with clean rooms.

One of the best hotels in San Vito is the Italian-owned **El Ceibo** *($$; pb, hw, ctv, ℜ; a few steps away from the municipal hall, San Vito, ☎773-3025).* The rooms open onto a small wooded area in back of the property (via a very small door), and have small, Italian-style balconies. They are very simply set up and not overly large, but clean. The hotel is partially hidden by a screen of vegetation (on the road that runs east of the main intersection), so be careful not to miss it.

You can stay overnight at the **Wilson Botanical Garden** *($$$$$ fb; ♿, pb, hw, laundry service; reservations through the "Organization for Tropical Studies", ☎240-6696, ⇌240-6783)*. In fact, it is one of the best places to stay in the area. The *cabinas* are lovely and impeccably clean, and the view from their windows is magnificent. A peaceful stay in the middle of the garden, and good food are guaranteed. In short, it's paradise! There are even two rooms specially equipped for disabled travellers. Reservations must be made early in the season, because this place is very popular.

**La Amistad Lodge** *($$$$$ fb guide incl.; sb/pb, hw; about 3 km from Las*

*Mellizas, northeast of San Vito, ☎233-8228 or 773-3193)* is probably the hotel most off the tourist-beaten path in Costa Rica. It is near the Panamanian border northwest of San Vito, near the little village of Las Mellizas. If you don't have a four-wheel drive vehicle, you might have to walk part of the way there. La Amistad is a family-owned lodge that was established to integrate ecotourism into the park. Thanks to the many trails and excellent guides, this is a great place to learn more about the flora and fauna that grows at this altitude of the primary forest. Part of the land is used to grow organic coffee. The combination of these two activities makes for an interesting and pleasant stay. The rooms are clean and simple.

## RESTAURANTS

### The Region's North

#### The San Isidro de El General Region

##### Cerro de la Muerte and San Gerardo de Dota

The roadside hotel-restaurant **Georgina** *($$; Cerro La Muerte, ☎771-1299 or 284-2760)* serves typical "rest-stop" fare at reasonable prices. Service is from the counter, but the appealingly furnished wood-finished dining room overlooks the surrounding mountains and has a superb view, with its high vantage point and large windows. A souvenir shop makes the place complete.

**Los Chespiritos** *($$; in the neighbourhood of Ojo de Agua, about 2 km north of the road to San Gerardo de Dota, Cerro La Muerte)* is a cafeteria that also serves as an *abastecedor* (convenience store). Its fruits and ready-to-eat treats (candies, marinated and conserved foods, etc.) are greatly appreciated by anyone stopping here between the Central Valley and San Isidro de El General. You can also buy souvenirs here. This clean and lively place is particularly welcoming in the chilly heights of Cerro de la Muerte.

At San Gerardo de Dota, **Los Lagos** *($$; San Gerardo de Dota, ☎771-2077)* is a charming restaurant whose menu features fresh trout from the area's many rivers. Breakfast is also served. Although the large dining room is quite plain, the restaurant's surroundings are spectacular, with the Río Savegre running right next to it. A fountain completes the attractive setting.

In addition to having a unique view of the Valle del General, **Mirador Vista del Valle** *($$; km 119 on the Interamericana Hwy., Cerro de la Muerte, ☎284-4685, ⇌771-2003)* serves typical Costa Rican food, and fresh trout is on the menu every day. You can also do some birdwatching, contemplate the restaurant's orchids, or shop for handicrafts.

##### San Isidro de El General

**Soda El Jardín** *($; San Isidro, ☎771-0349)* has the same name as the hotel, and serves good fast food, Costa Rican-style. You will recognize the restaurant by its orange tables and chairs.

#### The Dominical Region

On the riverbank next to Albergue Wildale, **Déli del Río** *(every day, Dominical)* is a relatively new delicatessen that sells pizza, baked goods, deli fare and other quality foods – and suntan lotions to boot! The place is very clean and friendly, with a North American look and attractive and inviting displays. You can have breakfast *(7am to 11am)* or dinner *(5pm to 8pm)* in the small restaurant *($$)* beside the delicatessen.

**Kardigui** *($)* is an inviting *tico*-style restaurant-bar situated on the ocean between Uvita and Dominical. It serves Costa Rican dishes at reasonable prices. The building has large open spaces with a red metal roof over the bar.

**Soda Laura** *($; every day, 6am to 9pm, Dominical)* sells inexpensive *tico* dishes.

A little past Buster's restaurant is **Soda Nanyoa** *($; Dominical)*, which serves inexpensive *tico* food. The setting is also typically Costa Rican.

**Buster's** *($$; Dominical)* is your standard North American restaurant in terms of the food it serves (pizza, hamburgers, and so on) and decor. Run by three friends who love to surf, Buster's is a favourite with Dominical's young surfer crowd.

Right beside the cabinas of the same name, the restaurant-bar **Punta Dominical** *($$; 4 km south of Dominical, ☎787-0016, ≠787-0017)* is a great place to go at sundown to savour Costa Rican or international food, or simply for a drink. The stereo sound of the sea lapping against the shores of the narrow point on which the restaurant is built is especially soothing and distinct at night.

Next to the Dominical Info Centre is Buster's alter ego, **San Clemente Bar & Grill** *($$; every day, 7am to 9pm, Dominical)*. With the same owners as the Cabinas San Clemente, which are on the sea, this place serves *tico* and North American cuisine, with grilled food as the house specialty. On Saturdays, the restaurant turns into a bar and nightclub. The atmosphere is very relaxed, with board games and billiards and a satellite television that shows all kinds of sports. Together with Buster's, the San Clemente Bar & Grill is the place to go in the evenings in Dominical.

## The Osa Peninsula

Because getting around is rather difficult on the Osa Peninsula, most hotels, inns and *cabinas* have their own dining rooms for their guests, and sometimes for people just travelling through, as well. Most restaurants, as well as several excellent, inexpensive small *sodas*, are found in Puerto Jiménez.

### Puerto Jiménez Region

Situated almost in the centre of La Palma, **El Rancho** *($; every day, 6am to 9pm)* is a vast and very airy restaurant whose varied menu features dishes such as *ceviche*, spaghetti, meat and chicken; most of the main dishes include a dessert. To quench your thirst, wine, beer and freshly prepared fruit juices are served.

South of La Palma, towards Puerto Jiménez, **Sabores del Golfo** *($; every day, 6am to 9pm)* serves excellent and inexpensive local food in a family atmosphere.

**Agua Luna** *($-$$; Puerto Jiménez, ☎735-5034)* is situated opposite the Golfo Dulce, right beside Cacao stream, near where the ferry from Golfito lands. Excellent local and international food is prepared at this very large, airy restaurant; the seafood is especially good.

In the heart of Puerto Jiménez, the **Carolina** *($-$$; every day, 7am to 8pm)* restaurant-bar is rarely empty. Drop by for a soft drink, a coffee or a beer, to chat with friends or simply pass the time. The Escondido Trex tourist agency is situated at the back of the restaurant. The food is also excellent, varied and reasonably priced.

Also on the main street, **Jossette** *($-$$; Puerto Jiménez, ☎735-5227)* is a *soda* and restaurant that serves grilled food, seafood and Chinese food, as well as fast food dishes.

## The Region's South

### Palmar Region

There are two reasonably priced restaurants at the crossroads of the Interamericana Highway and the road to Puerto Jiménez, on the way from Palmar to Golfito or Ciudad Neily: **Corcovado** and **Carratera Chacarita**.

#### Ojochal

**El Gringo Mike's Pizza & Café** *($$; a few km from the village of Ojochal)* is where vacationers from around Playa Tortuga go in the evenings.

The little **Rancho Soluna** *($$; Ojochal, ⇌788-8210)* is both a restaurant and a small inn (see p 367) to which the owners, Léo and Michèle originally from Québec, devote much time and energy. The cozy, relaxed restaurant serves spaghetti, pizza, hamburgers, and even *poutine*, as well as delicious North American desserts prepared by Michèle. An ideal place to feel at home away from home!

The Québec-run **Último Refugio** *($$$; 500 m south of the elementary school in Ojochal, ⇌786-6358)* comprises rooms, a restaurant and a souvenir shop. A very pleasant and charming place tucked away in greenery.

#### Playa Tortuga

Like the hotel itself, the restaurant of the **Villas Gaia** *($$; on Costarena Sur, Playa Tortuga, ☎256-9956)* is very well-maintained. Its international cuisine is so good, it is worth a detour.

### The Golfito Region

At Golfito, good daily specials for under $5 are served at **La Dama del Delfín** *(☎775-0235, ⇌775-0042)* restaurant and souvenir shop. The place has a good view of Golfito's Pueblo Civil district and of the gulf itself. The owner can give you all kinds of information about the area.

**El Barco** *($; Golfito)* is a friendly little *soda*, with *tico* prices.

The bar-restaurant **Alamedas** *($$; every day, 8am to midnight, Zona Americana de Golfito, ☎775-0126)* is right beside the hotel of the same name (see p 368). Its decor and service could use some improvement, but this might be because the place is for sale. The whole property is pleasantly shaded from the intense heat, for which this region, the Zona Americana de Golfito, is famous. The speciality is seafood.

**La Cazuelita** *($$; 200 m west of Depósito Libre, Golfito, ☎775-1621)* serves Chinese food in a simple, friendly setting.

The little **La Eurekita** *($$; Golfito, ☎775-1616)* restaurant is open on two sides, so it has views of both the gulf and the main streets of Golfito's Pueblo Civil. Costa Rican dishes and fast food are served in a friendly atmosphere. One of the largest restaurants in Pueblo

Civil, it is alsoone of the busiest at noon.

The restaurant of the hotel **Las Gaviotas** *($$; as you enter Golfito, ☎775-0062, ⇌775-0544)* is a very good seafood restaurant. Built outside but with an overhead covering, its open-air setting is very pleasant, and the view of the bay is marvellous.

**Centro Turístico Samo del Sur** *($$$; Golfito, ☎775-0233, ⇌775-0573)* is a restaurant-bar next to the hotel of the same name (see p 369). The food here is very good (pizza, seafood and *tico* dishes; try the *ceviche* or the *patacones con frijoles molidos*). The atmosphere under the large, inviting shelter is lively in the evenings, and you can have a drink while the TV and video compete for your attention. This is also a good place to sip delicious fruit juices in the late afternoon.

#### Ciudad Neily Region

On the banks of a small river running through the city, **Soda La Cuchara de Margoth** *($; Ciudad Neily)* is a very pretty, pleasant place for a light meal.

**Soda El Parque** *($; Cuidad Neily)* is a little closer to the centre of town than La Cuchara de Margoth. A clean place where the tablecloths are beautifully white and covered with plastic. Costa Rican cuisine.

**La Moderna** *($$; Ciudad Neily, ☎783-3097)* is one of the best restaurants in Ciudad Neily, with a varied menu that lists both *tico* and international dishes.

#### The San Vito Region

There are two prosperous and highly respected Italian restaurants in San Vito: **Mamma Mia** *($$)* and **Liliana** (*$$*). In our opinion, both are good restaurants, with slightly Italian decor.

For *tico* cooking, **Restaurant Neily** *($$; San Vito)* is highly recommended by the citizens of San Vito. The dining room is very clean, and its layout is simple but inviting. **Jimar** *($$; San Vito)* is a similar restaurant that is also very popular. The animated little terrace has a beautiful view of the surrounding area.

The restaurant of the hotel **El Ceibo** *($$; near the municipal building, San Vito ☎773-3025)* is owned by an Italian and serves decent Italian and *tico* food in a plain setting – with a television droning in the background, of course!

## SHOPPING

### The Region's North

#### The Dominical Region

In Dominical, **Dos Hermanos** *(right at the exit to town from the hwy. going to Uvita)* is a supermarket that specializes in quality products, and whose owner is very friendly. It is located in the Plaza Pacifica, an attractive complex perched on top of a little hill, with beautifully landscaped surroundings of lush and varied vegetation. **Del Mundo** sells clothing and jewellery in the same complex.

In the heart of Dominical, the **Dominical Info Center** is an information centre and souvenir shop that sells sunglasses, etc. There are also postal service and equipment rental for surfing.

Next to Albergue Wildale, towards the river, **Déli del Río** *(Dominical)* is a fairly new deli that sells pizza, baked goods, delicatessen products and other quality foods, as well as suntan lotion for the beach The place is clean, with tempting displays.

## The Region's South

### Palmar Region

**Tonio** is a little *abastecedor* (a kind of convenience store) in Palmar Norte, not far from the Interamericana Highway. The North American owners of the inns and restaurants in the Ojochal area shop here for supplies. Tonio sells different and exotic local products.

#### Ojochal

In Ojochal, **Ultimo Refugio** *(500 m south of the elementary school in Ojochal)* is the place to buy yourself presents from this region.

### The Golfito Region

Southern Costa Rica has a zone known as "free port" where you can buy all kinds of consumer goods for a little less than elsewhere in the country. This area was established in 1990, in Golfito's **Depósito Libre** district. However, there is an entrance fee to shop in the district. It is best to visit the Depósito Libre during the week, because the place – including hotels – becomes very crowded on weekends, when many Costa Ricans go there to shop, lured by the discounts. All sorts of products are sold in the Depósito Libre, and you will notice more and more billboards advertising the merits of this or that product as you approach the city of Golfito.

### The San Vito Region

English-language magazines are available at **Librería La Cruz**, in the centre of San Vito.

# GLOSSARY

**GREETINGS**

| | |
|---|---|
| Goodbye | *adiós, hasta luego* |
| Good afternoon and good evening | *buenas tardes* |
| Hi (casual) | *hola* |
| Good morning | *buenos días* |
| Good night | *buenas noches* |
| Thank-you | *gracias* |
| Please | *por favor* |
| You are welcome | *de nada* |
| Excuse me | *perdone/a* |
| My name is... | *mi nombre es...* |
| What is your name? | *¿cómo se llama usted?* |
| yes | *no* |
| no | *sí* |
| Do you speak English? | *¿habla usted inglés?* |
| Slower, please | *más despacio, por favor* |
| I am sorry, I don't speak Spanish | *Lo siento, no hablo español* |
| How are you? | *¿qué tal?* |
| I am fine | *estoy bien* |
| | |
| I am American (male/female) | *Soy estadounidense* |
| I am Australian | *Soy autraliano/a* |
| I am Belgian | *Soy belga* |
| I am British (male/female) | *Soy británico/a* |
| I am Canadian | *Soy canadiense* |
| I am German (male/female) | *Soy alemán/a* |
| I am Italian (male/female) | *Soy italiano/a* |
| I am Swiss | *Soy suizo* |
| I am a tourist | *Soy turista* |
| | |
| single (m/f) | *soltero/a* |
| divorced (m/f) | *divorciado/a* |
| married (m/f) | *casado/a* |
| friend (m/f) | *amigo/a* |
| child (m/f) | *niño/a* |
| husband, wife | *esposo/a* |
| mother | *madre* |
| father | *padre* |
| brother, sister | *hermano/a* |
| widower widow | *viudo/a* |
| | |
| I am hungry | *tengo hambre* |
| I am ill | *estoy enfermo/a* |
| I am thirsty | *tengo sed* |

**DIRECTIONS**

| | |
|---|---|
| beside | *al lado de* |
| to the right | *a la derecha* |
| to the left | *a la izquierda* |
| here | *aquí* |
| there | *allí* |
| into, inside | *dentro* |
| outside | *fuera* |
| behind | *detrás* |
| in front of | *delante* |
| between | *entre* |
| far from | *lejos de* |
| Where is ... ? | *¿dónde está ... ?* |
| To get to ...? | *¿para ir a...?* |
| near | *cerca de* |
| straight ahead | *todo recto* |

**MONEY**

| | |
|---|---|
| money | *dinero / plata* |
| credit card | *tarjeta de crédito* |
| exchange | *cambio* |
| traveller's cheque | *cheque de viaje* |
| I don't have any money | *no tengo dinero* |
| The bill, please | *la cuenta, por favor* |
| receipt | *recibo* |

**SHOPPING**

| | |
|---|---|
| store | *tienda* |
| market | *mercado* |
| open | *abierto/a* |
| closed | *cerrado/a* |
| How much is this? | *¿cuánto es?* |
| to buy | *comprar* |
| to sell | *vender* |
| the customer | *el / la cliente* |
| salesman | *vendedor* |
| saleswoman | *vendedora* |
| I need... | *necesito...* |
| I would like... | *yo quisiera...* |
| | |
| batteries | *pilas* |
| blouse | *blusa* |
| cameras | *cámaras* |
| cosmetics and perfumes | *cosméticos y perfumes* |
| cotton | *algodón* |
| dress jacket | *saco* |
| eyeglasses | *lentes, gafas* |
| fabric | *tela* |
| film | *película* |
| gifts | *regalos* |
| gold | *oro* |

| | |
|---|---|
| handbag | *bolsa* |
| hat | *sombrero* |
| jewellery | *joyería* |
| leather | *cuero, piel* |
| local crafts | *artesanía* |
| magazines | *revistas* |
| newpapers | *periódicos* |
| pants | *pantalones* |
| records, cassettes | *discos, casetas* |
| sandals | *sandalias* |
| shirt | *camisa* |
| shoes | *zapatos* |
| silver | *plata* |
| skirt | *falda* |
| sun screen products | *productos solares* |
| T-shirt | *camiseta* |
| watch | *reloj* |
| wool | *lana* |

**MISCELLANEOUS**

| | |
|---|---|
| a little | *poco* |
| a lot | *mucho* |
| good (m/f) | *bueno/a* |
| bad (m/f) | *malo/a* |
| beautiful (m/f) | *hermoso/a* |
| pretty (m/f) | *bonito/a* |
| ugly | *feo* |
| big | *grande* |
| tall (m/f) | *alto/a* |
| small (m/f) | *pequeño/a* |
| short (length) (m/f) | *corto/a* |
| short (person) (m/f) | *bajo/a* |
| cold (m/f) | *frío/a* |
| hot | *caliente* |
| dark (m/f) | *oscuro/a* |
| light (colour) | *claro* |
| do not touch | *no tocar* |
| expensive (m/f) | *caro/a* |
| cheap (m/f) | *barato/a* |
| fat (m/f) | *gordo/a* |
| slim, skinny (m/f) | *delgado/a* |
| heavy (m/f) | *pesado/a* |
| light (weight) (m/f) | *ligero/a* |
| less | *menos* |
| more | *más* |
| narrow (m/f) | *estrecho/a* |
| wide (m/f) | *ancho/a* |
| new (m/f) | *nuevo/a* |
| old (m/f) | *viejo/a* |
| nothing | *nada* |
| something (m/f) | *algo/a* |

| | |
|---|---|
| quickly | *rápidamente* |
| slowly (m/f) | *despacio/a* |
| What is this? | *¿qué es esto?* |
| when? | *¿cuando?* |
| where? | *¿dónde?* |

**TIME**

| | |
|---|---|
| in the afternoon, early evening | *por la tarde* |
| at night | *por la noche* |
| in the daytime | *por el día* |
| in the morning | *por la mañana* |
| minute | *minuto* |
| month | *mes* |
| ever | *jamás* |
| never | *nunca* |
| now | *ahora* |
| today | *hoy* |
| yesterday | *ayer* |
| tomorrow | *mañana* |
| What time is it? | *¿qué hora es?* |
| hour | *hora* |
| week | *semana* |
| year | *año* |

| | |
|---|---|
| Sunday | *domingo* |
| Monday | *lunes* |
| Tuesday | *martes* |
| Wednesday | *miércoles* |
| Thursday | *jueves* |
| Friday | *viernes* |
| Saturday | *sábado* |
| January | *enero* |
| February | *febrero* |
| March | *marzo* |
| April | *abril* |
| May | *mayo* |
| June | *junio* |
| July | *julio* |
| August | *agosto* |
| September | *septiembre* |
| October | *octubre* |
| November | *noviembre* |
| December | *diciembre* |

**WEATHER**

| | |
|---|---|
| It is cold | *hace frío* |
| It is warm | *hace calor* |
| It is very hot | hace mucho calor |
| sun | *sol* |
| It is sunny | hace sol |
| It is cloudy | *está nublado* |

| | |
|---|---|
| rain | *lluvia* |
| It is raining | *está lloviendo* |
| wind | *viento* |
| It is windy | *hay viento* |
| snow | *nieve* |
| damp | *húmedo* |
| dry | *seco* |
| storm | *tormenta* |
| hurricane | *huracán* |

**COMMUNICATION**

| | |
|---|---|
| air mail | *correos aéreo* |
| collect call | *llamada por cobrar* |
| dial the number | *marcar el número* |
| area code, country code | *código* |
| envelope | *sobre* |
| long distance | *larga distancia* |
| post office | *correo* |
| rate | *tarifa* |
| stamps | *estampillas* |
| telegram | *telegrama* |
| telephone book | *un guia telefónica* |
| wait for the tone | *esperar la señal* |

**ACTIVITIES**

| | |
|---|---|
| beach | *playa* |
| museum or gallery | *museo* |
| scuba diving | *buceo* |
| to swim | *bañarse* |
| to walk around | *pasear* |
| hiking | *caminata* |
| trail | *pista, sendero* |
| cycling | *ciclismo* |
| fishing | *pesca* |

**TRANSPORTATION**

| | |
|---|---|
| arrival | *llegada* |
| departure | *salida* |
| on time | *a tiempo* |
| cancelled (m/f) | *anulado/a* |
| one way ticket | *ida* |
| return | *regreso* |
| round trip | *ida y vuelta* |
| schedule | *horario* |
| baggage | *equipajes* |
| north | *norte* |
| south | *sur* |
| east | *este* |
| west | *oeste* |
| avenue | *avenida* |
| street | *calle* |

| | |
|---|---|
| highway | *carretera* |
| expressway | *autopista* |
| airplane | *avión* |
| airport | *aeropuerto* |
| bicycle | *bicicleta* |
| boat | *barco* |
| bus | *bus* |
| bus stop | *parada* |
| bus terminal | *terminal* |
| train | *tren* |
| train crossing | *crucero ferrocarril* |
| station | *estación* |
| neighbourhood | *barrio* |
| collective taxi | *colectivo* |
| corner | *esquina* |
| express | *rápido* |
| safe | *seguro/a* |
| be careful | *cuidado* |
| car | *coche, carro* |
| To rent a car | *alquilar un auto* |
| gas | *gasolina* |
| gas station | *gasolinera* |
| no parking | *no estacionar* |
| no passing | *no adelantar* |
| parking | *parqueo* |
| pedestrian | *peaton* |
| road closed, no through traffic | *no hay paso* |
| slow down | *reduzca velocidad* |
| speed limit | *velocidad permitida* |
| stop | *alto* |
| stop! (an order) | *pare* |
| traffic light | *semáforo* |

**ACCOMMODATION**

| | |
|---|---|
| cabin, bungalow | *cabaña* |
| accommodation | *alojamiento* |
| double, for two people | *doble* |
| single, for one person | *sencillo* |
| high season | *temporada alta* |
| low season | *temporada baja* |
| bed | *cama* |
| floor (first, second...) | *piso* |
| main floor | *planta baja* |
| manager | *gerente, jefe* |
| double bed | *cama matrimonial* |
| cot | *camita* |
| bathroom | *baños* |
| with private bathroom | *con baño privado* |
| hot water | *agua caliente* |
| breakfast | *desayuno* |
| elevator | *ascensor* |

| | |
|---|---|
| air conditioning | *aire acondicionado* |
| fan | *ventilador, abanico* |
| pool | *piscina, alberca* |
| room | *habitación* |

**NUMBERS**

| | | | |
|---|---|---|---|
| 1 | *uno* | 30 | *treinta* |
| 2 | *dos* | 31 | *treinta y uno* |
| 3 | *tres* | 32 | *treinta y dos* |
| 4 | *cuatro* | 40 | *cuarenta* |
| 5 | *cinco* | 50 | *cincuenta* |
| 6 | *seis* | 60 | *sesenta* |
| 7 | *siete* | 70 | *setenta* |
| 8 | *ocho* | 80 | *ochenta* |
| 9 | *nueve* | 90 | *noventa* |
| 10 | *diez* | 100 | *cien* |
| 11 | *once* | 101 | *ciento uno* |
| 12 | *doce* | 102 | *ciento dos* |
| 13 | *trece* | 200 | *doscientos* |
| 14 | *catorce* | 300 | *trescientos* |
| 15 | *quince* | 400 | *quatrocientoa* |
| 16 | *dieciséis* | 500 | *quinientos* |
| 17 | *diecisiete* | 600 | *seiscientos* |
| 18 | *dieciocho* | 700 | *sietecientos* |
| 19 | *diecinueve* | 800 | *ochocientos* |
| 20 | *veinte* | 900 | *novecientos* |
| 21 | *veintiuno* | 1,000 | *mil* |
| 22 | *veintidós* | 1,100 | *mil cien* |
| 23 | *veintitrés* | 1,200 | *mil doscientos* |
| 24 | *veinticuatro* | 2000 | *dos mil* |
| 25 | *veinticinco* | 3000 | *tres mil* |
| 26 | *veintiséis* | 10,000 | *diez mil* |
| 27 | *veintisiete* | 100,000 | *cien mil* |
| 28 | *veintiocho* | 1,000,000 | *un millón* |
| 29 | *veintinueve* | | |

# INDEX

INDEX

INDEX

INDEX

# OTHER ULYSSES GUIDES

Acapulco (Mexico)
Ulysses Due South guide offers a fresh look at Acapulco, the most famous Mexican resort: Acapulco Bay, its beaches, restaurants and captivating nightlife are all in there, but so are the neighbouring mountains, as well as an enlightened look at the people and history of this spot.
Marc Rigole, Claude-Victor Langlois 150 pages, 5 maps
$14.95 CAN $9.95 US £6.99 2-89464-062-5

The Islands Of The Bahamas
Vacationers will find extensive coverage of the big favourites of New Providence (Nassau) and Grand Bahama (Freeport) with their spectacular beaches, glittering casinos and great scuba diving, but they will also find the most extensive coverage of the Out Islands. Here island-hoppers enjoy world-class fishing, scuba diving and boating, friendly people and pristine deserted beaches.
Jennifer McMorran 288 pages, 25 maps
8 pages of colour photos
$24.95 CAN $17.95 US £12.99 2-89464-123-0

Belize
This tiny Central American country encompasses part of the ancient Ruta Maya and is rimmed by spectacular coral reefs. Its archaeological and natural treasures make it an explorer's paradise. Practical and cultural information will help you make the most of your vacation.
Carlos Soldevila 208 pages, 10 maps
$16.65 CAN $12.95 US 2-89464-179-6

Cancún & Cozumel (Mexico)
The entirely man-made resort of Cancún on the Yucatán Peninsula attracts visitors from the world-over. They come to enjoy a unique travelling experience with fabulous archaeological sites, the last remnants of the Mayan civilization, and the island of Cozumel, a scuba-diver's paradise, both close by.
Caroline Vien, Alain Théroux 200 pages, 20 maps
$17.95 CAN $12.95 US £8.99 2-89464-040-4

Cartagena, 2nd edition
Here is the new edition on this colonial jewel. Declared a World Heritage Site by UNESCO, Cartagena boasts historic charm, cultural riches, luxurious hotels, beautiful beaches and the possibility of exciting excursions, all the ingredients for an extraordinary vacation.
Marc Rigole 128 pages, 10 maps
$12.95 CAN $9.95 US £6.50 2-89464-018-8

Costa Rica
This fresh look at Costa Rica provides travellers with the most extensive choice of practical addresses, no matter what their budget while also placing special emphasis on eco-tourism, independent travel and the culture, history and natural wonders of this Central American gem.
Francis Giguère, Yves Séguin 368 pages, 35 maps
8 pages of colour photos
$27.95 CAN $19.95 US £13.99 2-89464-144-3

Cuba, 2nd edition
Already a second edition for this unique guide to Cuba. The island's spirit is revealed, from colonial Havana, to the world-heritage site of Trinidad and to Santiago with it Afro-Cuban culture. The guide also covers the famous beaches and provides travellers with countless shortcuts and tips for independent travel in Cuba.
Carlos Soldevila 336 pages, 40 maps
8 pages of colour photos
$24.95 CAN $17.95 US £12.99 2-89464-143-5

Dominican Republic
The most complete reference to this Caribbean hot spot: excursions, historical information, cultural details, addresses of restaurants, shops and hotels, road maps and city plans.
Pascale Couture, Benoit Prieur
250 pages, 20 maps
8 pages of colour photos
$24.95 CAN $17.95 US £12.99 2-89464-064-1

Ecuador and the Galápagos Islands
All the major sites of this South American country are explored including extensive coverage of the capital city, Quito, but also the extraordinary Galapagos Islands. Hundreds of addresses for all budgets as well as countless useful hints for discovering this fascinating and ancient land of the Incas.
Alain Legault 300 pages, 25 maps
8 pages of colour photos
$24.95 CAN $17.95 US £12.99 2-89464-059-5

El Salvador
This guide provides everything the traveller needs to discover this fascinating Central American country: explanation of cultural and political contexts, advice on how to travel in the area, descriptions of the various attractions, detailed lists of accommodation, restaurants, entertainment.
Eric Hamovitch 152 pages, 7 maps
$22.95 CAN $14.95 US £11.50 2-921444-89-5

Guadeloupe, 3rd edition
This is the only guide to provide such extensive cultural and practical coverage of this destination. The charm of this dramatically beautiful Caribbean island is revealed along winding picturesque roads through typical villages and towns. Magnificent colour plates help to identify Guadeloupe's birds and plants.
Pascale Couture 208 pages, 15 maps
8 pages of colour photos
$24.95 CAN $17.95 US £12.99 2-89464-135-4

Guatemala
Historic peace talks have once again allowed tourism to develop in Guatemala, providing a spectacular glimpse at a country whose native traditions are so strong and omnipresent.
Carlos Soldevila, Denis Faubert 336 pages, 30 maps
$24.95 CAN $17.95 US £12.99 2-89464-175-3

Honduras, 2nd edition
The prospects for tourism in Honduras are among the brightest – promising travellers a first-rate vacation, whether they are in search of spectacular deserted beaches, fascinating archaeological sites or supreme diving locations. This guide offers numerous suggestions for outdoor adventure plus practical tips and information on everything from A to Z.
Eric Hamovitch 224 pages, 20 maps
$24.95 CAN $17.95 US £12.99 2-89464-132-X

Martinique, 3rd edition
A perfect marriage of cultural and practical information provides the best coverage of Martinique. Numerous tours lead across the island of flowers, from Fort-de-France to Saint-Pierre, with stops in Grande Anse and Montagne Pelée. Everything you need to know about hiking and water sports. Magnificent colour plates help to identify birds and plants.
Claude Morneau 256 pages, 18 maps
8 pages of colour photos
$24.95 CAN $17.95 US £12.99 2-89464-136-2

Nicaragua
Once a headline-maker the world over, Nicaragua is more often featured in the "Travel" section these days. Besides the capital city of Managua and the popular resort of Montelimar, this guide traverses the whole country, discovering the touching cities of León and Granada, among other places, along the way.
Carol Wood 224 pages, 15 maps
$24.95 CAN $16.95 US £11.50 2-89464-034-X

Panamá, 2nd edition
Famous for its impressive canal, Panamá offers magnificent beaches on two different oceans, nestled in a diverse ethnic and cultural environment. This guide will help the traveller discover an infinite variety of landscapes, with unequalled flora and fauna.
Marc Rigole, Claude-Victor Langlois 208 pages, 16 maps
8 pages of colour photos
$24.95 CAN $16.95 US £11.50 2-89464-005-6

Peru
Ulysses reveals the stunning scenery of this varied land: the Inca Trail and the ancient Inca city of Macchu Pichu, the depths of the Amazon rainforest, the high reaches of the Cordillera Blanca, modern and bustling Lima and beautiful Arequipa. An insightful portrait and a thorough how-to section round out the guide.
Alain Legault 352 pages, 60 maps
8 pages of colour photos
$27.95 CAN $17.95 US 2-89464-122-2

Puerto Vallarta (Mexico)
What began as a tiny fishing village nestled between sea and mountains has blossomed into one of the Mexican Riviera's most splendid resorts. This guide reveals the splendour of Puerto Vallarta, from its luxuriant flora to its quaint tile-roofed houses and countless excellent restaurants.
Richard Bizier, Roch Nadeau 160 pages, 5 maps
$14.95 CAN $9.95 US £6.50 2-89464-039-0

Saint Martin - Saint Barts, 2nd edition
Jewels of the French and Dutch Caribbean, Saint Martin and Saint Barts offer a kaleidoscope of attractions – beautiful beaches, charming villages, first-class tourist facilities – and they have been combined for this guide. Whether it's international Saint Martin or tiny Saint Barts, or both, this handy pocket guide has all the great restaurants, luxurious hotels, outdoor activities, plus a glossary, maps and a historical overview.
Pascale Couture 192 pages, 10 maps
$16.95 CAN $12.95 US £8.99 2-89464-071-4

## ORDER FORM

### ULYSSES TRAVEL GUIDES

☐ Affordable B&Bs in Québec $12.95 CAN $9.95 US
☐ Atlantic Canada ....... $24.95 CAN $17.95 US
☐ Beaches of Maine ...... $12.95 CAN $9.95 US
☐ Bahamas ............ $24.95 CAN $17.95 US
☐ Belize .............. $16.95 CAN $12.95 US
☐ Calgary ............. $17.95 CAN $12.95 US
☐ Canada ............. $29.95 CAN $21.95 US
☐ Chicago ............. $19.95 CAN $14.95 US
☐ Chile ............... $27.95 CAN $17.95 US
☐ Costa Rica ........... $27.95 CAN $19.95 US
☐ Cuba ............... $24.95 CAN $17.95 US
☐ Dominican Republic ..... $24.95 CAN $17.95 US
☐ Ecuador Galapagos Islands $24.95 CAN $17.95 US
☐ El Salvador ........... $22.95 CAN $14.95 US
☐ Guadeloupe .......... $24.95 CAN $17.95 US
☐ Guatemala ........... $24.95 CAN $17.95 US
☐ Honduras ............ $24.95 CAN $17.95 US
☐ Jamaica ............. $24.95 CAN $17.95 US
☐ Lisbon .............. $18.95 CAN $13.95 US
☐ Louisiana ............ $29.95 CAN $21.95 US
☐ Martinique ........... $24.95 CAN $17.95 US
☐ Montréal ............ $19.95 CAN $14.95 US
☐ New Orleans ......... $17.95 CAN $12.95 US
☐ New York City ........ $19.95 CAN $14.95 US
☐ Nicaragua ........... $24.95 CAN $16.95 US
☐ Ontario ............. $24.95 CAN $14.95US
☐ Ottawa .............. $17.95 CAN $12.95 US
☐ Panamá ............. $24.95 CAN $16.95 US
☐ Peru ............... $27.95 CAN $19.95 US
☐ Portugal ............. $24.95 CAN $16.95 US
☐ Provence - Côte d'Azur .. $29.95 CAN $21.95US
☐ Québec ............. $29.95 CAN $21.95 US
☐ Québec and Ontario with Via .............. $9.95 CAN $7.95 US
☐ Toronto ............. $18.95 CAN $13.95 US
☐ Vancouver ........... $17.95 CAN $12.95 US
☐ Washington D.C. ....... $18.95 CAN $13.95 US
☐ Western Canada ....... $29.95 CAN $21.95 US

### ULYSSES DUE SOUTH

☐ Acapulco .......... $14.95 CAN $9.95 US
☐ Belize .............. $16.95 CAN $12.95 US
☐ Cartagena (Colombia) ... $12.95 CAN $9.95 US
☐ Cancun Cozumel ....... $17.95 CAN $12.95 US
☐ Puerto Vallarta ........ $14.95 CAN $9.95 US
☐ St. Martin and St. Barts .. $16.95 CAN $12.95 US

## ULYSSES TRAVEL JOURNAL

☐ Ulysses Travel Journal . . . . . . . . . . . . . . . . . . . . . . . . . . . . . . . . . . . $9.95 CAN
(Blue, Red, Green, Yellow, Sextant) $7.95 US

## ULYSSES GREEN ESCAPES

☐ Cycling in France . . . . . . $22.95 CAN
$16.95 US

☐ Cycling in Ontario. . . . . . $22.95 CAN
$16.95 US

☐ Hiking in the Northeastern U.S. . . . . . . $19.95 CAN
$13.95 US

☐ Hiking in Québec . . . . . . $19.95 CAN
$13.95 US

| TITLE | QUANTITY | PRICE | TOTAL |
|---|---|---|---|
| | | | |
| | | | |
| | | | |
| | | | |
| | | | |
| Name ___ | | Subtotal | |
| Address ___ | | Canadian postage & handling* | $4.00 |
| Payment : ☐ Cash ☐ Visa ☐ MasterCard | | Subtotal | |
| Card number ___ | | GST in Canada 7% | |
| Signature ___ | | TOTAL | |

**ULYSSES TRAVEL PUBLICATIONS**
4176 St-Denis,
Montréal, Québec, H2W 2M5
(514) 843-9447 fax (514) 843-9448
www.ulysses.ca
*$15 for overseas orders

U.S. ORDERS: **GLOBE PEQUOT PRESS**
P.O. Box 833, 6 Business Park Road,
Old Saybrook, CT 06475-0833
1-800-243-0495 fax 1-800-820-2329
www.globe-pequot.com